D0207734

The World of Prometheus

The World of Prometheus

THE POLITICS OF PUNISHING IN DEMOCRATIC ATHENS

DANIELLE S. ALLEN

BOWLING GREEN STATE UNIVERSITY DISCARDED LIBRARY

PRINCETON UNIVERSITY PRESS

PRINCETON, NEW JERSEY

BOWLING GREEN STATE
UNIVERSITY LIBRARIES

Copyright © 2000 by Princeton University Press
Published by Princeton University Press, 41 William Street, Princeton, New Jersey 08540
In the United Kingdom: Princeton University Press, Chichester, West Sussex
All Rights Reserved

Library of Congress Cataloging-in-Publication Data

Allen, Danielle S., 1971–
The world of Prometheus: the politics of punishing in democratic Athens / Danielle S. Allen
p. cm.
Includes bibliographical references and index.
ISBN 0-691-05869-5 (alk. paper)
1. Punishment (Greek law). 2. Punishment—Greece—Athens—History. I. Title.
KL4395.A43 1999 303.3′6—dc21 99-34848 CIP

This book has been composed in Times Roman

The paper used in this publication meets the minimum requirements of
ANSI/NISO Z39.48-1992 (R1997) (*Permanence of Paper*)

http://pup.princeton.edu

Printed in the United States of America

10 9 8 7 6 5 4 3 2 1

TO MY PARENTS

CONTENTS

PREFACE   xi

INTRODUCTION   3

PART ONE: THE PRELIMINARIES   13

CHAPTER ONE
What Is Punishment?   15

   Introduction   15
   "Revenge" versus "Punishment": Rereading the Oresteia   18
   Studying Punishment as Authority: Reading the Prometheus Bound   25
   Précis   35

CHAPTER TWO
Institutional Context   39

   Introduction   39
   Penal Institutions and Democratic Power   40
   The Lay Prosecutor and the Parameters of Judgment   45

CHAPTER THREE
Cultural Context   50

   Anger/Orge   50
   The Agon *and Honor*   59
   Reciprocity   62
   Social Memory, Social Knowledge   65
   Language   68
   Conclusion   72

CHAPTER FOUR
Punishment and Its Tragic Problems   73

   The Mythic Imaginary   73
   Method   75
   Disease and Remedy   77
   Power, Tyranny, and Law   86
   Conclusion   94

PART TWO: THE PROCESS OF PUNISHING   97

CHAPTER FIVE
Initiation, Part One   99

   Knowledge, Power, Action   99
   Investigation   102

Initiation: Metics, Proxenoi, *and* Xenoi   107
Initiation: Slaves   109
Initiation: Women   111

CHAPTER SIX
Initiation, Part Two   122

The Male Citizen Prosecutor   122
Back to the Bees and Wasps Again   128
The Household: Women and Men Together   134
City as Collective   141

CHAPTER SEVEN
The Negotiation of Desert, Part One   147

The Magic of Speech   147
Pity and Anger   148
The First Norm of Public Agency: Deserving to Punish and Dispelling
    Charges of Sycophancy   151

CHAPTER EIGHT
The Negotiation of Desert, Part Two   168

Introduction   168
The Second Norm of Public Agency: Using Social Memory and Law   168
The Rule of Judgment versus the Rule of Law   179
The Rule of Law in Plato and Aristotle   183
The Third Norm of Public Agency: Shaping the Democratic Community   190

CHAPTER NINE
Execution   197

War, Peace, and the Formalism of Punishment   197
The Details: Punishments and Their Executors   200
Two Forms of Memory: Remembering and Forgetting   202
The Symbolism of Remembering and Forgetting   205
War and Peace, the Body and Silence   213
Punishments of Reintegration   224
Punishments that Redefine the "Whole" Community   232
The Amnesty   237

PART THREE: INTERVENTIONS IN THE CONVERSATION   243

CHAPTER TEN
Plato's Paradigm Shifts   245

The Symbol of Leontios   245
Reform over Reciprocity   247
The Erasure of Orge   251
Undoing the Athenian "Principle of the Public": The Republic   257

The Just City and the Power of the Symbol   263
*The Incurables and the Necessity for Anger/*Orge *in the Just City of the* Laws   277

CHAPTER ELEVEN
Aristotle's Compromises   282
On Justice and Desert   282

EPILOGUE: The Reform of Prometheus and Promethean Rebellion   293

APPENDIXES
A. The Number of Magistrates in Athens   305

B. The Nature and Scope of Arbitration in Athens   317

C. The Relative Frequency of Penal Words within Each Orator   323

D. Further Argument about the Decree of Cannonus   324

E. Catalog of Cases of Punishing (or Attempts at Punishing) in
   Tragedy   326

ENDNOTES   333

BIBLIOGRAPHY   405

INDEX   431

THIS PROJECT began with an innocent question. In an undergraduate seminar I once asked a professor whether the Athenians had used imprisonment as a penalty. The teacher, always on the lookout for potential classicists, fired back: "You know, that would make a great dissertation topic." Little did I know what a dissertation entailed. Eight years ago, when I first asked that small question about imprisonment in Athens, I also had no idea that a chance curiosity about punishment would lead me to think about democratic politics, modern as well as ancient. Gernet called the study of penal systems a "walk through the garden of punishments."[1] I've found the exercise something more of a hike through the wilds. But now, as I introduce this project, having finally reached some sort of clearing, I should provide a map to those willing to join me in exploring punishment. In this book the path into Athenian punishment leads into Athenian politics, and then into the study of democratic politics more generally. Throughout the text, I investigate how the Athenians produced punitive judgments, but always with an eye to considering how that practice affected the Athenian political body as a whole.

As for the politics: the practice of producing and executing punitive judgments rests on a society's conceptualization of authority and desert (i.e., on its concepts of "what is deserved").[2] These political concepts of authority and desert are among the fundamental cultural and psychosocial elements supporting the operation of politics; they provide a framework on which to construct institutional structures.[3] In the punitive context, "authority" and "desert" are defined in terms of still other concepts that are also fundamental to the operation of politics (in Athens such concepts included anger, honor, reciprocity, law, judgment, the private, and the public). The conceptual relationships intrinsic to punishment inevitably lead from the topic of punishment as institutional and social control to the topic of punishment as politics. And so this book not only provides a thorough descriptive and analytic narration of the practice of punishment in Athens but also narrates a story of the relation between ancient punishment and ancient politics in order to speak both to classicists and to students of politics.

In what follows I aim to link historiography and political theory and to present ancient Athenian democracy in ways that may spur students of modern democracy (as well as students of ancient democracy) to new questions. It is sometimes thought that analytic history and normative political theory are not easily able to speak to one another. The limits set to the two disciplines derive from the conviction that historiography produces stories of "the way things were" while political theory advises on "oughts," and that these two projects should be kept distinct since the abuse of historiography by theory is notorious.

Historiography needn't be taken as providing models, but that doesn't mean it has no service at all to render theory. It can play handmaiden to theory by generating questions for theorists. In other words, historiography can do what theory doesn't always have time for: identify the problems, paradoxes, and tensions in the various phenomena that constitute democratic practice. Historians can nicely reveal the general political claims that underlie specific cultural forms of democratic practice, and they can delineate the forms of political authority inherent in the particular phenomena of historical democracies. I have tried to do this by specifically investigating a central modern concept and practice, "punishment," through an examination of its ancient equivalents. This is a study in "translation." I hope to shed light on the workings of punishment in Athenian democracy in order to contribute to ongoing discussions in the fields of classics, political science, and political theory about how to locate and understand the heart of democratic practice, whether ancient or modern.

In trying to find my disciplinary place between classics and political theory, I have passed through years of studentship and have at last embarked on a project of study that is only nominally independent. I have accumulated many intellectual debts and—more important—many, many gladly incurred debts of *philia.* First and foremost I thank my parents for everything, and to them I dedicate this book.

In gratitude for countless hours of instruction, innumerable suggestions, and ceaseless encouragement, I owe my wholehearted thanks to Paul Cartledge, who supervised my graduate dissertation, and equally to Josh Ober, who supervised my undergraduate thesis. This book would not exist without their insightful criticisms and their patience with my sometimes too tangled prose. I am also a thankful beneficiary of the copious and thoughtful advice of Simon Goldhill, Malcolm Schofield, Paul Millett, Chris Gill, Chris Faraone, Laura Slatkin, Melissa Lane, William Stull, Graham Burnett, Bernard Harcourt, Andy Wolpert, Colin Austin, and the anonymous readers of the Princeton University Press, all of whom read all or significant portions of one version or another (or more than one!) of the manuscript and who have all given me invaluable suggestions. My thanks also to those who had time to talk about the manuscript, especially Jill Frank, Patchen Markell, and Terry Aladjem, to Brigitta van Rheinberg at the Princeton University Press for her reliable support, to Brian MacDonald for efficient and helpful copyediting, and to Edith Foster and Fran Spaltro for proofreading and index preparation. Finally, my special thanks to Robert von Hallberg without whose careful editing and encouragement this project would not have reached completion. This book has not been easy to write; all of these people made the process easier.

On matters pertaining to the structure of Athenian institutions, I am more than grateful for the expert help of Stephen Todd and P. J. Rhodes, who had time to read sections of the manuscript in various stages of draft. My great thanks to them. I profited greatly from Dr. Todd's eagle-eye for my mistakes and from Prof. Rhodes's advice on how to characterize Athenian institutions; any errors or idiosyncratic interpretations are wholly mine.

I am aware of the risk of oversystematization in my presentation of certain legal procedures. My aim has been to write for the generalist and not only for the specialist and so I have tried to present as simple a picture of the institutional system as is possible within the bounds of the historical record. I encourage readers to turn to my notes if they wish to see the more complex picture. I think that in every such case the notes will be found to contain detailed analyses of the points where my systematization may break down and of the scholarly disputes that surround points of detail affecting the institutional procedures at issue. I have generally tried to build my picture of Athenian institutions on the basis of majority opinions about particular details, but in some cases I have signaled in the text where my opinions diverge from the majority.

In the same vein, it is worth noting here that I have employed Latinizations of Greek names where they are traditional and therefore more recognizable for the nonclassicist (thus Clytemnestra, and not Klytaimestra).

The World of Prometheus

INTRODUCTION

ONE OF THE most important but least acknowledged features of the modern world is that individuals no longer punish for themselves. By this I do not suggest, as so many have, that over time a dark Dionysiac and ancient age of mad blood vengeance has ceded to an era of rational, legally based state punishment and Apolline brightness. I refer rather to the quite specific fact that the modern age has produced the public prosecutor to replace the lay prosecutor as the person responsible for seeing that wrongdoing is dealt with. In the ancient world the victims of wrongs had to enter into judicial processes in order to prosecute their own cases. The modern age has produced the state representative who acts on behalf of wronged individuals and who is supposed to prosecute impartially, disinterestedly, and dispassionately. The invention of the public prosecutor is a small historical detail—small enough to slip out of most history books—but its consequences have been great and systematic.

Prior to the modern age, private prosecution was the norm in the ancient Greek *polis*, in the Roman Republic and Principate, in the pre-sixteenth-century French and Prussian monarchies,[1] and in the pre-eighteenth-century English monarchy. The use of public prosecution in modern states has come about more by evolution than by design. In Britain the attorney general prosecuted only cases that applied directly to the king until the end of the seventeenth century, and the justice of the peace prosecuted only cases without a private prosecutor.[2] Both types of official began to assume more power in the eighteenth century and the Crown Prosecutor's Service was introduced only in the 1980s. This office expands the state's prosecutorial powers to its greatest levels ever, but even so it remains institutionally possible in Britain for private individuals to bring criminal cases to trial—witness the recent Stephen Lawrence case in which the family of a murdered youth brought several defendants to trial after the Crown Prosecutor's Service had dropped the case.

The use of public prosecution in the United States has had a rather different history. Public prosecution came into use during the colonial period despite the fact that the mother country, Britain, had no such system. Historians have not been able to determine why the colonists adopted this institution, but whatever the case the public prosecutor was incorporated into the institutional structure of the United States at its founding.[3] To the best of my knowledge, the United States is the only pre-twentieth-century Western political regime to have come into being with the institution of the public prosecutor already in place. Moreover, in the United States private individuals cannot prosecute criminal proceedings. The public prosecutor (or district attorney) has jurisdiction over criminal cases to the point of a de jure exclusion of private individuals from the prosecutorial arena.[4] The U.S. public prosecutor, also often known as the district attorney, is therefore something of a historical anomaly, a curious product of colonial times. Whatever the reasons for its invention, the institution models a different understanding of the relationship between citizens and their government and of the use of political power than had been customary in the English-speaking world up to that point.

This is an important fact. The premodern citizen around the globe, including the ancient Athenian, was obliged, for safety's sake, to understand punishment: what it was, how it worked, how one "did" it. Athenians of democratic Athens who thought that they had suffered wrong usually had to be able to deal with that wrong for themselves. They themselves had to be able to bring the apparatus of authoritative political power to bear against the person who had wronged them. They had to see an act of power through from initiation to conclusion and carry out the process of punishing.

In contrast, the modern citizen generally has the luxury of being able to ignore the processes of punishment after he or she has memorized the emergency telephone number of the police department. In the age of democracy when "the people" hold political power, citizens have been insulated from considering what holding and using that power mean in practical terms. The degree to which modern democrats are content to pay little heed to the process of punishing is especially interesting, given that every step along the way to the institution of the public prosecutor was resisted as an erosion of the power of the citizenry.[5]

I do not mean—with my claim that modern citizens do not punish—to ignore the fact that modern parents punish, schools punish, and private institutions like clubs and sports teams set up systems of fines and mulcts to keep the behavior of members in line (although modern theorists often define these forms of punishment as "substandard" types of punishment).[6] But it is notable that the use of corporal punishment in these arenas has become increasingly limited with the growth of the modern liberal-democratic state and it is equally notable that corporal punishment (I include imprisonment in this category) is a prerogative that is now on the whole reserved for the state. In other words, the full power of punishment—the power to touch the body—resides only in the state. Despite much obvious good in these developments, one wonders too about the dangers that follow from changes that encourage citizens to think less about how the power to punish is used or should be used.

There is another key difference between what parents, teachers, and soccer coaches do and what prosecutors do. Parents, teachers, and soccer coaches who punish on their own authority only very rarely find themselves having to justify their punishments to the political community as a whole (generally they do not have to as long as they do not use corporal punishment). In contrast, legitimate punishments based on state authority must be justifiable at large within the political community. Punishments that make use of state power (or the power of the *polis* in the ancient Greek case) must be defensible according to definitions of fairness and justice that prevail throughout the polity and that arise from the rules and principles giving legitimacy to the political authority under which the citizens are unified into a society. This is true whether the prosecution that leads to the use of state/*polis* power has been carried out by a private citizen or by an "agent of the state." Those private and public actors who participate in a society's system of public punishment are forced to enter into, to use, and to shape its discourse of justice, desert, and fairness. Modern citizens are no longer obliged to participate in these sorts of discourses.

There is an exception to this. Modern citizens do participate in such conversations when they serve as jurors. The use of trial by jury is one of the key features of both ancient and modern democracy. In modern U.S. democracy, jurors have the final say on acquittal. In ancient Athens, the jurors of the popular courts had the final say on both acquittal and conviction. In both cases the jurors exercise a total power of some significance. But there is an important difference between how the ancient Athenians approached this power and how modern democrats do in the United States and the United Kingdom.

Ancient jurors had and modern jurors still have the power to hand down a decision that contradicts the letter of the law or the law as interpreted for them by judges, magistrates, or "legal experts" (in the modern case). Ancient jurors could not be punished for doing this, nor can modern jurors. In the Anglo-American legal world, juries who decide counter to the letter of the law are said to have exercised "jury nullification." Green organizes cases of jury nullification into three types: (1) systemic nullification in which the jurors acquit because they reject the law that criminalizes the wrong for which the defendant is being tried; (2) systemic nullification in which the jurors acquit because they reject not the criminalization of the act but the level of sanction attached to it; and (3) ad hoc, circumstantial nullification, in which the jurors accept the law and concomitant sanction but simply have no wish to see them applied to the particular defendant on trial.[7] Both of the first two forms of nullification have had significant impacts on politics.

Seventeenth-century disputes between the Quakers and the British government were significantly altered by the refusal of English juries to convict Quakers charged with violating the Conventicles Act for preaching at large non-Anglican gatherings. Similarly, colonial American juries regularly returned not-guilty verdicts against men like John Hancock and publisher John Peter Zenger, when they were brought to trial as smugglers by the British government during a period of prerevolutionary tensions. The crown responded to these colonial jurors with efforts to control jury selection and other procedures associated with jury decision making.[8]

In the nineteenth century, the U.S. federal government discovered that it could not enforce the Fugitive Slave Act because northern juries refused to return guilty verdicts against those who had helped slaves to escape. The federal government had to change its strategies for dealing with slavery because it could not enforce its legislation.[9] In the mid-twentieth century, the effect of jury nullification went in the other direction as far as the issue of racial justice is concerned. White juries in the American South practiced jury nullification in favor of white defendants. The southern juries failed to achieve the impartiality necessary for decision making in accord with political principles of the U.S.

government. Their verdicts challenged the federal government's claim to protect the rights of all citizens. The federal government had to intervene in the jury system by assigning new rules for jury selection in order for it to carry out its political goals.[10] Since the late 1960s jury selection has aimed at producing juries that are demographically representative rather than consisting only of the elite or "blue ribbon" members of a given community.

Jury nullification is also having an important effect on the politics of the 1990s. California's "three-strikes" legislation (which mandates a twenty-five-year prison sentence for a third felony conviction—three convictions of possessing marijuana would do it) is proving unenforceable because juries simply will not convict an offender to a twenty-five-year term for a minor felony, even if it is the third. Legislators are writing and rewriting bills to deal with the situation.[11]

These stories of jury nullification teach a relatively simple story: in their modern institutional role, juries are responsible for ensuring the integrity of legislation. They may affirm legislation by deciding in accord with it, or they may challenge it by deciding contrary to the guidelines laid out by the law. We generally take notice that the jury is political, however, only when it decides contrary to the law and highlights the legislative system's lack of integrity. In such cases, juries have an obvious and immediate impact on the political system and legislators scurry to find other means to carry out their projects. The jury is recognized as political precisely by asserting itself in opposition to the legislative power, but its affirmations of legislation are no less political.

The ancient Athenian jury also had the power to make decisions of great political significance, but the ancient and modern approaches to the ultimate power of the jury are rather different. The Athenian jurors were the same people who sat in the legislative assembly and made decisions on the laws and decrees that would govern the city. The decisions that they made in the courtroom, when they ran counter to the law, constituted a change of mind on the part of the legislators in a particular circumstance rather than a challenge to a separate legislative body or act of "nullification." Litigants in the Athenian courtroom regularly acknowledged the ultimate power of their jurors to decide even against the law and their complete authority as decision makers in the realm of prosecution. Modern jurors, in contrast, are encouraged to think of a decision to "nullify" as a violation of their assigned duty of adherence to the law. For that matter, the "principle of jury nullification" is not so much a principle as it is a statement of the fact that jurors cannot be punished for their decisions and therefore do exercise an ultimate power in the realm of judicial decision making. The Athenians stared this fact in the face, made no efforts to hide or to obscure the power of the jurors by encoding it in a legal formula, and breathed the bracing air of a world where people had to recognize themselves as the source of the authority by which they were to be governed.

The Athenian jury came into being with the right not to be penalized for its decisions. The same is not true of the Anglo-American jury. The principle of jury nullification was established in England in 1670 after a long struggle about whether juries could be punished for deciding contrary to the law as interpreted for them by the judge.[12] Until the late 1100s the Anglo-Saxon judicial system relied on trial by ordeal in order to determine guilt and innocence and to provide for the enforcement of community norms. In the early 1200s the English king organized the most notable men of local communities throughout England into "hundreds" in villages. These "hundreds" were called before the king's circuit court judges twice a year and were asked to report all of the criminals in the area who had violated the "King's peace" that year; judgments were made and punishments were imposed on the basis of the knowledge of these hundred-men.[13]

These groups of prestigious community members were the first criminal juries. They were self-informing, which is to say that they did not hear witness testimony, and they were not guided by instructions from a judge.[14] They were said to "speak the truth" (*vera dicere*), and hence their decisions were called verdicts. There could be no disagreement about the truth and so by the late fourteenth century, the verdict had to be unanimous.[15] Until the late seventeenth century judges used methods of coercion—restriction of food, inadequate accommodations—as means of forcing a stubbornly hung jury to come to a unanimous decision.[16] The institution of the jury thus arose from a combination of the king's desire to consolidate authority in the countryside and the country dwellers' desire to have some legal authority to enforce injunctions against thieves, murderers, arsonists, and the like.

In the sixteenth and seventeenth centuries, the jury took several significant steps toward its modern form. Before this period local justices of the peace had merely presided at the trial. The Marian Statutes, promulgated by Queen Mary in 1554, granted the justices of the peace the additional powers to investigate accusations, to take statements from the accused and any accusers, and to make indictments. The investigations carried out by the local justices of the peace and the knowledge that they produced began to preempt the local knowledge of jury members. Justices of the peace had to present evidence at trials, which afforded them the institutional latitude to advise juries on how to proceed. This advice was the forerunner to the "jury instructions" that the judge now provides at the beginning of a trial in order to explain to the jurors what their role is in relation to the law and judicial decision making.[17]

In the sixteenth century the Tudor royal house used the Star Chamber to extend control over juries even further. Individual jurors, or entire juries, could be bound over to the Star Chamber for corrupt judgments, with "corruption" being defined rather broadly.[18] A 1534 statute relating to the Welsh Marches (26 Hen. 8, c. 4) mandated fines for verdicts against "good and pregnant evidence." The statute "seems to [have] presumed subornation of perjury or browbeating of jurors by friends or relatives of the accused" as cause for the false verdict.[19] But examples of cases in which jurors were fined for false verdicts include those that, on the face of it, did not involve bribery or corruption.[20]

Early in the seventeenth century the courts under Chief Justice Hyde began to fine jurors more frequently (Green 1985, 209–10).[21] The matter was brought to a pass under Chief Justice Kelyng who began fining juries when they returned verdicts of manslaughter in cases where he had advised them to rule for murder. A member of Parliament was among the jurors fined by Kelyng. When the Parliamentarian protested, he was told by Kelyng "that he [Kelyng] would make him know that he was now his servant and that he would make him stoop" (Green 1985, 214, quoting *Diary of John Milward*, 162–63). Kelyng was brought before the House of Commons on charges of "introducing an arbitrary government" but was dismissed without further charges (Green 1985, 214). Nonetheless, Parliament decided to draw up a bill prohibiting further fining.[22] Future chief justice John Vaughan was on the committee for the bill and spoke to it in February 1668, but the bill was lost in a flurry of parliamentarian business and died in committee (Green 1985, 220).

The matter came to a head in the 1670 trial of William Penn and a codefendant on charges of violating the Conventicles Act with their public preaching. Penn had been preaching to a gathering of Quakers, a fact that he openly admitted. Penn urged the jury, however, to recognize that the law according to which he was charged was itself illegal and to acquit him on those grounds. The jury acquitted the men, contrary to the advice of the judge on how the law stood, and all twelve jurors were fined. One of them, Juryman Bushel, refused to pay the penalty. Bushel's case landed in the court of Chief Justice Robert Vaughan, who decided in his favor and wrote an opinion protecting juries from being penalized for giving verdicts according to their conscience. Vaughan thereby institutionalized the jury as being the body that has final say on matters of acquittal, even if jurors should find counter to the law.[23]

The Athenians never questioned the right of jurors to have final say on a matter, and even to decide counter to the law, but the power of the modern Anglo-American jury had to be carved out against efforts to keep the jury from having final say. Nor does the modern jury's power remain untrammeled or receive forthright acknowledgment. The 1992 Federal U.S. criminal jury instructions read: "You will . . . apply the law which I will give you. You must follow that law whether you agree with it or not."[24] And in forty-eight U.S. states judges and lawyers are not allowed to tell the jury that they have the power and legal right to set aside the law when they make decisions according to this principle of jury nullification.[25] Modern citizens typically do not punish within the public and political arena except as jurors, and as jurors they are sheltered from an awareness of how much power they may in fact exercise. Our practices in this regard disincline us from reflection on the relationships between punishment, power, and politics.

Many of us are lucky enough to be able to avert our attention from the question of how punishment is experienced by the individual actors (prosecutors and defendants) who must try to bring complex institutional and cultural phenomena under their control in their efforts to designate a wrongdoing and respond to it (or to deny and repudiate an accusation). From the perspective of such actors, the process of punishment always starts from a disruption in the flow of otherwise relatively stable social interactions. The disruption is followed by some contest or struggle that must be started, carried out, and finally brought to a conclusion in order to restore social peace. Prosecutors and defendants who have to deal with social disruption are situated within a whole "world"—an institutional, political, and social context—that they must understand how to "use" in order to produce an act of power. The story of punishment is in part the story of the nature of their efforts to use their "world" to carry out an act of power. Modern citizens are not obliged to consider directly and personally the implications of using power, of wielding cultural and institutional tools, in order to punish. Nor are we obliged to consider the components of the "world" or context within which punishment occurs and power is used. We have not been obliged (before Foucault) to notice that the institutions of punishment combine with a normative discourse that makes punishment a central component of sociopolitical order.[26]

What necessarily follows from these omissions is the further failure to ask questions about the *nature* of the concepts that constitute the system of value that underlies penal decisions. It is not only "political" concepts such as "justice," "fairness," "desert," and "law" that structure the realm of punishment and the system of value undergirding it. Concepts like passion, reason, anger, pity, free will, and necessity are also relevant although they are "ethicopsychological" and ostensibly nonpolitical. Ethicopsychological concepts are relevant to the system of value expressed by punishment because the *people* who initiate, carry through, and/or attempt to thwart a punishment are central to the process of punishing. Ideas about who can punish, about how they should behave and feel, about what kinds of knowledge they should use in the process, and about how they should structure arguments about desert are embodied in practices of punishment. If a punishment is successfully carried out, certain people and their forms of behavior have contributed to making that punishment a success. The norms governing their behavior are part of the punitive process. Punishment involves much more than penalties. We must also reflect critically on the sort of world and system of value that are constituted by the acts of power imposed with punishments.

A society's system of value is the dominant conceptual system or normative symbolic order that gives all members of a community some shared reality or habitual way of looking at things. The network of concepts underlying institutional and cultural practice can be given ideational articulation, and such conceptual systems are embedded even in customary linguistic usages (when, for instance, citizens of the United States switched from saying the "United States are" to saying the "United States is," they marked a sizable paradigm shift in the systems of value employed in the country). The central concepts of such systems of value appear in consistent patterns in institutions, cultural practices, and relatively less self-conscious forms of linguistic expression. They will also appear in a society's more self-conscious forms of linguistic expression, that is, in its literary productions, although perhaps with attempts at revision and redefinition. The relationships between the ideas about value found in institutions, cultural practices, and literary productions constitute a conversation about politics and social organization.

To think about punishment is to think about the definitions of justice and fairness that are embodied in institutions, acted out in cultural practices, and explicitly expressed in normative discourses. It is to think about the definitions of desert that sustain the authority that supports the legitimate use of force in a political society. Athens was a society in which, for the most part, citizens and city residents either punished for themselves or did not punish at all. Accordingly, any particular Athenian citizen or resident who wished to respond to a wrongdoing had to take a look around himself or herself, consider his or her social position and the institutional and cultural tools available for his or her use, and then make use of them to the best of that Athenian's ability. To succeed at punishing, Athenians had to understand the system of value employed by and embodied by the successful prosecutor. And then they themselves had to use that system of value. Accordingly, anyone who wished to punish or who tried to punish was forced to confront the nature of the political regime directly. Athenians regularly had to think about the systems of value underlying their political order. Modern citizens can avoid such modes of thought.

In Athens, the tragedians, poets, orators, and philosophers who wrote about punishment were well aware that reflection on punishment required thinking about a whole slew of concepts—such as anger, pity, desire, honor, reciprocity, gender, disease, the uses of vision and voice—that might well be assigned to private ethics or psychology rather than to politics. Of course the concepts of law, desert, and justice were also recognized as relevant. But all those who wrote about punishment in Athens recognized that one need not begin a discussion of punishment from a political concept like law or justice but could instead use a less obviously political concept as the basis for an examination of the Athenian social order. Those who identified the conceptual patterns structuring their society's system of value (as Plato did; see chapter 10) and self-consciously intervened in the system of value *as expressed linguistically and conceptually* were simultaneously intervening in the system of value as expressed institutionally and culturally.

My research here is essentially phenomenological. I am particularly interested in democratic phenomena—ranging from punishment to law to dispute resolution to property to judgment to citizenship identity. These phenomena exist within the context of institutional structures, cultural habits, and customary practices, but no given phenomenon can be split into, for instance, two parts institutional and one part cultural or vice versa. Like other phenomena a political phenomenon is a combination of institutions and culture and rests on an only intermittently stable conceptual system of value—a system by which dos and don'ts are established and particular social roles and places are assigned. In order to understand a political order, one needs to identify that conceptual system and to make the *phenomena* of human practice speak, so to speak.

We are used to reading religious ritual and cult practice and kinship structures—but not politics—in this fashion. And we are used to reading texts in order to find the conceptual tropes and "mythemes" that were crucial to a society's ways of thinking. I read Athenian politics by focusing on punishing in a similar manner in order to render audible—alongside tragedy and philosophy—certain conceptual claims inherent in the practice of Athenian democracy. My objective is to present in conversation a set of concepts like anger, desert, spectacle, and public memory that tragedians, poets, comedians, orators, philosophers, and institutions themselves all speak of as being at the heart of the Athenian system of politics and justice—and to understand the potential uses of this conversation for asking questions about modern democratic practice.[27]

PART ONE

The Preliminaries

What Is Punishment?

INTRODUCTION

Punishment has always been on someone's mind, and the ubiquity of the topic in literature affects my work here. Nearly every extant classical Greek author had something to say on the subject—so this book will be source rich. Every major political theorist since Plato has offered at least incidental comment on the topic, and many (including not only Plato but also Aristotle, Augustine, More, Hobbes, Locke, Beccaria, Kant) have seen punishment as indispensable to their study of politics and developed theories of "just punishment" to support their theories of politics. This book speaks *sotto voce* to that tradition and to influential twentieth-century studies of punishment, but especially to Foucault's *Discipline and Punish*, which has powerfully altered the self-understanding of those who practice a liberal-democratic politics. We will better understand not only Foucault but also our own ways of punishing and of doing politics if we sharpen our thinking about punishment on the stone of the unfamiliar ancient world and not always on the steel and concrete of our own modern and too intuitively familiar world.

Neither the ancient poets nor the pre-Enlightenment philosophers cared to catalogue sanctions actually imposed for particular offenses. They discussed punishment as a ubiquitous social phenomenon with significant political ramifications. The philosophers have been especially inclined to see punishment as a maddeningly persistent and unpalatable phenomenon intrinsic to the social fabric.

Historians of ancient penal practice, however, have indeed approached the topic with lists of crimes, their punishments, and the titles of those who administer them.[1] This "criminological" approach to the study of punishment asks how punishments are or were implemented in a given society.[2] This book, in contrast, investigates the ways the system of Athenian punishment interfaced with *polis* life more generally. Types of wrongdoing and their punishments are examined, but more generally I propose an understanding of punishment as a phenomenon that contributed to holding together the stable political community of ancient Athens. I start with questions about how the institutions and processes of punishment in Athens impacted other social structures, about how they served and expressed political power and authority, and about how they contributed to the construction of the web of meanings and symbols used by the Athenians to constitute democratic justice and injustice, social norms, and citizen behavior.

These historical-sociological questions have been asked in the context of modern penality with interesting results. Durkheim ushered in the historical-sociological approach to punishment with "The Two Laws of Penal Evolution." He situated punishment within other forms of social practice and explicated the cultural and symbolic functions of punishments. Weber did not write directly on punishment but he contributed to the study of authority and institutional practice and to the use of the phenomenological method in the social sciences. His work opened possibilities for thinking about the institutional and cultural forces that combine to make punishments authoritative in a given society.[3]

A pair of thinkers, Rusche and Kircheimer, took up these phenomenological tools in analyzing punishment from a Marxist perspective in *Punishment and Social Structure* (1939). They argued that a society's penal life reflects its economic life and hypothesized that societies have specific penal "tempers" stemming from economic conditions. These penal "tempers," they argued, are habitual modes of thinking about punishment and about the levels of intensity and severity with which it should be imposed. They made the claim that the ethical discourse that defines one arena of human practice (e.g., punishment) is inflected by events and changes that occur in other arenas (e.g., the market).

Foucault's 1975 *Discipline and Punish* combined these methodological paradigms to produce a quasi-Nietzschean genealogy of modern punishment that offers a comprehensive analysis of power in modern liberal-democratic constitutional regimes.[4] Foucault treated punishment not only as "repressive effects" but also as a necessarily symbiotic interaction of a society's conceptual deep structure and its political forms of authority (which he calls power-knowledge). Texts, culture, symbols, rituals, and the logic of institutions and economic practice combine in a "discourse" that articulates how a society structures a consistent reality on all fronts (bodies, subjects, practices, political orders) and enforces that reality on members of a community.

By the early 1970s, the dominant tendency in the historical-sociological study of punishment was to study punishment as a drama. The drama could be read for its symbolic meaning; its script could be parsed into roles assigned to different actors. One could consider the effect of the drama on the surrounding community before the curtain went up and after it came down. Foucault's own work is full of the metaphors of "theater," "drama," and "spectacle." Thus he argued that the "theater" of punishment expanded from the eighteenth to the nineteenth century to encompass the whole of society in a process that began as spectacle and became education. Punishment in this process turned into "forms of discipline" that function everywhere all the time.[5]

L. Gernet's work on Greek culture is a good point of departure for a historical-sociological analysis of Athenian punishment.[6] Gernet focused on specific penalties more than on the process of punishing, but he read their symbolic significance in terms of related social concepts. His analysis of "value," "prelaw and law," the "connections between punishment and religion," and "capital punishment" contributed to a body of work that treated the institutional, social, conceptual, and symbolic elements of punishing as parts of an integrated social structure. His paradigm for interpreting punishment derived from religious ritual, not drama.

My work draws on the insights of both Gernet and other twentieth-century theorists of historical and political sociology. This book takes up their questions—how can we study phenomena, how can we incorporate studies of the symbolic and ideological in studies of institutions and authority, and what is the force of punishment on social life?—more than their answers. I use Bourdieu's idea of practice, not drama or ritual, to analyze punishment. The concepts of drama and ritual imply a scripted event where the actors themselves have neither strategies nor power to affect the outcome of their activities. Bourdieu's insight is that many social experiences are driven by actors who strategically turn rules and norms of social practice to their benefit.[7] Those rules and norms are established both institutionally and culturally and have an ideational content that can be elucidated and analytically articulated—here I follow Durkheim, Weber, and Foucault.[8] That ideational content expresses some of the most deeply held conceptual structures according to which a society understands itself, defines justice to itself, and gives shape to its world. Some rules are less flexible than others or require greater effort to manipulate, but strategic actors may sometimes be willing to take on that work. The practice of punishing inevitably involves conflict over rules and norms and over consensual social organization. The concepts of drama and ritual become useful after we recognize the agency of strategic actors.

Accordingly, the present investigation of punishing in ancient Athens starts from the question, how *does* one punish in Athens? Where does the process start? What sorts of rules does a punisher engage? Where does the process end? And who is the "one" who is punishing anyway? The answers form a narrative about how different Athenians—male and female, citizen and foreigner, free and slave—moved in and out of the public and private spaces relevant to punishment in the city. For not only male citizens but also sometimes women, slaves, and foreigners wished to initiate punishment. This story follows quite different actors in diverse situations as they tried to initiate, carry through, and finalize acts of punishment. The process required first and foremost that those who wished to punish channel their anger into verbal formulations, stories, and definitions of an offender's "just deserts." Such desert claims generated and maintained the authority of public penal judgments in Athens. By examining the stratagems of these actors and the constraints they faced, as they acted on their anger and desire to punish, we improve our understanding not only of Athenian punitive space but also of Athenian justice and political culture. Athenian punishment has much to teach us not only about ancient practices of punishment but also about Athenian society, democratic ideology, and its practice. The definition of Athenian citizenship was thoroughly wrapped up in its system of punishment. My narrative thus tells two stories, one about Athenian punishment and another about its democratic politics.

"REVENGE" VERSUS "PUNISHMENT": REREADING THE *ORESTEIA*

Saunders' began *Plato's Penal Code* by dealing with the discrepancy between modern and ancient ways of thinking about punishment that has led some scholars to declare categorically that there are no punishments in the *Iliad*.[9] These scholars mean that in the *Iliad* responses to wrongdoing are not carried out according to laws and by legally instituted actors. It is true that methods of dealing with wrongdoing in the *Iliad* do not look much like modern methods, but how do we decide whether they count as "punishment"? What sort of practice are we trying to study? We must begin by asking what we mean when we say punishment.

Our intuition says that punishment resembles but finally differs from revenge; punishment is legitimate, but revenge is not. Our intuition finds quick support in analytical philosophy.

Just about everybody distinguishes punishment from revenge by arguing that revenge is focused on a personal wrong suffered; it is angry and passionate.[10] Passion is commonly thought to generate responses to wrongdoing that are neither impartial nor commensurate to the wrong. Punishment, on the other hand, is produced by an impartial judicial actor who is not personally involved in the matter and who acts in accord with law. Punishment is handed out with cool reason rather than passion. Thus the famous legal scholar H.L.A. Hart (following Flew) defines punishment in *Punishment and Responsibility* by including the criteria that "It must be for an offence against legal rules" and "It must be imposed and administered by an authority constituted by a legal system against which the offence is committed."[11] R. Nozick stresses the disinterestedness and dispassion of the agent of punishment as opposed to the agent of revenge:

1. Retribution is done for a wrong, while revenge may be done for an injury or harm or slight and need not be for a wrong.

2. Retribution sets an internal limit to the amount of the punishment, according to the seriousness of the wrong, whereas revenge integrally need set no limit to what is inflicted.

3. Revenge is personal, whereas the agent of retribution need have no special or personal tie to the victim of the wrong for which he exacts retribution.

4. Revenge involves a particular emotional tone, pleasure in the suffering of another, while retribution either need involve no emotional tone, or involves another one, namely, pleasure at justice being done. Therefore, the thirster after revenge often will want to experience (see, be present at) the situation in which the revengee is suffering, whereas with retribution there is no special point in witnessing its infliction.

5. There need be no generality in revenge . . . whereas the imposer of retribution, inflicting deserved punishment for a wrong, is committed to (the existence) of some general principles (prima facie) mandating punishment in other similar circumstances.[12]

The philosopher of punishment Cragg summarizes the several points:

> Vengeance, associated as it is with anger, bitterness, hatred, and resentment . . . takes as its focus the personal hurt caused by the wrong and is a response to that hurt and the anger it generates. Consequently, those seeking revenge frequently misjudge the harm or wrong to which they are responding. They over-react, with the results that the punishment that is inflicted is often excessive. Revenge also has a haphazard quality. . . . Just retribution requires that punishment should be in proportion to the seriousness of the offence. Punishment should not vary with the identity of the victim and it should be inflicted only for genuine wrongs . . . modern societies have delegated responsibility for infliction of serious penalties to formal state institutions. . . . Formal institutions, with a trained and impartial judiciary, would also be more likely to treat like cases alike.[13]

These definitions fortify our intuitions about the difference between "revenge" and "punishment" and seem at first glance to apply to the ancient world.

The distinction between revenge and "state punishment" is common in the historiography of Athenian politics and punishment. Ehrenberg, for instance, wrote: "When [the Greek nobles] renounced blood-vengeance and self-help, the road was opened which led to the legal supremacy of the state. Without that, there would have been no criminal jurisdiction by the state nor even a simple administrative organization." The idea that there was a historical shift from a system of revenge to one of punishment is central to many seminal analyses of politics in the ancient world. Thonissen had put it thus: "The change effected under the aristocracy was to transfer the initiative from the clan to the state. . . . The nobles said to the people, we are all one kin, and therefore all homicide is a crime against the kin to be dealt with by accredited authorities."[14]

Literary texts have been adduced to support the idea that angry private revenge was replaced by public and judicial dispassionate punishment as politics and Athens developed. The *Oresteia* has been an especially obvious target for historical interpretation because it is the only extant fifth-century Greek tragedy to give a significant dramatic role to a historical and specifically Athenian judicial institution: the homicide court called the Areopagus.[15] The *Oresteia* is a trilogy of tragedies written in the fifth century by the Athenian dramatist Aeschylus. It tells the story of the house of Atreus and its near destruction. The *Agamemnon*, the first play in the trilogy, relates how the queen of Argos Clytemnestra kills her husband Agamemnon upon his victorious return from the Trojan War. He had killed their daughter at the start of the war as sacrifice to the goddess Artemis, who had refused to provide winds for the voyage to Troy without the sacrifice.[16]

The second play, the *Libation Bearers*, makes clear that the trilogy concerns not just one act of revenge but a whole cycle. For it tells how Agamemnon's and Clytemnestra's only son Orestes comes of age, returns to Argos, and kills his mother and her lover Aegisthus in revenge for the death of his father. That play closes with the arrival of the Furies, divinities that avenge kin murder, to punish Orestes for the matricide (Aegisthus's death is irrelevant to them). They set upon Orestes as he turns away from the double murder and drive him and his blood guilt out of Argos. They pursue him first to Apollo's shrine in Delphi where he seeks shelter and then to Athens where he goes, on Apollo's advice, to supplicate Athena to judge the Furies' accusations that he is a matricide.

The arrival of Orestes in Athens, his trial, and the transformation of the Furies into the Eumenides or "well-minded" ones is the action of the *Eumenides*, the final play of the trilogy. Athena takes Orestes' case at first but then decides that murder cases are too weighty for even a goddess to decide. She refuses to render a judgment but founds a court, the Areopagus, to judge homicide in her stead thenceforth. The Furies and Orestes give speeches and the court votes, as does Athena who also declares that a split vote will mean acquittal for the defendant. Sure enough, the votes turn out to be tied and so Orestes is released from the accusations and from his blood guilt.[17] The Furies, however, are left furious by the acquittal and so the final third of the play consists of Athena's efforts to pacify them. This she manages to do and turns them into beneficent deities who will dwell in Athens ever after and work to protect the city.

Critics have argued that the institution of the Areopagus homicide court and the conversion of the Furies "constitute a permanent rejection of the precivilized 'justice' of the vendetta, and the victorious enthronement at Athens of a new Justice which is both legal and civic."[18] One commentator credits the invention of the Areopagus with establishing the rule that "punishment for wrongs done is to be inflicted, not by the person wronged or his/her representative, but by an independent authority not taking vengeance in a spirit of wrathful fury but hearing the arguments on both sides and then coming to a rational decision."[19] We hear that "blind retribution" finally becomes "justice, rooted in holiness, governed by reason" when the "Eumenides," the pacified goddesses, promise to bestow their blessings on the city forevermore.[20] The traditional reading of the trilogy presents a triumphalist advance from political systems of "revenge" to systems of "punishment." It is seen as depicting progress from a primitive stage of politics, linked to the concepts of anger, vendetta, self-interest, and self-help or private action and to a more developed stage of politics characterized by "punishment" linked to concepts of cool dispassion, impartiality, legality, reason, and public judicial forms of penal action. The distinction between "revenge" and "punishment" has seemed useful in thinking about historical process and literary texts. To our intuitions, the definitions of these terms seem settled.

But was punishment in Athens (or punishment by the Areopagus) a dispassionate, disinterested, wholly legal affair, carried out by state agents removed from the private passions and anger of those who had been wronged by a fellow member of the city? Virginia Hunter's *Policing Athens* (1993) persuasively makes the case that the developed Athenian democracy relied extensively on private action for the accomplishment of public order and conflict resolution. Private citizens could even execute some forms of punishment without passing through the court system at all. For instance, a private citizen was within the bounds of the law if he killed a thief or adulterer whom he caught in his house at night. He did not need to claim self-defense in order to justify his act (cf. Exodus 20.21). S. Todd has made a similar argument, that "the detection and prosecution of offences at Athens remained at all times the responsibility of private individuals."[21]

D. Cohen's *Law, Violence, and Community in Classical Athens* argues that in Athens political institutions developed precisely so as to provide public means of carrying on private wars of vendetta: "litigation . . . involved the opportunity to take revenge for wrongs, to display and validate one's claims to status, and to contest one's claims to honor with those of one's rivals."[22] Punishment in Athens was not the exclusive prerogative of public officials nor was it dispassionate, and at times it was not even in conformity with specific legal procedures. The arguments of Hunter, Todd, and Cohen are somewhat too one-sided, for they neglect the degree to which city officials *could* take punitive steps and the ways in which such private action was figured as having a public value. But they rightly stress the orientation of Athenian systems of penality on the victim, passion, and even noninstitutional procedures. Our intuitive distinction between "revenge" and "punishment" breaks down in face of the record.[23]

The "revenge" versus "punishment" reading of the *Oresteia* runs into similar problems. The conventional reading of the trilogy ignores at least two factors about the transition from pre-Areopagite to post-Areopagite justice that do not accord with the analysis established by the terms "prepolitical revenge" and "political punishment." First, judicial activity and judges are not actually a novelty when the Areopagus appears in the trilogy and, second, anger in no way disappears from punishment even after the Areopagus does appear.[24]

Electra does not need to know about the Areopagus before she can consider using a judge to resolve the city's problem of the murder of Agamemnon. Thus the chorus in the *Libation Bearers*, the second play, prays that some spirit or mortal will come to the aid of Argos, and Electra asks whether they are asking for a judge (*dikastes*, 120) or an avenger (*dikephoron*).[25] Apollo too sends Orestes to Athens precisely because he expects him to find judges there (*dikastas, Eum.* 81). Nor is Orestes surprised by the suggestion: he arrives in Athens with the supposition that he should find a judge there and accordingly asks Athena herself to judge him. He uses the standard legal phrase "judge the suit" as if he were well familiar with the process (*krinon diken*) (465–71). Athena also uses judicial language familiarly when she says that she will not act as a judge herself (*diairein dikas*) but will appoint sworn judges of murder (*dikastas phonon*) (472–83). In the *Eumenides*, it is not the activity of judging that is new, but rather its particular form in the Areopagus. The institution of the Areopagus is not the origin of judicial processes in general but of some specific kind of judicial proceeding.

This new type of judgment differs from the old in four respects: first, the Areopagus has Athena's mandate; second, judgments are left to a collective body, not to some single judge (as Electra expects); third, as Zeitlin has pointed out, after Athena's decision affairs of justice and anger are carried out by mortal men of significant reputation and not by ugly, haglike, unmarried (if immortal) women;[26] and fourth, after the institution of the Areopagus, decisions to act on anger no longer proceed automatically: the Erinyes followed the scent of spilt blood "mechanistically," but the court cannot guarantee the particular outcomes of its proceedings. The invention of the Areopagus and the use of the vote introduced a certain degree of uncertainty and indeterminacy in the system of responding to wrongdoing.

The Areopagite style of judgment, however, resembles the old forms of judgment in one crucial respect: it was not coolly distant from anger. Athena specifically assigns to her new court the characteristic of "a quickness to anger" (*oxuthumon, Eum* 705), an expression that Sophocles used later to describe the old and blind Oedipus who curses his sons for expelling him from Thebes (*OC* 1194) and Aristophanes used to describe the furious jurors of the *Wasps* (406).[27] Athena does not so much distance the new court from the Erinyes as draw a parallel between them. She describes the court's duties with a speech that closely echoes the earlier choral ode that the Erinyes sang to describe their own duties (*Eum.* 521–47). Like the Erinyes, the Areopagus is expected to inspire fear and dread in the citizenry and to ward off anarchy and tyranny, while being quick to anger (*Eum.* 696–710).[28] The "punishing" Areopagus takes over the work of the "avenging" Erinyes and is assimilated to them. They also take over their tasks of anger without actually being enjoined to heel to the laws. The relationship of the Areopagus to law is at best ambiguous.[29]

The Areopagus is not the only body that is allowed to persist in the use of anger for the "Furies" never really become "Eumenides" or the "Well-minded Ones." The title of the third play, *Eumenides*, is a post-Aeschylean invention, and the name "Furies" is a Latinization. Neither name is used in the trilogy itself: the goddesses are designated as Erinyes when they are pursuing Orestes and as Semnai Theai (revered goddesses) after they have left off their pursuit.[30] These names are less easily mapped onto a stark "revenge-punishment" dichotomy than "Furies" and "Eumenides." Nor are the Semnai Theai by any means entirely pacific creatures after they have been installed as deities in Athens. They retain their anger (*orge*), and Athena describes their new role without disavowing their earlier darker powers. She says:

> I do these things, and take forethought for these citizens, in settling here great and implacable spirits. The management of all human affairs has been allotted to them. Whoever has not found them weighty does not know where life's blows come from. The offenses of his ancestors lead him before these spirits; destruction comes silently and, with an enemy's anger [*echthrais orgais*], it levels the one who was boasting greatly. (*Eum.* 926–36)

The Semnai Theai remain deities who give song to some and tears to others (949–955).[31] The Erinyes abandon their anger toward Athens in respect specifically to the case of Orestes (*methistamai kotou*, 900), but they retain their anger in general and can apply it against other wrongdoers and against the enemies of Athens (984–86).[32]

What then is left of our distinction between "revenge" and "punishment"? And why has it been so easy to apply these categories to Athenian history and to the *Oresteia*? The one element that has survived our redefinition of punishment is the idea of "legitimacy." Acts of revenge are illegitimate responses to wrongdoing; acts of punishment are legitimate and therefore authoritative responses. The Erinyes' attempts to respond to wrongdoing did not carry authority; the Areopagus's response does. In the first two plays of the trilogy, first Clytemnestra, then Orestes, and finally the Erinyes claimed to punish a wrongdoer. The legitimacy of each penal agent's acts, however, was contested. The Areopagus is the first penal agent whose punitive decisions are uncontested. Each and every one of the characters agrees not to challenge its decision; the self-restraint of Orestes, Apollo, and the Erinyes makes the authority of the Areopagus conclusive.[33] For that matter, their self-restraint or acquiescence *makes* the authority itself. The trilogy models the transition from a situation where no particular method of responding to wrongdoing has authority to a system where one method of responding to wrongdoing can deal conclusively with social disruption.

The self-restraint of the Erinyes that "makes" the authority of the Areopagus is hard won, however. Athena labors through most of the last third of the *Eumenides* to produce this acquiescence. Immediately after the acquittal, the Erinyes are not willing to accept the decision. Athena threatens violence and promises rewards to get the Erinyes eventually to concede the finality of the court's decision, which they do.[34] The Erinyes become Semnai Theai only after and because they become acquiescent. The one fourth-century orator to refer to the mythical transformation of the Erinyes does not praise the goddesses for having ceded anger but for having become willing to accept "truths" determined by the Areopagus. Dinarchus rouses his audience by encouraging it to act like the "Semnai Theai [who] established themselves for all time as partners [*sunoikous*] in what resulted from the council's judgments and as partners in their truth [*autai hai semnai theai tei pros Oresten en toutoi toi sunedrioi krisei genomenei kai tei toutou aletheiai sunoikous heautas eis ton loipon chronon katestesan*]" (Din. 1.87). This fourth-century orator treats the trilogy as a story of how a single final and legitimate authority eventually arose out of a contest over authority and legitimacy. The act of the Areopagus, unlike that of the Erinyes, carries final authority.

The final authority of the Areopagus rests not on its use of law or on its dispassion but on divine mandate, collective judgment, male control, the use of a vote, and anger.[35] Athena appoints the court by claiming that she is making a rule (*thesmon*) for all time (*eis hapanta chronon*, 484); the Areopagus will always be the only body with authority to decide homicide cases. She intends the court to be not only a *final authority* but also a *permanent authority*. The authority that will sustain the court's punishments, however, is quite different from the authority that sustains modern punishments.

The modern definition of punishment as a legal, dispassionate, and disinterested response to wrongdoing is in effect a *species* definition of punishment.

A more general definition of punishment (or the *genus* definition) would call it "a response to a designated wrongdoing that has staved off contestation of its legitimacy and that has garnered acquiescence and thereby become authoritative and final." The authority used to support punishment differs from one political regime to another. (Saunders puts it thus: "What we must not do is to confuse the marks of a system of punishment with the marks of the concept of punishment; for there may be many systems . . . each embodying the concept.")[36] Criteria used in the Anglo-American context to constitute penal authority have to do with conceptualizations of legality, rationality, and the relationships between citizens, the state, and one another. The authority of the Aeschylean Areopagus is constituted by divine mandate, maleness, and the status accorded to majority vote or collective judgment. To study punishment (as opposed to revenge) requires attention to the ways that particular responses to wrongdoing become authoritative within any given society.

What does this mean for our present project? I accede to our intuitive need for a distinction between revenge and punishment and begin from the following definitions of revenge and punishment:

1. Acts of revenge are responses to acts designated as wrongdoing that are carried out by actors *without final authority* whose responses are also *without authority and whose legitimacy is contested*. (Acts of torture are, in some cases, comparable with "revenge" in this sense).

2. Acts of punishment are responses to acts designated as wrongdoing that are carried out by actors *with authority* whose acts are carried out *on the basis of authority and whose legitimacy is (largely and practically) final and uncontested*.

a. The authority that is the basis for punishment may be political, familial, or institutional (or something else entirely), and "punishment" is a term that can be applied to what parents and other agents do, as well as to what the state or political organs do.

b. The authority that supports "punishment" may (and probably will) be constituted differently in different societies and different social orders: for example, in the family, firm, classroom, or politics. This means that the authority supporting punishment need not be created with "laws" but may be created through other mechanisms of legitimation.

c. *Authority is created by acquiescence, but authority is also that which is capable of creating acquiescence.* As what creates acquiescence, *authority is a set of inducements (rational or otherwise) to acquiescence.* The inducements prod the acquiescence, until acquiescence in turn makes the methods of inducement authoritative and final. Every stable democratic punitive system depends on a set of inducements (e.g., legality, impartiality, public action) that are accepted by the greater part of the social group, with little or no prodding.

Punishment is about authority in the first instance and about law, dispassion, and disinterestedness only in certain contexts. Once we realize this, we have to study punishment as "a practice of constructing authority" and not as "the practice of applying laws disinterestedly." We therefore have to ascertain *how* to study practices of constructing authority.

Studying Punishment as Authority: Reading the *Prometheus Bound*

The *Prometheus Bound*, generally thought to be another Aeschylean tragedy, offers us a text on the construction of authority. The central issue is precisely whether Zeus's attempt to punish Prometheus will be taken authoritatively or treated as an act of torture against which all who look upon Prometheus must rebel. I now leave the *Oresteia* behind as a model for understanding the relation between punishment and democratic politics, not because *Prometheus Bound* is my model for studying punishment, not because I think that the narrative structure of individual tragedies maps directly on to the political situation in Athens (see chapter 3), and not because we need to take literary texts as theoretical models, but only because the *Prometheus* exquisitely illustrates my analytical framework.[37]

Prometheus Bound may or may not have been written by Aeschylus, but it was certainly written in the fifth century and known in Athens.[38] Like the *Oresteia*, the *Prometheus* concerns the problem of punishment and a *novus ordo saeculorum*. The story is based on the attempt of Zeus, ruler of the gods, to punish the Titan Prometheus for stealing fire from the gods and giving it to mortals. As the play opens, two of Zeus's thugs named Kratos and Bia have just escorted Prometheus to a desolate rock on "the edge of the world" and are now forcing Hephaestus, the divine blacksmith, to fetter him. The binding is complete by line 81.

The fact that Prometheus is in his fetters by line 81 has prompted some critics to suggest that the drama about Prometheus's punishment is over before the play has even begun. Schmid called the tragedy "the poorest in action of all Greek plays" because "a person chained to a rock has little opportunity for action."[39] These scholars treat the physical implementation of a punishment as the narrative telos of a story of punishment. The play, however, continues past this moment of implementation and thereby forces us to recognize that punishment extends beyond the implementation of a penalty to the struggle to convince a society that it is a penalty, not an act of violence. The binding may be complete by line 81, but we are not yet certain whether it is an act of punishment or an act of torture.

Prometheus is the only character on the stage for the duration of the play and spends his time arguing repeatedly that he does not deserve his punishment. The first words out of Prometheus's mouth are:

> O divine ether and sweet-winged breezes and running waters of the rivers, and infinite laughter of the waves of the ocean, universal mother earth and all-seeing orbit of the sun, I call you; look at me [*idesthe m' hoia pascho*], at the sort of things that I, who am a god, suffer from the other gods. Behold [*derchtheth'*] how I will struggle for thousands of years wasted away by such outrages [*hoiais aikeiaisin*]. (87–92)

Outrages (*aikiai*) were acts that could be subject to punitive prosecution in Athens. Prometheus claims that Zeus wrongs him and thereby interprets his binding not as just punishment but as a wrongdoing that is itself susceptible to punishment.[40] He so much desires to punish Zeus out of anger (*orgas*, 315, 377–80; *trachus*, 311)—Zeus had also punished him out of anger (*orge*, 80, 190; *cholos*, 29, 376; *trachus*, 35, 80, 186, 324)—that he determines to keep to himself information Zeus desperately wants to know: who is the hero who will eventually overthrow Zeus's rule unless Zeus manages to prevent his birth? By keeping this secret Prometheus "punishes" (*tinein poinas*) Zeus for binding him (167–77). Zeus has only recently won a war against the Titans for control over the universe, and he has punished Prometheus partly to stabilize his rule. Prometheus's rebellion threatens a young insecure regime. Throughout the play, Prometheus's arguments that he does not deserve his punishment are intertwined with arguments that Zeus does not deserve to rule. The challenge to his punishment is a straightforward challenge to Zeus's political authority.[41]

Prometheus's challenges to Zeus's authority provide the play a fixed focal point. Every character who appears on stage—Zeus's thugs, Kratos and Bia, the divine blacksmith Hephaestus, the divine messenger Hermes, and Prometheus's several visitors (his water-nymph cousins, the Oceanids, then Oceanus, the father of these water nymphs; and finally a tormented Io, the young woman who had been transformed into a cow by the lusty Zeus and driven on endless wanderings by his jealous wife Hera)—has to look at Prometheus and judge the nature and justness of his suffering. The audience of the play must also make up its mind how to judge Prometheus's suffering, a judgment that determines whether Zeus's act is authoritative and final.

The opening scene of the play poses the question of authority in its very iconography.[42] Zeus's minions, Kratos and Bia, or Sovereign Rule and Violent Force, have escorted Prometheus and Hephaestus to the edge of the earth where Hephaestus has been ordered to bind his equally divine relative to a craggy rock.[43] Of the two "Machtinstrumenten," it is Bia or Force who is silent.[44] Prometheus has been brought under physical control, and Bia can stand to the side, nothing more than a silent threat, her active work done. Kratos—sovereignty or authority—speaks the first lines of the play; its starting point is thus the idea that sovereignty or authority still has work to do, even as Prometheus is being bound.

Kratos straightway begins that work with a domineering announcement to the audience, to Hephaestus, and to Prometheus that Prometheus needs to learn to acquiesce in the rule of Zeus and to cease from his earlier man-loving behavior (1–11). Prometheus, he says, is a malefactor (*leorgon*), who has stolen (*klepsas*) and must (*dei*) suffer punishment (*dounai diken*) for his errors (*hamartias*) (1–11). Kratos paints the god as a wrongdoer who must be bound because he deserves to pay the price for "errors." Prometheus is a "*leorgon*" or criminal who has "stolen." Kratos has to name Prometheus as a wrongdoer to make him such, and his vocabulary of wrongdoing is perfectly consistent with the vocabulary of wrongdoing that is found in the mouths of Athenian orators when they make accusations.[45] Kratos thus opens the play by asserting and affirming both the legitimacy of Prometheus's punishment and the legitimacy of Zeus's authority with an explanation of why Zeus's treatment of Prometheus should be seen as legitimate and authoritative. Kratos provides a sort of official summary of Prometheus's desert that relies on a conventional vocabulary of wrongdoing, and his statement serves to tell the other characters on stage (as well as the audience) why they should acquiesce in and accept the binding of Prometheus as an act of punishment.

Hephaestus is the next character to confront the legitimacy of Prometheus's binding. He is the blacksmith who must attach Prometheus's fetters; the question of whether Prometheus's punishment will be completed, from a practical (or criminological) point of view, rests with him. The binding is delayed when Hephaestus is not convinced by Kratos's officialese; he is unwilling to bind a kinsman and fellow god (*sungene theon* 12–14).[46] His unwillingness is a challenge to the validity of the punishment and jeopardizes its completion. Hephaestus chews over the matter by rehearsing Kratos's reason why Prometheus should be bound: Prometheus gave honors (*timas*) to mortals beyond what was appropriate (*pera dikas*). But Hephaestus's analysis leads him to the conclusion that Zeus rules harshly (*trachus*) because he is a new ruler (*neon kratei*, 28–34). In tragedy only illegitimate rulers, tyrants in the negative sense of the word, are referred to as "new" rulers.[47] By remarking that Zeus is harsh, Hephaestus suggests that the punishment is too great for Prometheus's offense and undeserved. His assessment that Zeus's response is harsh evolves into a challenge to the legitimacy of Zeus's rule in general, the slur that Zeus is a "new" ruler. Again, an opinion on Prometheus's desert is enmeshed in a statement on whether Zeus acts with authority.

Kratos realizes that Hephaestus is unwilling to bind Prometheus and tries to bring him round to Zeus's side with concerns about status and divine solidarity. He counters: "Why don't you hate the god hated by all the other gods and who betrayed your honors [*geras*] to mortals?" (36–37). But Hephaestus again objects to having to punish a kinsman and companion (*to suggenes, he homilia*, 39). Kratos admits (40) that the claims of kinship militate against executing the punishment but argues boldly that the will of Zeus should be treated with greater reverence than the claims of kinship (*sumphem'· anekoustein de ton patros logon / hoion te pos; ou touto deimaineis pleon;*). Kratos thus reveals that his commission from Zeus is the task of authority: to make the subjects of Zeus, Hephaestus most immediately, simply acquiesce to Zeus's assessment of what Prometheus deserves. The question of whether Zeus's response will be treated as authoritative and brought to completion by his subordinates is shown to hang on the negotiation of "social" and "political" values: kinship, equality, status-honor, and respect for Zeus's will.

The contest over Prometheus's desert is staged as spectacle: how should he, fettered to the rock, be judged by onlookers? Hephaestus half-finishes the binding and then pauses to reflect:

The spectacle you look upon is not a pleasant sight for the eyes.
(*horais theama dustheaton ommasin.*)

(69)

Kratos responds:

I see a man who is getting confirmation about what he deserves.
(*horo kurounta tonde ton epaxion.*)
Throw the iron girdles around his chest!

(70–71)

Hephaestus and Kratos look at Prometheus half bound to the rock and each sees something different. Hephaestus sees an undeserved misfortune and unpleasant spectacle. He refuses to accept Zeus's formulation of desert, and so he does not even see a punishment before his eyes. His assessment of Zeus's behavior as "harsh" delegitimizes Zeus's punishment of Prometheus. Hephaestus continually interrupts and delays the binding by contesting Zeus's view of what Prometheus deserves.

Kratos, however, sees a wrongdoer whose desert (*epaxion*) is, in fact, confirmed by the act of punishment. To "see a punishment" is to accept the formulation of desert that underlies it. Kratos sees a punishment *because* he sees an appropriate application of a formulation of desert. He can therefore command that the punishment continue. "Throw the iron girdles round his chest," he says. Kratos's acceptance of Zeus's formulation of Prometheus's desert is what allows, and even requires, the iron bonds of punishment to fall into place. His judgment about desert leads straight to the penal action. Spectacle challenges consent.

Kratos never succeeds in soliciting Hephaestus's verbal acquiescence to the actual formulation of desert used by Zeus and his minions to legitimate Prometheus's punishment.[48] He has, however, revealed the methods employed in his effort to shore up Zeus's shaky authority. Kratos wants Hephaestus to *see* the same thing as he does when he looks at Prometheus. The negotiation is a contest over how to interpret the spectacle of someone's pain.[49] He tries to effect this by employing administrative conventions of a sort—the official language of wrongdoing—and by negotiating Hephaestus's social and political views of the world. Hephaestus's ethical norms and "ideological" positions, and not just his metallurgical skills, factor into Kratos's attempt to render Zeus's effort at punishing authoritative.

The debate between Kratos and Hephaestus clarifies what is required to make a punishment authoritative. Onlookers or participants in the imposition of force on an accused wrongdoer will acquiesce only if the act of force is sustained by a cogent argument about *desert* that the onlookers are willing to consider legitimate. Those who do not accept formulations of desert reject not only the "punishment" itself but also the legitimacy of the political power that administers the punishment. The action of the play consists of a series of characters who witness the spectacle of Prometheus and decide how to interpret what each "sees" in his binding and physical suffering.[50] Punishment presents a spectacle that forces the audience to contest or to accede to the definition of desert used to support the punishment.

The references to vision and visibility in the argument between Hephaestus and Kratos are recapitulated throughout the play (e.g., 144–52, 304–10, 235–44). "Sight" words predominate more in this play than in any other Aeschylean play.[51] Punishment involves not only the punisher and the punished—each of whom is likely to define what the wrongdoer suffers in a contradictory way—but also an audience of citizen onlookers who must inevitably take one side or the other.

The play progresses as one after another character has to assess Prometheus's punishment and, with that, Zeus's legitimacy.[52] The Oceanids, Oceanus, and Io stress the effect of the spectacle of Prometheus on them immediately upon arrival.[53] Thus the Oceanids: "I see Prometheus [*leusso Prometheu*]. A fearful mist replete with tears descends over my eyes [*ossois*] as I look at [*eisidousa*] your body withered away on the rock by these adamantine forms of maltreatment [*lumais*]. The rulers ruling Olympus are new, and Zeus rules despotically [*athetos*] with new laws [*neochmois nomois*]" (144–52). Like Hephaestus, the Oceanids reject the binding and simultaneously Zeus's authority. They term the binding maltreatment (*lumais*) rather than punishment, and like Hephaestus, they call Zeus a new ruler who rules despotically.

Then the Oceanids ask Prometheus why he is bound, why he deserves the punishment, and how he will respond to the punishment: "Reveal everything [*pant' ekkalupson*], and give us a speech explaining the reason for which Zeus has seized you and maltreats you thus dishonorably and bitterly [*poioi . . . ep' aitiamati / houtos atimos kai pikros aikizetai*, 196–99)."[54] Unlike Kratos, these characters arrive on the scene without conclusive conceptualizations of Prometheus's desert and ask to know the "reasons" (*aitiamata*) for the binding.

All the characters ask questions like this and the answers that they receive reveal that situations of punishment are susceptible to multiple narrative determinations.[55] Consider the following exchange (235–46) between Prometheus and the Oceanids:

> *Prometheus:* I delivered mortals from having to go to Hades in great destruction. For doing this, I am bent in miseries that are miserable to suffer and pitiable to see [*oiktraisin d'idein*]. Out of pity, I put mortals ahead of myself, but I myself am not thought to deserve [*ouk exiothen*] pity; unpitied I am brought into measure [*errhuthmismai*]; to Zeus I am a spectacle of ill-repute [*Zeni dusklees théa*].
> *Oceanids:* Anyone who does not grieve for your calamities is iron-hearted and made of stone. I never wanted to see [*eisidein*] such things, and my heart is miserable as I look on [*eisidousa*] them.
> *Prometheus:* To friends I am indeed pitiable to look at [*philois eleinos eisoran ego*].

Prometheus's single punishment affords two distinct views to spectators: the one of ill-repute favored by Zeus, or the pitiable one favored by friends of Prometheus. Punishments, if they are to be authoritative, must persuade onlookers to take the side of the person who punishes. The Oceanids resolve to pity Prometheus and remain his friends; their choice is a rejection of Zeus's formulation of desert and of his authority. The nature of Prometheus's bondage thus passes through several definitions during the course of the play: sometimes it is "maltreatment" and sometimes it is "punishment." This over-determination is what unsettles Zeus's attempt at authority and produces political ambiguity.

The Oceanids challenge Zeus's conceptualizations of desert on several grounds. They begin by basing their arguments on their opinions about law (148–52) and then on the basis of their opinions about anger (159–66). As we have seen, they say that Zeus rules with new and therefore illegitimate laws. They also argue that he is miserable-hearted (*tlesikardios*) since he is so angrily inflexible (*ho d' epikotos aei themenos agnampton noon*) in his attempt to subdue the offspring of Uranus. His inflexible anger is likely to continue such excesses until either his heart is sated (*koresei kear*) or someone seizes his stolen rule (*dusaloton archan*). The description of Zeus's rule as stolen is, of course, another challenge to the king's authority. The Oceanids finally challenge Zeus's conceptualization of desert on the basis of their opinions about reciprocity. Prometheus had helped Zeus to win the war against the Titans, even though he was himself a Titan. Zeus owes Prometheus a favor in return for this (*toiad ex emou ho ophelemenos*), but Zeus has nonetheless been willing to inflict evil penalties on him (*kakaisi poinais*) (221–25). In Prometheus's explanation of his plight this point leads the Oceanids to cry out in pity (244–45). The opinions of the Oceanids on these matters of anger, law, and reciprocity all contribute to their assessment of Prometheus's desert and their rejection of Zeus's authority.

It is at the point when the Oceanids begin to grant Prometheus their support that Prometheus's claims that he suffers "outrages" evolve into an increasingly rebellious threat against Zeus's rule. Prometheus tries to draw the Oceanids into a plot against Zeus, but to his dismay, the Oceanids' nascent rejection of Zeus's desert formulations and of the divine king's authority falters at this point. Their rejection of Zeus will be revived when they have to deal with his unjust treatment of Io, but for the time being they change their minds about Prometheus and switch over to Zeus's point of view.[56] One fact in particular is decisive in their change of heart.

Prometheus gave fire to *mortals*—an act that produced a drastic shift in the balance of the honors (*timas*) distributed between gods and mortals (247–58). For the sea nymphs, the issue of status ultimately overrides the issues of law, anger, and reciprocity. The Oceanids finally acquiesce to Zeus's authority because the social and political conceptions that they bring to bear in considering Prometheus's punishment eventually produce an assessment of desert that coincides with Zeus's assessment. The result is that they change their minds about how to interpret the spectacle offered to them by Zeus. They change their minds about what they see in Prometheus's punishment and say to him finally: "How can things be as [you say]? Do you not see [*horais*] that you erred [*hoti hema-rtes*]?" (259–60). The Oceanids are willing to accept the official vocabulary of desert—the vocabulary of *hamartia* that Kratos first introduced—once they change their minds about what they see. Like Kratos, they now use the term "error," and they emphasize their word choice: "To say [*legein*] 'you erred' [*hos d' hemartes*] is no pleasure for me and it is painful for you" (261). The Oceanids accept the official formulations of desert, and reinforce their acceptance by adopting the vocabulary of authority. The binding is now closer to being a final act of punishment and farther away from being a maltreatment that requires retribution in turn.

Zeus remained a "new tyrant" in the eyes of the Oceanids for as long they refused to accept Zeus's assessment of desert. The Oceanids equally remained unruly, potentially rebellious subjects and therefore a threat to Zeus's power for as long as they refused to accept his formulation of desert. Zeus's political power in general and not only his punitive power is made more secure by their final acquiescence. The Oceanids even encourage Prometheus to submit to his punishment: "The wise make obeisance [*proskunountes*] to Adrasteia [the spirit of Nemesis]" (936). Prometheus understands that what is at stake is not just the definition of his desert but also authority more generally. He shouts insults at the nymphs: "Revere, bow down, cringe before the perpetual ruler" (*sebou, proseuchou, thopte ton kratount' aei*, 937). Prometheus insults the nymphs with triple emphasis on their acquiescence—they revere, bow down, *and* cringe— and their meekness will allow Zeus to rule eternally. Prometheus thus reveals that he is well aware that to accept his punishment is to accept the legitimacy and authority of the power that is inflicting his physical pain.

How does Zeus respond to the contestation of his authority and the challenge to his assessment of desert? Initially his responses to the contestation are carried out through his ministers. Late in the play Zeus's messenger Hermes arrives on the scene to get matters under control.[57] Like Kratos, Hermes immediately declaims about Prometheus's desert in officialese: "You sophist [*sophistes*],[58] you bitterly bitter one, who erred [*exhamartonta*] by giving the honors [*timas*] of the gods to ephemeral creatures, I say [*lego*] you are a thief [*klepten*] of fire" (944–46). Hermes works from the moment of his arrival to shore up Zeus's authority by reexecuting Kratos's rhetorical pattern and by deploying the official vocabulary of value.[59] But Hermes also has another trick up his sleeve: more intense punishments. He threatens that Zeus will lock Prometheus up in Tartarus and eventually set an eagle upon his liver unless he reveals the secret of Zeus's potential conqueror (1007–35). Hermes has introduced another tool of Zeus's official power: the hierarchy of punishments and the threat of alternate or additional penalties.[60]

Throughout the play, Prometheus refuses to acquiesce in Zeus's attempts to generate authority whether those are carried out through verbal assertions of desert or through physical force—whether through *kratos* or through *bia*. In the beginning of the play, Prometheus had taken this position: "He will not charm me with his honey-tongued songs of persuasion [*m' outi meliglossois peithous / epaoidaisin thelxei*]; neither will his stubborn threats [*apeilas ptexas*] have an impact on me and make me speak before he releases me from these savage bonds [*ex agrion desmon*] and is willing to pay the penalty for this outrage [*poinas te tinein / tesd' aikias ethelesei*] (167–78).[61] At the end of the play, he continues in the same spirit: "It's as much good to bother me as to speak to a wave" (1001–6; cf. 987–96). His rebellion earns him further punishment.

The tragedy concludes as Zeus gives up on Kratos and his efforts to construct authority by means of verbal persuasion. He resorts to the force of Bia and blasts Prometheus with thunderbolts.[62] Amid the crash of thunder, Prometheus calls out: "The earth is shaken! Mother, sky, see what injustices [*ekdika*] I suffer!" (1094). The binding can still be called an injustice even in the play's final scene. Even at this point, Zeus's punishment is not authoritative, final, and uncontested.

We do not know what happened in the next plays of the trilogy for they are lost.[63] The mythological tradition, however, as well as some small fragments from a play called *Prometheus Unbound*, allow us to carry on with at least the outline of the story.[64] The thunderbolts strike just before Prometheus is hurled into Tartarus. Zeus locks him up there with the other Titans whom he has already imprisoned, but even in Tartarus Prometheus refuses to submit. Zeus eventually despairs of this second punishment and returns Prometheus, still shackled to his rock, to the upper world and sends the famous and horrific eagle to eat out Prometheus's liver every day (or every third day) as a third and final punishment.[65]

For the Zeus of the *Prometheus Bound* and *Unbound*, it was not enough, in light of his politically unstable situation, that formerly rebellious subjects like the Oceanids had acquiesced in his assessment of desert. He needed Prometheus's own acquiescence in order to legitimize his rule. Zeus tried two different methods, beyond the original punishment, to achieve Prometheus's acquiescence: imprisonment in Tartarus and the hungry eagle. Each new punishment increased the intensity of the physical violence applied to Prometheus. The three punishments therefore constitute a hierarchy of punishments. A lack of textual evidence prevents us from assessing Aeschylus's treatment of these punishments, but we can nonetheless read them as mythological symbols that played a role in the Athenian imaginary and its interpretations of the use of power and force by authority.[66]

Zeus's basis for choosing each different form of punishment is explicitly political. He decides to increase the level of punishment after Prometheus's challenges to his rule had evolved into explicit prophesies of overthrow. He resorts to the thunderbolt only after his ministers, Kratos and Hermes, have been unable, with assertions of desert, to establish his authority. Zeus's actions imply an expectation that different penal techniques, increasingly intense penalties, will have different political impacts. Each punishment handles differently the need to get acquiescence from the wrongdoer and the possibility that onlookers will repudiate Zeus's judgment.

The first punishment, the expulsion of Prometheus to the edge of the earth, gave Prometheus the opportunity to acquiesce in Zeus's punishment and to encourage others to do so as well, but he contests his punishment. The second punishment acknowledges Prometheus's unwillingness to acquiesce and shuts him away from public view, allowing him to be consumed in the bowels of the Earth where no one will see him.[67] The imprisonment of Prometheus with the Titans in Tartarus not only prevents Prometheus from encouraging other people to reject his punishment but also gives him an explicit and unambiguous status label.[68] He has been locked up with people who actually fought against Zeus in the war that has just been concluded. The acquiescence of the community in the punishment is thereby made more secure. The acquiescence of the wrongdoer, however, has still not been achieved.

Prometheus is a political threat to Zeus so long as he refuses to acquiesce, as is any wrongdoer whose principles for action stand in direct opposition to the principles defining the public sphere. Accordingly, Zeus needs another way to deal with him. For his third punishment, Prometheus is once again expelled to the outer edges of the world and there, removed from society, he is consumed by an eagle just as an unburied corpse would be consumed by scavenging animals. Triomphe sees the daily exposure of Prometheus to a bird of prey as the immortal equivalent to what happened to mortal wrongdoers when, after execution, their corpses suffered exposure. On Triomphe's view the exposure of the corpse utterly reconstituted and relabeled the wrongdoer.

It is significant that the eagle gnaws out Prometheus's liver, the organ considered to be the seat of both lust and anger in archaic and classical texts.[69] Prometheus' brother Tityus, who had committed an act of wrongdoing involving excessive lust, also had an eagle set upon him to consume his stomach or liver. The bird that consumed his liver consumed his lust.[70] In *Prometheus Bound* anger was the psychological power driving not only Zeus's punishment of Prometheus but also Prometheus's refusal to accept Zeus's authority. The bird devours Prometheus's anger when it preys on his liver. Zeus has found a punishment that will allow him to put an end to the very force—anger—that has led to the challenges to and contestation of his authority in the first place. Zeus is literally reforming Prometheus into acquiescence by re-forming and reconstituting his body. Zeus has to eradicate that force which leads to the irreconcilable conflict between him and Prometheus in order to establish his authority and to stabilize his unstable rule.[71]

The three levels of force illustrated in the punishments correspond to three different methods of stabilizing a conception of desert and making it final and authoritative. The punisher can allow the punished to acquiesce publicly in the assessment of desert. The punisher can dramatically label the punished with a certain status label and prevent the wrongdoer from having any say in undoing the label by locking the wrongdoer away. Or the punisher can get rid of that which is an irremediable threat to his or her penal and political authority. The less Zeus can afford contestation, the more severe and violent his penalties are.

I began this reading of *Prometheus Bound* in order to illustrate the investigative framework applicable to the study of "punishment" defined as "authoritative responses to wrongdoing."[72] Prometheus's punishment generates an entire drama based on his penal situation. The play in effect parses the mechanism of authority. It reminds us that obtaining physical control over someone designated as a wrongdoer is by no means the whole story of punishment. Looked at closely, any punishment is not a single final moment of execution but, and more important, an *unfolding drama about the attempt to establish a final moment as authoritative*. That drama is moved forward by *strategic actors* who contest one another's definitions of *desert*.

In order to understand the production of authority, we need to investigate the practice of punishing as an unfolding process with beginnings and middles, as well as ends. We need to look at the different tools and strategies deployed by actors in specific situations where they struggle to generate or administer punitive authority. Finding out what constitutes the "authoritative" requires analyzing social and ideological as well as institutional phenomena. This sort of analytical frame has rarely been employed in the context of a study of ancient Athenian punishment.

In scene after scene, the characters emphasize the experience of seeing Prometheus; their reactions to the question of whether the punishment should be treated as authoritative and final vary depending on whether the spectator is an "uninvolved" bystander and subject of Zeus (the Oceanids, Oceanus, Io, and Hephaestus partially) or a representative of Zeus's authority (Kratos, Hermes, Zeus himself, and Hephaestus partially).[73] The official administrators of the sovereign power (Kratos and Hermes) develop conventionalized claims about desert. They repeat the words "thief," "erred," and "stole." Their official assertions of desert, however, are insufficient to convince onlookers that this is a spectacle of "punishment." Punishment exists (as clearly distinct from torture, outrages, or revenge) only when the larger part of a group of onlookers considers a response to wrongdoing to be authoritative, final, and founded on desert. Accordingly, the socio-political conceptions or ideologies of bystanders (Hephaestus, the Oceanids, Oceanus, and Io) can contribute to or threaten the establishment of any particular assessment of desert as authoritative. In this play, those ideological conceptions that have had an impact on the negotiation of desert included opinions about anger, law, reciprocity, status, and honor. Furthermore, the larger political situation affects the way in which the sovereign power uses the hierarchy of penalties to achieve acquiescence.

Prometheus's penal "situation" teaches us that punishment is the drama of a particular attempt at punishing, whether successful or not; the drama is generated by the efforts of strategic actors to negotiate desert. In what follows, I break this drama into initiation, process, and execution. Any given punishment is a temporally extended drama situated within a larger institutional, social, and political context that mobilizes a society's conceptions about desert.[74] Combining the two elements, we can say that the practice of punishing: 1) begins in one place, with an event designated by someone as a wrongdoing; 2) progresses through a more or less complex negotiation of desert that engages social and political opinions about authority and desert; and 3) eventually ends in a finalized response of some kind—whether that is public acclaim, silence, or hemlock. In most cases, although not in that of Prometheus, the negotiation of desert occurs primarily before the physical execution of punishment. Strategic actors have to equip themselves with the institutional and cultural tools needed to move through such a sequence of events.

PRÉCIS

In Athens, various actors—citizen men and women, metics, and slaves—found themselves, as punishers and punished, in equally various punitive situations. But in almost all cases, it was private and self-interested individuals who undertook to bring about punishments with the city's institutional tools. Whether these individuals could succeed, however, depended on their ability to use the institutional tools in ways that coincided with Athenian cultural conceptions of desert, a set of publicly crafted, used, and contested terms that rested on ideologies of anger, honor, status, and reciprocity.

In chapter 2, I discuss the institutional tools and constraints that pertain to the practice of punishing. In chapter 3, I discuss the cultural tools and constraints. Then in a study of tragedy in chapter 4, I set out the conceptual parameters of legitimate punishment and the sorts of political problems that the Athenian imagination associated with punishment. In chapters 5–9, I discuss how each phase of a situation of punishment (initiation, process, and execution) was carried out with the institutional and cultural tools described in chapters 2 and 3 and within the constraints of just punishment as described in chapter 4. In chapters 5 and 6, I discuss the sorts of roles played by different members of the city in the construction of actionable accusations that allowed a wrongdoer to be named so that a punitive action could be initiated. Different members of the city had different means for turning their knowledge about a wrongdoing into the anger needed to legitimate a penal procedure. Chapter 5 is concerned with the powers of metics, slaves, and citizen women to initiate punishment. Chapter 6 considers citizen men. In chapters 7 and 8 I discuss how citizen men made arguments about desert in the Athenian courts in the process of trying to move from the moment of initiation to the moment of execution. In chapter 9, I turn to executions and consider the ways in which Athens tried to generate acquiescence in punishments.

In effect I claim that by orienting our investigation around "punitive situations" we will come to a new understanding of the operational character and ideological underpinnings of democratic Athenian society. We will discover first of all that in Athens anger and personal interest provided the only truly legitimate basis for an attempt to punish someone. Punishments inspired by anger provided a means of recalibrating status and honor in the city after a wrongdoing. This recalibration especially benefited the punisher.

Athenian punishment was in this sense oriented toward the private realm, but punishments nonetheless had to be carried out in a manner that benefited the city also. A punishment was carried out in a way beneficial to the city precisely when punishers, even those who acted most in their personal interest, displayed conformity to what I call "the norms of public agency."[75] All punishers had to place their private cases before the public eye and had to set their cases in the terms of a public language of "desert." The "norms of public agency" were generated by the will and judgment of the *demos*, employing a range of tools (from social knowledge, social memory, and law to extralegal communal action) in order to craft and maintain preeminent judgments and authoritative punishments. The process of punishing served to stabilize Athenian politics and legitimate civic authority.

Prosecutors who put their cases before the citizenry of Athens in terms of the public language of desert effectively reconfirmed community norms and the shape of Athenian politics. They also had opportunities to attempt a revision of prevailing definitions of "desert" in Athens, and sometimes they took them. The orator Lycurgus did so in a dramatic fashion. Plato and Aristotle also created and took similar opportunities for themselves in their philosophical works. Plato thoroughly revised Athenian punitive concepts, and Aristotle attempted a more moderate reform. The two philosophers shared a trenchant analysis of Athenian politics and of the nature of Athenian "desert" and "justice." They recognized the importance, for a project of political revisionism, of reformulating the concepts at the heart of a system of desert. Both self-consciously wrote texts that led explicitly from Athens and from its formulations of "desert" to two distinct philosophic "elsewheres." What was transferable from Athens to the philosophers' "elsewheres" was a recognition of the importance of contests over desert, and therefore of the significance of the Prometheus tale.

Taken together, chapters 2 through 9 also attempt to articulate the ideational content and political principles undergirding the Athenian practice of punishment. I read the institutions, cultural contexts, and behavior of individual strategic agents as constituting a conversation about democratic politics. I attempt to articulate the political principles underlying the practices of those who punished in the Athenian system. In chapters 10 and 11 I hold the Athenian conversation about punishment and politics up against Plato and Aristotle's discussions of the relationships between punishment and politics. I discuss the ways in which Plato and Aristotle contested the Athenian system of desert, and thereby Athenian politics, and reformulated elements of the Athenian system that were exceptionally unstable.

I bring up the philosophers with some trepidation for they posed a significant challenge to the democrats of their age, as Michel Foucault has recently to democratic-liberals. Plato and Aristotle criticized Athenian politics of honor and competition, and Foucault argues that the rhetoric of liberal democracies hides a modern unfreedom that is produced by pervasive mechanisms of discipline, which are not merely institutional but intrinsic to cognitive life. Plato, Aristotle, and Foucault all uncovered and critiqued the structures of authority underlying the politics of their age. All three teach a powerful lesson about how history yields concepts for theoretical discussion and about the ways that the conceptual "deep structure" supporting social phenomena reveals both systems of value and claims about how to order human life, which deserve theoretical analysis. We would do well to follow their close attention to the interrelation between history and concept that is at the heart of this investigation. Foucault has not accounted for the indeterminacy and possibilities for freedom inherent in that interaction between history and concept, and so I will return to this topic in the epilogue and here say only that my story about the ancient Athenian practices of punishing is intended to enhance our ability to think about punishing, politics, and freedom in the modern Anglo-American context. The narration about Athens should strike the reader as sufficiently unfamiliar to throw into relief the historical particularity of our current penal practices and our present thought about desert.

Let me tell two stories to illustrate the effect that the study of a modern concept through its ancient counterparts is intended to achieve. One you already know, probably even too well: the story of O. J. Simpson and his trial on charges of murdering his wife and a visitor in her house. All the evidence in the case was circumstantial, since Simpson never confessed and there were no witnesses to the actual crime. Scientists could not provide for a criminal jury of twelve citizens knowledge so certain as to be "beyond a reasonable doubt"; but they could prove enough facticity to meet the lower "in all probability" or "preponderance of the evidence" standards of proof required by a civil trial. In the criminal trial Simpson was acquitted of murdering his ex-wife and the visitor, Ron Goldman, and, therefore, not "punished." But in the civil trial, brought by the families of the murder victims, he was obligated to pay compensatory damages of $8 million to the families (including to his own children) and distinct penal damages, again to the families of the victims, of $25 million.[76] The latter penal damages are not, however, treated as "punishment" in philosophical and juridical texts. The case would probably have become legendary without extensive courtroom television coverage, but the spectacular coverage made the decision on guilt and innocence property of judges other than just the jurors in the room. The television spectacle provided masses of citizens with a sense that they were in a position to pronounce on the criminal verdict. The coverage realigned the relation between jurors and fellow citizens; in this case, one did not speak for the other. In this regard, the coverage and the verdict in the civil trial delegitimated any sense of permanence or finality that the criminal verdict was meant to convey. Why were we all so obsessed with the facts of the matter, and how did passion factor into what would seem possibly to have been a *crime passionnel*? How do we account for the difference between the criminal and the civil responses? How did the spectacle of the trial affect the larger political culture? What form of punitive authority shows itself in the case?

Nearly 2,500 years ago, Euphiletus was put on trial on charges that he had killed not his wife but his wife's lover, Eratosthenes. In one important sense his case is completely different from Simpson's. It is a fact that Euphiletus did the killing. Nonetheless, the two trials are worth comparing for they represent very different responses to relatively similar events. Euphiletus was prosecuted for murder not by "agents of the government" but by Eratosthenes' family. The "facts" were not at issue in his case for Euphiletus never denied the killing or his intentionality. In fact, he had gathered several friends for the very purpose of witnessing the act. These friends, who saw everything, testified to events. The facts were not at issue, only their interpretation. Did Euphiletus kill Eratosthenes as an act of cold-blooded and plotted murder after having lured Eratosthenes into a trap, or did Euphiletus execute a justifiable and angry response to adultery? Was the killing an act of justice or injustice?[77] Was it a private act of wrongdoing or a socially responsible act? In making his argument, Euphiletus claims to have followed the commands imposed by the law against adultery, and he makes a case for the value of that law. We do not know what happened to Euphiletus, but if convicted, he would have had no means of appeal. We do know, though, that because he was tried before a court whose jurors numbered in the fifties (although most Athenian juries would have numbered in the hundreds), his case, too, would have entered into the networks of social knowledge and memory in his city.

The stories have their resemblance—the sensationalism of crimes in the family, elements of "passion," trial by jury, and defense by argument. One resemblance in particular, "trial by jury," is generally taken to be one of the distinguishing institutions of democratic politics and ideology as practiced in both the ancient and the modern worlds. Nonetheless, the two jury trials and the two narratives that they generate are worlds apart, conceptually and historiographically as well as chronologically. The different emphases on factual and ethical arguments, the different treatments of passion, the different uses of "public" and "private" to legitimate different types of prosecution, and the different uses of law are all part of two very different constructions of democratic punitive authority. The particular form of punitive authority used in each case is thought to be crucial to the maintenance of democratic liberty and equality. We do not know what happened to Euphiletus, but that does not prevent us from analyzing the political significance of his speech. As we shall see, features of Euphiletus's case intersected with and impacted the conceptual system according to which the Athenian politics of liberty and equality operated. Similarly, the fact of Simpson's acquittal matters less, and can tell us less about democracy, than the practices used to accomplish it. Studying the practices that led to the judgment in his case would open up a vista on the conceptual foundations of modern democratic justice and authority. Foucault challenged us to think more about the nature of the networks of power-knowledge constraining life in liberal-democratic societies. In some sense, the challenge cannot be met until we have thought more about the ways in which authority is built out of an acquiescence that is itself engendered sometimes by persuasion and sometimes by threats of force. I hope that the close study of the punitive authority that operated in the democracy of ancient Athens will equip us, schooled more by the differences than by the similarities, better to see and study the punitive authority of our own democracy.

CHAPTER 2

Institutional Context

INTRODUCTION

Early in the sixth century, Solon, the much mythologized "founding" legislator of democratic Athens, carried out an overhaul of Athenian institutions.[1] He brokered an uneasy truce between elites and masses during a period of political instability. As part of that reform effort, he laid down the rule that the business of prosecuting crimes did not always need to be left to the offended victim, as was done before Solon's tenure as archon. Solon legislated that henceforth "whoever wished" (*ho boulomenos*) among the male citizenry could use a procedure called a *graphe* to prosecute certain specific types of wrongdoing.[2] It is difficult to say what sort of wrongs would have been tried by *graphe* under Solon, but by the fourth century the list included wrongs against the community such as military desertion, political bribery, temple robbery, and idleness on the one hand and, on the other hand, wrongs done to specific people such as theft, perjury, hubristic behavior, and sycophancy.[3]

The *graphai*—cases that could be prosecuted by any male citizen, victim or not—are therefore generally considered to have been "public cases" that stood in contrast to a set of private cases called *dikai*. Only the victim could prosecute in a *dike* (Isoc. 20.2), and the procedure was used for murder, nonhubristic forms of assault and sexual violence, and many forms of wrongs done in respect to citizens' property, including slaves. Scholars have also tried to map the two procedures onto the modern categories of criminal and civil law but such a comparison does not do justice to Athenian institutions.[4] Theft could be tried by both *graphe* and *dike,* and "murder" could be tried only as a *dike* or what modern scholars would call a civil suit. The differences between the two procedures are fundamental to Athenian penal institutions, but understanding them requires looking at how they were used, not at modern categories. This will be done in chapter 8. For the time being suffice it to say that Solon's invention of the *graphe* was a key moment in the development of Athenian institutions.

Many modern scholars, as well as some ancient commentators, have interpreted Solon's invention of *ho boulomenos* as the birth of a system of public prosecution and disinterested, even "senatorial," public-mindedness in the Athenian citizenry. Such a birth may be what Solon intended of his midwifery, but it was not to be. Solon certainly gave Athenian citizens the freedom and institutional tools necessary for them to act with disinterested "civic spirit." The Athenians, however, did not use them that way. Extant evidence reveals that the Athenians typically prosecuted only in cases where they were in fact victims or personally involved in the matter at trial.[5] The surviving oratorical corpus yields only four cases in which a prosecutor claims to act as a purely disinterested public actor (Hyp. 1, Din. 1, Lyc. 1; Lys. 22). The Athenians had institutional procedures for disinterested prosecution, but they used those penal procedures in private disputes instead. Institutional possibilities were limited by cultural norms. The dichotomy between what was institutionally possible in Athens and what happened in practice points up the need to understand both the city's institutions and the cultural practices and ideologies that constrained their use. In this chapter I outline the institutional contexts of Athenian punishment; in chapter 3 I take up the cultural context.

Institutions were the province of men, so this chapter analyzes how penal power was distributed within the male citizenry. Male Athenian citizens used their penal institutions to produce convictions based on communally acceptable formulations of desert. This required that they understand how the practice of "judgment" was constructed in relation to other practices within their political regime. Penal power was diffused throughout the male Athenian citizenry as was the citizens' need to understand the city's shared language for discussing punishment and arguing about desert.

PENAL INSTITUTIONS AND DEMOCRATIC POWER

Athenian institutions can not be neatly divided into the categories of legislative, executive, or judicial as are the institutions of modern democracies.[6] They are better distinguished according to how citizens took part in them—either gathered *en masse* (as in the assembly or on a popular jury) or as individuals holding one of the magistracies (*archai*) and taking their properly allotted turns at ruling and being ruled.[7] As to the first mode of participation, the quorum in the assembly was 6,000 and juries could be impaneled with anywhere from 200 to 6,000 citizens on them (*Ath. Pol.* 53; Din. 1.52). A citizen could participate as frequently as he liked in these mass gatherings and could participate year after year after he had reached the relevant qualifying age (eighteen for the assembly and thirty for the courts). The assembly primarily carried out legislative work and deliberative policy making—in the fourth century it was aided by a board called the *nomothetai* or legislators—but the assembly could also issue special decrees of punishment and until the 360s could sit as a court.[8] The assembly's power to punish by no means constituted the bulk of the penal power in the city, which fell instead to the jurors and to the allotted or elected magistrates.

A citizen's ability to participate as a magistrate was more limited than his ability to participate in the assembly—even the office of councillor could not be held more than twice—but a magistracy allowed him a greater direct exercise of power. There were probably between 700 and 800 magistrates in the city (this figure has been disputed; see appendix A). These 700-odd magistrates included, inter alia, the nine archons (*basileus, archon, polemarchos,* and six *thesmothetai*),[9] the 500 members of the Council of 500 (*boule*) that set the agenda for the assembly, "the Eleven" who were eleven men in charge of the prison, and the financial officers such as the treasurers of Athena, who supervised the city's public funds. Each member of the Council of 500 was considered to be a magistrate,[10] but a councillor might acquire another magistracy as well since the council filled various of the city's offices from within its own membership, for instance, the ten trireme makers (*trieropoioi*) who were assigned to build and review ships (*Ath. Pol.* 46); and the thirty "catalogers of the people" (*sullogeis tou demou*) who were empowered to discipline public slaves, oversee various religious matters, and receive certain types of legal indictment (*phaseis*).[11] The magistrates who were primarily in charge of maintaining order in public spaces such as the market and the city center (*agoranomoi*,[12] *astunomoi*) may also have been elected from within the *boule* (it is also possible that they were independent magistrates and the evidence is too sparse to prove the case either way; see appendix A). The council's jurisdiction in penal matters was primarily limited to commercial matters, matters of public finance, and matters of public order, although they could also hear cases of impeachment (*eisangelia*).[13] But its magistrates could punish people including with fines. I stress this point because the council's role in punishment has previously gone relatively unacknowledged. Most Athenian men would have been in the council at some point in their lives because of the principle of nonreiteration. Penal power was therefore diffused throughout the male citizenry as was a functional knowledge of how to use penal institutions.

Most magistracies were filled by lot, although some were filled by election, and terms were typically one year long. The 700-odd magistrates had slaves and citizens who worked as their subordinates and helped manage the work of social control.[14] For instance, the Scythian archers, a group of slaves who formed something of a police force in the city and who patrolled public meetings during the fifth century, worked under the council.[15] The magistrates and their subordinates—the foregoing list is by no means exhaustive[16]—had between them three forms of penal power: fining, arbitrating, and prosecuting or presiding at a trial. Only magistrates could register a case for trial or preside at trial, but both they and their subordinates could fine. Thus, we hear of a *choregos*—an official who was in charge of preparing tragic choruses, was not himself a magistrate, and reported to the *archon*—imposing a fine on a prospective chorus member (Dem. 21.179). Most magistrates and officials were subject to 10 or 50 drachmae limits on their powers to fine, but the *boule* could act as a court and fine up to 500 drachmae.[17] Presumably arbitrations were subject to the same sort of monetary limits as fines.

The power of punishment that was diffused throughout the citizenry was by no means weak. Even the magistrates who fined up to their limits could inflict severe disabilities on citizens. The cost of an adult male's food for a year was, on estimate, 36 drachmae, and the daily wage for an unskilled laborer at the end of the fourth century was 1.5 drachmae.[18] The power of the magistrates to fine up to 10, 50, and 500 drachmae and to arbitrate allowed them to impose penalties that would have been severe for any but wealthy citizens. The fact that the Athenians had some 700 magistrates who could fine to levels of 10 and 50 drachmae makes it likely that petty crime (and probably even more than petty crime) was handled by individual officials (and by means of private arbitration) rather than in the courts.

Arbitrations were of two types (see appendix B): *compromise decisions,* in which the arbitrator was not obliged to take an oath and where all parties involved stood to benefit or suffer equally from the decision (*dikazein, gnonai ta sumpheronta pasin; diallattein; dialusai*); and *judgment decisions,* in which the magistrate pronounced his decision on oath and where one party was thought to gain while the other party was thought to lose (*dikazein; ta dikaia diagnonai; gignoskein*).[19] In other words, magistrates could either work out a compromise on the basis of proposals put forward by both parties or, if a compromise seemed unlikely, they could carry out summary judgments. In both types of arbitration, any monetary penalty went to the prosecutor.

It seems probable that in the fifth century all of the magistrates, and possibly any of their subordinates who could fine, both could and did arbitrate (see appendix B),[20] but in the fourth century, a board of officials called public arbitrators who never acquired the status of being "magistrates" carried out the bulk of the arbitrations. During the fourth century, the power of arbitration nonetheless remained available to and was employed at least minimally by the magistrates as well (see appendix B).[21] A good deal of arbitration also took place outside the city center. Deme governments (akin to county governments) had officials and panels of citizens who acted as arbitrators.[22] The tasks of judgment—working compromises and rendering judgments—were by no means a duty that fell only to popular juries; the juries were situated within a wider culture of judging.

In respect to the power to use a jury trial, the magistrates would either preside over a case prosecuted by someone else or prosecute the case themselves.[23] A magistrate had to take a case to court if he thought that the wrong at issue merited a fine greater than he was legally allowed to impose, if one of the disputants refused to abide by an arbitrator's decision, or if the case could be tried only by a *graphe.* Likewise the Council of 500 had to turn the case over to a citizen jury if it wished to impose a penalty greater than a 500 drachmae fine.[24] This happened, for instance, in the prosecution of the generals who failed to collect the dead after the battle of Arginusae. After investigating and indicting the generals, the council moved that the assembly should appoint public prosecutors and passed the case over to the collected citizenry.[25]

Many social disruptions could have been and probably were resolved before ever reaching court. The disputes and accusations of wrong that did reach the courts would have been in a special class: they would have been those disputes which produced a form of social disruption too great to be subdued by individual magistrates. They would have been the disputes in which it was most important that the citizenry, acting as a collective body in the assembly or courts, confirm its authority over the establishment of norms that would govern and shape life in the city.

The courts imposed penalties far greater than those that the magistrates had the power to impose. Even relatively minor cases heard before the smaller juries could result in a penalty of up to 1,000 drachmae or approximately twenty-five times the average annual cost of a man's food. Jury trials, especially public trials, must therefore be seen as having been the province of the more elite citizens in the city, able and willing to forgo relatively less politically and financially risky procedural options.[26]

Verdicts and punishments were typically decided by courts called *dikasteria* manned by randomly allotted citizen jurors numbering anywhere from 200 to over 1,000. Verdicts and sentences handed out in homicide cases were an exception to this rule. These cases were handled by a special set of homicide courts, the most famous of which was the Areopagus Council, manned by former archons. The four other homicide courts—Palladion, Delphinion, Prytaneion, and Phreatto (each heard a different type of homicide case)—were staffed by a group of fifty-one judges known as *ephetai*, whose identity has not been determined. Only the *basileus*, the archon who was responsible for religious matters, could preside over the Areopagus and the other homicide courts.[27] The other magistrates presided only over the *dikasteria*.

A case of wrongdoing could be dealt with by more than one of the three procedures (fine, arbitration, or trial), and could be passed from one institutional context to another or from one citizen official to another, as is described here.

> The forty are competent to judge finally [*dikazein*] in those affairs concerning damages or penalties up to ten drachmae, but they hand over cases exceeding this penalty to the public arbitrators [*diaitetais*]. These arbitrators take them up and, if they are not able to work out a compromise [*dialusai*],[28] they judge them [*gignoskousi*];[29] if the judgments [*ta gnosthenta*] are suitable to both parties involved, they stop there, and the case [*he dike*][30] has an end here. But if either of the two litigants with conflicting claims appeals to a court, the arbitrator throws the testimonials and challenges and laws in a jar (those of the prosecutor separately from those of the defendant) and after sealing these and joining to them the judgment of the arbitrator written on a tablet, the arbitrator gives these to the four members of the forty who judge for the tribe of the defendant. And these, taking up the matter, lead it to court,[31] those cases for less than 1,000 drachmae to a court of 200 and those beyond 1,000, to a court of 400. (*Ath. Pol.* 53.2–3)

During the democracy, the Athenian effort to sort out communal disputes and to smooth over the disruptions brought about by injury was more than likely to turn out to be a communal effort, with citizens having to air their grievances before their peers on more than one occasion. In the preceding passage we can see the degree to which individual magistrates had to try to resolve disputes before sending them on to court. A citizen who wished to prosecute or who had to defend himself could expect to have to tell his story more than once and to a number of different audiences.

The character of his audience would be to some degree unpredictable, thanks to the system of filling magistracies by lot. This institutional system prevented citizens from interacting only within the confines established by whatever were their habitual patterns of friendship or business relations. The principle of non-reiteration would have intensified this effect. Prosecutors and defendants had to be able to speak some sort of common language that their fellow citizens would understand and to which their audiences would be sympathetic regardless of their composition. In order to engage the attention of his fellows, the male Athenian citizen had to understand what would *generally* be recognized as a social disruption and which forms of response would be seen as legitimate *by most of the citizens most of the time*. Such an understanding would have entailed not only an awareness of the ways in which the diffuse powers of the institutional structure functioned but also a sensitivity to definitions of desert and authority operative in Athens.

The story told thus far paints a picture of punishment in Athens as being largely under democratic control. But two other elite institutional bodies in the city also held important penal powers: the Areopagus Council and the ten military generals. The structure of penal power in the city of Athens changed as the relationships between the democratic institutions and these elite institutions changed. The Areopagus Council was viewed as being an elite body because it was staffed by former archons, all of whom received life terms as judges on the court. In the sixth century, archons had been selected only from among the wealthiest citizens of the city. In the sixth century, the city's wealthiest citizens therefore had the rare opportunity of life long service on a political body of sizable power. Originally the court not only tried murder but could also investigate and prosecute other wrongs. The Areopagus Council had traditionally provided the city's elites with a powerful and dependable political platform firmly in their control. Even after the archonships were made more generally open to the citizenry in the fifth century, the Areopagus retained its reputation as an elite stronghold.

The role of the Areopagus in the politics of democratic Athens has been much debated. It is at least possible to say that its extensive sixth-century jurisdiction was limited somehow—it is unclear exactly how—in the mid-fifth century. From that point on the council seems to have been reduced to being simply a court for homicide.[32] The limitations were associated with a politician named Ephialtes but, however they may have come about, they contributed to establishing the *demos* with its assembly, popular courts, and magistracies as the authoritative penal power in the city. The restrictions were crucial to the process of democratization that occurred from the sixth century to the fifth century, but they were only one part of the process.

The power of the generals also had to be reined in before the *demos* could truly hold all the reins of penal power. The generals had an elite status in that they held office by election rather than by allotment. Voting was a procedure that the Athenians (unlike modern democrats) considered antidemocratic, for it took merit and political standing into account and had the effect of keeping the generalships closed to the "common man." Nearly all male Athenian citizens served in the armed forces, land and marine, and fifth-century generals could punish soldiers in the field, even capitally, at their own discretion.[33] In other words, the entire male citizenry was subject to the generals' powers of capital punishment during the fifth century. Their penal power, however, was restricted to cashiering, fining, and handing wrongdoers over to the city's juries by the beginning of the fourth century (*Ath. Pol.* 61).[34] The *demos* thus eventually acquired full control over capital punishment and other major forms of punishment and, by early in the fourth century, had invested itself with the full force of the city's penal power.

Both the Areopagus and the generals seem to have chafed at the limitations on their powers, but neither body seems to have regained any punitive power until very late in the democracy (probably the 330s).[35] It is true that in the last half of the fourth century the Areopagus was once again permitted to investigate some wrongdoings (but not murder) either when requested to do so by the assembly or on its own authority.[36] But the restoration of power to the Areopagus was by no means unrestricted. In one case the fourth-century Areopagus tried to fine one of its members on its own authority (*autokratores*) for failing to divorce his criminal wife as was legally required of him, and the Areopagus acted in secret to do so. Their desire to impose the fine secretly at least suggests that the Areopagites were acting in a way that exceeded their legitimate authority when they imposed that fine (Dem. 59.80–82). In the fifth century, the *demos* was obliged to share punitive power with elites in the city, but throughout the fourth century penal power remained largely diffused throughout the citizenry. The Areopagites recognized that their penal authority remained subordinate to the authority of the *demos* even at a point in the democracy's life when the city was subject to the external threat of growing Macedonian power. It was in the fourth century that Athens was truly a radical democracy.

THE LAY PROSECUTOR AND THE PARAMETERS OF JUDGMENT

The powers assigned to the magistrates by no means precluded lay citizens from playing an active role in punishment in the city of Athens. As we have seen, the extant sources reveal that a high percentage of prosecutors were private citizens rather than magistrates. Power in the city was diffuse not only in that a large number of citizens participated in the apparatus of "bureaucracy" on a regular basis, but also in that judicial processes were more often than not initiated by private citizens. Every citizen could have his day as magistrate— and no doubt private citizens were to some degree equipped to initiate penal processes by serving as magistrates—but it was equally open to him to play the part of prosecutor. This he could even do on more than one occasion, and many of the famous orators prosecuted or were prosecuted repeatedly.

A citizen who wished to prosecute faced many institutional choices, and the success of his prosecution depended to large degree on whether he chose the right procedure. Usually, the citizen had to decide, first of all, how to catch a wrongdoer or how to bring an accusation against someone. Then he had to decide what form of prosecution to undertake. In certain instances the whole process might be collapsed into one event: a citizen could act on his own authority to kill any adulterer, traitor, nocturnal thief, or temple robber whom he caught in the act of doing wrong.[37] But a citizen might prefer to seek help from magistrates in dealing with a wrongdoing. A citizen who caught an adulterer but did not wish to kill him could "arrest" him and lead him before the Eleven. A citizen, however, who did not feel competent to arrest the wrongdoer, could get the Eleven to make the arrest in his stead. In either case, the Eleven were then responsible for killing those wrongdoers who confessed to a capital offense, but they had to arrange for courtroom prosecution in cases where the accused remained tight-lipped.[38] Either the private citizen or the Eleven might prosecute the case. The trial itself was called an "arrest" or *apagoge* when the citizen prosecuted, whereas an arrest by a magistrate seems to have been called an *ephegesis*.[39] The courtroom procedure was simply named after the method used to initiate it.[40] Thus a wrongdoer could also be "denounced" or "pointed out" in order to initiate a court process called the *endeixis*, which means "denouncement" or "pointing out," or in order to initiate a *phasis*, which comes from a word meaning "pointing out" or "making clear" (the processes of denouncement were probably somewhat different in the two procedures).[41]

Suits could be initiated not only by arrest or by denouncement but also by written indictment. In the fourth century *dikai*, in which only the victim could prosecute, and *graphai*, in which any male citizen could prosecute, both began with the combination of a written charge and an oral summons to the wrongdoer. The names of the two procedures, however, still capture a key difference between them. *Graphe* means "written thing" and this seems to refer to the fact that *graphai* always began with an act of writing: a publicly posted written indictment. In the fourth century written indictments were posted in public for *dikai* as well as *graphai*, but it seems probable that archaic *dikai* began only with oral pronouncements.[42] Thus the *dike* for homicide, a procedure with archaic roots, began with an oral, rather than a written, proclamation against the wrongdoer.[43] Moreover, judgments from *graphai* were publicly posted in writing for the whole citizenry to see, but judgments resulting from *dikai* were not.[44] The public inscription that followed on a conviction from a *graphe* memorialized the proven wrongdoing and its punishment, and so public cases, more than private cases, served explicitly as a crucible for the creation of shared public memories and helped maintain the city's ethical structure and orders of value. As we shall see in chapter 8, there was an important link between the *graphe* and a perceived need to memorialize certain kinds of wrongdoing publicly.

Two procedural distinctions were especially significant at trial. The first of these was the distinction between public suits in which anyone could prosecute—whether brought as a *graphe*, *phasis*, *endeixis*, *apagoge*, *eisangelia*, or *probole*—and private suits or *dikai*.[45] *Dikai* were heard before juries that had 200 or 400 citizens. Public cases were heard before juries of at least 500 and at certain points in the democracy's history some of the public procedures could be heard before the assembly.[46] Similarly penalties in *dikai* were smaller than in public cases, and in a *dike* the wrongdoer paid his penalty to the prosecutor. In public cases in general and in *graphai* in particular, the reverse situation obtained: the main penalty went to the city. In a *dike* the jury could decide to impose an additional fine or penalty that would redound to the benefit of the city, while in a *graphe* a minimal portion of the fine owed to the city might be paid out to the prosecutor.[47] *Dikai* have been considered private (*idiai*), if the penalty went only to the prosecutor, or public (*demosia*), if an additional penalty was in fact directed at the city.[48] Prosecutors in private cases risked no penalty for losing their prosecution, but prosecutors in many types of public case had to pay a penalty if they failed to secure at least 20 percent of the jurors' votes. *Graphai* have often been considered to be public (*demosia*) precisely because penalties in such cases always went to the city, even if not in their entirety. At least we can say that the stakes of prosecution were much higher in *graphai* than in *dikai* (the possible differences between *graphai* and *dikai* are treated further in chapter 8).

The second procedural distinction that was crucial to shaping a trial had to do with how a convicted wrongdoer was to be sentenced. Penalties were prescribed by law in some cases, but they had to be assessed by the jurors in a procedure called *timesis* if the penalty for a given wrongdoing had been left unlegislated. In the process of *timesis* both the prosecutor and the defendant would, after the vote for conviction, make new speeches proposing alternate penalties. These speeches would be followed by a second jury vote on the two penalties proposed. Plato's *Apology* memorialized the use of this procedure to condemn Socrates to death.

The practice of *timesis* bore a close resemblance to arbitrations in which each party offered a proposal for resolution of their dispute. Both *dikai* and *graphai* could be sentenced by either method, but the procedure of *timesis* was the more regular method of sentencing in *dikai*. For *graphai* it was more common to have sentences defined by law.[49] Private cases thus bore a closer resemblance to the practice of arbitration than public cases did. This resemblance of private cases to arbitrations is reinforced by the fact that the main penalty in a private case went to the prosecutor as in arbitration, but in public cases it went to the city. Private and public court cases were therefore distinguished from one another, to some extent, by the closer connection of private cases to arbitration. For that matter, a case of arbitration could be called a *dike*, even if it never came to court and was heard only before one of the public arbitrators. (This was true even in the fourth century, e.g., Dem. 40.16, 21.83ff. 52.30ff.; *Ath. Pol.* 53.2; cf. Isaeus 5.31; Dem. 34.21, 52.14–16.) In other words, the word *dike* denoted not a particular form of court procedure but rather the general practice of resolving disputes between two people, regardless of whether that dispute was resolved before a single magistrate or before a collective body of jurors.

The idea that the word *dike* referred generally to the procedures used for dispute resolution gains support from a look at the history of the judicial procedure. Prior to Solon's reforms the *dike* was the sole kind of judicial proceeding available in Athens. There were, however, two kinds of *dikai* at that time: homicide *dikai,* which were heard in courts like the Areopagus and the several other homicide courts from at least the time of Draco in the sixth century;[50] and *dikai* in other matters, which were heard before individual magistrates. The need to deal with homicide can thus be seen as providing the original impetus for establishing judgment by collective decision making. Solon's introduction of the *graphe* was an introduction of a new form of court case. Presumably the procedure would have been modeled, to some degree, on the homicide cases since they were the only form of court procedure already in existence.

Homicide cases continued throughout the course of the democracy to be tried in court as *dikai* or as private suits, a phenomenon that has puzzled modern scholars who expect murder to have been tried as a "public" and not a "private" charge.[51] But it seems probable that the status of homicide cases as *dikai* arises simply from the fact that there was already a way to take a murderer to court when the public suit or *graphe* was invented. The new *graphai* and the homicide *dikai* were, as court cases, like one another and distinguished from *dikai* heard before individual magistrates. By the sixth century, two forms of judgment had thus been established: judgment by collective body and judgment by individual magistrate.[52] Despite this distinction, the two forms of judgment— whether practiced in the homicide cases, in the *graphai,* or in the cases heard before individual magistrates—shared an important feature: the judges were always also the people who made laws. The archons (and the tribal kings) who adjudged nonhomicide *dikai* also promulgated decrees or laws for the city.[53] The judges in the Areopagus had formerly promulgated decrees. Solon legislated that his *graphai* should be heard by a court called the *heliaia.* This word was also used to refer to the assembly that he instituted, and the court is generally thought to have been staffed by 6,000 citizens just as the assembly was. The two types of court case and the *dikai* heard before single judges all gave institutional embodiment to the idea that it was legitimate for those who made laws also to be the people who pronounced judicial decisions.

Solon seems to have assigned jurisdiction over the new people's court (the *heliaia*) and over the new procedure to the *thesmothetai* ("establishers of judgments").[54] It seems likely that the assignment of the new *heliaia* and of *graphai* to the *thesmothetai* would have left the archons in a position to continue arbitrating or adjudging cases that were not subject to a *graphe.* In other words, they would have continued to hear *dikai* on matters other than homicide, and such *dikai* would have continued, for a time, to be procedures like arbitration in which two pleaders put their case before a single judge.

Solon's unitary court called the *heliaia* eventually evolved into a set of courts called *dikasteria.* One presumes from their name (which means "place for *dike*") that they came into being once it was possible for non-homicide *dikai* to be heard in court. This was possible only once appeal was invented and litigants could reject a judge's decision in a *dike* and take their case to court. It seems probable that the *dikasteria* arose in the fifth century after the reforms of Cleisthenes in 508 and following, which would make appeal a Cleisthenic or post-Cleisthenic invention (some scholars wish to argue that Solon invented appeal).[55] The new courts, the *dikasteria*, were no longer to be manned by the *heliaia*'s 6,000 citizens but rather by only a portion of the citizenry—a portion that, as we have seen, might be as small as 200. The introduction of the *dikasteria* thus established a set of judicial institutions that were nominally and formally distinct from the city's legislative institutions. Nonetheless, the invention of the *dikasteria* in no way violated or revised the principle that the powers of legislation and judicial decision making could be conferred on the same people. Even in the fifth and fourth centuries, the Athenians did not, as we shall see in chapter 8, establish a firm distinction between law making and judging.

The development of Athenian penal institutions between the seventh and fourth century thus suggests that cases that were first tried by means of court procedures were those which had been accorded some sort of special status: first murder and then a set of cases designated by Solon as open to "whoever wished" to prosecute. But a procedure used first only for murder and special "public" charges was gradually extended to the whole range of wrongdoing. Eventually not only murder but also private disputes had to be or could be submitted to the community monitoring provided by a court. The practice of submitting disputes not to a single judge but to communal monitoring was used ever more widely as the democracy grew older and more democratic. But the magistrates' power to make decisions and to give judgments was never completely obliterated. Arbitration continued, and magistrates retained the power to fine up to certain limits and to make initial attempts at brokering compromises and at pronouncing judgments. The method of judgment by jury and the method of judgment by magistrate were not utterly incompatible with one another. Rather the jury system was a reconfiguration of the archaic form of judgment wherein the people who made laws also judged. The powers of law making and judgment were intertwined and invested in a unitary institutional actor throughout the history of the democracy—the only question was whether that institutional actor would be a collective one or not.

Athenian prosecutors who stepped before a jury stepped before people who knew that they were legislators with the power to set down ethical norms for the city. As we shall see in chapter 5, the result of the pressure on citizens to narrate their stories before random audiences of judges *cum* legislators was a relatively consistent Athenian language for discussing politics, citizenship, and justice that would have been transferable from the courts to the assemblies and vice versa. The system of punishment forced citizens out of their local patterns of interaction and required that they act within the context of the political order, speaking always to their fellow citizens in general and not merely to those whom they knew best, speaking always to their fellow citizens as people with the power to establish ethical norms. In this sense, Athenian penality was structured in such a way as to make the democratic citizenry and its communally shared norms and expectations visible.

CHAPTER 3

Cultural Context

ANGER/*ORGE*

A citizen who found himself acting as magistrate, juror, prosecutor, or defendant in the penal system had to understand not only how his city's institutions worked but also how to represent himself and his actions to his fellow citizens in order to garner their support and legitimation. There were ideological and not merely institutional rules that established who could play each of these roles and how to play them. In most cases Athenian institutions defined the legitimate prosecutor as the adult male Athenian citizen, but Athenian ideologies specified that definition further. Ideologically speaking, the ideal prosecutor was not only an adult male Athenian citizen but also personally involved in the case at trial, acting as the angry defender of his and his family's honor, and timely in bringing his case (see chapters 6–7). The nature of *ho boulomenos* in Athenian politics was constituted as much by Athenian cultural conceptions about who could be a legitimate "democratic" prosecutor and who deserved to punish as it was by Solon's "constitution."[1]

The rules defining the legitimate prosecutor were established by a set of cultural norms that grew out of the Athenian treatment of anger. Those norms regulated not only the role of anger in citizenship and in personal and political action but also the roles of honor, reciprocity, and social memory in constraining citizens' behavior in the penal context. These four concepts (anger, honor, reciprocity, and social memory) played a foundational role in establishing behavioral norms in the city and the city's system of value; anger was the central concept.

In oratory, anger is the reason most frequently given by orators to explain why they, or someone else, or the city has tried to punish or wishes to punish.[2] This is true in stories about private noninstitutional acts of punishment, as when Lysias describes how a scorned lover initiated the punishment of her beloved because she had grown angry at him (*orgizomene*, 1.15). It is also true in mythical stories of punishment, even those told in the courtroom; Lycurgus, for instance, claims that the mythical king Codrus met his fate at the hands of soldiers full of anger (*orge*, 1.86). Such invocations were also central to punishments carried out in the courts. Isocrates has Lochites explain his desire to punish thus: "It is not on behalf of any injury from blows that I come to court trying to get justice from him but because I suffered indignity [*aikia*] and dishonor; and it is fitting for free men to be the most angry [*malist' orgizesthai*] at this and to inflict the greatest penalty [*timorias*]" (Isoc. 20.6). Even a defendant could put his case by claiming that he had never been angrier (*met' aganaktesai mallon*) (Aes. 2.4). Lysias sees in his jury an audience whose "wrath wishes to punish" (*ten orgen boulomenen timoreisthai*) (Lys. 29.6), and Demosthenes goes farther still and situates anger well within the context of virtue and political justice when he says: "The whole people, acting nobly [*kalos*] and acting justly [*dikaios*], were so angered [*orgisthe*] and annoyed [*paroxunthe*] that they voted against him with one mind [*miai gnomi*]" (Dem. 21.2; cf. 21.6).

The orators routinely operated in public spaces on the basis of claims about their personal passions, on the basis of their ability to distinguish between their own personal passion and the passion of the jury, and on the basis of their ability to manipulate cultural conceptions about the role of passion in politics. For an orator the process of speaking about anger and about the relationship between his desire to punish and the city's politics often culminated with an injunction to the jurors to display a public anger against wrongdoers (*phanesthai orgen; demosia orge*).[3] Litigant and jury would come together to make anger visible as a substantive thing that could be seen and recognized by other people in the city.

The language of anger was by no means merely a matter of rhetorical flourish. It was embedded in the language of ethical evaluation used in the Athenian courts (chapter 5). Speakers made ethical arguments by making reference to anger or, more particularly, to the Greek concept *orge*. For instance, Demosthenes could remark that whoever has voluntarily done wrong everywhere receives anger (*orge*) and punishment (*timoria*) (Dem. 18.274). The Athenians used definitions of what anger was, when it was legitimate, who could feel it and act on it, and how they should do so in order to define, structure, and give limits to the legitimate use of punishment.

Sophocles himself was explicit about the connection between anger and community regulation. In his famous "Ode to Man," the first choral stasimon in *Antigone*, his chorus praises the achievements of mortals and sings of how humankind tames the world and traps birds in the net of its mind, sails the seas, and plows the earth. Most important, people have learned how to build cities and practice politics. The chorus celebrates humankind for having been the architects of politics by teaching itself voice (*phthegma*), wind-swift perception and/or thought (*anemoen phronema*), and anger that is city-regulated and/or city-regulating (*astunomous orgas*) (354–55).[4]

Scholars have atheticized this Sophoclean line simply because they could not make sense of the comment that city-regulated or city-regulating anger (*astunomous orgas*) contributes to *polis* life.[5] Their mystification is understandable, for *orge*, an emotion connected to the famous *thumos*—the Greek spirit or soul—is almost never discussed in the sparse secondary literature on Athenian psychophysiological and passional concepts. The gap is startling because *orge,* variously translated as "nature," "desire," "passion," and "wrath," as well as "anger," was at the heart of the Athenian *polis* and appears over and over again at key narrative moments in the literature extant from the democratic *polis*. Anger was sufficiently central to Athenian ethical discourse that it turned up as a primary topic of discussion not only in the courts but also in the tragic theater (chapter 3), the comic theater (chapter 4), and the philosophical schools (chapter 7). Every citizen had access to a public conversation where concepts like anger could be defined and redefined in ways that might either confirm or challenge the city's structuration of punishment and politics. Students of Athenian history and politics should aim to understand the roles of anger, honor, reciprocity, and the construction of social memory in the cultural framework of value that gave meaning and structure to life in Athens.

Two caveats are necessary before undertaking a general anthropology of how anger functioned in the Athenian cultural context. First, the word for anger that appears most frequently in oratory is *orge*, but synonyms like *thumos* and the verb *aganakteo* (especially the latter) also appear.[6] Such terms are relevant to our discussion and I sometimes assume that the paradigms of thought that structured the Athenian experience of *orge* applied to other forms of anger as well. This book as a whole offers an analysis of anger in the place of Athenian life that should justify this assumption. Second, one must be wary of translating *orge* as anger. The need for such wariness is proved by anthropological studies of anger in other cultures.

> The anthropologist who reports on the Ilongot at first simply translated *liget* as anger, but then saw that through the ways in which it worked and the associations it held for the Ilongot, *liget* embodied a whole set of principles and connections underlying the entire way they conceptualized society, bodies, and world.[7]

The same applies to *orge* in the Athenian context—it does embody a set of concepts that contributed to conceptualizations of society, bodies, and the world. In the first place, the word *orge* referred not just to anger but also to sexual passions. Thus *orge* was characterized both by what I will call its *iretic* aspect—and by an *erotic* aspect. The iretic and erotic aspects of *orge* combine to generate a passion that informed Athenian understandings of self and body in the context of both the family and the *polis*. Translation of the word is therefore a tricky matter. I use the English translation "anger" only when I am referring exclusively to the iretic elements of *orge* or when the Greek word has been used to stress the iretic elements of the passion. I persist, however, in using the transliterated Greek word *orge* in cases where I wish the reader to keep in mind *both* the iretic *and* the erotic elements of *orge* and in cases where a text allows for the word to be read with a view to either aspect of the passion. I have attempted to keep Greek terminology at a minimum throughout the book, but this exception seems unavoidable.

The passional element of human experience called *orge* first appears on the scene in Hesiod's *Works and Days* and the Homeric *Hymn to Demeter*. It is entirely absent from the *Iliad* and *Odyssey*, both of which primarily use the words *thumos* and *menis* to denote anger.[8] In the Homeric *Hymn to Demeter*, the goddess Demeter is described as mourning for her daughter Persephone, who has been lost in the underworld, until she is at long last moved to smiles and laughter by the jokes of the "careful Iambe." Iambe is said to convert

Demeter from a grieving to a gracious spirit (*hilaon schein thumon*) (203–4). The poet adds that Iambe acted in a fashion "pleasing to Demeter's temper [*euaden orgais*] in later times also" (203–4). Demeter's transition from having a grieving to having a gracious spirit is thus depicted as involving a transformation of her emotions, or a mediation of them, through her *orge*. The word seems to refer not so much to an emotion as to some general element of the human psychological apparatus.

The same applies to the Hesiodic instance, where the word is used in a fashion equally underdetermined from the perspective of a modern reader. In the *Works and Days* Hesiod uses the word *orge* as part of a comparison between busy and lazy men, where the former are like bees and the latter are like drones. Hesiod writes: "Both gods and men are angry with a man who lives idle, for in respect to his passions he is like the stingless drones [*kephenessi kothourois eikelos orgen*] who waste the labor of the bees, eating without working; let it be your care to order your work properly" (*Op.* 304). Translators have generally rendered this instance of *orge* as "natural character," taking Hesiod to mean that the idle have the "natural character" of stingless drones.[9]

We might, however, take another step. The implication of the Hesiodic passage is that *orge* is something in respect to which one can be recognized as being either a good person or a bad person. The hardworking bee has its *orge* constituted one way. The lazy drone has its *orge* constituted another way. For Demeter, *orge* was something thanks to which she could, to put it crudely, be in either a good mood or a bad mood. In Hesiod, however, *orge* is constitutive not so much of one's emotional state as of one's ethical character. In both cases *orge* itself is treated ambivalently—it is capable of being either good or bad, of having a positive or negative effect on the person to whom it belongs.

The first connections between the passion *orge* and anger appear in Theognis and Herodotus. Both writers do use the word *orge* to denote the "natural character" of people, in some instances drawing parallels between *orge* and words that even by the fourth century will still refer to general elements of the human constitution (e.g., for Theognis *rhuthmos* and *tropos*, 964; cf. 214, 312; for Herodotus *paideusis*, *tropos*, and *andragathia*, 6.128). But both writers also regularly relate the passion of *orge* to quarrels and injurious behavior.[10] Theognis, for instance, draws an opposition between *orge* and "grace," "gratitude," or "favor" (*charis*, 1303), and links *orge* to the *thumos*, one of the physiopsychological organs of the Greek body that was a source of anger (1223, 1303).[11] For Theognis the passional power of *orge* produced an emotion central to conflicts and quarrels and one that stood in opposition to forms of social interaction that are smoothed over by *charis*.

Here then is the earliest explicit connection of the passion of *orge* to anger and competition. By the age of the orators, the association between *orge* and conflict had developed sufficiently to allow *orge* and enmity (*echthre*) to be treated as coextensive phenomena (e.g., Lys. 9.15). Aristotle was the first ancient writer to define *orge* explicitly and did so by drawing on the language of quarrels and punishment. He writes: "Let anger [*orge*] be considered as a desire [*orexis*], associated with pain [*lupes*], for a visible punishment [*phainomenes timorias*] [when that desire is] inspired by something that seems to be a belittling [*oligorian*] in regard to a man's own affairs or those of those people of concern to him, when the belittling is not appropriate [*prosekontos*]" (*Rhet.* 1378a30–32).[12] Aristotle defined *orge* as an emotion that led directly to a set of actions and in particular to quarrels of ambition fueled by the desire to respond to a belittling, an insult to honor, with some sort of observable response.[12] Anger thus led to the public *agon* or competition where claims of honor were contested.[13] It was also associated with pain and desire.

Pain, however, was not the only sensation to be associated with anger and punishment. There was also pleasure. Aristotle writes: "It is the case that a certain pleasure [*tina hedonen*], which derives from the hope of punishing [*timoresasthai*], accompanies every experience of anger (*kai pasei orgei hepesthai*) (1378b1–2; see also *Rhet.* 1370b29, 1378a1–29, 1380a34).[14] Aristotle adds heroic grandeur to this pleasure by citing Achilles' comment that anger (*cholos*) is "sweeter than dripping honey."[15] Again we are forced to recognize that the nature of anger is ambivalent—it is bringer of both pain and pleasure.

The relationship of anger in general and *orge* in particular to pleasure is complicated. It reflects not only the link between *orge* and the desire for punishment or revenge but also the link between *orge* and sexual desire. The English words "orgy" and "orgasm" come from *orge*, and modern Greek still uses *orge* to express concepts ranging from the iretic to the erotic. In the ancient context, the erotic aspect of *orge* first appears in a Pindaric text. Pindar, like Theognis and Herodotus, used *orge* to describe conflicts related to ambition (*P.* 2.77; *I.* 5(4).34), but he also used *orge* to describe Apollo's desire, his gentle passion (*meilichos orga*), to seduce Cyrene (*P.* 9.43).[16] The noun *orge* is related to the verb *orgao*, which connotes sexual passion and means "growing ripe, and (of men) swell with lust, wax wanton."[17]

The word *orgao*, when it refers to *female* sexual desire, is also connected to procreative fertility. The Hippocratic texts thus discuss remedies for infertility caused by situations where women "do not desire to mingle with their husbands because of dampness, and do not feel sexual desire [*orgai*], and grow thin" (*De Mul.* affect. i-iii, sec. 57, lines 5–6; cf. sec. 12, line 8).[18] A Hippocratic discussion of the effect of geography and environmental conditions on health is explicit about the relationships between *orge* and fertility. The author argues that people who live in locales oriented to the east rather than to the west have clear voices and are better off in respect to both *orge* and intelligence (*orgen te kai sunesin beltious eisi*). He continues to say that all of the natural productions in such a region are better as well (*ta emphuomena ameino estin*). For human beings this means that diseases are fewer and less powerful and that women are very fertile and give birth easily (*hai te gunaikes autothi enarikumones eisi sphodra, kai tiktousi rhedios*) (Hipp. *Airs and Places* 5.13–28). Ripe fruit could also be described as being full of *orge*, and the word *orgas*, a cognate of *orge*, was the name used in fifth- and fourth-century Athenian historical texts for the fertile, uncultivated land dedicated to a divinity at Eleusis (e.g., *IG* ii^2 204. 5–12).[19] Health and fertility reign where *orge* is rightly constituted.

Orge was therefore a passion that was central not only to political behavior (punishment and competitions over honor) but also to the constitution of the family (through procreation). The fact that a passion at the heart of enmity could also be central to sexual desire, and to the associated ideas of fertility and ripeness, will prove significant to understanding the Athenian system of punishment and politics—and, especially, the role of women within it. *Orge* was a fundamentally constitutive building block of human experience according to the Athenian understanding. It was both anger and *eros*. Its role in shaping Athenian life will be better understood if we examine how it relates to the rest of the Athenian psychophysiological apparatus.

First, another word about the bee-drone binary that Hesiod uses in the *Works and Days* to compare lazy with productive men. Hesiod also uses the image in the *Theogony* but to bemoan the presence of women, not lazy men, in society. Hesiod's description of the creation of Pandora and the birth of the race of women includes the remark that women are like the lazy drones (*kephenes*) who consume all the labor of men, who are the hardworking bees (*melissai*) (594).[20] As in the *Works and Days*, the bee-drone image separates the lazy from the hardworking, the bad from the good, the ethically impugnable from the morally respectable. But here the distinction turns around gender instead of around the positive and negative versions of *orge* possessed by the good and bad worker respectively.

The bee-drone dichotomy returns again and again in Greek literature—in Semonides' poem about good and bad types of women; in Aristophanes' *Wasps*, a comedy about angry jurors; and in Plato's *Republic*, when Socrates discusses the disintegration of the ideal city. In all three cases, the bee-drone opposition not only taps the language of *orge* but also is used to reflect on politics and social organization, with a stress on the roles of anger and sexuality in human experience. The use of *orge* in one of the Hesiodic bee-drone images and the use of gender in the other is not happenstance. Men and women were understood as having different relationships to *orge*, and women were the class of people who were most frequently depicted as being incorrectly constituted in respect to this passion. The *orge* of men was crucial to the political life of the city; the *orge* of women threatened it. The gender hierarchy in Greek thought that established the male as good and the female as bad maps onto a hierarchy where those whose *orge* is correctly constituted are superior to those whose *orge* is incorrectly constituted. Social, ethical, and passional concepts are overlaid in the image of the bee and the drone because, as we shall see, citizenship, for both men and women, was defined in terms of a set of social and ethical criteria grounded in the idea of *orge*.

The scholarly literature on Athens is littered with offhand comments to the effect that the "ancient Greeks" had conceptions of desire, emotion, and passion very different from those of the modern Anglo-American world, but very little work has been done to specify how and why those desires, emotions, and passions seem to be so different (the difference is usually explained in terms of the Greeks' being a "Mediterranean people").[21] Despite its eccentricities, Bruno Snell's *The Discovery of the Mind* provides a starting point from which to consider the issue.[22] Snell argued that the Homeric Greeks, and even the classical Greeks prior to Plato, did not draw a firm distinction between the rational and the emotional. Words referring to anger, passion, pride, or desire could also refer to thought, rational activity, or decision making (e.g., *enthumeomai*, *thumos*).[23] Both reason and passion seemed to be movements from within a person, frequently from an organ, called the *thumos*, of notoriously indeterminate location and qualities from the point of view of modern scholarship.[24] Insofar as reason and passion were both simply movements from "within" the body, the rational and passional were the same.

Padel has recently extended the trajectory laid by Snell (and taken up by Adkins) with analyses of Greek views of psychophysiological interiority and the "manifestations of consciousness in Greek thought."[25] She points out rightly that the modern prioritization of the "head" is an obstacle to our ability to understand Greek psychophysiological experience. Pre-Platonic Greeks did not employ an opposition between the head and the rest of the body but focused on the relationship between what was "inside" their bodies and what was "outside" them.[26] Padel therefore emphasizes the idea of the "innards" (*splanchna*)—especially heart, liver, lungs, gall bladder, and blood vessels—and the ways in which they were understood by the Greeks as being used for thinking and feeling.[27] In New Testament Greek, *splanchnizomai* simply means "I feel pity," and most of the organs constituting what we would call "the innards" were used by epic and tragic characters not only to think but also to feel, enjoy, get angry, and suffer desire.

In what follows, I rely heavily on Padel's work and adopt her focus on the opposition between what was inside and outside the body. I extend her focus on what was inside the body by suggesting that the ancient Greek conceptions of self, personality, and consciousness were shaped in crucial ways not only by the distinction between inside and outside but also by the desire to say something about *how* what was on the inside *got there* in the first place.

Three organs predominate in Homeric and pre-Platonic references to the human physiopsychological apparatus that produced thoughts, emotions, and actions: the *nous*, which is usually translated as mind but which the pre-Platonic Greeks generally located in the chest; the *phren*, which is usually translated as lungs or diaphragm; and the *thumos*, which has been translated as everything from liver to stomach to spleen to spirit to life force to, simply, *thumos*. There was also the *psuche* or soul and the *kardia* or heart, which seem to have overlapped in function with the *nous* and the *phren*.[28] The body was thought to consist of this collection of organs, but it was also conceived of as being filled with a mixture of air and liquid. The aerated, liquefied tumult inside the body produced, in conjunction with the organs, all of a person's emotive and intellectual responses, decisions, words, and actions.[29] According to Padel, the inner air and liquid mixture could be breathed out, spoken out, secreted out, or acted out.[30]

The mixture of air and liquid inside of the body consisted of what *got inside from the outside* and of what *sprang up on* the inside. Air and liquid seemed to get inside the body by means of sight, hearing, eating, breathing, and (for women) sex, but air and liquid also seemed to spring up inside the body—for instance, in the body's production of speech or "winged words" and in sweat, spit, and all the secretions of the sexual organs, and in the bloody mess that fell out of wounded bodies.[31] The liquids that sprang up on the inside included bile, "spore," and blood.[32] But the words for bile (*chole* and *cholos*) could also mean "anger" (hence the word "choler"), and so anger was itself one of the liquids that could arise within the body. Padel writes: "Many passions are represented as liquid, but the ones that particularly foam and flower are madness and sexual passion."[33]

The idea that emotion was an inner liquid persisted even after the fifth century; thus the author of the pseudo-Aristotelian *Problems* could write: "Those who have a large quantity of hot black bile become manic [*manikoi*] or clever [*euphueis*] or erotic [*erotikoi*] or easily moved [*eukinetoi*] to anger [*tous thumous*] and desire [*tas epithumias*]" (30.1, 953b34–36). As far as the author of the *Problems* is concerned, a single liquid (black bile) produces a pluralized psychological response, moving a person to erotic, intellective, and iretic responses all at once. The liquids provided for inner motion and, therefore, inner activity. In Aristotle's *Rhetoric*, one could be easily moved not only in respect to the *thumos* and in respect to *epithumia* but also in respect to *orge* (*eukinetoi pros orgen*, 1979a25–30).

The *nous*, *phren*, and *thumos* either *produced* the airs and liquids that provided for emotional and cognitive experience or *received* the air and liquid into themselves from elsewhere. The *nous* produced air in the form of speech (*logos*) or airy winged words (according to Padel, the *nous* was the only organ that was never itself treated as a liquid, although liquids could swell within it).[34] The *phren* was the organ most frequently characterized for its role as a passive receptor of sensations. It took in air from the outside (breath, perceptions of other people's words, sights, and smells), but it could also receive liquid from the outside or the inside—wine, for instance, was said to dampen the *phren* whereas *cholos* as anger or *chole* as bile could be said to stand in waves against the *phren*.[35]

The *thumos*, a word that derives from *thuo* or "I seethe" and could be "used of an angry man or the ocean," seems to have produced seas of inner liquids associated with the emotions.[36] The *thumos* was associated with the liver, spleen, and kidneys (the kidneys were also a euphemism for testicles) and with the sexual organs. All of these organs could be seen to produce liquid and were regularly associated with the production of both sexual desire and anger (although the latter association is less common for some of the organs).[37] The body could also be "full" of *orge*, a passion that was sometimes likened to the sea and that "swelled" when there was a boiling (*zesis*) of "blood or some other sort of liquid" around the heart.[38] Liquids such as *menos*, *cholos*, and *chole* could seize the *thumos*, and both the liquids and the *thumos* could also boil.[39] Anger was associated with heat.[40]

Anger in its different forms (*thumos*, *cholos*, *menos*) could get into the *nous* and *phren* as well as being in the *thumos*.[41] Once inside the organs the body's assorted liquids and airs mixed, entering the heart and *nous*, surrounding and filling the *phren*, or slashing, tearing, and eating the innards, and in the process produced someone's unitary responses to the world, responses that were inevitably a mix of air and liquid, or reason (*logos*) and passion.

One of the key words of Greek morality is *sophrosune* or moderation. Etymologically, the word *sophron* means "safe" *phren*. As Padel points out, we might understand the safe or secure *phren* as a *phren* that stays unshaken despite all of the inner ferment.[42] To be *sophron*, or self-restrained in respect to the passions, was to keep one's *phren* secure against the onslaught of the emotions. A state in which the passions, including the passion of anger, were aroused and flooding through the body stood in opposition to a state of *sophrosune* or temperance. *Sophrosune* or temperance was a character trait that, among other things, helped to keep *orge* under control. Temperance was therefore a habit of mind that guided a citizen's behavior in respect to matters having to do with punishment and with politics.

Social norms, as well as *sophrosune*, regulated the use and display of *orge*. Work done on the political aspects of the passional in the Athenian context has primarily dealt with the role of women in lamenting the dead and the erotics of marriage, seduction, pederasty, and homosexuality.[43] Three points have arisen from this work that are relevant to the present study: (1) from the time of the Homeric Greeks to that of the classical Greeks, the vociferous lamentations of both men and women occupied spaces assigned to public performances; (2) despite their apparently high level of comfort with such public displays of emotion, the Athenians also legislated funeral practice in such a way as to assert public control over emotional display and so as to define certain forms of display as "excessive"; (3) the legal limits set upon the citizens' emotional expressions were established on the basis of gender norms (the performance of emotional public lamentation was restricted to women in the classical era) and on the basis of the ideals of active citizenship.[44] Citizens' erotic lives were equally bounded by gender norms and ideals about the good citizen. Adult male citizens could legitimately have concubines, they could be the active partner in a pederastic relationship, and they could visit prostitutes. Women, in contrast, were not to behave in an equivalent fashion, and men who indulged their erotic desires "excessively" or at the wrong age or in the wrong manner risked not being allowed to speak in the assembly or in other public fora.[45] Passion was expected to be part of public life but was equally expected to be subject to public control.

Foucault has described the rules governing erotic passional behavior as an "economy" or set of ideological rules that regulated "expenditure" of the emotions. The Greeks accorded sexual desire a place among appetites like hunger, thirst, and exhaustion that were regularly labeled as "necessities" and needed to be controlled (e.g., *Clouds* 1075).[46] Someone might be "constrained" by a desire for food, drink, sleep, or erotic experiences, and whoever was so constrained had to follow cultural rules about when, where, with whom, how frequently, how openly, and with what intensity those desires could be exposed and satisfied. A temperate man had to limit his indulgence of his sexual desire so as not to weaken himself.[47] The man who failed to follow the rules of the economy that regulated dispersals of desire found himself restricted in his ability to function politically. In this sense, cultural norms for the passional were embedded in the structure of the political. The passional contributed to the constitution of public orders and spaces as with the funeral lamentation but was also restricted by the political order. This was true not only of *eros* but also of *orge*.

Orge was a complicated phenomenon encapsulating an emotion that could lead to destructive quarrels and competitions and also an emotional and cognitive experience associated with fertility, sweetness, and the "melting moods" of sexual desire. As anger *orge* concerned penal prosecution and the breakdown of human relationships; in its relation to fertility, *orge* concerned the creation of human relationships. These iretic and the erotic phenomena could be associated with a single passional concept because the organs of the Athenian physiopsychological apparatus produced a range of emotional and mental experience. There was no tidy division between the elements of the human constitution that produced erotic desire, anger, and mental activity. These sprang up together. What mattered was whether the liquid tumult of the passions was kept under proper control, a matter that the city as well as the individual saw to.

We have already seen that the "bee" could be used to make comparisons between *orge* that was rightly ordered and *orge* that was badly ordered. The bee also functioned as a symbol of Eros (e.g., Eur. *Hipp.* 563).[48] As we investigate systems of punishment in Athens, we will be drawn again and again to additional images of the bee. It was a symbol that captured the contrasts, tensions, and ambiguities inherent in the ambivalent passion of *orge*, and it will become clear that our investigation of Athenian punishment concerns not only the structure of Athenian institutions and not only the ideological norms defining the legitimate prosecutor or the legitimately angry actor but also the symbol world that was used to keep those norms in place. Symbols like the bee-drone image contributed to the Athenian cultural conversation about how to establish norms for conceptions of bodies, selves, and social relations. The symbols encoded networks of principles and comprehensive statements about the conceptual structure that supported ethical and social norms in Athenian life. They were therefore also sites of contestation.

THE *AGON* AND HONOR

Anger was not merely an emotion, nor merely a feeling of desire. It could also be a way of acting or behaving. As we have seen, Aristotle defined anger precisely in terms of the structure of action that it produced: it arose at apparent belittlings (*phainomenes oligorias*) and led to a desire for a punishment that would be visible (*phainomenes timorias*). Anger was made manifest in the world only when people responded to their desires in ways that would be recognized as punishment by onlookers. An emotion was designated as anger when it sparked actions that were meant to safeguard honor and status.

According to Isocrates, it was appropriate for an Athenian to grow angry (*orgizesthai*) at indignity (*aikia*) and dishonor (*atimia*) (Isoc. 20.6). In a certain sense, anger was recognized as existing only when it triggered phenomena crucial to Athenian politics—competitions over honor.[49] Accordingly, anger was defined in part by its interconnectedness with the phenomena of competition. We must consider how the competitions that anger inspired were structured if we wish to understand the penal actions that arose from anger.

It is a commonplace that Athenian communal life, and Greek life more generally, was marked by a vigorous competitiveness. We have all heard the lengthy litany of official competitions—stretching from the funeral games in epic (*Il.* 23.664–75; *Od.* 8.145–49) to the Panathenaic games, the Dionysiac festivals and other sorts of athletic and musical contests; there was even a contest for craftsman of the year (*IG* iii^2 6320). Honor (*time*) was the prize at stake in any Athenian contest.[50] The level of a citizen's honor reflected his position in the city—the anthropological concept of "status role" works here[51] —in two regards. It reflected the value of his personal characteristics to the city: the excellent warrior, the wealthy man who did good deeds with his money, those who were seen to exhibit excellence (*arete*) of character or ability in relation to any of the city's valued activities, like drama, sculpture, military action, and athletics, were all rewarded with honor. But honor or *time* was also a concept used to designate the specific political and legal status assigned to the different classes in the city such as slaves, metics, and citizens. To have political rights was to be *epitimos*; to have none—or to be deprived of some—was to be *atimos*. To hold office was to be *entimos*. Demosthenes calls citizens the class (*taxis*) in which the greatest amount of honor (*time*) is present (*taxis en hei pleistes an tungchanoi times*, 23.24), and so we can say that full *time* was for male citizens; demi-*time*, for female citizens; certain bits of *time*, for *metics*; while nearly none was available to slaves. All citizens were equal before the law and thus had the same level of honor in this one sense. But every public competition gave an Athenian citizen a chance to increase (or risk) the honor that he received due to his personal characteristics and thereby to raise his status-role in the community. The manipulation of honor thus allowed for rank and distinction within the citizenry despite the equality of citizens and allowed the Athenians to establish and maintain social hierarchies. The competitive ethos in Athens was fueled by this construction of honor, which provided simultaneously for equality and for rank.

The Athenian competitive ethos even reached into the courtroom, for the Athenians called judicial trials competitions (*agones*) and called the prosecutor and defendant "competitors" (*agonistai*).[52] Punishment, like reward, was the outcome of a contest for honor, but, a punishment was equivalent to a loss in a contest and a loss of honor.[53] Andocides explicitly treats punishment as the inverse of reward when he describes a trial with the comment: "This present contest [*agon*] is not for acquiring a crown [*stephanephoros*] but to determine whether it is necessary for one who has not wronged the city to go into exile [*pheugein*] for ten years" (And. 4.2). Lysias also recognized the importance of considering reward and punishment in relation to one another and suggested that both "honors and dishonors are distributed for those to come so that they know how to be good" (31.29–30).[54] The Athenians sometimes dramatized the fact that punishment resulted in a loss of honor, in one case, removing a man's honorary crown before executing him (Lyc. 1.122).[55] Anger not only led to efforts to punish but also provided opportunities for a public reassessment of the city's distribution of honor.

Every citizen who participated in a punitive competition was implicated in the struggle for honor. The defendant was not the only person in danger of losing honor in the competition. Isocrates points out that the unsuccessful prosecutor also suffered a reduction in honor: "It is a great penalty [*zemian*] that if the prosecutors are determined to have sued unjustly, they will afterward be seen by you as less estimable [*doxosi cheirous*]" (19.4).[56] Even the successful defendant could be said to have lost honor simply by virtue of having been accused, as Isaeus argues in a citizenship case (8.44).

When punishment stripped a convicted wrongdoer of honor, it simultaneously gave honor back to his victim, honor that the act of wrongdoing had taken away.[57] Several orators refer to the victims of wrongdoing as having been dishonored (*atimoi*) by the wrongdoer, and the victim's loss of honor could be given as a reason to punish. Thus Lochites, in a speech written by Isocrates, based his legal claim on the idea that he had to respond to a wrongdoer not because he had been physically injured but because the assault had brought him dishonor (*atimia*) (Isoc. 20.6). According to Demosthenes, a prosecutor in a public case should not expect to receive any benefit for prosecuting a wrongdoer other than the reassessment of honor (*timoria*); any fine imposed on a wrongdoer in a public case would go to the city (21.45). A penalty that was a diminishment of honor and an injury to the punished was a benefit or profit (*kerdos*) to the prosecutor (e.g., Lys. 1.5, 9.16).[58] Punishment thus provided for a redistribution of the honor relations left imbalanced by an act of violence.

Greek words for punishment reveal the centrality of honor to the process of punishing.[59] The most common word for "punishment" was *timoria* and for "to punish," *timoreisthai*, which we might translate as "to assess and to distribute honor."[60] The words *atimia* and *atimos* ("dishonor" and "dishonored") referred to the specific penalty of political disfranchisement and were originally used to describe the exile who had been cast entirely outside the community (cf. Hyp. fr. 118).[61]

A second set of common Greek terms for "punishment" captures the complementary idea that, for the Athenians, punishment was a process through which the punisher gained something and the punished lost something. The phrase *lambanein diken* meant to "take justice" or "to punish," while its complement, *didonai diken*, meant "to give justice" or "to be punished."[62] The practice of punishing transformed a moment of anger into a moment of justice. The movement from anger to justice or from the personal to the political occurred as a negotiation of honor and of status roles within the community. A punished wrongdoer not only lost honor but also "gave" or "handed over" justice to the punisher, and the punisher not only benefited or regained whatever honor had been lost during the wrongdoing but also took "justice." The definitions of anger and justice were thus constructed *through* one another and *in terms of* honor. The chain of actions generated by anger that led to the social negotiation of honor thus reached completion only in some final moment when "justice" was exchanged.

The competitions that arose from anger were shaped by norms of reciprocity. In order to understand the form of justice operative in Athenian penal situations, we will need to understand the nature of the competitive exchange that took place between punisher and punished and to consider the nature of the *dike* or justice that passed between litigants. Such an investigation will uncover the norms governing the reciprocity of penal exchanges.[63]

RECIPROCITY

The precept that one should "help friends and harm enemies" is heard in Greek texts from the *Iliad* to the fourth century, and norms of reciprocity were among the ethical rules that did the most to shape life in the Greek world. This applies to both "positive" and "negative" reciprocity, where the former term denotes the repayment of favors and the latter refers to the requital of wrongs. In epic texts and in the classical city, whoever had received a gift was generally expected to return the favor. The morality of positive reciprocity, which was crucial to Greek social relations, was shadowed by a morality of negative reciprocity—where one act of harm or suffering is exchanged for another. In Greek oratorical texts, orators described reward as "doing well" (*eupoiein*) and punishment as "doing badly" (*poiein kakos*) to those who had done well and badly to them in the first place.[64] We regularly hear that to the doer must be done.[65] Several scholars have investigated the importance of positive reciprocity to Athenian culture and to Athenian definitions of "justice."[66] But negative reciprocity is underexplored.[67] An exploration of negative reciprocity can, however, build on studies of the positive reciprocity involved in gift exchange.

The anthropological and sociological literature on positive reciprocity has produced two general categories of reciprocity: balanced (or specific) reciprocity and generalized (or diffuse) reciprocity. "Balanced reciprocity refers to simultaneous exchange of items of equivalent value, as when office-mates exchange holiday gifts," whereas "Generalized reciprocity refers to a continuing relationship of exchange that is at any given time unrequited or imbalanced, but that involves mutual expectations that a benefit granted now should be repaid in the future."[68] In balanced reciprocity, the reciprocal act, event B, will assuredly occur because the exchange depends on an explicit prior agreement to exchange items at the same time. In generalized reciprocity, in contrast, event B is produced by some sort of negotiation that begins after the fact of event A. "An effective norm of *generalized* reciprocity is likely to be associated with dense networks of social exchange," which provide for the process of negotiation of the transition from event A to event B.

The guest-host relationships of epic worked on the basis of "generalized reciprocity." A guest would receive hospitality on the unspoken or spoken promise to return the favor at some later date. The exchange would not happen instantaneously. Nor would such an exchange necessarily involve the return of equal favors. The aim was often to repay a favor by outdoing the original benefaction. In the *Odyssey*, for instance, one was supposed to give as much as one could when one returned a favor in order to display wealth and power.[69] In such acts of "unlimited reciprocation" the size of the reciprocal gift is not constrained by notions of equivalence. The model is that of the potlatch where chiefs and community leaders return gifts by striving to outdo one another with acts of reciprocity that aspire to an unstinting or unlimited generosity.[70]

Like the *Odyssey*, Hesiod's *Works and Days* contains a suggestion that a person who returns a favor should give more than he had previously received, employing the norm of "unlimited reciprocation." In Hesiod, however, the purpose of such extreme giving is not (or not only) to display wealth and power but to turn the tables of obligation (*Op.* 342–63, 709–11).[71] According to Hesiod, one needs to return favors with a generosity ample enough to leave one's creditors indebted in turn; they will then have to repay the second favor with a third. Such an approach to gift giving keeps the reciprocal exchange going in an open-ended fashion. The guest-host relationships that upheld the system of positive reciprocity in the world of epic were based on this idea. Systems of positive reciprocity could be used as much for the sake of tending to and nurturing social relationships as for clearing debt obligations or obligations of justice. Such relationships continued to matter in the classical era, especially for elites who built up friendship networks not just in their own cities but also beyond them.[72] The friendship patterns of elites were themselves the dense networks of social exchange that provided the context within which generalized reciprocity could be effected.[73]

Like positive reciprocity, negative reciprocity functioned according to the model of "generalized reciprocity."[74] A wrongdoing was committed (event A) and the attempt to respond to it with punishment (event B) typically followed after some delay and a period of negotiation. But what were the social networks that provided for the negotiation necessary to move a punitive event forward from the wrongdoing (event A) to the punishment (event B) that would complete an exchange of justice? And what kind of justice would be exchanged?

The language of negative reciprocity that echoed from the courtroom rang out with calls for unlimited reciprocity. The only specific punishment that we hear orators requesting for their opponents is death.[75] And the orators had a habit of saying that their opponents deserved to suffer the "last or most extreme things" (*ta eschata*) or the "greatest things" (*ta megista*) in reciprocation for their wrongdoing.[76] Such language was common enough that Aristophanes could make a joke out of it in the *Wealth* where two characters wonder what their fate at the hands of Poverty is likely to be and exchange the following remarks:

> *Blepsidemos:* Do you think that twenty deaths will be enough?
> *Wealth:* Enough for her. But two alone [i.e., one for each character] would satisfy [*apochresousin*] us.

(482–85)

A prosecutor almost always portrayed himself as wishing to respond to a wrongdoer with utmost force, and the competitive exchange involved in punishment was sufficiently dangerous that it could be described as making war or battling (*polemeo*) or as destruction (*apollumi*), regardless of whether the punishments were channeled through penal institutions or carried out by private citizens without help from the city's magistrates (e.g., Aes. 1.64).[77] This rhetoric suggests that prosecutors wished to exchange justice by imposing harms on the wrongdoer to the full extent that they were able. As in positive reciprocity, the language of negative reciprocity served the purpose of allowing citizens to express their power.

The orators who called for the greatest and most extreme punishments—death many times over even—did not necessarily get what they wanted. The Athenians did not punish everything with twenty deaths, nor even with one death. Instead, they employed a system of graduated penalties and could counsel one another against punishing excessively (see chapter 5).[78] Somehow the process of punishing transformed a prosecutor's unlimited desires for reciprocity into limited acts of reciprocity and a prosecutor's unlimited private anger into a limited public anger. The exchange of justice involved in the final moment of reciprocity was governed by the degree to which the city required prosecutors to restrain themselves. The process of moving from the act of wrongdoing to the response to it allowed the citizenry to negotiate the transformation of one citizen's unlimited private anger into a limited public act of judgment.

Anglo-American juridical writing tends to stress the idea that "punishment should fit the crime."[79] Thus Bedau writes: "Punishments should be graded in their severity according to the gravity of the crimes for which they are imposed." The law codes of the United States and the United Kingdom include a list of the graduated penalties to be applied to crimes. In this approach, a notion of equivalence sets the parameters for reciprocity and is embedded in law.[80] The Athenian approach to figuring out what sort of response B would be appropriate for event A involved no simple idea of "fit" that was comprehensively encoded in the legal order. As we saw in chapter 2, Athenian penalties were sometimes decided by law but also often had to be decided by *timesis* (a jury vote on the litigants' two proposals for a sentence). The Athenian effort to bring about event B in response to event A rested on a complex negotiation between the prosecutor's arguments for extreme penalties, the defendant's attempts to defend himself, and the jury's assessments of how to respond to the prosecutor's anger. Litigants drew not only on law but also on stories of past punishments to help their jurors make their judicial decisions, both when they made arguments about guilt and innocence and when they made arguments about what level of penalty to apply.

In his *Third Tetralogy* (4.1.5, 4.1.7) Antiphon argues that it is necessary to inflict such justice as is deserved for the suffering (*axia pathous*) caused by the deed done.[81] "Desert," however, is a contestable term, and so Antiphon's statement does not tell us whether the wrongdoer deserves an "extreme" penalty or a penalty that somehow "equals" the act of wrongdoing. The prosecutor, the defendant, and the jury had to negotiate between these two possibilities by discussing "desert." Which kind of punishment did a given wrongdoer deserve?[82] The litigants used the "dense social networks" of law and social memory in their efforts to push their jurors toward or away from unlimited reciprocity. Not only law but also social memory is central to understanding how the Athenians negotiated value and desert in order to move situations of punitive reciprocity from event A of the wrongdoing to event B of the punishment.[83]

In cases of positive reciprocity unlimited generosity expressed power but also helped to sustain social relations by ensuring that processes of exchange would continue ceaselessly. In cases of the negative reciprocity involved in punishment, calls for unlimited reciprocity also allowed citizens to express their power but had to be reined in in order to bring the exchange of ills to a halt and to *prevent* the exchange of negative reciprocity from continuing. Positive and negative reciprocity are not mirror images of one another despite what is implied by the phrase "help friends and harm enemies." Positive reciprocity allows for the cultivation of social relationships. Negative reciprocity, in contrast, aims to put an end to social disruptions and to disentangle social relationships that have gone awry. Like positive reciprocity, negative reciprocity aims to some degree at restoring normal relations in a community but positive reciprocity does this by enhancing and encouraging already existent and socially useful relationships. Negative reciprocity within the *polis* community aimed to generate harmonious social relations out of contexts where they did not exist or had been disturbed.

SOCIAL MEMORY, SOCIAL KNOWLEDGE

In Athens, any *agon*—whether a wrestling match or a footrace—was typically a spectator event, a communal experience of hearing and seeing in public space that linked competitors to their audience.[84] The penal *agon* that took place in the courtroom was no exception. A trial was a spectacle in which jurors, numbering anywhere from 200 to several thousand, watched and listened to litigants as those litigants tried to generate public anger (or public pity; see chapter 5) and public judgment from their private anger. Even arbitrations were often expected to have many, or too many, spectators (see chapter 4). In Athens, the public spectacle provided by a trial was a particularly good occasion to discuss the past, present, and future and to use and craft social memory, not least because public spectacles produced the greatest numbers of witnesses.

In using the phrase "social memory," I follow Fentress and Wickham who use the phrase to capture not only the idea that a community can share a set of narratives but also the idea that individuals can affect the narratives of their community. They write:

> An important problem . . . is how to elaborate a conception of memory which, while doing full justice to the collective side of one's conscious life, does not render the individual a sort of automaton, passively obeying the interiorized collective will. . . . How does one make individual memories "social" then? Essentially, by talking about them. . . . The production of spoken or written narratives about the past, will take form within the framework of the meaning given them by the group inside which they are told.[85]

The communal production of memories available for all to share occurs on public occasions or through public *media* in which the past, present, and future come under discussion. A trial was such an occasion.

In Athens social memory was especially important for crafting the citizenry's self-understanding because democratic Athens was a largely oral rather than literate culture.[86] Writing began to be used for public documentation on a regular basis only late in the democracy, and it seems to have been introduced to supplement rather than to replace other, primarily oral, technologies. The Athenians' distrust of the written document is no doubt partially explained by the fact that they began to use signatures and cursive writing relatively late, and so forgeries were a distinct possibility throughout most of the democracy.[87] For most of the classical period, oral and written modes of communication functioned alongside one another, but oral communication was accorded priority. Knowledge about the city's past was stored not in texts but in social memory. The content of the citizenry's social memory provided citizens with knowledge about themselves, about what their city had been, and about how to understand why they did what they did as Athenians.

The importance of social memories that were passed on orally led to a valorization of the eyewitness, the person who had actually seen the events caught in the narratives lodged in social memory. A witness's claim to have seen an event was the only proof that it had happened. Thus the eyes were generally treated as being the primary source of knowledge.[88] The verbs for "seeing" and "knowing" are the same (*horao*, "I see," has as its perfect form the *oida* that is "I know" ["I have seen"]). Writers like Herodotus and Heraclitus considered eyewitnessing or *autopsia* to be the best means of knowing something.[89] And pre-Socratic philosophers, Plato, and post-Platonic thinkers were all intrigued by the question of the relation between the senses, particularly that of sight, and knowledge.[90]

In the Athenian context, it took a series of moments of "witnessing" to construct social memory. Contracts undertaken without witnesses are extant only from the 320s on.[91] People and their bodies, and not texts, were regularly viewed as being the most trustworthy containers of knowledge about the past.[92] In the courts, witnesses were deemed more informative than either written documents or hearsay reports, even after approximately 380 when the Athenians began to require that evidence be presented in court in written form.[93] This idea appears in the following case from the mid-fourth century in which an orator, who was by profession a banker, admitted to relying on written evidence, and said: "Let no one be amazed that we have precise knowledge of this affair; for bankers are accustomed to write out reminders [*hupomnemata*]" (Dem. 49.5). The document is only a reminder; it cannot be proof. The speaker excuses his use of writing on the grounds that he is a banker and asserts that he himself, not the text, should be understood to be the container of knowledge. The practice of torturing slaves for evidence was another claim that truth about the past resided in the body of a witness, and that this person or body was the best source of information.[94]

There was one crucial exception to the Athenian distrust of the written document. This was the Athenian valorization of written law. This valorization, however, seems to have been based at least in part on an assimilation of law to the oral and visual modes of knowledge used to construct social memory. Thus in the *Rhetoric* Aristotle describes "law" as a form of evidence equivalent to the witness (1375a24–25). This is a reasonable formulation of the role played by law in the Athenian courts, and a study of law in Athens involves an examination of what and how the laws helped the citizens to remember (see chapter 8).

R. Thomas argues that social memory rarely extends farther than three generations or "beyond the grand-father" into the past in an oral culture.[95] In Athens the limits of human memory generally set the parameters for what could be proved as true. The oral poets who recited stories more than three generations old—like the story of the Trojan War—were an exception to this rule, and the poets—children of a muse named *Mnemosyne*, or Memory—had to be inspired by her in order to produce their "inhuman" knowledge "of the past." In oral cultures the truth about the facts of "past history" exists primarily in the living "social memory" of a populace and in those people who constitute the living "political body." History could be preserved in them and passed on through them without recourse to written texts.[96] But oral forms of communication were naturally also visual forms of communication in the ancient world. Social memory could be constantly recreated only through moments of spectacle.

Social memory needed to be re-created not only in order to preserve the past but also for the sake of the future. Social memory not only contains a community's history and the narratives it wants to remember but also (and more importantly) is a body of "knowledge" that is used in the *present*. Moreover, "social memory" is constructed in the *present* so as to generate sources of knowledge for the *future*.[97] In other words, social memory is always operationalized in the present, and it is operationalized in the present so as to provide a society with the information that it *presently* thinks will be worth knowing *in the future*. The Athenians of the classical era did not merely use or try to preserve the social memory bequeathed to them by their ancestors. They also decided what sort of social memories they wished to pass on to their own descendants.

In situations of positive reciprocity, the Athenians stressed the idea that they needed to find ways of constructing social memory so that favors could not be forgotten.[98] In situations of negative reciprocity, social memory was not needed for the purposes of reminding people of the wrongs they had suffered. These seem to have slipped the Athenian mind rather less easily than favors (see chapter 3).[99] In the context of negative reciprocity, social memory was needed to help a litigant prove that something that he remembered had in fact happened and that it was wrong. The easiest way to prove that an action was wrong was to refer to a decision to that effect made by the *demos* on an earlier occasion, whether that decision was encoded in law or in a story of an earlier punishment. A litigant invoked social memory before a large citizen audience. Thus he had the opportunity to impact social memory by offering his own interpretation of the past and by inserting his own judicial case into the social memory. When two litigants exchanged justice, a cycle of reciprocity reached its conclusion and, in addition, a new story about how to define justice was available for public consideration and consumption.

The punitive contests that were inspired by anger gave shape to anger by allowing it to be acted out. Anger was made real in the world precisely when citizens were able to speak to spectator audiences. When citizens spoke before their fellows, they engaged them in decision making about reciprocity. In the process, litigants and spectators invoked the social memories encoded in stories and laws and partook in crafting a set of communal norms, stories, and memories that established the city's formulations of value and that could be used to make decisions upon desert at later points in time. One citizen's effort to act on his anger thus gave rise to the constraints that would be set upon some other citizen's later efforts to do the same. Moreover, what was at stake in any given penal competition was not only the fate of a particular wrongdoer and prosecutor, not only the particular relation of each to his anger and honor, but also the definitions of reciprocity, desert, social memory, and law used to structure democratic political practice in Athens. When a particular citizen decided to act out or through or with his anger, he had to adhere to social norms but he also had opportunity to revise them. His anger put definitions of justice at issue. One of the central subjects of investigation that lies ahead is the relationship between law and social memory in Athens and the relative importance of each to the assessment of value, desert, and justice in the city.

LANGUAGE

Some of the social norms that were at stake in the system of punishment were embedded in the language of punishment itself. The different words for punishment—*timoria, didomi* and *lambano diken, kolazo, zemia*—encapsulated diverse conceptualizations of the practice and of desert. Orators mobilized distinctive ideas about how to punish legitimately when they chose one word for punishment over another. In the fourth century, all of the punitive words could be used for either public or private cases, all applied to every kind of penalty, and each could be used to describe acts of extrainstitutional self-help as well as punishment through the courts.[100] The differences between the words did not denote institutional distinctions and instead had to do with what was happening to the *people* (punished, punisher, and *polis* community) involved in any given situation of punishment.

We have already come across some of the words that were used for punishment: *timoria* and its verbal cognates, which stress the reassessment of honor and status in punishment;[101] the phrases *didonai* and *lambanein diken*, which highlight the exchange of justice between the punisher and the punished; and the phrase "doing badly" to a wrongdoer, which underscores the role of reciprocity in punishment and in the larger Athenian social context.[102] All of these words stress the importance of social relationships and relationality to the process of punishing. Two more words also appeared frequently in oratory but bear rather different connotations: *zemia* (penalty) with its verbal cognate *zemioo* and *kolazein* (punish).[103]

The words *zemia* and *zemioo* did not emphasize a set of relations between people or their roles in punishment but rather the effect of punishment on the wrongdoer. *Zemia* primarily meant "harmful loss" or "payment" and could also appear outside of the context of punishment, for instance, to characterize the impact of the death of a son on a father.[104] This word also linked the process of punitive exchange to the process of monetary exchange and to the status of citizens as economic actors.

Kolazein introduces a more drastic shift of perspective. *Kolazein* first appears in Lysias and in his speeches is always used in public cases where the penalty is going to the city. This seems connected to the fact that in the late fifth century, the collectors for the public treasury were known as *kolastai*. Also, in a late fifth-century decree, the word is used to describe what the Council of 500 did when it punished in a case of bribery.[105] In its early uses the word *kolazein* thus seems to have been associated with cases of punishment where the public, and not a private citizen, was understood to be the punisher. It would seem that the word *kolazein* originally applied to acts of punishment where what was at issue was the relationship of the wrongdoer to the community and not the relationship between two citizens.

Later uses of the word in oratory and uses of the word in nonoratorical texts associate the word *kolazein* with reformative approaches to punishment. The word was used to refer to the chastisement of children and slaves (Xen. *Oec.* 13.67) and even in one case to the chastisement of a man who was base but who had not yet actually committed a wrongdoing (Isoc. 20.14).

Theophrastus uses the vocabulary of *kolasis* to refer to a horticultural process that improves the quality of a tree's crop of fruit.[106] Thus he writes: "They drive an iron peg into the almond tree and, when they have made a hole, they replace it with a peg of oakwood and they hide this with earth; *this process some call chastisement* [kalousi kolazein] *because the tree was out of order* [*hubrizon*]. . . . In Arcadia they call this straightening [*euthunein*] the sorb" (*History of Plants*, 2.7.6–7).[107] Citizens could be prosecuted for *hubris*, the failure to behave as befit one's position in the social hierarchies structuring the world of the *polis*.[108] The tree might have pegs driven into it or it might have its fluid drained off with "blows," but whatever the case it was being cured of *hubris*. Removal of a problem within the tree, a problem of *hubris*, improved the entire tree. It is *because* the horticulturist needs to improve a tree that is out of order or hubristic that the process can be described as *kolasis* or a form of punishment. Similarly, the word for pruning, *diakatharsis*, comes from a word that connotes cleansing (*katharsis*) in the context of wrongdoing and pollution.

The word *kolasis* seems to refer to the effort to teach people their proper places in the city's social structure—most usually children and hubristic wrongdoers. The word *kolazein* thus directs the audience's attention to what must be done to the punished. For that matter, the word *kolazein* never appears in oratory without a direct object, and its object was always the wrongdoer. Moreover, the substantive *kolasis* is absent from oratory. The absence of the substantive, combined with the emphasis on the object-directed nature of the verbal forms, reveals that the word *kolazein* did not refer to a process that could be abstracted from particular contexts but always connoted the effects of punishment on some specific wrongdoer. Punishment, described this way, was inseparable from the context and the object of action. The word *kolazein* shifts the focus away from the idea of exchange between parties, away from the idea of reciprocity and victim-driven punishment, and to the idea of how the nature of the wrongdoer is affected by punishment. The switch of focus from the victim to the wrongdoer entails a switch in understandings of the social relations involved in justice.

Aristotle hit on an important historical and theoretical point when he defined the difference between *timoria* and *kolasis* thus: "The latter [*kolasis*] is inflicted in the interest of the sufferer, the former [*timoria*] in the interest of him who inflicts it, so that he may be satisfied [*hina plerothei*]" (*Rhet.* 1369b12–14). The verb *timoreisthai* appears without a direct object as often as it appears with one; this fact highlights the verb's status as referring to the process of punishing and to the subjects or agents who carry it out more than to the effects of punishment upon those who are acted upon.[109] The phrases *didonai diken* and *lambanein diken* establish a third set of relationships, and the phrase "give justice" constitutes the wrongdoer as an active subject or agent of punishment rather than as its object.[110] The flexibility of the relations described by the Greek vocabulary of punishment stands in marked contrast to the general tendency of Anglo-American English to speak of the criminal always as the direct object or passive subject of a verb of punishment. Even where the punished is "subject" or nominative, it is because: "She got twenty-five years."[111]

Timoria was the most common substantive used to describe punishment. The process of reassessing honor could be discussed as a thing in and of itself. In oratory, there were no substantives to go with the verbal phrases *didonai* and *lambanein diken* and *kolazein*. These activities could be discussed only with reference to subjects and objects, agents and those acted upon. While the word *timoria* was used to describe the process of punishing, the verbal phrases described the goals of a given act of punishment. The process of *timoria* could therefore be carried out, in any given context, for the sake of one of two different and incompatible ends: *either* in order to take justice from the wrongdoer (*lambanein/didonai diken*) *or* in order to teach a wrongdoer his or her place in the social order (*kolazein*).[112] Each orator favored one of these goals over the other, but eight of the ten orators preferred to deal with a wrongdoer by "taking justice." Only Hyperides and Lycurgus preferred the word *kolazein* to the pair *didonai* and *lambanein diken* (see appendix 4).

These two late-fourth-century orators seem to have gotten their taste for the language of reform from Plato. Plato is the earliest extant author to prioritize the language of *kolazein* and education to the language of reciprocity and exchange. Plato never employed the phrase *lambanein diken*; his Socrates refused to say that he or any one else should "take" justice "away" from the wrongdoer. Plato not only rejected the standard Athenian goal of punishment, but he also rejected the general agreement to treat punishment as a process of honor assessment (*timoria*). Plato introduced the substantive *kolasis* and used it and *kolazein* with greater frequency than he used *timoria* and other words derived from *time*. Unlike any of the orators, Plato wished to turn the whole process of punishment into a matter of educating the wrongdoer. For him that goal was too important to be a mere side effect of a process with other purposes. Plato thus rejected the language that described punishment as a reassessment of honor, chose instead to focus on punishment as education, and developed the first comprehensive theory of reformative punishment (see chapter 10).[113]

Aristotle's punitive vocabulary was equally idiosyncratic. He resisted the need to make a choice between Athenian and Platonic conceptions of punishment. Thus he regularly referred to punishment with a compound phrase: *he timoria kai he kolasis*.[115] Aristotle thought that punishment should pay attention to both a victim's anger and a wrongdoer's soul, and so he joined the Athenian word for punishment to the Platonic (see chapter 11). Like Plato, Aristotle used vocabulary to mark his philosophical commitments.

The very diversity of the Athenian vocabulary for punishment reveals how a unitary institutional and cultural structure could nonetheless be made to fit diverse political paradigms of authority and justice. The various words for punishment also show the way in which language is a site of contest over how to define the shape of human life. Plato and Aristotle recognized the political implications that were involved in making different decisions about how to punish. Both philosophers picked and chose from their society's linguistic tool kit as part of their effort to revise concepts at the heart of the Athenian punitive and political order. They wished to revise the conceptualization of desert, based on anger and honor, that was dominant in Athens, They thought that a new language would be necessary to express their new definitions of desert and justice. Their care reveals how much is at stake in even the everyday formulations of desert that undergird authority and also that the conceptual structure supporting punishment is contestable.

CONCLUSION

In Athens the ideological definitions of the legitimate prosecutor and legitimate punishment rested on concepts like anger, honor, reciprocity, and social knowledge that were central to the city's definition of the good citizen. The contest over how to define punishment grew out of conflicting understandings of how to handle anger in the community—out of conflicting analyses of the problems posed by anger to the *polis* and how to solve them. The debate over how to organize punishment touched the political life of the whole city, and the ideological construction of the good prosecutor and the good male citizen did not occur independently of the ideological construction of female citizenship and noncitizenship. There were norms governing the participation of all members of the city in anger, reciprocity, and the construction of social knowledge. These norms, it is true, defined women and slaves as nonpunishers and foreigners as people who could prosecute only in limited circumstances. But when women, slaves, and foreigners obeyed the social norms bounding their use of anger, their activities in the city complemented the activities of the male citizen prosecutor and made his status as prosecutor not only necessary but even practicable.

In chapter 4, I discuss tragedy in order to analyze the ways in which the Athenians thought of wrongdoing and anger as problematic for a community. The Athenian mythotragical imagination reveals what sorts of problems of human interaction were associated with anger and what sorts of problems punishment was expected to solve. The process of dealing with anger and of working reciprocal justice will be the subject of chapters 5 through 9. In those chapters, we can see how the penal institutions assigned different groups in the city particular roles in the system of punishment in order to address the problems posed to the community by wrongdoing and anger. All the members of the city had roles in punishment that allowed them to be integrated into a single system of punishment and into the unified system of ethics and value that established the male citizen as the city's primary prosecutor and structured Athenian politics.

CHAPTER 4

Punishment and Its Tragic Problems

THE MYTHIC IMAGINARY

Every year in late January the Athenians held a festival called Anthesteria, also known as the Older Dionysia. The Athenians broke out the year's new wine on the second day of this festival, which was called *Choes* after the wine pitchers. The Anthesteria was celebrated throughout Greece, but the Choes, only in Athens.[1] It was one of the "most polluted days" of the Athenian year because it was said to be the day that Orestes had arrived in Athens, bearing blood-guilt from the murder of his mother and seeking purification.[2] On this festival day, the Athenians varnished their house doors with purifying pitch, and whole households retired behind the blackened fronts to drink the new wine in one another's company.[3] Adults received individual drinking jugs (although it is impossible to say whether women participated as well as men). Even slaves might receive their own individual pitchers.[4] Children also received jugs, but it is unlikely that they drank wine from them.[5] The festival practice of using individual cups stood in strong contrast to the sympotic tradition of passing a shared cup. Those who participated in the festival, unlike sympotic drinkers, also drank without exchanging a word, competing to see who could drink the fastest.[6] The day was sufficiently important that the stages of an Athenian's initiation into the community could be listed as birth, *choes*, adolescence, and marriage.[7] On this day, all of the sanctuaries were closed except for one.[8]

In *Iphigeneia in Tauris*, Euripides gives an etiology of the festival that places its roots in Orestes' arrival to Athens and the response of the community to his guilt. Orestes recounts that when he arrived in Athens:

> At first no host received me willingly. I was hated by the gods. Some had respect and pity, and set a table for me as their guest: a separate table, alone, under the same roof as them. By their silence they built up the feeling that I couldn't be spoken to (or that I might not speak) so I was apart from them in food and drink. Each enjoyed the pleasure of Bacchus, pouring an equal amount for all, but into private cups. . . . I was my mother's killer. I hurt in silence, pretending not to notice. I cried. I hear my sufferings became a festival for the Athenians. And still the custom says: Athena's people honor a bowl made for the Choes. (947–60)

According to Euripides' fictionalized etiology, Orestes' arrival forced the Athenians to confront the problem of how to deal with wrongdoing and pollution. This the Athenians did, in the etiology, by reorganizing fundamental social relationships. Their guest was polluted, and so Orestes could not be accorded the welcome standardly given to guests. He was isolated, and the norms of guest-host relationships and friendship that facilitated alliances between strangers were thus broken. His presence was problematic enough that the Athenians could not talk and sing as at a symposium. While Orestes was in their midst, they sat silent, repudiating one of the most important forms of social interaction. But the norms of guest friendship could not be broken entirely. Orestes was given food and drink. Both isolation and integration were brought to bear in the attempt to solve the problem of wrongdoing.

The festival not only ritualized the problem of the polluted wrongdoer in the community but also dramatized the various roles that the Athenians would have to play in dealing with that polluted wrongdoer. The citizenry had to confront the problem of Orestes not merely as a collective whole but also as a set of individuals.[9] Most festivals took place in capacious public spaces. This one did not. The festival made the point that each Athenian had to face the problem of pollution as a member of an *oikos* or household. Each Athenian, however, also played another role as he sat drinking in silence. Callimachus described the *Choes* as the day when all festival drinkers drank from an Oresteian cup.[10] The drinkers were not only the citizens who had accepted Orestes into the city, not only members of households, but each was also Orestes, the lonely matricide. Garlands worn by citizens during the course of the ritual could not be hung in sanctuaries because they had been polluted.

In the festival of *Choes* citizens were annually initiated and reinitiated into an imaginative exploration of the problem of wrongdoing in the community, and the solution was figured partly in terms of their own behavior. With the ritual Athenians enacted the lesson that dealing with the problem of the wrongdoer required keeping in mind the overlapping penal roles of each Athenian: each was at once an isolated and competitive individual, a member of an *oikos*, and a member of the *polis* understood as a set of isolated households. The solution modeled by the festival also drew on conceptual relationships established in the tragic and mythical imagination, and so Athenian litigants and jurors entered the courtroom having participated in communal explorations of the role of the citizen in punishment as figured in the community's mythotragical imagination.

In this chapter I explore the conceptualization of punishment made present to the Athenian citizenry in their tragedies.[11] I do this by investigating the poetic and linguistic tropes that appear over and over again in the tragedians' narratives of punishment. The trope of "anger" is repeatedly tied to the themes of "disease," "necessity," and "visibility" in many of the extant plays.[12] These tropes function as part of the figurative "grammar" used to talk about punishment in tragedy, and an investigation of this grammar elucidates what kind of process the Athenians thought that "punishing" was. It also reveals the problems that "wrongdoing" and "punishing" entailed for the Athenians. In chapter 3, I laid the foundation for an exploration of the processes of anger, competition, reciprocity, and visuality. These "ideological elements" were not separable and discrete in any given punishment. Rather they were different aspects of a composite process. This chapter explores the intersection of anger, vision, reciprocity, and competition in the Athenian tragic imagination in order to see how the Athenians understood the practice of punishment taken entire and in order to see what problems, to their minds, arose from the intersection.

METHOD

A word about method. I am investigating the conceptual "deep structure" underlying tragedy, employing a methodology akin to that of structuralism, which attempts to reconstruct the fundamental ideational "codes" according to which a society is organized.[13] "The idea [is] that certain concepts are not merely understood intellectually; rather they are used automatically, unconsciously, and without noticeable effort as part of normal functioning. Concepts used in this way have different, and more important, psychological status than those that are only [sic] thought about consciously."[14] As a theory of language and cognitive linguistics, structuralism does two things: it looks for categorical patterns in the ways members of a culture connect ideas; and it looks specifically for patterns of opposition (like the raw and the cooked, male and female, inside the city and outside). Structuralism does not invest itself simply in uncovering oppositions. Structuralists also show how the rhetorical power of these oppositions is deployed and how the tensions inherent in the dichotomies are negotiated institutionally and socially (e.g., in festivals, in drama, and in politics).[15]

The approach of the structuralists is useful but, on one front in particular, inadequate. Language does to a large extent function by means of categorization, but this categorization is by no means exclusively oppositional or dichotomous.[16] Any "conventional linguistic expression" encodes ideas or opinions about the world.[17] English speakers, for instance, tend to describe their feelings of anger by using a vocabulary of heat and mass. Those metaphors reveal something about how we (subconsciously) understand and define anger.[18] The conceptual metaphors that generate the linguistic expressions, tropes, and clichés regularly associated with a concept constitute the "grammar" of that concept.[19]

A grammar of a concept is produced by compiling the maximum possible number of conventional linguistic expressions associated with it.[20] One can list all the descriptors that members of a culture might normally use for anger just as one can list the items one might "typically" take along to a baseball game. After compiling what English-speakers say about "anger," one can say that the "grammar" of anger uses the vocabulary of heat and mass. The catalogs, however, are not complete at this point. Like "anger," the tropes of "heat" and "mass" will in turn have a set of tropes associated with them that constitute their own grammars. One "grammar" leads to another in a phenomenon called "chaining."[21] The chains that lead from one grammar to another reveal the "deep structure" or conceptual framework of a language by revealing the ways in which a culture's conceptual categories are connected to one another. This phenomenon underlies the interest that we all take in the familiar game of word association. But is the game of word association a game that can be played on the surface of literary texts?

The tragedians were quirky playwrights who imposed idiosyncratic linguistic patterns and ideas on their native language. To some extent, however, they had to leave in place the category structures bequeathed them as raw material by their language regardless of how brilliant and unconventional each may have been.[22] Linguistic patterns and repetitions of usage do appear across the texts of Aeschylus, Sophocles, and Euripides. I use their tragedies to find a "grammar of punishment" for Athens but only by drawing on expressions that are repeated across tragedians and across several plays. Nor do I take the language of tragedy, not even the conventional language of tragedy, as representing the day-to-day language of the Athenians. The playwrights could have been deploying a set of conceptual conventions restricted wholly to the genre of tragedy. My approach has been to consider the grammars of punishment and anger that turn up in tragedy as relevant to an exploration of Athenian culture only when the tragedians are using discourses that also appear in oratory, whether expanding on them or treating them differently.

The language of Greek moralizing does in fact betray a remarkable consistency across genres, as Halliwell found in his study of the uses of laughter in Greek culture.

> It will emerge, I believe, that the forces contained in or expressed by laughter were a recurrent subject of Greek moralizing. One incidental result of the inquiry will be to demonstrate just how pronounced an inclination to moralizing patterns of thought existed within Greek attitudes to personal and social behavior. Thus it will prove consistently possible to cite alongside one another as confirmative of the existence of certain habits of mentality, sources such as comedy, oratory, tragedy, history, which in other respects are so disparate.[23]

The same proves true in respect to punishing. The conceptual framework that undergirded discussions of punishment in oratory proves to have been central to the ideational systems that functioned in all Athenian literary genres and confirms the existence of certain habits of mentality in Athenian culture.

The grammar of punishment found in fifth-century tragedy, like that found in fourth-century oratory, turns substantially around the concept of anger (especially *thumos, menis, cholos, orge*). The associative "chains" that lead from the grammars of "punishment" and "anger" in tragedy, produce an accumulation of mutually referential grammars, and the tragic grammar of punishment turns out to rely heavily on four sets of metaphors: a grammar of "vision," a grammar of "memory," a grammar of "disease," and a grammar of "necessity." The grammar of "vision" and the grammar of "necessity" converge in a grammar of "power." This chapter examines the significance of these tropes with a view to uncovering what the Athenians worried about when they embarked on an effort to respond to wrongdoing.

DISEASE AND REMEDY

Situations of punishment as represented in tragedy are regularly characterized with the medical terminology of disease and cure (*nosos, pharmakon, iasis, akos, alexema*).[24] In tragedy, these terms rarely denote biological sickness. They serve as metaphorical concepts used by the tragedians to denote disorders at the level of both the individual consciousness and the social order, just as the phenomenon of pollution was used to discuss such problems in the historical city.[25] The disease involved in or produced by cases of wrongdoing and punishment could be located in the victim of a wrongdoing, in the would-be punisher, or in the wrongdoer. In Euripides' *Electra* (318), Electra says that the spilled blood of Agamemnon, the victim, is a "festering within the house." In the *Eumenides* (478–79), Athena ponders what to do about the fact that the Erinyes, who are would-be punishers, will leave behind poison (*ios*) and intolerable, horrid disease (*nosos*) in the land (*chorai, pedoi*) if their desire to punish is left unsatisfied.[26] In the *Orestes*, Euripides gives the trope of the diseased wrongdoer especial prominence by showing us Orestes literally on a sickbed pondering the nature of his illness.[27] The wrongdoer Orestes not only has a disease, which is dreaded but curable (395), but is also a disease for the land (*kata gen*) (831). All the parties to a wrongdoing—victim, punisher, wrongdoer, and community—could be implicated in the trope of disease and its cure.

The disease in which all were implicated was anger.[28] Both the victim of wrongdoing and the would-be punisher needed to be cured because they *felt* anger.[29] Thus, Prometheus is said by the chorus to suffer from "diseased anger" (*orges nosouses*) because of his desire to punish Zeus (Aesch. *PB*, 379),[30] while the disease brought by the Erinyes emanates from their hearts or spirits, and these are wrathful (*ek phronematon*; *mainadon, kotos, Eum.* 480; 499–506). Passions, like diseases, were said to "fall upon" people. Girard formulates the problem of violence within the community in similar terms: "The truth about violence is that if left unappeased it will accumulate until it overflows and floods an area." Apollo similarly explains leprous ulcers and plagues as attacks made by the wrath of malignant powers that rise up underneath the earth (*menimata, Lib.* 278–84). And Apollo himself is the god not only of revenge but also of medicine and purification.[31]

The language of passion as disease is a common trope in Greek literature. *Eros* was subject to "the belief [that] runs deeply through ancient medicine, social practice, and literature that intense desire is a diseased state affecting the soul and body, an illness that up to a point can be discerned and analyzed but that is remarkably difficult to treat."[32] The same was true of anger, which was often described with the word *ome*, a medical term for raw wounds. The trope of disease expressed the idea that the angry person suffered an invasive attack, or what Padel calls a "dangerous intrusion on life and self," which could be cured only with difficulty.[33]

Tragic characters will pray for a cure to this intrusion, as Medea's nurse does in the opening of Euripides' *Medea*, a play about the efforts of the non-Greek princess Medea to repay her husband Jason for violating their marriage bonds by marrying the daughter of the king of Corinth. Medea's nurse prays that there will be a cure for the strife between Medea and Jason that has led to a situation where "all is enmity and the strongest bonds of *philia* suffer disease" (*nun d'echthra panta, kai nosei ta philtata*, 16). At this early point in the play, the nurse still hopes for a reconciliation between Medea and Jason, but the members of the chorus eventually let it be known that the anger that motivates Medea's conflict with Jason will be extremely difficult to cure because when lovers (*philoi*) meet in strife, their anger (*orge*) is fearsome and hard to remedy (*deine, dusiatos*) (520). *Orge*, they recognize, undoes social bonds.

In the *History of the Peloponnesian War*, Thucydides places the concept of *orge* at the heart of his analysis of the civil war in Corcyra (book 3). Thucydides argues that unbounded and spreading passions, insubordinate to the idea of justice, destroyed the city (*para tous nomous*; *akrates orges*; *kreisson de tou dikaiou*; 3.84.2). He concludes his analysis with the remark that the people of Corcyra were the first among the Greeks to display "such tempers [*toiautais orgais*] in their city" (3.85.1). Innumerable commentators have taken the description of the Corcyrean civil war to be an analogue to the book 2 discussion of the deadly plague in Athens. Following their lead, we might add that Thucydides' narrative suggests that *orge* did to Corcyra what disease did to Athens. Both brought about the disintegration of the community.

Tragic characters who suffer from the disease of anger regularly betray their state in their eyes. In this they are like Iliadic heroes who "looked darkly" at those who angered them.[34] The Aeschylean Erinyes, who punish out of hate and anger, drip hateful liquids from their eyes, and Medea's nurse notices that Medea's eyes flash like a bull's (Eur. *Med.* 92). This is a warning to the nurse that Medea's angry emotions will have an effect not only on herself but on those around her; they will extend from Medea to touch the rest of the world like the liquids that drip from the eyes of the Erinyes. The gaze represents human intersubjectivity and relationality. The materiality of the Erinyes' gaze represents the concrete impact that emotional engagements have on the world. The figure of the diseased glance marks the fact that something has gone wrong with human interactions. An angry gaze might even be murderous. In Euripides' *Madness of Herakles*, the warrior hero at last returns home from his labors only to find his wife and children at the mercy of a tyrant. After killing this tyrant, Herakles is not able to cease fighting. In a fit of "madness" sent by Hera (969–71, 982–83, 989), Herakles mistakes his wife and children for relatives of the tyrant and kills them in "anger" and with a Gorgon-eyed gaze (anger, 549, 562, 526; *ho d' agriopon omma Gorgonos strephon*, 990; cf. 868). Herakles' anger, his madness, and his desire to kill are expressed with a metaphor that gives his gaze the fatal power of the Gorgon Medusa, who turned to stone those who looked upon her and upon whom she looked.

The trope of angry visuality interfaces with that of bestiality not only in the *Medea* but also in Euripides' *Hecuba*. After the Trojan War, Hecuba, the former queen of the fallen city, blinds her son's guardian Polymestor and kills his sons because he has killed her son despite promising to keep him safe during the war. As he is being blinded, Polymestor prophesies Hecuba's death: she will fall from a ship's mast into the sea and then turn into a dog whose eyes blaze fire. She will become a sailor's beacon, a sign permanently warning travelers about unseen dangers (Eur. *Hec.* 808).[35] Her anger at Polymestor will be refined into a warning sign.

Tragic characters did not merely reveal their anger in their eyes but were also initially aroused to anger or inspired to angry action by moments of viewing. For instance, Medea's nurse fears letting the children be seen by the angry Medea, because she is afraid that the sight may trigger some act of rage (Eur. *Med.* 100). And a guilt-ridden Helen moves through Argos at night for fear of being seen and stoned (Eur. *Or.* 57).[36] People were roused to anger and the desire to punish when they caught sight of the people and things that reminded them of wrongs that they had suffered.

Sight was a key part of the process that inspired people to anger and punishment. In chapter 3, we saw that, in the Athenian conceptual world, knowledge was thought to be generated out of visual experience. Now we have seen in addition that the transfer of emotion, especially the emotion of anger, ocurred in moments of viewing or spectacle. This was possible because seeing was thought of as a process of two-way exchange between seer and seen. Frequently in Greek thought, vision was treated as the mutual transfer of "particles" or "fire," from seer to seen and vice versa. "According to early Greek theories of perception, the eye was the source of a ray of light—of fire—that was necessary for vision. As eyes beamed, so they saw; hence the single act of beaming and seeing could not fail to affect the person who was the object of the illuminated/illuminating gaze."[37] Aristotle provides a graphic example of the idea that vision could be understood as a physical transfer of properties from seer to seen when he remarks that mirrors ended up covered with blood whenever a woman who was menstruating looked into them (*On Dreams* 2.459b25–35).[38] To see was to be seen and to be seen was to see. The processes of vision entailed a two-way physical exchange of what was inside, or in the innards of, both seer and seen. In the context of punishment, what was inside when people looked at one another was anger—for instance, the Erinyes' hateful liquids—and this was exchanged in the crossing of glances. The latter occurred in moments of spectacle.

We are accustomed, thanks to Aristotle's theory of tragedy, to the idea that spectacles can generate emotions. On his account, the experience of watching tragedy should produce feelings of pity and fear in the viewer. Herodotus relates a particularly striking historical example of the emotive effect of spectacle when he reports that Phrynichus's tragedy presented in 493, the *Capture of Miletus*, moved the "theater" (or better, the spectators, those engaged in seeing as a collective group) to tears (*es dakrua te epese to theetron*, 6.21). Segal remarks on Herodotus's story that "in tragedy, it is the eye that permits the strongest and most complex play of emotions. . . . The [Herodotean] passage indicates the emotional involvement of the Athenian audience in the tragic performances, but it also shows the recognition of the special category of collective emotion. . . . Important as the aural experience is for memory and the transmission of culture, Greek thought tends to privilege vision as the primary area of knowledge and even of emotion."[39] Moments of spectacle not only motivated but even necessitated an exchange of some sort—whether of glances, of emotion, or of justice.

The eyes were associated not only with knowledge and the arousal of emotions but also with justice and properly ordered reciprocity. Medea, for instance, argues that justice does not inhabit the eyes of a person (*dike gar ouk enest' en ophthalmois broton*) who hates on sight *without* having been wronged (*hostis . . . stugei dedorkos, ouden edikemenos*) (Eur. *Med*. 219–21)."[40] The idea is that the exchange of anger and hate between seer and seen had to be based on a legitimately designated wrong and on the legitimate need for reciprocity. Only if these criteria were met could it be said that justice "inhabits" or "is in" somebody's eyes. Justice could be located in the eyes because seeing was a form of reciprocal interaction that could function as an analogue for other forms of reciprocity. In other words, the justice of punishment, the right response to wrongdoing, inhabits or takes place in the realm of human intersubjectivity marked out by the gaze. The wrongdoer and punisher, the two contending parties, exchanged "glances" when they exchanged justice. Acts of reciprocity implicated them in one another's emotional state and did so through spectacle and the experience of seeing.

Medea's remark is wise if also replete with irony. She makes this statement about the nature of justice before taking revenge on her husband Jason and his new wife by killing not only the wife but also the two sons she has had with Jason. She kills innocents who have done her no wrong, turning her angry glance, as the nurse feared, on the innocent children without justification and thereby violating the rules of reciprocity that she herself has laid out. Medea's destructive behavior results from her violation of her own rule that norms of reciprocity must be followed for "justice" to inhabit the eyes.[41]

The victim, punisher, and community suffered from a disease of anger that made them wish to punish. Their eyes revealed their need to be cured and the need for a remedy for diseased intersubjectivity. The wrongdoer, however, was diseased in a different sense. The wrongdoer was treated as someone who not only had a disease but also could spread disease within a community. The wrongdoer was thus the bearer of pollution (e.g., Orestes in the *Eumenides* 470–80, 505; and Orestes in *Orestes* 35, 570), and in the case of murderers, it was precisely their "look," which involved the murderer in an exchange relationship with the onlooker, that spread pollution.[42] To be seen by a murderer was also to see the murderer with one's own eyes. This in turn meant being inspired to anger. The murderer's look thus inspired anger in the community. The word "glare" (*derkesthai*), to look angrily, comes from the word for snake (*drakon*), and the "glance" of snakes, like the glance of the "murderer," was said to spread poison.[43] The wrongdoer brought disease into the community because the sight of the wrongdoer inspired the community to anger. The wrongdoer was thus diseased not in *having* but in *being* an infection, and the wrongdoer's disease was his or her ability to introduce negative forms of inter-subjective exchange—glares and glances of anger—to the community.

The disease with which the wrongdoer infected the community was persistent because anger triggered memory. Knowledge and anger were both the products of vision and, thanks to the connection between anger and memory, even collapsed into one another. The Furies often bear the epithet "those who remember" (*mnemones*); and wrath is said to be ever mindful and to be a "reminding bitterness."[44] We hear that anger has no old age but only death and that people nurse their wrath.[45] Plato, in his work on etymologies, reports the standard view that the goddess Leto's name, which implies a readiness to forget (linked as it is to *lethe*), comes from her slowness to anger (*Crat.* 406). For Aristotle, memory is specifically a passion (*pathos*) that is able to produce a disposition to remember that lasts over time.[46] Anger was thus thought of not only as an inspiration to action but also as a powerful motor for the production and maintenance of systems of knowledge. The disease of anger transmitted by the wrongdoer was hard to cure not only because it might engender reactions as violent as Medea's but also because it lasted.

Still, it was necessary to search for a cure for the disease of anger, despite its longevity. After the wrongdoer brought to a community a persistent or memorable invasion of destabilizing emotions, the community had to be re-stabilized. According to Parker, Greek cathartic and purificatory medicine "aims to restore the sense of personal wholeness that has been disturbed by attack from outside."[47] The integrity of both the punisher and the community was violated by the invasion of anger. Both punisher and community had to be made whole by a remedy.

Tragic methods of curing a diseased wrongdoer or diseased punisher turn out to map onto, and can be indistinguishable from, tragic methods of punishing and of curing anger. In Euripides' account of the Orestes story, Tyndareus thinks that Orestes should be exiled for the killing of Clytemnestra, which has brought about his illness. Tyndareus argues that exile is a good way to deal with a wrongdoer because it solves the problem of pollution by removing the wrongdoer from the *sight* of those who are angry and who desire to carry out an angry response of reciprocation. He says:

> If the wife who shares his bed kills a man and the son of this one kills the mother in turn, and afterward the one born of this one does away with murder by means of murder, where will a limit of these evils be reached? The ancient fathers handled these matters nobly: whoever was stained with blood, they did not allow to come near to the sight of their eyes [*es ommaton men opsin ouk eion peran*] nor to encounter them—but rather required such a person to make matters holy [*hosioun*] by exile and not to exchange blood for blood. (Eur. *Or.* 508–16)[48]

Exile fends off pollution precisely by warding off sight of the wrongdoer and an angry response to a wrongdoer.[49] Euripides' Herakles is offered the same remedy after he kills his wife and children. He asks whether anyone will be able to cure him (*tis eggus e proso philon emon / dusgnoian hostis ten emen iasetai*; 1106–7), and Theseus—after promising to remedy Herakles—then suggests that the hero leave the city. Once Herakles and Orestes are exiled and each is no longer able to be seen, each will no longer inspire the disease of anger. Only at this point will each killer be cured.[50] Exile—punishment by expulsion, removal of the infectious disease from the community—will cure the community and simultaneously cure the wrongdoer by curing him or her of being an infection.

But the wrongdoer's disease could also be overcome with friendship or *philia*. In the *Orestes* Orestes remarks that he cannot purify himself—and the scene is evocative of the Athenian festival of *Choes*—because everyone's doors are closed to him (Eur. *Or.* 430). He complains, in effect, that he cannot purify himself because no one looks upon him with friendly eye or stands in the relation of *philotes* to him. At last, however, one friend appears for Orestes. Pylades offers to tend to him, but Orestes warns Pylades to stay away in order not to catch his madness. Pylades responds: "Banish such a thought . . . shrinking away from friends is a grave wrong" (*oknos gar tois philois kakon mega*, 790–94). Friendship or *philia* is precisely the emotion that restrains anger, precludes its presence in a relationship, and may therefore be considered to be an antidote to anger.[51] Friendship prevents disease.

Theseus is more explicit about this idea when he has to assuage Herakles' fears that the sight (*omma*) of him will pollute Theseus (*MoH* 1215, 1231). He argues that no destroying curse (*alastor*) can pass from friend to friend (*tois philois ek ton philon*, 1234).[52] Similarly, in the historical city the *philia* of marriage was expected to reconcile differences between citizens, and the fourth-century orator Isaeus remarks: "It seems that marriages [*epigamiai*] reconcile [*apallatein*] relatives, and people in general, who have serious rifts [*megales diaphoras*]" (Isae. 7.12).[53]

Friendship can be an antidote to anger not only because friends have certain obligations to one another but also because they have the powers of persuasion necessary to talk one another out of being angry. In Sophocles' *Oedipus at Colonus*, the self-blinded Oedipus curses his sons for having driven him out of Thebes, but his daughter Antigone chastises him with the remark that he should allow himself to be charmed out of (*exepaidontai phusin*) his sharp anger (*thumos oxus*) by the persuasions of his friends and relatives (*philon*) (Soph. *OC* 1194, 1195).[54] Helen, who is Orestes' maternal aunt and therefore is in a relationship of *philia* to him, is like Pylades willing to remain in Orestes' presence. She also claims that she will not be affected by Orestes' disease but gives a different reason from Pylades' for thinking that she can escape his pollution. Helen claims that she can look upon Orestes without herself becoming polluted because she does not think that he is guilty (Eur. *Or.* 71).[55]

Exile, amity, persuasion, and a conviction that the accused wrongdoer was innocent could all restore healthy relations between people in tragedy. But such cures as these would often not prove strong enough. Prometheus is enjoined by the Oceanids to treat words as "doctors" (*iatroi*) to his diseased anger (*orges nosouses*) (Aesch. *Prom.* 379–80), but the Titan warns the chorus that words can cure anger only if one softens the heart (*malthassei kear*) in the right moment (*kairoi*) and does not instead use violence (*biai*) to dry out (*ischnainei*) ripe and bursting (*sphrigonta*) anger (381–82).[56]

Too often in tragedy it takes the violent process of punishment to reduce a victim's or a would-be punisher's bursting rage and to cleanse the character.[57] This was the case in the *Oresteia* when the woes of the house of Atreus could find their cure (*akos*) only in a savage and bloody strife (*di' oman erin haimateran*) (Aesch. *Lib.* 470). In Sophocles' *Electra*, Orestes arrives to kill his mother just after the women of the chorus have told Electra that they are not sure that she will ever find any relief (*arexin*) from her troubles (*pematon*) and that they can see no possibility of a cure (*iasis*) (*El.* 874).

The violence of punishment that brings an end to anger might be said to tame the tumult within the innards of the angry punisher. In Euripides' *Andromache*, Menelaus accuses Neoptolemus's Trojan concubine Andromache of having used her barbarian arts to prevent his daughter, Hermione, Neoptolemus's wife, from bearing children. Menelaus claims that he and Neoptolemus will interact with rage (*thumoumenos de teuxetai thumoumenon*) as long as Andromache goes unpunished; with her punishment (*kolazei*), the two men can be temperate (*sophron*) to one another (Eur. *And.* 742).[58] The act carried out against the wrongdoer restores the angry person to a state where his or her *phren* is safe again and no longer slashed up by anger (see chapter 2). Both Medea and Ajax are released from their anger (*cholos*) after their "lightning has struck," and Ajax is temperate again (*phronimos*).[59] Zeus's lightening bolt, the ultimate tool of punishment, is thus an icon for the emotional and social relief paradoxically provided by an act of violence.

A moment of spectacle is frequently needed to complete the cure of anger effected by punishment.[60] Several characters suggest, upon undertaking to punish, that it is pleasure (*hedone*) to see enemies suffer (Eur. *MoH* 733; *CoH* 885). The Aeschylean Aegisthus thinks that he will be able to die happy, if only he can see Orestes in the toils of justice (*idonta touton tes dikes en herkesin*) (*Ag.* 1611). Sophocles depicts even Philoctetes, whose disease *is* biological for once and stems from a snake bite, as nonetheless expecting that he will escape his disease (*tes nosou pepheugenai*) if he may see Agamemnon and Menelaus ruined (*eid' idoim' ololotas*) (*Philoc.* 1043).[61] The spectacle of punishment is so important to the angry punisher that in one case, dramatized in Euripides' *Children of Herakles*, a would-be punisher refrains from killing a wrongdoer on the battlefield precisely in order that he may kill him in front of the queen who wishes to see the punishment with her own eyes (*hos nin ophthalmois idois*) (Eur. *CoH* 883–85). Anger was not only begun by a moment of spectacle but also finally resolved by a moment of spectacle.

The punitive process that led from one moment of spectacle to another was frequently described as "necessary," and the anger that drove a situation of punishment as having the force of "necessity."[62] In Sophocles' *Electra* the chorus tells Electra, daughter of Agamemnon and Clytemnestra and sister of Orestes, that she ought to stop contending against Clytemnestra, and she answers: "I am forced by necessity [*enangkasthen*] in these fearful affairs. I am well aware that I have not escaped the clutches of wrath [*orga*], but while I still live I will not restrain the passions [*atas*] that are aroused by these fearful affairs" (Soph. *El.* 222).[63] Anger was described as a necessity that, like an invasion of the body, subverted the individual's control over the situation. In this, anger was like sexual desire, thirst, hunger, and exhaustion. The rhetoric of necessity enters tragic discourse at crisis points, when human beings no longer wish to assume responsibility for the situation in which they find themselves and wish to allow a crisis to build to its conclusion rather than being interrupted. When Athenian orators claimed anger as the basis for their punishment, they were also claiming that matters had reached such a pitch that there was no turning back. Speakers used anger to justify a claim that it was time to act. Their claims of anger also warned the community about impending social disruptions and that it was no longer possible for the citizenry to avoid dealing with the contest of wills that was about to occur among some of their members.

The language of anger is also imbedded in discussions of how to restore social order. In tragedy gods and mortals most often attribute their attempts to punish to wrath (*orge, thumos, menis, menos*) and hate and, nearly as frequently, to a desire to make their "enemies groan."[64] But almost as frequently again, mortal characters explicitly adduce honor, duty, or a desire to maintain political power as the motivation for their efforts to punish. (Gods only very infrequently adduce political reasons for their punishments, and it seems that the difference between mortal punishment and divine punishment is that mortals who punish must self-consciously acknowledge that they impact power structures when they punish.)[65] Anger functioned not merely as a simple personal passion, but rather as a social phenomenon that inspired actions with social consequences and purposes. Punishment was no merely personal matter.

Not only victims, punishers, and wrongdoers but also the community as a whole had to be cured after anger spread. Thus the general public is often required to witness acts of punishment. This occurs in Sophocles' *Ajax*, after Ajax, who thinks himself wronged by Agamemnon and Menelaus, grows angry and sets out to kill his enemies to repay them for the dishonor. Athena afflicts him with a fit of madness that leads him to kill a flock of sheep instead of the Greeks, and when Ajax finally comes to his senses amid all the slaughtered sheep and feels the shame of his action, several characters take it upon themselves to see that Ajax is displayed to his compatriots in his dishonor. Athena charges Odysseus, for instance, with the task of telling all the Argives about the sight of Ajax in the middle of the dead sheep, and Odysseus carries out the task (Soph. *Aj.* 65, 130). Ajax's slave Tecmessa also offers the sight of Ajax to the public (Soph. *Aj.* 345), and Hippolytus receives similar treatment in Euripides' play of that name (Eur. *Hipp.* 940–50). Sophocles' Oedipus displays himself to the people of Thebes (Soph. *OT.* 1290), thus concluding a play that began with the need to cure Thebes of plague. Oedipus remedies the city by making himself a scapegoat or *pharmakos*.

One Greek word for "remedy" expresses particularly well the paradoxical idea that spectacular acts of violence could cure anger and that they could cure not only personal but also social forms of anger. This is the word *pharmakon*, and it meant not only "remedy" but also "poison."[66] Creusa tries to punish her husband by using a *pharmakon* that is made out of the Gorgon's blood and of which it is said that one drop deals death while the other heals disease (*noson*) (Eur. *Ion* 1005, 1221, 1225).[67] The *pharmakon* symbolizes the idea that destruction and healing can be two halves of one concept.[68] The same idea appears when Cassandra predicts her death at the hands of Clytemnestra before entering the palace of Agamemnon. Cassandra, Agamemnon's prisoner-of-war prophetess concubine, describes Clytemnestra as preparing a penalty (*misthon*) for her in wrath (*kotoi*) and also as brewing a remedy (*pharmakon*) (*Ag.* 1261). Cassandra's death under Clytemnestra's ax is a poisonous penalty that cures Clytemnestra of her wrath, although it cures no one else.

The Athenians employed one form of "remedy" that was meant to benefit the whole community. As a city, they drove scapegoats out of Athens once a year. In a ritual that resembled a stoning, the Athenians "cleansed" the city by driving out two of the city's least significant citizens after decking them with dried figs. This event took place during a festival held on Thargelion, the last day of the Athenian year, and so, the ritual expulsion of the scape-goats rang in the new year. As myth had it, the festival had begun at a time when the city had killed a Cretan man named Androgeos and had afterward repented of the deed. The *pharmakoi* were human remedies for the city's anger at itself. More important, the citizens' participation in the stoning reminded them, at the beginning and end of every year, that all the citizens were mutually implicated in the processes of violence that were involved in curing the problems of wrongdoing, passion, and punishment that arose in the community.[69] The festival implied that the new year could not start until this act of cleansing and the communal admission of responsibility had taken place.[70]

Endeavors to cure personal and social anger were not uniformly successful. The idea of the *pharmakon*, which was both poison and remedy, not only signified the paradox that violence could cleanse the community but also warned the community about the dangers involved in trying to remedy anger. The dangerous dynamic involved in trying to cure anger is perhaps best encapsulated in Sophocles' depiction of how Deianira, the wife of Herakles, tries to deal with her anger at her husband for bringing a new wife home after his labors and journeys (after the manner of Agamemnon). As the story is told in the *Trachiniae*, Deianira decides that it is a mistake for her to be angry at Herakles since: "it is not noble [*kalon*] for a woman who has any sense [*noun echousan*] to grow angry [*orgainein*]" (552–53). It occurs to her that she needs a curing or remedial pain (*luterion lupema*).[71] The remedy that she devises is a love potion to win back Herakles' love (*philtrois, thelktroisi*, 584–87; *pharmakon*, 685–86; also, Deianira is *pharmakeus*, 1140). The potion is made from the blood of the centaur Nessus whom Herakles had killed, and the centaur, it turns out, has played a nasty trick on Deianira. He had told her that the potion was an aphrodisiac, but it is actually a poison that kills Deianira's hero-husband. Deianira's "remedy" transforms her from a despairing but hopeful wife into an unwitting murderess.[72] She had wished to avoid acting on her anger in any way that would amount to punishment but her attempt to remedy her anger nonetheless led to violence. The ambiguous nature of the *pharmakon* or remedy available in situations of punishment indicates how easily the Athenians thought that a punishment and the attempt to remedy anger could go wrong.

Power, Tyranny, and Law

In tragedy, punishments were especially thought to have gone wrong when they involved an abuse of political power. The presence of anger in the community indicated that the peaceful relations between citizens had been disturbed. Anger was cured when peace and order were restored. Tragic punishers used punishment not only to cure anger but also to establish a stable power structure in the city. In tragedy, this typically meant that punishers used punishment to establish their personal authority. The queen Alcmene, for instance, is expected to want to see the punishment of Eurystheus precisely so that she can see that he has been mastered by her hand (*sei despotoumenon cheri*) (Eur. *CoH* 885). The punisher wished to see the punishment of the wrongdoer in order to confirm his or her power and not only to satisfy anger.

The queen Alcmene exults above her enemy Eurystheus when she finally does see him mastered by her hand, and an attendant slave describes Eurystheus as having been yoked to force by necessity (*alla pros bian / ezeux' anangkei*) (Eur. *CoH* 885–86). The slave knew what it meant to be yoked, for the figure of the yoke, which signified the domestication of oxen, also signified slavery, the total subjection of one human being to another. Punishment and slavery were not utterly distinguishable experiences. If the moment of spectacle gave tragic punishers the opportunity to prove that they were master (*despotes*), by implication such moments made the punished slaves. The use of the image of the yoke to figure situations of punishment indicates that an act of punishment not only cleansed the punisher and the community of anger but also separated the powerful from the powerless.[73]

The yoke was generally a symbol of necessity, and on fifth-century vases, the divinities who represented punishment—the Poinai, Anangke (Necessity), and Erinyes—were personified with goads or whips in their hands, instruments of torture and subjection analogous to the yoke.[74] Yokes, goads, whips, and bridles were symbols of punishment precisely because they expressed the ways in which punishment aimed to impose the force of necessity or total power upon a wrongdoer. Punishment involved not only the necessity of anger that left the victim and would-be punisher feeling as if they had suffered an invasive attack. It also involved the transfer of that attack from the angry punisher to the punished wrongdoer. The punisher resolved the problem of the disease of anger, of anger's necessity, and of its "unwanted violation" of his or her independence by transferring the force of necessity to the punished. In so doing, the punisher reasserted control over the situation, vitiated the constraints under which he or she labored, and reestablished mastery over necessity (the same thing could happen with *eros*).[75]

Prometheus calls out from the fetters in which Zeus has had him bound that he is "wretched and yoked with these necessities [*anangkais taisd' enezeugmai*] for having distributed gifts to mortals" (Aesch. *Prom.* 106–8, 103–4).[76] His suffering leads the chorus to wonder out loud about who the steersman of necessity is (*oiakostrophos anangkes*), and Prometheus answers its question: necessity is controlled by the "triform fates and the remembering Erinyes [or Furies] [*mnemones Erinyes*]" (515).[77] Prometheus thinks that he has done a good deed in helping mortals, but Zeus disagrees. Zeus's punishment of him is an attempt to force a different interpretation of events on Prometheus. The idea of necessity is used to express what happens when one citizen is forced against his or her will to submit to the will of another citizen and to accept another's interpretation of the world and its norms. Such submission is often the result of conflicts between actors who refuse to interpret a situation in the same way. Such conflicts are driven by anger and its progeny, memory, the guardian over interpretations of past events. Anger is problematic for the community because it inspires clashing interpretations of events. The effort to resolve such conflicts often leads to one citizen's having to submit to another's view of reality and the just social order.

Like Alcmene, the Sophoclean Aegisthus believes that the spectacle of punishment expresses his power. He also thinks that punishment will teach those who have been rebelling against him to accept "the bridle" of his rule in Mycene and Argos. In a late scene in the play, Aegisthus, upon hearing screams from within his palace, interprets them as indicating the death of Orestes and shouts to the chorus:

> Be silent and throw open the gates so that all the Myceneans and Argives may have a look [*horan*] and so that those who may have been seized by vain hopes for Orestes earlier may now see [*horon*] him dead and therefore welcome the bridle [*stomia*], thereby avoiding having to acquire wisdom by happening upon the force of my punishment [*emou kolastou*]. (Soph. *El.* 1458–63)

Aegisthus claims to have total control over the paraphernalia of subjection (the bridle) as part of an effort to get the citizens of Mycene and Argos to accept a city organized on his terms.[78] In tragedy, punishment is depicted as being inspired not only by the necessity of anger pure and simple, but also by a desire for power.

Punishment established structures of power.[79] In addition, those people who claimed to hold power could only prove that they did by punishing and by forcing their world views on someone who had rejected them. While Sophocles' Aegisthus intends to use punishment in order to assert his power, Aeschylus's Aegisthus is mocked for failing to do so. Because he lets Clytemnestra kill Agamemnon rather than carrying out his own punishments, the chorus ridicules him: "As if you could be master of Argos, who cannot even carry out his own punishment!" (*Ag.* 1635). Even the gods had to punish in order to prove their power because, as Oedipus says, the gods must punish or else they do not exist (*OT* 7, 903). Prometheus puts it thus: "No one is free except for the gods, who are required [*chre*] to punish" (Aesch. *PB* 50).[80] And other Aeschylean and Euripidean characters also make the same point.[81] The possesion of power and the ability to impose necessities on others brought with them their own necessities.

Punishment introduced to the community not only the problems of anger and of disputes between citizens but also the question of what sort of power would prove authoritative by the end of a struggle over how to resolve a social disruption. It was not always the case in tragedy that the punitive spectacle gave relief to, or "cured," everyone who looked upon it. The various tragic choruses who regularly represent "the masses" in the tragic city frequently find the sight of an exhibited wrongdoer painful, especially in cases where they deem the punishment excessive.[82] Their reactions to the spectacle of punishment are often a criticism of the act of power reflected in the punishment. Punishment addressed one problem, the problem of spreading anger, but in so doing it caused another problem: that of power.

The gods were supposed to be ideal punishers—all-seeing, never sleeping, and having all of eternity in which to punish—and yet even they could be criticized for their punishments.[83] In Euripides' *Hippolytus,* Aphrodite, goddess of love, punishes Hippolytus, who is the son of Theseus and an Amazon queen, with death because he has managed to resist the impulses of *eros* and remain a virgin. As he comes near death, Hippolytus expostulates against his punishment, crying out in his agony: "Zeus, Zeus, do you see these things? . . . . Some bloodstained family evil of ancient ancestors breaks the bounds [*exorizetai*] and does not rest but comes against me. Why, when I am in no way guilty of evils?" (1381). The treatment that he is receiving "breaks the bounds" insofar as it exceeds the norms of reciprocity.

Characters in tragedy often offer criticisms of the acts of power enacted in tragedy. Their criticisms give us a window into the language that the Athenians used in order to discuss the border between legitimate and illegitimate acts of punishment and forms of power. The most general criticism that is leveled against a punishment by characters in tragedy is that it has somehow been carried out to excess.

In the *Oresteia* this divine excess is described as arising from divine "unlawfulness." The chorus of the *Agamemnon* is resentful of the lengths to which the gods go in punishing mortals and is tired of the cycle of murderous violence that the goddess Artemis has inspired in Argos as a way of punishing Agamemnon. The chorus wishes that it did not have to participate in the bloody cycle of reciprocity and prays for a state of affairs that would be free from excessive pain (*periodunos*) (1448). The chorus acknowledges that the requirement that "to the doer something must be done" is a *thesmion* or decree from Zeus (1560), but the old men also wish that someone could end the curse and vengeful calamities (*ata*) afflicting the house of Atreus. Their wish indicates a desire that the house of Atreus be punished in some more minimal fashion. "If Agamemnon must pay for earlier murders and will in turn require further penalties and other deaths after he dies for the dead, what mortal could claim to have been born under a happy spirit once he has heard this?" (1335). The chorus thinks that the cause of its woes is Artemis's "unlawful" desire (*anomon*) to have Agamemnon sacrifice his daughter (151).

Tragic characters' criticisms and approbations of particular acts of punishment often turned around an idea of excessiveness that was connected to lawlessness. A study of the tropes of excessiveness and lawlessness gives us a way of fleshing out how the idea of "lawfulness" was understood in the Athenian context. This will help us to understand the constraints that the Athenians set upon penal power even in the historical city.

Characters who are said to punish excessively or lawlessly are often accused of three other violations: of impiety, of introducing novelty to the laws, and of treating law as a private possession.[84] Thus in Euripides' *Madness of Herakles* Herakles' enemy, the tyrant Lycus, is called a new ruler (*kainos anax*) who has overturned the ancient line (*palaios*) and who acts "in lawlessness [*anomia*] flouting the gods, and saying that the gods are not strong [*sthenousin*]" (755, 768).

As we have seen, the chorus of the *Prometheus* also accuses Zeus of being a new ruler. The Oceanids then add that he rules with private laws, and are upset because "new rulers [*neoi gar oiakonomoi*] rule in heaven and with new-fangled [*neochmois*] laws; Zeus rules arbitrarily and the things that were great before he makes nothing of" (148–151). Later, the Oceanids amplify their critique thus: "Zeus, ruling with private laws [*idiois nomois*], displays toward the earlier gods [*tois theois paros*] an overweening [*huperephanon*] scepter" (Aesch. *Prom.* 402–6).[85] The charge that Zeus is arrogant or overweening taps the rhetoric of "hubris" that is so frequently associated with tyrants and with "excessive behavior" in tragedy.[86] The criticism of Zeus and his punishment as excessive and overly severe brings together the charges that he has mistreated the gods, that he has introduced bad laws, and that those bad laws are both "new-fangled" and "private." Prometheus has introduced the theme of Zeus's possessiveness of the law earlier in the play. He remarks that Zeus is harsh (*trachus*), angry without limit (*ateramnon . . . orgen*), and possesses justice for himself (*kai par' heautoi / to dikaion echon Zeus*) (186–95). The injustice of Zeus's attempt to punish Prometheus somehow lies in the connections between his personal possession of law and his limitless, harsh anger.[87] Prometheus thus implies that the just or lawful puts limits on anger. Zeus's attempt to punish Prometheus, however, is unjust not only because his anger is limitless but also because he has used private laws or a private justice to justify and explain the exercise of his anger.

But what exactly are private laws? And what is wrong with them? The best way to examine the issue of what that "personal possession of the law" means is to examine a discussion about law in Euripides' *Suppliants*. Aethra, the mother of Theseus, wants her son to help a group of suppliant women who have come to Athens to seek support in reclaiming the bodies of relatives lost in a war. She bases her argument on the importance of preserving the laws of Greece (*nomima Hellados*): "I would have held my peace . . . But now know that this duty falls upon you, . . . to stop the people who confound the laws of Greece [*nomima Hellados*]; for the bond [*sunnechon*] of the cities of all men is this: that each preserve the law nobly [*nomous soizei kalos*]" (296–313). The chorus agrees with Aethra but casts its arguments as having to do not with the laws of Greece but with "the laws of mortals (*nomous broton*)." These "must not be made polluted" [*miainein*] (378). Theseus agrees both with his mother and with the chorus about the need to preserve law but he discusses the matter by referring neither to the Greek laws nor to the laws of mortals but to the need to preserve the laws of the community or publicly possessed laws: "No worse foe has a city than a tyrant from whom there are first of all no common [*koinoi*] laws, and who rules [*kratei*] by possessing [*kektemenos*] the law [*nomon*]. When this happens, equality [*ison*] is no more. From written laws the weak and wealthy have equal justice [*isen diken*], . . . thus freedom speaks" (430–34).

On Theseus's account the tyrant's personal possession of the law violates equality and freedom. Such violations may be said to bring pollution to the city.[88] As we saw earlier, not only lawlessness but also excessive anger brought pollution to the city. Excessive anger played a role in Zeus's tyrannical behavior and in his use of private laws. Acceptable forms of law keep excessive anger under control. But what does it take for law to do this?

Later in the play Theseus amplifies what he says here by returning to his mother's topic—the laws of Greece. He says: "All Greece's law I preserve. . . Never let it be said that when it came to me to uphold the ancient [*palaios*] law of the gods, it perished [*diephthare*]" (526–64). Theseus thus makes explicit the way the play has established parallels between different types of law. On his account here, the laws of Greece and the law of the gods are one and the same.[89] Throughout the play the laws of Greece, the laws of mortals, the laws of the community, and the laws of the gods are synonymous and all represent forms of law that uphold equality and freedom. Thus the violation of equality and freedom itself is what brings pollution to the city.

The laws of Greece, the laws of mortals, the laws of the community, and the laws of gods have another feature in common in addition to all supporting freedom and equality. If the tyrant's law is personally or privately possessed, then all four of the good types of law must be a public possession. The word *koinos* was used by Theseus to describe valid law that stands in opposition to the tyrant's law and designates legitimate law as public or communal or a shared possession. The laws of Greece, the laws of mortals, and the laws of the gods must all be different types of "common law" or "law of the community."[90] These types of law are publicly possessed in that not one of these types of law has a specific, nameable mortal author; they seem to come from the community as a whole. In a society whose religious laws were not based on a single divinely inspired text, even the laws of the gods took their authority from the community's valorization of religious beliefs. The tyrant's laws, in contrast, are issued by some specific and nameable person, who claims to be the author of the law and who claims authority on the basis of that authorship.

The distinction between laws written by one person and laws written by the community or based on the consent of the community was crucial to the development of law in Greece. Ostwald and Shipp have argued independently that in the archaic period, when laws were called *thesmoi*, *thesmos* denoted the decree or decision of a single, authoritative person. The classical period used the word *nomos* for law and rule that "was motivated less by the authority of the agent who imposed it than by the fact that it is regarded and accepted as valid by those who live under it."[91] The laws of the tyrant were written by one particular and identifiable person, they had an author, whereas pan-Hellenic law, the common law, and divine law did not but were acceptable to those who lived under them.[92] Even outside of tragedy, tyrants were criticized for treating law as their own possession.[93] Athenian tragedy thus treats the archaic version of "lawfulness," rule by *thesmos*, as tyrannical. In its place, tragic characters valorize the idea of lawfulness that dominated in the classical period where laws gained their legitimacy when they were accepted by those who lived under them.

In *Oedipus Tyrannos*, the chorus draws a contrast between legitimate law— in this case divine law— and the tyrant's laws in terms of authorship:

> May such destiny abide with me that I win praise for a reverent purity in all words and deeds sanctioned by the laws that stand high, generated [*teknothentes*] in ethereal heaven, and whose only father is Olympus. The mortal nature of men did not give birth to them, neither shall they be lulled to sleep by forgetfulness. Great in these laws is the god, nor does he ever grow old.
>
> Hubris gives birth to the tyrant [*hubris phuteuei turannon*] / if it is sated with many things without reason [*ei pollon huperplesthei matan*]. (863–74)

The chorus praises the divine laws because they have no anthropomorphic parent or author, whether divinity or mortal. Their only progenitor is Olympus, not even a specific god but only the "realm" or "place" of divinity. The chorus follows that with the remark that the god never grows old and then the antistrophe begins with the comment: "Hubris gives birth to the *turannos*" (863–73). The juxtaposition of the two strophes sets divine law and its birth in ethereal heaven in contrast to hubristic tyranny.[94] The Sophoclean passage valorizes not only laws that arise from no particular mortal author but also laws that never grow old. If the laws of the gods do not grow old, neither can they be said to be new. They simply exist eternally. Like the gods they live forever and are simply ageless.

The famous dispute between Antigone and Creon in Sophocles' *Antigone* also invokes a distinction between legitimate and illegitimate law, and once again the questions of both age and authorship come up. In the play Creon, the king of Thebes,—and according to the chorus he is a "new kind of man [*neochmos*] for new conditions" (155, cf. 735)—decrees that no one may bury the body of Polyneices, a former prince of the city who had recently attacked the city and who had killed and been killed by his own brother, a soldier fighting in the city's defense. Polyneices' sister Antigone decides to bury him anyway, in defiance of the order. Each of the protagonists, Antigone and Creon, is a character with a powerful will who desires to impose his or her own interpretation of law on the general community.[95]

When Antigone gets caught burying her brother, she explains herself by questioning the validity of Creon's laws:

> *Creon:* You dared to step beyond the bounds of these laws?
> *Antigone:* Yes, for Zeus was not the herald of these, nor did Justice who is fellow administrator with the gods below draw up such laws, and I do not think that your proclamations, being mortal, are strong enough to overrule the unwritten and unfailing customs of the gods. For these live not just now and yesterday, but always and forever [*aei pote*] and no one knows when [*otou*] they appeared.

(449–470)[96]

In tragedy, laws are called "old" or are seen as displaying "longevity" only when they have no identifiable mortal author insofar as no author can be remembered within living memory.[97] In contrast, laws with a specific and nameable human author, who can still be remembered, also have a specific birth date (or can be dated in relation to the author's life). The new man Creon who is author of his own laws writes new laws. They can be called new because it is possible to remember when and where they were introduced. Laws that are not born from specific authors do not have specific birth dates and therefore do not seem to have arisen at some specific point in time. The valorization of the "age" or "antiquity" of laws derives from the importance of custom and consensus to the production of political legitimacy. But that valorization did not require that laws in fact be old. All that was required was that a law *seem* to have existed forever, which also occurred when a law or principle of justice had been authored by the people in general and not by some one specific person.[98] The attribution of age to divine law, and pan-Hellenic laws, and to the common laws confirms that these forms of law are a "public" possession over which no single individual could or might claim personal authority. Antigone objects to Creon's rule because he is the author of his own proclamations and punishments.[99]

The problem that is at the heart of the struggle in the *Antigone* is that both Antigone and Creon want to act on the basis of laws that they have written for themselves in violation of community norms. Creon violates religious prescriptions about the burial of relatives. Antigone violates political norms about the place of women in politics. The chorus explicitly argues that Antigone has wound up in trouble because she is the author of her own laws. As the chorus sees it, Antigone is dying because she is autonomous or self-legislating (*autonomos*, 821).

The chorus not only calls Antigone autonomous—the earliest appearance of the word *autonomos* in extant Greek literature—but adds fifty lines later that she has destroyed herself with *autognotos orga* or "self-chosen or independently chosen anger" (875). The remark puns easily on both the accusation that

Antigone is autonomous and on the idea, expressed earlier in the "Ode to Man," that a successful politics depends on *astunomous orgas* or "city-regulated angers." Antigone acts autonomously or according to her own laws in that she does not act in accordance with the laws used by the city to regulate anger and repudiates the *astunomous orgas* that the chorus had praised earlier in the play.

Antigone has refused to adhere to norms of justice generated by the consensual community of the citizenry and has claimed, in her own a name, a right to push off into new moral territory. Creon does the same. Legitimate law is thus set in contrast to individual wills. In the *Antigone* those wills are described as involving forms of anger and desire that lead to a violation of community norms.[100] Tragedy puts the case over and over again that punishment must work to control anger by allowing anger to be exercised only in accordance with norms that are based on the community's consensually established authority. Antigone and Creon ignore that argument, and the result is that instability and disorder spread through Thebes until the royal family is ruined almost in entirety.

Stability in the *polis* is achieved when characters are willing to accept the community's injunction to adhere to laws that have arisen within it. In the *Oresteia* Orestes can win back rule of Argos from his mother precisely because he, unlike her, is willing to reinstate the communal laws. His willingness to do so allows him to effect a transition from the rule of a tyrant to the rule of a just king, or from the rule of the "new" to the rule of the "'old" and a reinstatement of the communal laws. This idea is built up in the trilogy's first two plays.

In a passage layered with a typically Aeschylean level of narrative overdetermination, Clytemnestra welcomes Cassandra to Argos saying: "If necessity should allot to one a slave's fortune, one should be very grateful [*polle charis*] for masters [*despoton*] of ancient wealth [*archaioplouton*]; those [masters] who have amassed a noble fortune against their expectations are in all things savage [*omoi*] to their slaves [*doulois*] beyond measure [*para stathmen*]. From us, you will receive what is customary [*nomizetai*]" (*Ag.* 1042–46). Clytemnestra sets up a distinction between "old" money, which acts with moderation, and "new" money, which acts beyond measure and with a raw savagery.[101] But Clytemnestra is not merely a wealthy woman speaking to a poor refugee. She is also the ruler speaking to the slave. She links the class distinction of old money versus new to political questions by introducing the terms "despot" and "slave" (*doulos*). Clytemnestra says that she will treat Cassandra as is customary but essentially leaves open the question of whether she will act as is typical of an "old" ruler (i.e., justly) or as is typical of a "new" ruler (i.e., unjustly). She thus figures herself as potentially being a new ruler who will punish excessively.

Her next action turns this possibility into actuality. Clytemnestra kills Agamemnon and murders Cassandra despite the words of welcome. She thereby shows herself to be not the successor of Agamemnon's old rule but a truly new and tyrannical ruler in the city. From the perspective of the chorus, Clytemnestra's newness is better described as "angry excess." It laments: "O Fiend that falls on this house and wields a power [*kratuneis*] through women that matches their temper [*isopsuchon*], it is bitter to my soul. Beyond the law [*eknomos*]—she screeches her triumph like a raven" (*Ag.* 1468–75). Clytemnestra is a punisher whose temper, bitter to the heart of those who feel its force, leads her to act excessively or beyond the bounds of the lawful. Her temper and her act of punishment are central to her attempt to establish a rule that will be called unlawful.

It will require an act of punishment—Orestes' killing of his mother—to replace Clytemnestra's excessiveness and newness with a restoration of communal laws and a politics based on the wider consensual community. The chorus makes known that it sees Orestes' return as a restoration of the old order: "Where shall I start my appeal? How find words to match the need? Now is the moment when either the bloodstained edges of the blades forevermore destroy the house of Agamemnon, or else, kindling a flaming light for freedom [*eleutheria*], Orestes will win rule [*archas*] and the management of the city and/or the city's laws [*polissonomous*] (*Lib.* 855; cf. 480). Orestes will restore his father's older rule and will have to employ "city laws" (*polissonomous*) or public laws to do so. He will stand in contrast to his mother who is "beyond the law."[102] Her temper was bitter and like that of a raven; his must be what the community wants. The chorus has given Orestes a mandate to act and to punish and so has given him the authority to claim that he uses "public laws." Orestes will restore the city's freedom in the process of using his anger in accordance with the mandate of the citizens. The term "city laws" (*polissonomous*) should call to mind the term *astunomous orgas* as well as the idea that legitimate law is "communally based" (*koinos*). Punishment can do the work of restoring the city but only when it is based on laws that are generated and authored by the "city" as a whole.[103]

CONCLUSION

The tragic tropes of sickness and remedy reveal the Athenian concern with problems of personal interrelation and the mutual implication of citizens in one another's affairs and emotions. The tragic grammars of anger, disease, necessity, and law represent punishment as a response to diseased forms of intersubjectivity and problems of excessive power and passion in the community. These problems of disease and power were solved when passions were acted upon according to the terms established and approved by the community in its "public" laws, whether written or unwritten. The punitive spectacle was acceptable, and reciprocity and equivalence were rightly carried out only when no citizen had more personal authority than another over the processes of anger and punishment. Punishment based on this idea could remedy anger. *Astunomoi orgai* existed in the healthy city that had escaped the pollution of the laws by containing conflicts and angers with public laws that channeled power into the achievement of freedom and equality.

This chapter began with a discussion of the festival of the *Choes* and examined how it modeled the Athenians' conviction that communal norms and behavior had the power to keep anger under control and to keep the city purified. On the festival day, when all Athenians drank from an Oresteian cup, the problem of pollution was ritually solved by a kind of internal exile of Orestes from all the citizens and of all the citizens from one another. No Athenian was implicated in the emotional affairs of another; each was equally isolated within the superordinate frameworks of city and household. Each was integrated into the city in exactly the same way. Anger and pollution could not spread without conversational exchanges and with all households removed from public view. The problem of the mutual implication of citizens in networks of anger was solved.

Lysias tells a story about a group of historical Athenians who treated a wrongdoer in precisely such a fashion. When Agoratus, a man who had ambiguous ties to the oligarchs whose behavior had brought about numerous Athenian deaths, went to join the democratic troops at Phyle, the prodemocracy forces treated him as Orestes was treated in the festival:

> [Agoratus] had the nerve to go to Phyle [the democratic holdout during the fight against the oligarchs] where some of those who had been banished [by the oligarchs] were. As soon as they saw him, they laid hold of him and dragged him straightway to be killed where they execute whichever other people they capture as a pirate or wrongdoer. Anytus said that they ought not to do that on the ground that they were not yet in a position to punish certain of their enemies. At that moment they should have peace. But if they ever returned home, they would punish the guilty. So they did not kill him at Phyle, but no one would share table or tent with him, he received no tribal place, and no one talked with him, considering him polluted. (Lys. 13.79)

Lysias explicitly treats this method of punishing Agoratus, which is so much like the method taught by the festival of Anthesteria, as the product of exceptional circumstances. According to Lysias it was only because the democrats were out of power that they could not avail themselves of the normal punitive mechanisms in the city. He says that when they "returned home" or returned to their ordinary institutional and cultural frameworks, they would be able to punish differently.

The solution to the problem of anger modeled by the festival of the *Choes* was similarly exceptional, functioning in the context of a festival that happened exactly one day a year and not in the context of day-to-day Athenian life. In day-to-day Athens, the strife-ridden interactions between citizens could not be stopped by means of silence and isolation. And, in day-to-day Athens, resident aliens and foreign visitors had to be taken into account. The festival of Anthesteria, the myth of Orestes, and the imaginative frameworks of tragedy are useful for *exploring the problem* posed by the presence of a wrongdoer and the spread of anger in the community, but they are not necessarily so useful for uncovering the city's everyday *solutions* to the problems posed by wrongdoing and anger in the community. Neither a day of festival nor the events of tragedy happened "at home." In the festival of the *Choes* all the citizens were taught about the problem of pollution—about anger, power, and the community need to control anger—but it was in the day-to-day workings of the city that the Athenians learned both their roles in solving the problem of pollution and the community's norms for regulating anger.

PART TWO

The Process of Punishing

Initiation, Part One

KNOWLEDGE, POWER, ACTION

A would-be punisher's attempt to initiate a punishment was generally an effort to use the avenues of action open to him or her in the most powerful and authoritative way possible. In attempting to initiate a punishment, individual men and women in Athens, free and slave, foreigner and citizen, probed the possibilities for action open to them personally within the institutional and cultural contexts of the city. A person who wished to punish needed to know that he or she was introducing a social disruption to the city, enacting the disease of anger, and putting the city in need of a cure. Moreover, the would-be punisher needed to ascertain exactly how to use the array of available institutional tools so as to craft a competitive arena where a fight for honor would lead to success at the game of reciprocity. When residents of Athens attempted to initiate a punishment, they were also initiated into the social roles assigned to them in the city's attempt to deal with social disruptions.

It is a well-known fact that male Athenian citizens could bring cases to court and that slaves and citizen women faced severe legal limits on their institutional ability to punish, including the lack of a right to prosecute on their own behalf. Metics (resident aliens) and other foreigners in the city also faced limits on their prosecutorial powers, even if these limits were less severe than those faced by women and slaves. The fact that "punishing" was primarily the prerogative of male citizens does not, however, mean that slaves, metics, and women were not incorporated into penal processes in the city. These groups were constituted as "nonpunishers" in ways that not only offset and complemented the role of the male citizen as punisher but also made that role practicable and addressed the fears of male citizens about the spread of anger and the structure of power in the Athenian *polis*. All of the different Athenian social groups (citizen men and women, metics, slaves) had very specific roles to play in the practice of punishing in the city, and these roles are the subject of chapters 5 and 6.

The initiation of a punishment took place in two steps. First, the punisher had to be able to produce an actionable accusation or a story of a wrong suffered with a narrative power sufficient to secure the narrator access to the city's institutions of reciprocity. The person who wished to punish had to say that he or she knew that a social disruption had occurred and needed to be addressed. The argument involved claims about both factual knowledge (the claim that something had happened) and ethical knowledge (the claim that what had happened constituted a social disruption). The would-be punisher (or would-be public actor) therefore had to know how to legitimate knowledge claims made in the public arena.

The following story is not about punishment, but it nonetheless makes the point that public action began from an assessment of what a public actor could legitimately claim to know. Plutarch tells a tale at the end of the *Life of Nicias* (30.2–5) about an unnamed and unfortunate barber from the Piraeus, probably a slave, who hears that the Athenian expedition to Sicily of 415 has met an unfortunate end. After he hears the news he rushes straight to the city to spread the story around the agora (*euthus kat' agoran enebale ton logon*).[1] The Athenians take him on his word and begin to query him about the loss of the expedition. Plutarch depicts the male Athenian citizenry as being willing to act on a slave's information in order to secure the *polis*; the citizens' willingness to question him testified to the dependence of the city's preservation even on slaves. The barber, however, is unable to provide any further details of the defeat, and so the citizens decide that he is "an inventor of stories and teller of gossipy tales" (*logopoios*). They punish the hasty but falsely accused rumor-monger with torture. The male citizens thus repudiated their dependence on the slave, deciding which stories to take as true and punishing the man whose knowledge they were unwilling to validate. The fury with which the Athenian citizenry reacted to being shown up as dependent on unfree members of the city reveals a painful ambiguity in Athenian political practice: the male citizenry was dependent on other social groups in the city, not least for knowledge and information, but at the same time wished to claim total control of the preservation of the city. The system of punishment was itself structured so that male citizens could make use of other classes in the city but at the same time mark themselves as the ones who controlled the stories that could be told in the city for the sake of its preservation.

The second step in punishing, for a prosecutor who had been able to produce a convincing accusation, was to carry the penal process forward from the accusation to a moment of judgment. A story told in Pindar's fifth *Nemean Ode* reveals the complexity of the social relations involved in that transition. In this story yet another ruler (this time the king Akastos) is shown to have an ambiguous relationship to a teller of tales. This time the tale-teller is the king's wife Hippolyta and she, unlike the barber, truly does tell lies. Hippolyta tells her husband Akastos that their houseguest Peleus has tried to seduce her. In response, Akastos sets up an ambush for Peleus with the intention of killing him despite the fact that he has but recently extended hospitality to him and has purified him of murder. Akastos's action, however, is illegitimate, for Hippolyta has lied about what happened between her and Peleus. Hippolyta is trying to get back at Peleus, not for having tried to seduce her as she had claimed, but for repudiating her own amorous advances. The scorned woman had gone to her husband with a false tale (*pseustan de poieton sunepaxe logon*) in an effort to punish the man who had slighted her (25–30). The woman wishes to punish, and does so by turning Akastos into her unwitting accomplice in a tricky plot (*doloi*) thanks to her seemingly actionable accusation (26). Akastos takes Hippolyta at her word and the result is that he punishes wrongfully.

In Pindar's version of the story, the whole affair turns out as badly as it does for Akastos because Hippolyta has not been able to control her *thumos*. She became enamored of Peleus and then sought his adulterous affections by trying to win him over with all her *thumos* and numerous speeches (*polla gar nin panti thumoi parphamena litaneuen*, 31–32). Hippolyta's *thumos* inspires her hasty words (*aipeinoi logoi*) to Peleus, and these in turn provoke (*knizon*) his *orge* (*organ*) (32–33). The result of Hippolyta's efforts at seduction are ambiguous since *knizein* could refer to sexual intercourse as well as to provocation and *orge* could refer to either anger or sexual lust.[2] A woman's involvement in punishment brought the ambiguity of *orge* to the fore. Peleus proves to be a man in control of necessity, regardless of how Hippolyta had provoked him, and straightway (*euthus*) rejects the nymph (*numphan*) out of fear of the wrath (*cholon*) of Zeus, the father of hospitality (*xenia*) (33–35). Peleus's personal reaction to Hippolyta may be unclear, but what is clear is that he recognizes that he would be violating the rules of hospitality (*xenia*) if he were to join her in adultery.

The rules of hospitality were norms of reciprocity governing how men interacted with one another beyond the borders of their households.[3] Peleus's reaction to Hippolyta prevents the female *thumos* from overturning male rules of reciprocity, and his success is figured by Pindar as depending on his response to his *orge*. Peleus's desire to maintain the rules of male reciprocity is rewarded when Zeus rescues him from Akastos's ambush and then gives him the sea nymph Thetis as his bride. Man and nymph give birth to Achilles, and Peleus therefore becomes a symbol of that which engenders all that is heroic and worthy of imitation in Greek culture. This is his award for shying away from female *thumos* out of respect for divine wrath and the accords between men.

Akastos, husband of Hippolyta, is Peleus's antithesis, and his misconceived attempt to punish Peleus is a double story of what makes punishment either legitimate or illegitimate. Akastos thought that he was acting rightly: his wife had brought her complaint to him; it seemed his guest had violated the rules of the household and of *xenia*; he, Akastos, would punish for it, representing both himself and his wife and securing the rules of the *oikos* and of the male world of guest-host relations. His act turned out not to be legitimate for two reasons: first, because he could not recognize false stories when he heard them;[4] second, because he had inappropriately trusted a wife who had violated the norms of the *oikos* in her use of her *thumos* and in her relation to the *orge* of Peleus. Akastos's public actions, and therefore his public reputation, hung not only on his inability to control the truth operative in his household, not only on his understanding of the rules according to which men interacted, but also on Hippolyta's behavior. Akastos was able to regulate neither the narratives operative in his household nor the forms of behavior that arose from *orge*. Akastos was painfully reminded that the legitimacy of his role as punisher depended not solely on his own position as head of an *oikos* but also on the roles played by those around him and on his control over those roles.

The stories that I have used are told by non-Athenians, but what applied to the Athenians in the Plutarch tale and to Hippolyta, Akastos, and Peleus in Pindar's poem also applied to punishers in the Athenian city: the definition of the legitimate prosecutor or public penal actor depended on ethical norms for how knowledge and anger could be legitimately used, and the legitimate prosecutor did not act in a vacuum or in a world constituted solely of men.

Let me also briefly explain why I have used stories—and stories written by non-Athenians at that—to elucidate my argument about punishment in Athens. An attempt to understand the concepts that provide the foundation for a society's system of value cannot depend merely on catalogs of the words, concepts, and ethical claims that appear most frequently in arguments about justice. Stories, unlike definitions, show how human actions and social relations were defined and evaluated in terms of these concepts. Stories or, better, dramas are a necessary tool in the effort to trace the sets of relations among the concepts that are most central to the system of value. As for the use of non-Athenian stories, I present them only when they exemplify the same conceptual dynamics as are found in the Athenian texts. These stories suggest that some of the cultural paradigms discussed here permeated beyond the boundaries of Athens.

In this chapter, I first of all examine the roles played by all the members of the city in the production of the forms of knowledge that could support penal accusations. Then I examine the capacity of metics and other foreigners, slaves, and women to move beyond accusation and to the point of judgment. This allows me to describe how the norms for reciprocity and anger constrained the behavior of members of these groups. In chapter 6 I consider, in contrast, the capacity of male citizens to move beyond accusation and to the point of judgment and the ways that the norms for reciprocity and anger guided the behavior of citizen men. These two chapters provide basic information as to how different members of the city could initiate punishments, but they also offer analysis of the ways that the social roles assigned to the various members of the city drew upon the system of value underpinning political authority in Athens. By the end of these two chapters, we should have a better idea of how anger, honor, reciprocity, and social memory worked together to give the different classes in the city their complementary roles in maintaining not only the system of punishment but also the Athenian political order.

INVESTIGATION

Anger must have its object, for one is always angry at someone in particular. To paraphrase Aristotle in the *Rhetoric*, one grows angry "at Cleon, for instance, and not generally at the nonspecific category of *anthropos*" (*Rhet.* 1378a31).[5] Punishments based on anger could not begin until the cause and object of the prosecutor's anger had been identified. The gods could see everything, including who had done the acts that made them angry, but mortals had to carry out investigations to uncover wrongdoers. Usually private citizens had to undertake their own investigations (e.g., Lys. 23), but city officials were required to help the investigation of murder to a certain extent. In one case (Lyc. 1.112) the prison officials, for instance, were described as carrying out an investigation.[6] And at least after the mid-fourth century, the Areopagus could investigate political wrongdoing on its own authority (or upon having been asked to carry out an investigation by the assembly) (Din. 1.5–6). The Athenians rarely employed "real" forensic evidence in court (such as documents, objects, etc.), and the main work of an investigation was therefore the task of gathering witnesses.[7] These witnesses would be a crucial support to a prosecutor's efforts to produce an actionable story about a wrongdoing. Gathering witnesses, however, was not a simple matter of accumulating a list of the people who had in fact witnessed a wrongdoing or who had information pertaining to a case. There were rules governing who could be a witness, and the process of producing actionable stories depended on the ability of a would-be punisher to adhere to certain rules governing the use of social knowledge and social memory.

Women could provide evidence in arbitrations, but neither women nor children could appear in court as witnesses.[8] A male prosecutor might nonetheless wish to introduce the testimony of a woman into court. If so, he had to use a process called "oath challenge" (*proklesis eis ton horkon*).[9] In an oath challenge the male litigant presented his would-be witness (not only women but also men who were not willing to testify voluntarily) with a statement concerning a point at issue in the case, and he challenged the witness to do one of three things: to swear to the facts as written up by the challenger, to swear that he or she was not present upon the relevant occasion, or to swear that he or she did not know the truth of the statement.[10] These challenges took place only during the arbitration stage of a *dike* or during the preparatory stage of a *graphe* (*anakrisis*), and the witness's response to the challenge would be reported in court and her testimony thereby incorporated into the trial. These challenges allowed for women's testimony to be solicited on points that male litigants considered to be at issue in a case.[11] Women's testimony had to be connected to the structure of male social memory in order to be useful for punishing. Women are, it is true, sometimes described as volunteering to take oaths in order to make their testimony available, but such an offer was frequently rejected (e.g., Isae. 12.9, Dem. 29.25–26, but not Lys. 32.1–18). A woman's knowledge could enter the courtroom, and a woman could tell tales that would play a role in the social memory of the penal system, but she could usually do so only if her knowledge and her story had been legitimated by a male request to hear the story.[12]

Male citizens faced a quandary in situations where the only witnesses were women, as in a speech of Demosthenes depicting a prosecutor who could muster no testimony about a murder that had occurred in his house other than that of women and children. The citizen claims that he never initiated a prosecution for that murder because of the lack of testimony from a male citizen. He went to the interpreters of religious law to find out how to deal with the murder and their advice was the following: "Here is what we counsel you: since you yourself were not present, but your wife and children were, and there are no other witnesses, do not proclaim against somebody by name [*onomasti medeni*], but against 'doers' [*tois dedrakosi*] and 'murderers' [*kai kteinasin*] in general" (Dem. 47.69–70). A woman's knowledge, a woman's tale, could support a general proclamation against wrongdoing but not a particularized, and therefore actionable, accusation against a specific and named wrongdoer.[13] Women were cut off from systems of anger not merely by being excluded from prosecuting but also by being prevented from naming the object of their anger.

The evidence of slaves, like the evidence of women, could be introduced to court only after male citizens had mediated the telling of their stories. As with women, male citizens used a "challenge" to introduce the testimony of slaves to court, but the challenge used to solicit the evidence from a slave involved physical torture instead of an oath.[14] Like the citizen woman, the slave was asked to confirm or disconfirm a point of fact at issue in the testimony of one of the male litigants but had to do so while being tortured.[15] One litigant would challenge another to hand over his slave for torture, and the citizen who accepted a slave challenge agreed to abide by the outcome of his slave's testimony in respect to the point of fact at issue. The litigants sometimes even exchanged sureties, such as rings, to seal the deal, thus guaranteeing the decision to use slave torture, as if making a mercantile contract.[16]

The city, *qua* male citizenry, admitted that it needed the knowledge of slaves, and the male citizenry thus grudgingly granted slaves a certain minimal means of employing the power of knowledge in the penal context.[17] Nonetheless, orators frequently argued that slave torture produced nothing but lies from slaves whose only concern was to save their skin.[18] The system of torture simultaneously granted slaves status as knowers and invalidated any claims that their knowledge had to objective truth. Aristotle's analysis of slavery, with its tension between an acknowledgment of slaves as rational actors and an insistence that they are nonetheless unfit for the political realm, resonates richly in the context of the Athenian practice of slave torture, a practice that acknowledged the agency of slaves and the value of their memories while also undoing them.[19]

Orators did not, however, always describe slave torture as producing lies. Some orators described the torture of slaves as being the best means of producing truth.[20] This inconsistency reflects the fact that slave torture was embedded in two different systems of assessing "truth." The citizens had contracted to take the testimony as true, regardless of its content. As a result, a slave's testimony always resolved whatever point was under dispute between the two litigants. The slave's testimony thus had a *pragmatic* truth value—it settled the question, regardless of how *objectively* true it was. The slave's testimony was in effect made true by the citizen's contract, and the practice of slave torture reveals how citizen men could and did establish different modes of truth in the city.

Slave torture also allowed male citizens to ritualize their ability to construct truth and meaning on the basis of political agreement, a significant aspect of their political practice. There was no way to appeal a jury's decision, and so the Athenian court system depended for its efficacy on the willingness of citizens to accept judicial decisions as "final and authoritative" regardless of their substantive content. The process of slave torture not only provided Athenian citizen men with information for their cases but also allowed them to ritualize their ability to accept "final authoritative decisions" on the basis of social agreement and provided a symbolic statement of the ways in which Athenian political systems of power and the networks of knowledge that defined social reality were built on some moment of citizen consensus. Litigants agreed to submit themselves to the lowest of the low when they agreed to take the testimony of slaves, whatever it might be, as true. Such submission provided a dramatic way of representing the submission of all citizens to the *demos*'s decisions on justice. Slave torture modeled a trenchant political irony: male citizens were free because of their complete subjection to democratic judicial authority.[21]

There was one exception to the rule that a slave's testimony could be admitted to court only after torture. Slaves could proffer unsolicited information (*menusis*) and give evidence in court without being tortured in cases of impiety (and possibly in cases of treason and attempts to overthrow the democracy).[22] Slaves who informed about the late fifth-century mutilation of the herms were not tortured but received freedom for their service.[23] There was, however, a great risk involved in giving information in this way because slaves were put to death if their stories turned out to be "false." Citizens themselves sometimes killed their slaves after they had testified against them, even if the testimony had been true. For that matter, some citizens killed their slaves even before they had given evidence in order to block the testimony.[24] Aristophanes' *Wasps* depicts a slave being punished for eavesdropping in the first place (760–69). Like citizen women, slaves had to live with having male citizens constantly patrol their knowledge and the memories that might grow out of their anger.

Unlike women and slaves, *metics* (resident aliens), *proxenoi* (foreign ambassadors), and *xenoi* (foreign visitors to the city) could testify in court, although it is ultimately rather difficult to ascertain the status granted to their testimony.[25] Moreover, metics could initiate a punishment by putting forward an actionable accusation—but the degree of success that they could expect to achieve with that accusation remains obscure. One account suggests that the power of metic grain traders to generate acceptable testimonial narratives was contested and that a citizen's word probably won when set against a metic's (thus Lys. 22.18).[26]

The testimony of male citizens could enter the courtroom without having been so rigorously monitored prior to trial, but once at trial their testimony did come under scrutiny.[27] The quality of a prosecutor's testimonial story was judged to a large extent according to who out of the citizenry supported it. As Isaeus puts it (3.19–22), a speaker needed to choose for his witnesses the most reputable among his fellow citizens (*tous epieikestatous ton politon kai tous hemin gnorimotatous*). The litigant's evidence was embodied in his group of assembled witnesses. Todd argues that courts were more interested in witnesses' identities than in the evidential details provided by them.[28]

The rule "help your friends and harm your enemies" disinclined citizens from serving as witnesses for any but their friends, and so litigants typically gathered their witnesses from within their support networks.[29] Gathering proofs and witnesses in preparation for a situation of punishment could be expressly described as gathering one's supporters, as when Isaeus says that a litigant preparing to go to court must not only procure orators and muster all his forces, but also gather friends (1.7; cf. 3.19–22).[30] The jurors assessed a litigant's claims on the basis of the nature of his support group and friendship network and thereby assessed not only the content of social memory but also the structure of social relations in the city.

The refusal of the male citizenry to grant full evidential status to the knowledge of women and slaves restricted the store of social memory and knowledge available to male citizens for penal purposes.[31] As a result, male Athenian citizens and noncitizens had to worry about "making," as well as about "finding" witnesses, especially male citizen witnesses. Victims of wrongdoing are frequently depicted in the act of calling out for witnesses or attempting to create witnesses through storytelling. Lysias reports such an instance in telling the story of a young man (possibly a slave but more likely a free metic) who found himself in the middle of a violent dispute over which of two citizens had a right to be his lover: "These men seized him and led him by force, and the boy shouted and screamed and called people to witness [*marturomenon*]. And many people came running up [*sundramonton*] and were angry [*aganaktounton*] at the deed, which they were saying was terrible [*deina*]" (Lys. 3.15–16). The boy implicated bystanders in a network of social knowledge and collective emotion immediately upon being attacked. Some victims did this work of knowledge generation after the fact. For instance, a citizen named Callimachus "went to the agora and mixed with the crowds, sitting in the workshops, and relating again and again" the story of a wrong that he claimed to have suffered earlier. According to his prosecutor Callimachus was behaving as people do when no one knows about the wrong that they have suffered (*oudenos suneidotos*) (Isoc. 18.9).

In a third case, Pittalakos (a state slave) also tried to implicate bystanders in a network of social knowledge after having his house broken into and being whipped himself by the intruders. Aeschines emphasizes precisely the regularity of such attempts to generate social knowledge when he relates the story (Aes. 1.60): "The next day Pittalakos, exceedingly angry over the matter, came to the *agora* nude [*gumnos*] and sat at the altar of the mother of the gods. As usual [*hoion eiothe gignesthai*], a mob [*ochlou*] ran up and gathered around [*sundramontos*]." The agora, acknowledged center of gossip and knowledge generation, was the place to do the work of "making" witnesses, and in it the mob (*ochlos*) became the witness.[32] Anyone standing around in the *agora* was available to become the bearer of social knowledge.[33] This figure of the mob that runs up "as usual" obscures whether those who were witnessing were slaves, metics, citizens, men, or women. Anyone could be a bearer of social knowledge as part of the mob. But the mob had no standing in court.

Members of the mob who wished to report their personal knowledge of an event had to be willing to have their stories monitored by male citizens. Slaves who were part of the mob sometimes worked—for self-protection, presumably—to ensure that citizens were drawn into conflicts in the city and the networks of knowledge that served to regulate them. This happens in a burglary described by Demosthenes (47.60) where the slaves in the houses adjacent to the target of the burglary called out to passersby to bear witness.[34] Some slaves even went out into the streets to look for witnesses, bringing back a citizen (Hagnophilos).[35] The slaves in this story spread social knowledge and use social knowledge and do so legitimately as long as they remain unnamed members of the shouting mob and as long as they make sure to attach their knowledge to that of a citizen. Slaves who acted thus did not threaten the control of the male citizenry over the realm of social knowledge, but rather played a necessary role in establishing male citizens as the actors who were ultimately in control of the content of social knowledge.

One of the most important and dramatic cases of public punishment in Athens was the prosecution of a case known as the Mysteries, in which several elite Athenian citizens, among them Alcibiades, were accused of having vandalized phallic boundary stones called herms located throughout the city. These elite citizens were also accused of having violated the provisions of the Eleusinian Mysteries, and the wrongdoing was taken as a challenge to the very foundations of democratic Athens, a case of elite mockery of the democratic community (Thuc. 6.27–28). The citizen who first accused Alcibiades of holding the Mysteries in a private house recommended that the assembly hear the evidence of the slaves, and the assembly decreed that anyone who wanted to, even slaves and metics, could testify on the matter (Thuc. 6.27). Most of the initial information in the case was then provided not by citizens but by two slaves, a metic, and a woman. The slave whose information began the case did not volunteer to testify but was volunteered by a citizen who had secured his immunity (And. 1.11–16).[36] He was offered up as a vessel of knowledge to which citizens had a right. The metic who testified did come forward on his own accord, but not before withdrawing to Megara and securing a promise of immunity from that safe distance. Some of the most damning and dangerous testimony ever given in the city thus appears only in the mouths of those whose testimony was most under control of the male citizenry as a whole, nor were these witnesses exactly eager to testify. The citizen who made the original denouncement had to put himself in the position of being a "slave" before the *demos* in order to get away with it. He made the denouncement with the following rhetorical gesture: "If it is not so, if I do not speak the truth, treat me as you will."[37]

INITIATION: METICS, *PROXENOI*, AND *XENOI*

Once the story of a wrong was abroad, it had to be dealt with. There were rules governing the exercise of anger in the city, and these rules were different for each class of people who lived in Athens. These rules were represented by the trial system as a whole, a system that allowed citizen men to prosecute in all cases, allowed metics and foreign visitors to prosecute in some cases, and forbade women and slaves from prosecuting at all. Periods of war, from the Persian Wars to the Peloponnesian War to the Corinthian War, were periods of hiatus in judicial action.[38] During these wars the democrats set extreme limits on the kinds of cases that could come to court in order to minimize the numbers of trials in the city.[39] The normal system of punishing was generally restored when peace was restored. The trial system was therefore not simply an institutional structure but also a form of cultural life that obtained in Athens specifically during times of peace.

Metics and foreign visitors, who could prosecute only in a limited number of cases, were therefore never allowed to make a full transition from wartime to peacetime.[40] The *polemarchos* or "war archon" had jurisdiction over legal issues involving foreigners. This is the first indication that metics and aliens were treated according to the terms of war rather than according to fully developed terms of peace. Metics appeared before the *polemarchos* to initiate *dikai* and some forms of *graphai* on their own behalf;[41] they, and also foreign visitors, could bring *dikai emporikai*, or suits having to do with the market and harbor (and possibly *emmenoi dikai*);[42] and they could initiate arbitrations (whether private or public) and act as arbitrators, although one orator suggests that they could do so only with their fellow countrymen.[43] Unlike metics, temporary foreign visitors received the right to bring a case before the *polemarchos* only as a reward dispensed by honorific decree of the Athenian citizenry.[44] Like metics, foreigner visitors were not granted the peacetime privilege guaranteed to citizens of having a full right to prosecute a trial.

Even when noncitizens could prosecute, they did not have a right to take full part in the world of reciprocity. Metics were not allowed to respond to murder to the same degree as citizens: the *premeditated* murder of a metic was legally considered to be equivalent only to the *unintentional* murder of a citizen.[45] Like the defeated who are not capable of paying back their enemies, metics and foreigners in Athens could pay back their enemies only if granted the privilege to do so by the Athenian *demos* under whose total control they fell.[46] The question of exactly how much prosecutorial power metics in the city had must remain open, but the situation was at least such that one speaker could argue: "Callipus was one of your citizens and, therefore, a man able to do both well and badly [*poiesai kakos*] to someone [i.e., he was able to do the work of reciprocity], while Cephisiades was a metic and not able to do anything" (Dem. 52.25). Full reciprocity was a practice that was reserved to citizens under peacetime protections.

The Athenian treatment of acts of wrongdoing that arose in their allied cities and colonies reflects the same sort of relationship between the Athenian citizenry and the foreigners with whom they interacted. After the mid-fifth-century, capital cases in allied or subject cities had to be transferred to Athens on the basis of the treaties that established the relationship between Athens and the other city. The Athenians exercised the prerogative of the military victor when they peremptorily claimed the right to preside over the important penal proceedings of their allies.[47] In the eyes of the antidemocratic author of the pseudo-Xenophantic *Constitution of Athens*, this use of imperial power allowed the Athenians to acquit democrats in other cities and to make the allies more the slaves (*douloi*) of the Athenian people ([Xen.] *Ath. Pol.* 1.16–18).[48]

Not only did metics face limits on their abilities to prosecute, but their right to defend themselves at trial was also on shaky ground. In fourth-century sources the Council of 500 appears willing and able to execute metics without a trial in two cases, despite the legal right of metics to a trial and despite the fact that the council was not supposed to punish to an extent greater than imposing a 500 drachmae fine (Lys. 22.2–4; Isoc. 17.42). (There is a third report of a fifth-century incident in which a metic was at risk, although it is unclear if he was being threatened with death by the Council of 500, Lys. 6.54–55.) In both cases citizens were eventually able to convince the council that it should try the metics instead of executing them without trial, but it took a great deal of arguing. Epigraphical evidence also reveals that the council did in fact execute a foreigner in at least one instance (*IG* ii²111. 37–39 (= Tod 142) [364/3]).[49] Moreover, those who defended the metics in these cases did not argue a "justice for the sake of the metics" line. They argued that a trial would be to the practical advantage of the city, and their arguments resemble those made by Diodotus in the famous Mytilenian debate in Thucydides' *History of the Peloponnesian War*. In that debate Diodotus argues against putting the Mytilenians to death on the basis of claims about advantage and harm.[50] The Athenians treated the life and death not only of the Mytilenians but also of metics in the city as being a matter of Athenian "benefit." Such an attitude asserted the totality of Athens's power over those whose fates hung in the balance of their decisions. Even in the peaceful city, foreigners were treated, to some degree, according to the wartime terms governing the relation of conqueror to defeated: there seem to have been no secure limits that were able to restrict the citizens' treatment of foreigners in any practical or predictable way. The contrast between the positions of foreigners and citizens in the city's punitive process reveals what "peacetime" meant for an Athenian citizen.

INITIATION: SLAVES

Slaves were sometimes credited with having one limited form of penal or prosecutorial power despite their overall institutional weakness. Citizens occasionally argued that slaves' knowledge of their owners' private lives gave them the ability to punish (*timoreisthai*) their owners by informing in regard to the owners' wrongdoing and thereby providing for the initiation of a case.[51] Thus one defendant argues that it would be unreasonable to think that he had acted wrongly on his own property where his slaves would have been able to witness his wrongdoing: "How would I not be the most miserable of all men if my own servants were to be no longer my servants but my owners for the rest of my life, since they would also know about my act, so that even if they carried out the greatest wrongs against me, it would not be possible for me to take justice [*diken lambanein*] from them; I would be well aware that it was possible for them to punish [*timoreisthai*] me, and to free themselves by informing on me" (Lys. 7.16–17). Is this citizen being facetious? Oratory does in fact turn up stories where a slave's act of informing precipitates a response to wrongdoing. For instance, Euphiletos kills Eratosthenes for adultery after a concubine of Eratosthenes (presumably either a former slave or a metic) had one of her servants inform Euphiletos that Eratosthenes was now having an affair with Euphiletos's wife (Lys. 1.15).[52]

Slaves may have informed on their owners, but rather little power ultimately lay in this ability. We have already seen that citizens sometimes killed their slaves to prevent them from testifying or after they had testified. There was also a law against slaves who slandered freemen or spoke badly of them (*Ath. Pol.* 59). It is surely significant that this law is the only one that we know of as having been directed specifically against slaves. It seems highly possible that the measure would have been used against slaves who tried to make accusations on their own authority. Such a prosecution of a slave would no doubt have led to his or her torture for testimony.[53] As a slave says in Menander's play, *Arbitrators* (575), "But if he catches me as a busybody or babbling, I'll give him my testicles to cut off" (cf. 500–506). The threat of torture taught slaves not to talk and not to have a good memory. The exception to this rule, as we have seen, entailed those cases against acts of public wrongdoing that were so great that the testimony of slaves was necessary. In the context of punishment, slaves were turned into purely public actors without private memories; their private purposes paid off only if fully coincident with public need. Private memories were the privilege of the angry citizen.

Slaves may have had this putative ability to inform on their owners, but they generally had to look to their owners for protection from wrongdoing. Their owners could initiate three kinds of legal proceeding in order to redress wrongs done to them. A slave was property, and so an owner could initiate proceedings for property damage for any wrong done to one of his slaves. Second, slaves were said to be protected by the procedure *graphe hubreos*, a public charge that allowed for the prosecution of *hubris* or wrongs carried out in violation of someone's status or honor.[54] According to Demosthenes, the legislator had, in this instance only, made an exception to a general principle that slaves were not to be granted legal protection. The reason for the exception was quite simply the gravity of *hubris* and the degree to which violations of honor were considered problematic in the city (Dem. 21.47–50). The fact that citizens would be punished for failing to respect even the small bit of honor accorded slaves makes the point that the system of punishment in Athens was based not only on citizens' individualistic pursuit of honor but also on the city's assessments of honor and on the citizenry's need to make individual citizens adhere to those assessments.

There was a third way that slaves were granted legal protection. Slave owners, and probably only owners, could initiate murder charges against those who had killed a slave.[55] Legal recrimination was therefore unlikely when the murder of a slave was carried out by the slave's owner. Nonetheless, the protection of slaves in respect to murder was supplemented by religious prescriptions about how to respond to murder. According to Antiphon (6.4–5), the murder of a slave required rites of cleansing as much as did murder of a citizen, even when the murderer was the owner. Religion seems to have provided other protections for slaves as well. Sinclair points out that slaves could seek shelter from beatings at the shrine of Theseus or altar of the Eumenides.[56]

The citizens of the classical democracy saw limits to the slave's degradation on these two fronts: in the importance of maintaining a rule of respect for other people's honor and in religious prescription. These two concepts had the power to impose limits on citizen behavior and therefore on the political sphere. The limits were generative of "civic restraint," to use G. Herman's term, and as such they were among the terms of peace that defined the political order in the city during peacetime. The religious protection of slaves probably resulted not so much from a theological universalism that ignored the difference between slaves and citizens as from the historical development of the slave-citizen boundary. Draco wrote his homicide laws before citizens were protected from being sold into slavery for their debts. Draco's murder laws were therefore written at a time when murdered slaves would frequently have been murdered "ex-citizens" who had citizen relatives. The power of kinship networks would probably have necessitated that these "ex-citizens" also be protected from murder despite their slave status.[57]

INITIATION: WOMEN

Slaves were turned into wholly public actors when they played a role in punishment, but the "terms of peace" in the city turned women into almost wholly private actors in the penal context. Able to punish within the household, citizen women seem to have had their greatest punitive freedom in respect to slaves. Nonetheless, the power of women to punish slaves in the household is usually figured as resulting from a transfer of power from husband to wife. One husband claims to have told his wife to be *nomophulax*, or law guard, in regard to the slaves in their home (Xen. *Oec.* 9.14). Elsewhere we hear the following: "The slaves, seeing their owner in weak condition, knew their mistress would soon rule, and that they would be punished if they displeased her" (Hyp. 1.B, fr. 1).[58] The citizen woman, as described by citizen men, could rule over slaves, but only in the absence (or illness) of men. This was an occasion that the Athenian male citizenry aspired to have arise infrequently, since most women had male legal guardians (*kurioi*) who were responsible for representing them in financial and legal matters.[59]

Citizen women had two options when they wished to take punitive action against other free members of the city. They could (possibly) act for themselves by initiating divorce proceedings, despite the tight rein that the *kurioi* had on the affairs of women in their *oikoi* or households.[60] Women could also initiate and participate in arbitrations, whether before friends or before public arbitrators.[61] But women who wished to have grievances heard in court had to have a male citizen prosecute on their behalf (e.g., Isae. 3.3).[62] Likewise their *kurioi* had to speak in their defense should they be accused of wrongdoing. The terms of peace operative in the city included the rule that women restrain themselves from acting publicly on the basis of their own anger and channel their anger through men.

Women could, however, speak for themselves in arbitrations because the practice of arbitration provided a liminal space on the border between the private realm and the public realm. Arbitration was also a liminal space between the realm of compromise and reconciliation and the realm of anger and competition. As we have seen, arbitration could be carried out in two forms: either as a compromise resolution or as a judgment decision about "justice."[63] The first type of arbitration could be carried out without the arbitrator's having to take an oath and led, if successful, to a ceremony of reconciliation (on the Acropolis or in another temple). Litigants would promise not to remember the ill will that had passed between them and "to treat each other well [*eu poiein allelous*] for the rest of time, accordingly as [they] were able, both in word and deed" (Isae. 2.31–32).[64]

No such ritual of reconciliation followed on arbitrations where the arbitrator "judged the justices" (*diagnonai dikaia*) of the matter on oath after attempts at compromise had failed. The decision to take an oath and "judge the justices" was precisely a decision not to reconcile the angry parties but to reassess their relative status positions in the city by deciding who would "give" and who would "take" justice. The arbitrator *qua* judge reordered the relationships of the city, made enemies of friends, and made the changes permanent and remembered. His oath was used to distinguish between the two types of arbitration and swearing it marked the movement from efforts at reconciliation to competitive decisions, and established the world of arbitration as a transitional or liminal juridical space where citizens stood on the border between cooperation and competition.[65] In our historical sources, the arbitrations in which women appear are inevitably compromise arbitrations. Women could enter the world of reconciliation but not the world of anger. The liminal space provided by arbitration gave them the institutional context in which to do that.

Men as well as women were expected to be careful in crossing the boundary from the realm of reconciliation to the realm of anger.[66] One citizen glosses the nature of the good citizen thus: "He came up to me in front of the courtrooms with Polyeuctus of Crioa and some others, and begged me first to have a conference with him regarding a settlement, assuring me that he would do everything right. . . . I on my part was persuaded because I think it becomes a good citizen who wishes to avoid quarrels not to rush headlong into court" (Dem. 42.11). Arbitration, especially when it occurred before friends, did the additional service of providing for family privacy. The realm of arbitration not only kept women from the world of angry competition that dominated the courts but it could also keep women's knowledge out of the general reach of social knowledge and public spectacle.[67] The courts were for anger, competition, and public spectacle but only as a last resort and, of course, only for men.

The extent of the ideological exclusion of women from the sphere of anger and competition is evident from the approach that the orators took to the presence of women even in the liminal space of arbitrations. Lysias describes one case where a man who is helping his mother-in-law to initiate an arbitration justifies himself thus: "Finally, their mother begged and beseeched me to bring together her father and friends, saying that even if she had not before been accustomed to speak in the presence of men, the greatness of their misfortune forced [*anangkasei*] her to make clear all of the evils" (Lys. 32.10–18). The son-in-law makes clear that the woman's appearance in public in this case is an exception brought about by conditions of extreme duress, permitted only because it is a necessity (*anangke*).[68] It is as if he is excusing himself for helping a woman punish.

Similarly, in Aristophanes' *Wasps*, the female bread seller Myrtia issues Philokleon a summons to appear before the market officials. She arrives with a male witness, who is then roundly mocked by Philokleon for supporting a woman's summons (1388–1414). Women had to channel their anger through men, but Philokleon implies that they should be restricted in doing even this because "real men" should be reluctant to allow even this much expression of women's anger. Not only institutions, but also an ideology of the proper use of anger functioned to keep women out of the realms of punishment and politics, honor and angry competition.

There were always violations of the rule that women should not act on their anger. One is found in a case called *Against the Stepmother*, written by Antiphon. A stepson is prosecuting his stepmother for the murder of her husband, a murder which the stepson claims was her attempt to punish her husband for wrongs done to her (Ant. 1.14–15). This is the only case to be found in oratory where a citizen woman is described as going so far as to respond to a wrong done to her. The speaker refers to his stepmother as "this Clytemnestra" (*tes Klutaimnestras tautes*) (Ant. 1.17). The tragic reference reveals the force of women's anger in the city. Moments when women acted on their anger bespoke crisis in the social order. In general, "anthropologists have noticed that women's attempts to exert power, of necessity affecting close kin and affines, are universally perceived as tragedies."[69] In fact, extant Attic tragedies frequently revolve around the character of an angry and punishing woman, and a look at the trope of the angry and punishing woman as it appears in tragedy will elucidate the norms applied to female anger and enrich our understanding of the exclusion of women from punishment and politics.

The moral universe of Attic tragedy employs, as one of its central components, an ideology of anger that is extremely gender sensitive. Several tragic characters explicitly state that women should suppress their anger, and the plots of a significant number of plays turn around the problem of female anger. As we have seen, Deianira in Sophocles' *Trachiniae* bases her efforts to control her anger at her philandering husband on the rule that: "it is not noble [*kalon*] for a woman who has any sense [*noun echousan*] to grow angry [*orgainein*]" (552). Likewise, a Sophoclean chorus reminds Electra, the daughter of Agamemnon and Clytemnestra, that she should control herself and commit the wrath (*cholon*) that she feels toward her mother to Zeus (Soph. *El.* 177, 178). Athena tries to calm the Erinyes in the *Eumenides* by making a similar argument about leaving anger to Zeus: "You are not dishonored, so don't, goddesses, give us a land of mortals that is past remedy because you are overly angry [*huperthumos*]. Even I give in to Zeus—why is it necessary to speak of that? I, who alone of the gods know the keys of the house in which the thunderbolt is fenced. . . . Lull to rest the bitter rage of the black wave [*koima kelainou kumatos pikron menos*]" (824–32). Even Athena, who has access to the ultimate tool of punishment, the thunderbolt of Zeus, is willing, woman and supporter of male superiority that she is, to be persuaded away from wrath and to leave punishment to Zeus.

Euripides' *Medea* focuses on the tensions that arise when women refuse to channel their anger through men and act for themselves. The play describes women's anger as upsetting peace and introducing conditions of war to the city. The play begins, as we have seen, with the nurse's despairing assessment that the conflict between Medea and Jason is destroying what is most beloved (*philtata*); it is destroying the peaceful bonds of *philia* that should exist between husband and wife and that should be an antidote to anger within familial relationships. Enmity has replaced *philia* (467). The nurse of Medea's children is distraught because Medea will not put aside her anger (*cholon*, 171), and the chorus agrees (178), wishing that Medea would allow its words to turn her away from the angry wrath (*baruthumon orgen*) that she feels toward Jason.[70]

Medea herself discusses the topic of the destructive effect of her anger and couches her discussion of anger between husband and wife in terms of the enmity that can exist between a foreigner and a head of state. She makes a pretext of asking Jason for forgiveness, saying:

> Jason, I beseech you to forgive the things that I have said. . . . I have reached the point of railing against myself because of my speeches. "Wretch, why am I mad and why I do I harbor ill will [*ti mainomai kai dusmenaino*] against those who give me good advice, and why do I stand in enmity [*echthrais*] with the heads of the land [*gaias koiranois*] and with my husband, who does things that are most beneficial to us . . .? Shall I not be released from wrath [*ouk apallachthesomai thumou*]?" . . . When I think these things, I recognize that I have been very foolish and that I have been angry without reason [*maten thumoumene*] . . . but we are only what we can be—I cannot speak a worse word—women. (869–90)

It is always the case, when the crafty Medea speaks, that her speech is full of ironic overdeterminations of the situation that obtains in the play. This speech is no exception, for Medea is playing on the idea that there is a parallel between her status as foreigner in Corinth and her status as a wife at odds with her husband. Medea is from Colchis and is a foreigner in Corinth. Her husband is also a foreigner but is in the process of trying to naturalize himself by marrying into the royal family. As a foreigner in Corinth, Medea can never truly be at peace with the heads of the land. Medea's anger has made her relationship to her husband analogous to her relationship, as a foreigner, with enemy heads of state, and Medea makes the coy point that Jason should have expected her to act as she has because she is, after all, a woman (and, as she implies, "women are bound to get angry"). Her coyness insinuates that the terms of peace are always as shaky in the household as they are between the foreign guest and heads of the land.[71]

Jason is oblivious to the many ironies in Medea's speech[72] and responds to his wife by commending her for remembering her role: "Woman, I praise what you've said, but I do not blame your earlier behavior; for it is natural that the female kind will be angry [*orgas poieisthai*] with a husband when he smuggles other marriages. But now your heart has turned to something better, since you have perceived, albeit with delay, the winning counsel. These are the acts of a prudent [*sophronos*] woman." (908–913)

The woman who gives up her anger restores the peace, and the woman who acts according to the terms of peace rather than according to the terms of enmity is the temperate (*sophron*) woman, the model of female virtue. Medea's speech, like Deianira's, indicates that she knows what it is to be a prudent woman or a woman with a "safe *phren*" and chooses not to act according to those norms.[73]

The ideology of anger to be found in tragedy not only prescribes that women must restrain their anger if they wish to be *good* women. It also suggests that they must restrain their anger if they wish to be women at all. The conditions of being female and of being angry are depicted as mutually exclusive. The punishing Clytemnestra is man-counseling, and Herakles describes Deianira as having a nonwomanly nature because he thinks that she has killed him intentionally and out of anger (1062–63, 1075). The Sophoclean Electra contemplates revenging herself on her mother, speaking of herself as having *andreia* (983) or manly courage. She even dreams of her heroic *kleos* but only until the chorus reminds her that she is a woman, not a man (997–98).[74] Euripides' punishing women are also called manly.[75] Women lose their position as "women" in the city when they fail to put aside their anger and decide to punish, evolving from real women or women with "sense" and a secure *phren* into manly creatures.[76] When women violate the terms of peace, the result is not merely tragedy but even an inversion of normative gender relations.

Not only do female bearers of justice evolve into men—and into Sophoclean heroes only if they are lucky. They also turn into manic tragic monsters. Schlesier has shown the frequency with which the trope of the Maenad and words like *mainomai* are applied to women in tragedy.[77] But the transformations can go even farther. In the *Hecuba*, Hecuba punishes the man who has killed the son that she sent to him for safekeeping. She and other characters describe her act with the vocabulary used in the city to designate legitimate acts of punishment (including the words *timoreo* and *didomi diken*).[78] Nonetheless she and her female accomplices are likened not to legitimate citizen prosecutors but to a pack of hungry dogs.[79] By the end of the play, Hecuba will herself become, according to a prophecy in the play, childless, cityless, abandoned, and the most wretched of human beings (Eur. *Hec.* 808), the exact formulation used in oratory to describe the male *atimos*, the dishonored or cityless man.[80] But she will also become a dog with glaring eyes. As Gregory argues: the text, itself, "posits a link between her vengeance and transformation [1173–74]."[81] Medea, too, is bestial by the end of her tragedy, like a lioness and like the Scylla (1342–43). Carrying out punishment takes her outside the boundaries of her species.[82]

"Manlike," "manic," "monstrous"—women become all these things when they punish in tragedy. At the same time their acts of punishment become "murder." Tragic characters who have punished or who have tried to punish are accused of murder seven times (if we leave out cases where Orestes is called a matricide) in the extant plays. Of those seven accusations, five are directed at women, despite the fact that women in extant tragedy "punish" or try to "punish" roughly eighteen times to men's (roughly) seventy-one.[83] Tragic women who kill people who have done them wrong become "murderesses" in situations where men, acting analogously, do not become murderers.

Two phenomena that are typically used to define murder in tragedy are especially associated with female characters.[84] In tragedy an act designated as murder rather than punishment is typically defined as an act of deceit or calculated plotting and is often marked by a temporal delay between the initial recognition of a wrong and the final attempt to punish. These two characteristics of murder are also related since delay is suggestive of calculated plotting. In tragedy, accusations of both guile and delay are made against women with disproportionate frequency. Creusa wished to punish her husband for seemingly disinheriting her and her children by adopting Ion, priest of Apollo, as his son, and is told that she will be murdering (*phonous*) if she waits and fails to kill (*kteina*) Ion immediately (*nun*) (Eur. *Ion* 1026). Similarly, Iolaus's delay in killing Eurystheus makes the act one that no one would do any longer and opens Alcmene to much blame (*pollen mempsin*, Eur. *CoH* 972). Every tragic woman who fails to control her *thumos* and who punishes is accused of using guile in her attempt to punish (Aphrodite in her punishment of Hippolytus, Eur *Hipp.* 1312; Creusa, Eur. *Ion* 844, 985, 1481; Hecuba, Eur. *Hec.* 1269; Clytemnestra, Soph. *El.* 279; Aesch. *Ag.* 155, 1129, 1495, 1519, *Lib.* 1003; and even Electra, Eur. *El.* 9, 830). The same was true of the Pindaric Hippolyta with whom we began this chapter. Medea, who is always extraordinarily self-conscious about the way in which she is treading on taboos, says explicitly that she will use guile (*dolos*) to punish Jason. For that matter, she even goes so far as to call her own act of punishment a "murder" (*phonos*) (*Med.* 391, 783). Murder was "deceitful" and "calculated." Rightful acts of anger were, in contrast, straightforward and open. A Sophoclean chorus defines the "fated principle of justice" (*moiridia tisis*) in these terms. It sings: "The punishment of fate never falls upon the person who makes the person who's done him wrong suffer in turn [*propathei to tinein*], but if they pay each other back [*antididosin*] by setting guile against guile, they will suffer burdens [*ponon*] rather than grace [*charin*]" (*OC.* 229–33).

Even a hero such as Herakles could turn punishment into murder by using deceit and failing to act openly. Herakles's punishment for such deceit is interesting precisely because his guile was gendered female despite his hero status. Herakles was punished for sneaking up on a man from behind and pushing him off a cliff to his death (*Tr.* 248–90). He had to serve one year as a serving woman for the queen of Lydia. The queen spent the year dressed in Herakles' lion-skin and carrying his famous club. The hero changed places with the female as a result of his deceit and left the female in charge of the heroic realm.

Punishment was therefore distinguished from murder in that it was effectively expected to be an open, spontaneous act of "hot blood." According to Aristotle, anger was defined not only as a desire to return pain for pain, but also as "a boiling of the blood or warm substance surrounding the heart" (*zesis tou peri kardian haimatos kai thermou*; *De Anima* 403a29–b1). The modern phrase, "in hot blood," captures not only the materialist definition of anger discussed by Aristotle in this passage, but also the ethical criteria used by the Athenians to determine what types of action were legitimate vehicles for anger. Anger had to be made manifest in open hot-blooded (and not deceitful or calculated cold-blooded) actions if it was to be considered legitimate—if, in fact, it was to qualify as anger.

The definition of punishment as an open act of anger necessitated a complementary definition of the legitimate punisher as someone who could act on his anger by acting in hot blood. Aristotle thus purports to prefer hot-tempered (*oxuthumoi*) men to mild (*praoi*) men precisely because the former will be outspoken (*parrasiastikoi*) and will let you know what they are doing while the latter will dissemble (*eirones panourgoi*) and it will never be clear what they will do (*adeloi, oudepote phaneroi*) (*Rhet.* 2.5.11–12, 1382b18–21). Note that the word translated here as "hot-tempered," *oxuthumoi*, and standing in contrast to "mild" is the same word as was used for the Aeschylean Areopagus. Punishment had to be openly angry and confrontational, not coolly calculated and guileful.

This definition of legitimate anger generated a context for punishment where punishers and wrongdoers had to pit strength against strength in an open contest.[85] The physically weaker, including women, were necessarily excluded from this contest of strength. As Detienne has shown, the association between women and guile had to do with their physical weakness relative to men. Children and the aged were also regularly expected to use guile.[86] In using guile, women, children, and the aged equipped themselves to be competitors against those who were understood as being stronger. But in this test of strength, "hot blood," figured as essentially male, was the only legitimate vehicle for anger.

Two plays in which Orestes and Clytemnestra are both the focus of accusations of guile make this point. In Sophocles' *Electra* (1392) and Aeschylus's *Oresteia*, both Clytemnestra and her son act deceitfully. But in each play Orestes' deceit is neutralized. In the *Electra* Orestes is said by the chorus to be a guile-footed defender (*doliopous arogos*). The use of the term *arogos* for Orestes associates him with divine punishers because the word is used of Zeus in the *Iliad* (4.408). Orestes' use of guile makes him the very image of piety; he punishes like Zeus himself. Clytemnestra, in contrast, is said by the chorus to carry out godless trickery (*ek doleras atheotata matros apatais*, 124). Similarly, in Aeschylus's *Agamemnon* (1129), Clytemnestra is accused by Cassandra of being about to carry out guileful murder (*dolophonou*). Orestes, however, is said by the chorus of the *Libation Bearers* (947) to bring crafty-minded punishment (*doliophron poina*) and later (955) to use guile guilelessly (*adolos dolois*).[87] Orestes' guile, unlike Clytemnestra's, does not transform his act from *poine* (punishment) to *phonos* (murder). The idea that Orestes, but not Clytemnestra, could use guile "guilelessly" suggests that his action remains a "legitimate act of punishment" or an act of "hot blood," *despite* his use of deceit to punish.

It is, therefore, not always the method of punishing that establishes the distinction between murder and punishment. In these three examples, it is simply the status of the punisher that justifies the distinction. A woman and wife cannot be said to act in hot blood. Their acts of punishment are inevitably murder in tragedy. It turns out that it is not only guile but even gender per se that redefines an act from punishment to murder. Gender thus turns out to be an important criterion used to organize not only the penal structure in the city but also the ideology of anger supporting it. Not only may women not punish; but they actually become the focal point of a nexus of concepts concerning what punishment should *not* be.

In chapter 3, I introduced the concept of the *pharmakon*, a word for remedy that was also a word for poison. Punishment by poison, like punishment by *dolos*, is more often associated with women than with men in ancient texts. Medea, for instance, punishes Jason by smearing poison on the fine robes that she sends to Jason's new wife. Creusa tries to use poison against Ion (Eur. *Ion* 1221, 1225), and the love philter that Deianira smears on the robe that she sends Herakles turns out to be poison instead.[88] (It is perhaps worth noting, although it is far afield, that the only woman to be executed in the United States between 1976, when the Supreme Court permitted states to restore capital punishment, and 1996 had been convicted of putting poison in her boyfriend's beer.)

The word *pharmakon* was also used to denote aphrodisiac love philters, potions halfway between remedies and poisons. Deianira's poison had been intended as a love potion. The stepmother prosecuted for murdering her husband in Antiphon's *Against the Stepmother* offers a defense that is the same as Deianira's. She claims that the poison that killed her husband was intended as an aphrodisiac. Death by poison (*pharmakon*) was the guileful action par excellence because it was death dealt in guise of remedy and destruction dealt in the dangerous dress of seduction (*pharmakon*).[89] The Greek concept of the *pharmakon* tapped a fundamental ambiguity in the concept of *orge*: did it refer to the forces of anger or *eros*? Punishment, the remedy for anger, could be disguised as seduction, the remedy for dysfunctional *eros*. The trope of the *pharmakon* captures not only this ambiguity but also the idea that *orge* and punishment, the remedy for anger, were expected to turn deadly, deceitful, and tragic when handled by women. In order that tragedy in the city be avoided, the terms of peace dictated that women channel their anger through men. The "terms of peace" in the city required that women not tell stories about anger, not make claims about desert, and not act as punishers; the "terms of peace" required that women employ neither public openness nor guile as vehicles for their anger.

The overlap between anger and *eros* was a central element of the Athenian conceptual order. The link between anger and *eros* increased the importance of using the norms of anger and of gender to define one another. In chapter 3 we saw that Hesiod used the negative-positive dichotomy drawn between drones and bees to make a comment on *orge* in one case and a comment on gender in another. On Hesiod's account lazy men, whose lives were not rightly ordered in respect to their *orge*, were, like drones, a curse upon beelike busy men, whose lives presumably were rightly ordered in respect to *orge*. Women, like lazy men, were also drones who are a curse to men, and so they too, presumably, were not rightly constituted in respect to *orge*. Hesiod was not the only author to mobilize the drone-bee dichotomy for the sake of making his own comment on his society's system of value vis-à-vis matters of gender and anger. The seventh-century poet Semonides also based criticism and praise of women on their use of their *orge*. Semonides, who is reputed to have participated in the archaic Athenian literary scene, wrote a poem about ten different kinds of women by describing each type as an animal or natural phenomenon. There is the pig woman, the fox woman, the dog woman, the earth woman, the sea woman, the donkey woman, the cat woman, the mare woman, and finally the bee woman. According to Semonides, the bee woman is the only praiseworthy type. The bee thus retains its Hesiodic position as a signifier of that which is valued positively.

The bee woman is praiseworthy because she loves her husband, is beloved by him, and grows old with him. She bears fine children and never takes pleasure from sitting among women and speaking about sexual matters (*aphrodisious logous*) (fr. 7.85–95). She stands in opposition to the fox woman, among others, who knows of all things (*panton idrin*), who forgets nothing regardless of whether it is good or bad (*oude min kakon lelethen ouden oude ton ameinonon*), who often calls things first bad, then good (*to men gar auton eipe pollakis kakon, to d' esthlon*), and who has one sort of *orge* after another (*orgen d' allot' alloien echei*) (7.7–11). The bee woman thus stands in contrast to the woman who not only has many different kinds of *orge* but also makes claims to knowledge, refuses to give up her power of memory, wishes to argue about value, and insists on telling her stories about desert and what is good or bad. All of these practices would have wreaked havoc in the system of punishment that functioned in Athens. The bee woman does none of them.

The bee woman also stands in contrast to the sea woman. The sea woman, who is nonanimal as well as nonhuman, is sometimes laughing and joyful but has two different kinds of *phren* (*du en phresin noei*). She is unbearable to behold with the eyes (*en ophthalmois' idein*) when she rages like a bitch with her young (*mainetai*) and has an *orge* that is like that of the raging sea (7.30–

42). It cannot escape our notice that Semonides' pithy and highly judgmental summations of the characters of women regularly employ a familiar set of associations. Semonides links *orge*, rage, the sea, fertility, an opposition between prolific and restrained speech, vision, memory, and the difficulty of dealing with both anger and lust. In contrast to the sea woman, the bee woman is praiseworthy because she has got matters relating to fertility and lust well under control. Moreover, she is at peace with her husband and avoids bringing war into the household. She can be called a bee because her *orge*, especially as that term denotes the erotic passions, is rightly ordered. In Semonides' poem, the symbol of the bee retains its Hesiodic role as a signifier of forms of *orge* that are rightly ordered and as a symbol for the comprehensive and coherent network of concepts used to construct a system of value.

Semonides' use of the bee trope tells us three things about the self-conscious conversation about systems of value that took place in Athens and the role of this conversation in establishing normative social roles in the city. In the first place, Semonides' use of the bee trope simply emphasizes the capacity of symbols to provide comprehensive statements about value hierarchies and systems of norms. Students of rhetoric have long been able to express the ways in which symbols speak volumes. Kenneth Burke wrote: "There is a difference between an abstract term naming the 'idea' of say, security, and a concrete image designed to stand for this idea, and to 'place it before our very eyes.' For one thing, if the image employs the full resources of imagination, it will not represent merely one idea, but will contain a whole bundle of principles, even ones that would be mutually contradictory if reduced to their purely ideational equivalents."[90] A symbol, quite simply, is worth a thousand words, and the symbol of the bee seems to have tapped the conceptual registers that related anger to desire and both to memory, knowledge, public speech, and peace in the household. In the context of the symbol of the bee, these concepts were all treated as being central to ethical and social principles that structured human relationships and social organization. The conceptual structure mobilized by the symbol is complex and comprehensive and expresses a whole "bundle of principles." These principles were taken to be relevant to thinking about social organization by Semonides in his archaic context, but they were also central to the classical Athenian penal system and Athenian life.

The bee is a symbol and it is a symbol of (positive) value. As such, it can be used to attribute positive values to certain forms of human behavior. The symbol makes its arguments about value by mobilizing a complex of ideational concepts. This it can do not only because a symbol can be constructed so as to express a whole set of principles but also because orders of value consist of conceptual networks and bundles of principles in the first place. The second thing that Semonides' use of the bee trope shows us is that a symbol speaks to a society's system of value by mobilizing *a set of interrelated concepts that are already interrelated within that society's system of value*. The concepts are interrelated insofar as their definitions overlap one another, insofar as they are used to define one another, and insofar as they are given positive and negative values based on their relationships to one another. Semonides' use of the bee trope makes the point that the various concepts at the heart of the cultural context of Athenian punishment—for instance anger, vision, and memory—cannot be separated from one another but are already connected in sets of conceptual linkages crucial to the culture's ability to talk about human actions and interactions. Each of the terms can be used to define the terrain of legitimacy that constrains the use of another term.

There is little reason to think that Semonides was necessarily reflecting the precise relationships between vision, anger, *orge*, speech, and memory that were established in the deep structure conceptual order of archaic Athens. He may have developed his own ways of thinking about the relationships between vision, anger, *orge*, speech, and memory, or he may have taken concepts at the heart of the archaic Athenian value system and rearranged them. An author is not bound to use a symbol merely to reproduce a society's system of value. "The symbol may also serve to force patterns [of experience] upon the audience, . . . the universal experiences being capable of other groupings or patterns than those which characterize a particular reader."[91] Semonides' use of the bee trope constitutes a self-conscious attempt to present his own evaluations of different personality types and forms of behavior in terms of a standard set of concepts.

Such self-conscious attempts to assign values to different forms of social behavior should by no means be treated as a nugatory element of a given society's political life. They highlight the elements of a society's system of value that appear most contestable or revisable to members of the community (we shall see this more clearly still in Aristophanes' and Plato's use of the bee-drone trope). The use of such symbols offers us a way to read the shape of a cultural conversation about how to articulate, how to contest, and how to maintain the society's dominant system of value. We can read the normative content of a society's system of value from the structure of its institutions and cultural practices. We typically find relatively stable or static systems of value when we do this. But a third element of the conversation about social norms is to be found in the self-conscious expressions of normative values that make use of, respond to, and revise the coherent conceptual patterns inherent in the system of value. This portion of the conversation provides evidence of moments or places where the system of value was unstable or was treated as being unstable.

These self-conscious efforts introduce an element of potential instability to the normative structure of a society's social and political space. To understand the dynamism of a system of politics (or a system of punishment), we need to analyze both the patterns of stability and the potential for disruption within that system. Thus we must triangulate our examination of a society's system of value to take in not only institutions and culture but also the idiosyncratic interventions in the cultural conversation made by particular speakers who are attempting to use symbolic orders in order to recast relationships between key elements of the conceptual structure that underlie the ethical rules of their society.

CHAPTER 6

Initiation, Part Two

THE MALE CITIZEN PROSECUTOR

Slaves were almost entirely public actors in respect to punishment; women were essentially private actors. The anger and tales of wrongdoing of both slaves and women had to be mediated by citizen men, who were the city's vehicles for punitive action. Citizen men, as the city's prosecutors and as spokesmen for their households, regularly had to negotiate a transition between private and public. This transition amounted to moving from the space of the *oikos* or household to the space of the *agon* or competition. Male citizens entered into the competition out of anger and a sensitivity to honor. But the trial was a competition in which the competitors were always ultimately subject to the judgments of their peers. They competed to defend their independence and social standing in the context of private feuds but had to do so by submitting their feuds to the control of the *demos* and its citizen juries. Men initiated punishments as competitive private actors but always with an eye to the public's rules and to "civic restraint."[1] Competitiveness was thus made compatible with peace.

Different methods of punishment were available to the male citizen for use against slaves, female relatives, and fellow citizens. The male citizen could legitimately act outside of institutional channels to do almost anything to his own slaves. A citizen could also beat any slave caught stealing, even if the slave belonged to someone else.[2] But citizens sometimes restrained themselves from punishing slaves too severely for fear of damaging valuable property.[3] As we saw in chapter 5, the male citizen also faced minimal limits on his behavior toward slaves imposed by religious prescription and the laws of *hubris*.

The male citizen had a similarly far-ranging power over the female members of his household and was expected to punish the women in his household. Mythology is full of stories of daughters subjected to confinement as punishment for violating norms of chastity, and Aeschines claims that a daughter of an Athenian citizen was once not only walled up in a house for having broken sexual norms but was also walled up with a horse that trampled her to death (Aes. 1.182).[4] Husbands were expected to divorce their wives for sufficiently noxious wrongs (such as adultery or pretended citizenship). They could even be brought to court for failing to punish their wives.[5] Men had to act not only as the representatives of women in relation to the city but also as the representatives of the city in relation to women.[6] Even in dealing with the private world of their household, male citizens had to have an eye to the public world.

Male citizens who wished to punish fellow citizens had a range of procedural options, as we saw in chapter 2. Orators regularly displayed a sensitivity to the fact that they could be evaluated for their procedural choices and that their prosecution might be invalidated by the argument that they had used the wrong procedure. Demosthenes discusses this phenomenon thus:

> I think for the defendant, the man who has committed a wrongdoing, the thing to do seems to be to shuffle out of the procedure being used to make him pay a penalty and to say that these procedures should not have been used. It is clear that when he speaks he will say that it would have been fitting for me to start a private suit against him but not, by Zeus, to start a public trial if I had truly suffered the things that I say I have suffered. (Dem 21.25)[7]

Several criteria determined whether a litigant had chosen the appropriate procedure. The relative social positions of the prosecutor and defendant were an initial determinant of how a prosecutor should act, and one speaker claims to have opted for arbitration because he is afraid that a decision to go to court will mean confronting people whom he had injured during the course of his public life (Dem. 39.3). Some speakers simply claim that a general hesitancy to speak on public matters (*ton koinon*) induces them to stick to arbitration (e.g., Dem. 23.5). Arbitration was the easiest, least risky procedural option for those who were worried about their public stature.

Arbitration was also the appropriate procedural choice if a litigant found himself in conflict with kin, male as well as female, since compromise and reconciliation were possible in the context of arbitration.[8] According to Demosthenes and other orators: "Punishment [*timoreisthai*] and prosecution [*epexienai*] should be left to victims [*peponthosi*] and enemies [*echthrois*]," and not taken up by kin and friends (*philoi*) (Dem. 21.118). Demosthenes continues by arguing that it is inappropriate to punish friends any more extensively than by withdrawing from their friendship. Again we see that friendship is meant to be an antidote to anger or to restrain the full expression of anger. In the same vein, problems within secret societies were best taken to arbitrators.[9]

The oratorical corpus provides clear evidence of a general ideological antipathy toward the public exposure of cases involving kin, but the extant oratorical corpus also includes 28 cases (out of approximately 120) in which disputes between male kin, usually property disputes between sons of deceased fathers and their uncles, did reach court.[10] The ideological norms attached to kinship were insufficiently powerful to rein in the competitive ethos of the male Athenian citizen completely.

In *graphai* before the *thesmothetai* (and in *apographai*) the prosecutor risked a fine of 1,000 drachmae for failing to win at least 20 percent of the votes, and a trial could last as long as a full day. A prosecutor needed to have the safeguard of wealth and confidence in his ability to manage a full day of verbal combat before he could undertake a case. Only the strongest citizens would have been wise to undertake a public case, or *graphe*—regardless of whether their strength was measured in the number and kind of their friends, in drachmae, or in reputation.[11] Likewise, only those with the greatest physical strength or the most powerful support group would have been wise to exercise their right to kill nocturnal thieves, adulterers, temple robbers and highwaymen rather than getting an official to arrest the wrongdoer.[12]

The institutional procedures were sufficiently diverse that Demosthenes could describe the range of choice as an intentional means of providing equality to citizens with varying abilities, strength, and status:

> For Solon knew, I think, that it could not happen that everyone in the city would be alike, whether in respect to cleverness, courage, or moderation. . . . But he thought it necessary that no one should be robbed of the chance for justice, insofar as he may be able. How could he achieve this? By using the laws to provide many routes to be taken against wrongdoers. Take theft. Are you strong and do you have confidence in yourself? Arrest him. The risk is a 1000 drachmae. If you are weak, guide the archons to him and they will do the rest. (Dem. 22.25–26)[13]

Demosthenes effectively argues that equality is achieved in the city when every citizen can punish. The variety of procedures provided for that sort of equality. But it was also a hierarchical form of equality. Each citizen could punish only in a way that accorded with his position in the city, a position that was in part determined by his fellow citizens.[14]

The male Athenian citizen might choose any of the available penal procedures, but regardless of his choice, he had to carry out his punishment by acting according to the rules of honor and anger and also according to the rules of civic restraint. This point is made clear by four stories in the oratorical corpus in which litigants are explicitly debating where to place the boundary between legitimate and illegitimate punishment. We have one speech that deals with a situation in which a citizen who claimed to have killed someone in order to "punish" was nonetheless prosecuted for murder and three brief descriptions of similar cases. These include two stories told by Demosthenes about men who killed people who insulted them at parties (21. 71–72), and a story told by Dinarchus about a miller named Menon, who was executed for imprisoning a free man in his mill (1.23–24). The speech is Euphiletos's defense against the murder charges brought against him for killing his wife's lover (Lys. 1). In all four of these cases the defendants and prosecutors would have debated the distinction between punishment and murder; their stories reveal the criteria used in Athenian courts to define punishment. In tragedy, an act counted as punishment only if it was carried out openly, quickly, and by a man. It qualified as murder if it was carried out with guile, after some delay, and/or by a woman. The same was true in the city, but "hot blood" was not the only feature of a legitimate act of punishment. Citizens had to act on "hot blood" but also within limits set by the city if their punishments were to be valid.

Demosthenes tells a story about a man called Eueon (21.71–72). Eueon was insulted at a party, killed the offender, was tried for this, and was executed. Demosthenes is a wealthy politician in Athens, and he reports Eueon's story during the course of his prosecution of Meidias, another wealthy politician in the city who had punched Demosthenes in the theater of Dionysos when the latter was the official producer of a tragic chorus. Demosthenes is trying to argue that not only his own honor but also the city's has been insulted (21.1–12), and he is using the Eueon story in order to be able to put the strongest possible case for the importance of honor in Athenian life.

According to Demosthenes, Eueon was almost acquitted, convicted by only one vote, even though his response to the insult was so extreme (21.75). Demosthenes describes what happened thus: "The judges who condemned him did not vote against him for retaliating [*hoti emunato*] but because he retaliated in such a manner as to kill. And those who acquitted him permit such an extent [*huperbolen*] of *timoria* for someone who has suffered *hubris* [*hubrismenoi*]" (21.75). Eueon's desire to defend his honor was considered legitimate by all the jurors. The only question was how much of a response constituted a legitimate defense of honor. For 49 percent of the jurors the need to defend one's honor validated even the most extreme response to an insult. But at the end of the day, honor justified the killing in the minds of only a minority of the jurors. Honor alone could go a long way to constituting a punishment as legitimate but it could not quite carry the day. Eueon went too far by killing his opponent and by failing to make use of the legal institutions available for punishing the offender. He was convicted for failing to restrain his anger within limits set by the city.

Demosthenes' word choice in describing the incident and the conflicting views of the jurors is informative. Demosthenes describes Eueon's act with the word *amunomai* when discussing those who thought the retaliation was unjustified and accordingly voted for the condemnation. He uses the word *timoria* when he discusses the opinion of the jurors who thought Eueon's response was acceptable and therefore voted to acquit Eueon. *Timoria* refers to legitimate and legally sanctioned "punishment," but the word *amunomai* refers to acts of revenge, or to responses to wrongdoing that are not final and authoritative. In Thucydides' *History of the Peloponnesian War* the word *amunomai* appears frequently to describe wartime acts of negative reciprocity.[15] The word denotes a return of ill for ill that does not have final authority and is carried out within an unbounded or warlike context. Demosthenes' use of *amunomai* highlights the fact that, as far as the jurors who condemned Eueon were concerned, the killing appeared to be an act of war. Eueon's action was equivalent to an act of war because he had failed to initiate a punishment according to the terms of peace. Civic restraint had been missing from Eueon's behavior. The jurors who acquitted Eueon thought of his act as a legitimate act of punishment, as *timoria*, but a male prosecutor had to combine a defense of his honor with "civic restraint" and respect for the city's assessment of how much punishment a given act of wrongdoing deserved.[16] In Eueon's case, the outer limits of the importance of a citizen's personal honor was that it could get enough votes to matter—49 percent of them—but not enough votes to be conclusive. He would have needed to have responded somewhat less drastically if he were to have won his case.

The citizen was simultaneously encouraged to act angrily and required to accept restraints on his anger imposed by the city. Those restraints were established by the city's assessments of particular levels of status to different members of the city, as made clear by the story that Dinarchus tells about Menon, the miller, who was executed for putting a free man in a mill, during his prosecution of Demosthenes. Dinarchus wishes to argue that Demosthenes should be punished for mistreating the Thebans and is therefore concerned to discuss how Athenians should treat foreigners. The nature of Demosthenes' wrongdoing lies in the fact that he had not granted the Thebans the pity (*eleese*) that an ally (*summachos*) deserves (Din. 1.24). Dinarchus draws a rhetorical parallel between Demosthenes' behavior toward the Thebans and Menon's enclosure of the free man (presumably a metic) in a mill. Demosthenes' treatment of the Thebans and Menon's treatment of the freeman both violated norms that the city had established for the treatment of foreigners. The Thebans were to be pitied because an official alliance had been drawn up between Athens and Thebes. The free man was not to be put in a mill because (presumably) that was a punishment otherwise used only on slaves.[17] Putting a free man in a mill, even a metic, was a violation of his status as determined by the city and by its system of alliances with foreigners. Menon was punished for acting in a way that failed to acknowledge the city's determinations of status vis-à-vis foreigners. The *polis* as a whole might treat metics according to the terms of war, but individual citizens had to respect whatever alliances had been drawn up by the city. Demosthenes was accused of similarly failing to respect the guidelines for behavior established by the city's hierarchization of *time*; for that he deserved punishment, argues Dinarchus.

Eueon and Menon were both punished for their failure to obey the city's assessments of honor and social status and therefore for a lack of civic restraint. Euphiletos, in contrast, stood accused of murder because he had failed to obey the norm of "hot blood." As we saw in chapter 1, Euphiletos was a cuckold who caught and killed his wife's lover Eratosthenes, after Euphiletos was tipped off by various servants. Euphiletos claims that he killed Eratosthenes as punishment for adultery, but he does not defend himself on the basis of his honor. Euphiletos argues that his killing of his wife's lover displayed a socially responsible desire to act according to the city's laws. He acted for the laws, Euphiletos argues, and not he but the laws may be said to have killed Eratosthenes. But Euphiletos's emphasis on civic responsibility and his refusal to make an argument based on anger and honor is not straightforwardly well intentioned.[18]

According to Eratosthenes (Lys. 1.23–24) the events of the fateful night unfolded as follows. A servant woman in Euphiletos's household had betrayed his wife's secret to him; Euphiletos arranged that the servant should tell him the next time that Eratosthenes came to visit. She does and promises to leave the door to the women's quarters unlocked while Euphiletos goes out to find friends to act as witnesses to his capture of Eratosthenes. He returns with friends, passes through the door left open by the serving woman, finds Eratosthenes with his wife, and kills him in front of his friends.

The arguments that Euphiletos makes in his own defense reveal that the prosecution must have charged him with having arranged the murder in advance and with having laid a calculated plot with which to catch Eratosthenes. For instance, Euphiletos tries to refute accusations that the tryst between his wife and her lover had been set up by the serving woman at Euphiletos's request in the first place (Lys. 1.37).[19] He also tries to refute arguments to the effect that he had gathered his witnesses much earlier in the afternoon rather than at the last minute (Lys. 1.41–42).[20] Euphiletos, it would seem, has been accused of having plotted the killing in advance of the evening and of having carried out a delayed, calculated, and plotted act rather than a "hot-blooded" defense of honor.

Euphiletos cannot deny that he made some preparations for the killing. By his own admission, he had learned about his wife's infidelity four or five days in advance of the events (Lys. 1.22). By his own admission, he did not kill Eratosthenes immediately upon discovering him in his house. Euphiletos also self-confessedly took the time to arrange for the servant to let him in, and also to go get his friends instead of rushing in on his own to catch the adulterers in a fit of hot blood.[21] Euphiletos acted with guile and deceit and omits claims about honor and anger from his defense not because he *chooses* to omit them but because he *cannot* make such arguments. He has no evidence that he acted in hot blood and can argue only that he has adhered to and carried through on the city's legislation about adultery. We do not know what the result of Euphiletos's rhetorical strategy was—the outcome of his trial is not reported—and so we have no way of knowing how his argument fared without the 49 percent of the votes that arguments about honor could bring a defendant.

Euphiletos's story is at the center of the current debate between D. Cohen and G. Herman over the nature of the Athenian legal order and the role of honor in Athenian politics and conflict resolution. Cohen has argued that codes of honor and patterns of vendetta were central to Athenian conflict resolution. Herman, in contrast, has argued that a democratic civic ideology of "civic restraint" invalidated or restrained the Athenian competitive ethos and prevented the excessive sensitivity to honor that is found in other "Mediterranean" societies. He takes Euphiletos's speech as his central example of the "code of civic restraint" that existed in Athens.[22] The debate between Cohen and Herman derives from the fact that each scholar has founded his analysis of Athenian judicial behavior squarely and solely on *one* of the *two* criteria that circumscribed Athenian judicial activity. The terms of peace in the city included no overarching prescription against anger in citizen men and no general injunction for men to make sure that their innards were always undisturbed by anger. But the terms of peace did include a limit on the male use of anger and thus produced a twofold ethical norm: the male citizen could and should pursue his own honor out of anger when he punished (Cohen's point); *but* he had to do so while also respecting the honor of others as determined by the city and its institutions (Herman's point). A male citizen could be considered to have initiated punishment according to the terms of peace only if he had acted according to *both* norms. He could, however, pursue both norms at once simply by paying attention to *time* and thus both to his own sensitivity about status and also to the city's distributions of status and honor. He had to safeguard his honor, but doing so required acknowledging the city's overarching control over citizens' honor. The male citizen, in other words, was expected to pursue both his personal interests and the city's interests.

BACK TO THE BEES AND WASPS AGAIN

It is clear why "the terms of peace" might include the prescription that male citizens act with "civic restraint:" to some degree social stability rested on the city's ability to put limits on strife within the citizenry. It is perhaps less obvious why "the terms of peace" dictated that male citizens should carry out their defenses of honor as vigorously as they did, but a look at Aristophanes' *Wasps*, a comedy produced at the Lenaea festival of 422, will help us to answer that question. That play is the story of what happens in one Athenian family when a son (Bdelycleon) decides that his father (Philocleon) is addicted to jury service and needs to be broken of his habit. He tries to lock his father up in their house to prevent him from returning to jury service. A chorus of Philocleon's fellow jurors tries to rescue him. The member of the chorus are represented as wasps and the play is named after them. These wasp-jurors are very angry, and throughout the play the characters discuss the ways a juror's anger may or may not be useful to the democracy.[23]

The play begins by revealing that the son Bdelycleon thinks that his elderly father Philocleon has some sort of disease (*nosos*) (69–72, 114). All we know about the disease early on in the play is what the slaves tell us: the disease is of a strange nature (*allokotos*). A word for anger, *kotos* is used in the compound, and the slave has therefore already introduced a pun on the relation between anger and disease (71). In short order the audience discovers that the *nosos* is Philocleon's addiction to jury service (*phileliastes*), his propensity to a juror's anger (*duskolias*) (106), and his fondness for convicting people. Bdelycleon wants to cure his father of these symptoms. He would like his father to retire into a leisurely life of luxury and to be cured of his excessively harsh disposition (*to lian struphnon kai prininon ethos*, 877) and of the ill-temperedness of his anger (*pausamenon tes duskolias / apo tes orges*, 883–84). Despite Bdelycleon's efforts, Philocleon makes regular attempts to escape from the house and get to court, hoping to get out before he "bursts" (*diarrago*, 162). Aristophanes is evidently playing off the tragic trope of diseased anger in his treatment of Philocleon.[24]

Not only Philocleon but also the wasps are consumed by anger. They come to the rescue and arrive on the scene, announcing they are on their way to court bearing three days' worth of troublesome anger (*hekein echontas hemeron orgen trion poneran / ep' auton*, 242–44). Bdelycleon remarks that, "if anyone should anger (*orgisei*) this tribe of old men, it's the same as in a wasp's nest [*homoion sphekiai*]" (223–24). *Orge* is one of the focal elements of the chorus's performance as both jurors and wasps, and the wasps' discussion of the difficulties of Philocleon's situation allows them to provide an anatomy of the political role of anger in the democratic city. The wasps claim to punish with a sharp *thumos* (*touxuthumon, hoi kolazomestha*, 406, also 408–25, 1101–12). This is a claim that they punish like the Aeschylean Areopagus. The wasps also produce a comic formulation of the standard association between visuality, anger, and punishment when they say they fix people with sharp and just angry glances of "mustard" (*oxuthumon kai dikaion kai bleponton kardama*, 455).

The wasps represent their anger as having an important function outside of the courtroom as well as in it. It is constitutive of the proud spirit that allowed them to overcome the Persians and to achieve their city's independence (cf. 383; 1071–88), while their *orge* helps them to secure their city against external enemies in wartime, in the peaceful city it allows them to equalize the city's internal power structure by engendering fear in the wealthy and aristocratic (1107–11). The wasps place a great ideological weight on the concept of anger inasmuch as they treat anger as the source of Athenian independence, greatness, and egalitarianism. The case put by the wasps leads to the following idea: anger plays a positive role in the city insofar as the individual citizen who was sensitive to his honor and guarded it with anger was also guarding his personal independence, greatness, and equality. His efforts to guard these aspects of being a democratic citizen in turn contributed to the preservation of the city. Anger simultaneously preserved both the democratic citizen and the democratic city.[25] Local and personal practices were seen as having political ramifications.

The wasps, despite their desire to help the elderly Philocleon escape, prove unable to effect his return to the angry arena of the courtroom and are obliged to accept a compromise agreement between Bdelycleon and Philocleon, between son and father, instead. The two men have decided to hold an arbitration in good Athenian familial spirit (471–72, 521–47), and each will give a speech that the wasps will judge. Each man has to make a case for why Philocleon should or should not participate in the arena of anger that functioned in the courtroom. The arbitration therefore gives us the opportunity to hear not only more arguments (Philocleon's) in favor of the use of anger but also Bdelycleon's arguments against jury service and against anger.

Philocleon's arguments about why he should keep going to court parallel the wasps' arguments (548–630). He claims that his anger makes him powerful as a king (*basileia*, 549) since great and tall men supplicate him (552–55). His ability to raise and lower the pitch of his anger allows him to mock at wealth (*tes orges ton kollop' aneimen, tou ploutou katachene*, 575). He does not have to face an audit for his decisions and so has more freedom than if he were serving in a magistracy (587, 590–602, 605–30). He shoots a lightening bolt like Zeus (619–30) and, to top it all off, gets his three obols of jury pay. The fact that Philocleon gets paid for a form of behavior that makes him free, independent, and powerful is the final comic touch on what is otherwise a rather serious argument. Nonetheless, most commentators have taken this last point to be the main issue in the play and have read the play's political argument as turning around the issue of jury pay. But the wasps and Philocleon have focused the discussion more generally around the benefit of having citizen jurors. As their argument runs, the value of jury service rests not on the fact that it provides financial support to elderly citizens but on an acknowledgment that the democrats exercised their fullest power in the practice of punishing, where they acted on anger and regulating anger, without having to face audits.[26] Such practices preserved their freedom and independence, even if they also happened to get the jurors paid.

Bdelycleon's countercase also addresses the jury system as a whole (655–724). He disputes the extent to which his father's anger is actually generative of freedom, power, and equality for him and the other citizens and presents three central objections to courtroom processes of anger. First, Bdelycleon argues that the demagogues like Cleon, Theorus, Aeschines, and Phanus, who appear regularly in court as litigants but who never participate on juries, have duped the citizens into accepting a minuscule three obols of jury pay while they pocket the bulk of the money pouring into Athens in the form of tribute money. Worse still is the fact that this arrangement means that the demagogues make enough money to buy off jurors. On Bdelycleon's account, the elderly Philocleon needs to recognize that he does not control the litigants he sentences, despite what he may think. Rather he is a slave to the demagogues he worships, even when they are the litigants he is judging (512–3, 518–20, 666–79, 682–95, 698–712). Third, Philocleon should recognize that his judgments are meaningless not only because he has been bought off but also because in his harsh spirit he prejudges cases and does not actually assess the merits of each litigant's arguments. According to Bdelycleon, the jurors convict with regularity merely to satisfy the desires of their anger and cannot take pity on defendants when necessary (158–60, 322, 880–84, 919–20). In sum, Bdelycleon argues that the problems with the jury system are the following: the demagogues have opted out of the processes of anger: they neither serve as jurors nor submit to the regulation of the jurors; the citizens are pawns of the demagogues and have been bought off with a disgracefully small portion of the tribute money; and the citizens are simply bad judges.[27]

The structure of the arguments for and against the jury system reveals that the whole debate concerns the problem of demagoguery. The names of the father and son respectively mean "lover of Cleon" and a "hater of Cleon," a clear reference to a real-life politician with whom Aristophanes had found himself at odds in his own business dealings in the city and who has generally been accused of being a demagogue. All the arguments presented by the wasps, Philocleon, and Bdelycleon are arguments against demagoguery, and the protagonists differ only on the question of how to deal with elite politicians who tried to control the masses. The wasps and Philocleon think that they are in control of what happens in the courtroom; they think that their anger is sufficient to keep the city operating on democratic principles. Bdelycleon argues in contrast that their love of the demagogues, evidenced in their devotion to jury pay, has corrupted their ability to use anger productively. The wasps are ultimately convinced by the argument that the demagogues are passing only a small portion of the tribute money onto the citizenry. That thought persuades the wasps that their juror's love of anger is not such an all-powerful weapon as they had imagined. At the end of the arbitration, they decide that the elderly Philocleon should keep to the house after all, and they "loosen" their hold on the anger that was inspiring their resistance to his son (*ten orgen chalasas*) (725–49). The importance of money to their final decision does not shift the focus of the play from the question of anger to the question of jury pay but ensures that the *Wasps* is a comedy and not a political morality fable. The son Bdelycleon has accused the jurors of being too influenced by money; his victory proves him right. But his father is not yet cured by the wasps' decision. One more cure awaits.[28]

Philocleon agrees to stay home but begins to set up a court there (776–804). He decides to play-act his life as a juror, beginning with a case in which the family dog Labes is being tried for cheese stealing (764–862). Philocleon wishes to convict the dog but is tricked into an acquittal by his son (who confuses him as to which voting urn is to be used for conviction). Upon discovering his acquittal, Philocleon collapses and says that he is no more (*ouden eim' ara*, 987).[29] Philocleon's cure is complete with this acquittal but only with this acquittal. He had to break his addiction to the heliastic anger that disinclined him from acquitting people (and not merely his addiction to jury pay) in order to be healthy. With the forced acquittal, he has at last been freed of all his heliastic anger, even that which would keep a mock court going in his house.

Now the characters have finally completed the original search for a cure of Philocleon's anger, and the old man is freed from court business so that he can finally attend symposia. He and his son turn directly to such indulgences (1008). Bdelycleon prepares his father for his sympotic experience by talking him through a hypothetical party. He asks Philocleon to imagine himself as being about to go join the revels of Cleon, Theorus, Aeschines, Phanus (1219–21), precisely the four politicians who were criticized earlier in the play. It should give us pause to think that Philocleon's cure has made him ready to hang out with them. Perhaps curing his anger has not been for the better after all.

Our suspicions are soon confirmed. Philocleon goes off to his real symposium, and his behavior disintegrates with embarrassing dispatch from silly and pleasantly entertaining to downright socially maladapted and offensive. Philocleon insults people, mocks them, and steals a flute girl for his wanton purposes. Three different people present him with summons to court for his behavior by the end of the play (1332–41, 1387–1414, 1417, 1441). The third prosecutor even charges Philocleon with *hubris*, and Philocleon responds not only by taunting him but also by hitting him over the head with a water jug. In response the prosecutor shouts "Go carry out your *hubris* until the magistrate calls your suit on" (1441). MacDowell has described *hubris* as a form of behavior whose "characteristic manifestations are eating, drinking, sexual activity, larking about, hitting and killing, taking other people's property and privileges,

jeering at people and disobeying authority both human and divine." Mac-
Dowell's definition might equally well be a synopsis of Philocleon's behavior at
the end of the play. The man who had once been a proud upright and angry
Athenian wasp has become just another demagogic and hubristic Cleon. Philocleon was supposed to be cured of a disease when he abandoned his anger,
his desire to be a juror, and his devotion to the courts and to their ability to
foster equality in the city, but instead of being cured, Philocleon has become the
prime example of the hubristic Athenian who fails to take account of anybody's
honor but his own. This is the cure Bdelycleon had to offer. Even the slave
thinks that matters have gone from bad to worse (1483).[30]

Padel describes the angry Erinyes by stressing that "The center of their persona is self's *awareness* of *other's anger*."[31] In other words, the threat of the
Furies reinforced the idea that citizens had to be aware of other people's anger
and of other people's desire to defend their honor. The same might be said
about the persona of the wasps. Philocleon's participation in the processes of
anger was about his own honor, but it was also about his awareness of other
people's anger and honor. He gave up that awareness and became hubristic
when he was cured of his own anger. Prior to his cure, the combination of his
personal sensitivity *with* his awareness of other people's sensitivity had kept
him an upright democrat.

By the play's conclusion Philocleon is in such a bad way that his *nosos* has
been replaced by a mania (1485, 1491, 1496). Aristophanes is indeed playing
off the tragic trope of diseased anger, for in his state of mania, Philocleon
spouts endless drunk and lusty nonsense about going off to compete in dancing
competitions against tragic performers (1474–81, 1497–1500).[32] Philocleon has
become something of a manic tragic monster. The play began, after all, with
Philocleon's seclusion in a house wrapped in a net, an explicit statement of
maleness having been subsumed within the feminine (131–32, 368). We might
therefore even go so far as to say that Bdelycleon has made a manic woman out
of his father, by stripping him of his juror's *orge*.[33] When Philocleon was devoted to juries and to anger, he was precisely what he was supposed to be: an
honor-sensitive and male Athenian citizen. Now "cured" of his anger, he has
become a feminized and tragic monster.

Bdelycleon's cure of his father's disease may have been overhasty, but the
son's criticisms of Athenian penal practices, of Athenian processes of anger, of
the demagogues who opt out of the processes of anger, are not themselves
refuted by the play's finale. In fact, the chorus, which had opposed Bdelycleon
earlier in the play, latches on to his criticisms and repeats them toward the end
of the play. This occurs in a speech where the wasps set out to explain the
"meaning of their sting" (*hetis hemon estin he 'pinoia tes engkentridos*, 1073).
As Reckford argues, "the sting is a weapon of sexual as well as judicial aggression and it symbolizes the potency which Bdelycleon would take away from his
father."[34] In explaining their sting, the wasps explicitly undertake to explain the
relevance of their anger to their role as jurors and citizens. At this point in the
play, the wasps echo Bdelycleon's criticisms of the demagogues, making use of

Hesiod's bee-drone imagery. They resent those "who sit among us as drones [*kephenes*], not having a sting [*ouk echontes kentron*], and who sit at home eating up the tribute crop without working for it" (1102–21). The dronelike demagogues commit two wrongs: they not only eat up the tribute crop, but they are also stingless. They do not participate in the processes of anger nor do they behave in the courts the way the wasps do. Their refusal to use stings and to participate in the processes of anger is a refusal to acknowledge other people's claims to honor. The demagogues are a political problem for this reason.[35] According to Hesiod, such a stingless drone behaves badly in numerous ways—for example, by abusing his old father (*gonea geronta . . . neikeiei*) and attacking him with harsh words (*chalepoisi . . . epeessi*) when he is at the evil threshold of old age (*Op.* 331–32). Bdelycleon the son thus turns out to be one of the demagogic drones without knowing it. After all, he wants to hang out at symposia.

Aristophanes' treatment of the bee (wasp)-drone dichotomy has amplified the Hesiodic description of the stingless drones. In his play, not only do the drones not work and abuse their elderly fathers, but they also refuse to act like the rest of the Athenian jurors. They refuse to contribute to the regulation of the city by means of straightforward democratic anger. The wasps are hardworking not only because they take care of provisioning the community but also, by implication, because they look out for the city's political and judicial order. In the parabasis, the chorus once more reiterates the point that some people in the city have inappropriately opted out of the system of punishment (1450–61).

Two of Bdelycleon's criticisms are not refuted by the end of the play: the demagogues have the citizens under their thumb and are thereby gutting the power of the judicial system to sustain the democracy; the anger of the jurors should be preventing that but it is not. Despite Bdelycleon's lack of self-knowledge, his analysis of politics in the city turns out to have been correct even on the wasps' account. Nor does any character ever refute Bdelycleon's argument that the jurors fail to judge carefully enough. Moreover, the action of the play has shown, Bdelycleon to be correct in his argument that the wasps are not very good judges. After all, he managed to talk them into making a decision in his father's case that resulted in the hubristic behavior that concludes the play.

Bdelycleon is thus portrayed as having provided a trenchant analysis of the city's penal system, if from a point of view antagonistic to the democratic city. He failed, however, when it came to devising a solution for the problem of his father's participation in a degenerate jury system. Philocleon should not have been taken out of the publicly controlled processes of anger and contests for honor, but demagogues like Cleon (and Bdelycleon) should have been brought into them and required to submit to them. The wasps had argued that the processes of anger allowed for the maintenance of equality in the city and a reasonable distributions of honor. For these processes to work, all male citizens had to participate in and submit to the institutionalized processes of anger. Only in this way could the *demos* keep reasonable control over the competitions between men in the city.

THE HOUSEHOLD: WOMEN AND MEN TOGETHER

Participation in every Athenian political institution involved some participation in the city's penal practices. As a result, Athenian citizenship itself was in part defined in terms of the male citizens' ability to participate in public prosecution and open contests of anger. The Athenian "principle of the public" or principle according to which political life was organized depended on a communal commitment to the right of all male citizens' to judge, collectively, the spectacle of their angry honor-sensitive fellows competing with one another although within the bounds set by standards of public utility and with women excluded from the realm of anger in the ideal case. The Athenian political world was constituted by a valorization of anger as socially useful, even if that valorization was limited.

Tragedy, however, reveals a communal fear that anger might be dangerous as well as useful. Useful in the *polis* context, anger is regularly portrayed as destroying familial relationships in tragedy. In fact, the fear of the anger of women is thoroughly tied up with a fear that anger will enter the sphere of the household. Clytemnestra killed her husband, Agamemnon, and his death led to her own death at the hands of her son. Her act ultimately resulted, therefore, in a complete inversion of normal family relations. Medea's violation of household bonds is the most dramatic, since she kills not only her husband but also her children. As we saw in chapter 3, her anger was a disease that destroyed what was most beloved (*philtata*) or that to which she was bound with the strongest bonds of *philia*. Creusa sets out to kill Ion, whom her husband is about to adopt as his own son, without realizing that Ion is actually her own child borne after her rape by Apollo. Deianira and Antiphon's stepmother were also depicted as destroying their households when they acted on their anger.

The valorization of anger in the public sphere thus introduced a peculiar sort of political problem to the Athenian polis. A political community is constituted with a view to its own survival. A precondition to the constitution of a political community is an implicit claim made by those who constitute it that the principles in accordance with which they constitute the political community will preserve the lives of and provide for the flourishing of those who live in the community.[36] In the Athenian context, this meant that the principles that shaped the public sphere also had the task of ensuring the preservation of private households.[37] Men could carry out a politics based on angry punitive competition only on the condition that their activity would not bring about the ruin of the family. But the activities in which citizen men engaged in their political lives—anger and competition over honor—were by definition those activities that would destroy the family if transplanted into the household.[38] To the degree that anger threatened the household, it invalidated claims about its social usefulness made by male citizens and made irrelevant arguments that it provided male citizens with freedom, equality, power, and renown in Greece.

The political valorization of anger thus brought with it a worry that people would act according to the norms of anger in contexts like the household where such action would be socially destructive. Modern worries about vendetta are based on a similar anxiety about the valorization of anger. For that matter, we moderns generally expect that vendettas will arise when anger is made the basis for responses to wrongdoing. Where anger is a legitimate ground for punishing, one act of punishment will constantly lead to another, since those who are punished will become angry at the loss of honor entailed in their own punishment and will then try to punish in turn. This return of one act of anger for another can lead to the destruction of families and social groups alike, but vendettas are especially destructive when they arise not between families but within them. Greek tragedy emphasizes this point over and over again. Like modern democrats, the Athenians also recognized the problems associated with anger and feared that it could lead to vendetta, even involving angry disputes between women and men. Anger had to be kept out of the family if its valorization in the realm of politics was not to have negative implications.

There are two ways to stave off the threat posed to social groups by the practice of reciprocal anger: anger can be delegitimized as a basis for punishment; or punishment may be localized in a limited set of "legitimately angry punishers." Most theorists of punishment from Plato onward have chosen the first method. Punishment, they argue, must be based purely on reason and must be cool and dispassionate. Most Enlightenment and twentieth-century political theorists have defined "acting in anger" and "punishing" as mutually exclusive. This approach invalidates the idea that a person who has suffered wrong should treat his anger as a reason to respond in kind. It also invalidates the idea that someone punished might legitimately try to pay back his punisher for the punishment. This disqualification of anger as a basis for punishment is the move traditionally labeled as a transition from "vendetta" to "rule of law" or from "revenge" to "punishment."

The Athenians, however, chose the second method. Their decision, to put it crudely, was to establish one angry punisher per household—the male adult—and to regulate the contests between households.[39] The Athenians could not choose the first method, the general invalidation of anger, because anger was ideologically necessary to the self-understanding of male citizens as political actors. Anger, even anger arising from one's own punishment, remained a valid basis for punishment throughout the democracy for those who were allowed to punish: fathers, brothers, and sons.[40] When a vendetta began between father and son or brother and brother, a new family was created. This moment is dramatized mythologically when Polyneices and Eteocles fight over the rule of Thebes. The historical city, unlike the tragic city, developed means for regulating contests between households and men. In the city, the death of a father frequently resulted in a competition between his sons and his brothers over family property, and these conflicts frequently found their way into court.[41] Vendettas between households were explicitly granted the status of public competition; they were preserved, fostered, but also and importantly regulated for the sake of public and democratic political life. This was achieved by establishing one angry punisher per household.

Anger could be kept out of the household, however, only so long as women were prevented from acting upon their anger. The only way to ensure that there was only one punisher per household was to develop an institutional and ideological regime that not only kept women out of political institutions but also kept them from learning how to act successfully on anger. The institutional boundaries to women's participation in politics kept them from becoming habituated to practicing the forms of competitive behavior that qualified as political. The female morality of anger instructed women not even to try to breach the boundary between the private and the public lest they become hateful, monstrous drones. Thus the female morality of apolitical temperance or *sophrosune* stood in contrast to and complemented the morality of male *orge* that stressed hot-bloodedness.[42]

This female morality, which was crucial to the maintenance of the Athenian public order, was stabilized by the distinction between public and private worlds. Women were restricted to acting in contexts where they could act "apolitically" or without anger and competition: the household, the water fountains, assorted religious festivals. They were restricted to "private places" in other words. "Private" does not so much denote a geographical locale—and the water fountains were certainly "in public"—but a context for action requiring a specific (nonangry) mode of behavior. Likewise "public" refers not to specific sites but rather to contexts in which the principles of anger, honor, and competition governed behavior. The public forms of behavior based on anger were not only left entirely to men but were also, it is true, assigned to specific locales like the assembly, the courts, the athletic grounds, and the military camps. In these spaces men would sometimes compete and sometimes cooperate, but competition was always legitimate.[43] The exclusion of women from political institutions was not so much an exclusion from specific places as a restriction from contexts where certain forms of behavior would be required. Both men and women could frequent the streets of Athens and its agora, but presumably they behaved differently in those places. Female forms of behavior would have had to have been compatible with the norms of the "private" realm, even when they were acting before the public eye; male forms of behavior in the streets and agora would have been compatible with the norms of the "public" realm.[44] The categories of public and private were coextensive with the categories of gender precisely because the concepts of "public" and "private" were used to stabilize the rules established for interaction between genders and the nature and social role of each gender.

The very viability of the male citizen's project for a society made secure by a politics based on competition and honor required the radical ideological disjuncture between public and private—one a realm with anger, the other a realm without anger. If male Athenian citizens had proved unable to maintain the split or disjunction between the private realm without anger and the public realm with it, they would have been proved wrong in their (implicit) claim that a stable society could be built on the basis of the angry pursuit of honor extended to all male citizens; the logic of a democratic politics based on competition would have been refuted. A tremendous ideological apparatus was layered on top of institutional structures to keep women out of situations of punishment and to keep private differentiated from public and male-male relationships differentiated from male-female relationships. This ideological apparatus was aimed at solving a conceptual problem underlying institutional practice: anger could not be the principle of interaction in all areas of human life. The very viability of the male Athenian citizen's project required the exclusion of women from politics.[45]

The Athenians were self-conscious about the fact that their approach to punishment depended on a particular organization of the relationships among members of a household and of the relationship between household and the city, as the *Oresteia* shows. The whole trilogy addresses the question of how to deal with the presence of anger in the household. Thus the Erinyes claim that they have made the overthrow of houses their job (*Eum.* 354). They add that they are called curses in homes (*oikoi*) (415). And the chorus of the *Oresteia* regularly bemoans the dangers introduced to the household by the presence of angry women.[46] Thus in the *Libation Bearers* the chorus tells the story of Althaea, who murdered her son for having murdered her brothers. The chorus concludes with this comment: "The female power of unerotic [or unloving] eros completely defeats the wedded unions of beasts and mortals" (*xuzugous d' homaulias / thelukrates aperotos eros paranikai / knodalon te kai broton*, 599–601). Althaea's desire to punish is inspired by an "unerotic eros." Her desire to punish negates her familial *eros*, her marriage bonds, and her relationships of *philia*. (Notice that anger might therefore be called "unerotic eros.")[47]

Athena resolves the Atreid familial woes in the *Eumenides* by casting her vote in favor of Orestes, acquitting him for the murder of Clytemnestra. She explains herself with the comment that she is in favor of the man with her whole *thumos*. She says: "I acquiesce to the man in all matters [*to d' arsen aino panta*] (except that I choose not to marry) and I take the father's side with my whole *thumos* [*hapanti thumoi*]" (737–38). After Athena votes, Apollo notes that she has restored the household with one vote (*balousa t' oikon psephos orthosen mia*, 751), casting a vote to allow men, but not women, to punish.[48]

The trilogy concludes not, as is often thought, with the institution of the Areopagus but rather with the reorganization of the relationship of the Erinyes to the city. They become Semnai Theai and are led off to their new underground home by women from the city of all ages. The Semnai Theai have agreed to be *sunoikoi* (housemates or "with-dwellers," *Eum.* 916), and so they are led into the earth or "inside" (1004, 1026, 1033). The goddesses wear new red robes as they are led off (1028–30), just as metics did who processed at the Panathenaic festival (and notice that *metoikos* is close in meaning to *sunoikos*). Like the metics, the Erinyes are treated as foreigners who are being given a place in the peaceful city. But the word *sunoikoi* also casts the Semnai Theai as wives, for *sunoikos* is the word for spouse.

The Semnai Theai are finally led off to their cave, but only after they pray that the people in the city will "reciprocally exchange favors [*charmata d' antididoien*] in a spirit of communal friendship [*koinophilei dianoiai*] and hate with one mind [*stugein miai phreni*]" *Eum.* 985–87). The processional chorus closes the trilogy, saying in the final antistrophe: "May these peace treaties [*spondais*] persist for all time [*to pan*] between the citizens [*astois*] of Pallas and those who dwell with them [or those who have changed their residence] [*metoikon*]" (1045–47).[49] A peace treaty has been established between the female foreigners and the citizens. Notably Aeschylus chose to refer to the citizens not with the word *polites*, which referred to male and female citizens, but rather with the word *astos*, which often meant a male citizen in contrast to his female equivalent, the *aste*. But Loraux has made the broader point that Athenian women were simply never discussed as citizens. Citizenship and references to it were references to men.[50] The treaty might therefore be read as simply being between women and men.

The scene depicts the following situation: the "foreigners" have become the female partners of the male citizens; the women will dwell "inside" and are joined to the men by means of peace treaties; they are incorporated in a system of punishing that requires that acts of anger be channeled through men so that everyone can love and hate with one accord in collective unity. As we saw in chapter 1, these are precisely the terms in which the fourth-century orator Dinarchus summarizes the play. He says, "The Semnai Theai established themselves for all time as housemates [*sunoikous*] sharing in whatever resulted from the council's judgments and in their truth [*krisei genomenei kai tei toutou aletheiai sunoikous*]" (Din. 1.87). Throughout the trilogy, the problem of women's place in the house has been much discussed. It finds resolution when the women have been taught the job of being *sunoikoi* and when they are willing to except the truths generated by male judgment.[51] With the one lesson comes another: by the end of the play, not only have women been taught to be housemates but men have been taught to be citizens.

Aeschylus thus offers a dramatization of the institutional solution attempted in Athens in response to the problem of anger. But the *spondai* or peace treaties established in his play between angry men and women are continually depicted in later Sophoclean and Euripidean plays as disintegrating.[54] Anger simply keeps cropping up in literary representations of the tragic household, despite Aeschylus's literary attempt and the Athenians' political attempts to get rid of it. And how could it not? After all, *orge* denotes not only the necessity of anger but also sexual necessity. *Orge* therefore had a permanent place at the heart of the private sphere, whatever the power of *philia* might be to regulate and restrain it.[53]

The *polis* tried simultaneously to encourage iretic *orge* in men and to discourage iretic *orge* in women while also encouraging or at least making space for their erotic *orge*. To protect the family, women needed to be ripe with children or full of erotic *orge*.[54] The norms of the *polis* to some degree contradicted one another, and the fundamental ideological propositions of the Athenian system of value suffered this notable perplexity. *Orge* entered into interactions within the household as sexual necessity; once there it evolved easily into an anger that made *eros* "unerotic." The Athenians could not establish enough of a distinction between sexual desire and anger to allow them to control the latter. Thus time and time again in tragedy, female anger arises because of male erotic violations. It is by taking a new bride that Jason has, according to Medea, become her enemy (*echthros*; *Med.* 467). Jason considers it natural that women grow angry when their husbands stray sexually (*eikos gar orgas thelu poieisthai genos / gamou [parempolontos] alloiou posei*) (909–10). Sophocles' Deianira grows angry at Herakles at the prospect of having to share a marriage with his new bride (*Tr.* 545), and explicitly argues that those who are angry are not able to live together (*thumousthai* and *sunoikein*) (545–46; see also 574–81).[55] At the end of the play, we are left with the scene of the agonized, dying Herakles wrapped in the poisoned robe sent as a well-intentioned gift by his wife, and he is said to dwell with (*xunoikoun*) the poisoned robe (1055), a robe that is also said to be the woven net of the Erinyes (1051–52).[56] Herakles no longer has relations of *philia* with his wife now unable to be his wife's "housemate." This destructive dwelling with anger and punishment has supplanted the "dwelling together" of marriage. As Pozzi says, "[Deianira's] gift is eros gone awry, *sunoikoun* gone wrong, perverted marriage that feminizes Herakles and makes Deianira like Clytemnestra (1062–63, 1075)."[57]

A Euripidean Clytemnestra argues that she would not have raged (*egriomen*) and would not have slain her husband, even having being wronged by her daughter Iphigeneia's death, if Agamemnon had not also brought a new bride home (*El.* 1031–40). Although Electra (or possibly the chorus) responds by arguing that her mother should nonetheless have restrained herself—because it is necessary for the woman to give in to her husband in all things (*gunaika gar chre panta sungchorein posei*, 1052)—it is already too late. Competition and anger had already spread from the ramparts of Troy to the palace in the city.[58]

The isomorphism of anger and lust connoted by the word *orge* meant that the step from one form of Athenian *orge* to another was not exactly very great.[59] *Orge* was always at the heart of the Athenian *polis*—not only in respect to the political sphere but also in respect to the family. As we have seen, the chorus of the *Libation Bearers* tells a tale of the unerotic eros of Althaea. It follows that story with two other stories of punishing women, and then sums it all up with the following remark:

> But since I have remembered stories of unsoftened troubles [*epei d' epemnesaman ameilichon ponon*], it is the right time [*kairos*] to sing of a loveless marriage and an abomination to the house and of woman-plotting cunningness of mind turned against her shield-bearing husband [*dusphiles gameleum' apeucheton domois gunaikoboulos*]. I honor in contrast a hearth and home that are not boiling [*athermanton*] and a womanly spirit that does not dare audaciousness. (Aesch. *Lib.* 625)

The subject of punishing women leads straight to talk about honeyless troubles and loveless marriages, about the minds of women turned against men, about women who thwart shield-bearing political actors, and about the unfortunate presence of too much hot blood in the home. Stories of female punishment rehearse the downfall of political order. The social norms that operated against women's anger were all that kept erotic *orge* from becoming its inverse, an anerotic and iretic counterpart. Everything hinged on how a woman decided to act in face of the norms about private and public realms and about male and female anger.

Parallel attempts to isolate and contain the *eros* of women supplemented the ideological work done by the norms of anger and by the private-public distinction:

> Both as subject and object of love, the unstable female presented Greek society with a set of tactical and moral problems that it never quite solved but which it sought to clarify, during the archaic and classical periods by recourse to pollution beliefs and the code of conduct governing *miasmata* ("defilements") in general. To isolate and insulate female *eros* from society and from itself was demonstrably the strategy informing many of the notions, conventions, and rituals that surrounded female life in the ancient world.[60]

Eros had to be isolated and insulated because, among other reasons, it was too directly linked to anger. The valorization of anger destabilized not only structures of punishment but also the structures of sexual relations.

The exclusion of women and slaves from the spheres of anger led to fears that women and slaves would use not only deceit and false tales but also poisons as the vehicles for the anger that the legal and political institutions were trying to suppress. The figure of the *pharmakon* is evidence of the worry men had that their subordinates might try to evade their control. But the figure of the *pharmakon* also reflects the particular fear that women would hide their desire to act angrily behind the mask of the erotic action. Thus the trope of the poisonous woman is also evidence of male worries about the ambiguous relationship between anger and lust that the concept of *orge* pointed out with especial clarity. In worrying about female deceit, male citizens admitted to their efforts to control women. The author of a fragmentary play called *Sisyphus* discusses precisely this type of fear as the reason that societies supplement institutions and laws with ideologies and normative orders.[61] The playwright wrote that mortals first established laws to define what was good and what bad, and then they realized that the law prevented open wrongdoing, but it did not prevent deceit and "false tales" (*pseudei logoi*) (fr. line 26). To prevent false tales, he argued, mortals invented the gods and fear of them.

The ideological constructions that we have been investigating—the norms of anger for men and women, the distinction between public and private—functioned as a way of controlling the ambiguities inherent in the concept of *orge*. But the ideological controls sometimes failed. A woman's erotic *orge* might evolve into iretic *orge*, and when it did, the norms established by distinctions between private and public realms, male and female versions of anger, and legitimate and illegitimate uses of *eros* had ceased to do the work of keeping anger out of the household. The male Athenian democrats were unable to invent an ideological construction of anger powerful enough to solidify their control over individual actions based on anger. Faraone has shown that the figure of the *pharmakon* was used to express the male fear not only that women would be able to punish if they used poison but also that women could use deceit to undo the political nature of men.[62] Hippocrates (*Top. And.* 45) defines *pharmaka* as things that shift the present state of things (*ta metakineonta to pareon*). The rhetoric of the *pharmakon* made vivid the degree to which women's behavior had the power to shift the city's hierarchy of values and social norms and thereby to subvert the social order that made the men the active citizens.

The cultural tension reflected in the tragic stories of female punishers and in the rhetoric that women cannot control their passions was founded on a communal Athenian recognition that their politics was based on a self-contradictory proposition: the proposition that *orge* could function in the public political realm as "anger" while functioning in the private realm of the household only as "sexual desire." Athenian tragedy, taken as a genre, makes manifest an extreme cultural unease about anger.[63] This unease reveals the degree to which the work done by the ideological concepts could not be trusted to generate the forms of behavior required for the stability of the political order.

This unease was as powerful as it was—and it was powerful enough to come up over and over again in literary evidence—because the logic of Athenian politics, which claimed that anger could be valorized as a basis for politics without leading to an excessive use of anger and the destruction of the family unit, rested on a fundamentally untenable idea: the idea that male citizens could completely control the ways in which female *orge* functioned. The woman who introduced anger to the household in the guise of erotic seduction refuted the democracy's political logic. Literary texts thus betray an extreme unease among male Athenian citizens about the power of their society to generate perfectly stable ethical and ideological norms. The texts reveal not only the ways in which ideology worked, a necessary complement to institutions, to produce a peaceful and stable regime but also the ways in which even such an ideologically homogeneous society as Athens expected that local actions could undermine socially dominant social and ethical principles and the socially dominant system of value.

CITY AS COLLECTIVE

The major threats to Athenian life that arose during the course of the democracy did not, at the end of the day, come from women but from the oligarchs (chapter 9) and from Plato (chapter 10). The democracy was relatively stable throughout the fifth and fourth centuries despite its ideologically shaky foundations. Its structures of authority for the most part succeeded in sustaining a limited politics of anger and honor as the privilege of citizen men. Moments of collective action—moments when all the members of a community have been given and are willing to carry out complementary, integrated roles that are aimed at achieving a single goal—made this structure of authority especially clear. In moments of collective action, the principles establishing social roles were made visible.

The city of Athens had three ways of acting as a collective unit.[64] First, social memory and knowledge provided for some forms of punishment The wrong-doer could be made *atimos* (without honor or political rights) without a trial for maltreatment of parents, prostitution, adultery, failure to repay public debts, impiety, murder.[65] Those who were *atimoi* had to stay out of the city's political and religious spaces. Women could be kept out of the religious spaces and agora.[66] This means that citizens who were generally recognized as having committed one of these forms of wrongdoing were kept out of the political and religious spaces and the agora solely on the basis of their reputations as wrong-doers. Any citizen could tell anyone generally acknowledged to have done such wrongs to leave the forbidden areas and, if necessary, could force them to leave or else bring a capital suit. This punishment maintained the propriety of specific communal spaces in the city and was worked by rumor or *pheme*.[69] Rumors could be transported by anyone in the city, by all of the unspecified members of the mob—slave, foreign, free, or citizen—without detracting from the power of the male citizen. Social memory was intrinsic to the functioning of punishment in Athens and drew slaves and women into the practice of punishing.

The second method of initiating collective punishment was carried out by the officials who functioned with the name of the collective (*ho demos*) to maintain communal spaces. Magistrates, like the market officials, were frequently named after and responsible for the specific public spaces in which they fined, arbitrated, and adjudged—for example, *agoranomai* and *astunomai*. But the powers of the magistrates, assembly, and Council of 500 to punish were limited, as we have seen (chapter 2). Magistrates and the Council of 500 could fine only up to legally established limits, and the magistrates and the council had to depend on courtroom jurors to make final decisions.

Third, the collective of the citizenry could initiate punishment in the assembly or council by voting that some specific citizen prosecute a known wrong-doer.[68] Also, the assembly could pass special decrees of punishment.[69] The city did this especially in relation to cases involving politicians and finance, such as bribery or misuse of public funds (e.g., Cimon; see also Dem. 21.1–2).[70] The assembly had to appoint private citizens to act as prosecutors before it could try a case. Even the institutions of collective power and public punishment could not depend entirely on public officials to initiate an act of punishment but needed private citizen men to carry out acts of punishment on their behalf. The citizens who initiated acts of collective anger thus prosecuted as individual members of the "citizenry" and as members of the *demos*, rather than as permanently appointed agents of a "state."[71]

Herodotus in the fifth century and then Lycurgus and Demosthenes in the fourth all report the extraordinary case of Athenian collective action: a brutal stoning carried out during the Persian Wars, when the whole city had fled to Salamis. A stoning is a paradigmatic form of collective action, and in the events involved in the story of this stoning we can see quite clearly what kinds of roles in punishment were assigned to the various members of the city. In this story, we can also see what happened to the system of peacetime punishment when inverted by the context of war.

Here first is Herodotus's story about what happened during one particularly memorable council meeting while the Athenians were on Salamis in 479 during the Persian Wars:

> For the sake of [a peace offering requiring Athenian submission to Mardonius], Mardonius sent Mourychides to Salamis, and he went before the Council of 500 and spoke about Mardonius's business. One of the councillors, Lycidas, said that he thought that it seemed better to consider Mardonius's offer, as conveyed by Mourychides, and to bring it before the *demos*. He made clear that this was his opinion, whether because he had received bribe money from Mardonius or because the plans pleased him. But the effect was to make the Athenians menacing [*deinon*] immediately, and both the Athenians who were members of the council and those who had learned about the matter from where they were outside [the council chamber] encircled Lycidas, threw [stones] at him, and stoned him to death, but they sent away the Hellespontian Mourychides uninjured. Then a hue and cry [*thorubos*] about Lycidas arose in Salamis, and when the women learned what had happened, one woman called out to another and took her along as they went to the house of Lycidas on their own authority [*autokelees*], and stoned his wife and children. (9.5)

In the year 330, Lycurgus attempted to rally his jurors to punish Leocrates as a traitor with a version of the same story:

> It is appropriate for you to hear the decree about the man who died in Salamis, whom the Council of 500 killed with their own hands after taking off their crowns because he had tried to betray the city, even if only in speech. The decree was noble, men, and justly worthy [*axion*] of your ancestors. For they possessed nobility not only in their souls but also in their punishments [*timorias*] of wrongdoers [*adikounton*]. What then, gentlemen? Does it seem to those of you who wish to copy your ancestors that it would be in the spirit of your country *not* to kill Leocrates? (1.122)

Later that same year, Demosthenes incorporated the story into his speech *On the Crown*:

> You take these actions [of your ancestors] to be so estimable and so suitable to your national character that you praise those of your ancestors who were most especially [*malista*] doing these sorts of things. And rightly so. Who would not praise the virtue of those men, who left their fields and their city and took to triremes in order to avoid giving in to commands, who chose Themistocles to give them advice as their general, who stoned Cyrsilos because he had declared they should obey the orders [of Mardonius] and they not only stoned him, but your women [*hai gunaikes hai humeterai*] stoned his wife. (18.204) [Notice that Demosthenes has transposed letters in Lycidas's name.]

Lycurgus and Demosthenes both use the exceptional event to praise the virtue of the ancestors and to enjoin the Athenians to exercise the same kind of virtue.

The two orators take the story as a paradigmatic example of public punishment, despite its idiosyncratic nature and wartime context. The exceptional is paradigmatic when it is the supranormal or ideal form (for instance, the A+ student is paradigmatic despite being exceptional), and so Lycurgus and Demosthenes are using the story to represent public Athenian punishment in "pure" or idealized form.

The stoning takes place during wartime. This circumstance already makes the stoning unusual, and the stoning, as described by these three authors, is in fact characterized by three major deviations from the institutionally established methods of punishing that obtained in peacetime. First, after deciding to punish, the Council of 500 while punishing a citizen with death without a trial, dismissed a foreigner unharmed. Second, the council carried out the punishment with their own hands, and thereby violated not only the rule that they could not punish above certain limits but also the established procedures for handing wrongdoers over to the public executioner. Third, the women of Athens punished, which makes this story the only instance in Athenian sources in which we see the women of the city actively participating in the processes of anger and punishment. And yet the story is taken as paradigmatic. As it turns out, the punishment can be taken as a paradigm because all of the exceptions were carried out precisely in ways that confirmed the peacetime norms. Wartime required inversions of peacetime legal procedures in order to maintain the peacetime system of value. Institutional rules were ignored, but ideological norms were not.

In this council meeting, the foreign ambassador was sent away unharmed. The foreigner received more restrained treatment than the citizen did in an inversion from the city's standard practice—where the foreigner was always treated according to terms of war that led to harsher treatment for foreigners than for citizens. But it was precisely according to the terms of war that the Athenian could not kill the ambassador. The foreign ambassador was protected because he was the subject of a king who was making war on and, momentarily, defeating Athens. A shift in context from peacetime to wartime required that the application of the usual norms—that metics be treated according to the terms of war—be carried out in unusual ways. Wartime increased the safety of the foreign ambassador but robbed the citizen of privileges and protections, that were precisely the fruits of peace.

The council members' decision to carry out the punishment with their own hands was also done in such a way as to confirm the structure of peacetime norms. As Lycurgus emphasizes, they removed their crowns of office before acting. In removing their crowns, the councillors handed their power back to the *demos* as a whole and acted not as magistrates with "extra" *time* or status but merely as citizens, as "Athenians" in general, and as an instantiation of the *demos*. As such, they did not abuse their magisterial power by punishing beyond the limits allowed to magistrates.[72] Moreover, they were joined in the stoning by the nameless democrats standing around outside the council house who had "learned about the matter from where they were" and who were roused to a menacing "fearsomeness." As in peacetime, the *demos* as a whole, and not state agents, was punishing and it was punishing only after it had been constituted by social knowledge and by collective emotion.[73] Lycurgus even claims that the council issued a decree of punishment, so legitimate does he conceive the council's act to have been, and Aeschines and Apollodorus both are able to compare the experience of being in court to a stoning (Aes. 1.163). The image of the *demos* circling Lycidas is powerfully evocative of the way in which individual Athenian citizens were embedded in and at the mercy of the network of social knowledge and communally possessed norms. The Athenian *demos* was a community with final authority to control the behavior of individual citizens, even in wartime when trials were restricted.

The women's participation in the stoning also confirmed the peacetime political order. After the men had stoned Lycidas, social knowledge in the form of the autonomous and impersonal *thorubus* or hue and cry spread through Salamis, obscuring whether its bearers were slave or citizen, male or female. The spread of social knowledge and public anger bore with it the command that the city restructure its networks of friendship and *philia*. In order for the city to complete its judgment, to make itself secure in the face of a threat, and thereby to reconstitute itself, the women had to be implicated in the same emotional relationships as the men; all the members of the city needed to love and hate with one mind. The men had stoned Lycidas, and so the women stone Lycidas's wife and children. For once, the city's women exercised anger publicly and explicitly "on their own authority" (*autokelees*). They did so, however, in such a way as to confirm both that their passion was specifically limited to the private sphere and that their passion was directed precisely at controlling and assuring the proper constitution of the household. Their project was the destruction of Lycidas's family, the realm of his sexual *orge*. The women did not merely stone Lycidas's wife and children, but even enacted the idea that if a man's political practice was harmful to the *polis*, then it was also harmful to his family. They also confirmed the painful dependence of women and children on male political activity.[74] Thus they angered and punished in a manner that consolidated the political order and their place in it rather than in a way that threatened it.

The story of the stoning is narrated by Herodotus, Lycurgus, and Demosthenes in ways that did not require the Athenians to make exceptions to their systems of value and symbolic orders. We can therefore see how much power conceptual systems of value and symbolic orders have to give meaning and shape to legitimate action within a society. Institutions are only one source that can be drawn upon for the norms that legitimate an act of power and render it authoritative. It is not merely institutions that legitimate collective action but rather the norms governing the forms of social organization that are embodied by those institutions.

All the members of the peaceable and stable city of Athens had their legitimate roles in punishing. Each role, whether that of male or female, of free, slave, or citizen, helped to constitute the male citizen as the person who "deserved" to punish and to act publicly on anger. The word "citizen" denoted a set of men and women who were at peace with one another and who simultane- ously valorized public contests of honor and limited them in such a way as to provide for the stability of the *polis* as a set of families. The male citizen, as legitimate punisher, was someone who pursued honor and participated in its angry defense in order to ensure freedom and equality. The female citizen was someone who behaved so as to ensure that passions within the household were ordered in such a way as to maintain the integrity of the family unit. Anger could not appear in the household, nor could the competition in the city be allowed to reach the levels of war. The female citizen had to submit to the city's ethics of anger. The male citizen had to submit to the city's assessments of honor. In assuming their day-to-day roles in the city, the Athenians (male, female, free, citizen, slave) initiated punishments and entered into penal spaces by working within a set of institutions and cultural norms constructed in such a way as to preserve anger and honor as political principles while dissolving the threat that they posed to the coherence of social groups. In the peacetime city, those who deserved to punish, including women when they punished, were those who understood how to do the peaceful work of politics rather than the disruptive work of war. The inverse was the rule during wartime.

CHAPTER 7

The Negotiation of Desert, Part One

THE MAGIC OF SPEECH

Lycidas probably never got a chance to try to talk his way out of the sticky situation in which he found himself when he was face to face with the mob that was ready to stone him. His only hope of escape would have been to talk his fellow citizens into taming their anger, but he was not given much opportunity to plead that he did not deserve to be stoned. This chance to avoid punishment was made available to male citizens when they stood trial. Winkler remarks: "Competitive success is regularly joined not only with personal charisma but with the power to soften and restrain the anger of one's enemies."[1]

Male citizens initiated punishments by marshaling narratives from witnesses, by choosing procedures that proved their sensitivity to social status, and by obeying the norms governing the use of anger. But they had to advance beyond that moment of initiation to the moment of judgment. This they could do only by means of discourse, by convincing their fellow citizens to accept their arguments about desert, law, and justice. The city's definition of justice and its system of value were contestable between the moment of initiation, when some social disruption had unsettled the established system of authority and social roles, and the moment of judgment, the moment when that order was reestablished. That contest was carried out by means of argument, and the Athenian fame for litigiousness was equally a reputation for "talkativeness." Thus for Plato the Athenians were word lovers (*philologoi*) and gabbers (*polulogoi*) (Plato *Rep.* 641e). The power of speech was central to constructing the authority necessary to sustain punishment.

Like Lycidas, Athenian women probably never had the chance to deliver carefully crafted courtroom orations in order to remedy the problems caused by their anger and by the anger of other people. Nor could they turn to rhetoric to give public expression to their conception of how social roles should be ordered. Some fourth-century Athenian women turned instead to the power of magic in order to accomplish their punitive ends. Women both cursed those who had done them wrong and were the objects of curses in punitive curse tablets from the fourth century. On such tablets women called on the gods to punish those who had done them wrong.[2] (Women in other Greek cities and at later dates also used these tablets. On thirteen late vengeance tablets from Cnidus in Asia Minor and on similar tablets from Corinth, the plaintiff is almost always a woman.)[3] Those who used curses, like those who used rhetoric, expected to obtain power and carry out actions by means of the effective force of words.

The women of Athens were not alone in using such curse tablets. Male Athenian litigants treated magic spells as an extension of courtroom rhetorical efforts. They not only made speeches in their own defense but also used binding spells to protect themselves from the power of their opponents' speeches. Before coming into court, they would name their opponents on curse tablets and beseech divinities to tie the tongues of their opponents. On one late curse tablet, the suppliant used a magic spell to request "protection against failure, plots, harmful drugs, exile, and poverty that come from other people's *thumos*" (*Papyri Graecae Magicae*, 36:211–30).[4] The Erinyes curse Orestes before the trial scene in the *Eumenides* (306),[5] and similarly litigants used the magic words of binding spells to prevent what their opponents were "doing and plotting against" them.[6] The use of the curse tablets reflects an awareness that only the magical power of words—whether they took the form of a curse or of rhetoric—could restrain the far-reaching power of punishing anger.[7]

PITY AND ANGER

Pliny reports that the fifth-century Athenian painter Parrhasios in an allegorical picture of the Athenian *demos* depicted the character of the *demos* as consisting of a set of emotions. Anger (*iracundam*), pity (*clementem, misericordem*), and a susceptibility to being swayed by argument (*exorabilem*) were among the emotions that Parrhasios used to characterize the Athenian people (Pliny 35.(36).68–71). Pliny's description of the painting, with its emphasis on anger and pity, mirrors what intervening centuries have chosen to tell us about how Athens worked. In the extant oratorical corpus, calls for pity for the speaker, and injunctions not to pity the other party, along with statements by the orators enjoining their audiences to anger are among the most often repeated arguments. Regularly the orators remonstrated their audience: pity us (*eleesate hemas*).[8] Or show your wrath (*phainesthe orgizomenoi*).[9] The discourse of anger and pity is littered with the vocabulary of desert (*axia*). In oratory, requests like "I deserve to be pitied" (*axios eleethenai*, Ant. 5.73) are as frequent as injunctions to hand out "deserved anger appropriately" (*orthos axian orgen*, Dem. 21.127).[10]

The language of anger and pity defined the contours of the competition between prosecutor and defendant. Thus Demosthenes argues: "Which of us is more deserving of pity?" (Dem. 54.43). A litigant's request that a jury pity him or those whom he was defending was equally and simultaneously a request that the jury feel anger toward his (or their) opponent. Lysias makes this clear when he says: "You should pity these young ones . . . [but] this man is worthy [*axion*] of the anger [*orges*] of all the citizens" (Lys. 32.19). Anger and pity, as painted by Parrhasios, represented the two faces of judicial power; pitying one party required being angry at the other.[11] The status of the two contenders in a court case was not expressed in any abstract or objective fashion but instead was made dramatically dependent on the collective emotional subjectivity of the *demos*. Each contender had to use his speech to define the pitiable and that which was worthy of anger in order to make a claim on his jurors' votes.

Other emotional concepts could be used to flesh out the core ideas of "anger" and of "pity" in the process of trying to establish desert. The ideologies of hate, envy, and fear (*misos, phthonos, deos*) could be grafted onto the ideology of anger. Thus Demosthenes could replace the concept of anger with the concept of envy and argue: "Have I not suffered great wrongs from the beginning, great indeed! And now I am harmed by them because I seek to take justice; who of you would not justly begrudge [*phthoneseie*] them and pity [*eleeseien*] us?" (Dem. 28.18). On the other hand, the ideologies of forgiveness, grace and gratitude, and philanthropy (*suggnome, charis, philanthropia*) could be grafted on to pity.[12] Nor did the orator need to scrimp on his use of emotional vocabulary; the following remark from Lysias is one of the most baroque: "If someone of you either pities [*eleei*] those who died in the naval battle, or is ashamed [*aischunetai*] on behalf of those enslaved to the enemy, or is annoyed [*aganaktei*] at the destroyed walls, or hates [*misei*] the Spartans, or grows angry [*orgizetai*] at the thing, it is necessary [*chre*] for him to think this man's father is to blame [*aition*]" (Lys. 14.39).[13]

Each speaker couched his argument about "desert" in terms of the claims that he could make on the jury's pity or anger. These concepts and phenomena were thoroughly contestable in their definitions, and the claims to anger and pity were embedded in a language of communal ethical evaluation. We shall examine the nature of this contest over the course of the chapter, but let me briefly point out its significance in advance.

The Athenian approach to judicial desert—according to which citizens made claims on one another by arguing about anger and pity—contrasts markedly with the modern use of "rights" language to establish protections for citizens.[14] "Rights claims" function as argumentative "trumps," to borrow Dworkin's term. If I claim that I have a right to free speech, I do not have to defend my desire to speak but only my right to give expression to the particular thing that I want to say. I can take the first point as already argued for and won. A language of rights thus puts an end (on some level) to discussions of what sort of behavior is meritorious, deserving, or acceptable and shifts the argument to the question of whether a given act falls in the category protected by a right. Rights claims ostensibly establish a shared ethical bedrock for citizens to draw upon in making their arguments and provide a political discourse in which a certain bare minimum of equality and protection is guaranteed to citizens at all times. Athenian judicial argument had no such "trumps" for litigants to use. Athenian orators might well have to argue their positions from the ground up. If an orator wanted to protect speech, for example, he might have to argue not only for what he wanted to say but also for the importance of open speech to a democracy. No word in classical Greek translates directly into "right," but F. Miller has argued that the word *to dikaion* ("justice") and with it *ta axia* ("deserts") also functioned as trumps in Athenian ethical arguments and should be understood as equivalent to "right."[15] Miller is correct to point out that the Athenians *made claims on* their fellows by using the language of *to dikaion* and *ta axia*, but he is incorrect to argue that such claims had to be *honored automatically.* An Athenian's claims about justice and desert were not, unlike rights claims, automatically determinative of a given point in the debate. No modern prosecutor has to justify the right to free speech. He or she has to define "speech," but we know in advance of any courtroom argument that *some* kind of speech will end up being protected by the end of the case.

We would not be able to make similar predictions about the decisions made in Athenian courts. It is true that the final outcome of any judicial decision would be said to be in accord with *to dikaion.* But the substantive content of that justice, the specific protections provided for by the judgment, could not be predicted in advance of the courtroom arguments. In Athens, each litigant had the tasks of giving *to dikaion* and *axia* substantive meaning and convincing the jury to accept his definitions of those terms. Claims based on *to dikaion* were totally contestable.[16] Not even the written laws of Athens were granted a status sufficiently binding as to preclude in-court debate over the morality of actions. Athenian jurors simply made a choice between the litigants' two interpretations of what would accord with *to dikaion* and "desert," and whatever could produce anger and pity were, like "rights," the magic words that had an effective force in respect to the jury's judgments. The only "incontestable" right that an Athenian had was the right to a trial by jury, and this was simply a right to speak in one's defense and to put an argument about justice before one's peers.[17] The arguments used to sustain claims to *to dikaion* or to desert were structured around claims for anger and pity. Consider this Isocratean comment: "It would be just [*dikaios*] that I should be pitied [*eleetheien*] by you on the basis of the facts themselves [*ex auton ton ergon*], even if I am unable to lead you [*agein*] [to pity] with speech [*toi logoi*], since it is necessary to pity those who are unjustly endangered, and . . . who are in a situation such as they do not deserve [*anaxios*]" (16.48). Isocrates defines justice by invoking the jury's pity and by making an argument about how to decide who should receive pity: those who are unjustly endangered.

The Athenians did not develop a rights-based judicial order other than generally maintaining the right to trial and the right to participate in the city's political institutions. It should, therefore, not be surprising (although commentators have found it surprising) that the Athenians did not develop a corpus of legal handbooks—akin to the handbooks written by students of Roman law or by students of modern legal systems—to explain the penumbras of given rights. They did, however, produce rhetorical handbooks (as did other Greeks). These were treatises on how to construct successful arguments about desert by making use not of a rights language but of the language of anger and pity. Aristotle in his *Rhetoric* spends one of three books discussing the rhetorical technique of *pathos*, defined broadly as "creating a certain disposition in the audience," and anger and pity are central to his discussion (*Rhet.* 1356a, 1377b1). Other rhetorical handbooks also explored *pathos*, and in all of them the creation and destruction of anger and pity are stressed.[18] The handbooks served a purpose in the Athenian context equivalent to the purpose of the legal handbooks used in the Roman and modern context: they taught citizens who had to engage in situations of punishment how to construct arguments about desert so as to obtain the sought-after outcome.

The effort to construct a formulation of desert that would produce anger for one's opponent and pity for oneself consisted primarily of three strands of argument. These and their implications are the subject of this chapter and chapter 8. First, the orator had to prove that he deserved to prosecute by showing that he understood the "economy of spending anger" or the norms according to which his *private anger* could be "used" or acted upon. In particular, this required displaying an understanding of the ways in which the rhetoric of sycophancy served to invalidate certain forms of prosecution. Second, the rhetorician had to display a judicious use of *nomos* (understood both as social memory and as law) in his effort to identify an action deserving of public anger and public judgment.[19] Third, a speaker had to show that he had used public institutions— and was trying to rouse public anger—with sensitivity to the ways in which public judgment contributed to the constitution and preservation of the *polis*. A litigant's effort to prove "desert" functioned as a test of whether he understood the operational structure and aspirations of the Athenian democracy and his role as democratic citizen. In examining the ways in which the *demos* regulated assessments of honor and the ways in which a citizen could build an argument about desert, we uncover not only the parameters given to desert in the Athenian context but also the norms, rules, and politicoethical criteria with which the *demos* controlled angry penal competitions. These "norms of public agency" constrained the public (penal) behavior of citizen men when they took part in the limited forms of competition intrinsic to Athenian punishment and politics.[20]

THE FIRST NORM OF PUBLIC AGENCY: DESERVING TO PUNISH AND DISPELLING CHARGES OF SYCOPHANCY

A litigant was attempting to transform his private anger into public anger when he tried to make an argument that would inspire his jury to be angry at his opponent and to pity him. The first step of this process was for the litigant to prove that he himself was personally angry at the defendant and that he understood the norms according to which his anger should be spent.

We have seen how important anger and competition were to Athenian punishment and with what regularity the prosecutor was personally involved in the matter at hand (chapter 2). Not only were Athenian litigants personally involved in the matter at hand, but they made a point to demonstrate that fact in their speeches. In speech after speech, whether in private or public cases, the orators include long stories explaining their anger, hatred, or enmity for their opponents. The speeches written for disputes over inheritance, which had frequently passed through several legal stages by the time they reached court, virtually required such argumentation. One speaker, for instance, begins thus:

"Since we have already brought suits against these very men, regarding the estate of Hagnias, men of the jury, and since they do not leave off their law-breaking and violence in their effort to hold by any method at all what does not belong to them, it is perhaps necessary to explain what has happened from the beginning; . . . These men will be seen for what they are, as people who began to behave this way long ago and who are still continuing in their nasty schemes" (Dem. 43.1–2).[21]

Speakers provide narrations of personal involvement even where they are not germane to the facts of the case. The speaker of Lysias 13 does this when he brings a homicide prosecution against Agoratos, a supporter of the oligarchs who took over Athens at the end of the fifth century. The speaker does not rely on Agoratos's wide wrongdoing against the community in making his case but emphasizes his personal relationship to Agoratos: "It is fitting [*prosekei*], men of the jury, for all of you to punish [*timorein*] on behalf of those supporters of the populace who were killed, and it is especially fitting for me to do so [*prosekei de kai moi ouch hekista*] since Dionysodorus [one of the victims] was my brother-in-law and cousin. Because of the things that Agoratos [the defendant] has done, it is fitting [*eikotos*] that I hate him" (13.1). Agoratos's behavior toward the speaker's brother-in-law has inspired his hate of him. The personal connection ensures that Lysias is emotionally involved.

Even in public cases, the orators spend time detailing private grievances that are, from a modern perspective, irrelevant to the facts of the case. In a speech written by Demosthenes for one Diodorus, who, with his friend Euctemon, was prosecuting Androtion for having passed an illegal law, the speaker begins by pointing out that his coprosecutor Euctemon has undertaken the public case in part because of a private grievance: "Because, gentlemen of the jury, Euctemon was treated badly by Androtion, he thought it necessary to take justice on his own behalf and to help the city at the same time [*hama*]." The prosecutor Diodorus then continues: "And I will also try to do this if it is possible. Although the things that befell Euctemon were many and fearful and wholly against the law, Euctemon was nonetheless treated with *hubris* by Androtion to a lesser degree than I was" (22.1–3). Diodorus not only justifies Euctemon's participation in the prosecution in terms of personal involvement but also justifies his own participation in such terms. He even claims that his prosecution is more justifiable than Euctemon's. After opening in this fashion, Diodorus explains what Androtion has done to him in a paragraph and a half. He finally turns to the topic of Androtion's public wrongs, but only after he remarks that he could say many more things about the wrongs that he had suffered privately. He makes sure that his audience knows how much he has personally at stake in the case.

Aeschines gave accurate expression to a consistent theme in Athenian opinion when he said:

When I saw [*horon*] that Timarchus was, though disqualified by law, speaking in your assembly, and when I myself was personally being slanderously accused [*autos idiai sukophantoumenos*] [by him], I decided it would be most shameful not to help the whole city and the laws and you and myself . . . It would seem, O Athenians, that the usual saying about public trials [*tois demosiois agosin*] is not false: that is, the saying that private enmities [*idiai echthrai*] do indeed correct many public matters [*epanorthousi ton koinon*]. (1.1–2)[22]

Aeschines asserts that he has a private interest in prosecuting Timarchus's acts of self-prostitution on a public charge. The facts of the case do not require that Aeschines introduce the topic of his enmity for Timarchus, but he does anyway. The frequency with which speakers narrate feuds and disputes reveals not only that orators *were* usually personally involved in the case at bar, and not only that they *felt obliged to be* personally involved in the case at bar, but also, and more important, that they felt obliged *to show* their audiences that they were personally involved and to explain that personal involvement.

Several orators explicitly address the unspoken requirement that one be able to prove one's personal involvement in the matter at hand.[23] Lysias, in a highly political speech against Eratosthenes who had aided the oligarchs, says:

At other times [*poteron*] it is necessary to ask the accusers to explain their enmity [*echthran*] toward the defendants, but in the present case [*nuni*] it is necessary to learn from the defendants why they showed such enmity to the city. I do not speak this way because I do not have my own private enmity and misfortunes [*oikeias echthras kai sumphoras*] but because for all of us there is great reason to be angry [*orgizesthai*] [against Eratosthenes] whether about private matters [*idion*] or about public matters [*demosion*]. (12.2)

In a blatantly rhetorical maneuver, Lysias first of all asserts that in this particular case he should not have to explain his enmity given how infamous Eratosthenes is. But he does not leave matters there, using 20 paragraphs (out of a 100-paragraph speech) in order to explain his enmity toward Eratosthenes. Lysias's two-pronged argument—on the one hand he argues that he does not need to meet the standard ideological requirements constraining speakers but on the other hand he goes ahead and meets them anyway—reveals how powerful the norms were that the *demos* established for speakers. As we will see again, a speaker might indeed try to challenge one of the norms of public agency, but he would also protect himself by meeting it.[24]

Orators also went to especially great lengths to prove rhetorically that they had personal grievances against the defendant in cases where they were not actually the victim of the wrong under trial but were speaking on behalf of the actual prosecutor.[25] A victim-prosecutor (Theomnestus) therefore introduces his supporter, Apollodorus, with the following words: "I beg you [*deomai*], o jurors, to allow me to call to this trial as a cospeaker, Apollodorus, which I think is fitting because I am young and inexperienced at speaking. For he is older than I and has more experience with the laws, and he also is wronged by this Stephanus, so no one can begrudge him the act of punishing [*timoreisthai*] the one who began this affair" (Dem. 59.6–15). Theomnestus claims that he is too young and weak in respect to speaking ability to prosecute his own suit. His purported weakness itself functions as a justification of Apollodorus's presence. But his introduction of the second speaker is not complete until rounded out by the argument that Apollodorus is in fact personally involved in the case.[26]

Arguments about personal involvement proved that a speaker was acting in "hot blood." The proof of hot blood also rested on arguments that an orator's timing in dealing with a "wrongdoing" was appropriate.[27] Repeatedly we hear that the only appropriate time to be angry is "immediate" to the event that causes the anger (*euthus*) (e.g., Isae. 3.48; Dem. 36.9, 37.2). Lysias, discussing a dispute over a scuffle about a slave boy, chastises his opponent for having waited to bring a charge and says: "Other people in their anger [*orgizomenoi*] would immediately [*parachrema*] seek to punish [*timoreisthai*]" (Lys. 3.39). Institutions gave support to this norm. The statute of limitations was set at five years for all types of cases except for homicide (which had no statute of limitations) and for prosecutions against unconstitutional laws (the proposer of the law could be brought on trial only for a year but the law itself could be impeached at any time).

A number of orators fault people for having waited to make their claims,[28] and, according to Isaeus, a delay was sufficiently problematic that it could be used to challenge the truth of the charge. Thus, he argues: "And if it were true [*alethe*], the things which you now have dared to testify, you would have punished [*etimoreso*] the wrongdoer then [*tote*] on the spot [*parachrema*] immediately [*euthus*]" (Isae. 3.48).[29] A seeming absence of anger—whether evidenced through a lack of personal involvement in a case, through delay in bringing a charge, or some other cause—was seen as a sign of lying and scheming and invalidated punishment (see chapter 4 on *dolos*). Delays in prosecuting were associated with attempts to take advantage of wrongs only vaguely remembered.[30] Behavior that produced delays of such exceptional length that relevant witnesses were dead by the time that the case was brought on might be called shameless (*anaischuntias*) (Dem. 38.6).[31] As we have seen, knowledge and proof depended on memory (from anger) and witnesses. Delay weakened the strength and power of both of these, making wrongdoings "stale [*heola*] and cold [*psuchra*] when they arrived before the jury" (Dem. 21.112). Delay evidenced a crucial lack of "hot blood" that was also capable of subverting the city's procedures for managing public knowledge.

Orators, when they are in position of having to justify some delay, commonly claim that they have acted as soon as they were actually physically and institutionally able to act. Several orators argue that they were forced into delays because the city had restricted judicial activity during wartime.[32] Isaeus provides us with a telling passage in which an orator simultaneously tries to challenge the prejudice against delays but nonetheless also explains how his particular delay came about:

> Perhaps, someone among you, men, marvels at the amount of time [*ton chronon*], at how we have allowed so much time to pass and at how we did not proceed in these

matters when [*pos pote*] we were robbed but are only now [*alla nuni*] taking action concerning them. But I think it is not just [*ou dikaion*] that someone should have less [than his due] because he was unable to carry out his business or neglected to do so. *For it is necessary not to consider this [delay], but only whether or not the case is just. . . . But that aside, we have a reason for these delays, men . . .* there was the Corinthian War and when peace came some bad luck with the public treasury fell upon me [so I could not bring a suit]. (Isae. 10.18, 20; cf. 11.27)

Once again, the speaker makes a two-pronged argument in order to confront his audience's expectations—on the one hand he tries to undermine the problematization of delay but on the other hand he nonetheless tries to meet the standard requirements that orators justify delays. The double effort again reveals the power of the norms guiding efforts to speak before the people.[33]

"Hot blood" was for those in the prime of life, and young men risked seeming presumptuous or out of order when they tried to prosecute.[34] The speaker of one Lysianic speech treated this communal norm as a given when he prosecuted a speech at a young age: "Already I have perceived that because of this affair some people are annoyed [*achthmenon*] with me because I am too young to be trying to speak before the people" (Lys. 16.20).[35] The norms of public agency in the city controlled the entry of the young into the full citizenship of anger, honor, and competition just as institutions of initiation and enrollment in citizens lists did. Every orator had to be ready to defend himself against arguments made about his involvement or his timing in bringing a case, but a young speaker also had to defend himself against charges that he was acting in a presumptuous fashion.

Antiphon was one orator who appeared in court at a young age. He claims that it is "necessity" that has led him to assume the role of orator. He argues: "It is necessary [*dei*] for me to argue on behalf of my father, even though it would have been much more fitting for him to argue on my behalf, since he is my father. He is much older and knows what has happened to me, but I am much younger than the events of his life. I know them only by hearsay. My father is too old to help me, and I am not yet of an age to punish [*timorein*] effectively for myself" (Ant. 5.74, 80). Mantitheus, the speaker in the Lysias speech quoted earlier, also deploys the idea of necessity. The young man claims: "Many of you are annoyed with me merely for attempting to speak before the people at too early an age. But I was compelled [*anangkazomenos*] to speak in public to protect my own interests" (Lys. 16.20).[36] Similarly, people who have come to court against family members regularly make use of the concept of necessity to excuse their violation of a community norm.[37] The concept of necessity (*anangke*) contributed to the tricky work of the construction of the pitiable. It was used especially by the young and by litigants involved in family conflicts. As we have seen, in tragedy anger was itself figured as a "necessity" that legitimated attempts to punish. The concept of "necessity," whether derived from anger or otherwise, provided people with an excuse to talk and act.

Wealthy orators use the concept of *charis* in a similar fashion.[38] Elite speakers had to work hard to avoid appearing to harbor attitudes that were antithetical to those of the *demos*.[39] One tactic was to remind the jurors of the liturgies (public works projects) that they had paid for out of their own pockets. Wealthy orators argued that they deserved public gratitude or *charis* for having benefited the city in this way, and such speakers, who might otherwise have been excluded from the realm of the pitiable, could thereby reenter its field of influence.

An orator was most in need of rhetorical means of reinscribing himself within the realm of the pitiable when faced with charges of "sycophancy," that mysterious and vilified form of prosecution, whose name literally means "pointing out" or "displaying figs." In classical Athens the term "sycophancy" did not refer to flattery but to some method of prosecuting that was not socially acceptable. The sycophant was somehow the opposite of the upright legitimate democratic prosecutor. Accusing one's opponent of being a sycophant was one of the most powerful weapons in the rhetorical arsenal because the word sycophant specifically directed the audience to consider the degree to which a prosecutor had veered from the city's system of value. But what exactly was the sycophant if he was not the modern flatterer? How did he violate the norms of anger, honor, and peaceableness used to regulate male political behavior? As Todd has noted, "It is easy enough to describe the sycophant as a perversion or perhaps inversion of the ideal of the volunteer prosecutor, but there has been considerable recent dispute as to what it is about him that is perverse."[40]

The traditional view was that the sycophant prosecuted for the sake of making money. Osborne, however, has argued that the term sycophant denoted a "vexatious litigant," one who was excessively eager to prosecute.[41] More specifically, Osborne uncovered an association between sycophancy and violations of the requirements that people prosecute without delay and only in cases where they are personally involved. "The orators . . . frequently take the fact that the prosecutor was not himself wronged as a sign that the prosecution is sycophantic. . . . The sycophant characteristically acts after the event and rakes up old charges. . . . If men do not contest charges immediately but later, they are regarded as sycophants and *poneroi*."[42] Prosecutors who do not follow the normal guidelines for "hot blood" end up being called sycophants.

Sycophancy is, in fact, a central issue in both of the two cases in the extant oratorical corpus (excluding administrative cases like *euthunai*, *dokimasiai*, and cases of wrongdoing involving public finance such as the Harpalos affair in which the city appointed prosecutors) that are prosecuted by citizens who were not personally involved with the defendants: Lysias's *Against the Grain Dealers* and Lycurgus's *Against Leocrates*. In the Lysias speech a private citizen is prosecuting metic grain dealers against whom he holds no personal grudges, for having fixed grain prices. Lycurgus's speech, in contrast, is a treason prosecution, against a citizen, Leocrates, who moved away from Athens after the Battle of Chaeronea in violation of the generals' command that all Athenian men of military age gather in the assembly to be redeployed. Lycurgus does not have any personal involvment with Leocrates and is also prosecuting him eight years after the purported offense.

The speakers in both cases acknowledge that they must defuse the charges of sycophancy brought about by their lack of personal involvement with the defendants. Their diverse approaches to the matter are enlightening. The speaker in *Against the Grain Dealers* cuts to the chase, and opens the speech by directly addressing the problem of his failure to follow the norms of public agency:

> Many people have come to me, gentlemen of the jury, surprised at my accusing the grain dealers in the Council of 500 and telling me that you, however sure you are of their guilt, nonetheless regard those who make speeches [*logous poioumenous*] against them as sycophants [*sukophantein*]. I therefore propose to speak first on the grounds on which I have found it necessary to accuse them. (Lys. 22. 1–3)

The defendants' guilt is purportedly evident to everyone but that is not enough to justify a prosecution. The prosecutor's right to act is a separate matter from how guilty the defendant is.

The speaker explains himself by telling the following story. When the grain dealers had first been accused of wrongdoing in the council chamber, the councillors had wanted to put them to death without a trial. Our speaker had defended their right to trial and had prevented their illegal execution. Then no one had stepped forward to prosecute the metics, and it began to look as if our speaker had defended their right to trial in order that the metics might get off scot-free. He defends himself thus: "While the others were holding their peace, I stood up and accused them and made it clear to all that I had not spoken on their behalf but was only trying to uphold the law. I undertook this case for the sake of those reasons and fearing censure [*dedios aitias*]" (1.3–4). The prosecutor claims to have brought charges lest his reputation in the city be tarnished with "censure," lest he seem to have sided with metics and against the citizenry. Our speaker has managed to turn a case in which he had no private interest into one in which his entire honor and status in the city are at stake, thus revealing how important it was that a prosecution be motivated by acceptable, discussible private interests.

Lycurgus, in *Against Leocrates*, does not, in contrast, try to turn himself into an interested, personally implicated prosecutor. His speech is interesting because it is the only extant oratorical text in which a speaker actively repudiates the principle that one should prosecute only in cases in which one has a personal interest. Like the prosecutor of the grain dealers, Lycurgus opens the speech by moving directly to the question of his lack of personal involvement in Leocrates' affairs and actions; he expresses the ambiguous nature of his position as disinterested prosecutor explicitly:

> Since it is to the advantage of the city that there are those who accuse [*krinontas*] traitors in it, it would be nice to receive the appropriate gratitude. But as things stand it is the case that whoever risks his private well-being and incurs hatred on behalf of

the community [*koinon*] [by prosecuting] is not considered a lover of the city but a meddler, and so things stand neither justly nor beneficially for the city. . . . I brought this public case [*eisangelian*] not because of any hatred nor because of a love of strife nor taking up any other matter of competition, but because I think it shameful to look askance while this man intrudes on the marketplace and shares in communal religious activities, when he has been a disgrace to the fatherland [*oneidos tes patridos*] and all of you . . . For it is not the mark of a just citizen to bring forward cases about public matters because of private enmities when the wrongdoings are not against the city. Instead a just citizen thinks [*nomizein*] that those who violate the laws of the fatherland [*tous eis ten patrida ti paranomountas*] are private enemies [*idious echthrous*], and holds that wrongs done to the community are communal reasons [*prophaseis*] for being at odds with those who do them. (1.3, 5, 6)

Lycurgus repudiates the role of the Athenian prosecutor who was personally involved in the case and acted out of enmity and thereby rejects a fundamental element of Athenian public life. Unlike the speaker in *Against the Grain Dealers*, he does not try to represent himself as having a personal stake in the matter "after all." Instead, he redefines personal interest as an interest in the good of the community and calls this the only legitimate grounds for prosecution. Lycurgus's rhetorical task is therefore to take a concept that usually has negative connotations and is associated with sycophancy—"disinterested prosecution"—and to turn it into something with positive connotations. Thus he uses words like *patris* at an unusual frequency and inverts the normal relationship between private enmity and the good of the city.[43] Later in the speech he will point out that people are calling him a sycophant, but here in his opening he uses only the term "meddler." This choice of vocabulary allows him to distance himself rhetorically from the accusations of sycophancy that will be made against him.[44]

Later in the speech Lycurgus fleshes out his description of the disinterested public prosecutor and deals explicitly with the possibility that he will be called a sycophant. He argues:

Leocrates will immediately cry out that he is a private citizen who is being preyed upon by a fearsome orator and sycophant. But I think that you all know [*ego d' hegoumai humas eidenai*] what kind of work is done by those terrible [*deinon*] people who try to "sycophant." . . . They choose a point and seek out grounds on which to derail the arguments of those on trial, but the work of those who bring suits with justice, as I do, is just the opposite [*tanantia toutois poiountas*]. (31–32)

Lycurgus's comments depend more on what is unsaid than on what is said. He assumes that his audience will simply know, without being told explicitly, what it is that a sycophant does, and treats himself as an example of the positive ethical values that can be contrasted to the negative ones associated with a sycophant. Sycophant is a word of opprobrium that leaves audiences the task of filling in its meaning, with the help, of course, of the speaker's definition of the term. Lycurgus taps a network of ethical concepts that are salient to his audience, and tries to establish the disinterested prosecutor as the opposite of a sycophant. Lycurgus sets himself the project of redefining the ethical hierarchies maintained by the discourse of "sycophancy."

The Athenian norms of public agency required that prosecutors speak personally and in tones of anger. Because Lycurgus rejects this norm, he must develop a new form for the "prosecutorial voice," and the result is that Lycurgus's speech is one of the strangest in extant Attic oratory. In the first place, it contains by far the lengthiest section of quotations from the city's literary and historical texts. Paragraphs 75–132 of Lycurgus's 150-paragraph speech consist of a discourse on the ephebic oath (an oath taken during the mandatory military service of youths 18–20 years old and known by all Athenian men), the Delphic oracle and a story about Codrus (a mythical king of Athens), a story about the punishment of one Callistratus, the myth of the "Place of the Pious," fifty-five lines from Euripides' *Erectheus*, a quotation from the *Iliad*, thirty lines from Tyrtaios, the inscriptions from Marathon and Thermopylae, four more stories of punishment, quotations from two anonymous poets, and one Spartan law. Before Lycurgus orators were not wont to quote at length from the poets at all (nor from Spartan laws, for that matter).[45] No other Athenian orator comes close to quoting "the greats" as much as Lycurgus.

This section of the speech is central to Lycurgus's rhetorical strategy, for it reveals the method by which he intends to redefine the city's system of values and its symbolic orders. He draws on poetic and historical authorities whom jurors are already used to hearing on political subjects to justify his ethical claims, and quotes at such length that he effectively substitutes the voice of the city's poets and historical monuments for his own.

Lycurgus concludes his speech with another move of substitution. Most orators concluded their speeches with a personal appeal for pity and anger. Lycurgus, however, erases his own presence and tells his jurors that the Athenian countryside, the trees, the harbors, the dockyards, the walls of the city, the temples, and the shrines are begging for help (*nomizontes hiketeuein humon ten choran kai ta dendra, deisthai tous limenas [kai] ta neoria kai ta teiche tes poleos*) and that the ships and temples think themselves worthy of help from the jurors (*axioun de kai tous neos kai ta hiera boethein autois*) (1.150). Lycurgus claims to speak not with his own voice but with the voice of the whole countryside. Lycurgus, as a disinterested prosecutor, could not formulate claims of desert in the standard form of personal requests for pity and anger. He could not offer the jurors the voice of the offended angry victim asking for pity; and so he replaced his own voice with several of the different voices that played important roles in constituting social knowledge and communal memory. He lost the case by one vote, which perhaps reveals both the power of the norm of personal involvement and the degree to which it was possible to change it. Echoes of Lycurgus's speech turn up in two speeches given later that year, suggesting that his new and dramatically public voice did have a noticeable impact on Athenian politics.[46] The key point here is that Lycurgus's speech, through its oddity, reveals that there was a typical prosecutorial kind of voice, which resounded with a commitment to the idea that punishment should be the business of citizens who had personal stakes in one another's affairs. The justice that was meted out in the courts took on its meaning according to how the Athenians defined the legitimate speaker and prosecutor.

Throughout his speech Lycurgus never tells us exactly who or what the sycophant is, despite tackling the topic head on. According to him, "everyone knows what the sycophant does." Todd, notably, refers to the sycophant as a "perversion." It is as if the matter is slightly obscene. Scholars have generally dismissed the etymology of the word "sycophant"—revealer of figs—as meaningless, but that is where the answer lies. The figure of the "fig" served primarily as a metaphor for sexuality and taps the eroticism of *orge* brought into the public sphere by the valorization of anger. A comic fragment defines the sycophant (*sykophantein*) as one who "screws or provokes [people] erotically" (*knizein erotikos*).[47]

The fig tree with its pendant fruit (*suke, suka*) represented the male reproductive organs; the single fig (*sukon*) represented the female genitalia (cf. *Peace* 1351–52).[48] Dried figs (*ischadas*) sometimes represented female genitalia (primarily outside Old Comedy) and sometimes represented spent and satisfied male genitalia (in Old Comedy).[49] The petals of the fig (*thria*) were a euphemism for the foreskin. To draw back the "fig leaves" was equivalent both to preparing for sexual activity and to being overly virile and violent.[50] "Figs" did not represent only sexuality. They also represented anger, in Aristophanes' *Wasps*, for instance, and a ripe fig was a fig that was swollen with liquid or, one might say, that was full of *orge* (Xen. *Oec.* 19.19). Notably, the Athenian scapegoat, the *pharmakos*, the remedy to the city's ripe anger, was driven out of the city with dried figs hanging around his neck; scapegoats in other cities were beaten around the genitals with fig wood.[51] The sycophant returns us to the overlap between the iretic and the erotic and an exploration of this figure will help us understand the effect of the isomorphism of anger and *eros* on how the Athenians practiced punishment and politics.

In *Wasps* Aristophanes first deploys the figure of the fig in his description of Philocleon, the old angry juror who tries to escape his son's house arrest (see chapter 6). In one escape attempt, Philocleon climbs out the chimney, gets caught, claims that he is smoke coming out of the chimney, and is mocked by his son for being the stinging kind of smoke (*drimutatos*) that comes from fig wood (*sukinou*, 145).[52] Bdelycleon wryly notes the arrival of the chorus of wasps at his house with another fig metaphor: he knows the jurors have arrived, he says, because he recognizes the sound of fig leaves crackling as they open (*thrion ton psophon*) (436). Does it matter that the genitive of "wasp," *sphekos*, is so close to the word for "string of figs," *sphêkos*? The jurors are like men preparing for sexual intercourse; they are also men preparing to be "violently virile." The *Wasps* thus explicitly (and obscenely) draws a parallel between the iretic and the erotic passions. In court the jurors will "eat" lawsuits, they say (*phagoimi*, 511; *phagois*, 1367), and "eating" was another metaphor frequently applied to sexual intercourse.[53]

The wasps' stings are a sign of their anger, but the word for their stings, *kentra*, is also a euphemism for *phalli* (408, 1115, 1121).[54] Reckford has argued: "The sting is a stand-in not just for anger, but for anger as a sexual surrogate."[55] Philocleon himself links his anger to his sexual potency. He is afraid to acquit anybody for fear that he will wither away and/or dry up if he does (*aposklenai*, 160). Philocleon's fears are justified, it seems, since after Philocleon gives up on going to the courts, Aristophanes begins to incorporate jokes about Philocleon's elderly impotence (808, 1343, 1379ff.). The norms that regulated the male Athenian's use of anger were implicated in the norms that regulated his sexual self-representation. In tragedy women who punished were called manly and unwomanly. Men likewise affirmed their virility when they punished.

This is made especially clear in one scene of generational conflict in the *Wasps*. One of the older jurors offers to give his young son a present and is dismayed when the boy asks for dried figs (*ischadas,* 297). The boy's father swears by Zeus and says that he would never grant his son the request for dried figs, even if the boy were to hang himself out of disappointment. The elderly juror concludes his refusal by reiterating his amazement at the request for figs (*suka,* 302).

The word for dried figs, *ischada*, which could be used of female genitalia or spent male genitalia, comes from *ischnos* ("withered, lean, meager") and the verb *ischnaino* ("to make dry or withered, to dry up"). The verb could also be used to denote what happened when the *thumos* was tamed or satisfied or when a ripe and bursting feeling of anger (*sphrigonta thumon*) (*PB* 381–82) had been dissolved.[56] The boy's request for dried figs (*ischadas,* 297) can be read in triplicate: it can be read as a request to have his own youthful anger/lust satisfied; and it can be read as a request for female genitalia; but, it can also be read as desire to see his father's anger spent and used up. The son's request for "dried figs/satisfied genitalia/spent lust" is both a request to be allowed to enter into public and sexual life and a request that his father retire from both forms of adult male behavior.[57] The boy is asking to be initiated into the adult world. The boy's father responds by shifting the focus of the conversation from dried figs to *suka*, a euphemism for testicles, and so the older juror is turning attention away from what is dried out and used up to what is fresh and ripe. He shifts the focus from spent anger and lust to anger and lust that have yet to be spent. In other words, he turns attention away from the question of whether his own anger must come to an end and turns it toward the question of whether his son should be allowed to begin the lustful experiences of sexuality and anger. But "boys" are by definition too young to be asking for sexual or punitive satisfaction.

Anger, as the desire to punish, was a desire to rearrange human relationships according to the norms of reciprocity. *Eros* was also a desire to rearrange the structure of human relationships. The isomorphism of the two passions therefore rests on the fact that each produces a powerful desire to destabilize the *status quo* that obtains in respect to social relations. The political order established control over those destabilizations to the degree that it regulated the practices and forms of behavior that were inspired by anger and *eros*. In his father's eyes, the boy who requested figs was simply too young to be playing with the politically volatile practice of rearranging human relationships. Like wrongdoing and marriage, generational transitions had the power to destabilize the status quo and had to be regulated with rigor. Athenians were educated simultaneously about how to act upon their anger and about how to respond to their *eros* since the concepts overlapped with such regularity.

Orge, insofar as it referred to both anger and sexual lust, was a passion that motivated a desire to change social relationships, whether by destroying them (when *orge* meant anger) or by creating them (when *orge* meant sexual desire). The passion signaled the fact that a social disruption had arisen because an individual's desires were not in harmony with the structure of relationships in which he or she was situated and had inspired the individual to bring social relations into harmony with his or her desires. If such a desire manifested itself as a wish to end or do damage in a relationship, the desire was anger. If it manifested itself as a wish to create relationships, the desire was *eros*. The impulses to destruction and creation are not easily kept separate nor are they wholly separable, and so anger and *eros* were inextricably connected to each other.

Figs (*suka*), as a euphemism for the testicles, represented both the iretic and the erotic elements of *orge*. The vine (*orchos*) was another euphemism for and even pun on the word for testicles (*orchis*), which was also the name of a flower (the orchid) that was thought to have both aphrodisiac and anaphrodisiac properties. The orchid could, as an aphrodisiac, inspire people to create new social relationships or, as an anaphrodisiac, to end old ones. The orchid itself did the work of both halves of *orge*.

The multiplicity of meanings attached to the figure of the fig in Athenian thought allowed Aristophanes to explore anger, sexual desire, and generational transition simultaneously.[58] Speaking about one form of destabilization implicated another by means of metaphorical association. Conversations about anger ultimately concerned the possibility of achieving order and peaceableness in the relationships between people, but the topic of order required thinking about *eros* as well.

The meaning of the word sycophant, the person who pointed out figs, thus depends on the symbolic weight of the fig as representing the intersection of anger and sexual lust. The sycophant, as someone who screwed or provoked violently, somehow violated social norms that constrained the iretic and erotic behavior of citizens. As we saw in chapter 3, Foucault argued that the Athenians (or Greeks in his terms) attempted to control appetites like eating, sleeping, and sexuality denoted as "necessities" by establishing an "economy of spending" them; the arousal and dispersal of desire had to be controlled. As we saw in chapter 4, anger was among the emotional forces of desire and appetite that could be labeled as a "necessity." Like the other desires, anger was also regulated by an "economy of spending," the rules of which are analogous to those regulating sexual desire. In respect to sexual desire, a man had to be temperate (*sophron*) and limit his indulgence so as not to weaken himself.[59] The norms bounding sexuality also prescribed more specifically that the citizen indulge his desires neither for payment, nor for overly sensual purposes, nor (in the case of homosexuality) as the passive partner.[60] The norms for the prosecutor were parallel. He was expected to eschew prosecuting for payment, avoid indulging an excessive taste for provoking people and disrupting social relations, and reject serving as someone else's flunkey. The man who followed these rules would be not only a good citizen but also, on the analogy to sexual norms, a temperate man.

Norms for the "right use of *eros*" were transferable to the realm of anger. As it turns out, the metaphorical association between the passions and plants like the fig and the orchid was based on the fact that the rules for using these fruits were themselves transferable to the use of the passions. In the *Oeconomicus* Xenophon portrays Ischomachos as giving Socrates a lesson about the proper way to pick grapes, figs, and other fruit. The advice that Socrates receives helps to explain why "timing" was so important to determining whether a prosecution was legitimate. Xenophon writes:

> The vine herself [*aute*] teaches you many things about how best to treat her [*autei*] . . . when her clusters of grape are still tender, the vine, by spreading leaves, teaches you to shade what is exposed to the sun during this time [*didaskei skiazein ta helioumena tauten ten horan*]; but when it is the right moment [kairos] for her bunches of grapes to be sweetened by the sun, the vine, by shedding leaves, teaches you to strip her [*heauten*] and to ripen [*pepainein*] her fruit [*ten oporan*]. Because of her great fertility, the vine reveals [*deiknuousa*] some clusters that have ripened [*tous peponas*] while also still bearing others that are raw [*omoterous*], and thus teaches you to gather [*trugan*] her fruit as men pick figs [*hosper ta suka sukazousi*]—always take one of the luscious/ripe/fertile/angry ones [*to orgon aei*]. (*Oec.* 19.17–19)

The passage presents the rules for fruit gathering and nothing more. But the norms established for the farm are the same as the norms that sycophants violated in the courtroom. The Athenian system of value included an ethics of proper use that applied to the use of plants, objects, money, and passions. Xenophon's maxim, if read with an awareness of its dense metaphoricity, reveals fundamental Athenian ethical principles and also the fact that cultural building blocks could be discussed under any number of guises. The use of the fig as a symbol for the sycophant is rooted in its actual use and treatment by the farmer.

Gathering figs is gathering what is ripe and soft or full of *orge*. For that matter, *pepaino*, or ripen, is also used as a metaphor for anger that needs to be softened or assuaged.[61] If one gathers too early, one gathers fruit that is raw (*omos*); remember that rawness was a typical feature of diseased *orge*. Ripeness and fruit gathering, *opora*, were also tropes used to discuss sexual readiness and intercourse. Aristophanes was well acquainted with this metaphor. In the *Wealth* his character Trygaios, "the fruit gatherer," marries Opora, "the ripe fruit," in order to "produce grapes" (706–8).[62] The activity of gathering that which is full of *orge* is thus homologous both to dealing with anger (punishment) and to sexual intercourse, and several forms of human behavior were all subject to what was effectively a single ethical system involving the idea of proper use. Gathering from the vine was like gathering figs, gathering testicles, gathering female fertility, gathering what is ripe and full of *orge*, gathering anger. The relation of fertility to both *eros* and anger allows for the metaphorical transfer of the rules of viticulture, fig gathering, heterosexuality, and homosexuality to processes of anger and punishment and makes punishment itself an analogue to sexual intercourse.

The Athenians had a number of fig-related words that could be used to insult those who misspent their erotic passions. In the *Peace* (1351), *sukologein* and *sukazein* are used to describe excessive homosexual intercourse. In another play Cleon is essentially accused of being a homosexual rapist with a word that means "squeezing figs" (*aposukazein*, *Kn*. 259). He treats other people's "testicles" too aggressively and too lustily. Negative forms of sexual behavior included not only "fig squeezing" (*aposukazein*) but also "fig gathering" (*psenizein*), another euphemism for homosexual contrectation.[63] Cleon violated the norms of *eros* by acting too aggressively.

But how did the sycophant, who "pointed out figs," violate the norms for standard use of the passions? According to Xenophon, the vine is supposed to point out to the farmer which fruits to pick and only those. There is therefore a right time and method for the exposure of ripe figs or of *orge*. There were rules against improper exposure in the sexual context. According to Henderson, the desire to "expose what should be hidden" was a fundamental part of sexual aggression. Calling attention to one's opponent's genitals was an act of violence, and according to Henderson, "references to testicles in Aristophanes almost always occur in threats (to rip out someone's testicles) or in violent erotic advances (seizing the testicles in preparation for sexual contact) (e.g., *Clouds* 713, *Birds* 442)."[64]

Presumably the sycophant "showed his own figs" or manly vigor inappropriately and also denigrated other people both by pointing out facts about their lives that should have been kept out of the public eye and by shaming them too agressively. As Isocrates wrote (15.314), the sycophant "shows to all [*epideiknusthai*] his rawness [*omoteta*], his misanthropy, and his fondness for making enemies [*philapechthemosune*]." In misspending in the economy of pleasures, the sycophant stood with *moichos*, the male prostitute, and the citizen who violated the norms of homosexual love—an exclusive club for those *poneroi* or base men who did not deserve to be active citizens.[65] The intersection of anger and sexuality in the trope of figs does not allow us to produce an epigrammatic definition of who or what the sycophant was but it does allow us to see the web of meaning within which the sycophant's bad reputation and dirty name were established. That web of meaning is based on an ethical system that coalesced around the problem of trying to deal with desire. The sycophant violates the economy of desire by initiating processes of anger when the time or situation is not appropriate.[66] Thus, Demosthenes describes the statute of limitations as having been drawn up specifically so as to prevent sycophancy (36.26–27).[67]

The ban on the sycophant's acts of "exposure" limited excessive aggressiveness in the judicial system. The Athenian requirement that speakers explain their personal interest ensured that prosecutors had only an "honest" interest in sating a "ripe" anger and were not acting for some more savage and unseasonable ulterior motive. The economy of anger put limits on the number of public conflicts and disputes in which any individual could be legitimately involved, just as the economy of desire put limits on the number and kind of homosexual love affairs an Athenian citizen could have and still maintain a political role in the city. The need for prosecutors to prove and justify their personal anger was guard against the much decried oligarchic activity of too frequent and too comprehensive punishment.[68]

The city's drive to put constraints on desire operated in all arenas and on the basis of a consistent set of norms for "proper use" that were at the heart of Athenian culture. The slurs against sycophants contributed to the constraint of desire. The word "sycophant" was used to mark the moments when the Athenian normative structure seemed to have failed to constrain a particular individual's will. Orators who made charges of sycophancy and defended themselves from charges of sycophancy involved themselves in a conversation about how to manage the diverse and conflicting wills of the citizenry, about how to define the Athenian system of value, and about how to regulate behavior that impacted social relationships. Lycurgus's attempt to redefine sycophancy by validating disinterested prosecution was an attempt to effect a cultural paradigm shift and to redefine the rules for using political insititutions.

The word sycophant could also be used to mobilize citizens into acting more aggressively to impose their norms upon their fellows. The oligarchs began their late fifth-century attack on Athens by claiming that they would rid the city of its sycophants.[69] Xenophon reports:

> First of all they arrested and brought to trial on capital charges all those persons who were known to have made their living by acting as sycophants [*apo sukophantias*] and by being offensive to the aristocrats. The Council of 500 and all other citizens were glad to vote against these men, and whoever thought he himself was not like these [sycophants], was in no way troubled. (*Hell.* 2.3.12–13)

The so-called sycophants were vulnerable to the attack of the Thirty because they had failed to meet the norms of the good man and good citizen. The democrats, who understood themselves as distinct from the sycophants, were willing to let the oligarchs eliminate them. The citizenry's acceptance of the Thirty's generalized attack on people labeled sycophants indicates the power of the word to regulate the norms of public agency and boundaries of the city's ethical system and to legitimate moves against members of the citizenry who failed to live up to these.

The Thirty did not ultimately restrict their attacks on Athenian citizens merely to people whom the citizens already called sycophants. Xenophon writes:

> Then the Thirty began to take counsel as to how they might use the city as they saw fit. . . . they arrested those whom they wished—not now the base people and those of little worth [*tous ponerous te kai oligou axious*], but from this point on those people whom they thought were least likely to submit to being ignored, and who would gather supporters together in the greatest numbers, if they tried to fight back against the Thirty. (Xen. *Hell.* 2.3.13–14)

The Thirty attacked all those whose wills might disrupt the newly installed oligarchic social system. Ultimately, Xenophon says, the oligarchs' extermination of the sycophants was not about getting rid of all the people whom the democratic masses normally identified as sycophants (*tous homologoumenous sukophantas*, Xen. *Hell.* 2.3.38). Instead, the Thirty used the label "sycophant" to expand the category of the socially unacceptable according to oligarchic terms.[70]

Theramenes, who was initially a member of the oligarchic faction, eventually came to the conclusion that things had gone too far and expressed his dissent by saying that the Thirty, with their extensive "punishments," were worse than the sycophants whom they had set out to destroy in the first place (*adikotera ton sukophanton*, Xen. *Hell.* 2.3.22). The oligarchs had been able to begin their attack on Athenian democrats by deploying the word sycophant. Theramenes tried to end their attack with the same word. Both he and the other members of the Thirty recognized the power of the word sycophant, with its capacity to delineate "common knowledge" distinctions between the socially acceptable and the socially rejectable. The Athenian orator who called upon his jurors to recognize someone as a sycophant was likewise calling them to a more vigilant defense of the city's system of value and the distinction between forms of behavior which were and were not socially desirable.

The use of a near obscenity, the term sycophant, to establish the contours of the practice of legitimate prosecution reveals the power of ideology to regulate democratic norms. On the topic of obscenity, Henderson writes:

> The great majority of obscene words are those which, although they may be unmistakably direct in their reference, neither attain to the absolute and exclusive explicitness of primary obscenities nor possess their hallucinatory and repressive power, but which distance the listener in a greater or lesser degree. They are products and components of the capacity for abstract and metaphorical thinking characteristic of latency. *Unlike the primary obscenity, valuable only for its directness and primitive force, the value of metaphorical obscenity lies precisely in its flexibility and nuance.*[71]

The word sycophant functioned in the following fashion: all Athenians knew in general that a sycophant essentially misused the lust of prosecutorial anger (whether by faking it, overindulging it, or accepting money for it) and thereby violated democratic norms of public agency. No Athenian, however, would (or perhaps could) specify precisely the full set of terms that delineated the sycophant's misuse (despite modern efforts to write up "economies" of spending desire). And, anyway, the whole matter was slightly obscene. Nonetheless, the word sycophant was widely recognized as a word that straightforwardly separated the socially respectable from the socially rejectable despite, or rather because of, its vagueness, its metaphoricity, and the tinge of obscenity. The word sycophant captured, in general, what was beyond the pale established by the norms of public agency.

E. Csapo writes: "It is often said that symbols are interesting because they encompass contradictions. But symbols are also contradictory because they are interesting. . . . [they are] the loci of struggle between competing social groups, and necessarily ambivalent, because the language of the debate must be common, even if competing groups ascribe different values to the terms."[72] The word sycophant was vague, so the fence between the respectable and the rejectable could be moved easily with a simple shift in definition (or resignification) of the term sycophant. The word sycophant was available for those like Lycurgus who wished to attach new definitions to it and thereby change the "norms of public agency" in the process. Does this explain why the modern definition of sycophant could have strayed so far from its ancient origins? More important, the vagueness of the word sycophant reveals the degree to which the city's norms were contestable and the system of value susceptible to being revised over time, despite its consistency across diverse social spaces. The "norms of public agency," and the symbolic language that expressed those norms, were powerful ideological tools. In the context of democratic Athenian punishment, they primarily allowed for the controlled indulgence of anger; but they also provided orators like Lycurgus with the means with which to contest socially dominant definitions of politics, the public sphere, and the good citizen. The orators speeches for the prosecution and defense helped to establish a consistent set of norms throughout the citizenry *at a given moment in time* but also made it possible for that consistent set of norms to be shifted *over* time. The symbolic rhetoric associated with the sycophant reveals the nature of the media in which the orator worked. Speech could be used both to refer to already existent systems of value and to make those systems malleable and fluid.

But this malleability is not the whole of the story for there was also a written law. Written law aspires not to establish norms that are malleable and fluid but rather norms that are consistent *over* time. There was a tension, in Athens, between the power of speech to set and revise communal norms and the power of law to fix them. That tension appears in any society that tries to use law, but the Athenians dealt with the tension differently than do modern democrats. The use of law in the courts and the tensions involved in that are the subject of the next chapter.

The Negotiation of Desert, Part Two

INTRODUCTION

Athenian prosecutors initiated penal processes and stepped into the courtroom in order to try to generate final and authoritative judgments in their favor. To pull this off they first of all had to prove their right to prosecute. As we saw in chapter 7, orators usually made remarks about their personal involvement with the wrongdoer, about their timing in bringing the prosecution, or about the necessary straits in which they found themselves. Fairly frequently they might also have to broach the topic of sycophancy. The prosecutor's opening arguments thus immediately turned the jurors' attention to the question of what legitimate public speech was and who could legitimately be a public actor. These were political questions, for those who could legitimately speak in public were in a position to confirm the city's system of value or to try to gain acceptance for revised norms. After an orator legitimated his prosecution, he argued about what his opponent deserved and about how to define justice. To do this he drew on both social memory and law. The first norm of "public agency" was that orators follow the guidelines of "hot blood" for spending anger. The second norm of "public agency" required orators to cast their arguments about anger in terms of the city's authoritative definitions of desert and justice—whether those norms came from social memory or from written law. There was also a third norm of "public agency" that applied only to *public* (and not private) prosecutions and distinguished cases like the *graphe* from the *dike*. Prosecutors of public cases had to acknowledge explicitly that their speech acts would impact the city's ethical structure. The public realm thus turns out to be the conversational arena in which citizens were self-conscious about engaging the ethical structure of their world. In this chapter, I explore the second and third norms of public agency. The exploration reveals that the Athenians conceptualized law and judgment in a way that challenges habitual modern assumptions about what law is.

THE SECOND NORM OF PUBLIC AGENCY: USING SOCIAL MEMORY AND LAW

For the Athenian jury, attempts to answer the question of whether a defendant deserved the jury's anger or pity required both factual and ethical evaluation. An orator made both types of argument by drawing on *nomos*: the audience's customary memories and the laws written by the people. An orator could successfully transform his private anger into public anger only by following the second "norm of public agency" and arguing about the defendant's desert in terms that were relevant to the *demos*, represented by the body of jurors sitting in the court.

As we have seen, the Athenians generated the knowledge needed for a prosecution by gathering witnesses, calling bystanders to witness events, and allowing knowledge to spread by means of rumor, gossip, and the hue and cry. Many of the orators, in putting the facts of their cases, expected to rely on the jury's own knowledge of events and counted the jurors as witnesses.[1] Thus Dinarchus asks his jury: "Are you not eyewitnesses [*autoptai*] to this man's wrongdoing?" (Din. 3.15).[2] Orators regularly claim that they have the job of "reminding" their listeners of facts that the jurors already know, and Aeschines remarks: "You yourselves are both judges and witnesses [*autoi dikastai moi kai martures*] to the matters discussed in my speeches; it is fitting for me to refresh your memory [*prosekei anamimneiskein*]" (1.89). The orators thus made explicit the fact that they were frequently triggering social memory (or constructing it) rather than trying to "prove" facts to a jury that knew nothing about the matter at hand.[3]

This approach to evidence made orators highly dependent on what their jurors "already knew" when they arrived in the courtroom. Victims who tried to spread their story, whether in the agora or elsewhere, were trying to control this body of knowledge. The *demos* was anywhere and everywhere and always ready to play witness. One orator speaks thus to his jury: "Witnesses I will not lack, men of the jury; for I see many of you here to judge who were also present at the trial where Lysitheus was prosecuting Theomnestus . . . during the course of which he said that I had killed my father" (Lys. 10.1). Those citizens who were witnesses in one time and place could pass on their knowledge to other citizens so that the *demos* as a whole never lacked for information.

The jurors were regularly asked to remember not only "facts" about events but also information that would factor into the ethical evaluation of the wrongdoer. Lysias argues to his jury: "It is your duty to remember his ancestry and his actions and punish him" (Lys. 30.1–6). Communal knowledge of the defendant's social position affected ethical valuation of his actions. As we saw in chapter 3, the Athenian notion of reciprocity did not necessarily include a commitment to any kind of equivalence, and juries had to negotiate orators' requests that they inflict the "last or most extreme penalties" (*ta eschata*) or the "greatest penalties" (*ta megista*) on the defendant. The prosecutor's and defendant's relative social positions and characters were among the factors used to determine how to graduate punishments.

As we have seen (chapter 2), about half of the penal sentences in Athens could be decided by a process called *timesis* in which the prosecutor and defendant both had to suggest a penalty, and the jury voted on the two options. Relative social status was crucial to determining what sort of penalty to propose, as in this extreme example:

During *timesis* when the jurors were wishing to sentence him to death, I begged the
jurors not to do that sort of thing on my account, but I agreed to a talent fine [as
punishment], which the defense themselves suggested, not in order that Arethousios
not die (for he did things to me worthy of death) but in order that I, son of Pasion, a
citizen by decree, should not have killed any one of the Athenians. (Dem. 53.18, cf.
Dem. 59.6)

This prosecutor acknowledged his status in the city as a former slave and therefore asks for a more lenient penalty. A litigant had to assess carefully what he
could expect from the jury, given his position in the city. Pasion's opponent got
off with a fine thanks to his greater social status.

Another litigant argues that a very large fine that had been imposed on him in
the past was caused not by the offensiveness of his action but because his
prosecutors found him weak and without support (Lys. 20.18; cf. Lyc. 1.65–
66). In another Lysianic speech, however, the speaker uses a defendant's weak
status to justify a small rather than a large fine. The orator argues: "It is a just
custom established for all men that in face of the same crimes, we should be
most angry [*malista orgizesthai*] with those men who are most able to avoid
criminal action but should be indulgent to the poor or disabled because we
think that they err unwillingly" (31.11). Even intentionality could be ethically
assessed on the basis of the social status of the defendant and on the basis of
what his fellow citizens knew about him. Orators might put different constructions on what a given social status meant but they all treated social status as a
reasonable criterion on which to base a penal decision.[4] The ability of litigants
to manipulate the networks of social knowledge that controlled reputation affected his chance of victory.[5]

In moments of defeat orators were forced to recognize their inability to control the force of social knowledge. Thus Andocides admits: "I saw the hue and
cry [*thorubos*] against me and knew I was destroyed" (And. 2.15). Andocides
knew he was destroyed when the *thorubos*—a characteristic courtroom outburst
of social knowledge and collective emotion—rose against him, announcing his
inability to sway his jurors.

The social knowledge relevant to public judgment was stored in rumor, gossip, and evidence and embodied in the *thorubos* but it was also embedded in
collective emotions. Tragic characters, as we have seen, saw anger as being a
phenomenon that generated memory (chapter 3). The same applied to the courtroom. Anger was expected to endure over time,[6] and to generate memories that
would benefit both the individual and the city. Thus one orator argues: "If they
were in fact wronged, the sorts of deeds [they accuse me of] should have been
sufficient to remind them and to keep the matter in their *thumos* [*enthu-
methenai*], both for themselves and for the sake of the city" (Ant. 6.46). In
moments of reconciliation people put aside their anger and also promised not to
remember evils (*me mnesikakei*).[7]

The power of memory was triggered by anger, and so the Athenian litigant,
who roused his jury's anger, simultaneously mobilized their communal memo-

ries and social knowledge. The social knowledge triggered by anger could be factual, as when Lysias exhorts his jury thus: "Be angry [*orgisthete*] and remember [*anamnesthete*] the other bad deeds you have suffered from them" (Lys. 12.96). But anger was also used to produce ethical assessments of how the defendant should be treated as when Demosthenes writes: "Remember [*mnesthentes*] all these other cases and apply that same anger to this case [*labete tauten ten orgen*]" (Dem. 24.138). Athenian litigants regularly treated the passional as playing a role in the rational, and they used social memory, whether linked to anger or not, to help decide questions of both fact and ethics.

In some cases, it is impossible to dissect factual from ethical argument. Take, for instance, the following supremely embellished Lysianic period volleyed at Agoratus, a supporter of the Thirty whom Lysias here sarcastically calls deserving of pity:

> I am much pained by remembrance of the misfortunes that befell the city, but at the present moment it is necessary, gentlemen of the jury, in order that you may know what a great deal of your pity Agoratus deserves! For you know the nature and number of the citizens who were brought from Salamis and you know how they were destroyed by the Thirty. . . . you remember . . .; now remember, each one of you, your private misfortunes and the communal misfortunes of the city and punish [*timoreisthe*] the man who caused them. . . . Remember all the horrors [*apanton deinon*], both those of the community in the city and your private horrors, and punish [*timoresate*] the one who is to blame [*aition*]. (Lys. 13.44–48, 95)

It is difficult to say whether Lysias is rousing his jury's memories in order that they can make factual assessments about what Agoratus did or ethical assessments about whether what he did was horrific.

The modern courtroom treats the distinction between matters of fact and matters of law as a cornerstone of judicial argument.[8] In U.S. courts, for instance, there are "genuine issues" for the jury to decide only if there are issues of "material fact" to be decided. There is only an "issue of law" in cases where "evidence is undisputed and only one conclusion can be drawn therefrom," and a litigant can move for a "summary judgment" that allows for "prompt and expeditious disposition of controversy without trial when there is no dispute as to either material fact or inferences to be drawn from undisputed facts . . . [and the party] believes that he is entitled to prevail as a matter of law."[9]

In the Athenian context, there was never a suggestion that only one conclusion might be drawn from a given set of facts, and it was factual argument, not ethical argument, that was sometimes dispensable from judicial argument. In some cases the two litigants themselves arrived in court already in agreement on the facts, and the only issue to be decided was whether the defendant deserved punishment for what he admitted doing.[10] Similarly, litigants sometimes came to court only after the assembly or the Council of 500 had already voted on the factual guilt of a defendant; they started their arguments with a decision of the *demos* on matters of fact already before them.[11] In still other cases there was no way to decide a matter of fact other than to weigh one litigant's word against that of another, and in such cases the decision between the two versions of the facts ultimately depended more on a social assessment of the litigant's character than on evidence.[12]

The modern distinction between arguments on facts and arguments on matters of law or ethics breaks down when applied to the Athenian courtroom, as many scholars have found.[13] The distinction also breaks down in the modern context and in modern courtrooms, but unlike modern democrats the Athenians never really tried to make a rigorous distinction between factual and ethical assessments in the first place. The extant oratorical corpus offers only one example of an Athenian orator adopting a stark distinction between "matters of fact" and "matters of law" to frame his courtroom arguments. Only Antiphon argued: "The law and decrees are *kurioi* of the whole *politeia* and they decide [*krinein*] in cases where the facts are agreed upon; in matters where facts are disputed you have to judge [*diagnona*]" (Ant. 3.1.1). Antiphon was also the sole orator to disavow anger unilaterally. Where Antiphon asked jurors to orient themselves around questions of fact, all the other orators oriented jurors around the question: Does the defendant deserve to feel our anger? This single question required both factual and ethical evaluation, and there was no need to compartmentalize the two types of argument. Anything that roused the jury's anger or pity was relevant to the orator's argument, as the rhetorical handbooks make clear.

The vocabulary of anger used by the orators was neither ornamental nor "demagogic rabble-rousing" but constituted the heart of the analytical framework that guided public decision making and decisions about what justice was. Demosthenes, for instance, remarks that after jurors hear a case, they should adjust their condemnation to what is necessary for their anger (*orge*): "Great for great, small for small" (*chresthai tei orgei mega megalei, mikron mikrai*) (Dem. 24.118; cf. Isoc. 20.3). Anger was a good or commodity, that could be stored up and measured out in ways that fit the circumstances of a particular case. Aeschines describes the moment of sentencing as being when "the third water is poured in [to the water clock to time speeches] about the penalty and the extent [*to megethei*] of your anger [*tes orges tes humeteras*]" (Aes. 3.197). The juxtaposition of the water in the water clock which measures time, to the anger in the jurors, which measures justice, underscores the way in which anger was thought of as being measurable, assessable, and finally dispensable. This idea was expressed by Aristophanes' wasps when they claim that they are on their way to court bearing "three days' worth" of troublesome anger (242–44) and when Philocleon claimed to "raise and lower the pitch" of his anger (*tes orges oligon ton kollop' aneimen*, 574).

Not only the individual orator but also the city as a whole had to follow rules for spending anger. For instance, Lycurgus argues that "It will be easy [for people] to commit the greatest wrongs [*megala adikein*] if you jurors show that you are more angry at the small ones [*epi tois mikrois mallon orgizomenoi*]" (Lyc. 1.78). His remark reflects the idea that different acts of wrongdoing should engender different levels of anger.[14] As we saw already, Lysias suggested that the jurors should be most angry (*malista orgizesthai*) with defendants who could easily have avoided doing wrong (31.11).

The discourse of anger was, as I have pointed out, littered with the vocabulary of "desert," and the orators refer often to due, fitting, and appropriate anger.[15] Demosthenes criticizes the Athenians in such terms for failing to mete out appropriate levels of anger. He says: "It is not your habit to store up matters [*all' ou tithetai tauta*] for accurate remembrance [*akribe mnemen*] and due [*proseken*] anger. You are too swayed by the calumny of the moment" (Dem. 18.138). The notion employed in Athens for judging "desert" and "equivalency" was not that the punishment should fit the crime but that anger should. Anger arose with varying degrees of force and in proportion to the relative significance of the acts that inspired it. Punishment in turn fit the anger that had been aroused in the case. As Demosthenes says, "The laws permit the jurors, after hearing the case, to adjust the punishment to what is necessary for their anger" (Dem. 24.118).

Orators developed the criteria for establishing equivalencies between wrongdoing and levels of anger by comparing and contrasting different cases. One knew how much anger (and punishment) fit a wrongdoing on the basis of how punishments had been handed out in the past. Demosthenes instructs his jury: "I will tell you what other people have done previously to incur your anger [*orges*]. Let me begin then with the most recent condemnation against Evandrus for violating the mysteries. . . . Do not act angry when someone speaks counter to the law and, then, treat people gently when they do not speak but act counter to the law" (Dem. 21.175, 183). Orators made appeals to social memory for the sake not only of inspiring public anger and refreshing the public's memory, but also for the sake of making sure that anger was meted out consistently, as when Demosthenes exhorts his jury: "Remember [*mnesthentes*] all those other cases; apply that same anger [*labete tauten ten orgen*] to this one" (Dem. 24.138). Not only was anger a passion of graduated force, but it was also a passion that arose to the same degree in similar circumstances. The desire to maintain at least a nominal continuity with the *demos*'s past decisions proves to have been a core goal of Athenian judicial decisions. Thus, Lysias argues: "Before, when you rejected Leodamas, they thought you did it out of anger, and if you do not reject this man also and show yourselves still angry, they will think it was unjust" (Lys. 26.13–14).

Justice itself was defined by the two principles of gradation and consistency. To know how much anger was fitting in a given circumstance, a speaker had only to figure out how much anger had been thought fitting when such circumstances had arisen previously.[16] The stories of earlier punishments were used as a form of informative but nonbinding precedent, and stabilized the gradations that set up a framework of equivalencies for dispensing anger.[17] Orators did, however, sometimes use the method of compare and contrast for the sake of exaggeration, as does Lysias who argues about one opponent that he deserves to feel the jury's wrath (*prosekei orgizesthai*) more than the Thirty did (Lys.

28.13–14).[18] Nonetheless, in general the analytical framework attached to anger allowed for the regulation of reciprocity and made it possible to limit litigants' requests for the "most extreme" punishments. The norms for spending public anger were established by the practices of oratorical storytelling and social memory, the artisan of custom.

In Athens custom was the stuff of *nomos*, a word that meant not only custom but also law.[19] The written laws of Athens played a role in the courtroom similar to that played by social memory: they established memorable guidelines for the use of anger. Aeschines describes legislation as the process of being angry in advance (1.176), and Demosthenes explicitly describes the laws as a code delineating how much anger should be attached to each kind of wrong: "Observe that the laws treat the willful and hubristic wrongdoer as worthy of greater anger [*orge*] and punishment [*zemia*] . . .; this is reasonable because while the injured party everywhere deserves support, the law does not establish that the anger [*orgen*] against the actor should be always the same" (Dem. 21.42, 43). Lysias also characterizes written law as a system that helps set up the public economy of anger when he describes a misguided prosecution as an act of excessive anger that is contrary to the guide of the law (*paranomia prothumos*) (Lys. 12.23–24). The written laws of Athens encoded a body of past opinion about how much anger should be meted out for any given act of wrongdoing. *Nomos*, whether in the form of communal memories or written laws, provided the Athenians with information about how to measure and apply anger.

The insight that written laws equipped the Athenians with information on how much anger to dispense in any given instance allows us to explain a peculiarity in the Athenian use of law: The Athenians treated law as evidence or "proof" analogous to a witness's testimony.[20] Aristotle, in the *Rhetoric*, provides the most direct articulation of that notion. He writes that there were two kinds of rhetorical proof to be used in courtroom speeches: "technical" proofs and "atechnical" or (more typically) "artificial" proofs (1375a24–25). The "technical" proofs were proofs of argument that the speaker had to come up with by means of his own rhetorical art. The "artificial" proofs were ready-made forms of proof that the litigant could simply introduce into his argument; they include the testimony of oaths, witnesses, and the laws.[21] Aristotle's formulation captures Athenian practice because orators frequently asked their jurors to listen to the testimony provided by "oaths, witnesses, and laws" or complained, as Isaeus does, that an opponent had "given no answer [*apokrisis*], offered no witnesses, sworn no oaths, and read out no laws" (11.6).[22]

The Athenian categorization of law as proof has been found confusing by modern scholars because it flies in the face of modern expectations about how law works. As Todd puts it, "we would speak of evidence as establishing issues of fact, and of law as setting the rules under which those facts are to be considered."[23] In modern judicial argument, law is used to frame the case, to establish the issues of "material fact" that need to be proved, and to establish the burden of proof, but it itself does not "prove" anything.

Athenian law was not used to establish burdens of proof and to allow a case to be cast in terms of decisions on facts. Law helped answer the question of whether the jurors should express anger at a person, and the key to its status as proof lies here. Antiphon describes the role of the law by arguing that jurors must "learn from the laws" when they are judging. He argues: "You must not use the speech of accusation to study whether the laws are well laid out or not, but treat the prosecution speeches by learning from the laws [*katamanthanein ek ton nomon*] whether the prosecutors teach you rightfully and lawfully [*orthos kai nomimos didaskousi*] about the matter at issue" (Ant. 5.14 [6.2]). Prosecutors tried to teach their juries how to judge a given defendant; the law was a guideline that jurors could use to assess a prosecutor's arguments about anger and justice. Anything, including law, that could help prove that a defendant deserved to feel the jury's anger constituted proof. For Lycurgus law was a measuring rod (*kanon*) against which to judge someone's actions (1.9).[24] Written law helped Athenian jurors to assess whether a wrongdoer and his action deserved their anger, but it was only one of many tools.[25] According to Plutarch, Thucydides praised Antiphon for his ability to orient his speeches in regard to both the laws and the emotions, aiming at what was fitting (*epi tous nomous kai ta pathe trepon tous logous*, *Mor.* 832E-F). Isaeus argues: "Do not let him win without law or justice [*aneu tou nomou kai tou dikaiou*]" (9.35),[26] and Demades could write: "Without the jurors' well wishes [*he ton akouonton boulesis*] neither speeches nor laws nor the truth of deeds can save a man unjustly tried" (1.6).

An Athenian litigant wove the text of the laws into arguments constructed out of his own opinions about how pity and anger should be applied, and sources reflect the close connection between law and opinion. Although Aristotle treated oaths, testimony, and laws as parallel forms of proof, Anaximenes drew a parallel between oaths, testimony from witnesses, and the opinion of the speaker (*Rhet. ad. Alex.* 14.8–17.2). What Aristotle thought the laws did, Anaximenes thinks a speaker's opinion does. The comparable positions of the "opinion of the speaker" on Anaximenes' list and "law" on Aristotle's list underscore the idea that in Athens written law functioned as an important *body of opinion*. Each law characterized a particular action as deserving anger, and the speaker incorporated the opinions of the laws about wrongdoing into his own arguments about anger, pity, and justice. As Todd puts it, "statute law has only persuasive and not binding force on an Athenian court."[27] The juror's job was to assess a litigant's argument about justice—put together with reference to several forms of proof. Only one orator, Antiphon, ever enjoined his jurors to decide the legal (*ta nomima*) things (Ant. 5.85). All the other orators told their jurors to decide, simply, the just things (*ta dikaia*).[28]

Law was an important form of proof but it was still one among several forms of proof and could be weighed against other forms of proof.[29] The juror judged "the just things," subordinating law to judgments about how to define justice. This practice led to a form of judicial decision making that have been considered strange by modern scholars on three fronts. First, speakers stopped to evaluate whether the laws encoded "good opinions," as if the validity of any given law might be open to question. Antiphon, for instance, evaluates the law on murder thus: "I say that the law speaks rightly [*orthos agoreuein*] to say that those who kill should be punished" (Ant. 3.3.7).[30] Litigants and jurors regularly commented on the reasonableness of the laws as part of the process of weighing the diverse opinions about how a particular wrongdoing should be treated. Lysias writes: "For I think all cities establish laws for this reason: in order that concerning affairs about which we are perplexed, we may consider what we need to do by turning to them. The laws then command those who have been wronged to take a certain form of justice in each type of affair. . . . I think it is appropriate for you to be of the same opinion as the laws" (Lys. 1.35–36).[31] Lysias's exhortation to the jury to have the same opinion as the laws reveals the degree to which the jurors were expected to decide for themselves whether they would in fact take their opinions about desert, justice, and anger from the laws.

Second, orators were willing to argue that a prosecution could be valid even if no specific law criminalized the act being prosecuted.[32] Thus, Demosthenes remarks that: "For those cases for which there are no laws, you have sworn to judge with what is most just in your judgment [*gnomei*]" (Dem. 39.40), and Lysias reaches back to Pericles for the idea that the jurors should act on unwritten law: "You should enforce not only written laws but also the unwritten because that way not only men but also gods are given justice" (Lys. 6.10–12).[33] Comments like this were made throughout the fourth century despite late fifth-century attempts to legislate against using unpublished laws as the basis for a prosecution (And. 1.89). Thus in 330 Lycurgus can still exhort his jurors to be legislators:

> The reason why the penalty for such offenses has not been recorded is because this kind of wrongdoing has not happened before; nor did anyone think it was likely to happen in the future. Because of this, men, it is especially necessary for you not only to be judges [*dikastas*] of present wrongdoings but also to be legislators [*nomothetas*]. For whenever the law defines a wrongdoing, it is easy to punish the lawbreakers using that standard; but [in other cases] it is necessary for you to leave your judgment as an example for your descendants. (Lyc.1.9)

The orators themselves were willing to encourage their juries to look to standards outside the written law as a basis for their judgments.

The third type of argument that looks unusual from the modern perspective is that litigants regularly acknowledged that the jury's power of judgment included not only the power to judge where there were no laws but also the power and right to decide contrary to the laws. Orators both encouraged their juries to overrule the law and argued against their doing so—but everyone acknowledged that the jury could overrule the laws if it wished.[32] Demosthenes responds to an opponent who (according to Demosthenes) is asking the jurors to set aside the law by conceding that "The plea that, although it is illegal, it is to the public's benefit has reason in it" (23.98–101) and then arguing that his opponent's proposal is not only illegal but also harmful to the city. He makes a similar argument in another speech: "And even if [their case] turns out not to be supported by the laws, but they are nonetheless seen to be speaking with justice and philanthropy, we will withdraw from the case" (Dem. 44.8).[35]

Aeschines and other orators complain about the fact that the jurors would allow litigants to bring cases contrary to the requirements of the law: "There are men who are enslaving private people and making dynasties for themselves. They set aside judgments from the laws and carry verdicts at the vote, using anger [*met' orges*]" (Aes. 3.3–4; cf. Aes. 1.178–81). A Lysianic speech betrays a similar fear that the jurors will act as legislators: "If the penalty seems to be too heavy and the law too powerful, it is necessary to remember that you have come not to be legislators about these matters, but to vote according to the established laws, not pitying [*eleesontes*] wrongdoers but rather being angry [*orgioumenoi*] with them" (Lys. 15.9).[36] The speaker recognizes that his jury might disagree with the opinion encoded in a law—it might consider the law to be too heavy and too powerful—and so he abandons arguments from the reasonableness of the law in order to make a case for the general bindingness of law. But the litigant in another Lysianic speech is perfectly happy to encourage his jurors to act as legislators (*nomothetai*, Lys. 14.4–5; cf. Dem. 19.232).

The rhetoric heard in modern courts is drastically different. As we have seen, the 1992 Federal U.S. criminal jury instructions read: "You will . . . apply the law which I will give you. You must follow that law whether you agree with it or not."[37] No Athenian orator would have dared to say this to his jurors. Athenian juries took for granted the idea that they could overturn the law if they disagreed with it. Unlike them, modern Anglo-American juries are also kept in the dark about the principle of jury nullification. In the United States the effort to prevent the jury from making findings on law rather than on fact goes back to the end of the eighteenth century. Abramson writes that "within a generation" after the American Revolution a line of cases "stripped the jury of law finding."[38] The effort to give law a binding authority has played an especially important role in the twentieth century in efforts to rein in segregation-era white southern juries that bent legal principles for the sake of racial ones. Anglo-American legal systems have increasingly tried to secure the psychologically binding force of law on citizens, and analysts like the American Civil Liberties Union believe that "jurors often manage to control their own strong prejudices because the judge tells them they must."[39] Athenian courts were ruled by the judgments of the jurors. Modern courts do what they can to make sure that jurors' judgments are always ruled by the law.

A brief consideration of the concept of "equity" gives us another way of framing the difference between modern Anglo-American courts and ancient Athenian courts. "Equity" is the principle according to which modern judges are able to bend the law ever so slightly in the name of justice when they hand out sentences. Thus in Webster's *Third International New Dictionary* "equity" is defined as follows:

> a. system of law (as in England and the U.S.) originating in the English chancery and comprising a settled and formal body of legal and procedural rules and doctrines

that supplement, aid, or override common and statute law and are designed to protect rights and enforce duties fixed by substantive law.

b. trial or remedial justice under or by the rules and doctrines of equity administered in a separate court.

c. a body of legal doctrines and rules (as the Roman praetorian law) developed to enlarge, supplement, or override a system of law that has become too narrow and rigid in its scope (*s.v.* equity).

Black's Law Dictionary (s.v.) tells us that equity is:

> Justice administered according to fairness as contrasted with the strictly formulated rules of common law. It is based on a system of rules and principles which originated in England as an alternative to the harsh rules of common law and which were based on what was fair in a particular situation. . . . A system of jurisprudence collateral to, and in some respects independent of, "law"; the object of which is to render the administration of justice more complete.

Harris points out that appeals to equity or fairness (*epieikeia*) never found a place in the extant speeches of the Attic orators.[40] He argues that such pleas were actually made illegal. The case, however, was that the Athenians simply never needed the concept of equity to support their judgments when they ruled counter to law. Athenian jurors always made decisions that were about justice or fairness in the first instance and so their decisions never had to be revised to "render the administration of justice more complete." As Paoli argued, "the basis of judgment is the public concept of what is equitable."[41]

The orators' recognition that the *demos* had power even over the law testifies to the ways in which law was generally subordinate to the power of judgment in the Athenian courts. The tension between the two activities of law and judgment—of setting ethical norms by law and setting ethical norms by judgment— was natural given that the *demos* sat in both the assembly and the courts.[42] At the end of the day, a judicial decision was legitimate as long as it had come from the *demos*, whether that was the *demos* as represented in court by jurors or the *demos* as represented by law. The Athenian *demos* saw itself as the source of the ethical norms that structured social relations; this applied to the *demos* embodied in the assembly, to the *demos qua* mob in the marketplace, and to the *demos* embodied in an assemblage of jurors. The jurors recognized that there was no authority existing outside of them that would define justice. The jurors leaned heavily on the tool of *nomos*—social memory and laws written by the people—in order to make their judgments, but ultimately a judgment consisted of the people's decision to say either yes or no to the litigants' arguments about desert and justice. In the courtroom there was no appeal from the jury's decision since the citizens accepted the principle of majority vote, and not the laws, as the final authority. (Athena in the *Eumenides* did not, after all, establish written law as authoritative but rather the rule that a tied vote goes to the defendant.[43]) The Athenians treated law as a wise advisor but as an advisor whose wisdom was ultimately of second rank to that of the judge. Athenian citizens breathed the heady empyrean air of knowing that they gave shape to their own reality every time they spoke as a collective body, and their commitment to judging the "just things" over and above the "legal things" stands in marked contrast to the modern commitment to constitutionalism and to the idea that judgment should always conform to and to confirm the law.

THE RULE OF JUDGMENT VERSUS THE RULE OF LAW

This argument that the Athenians subordinated law to the decision-making capacity of the democratic collective contradicts an important tradition in the interpretation of Athenian history and politics, which argues that the Athenians invented the "rule of law." Barker, for instance, wrote: "Freely as the spirit of Socrates ranged, he acknowledged himself the slave of the law. And what is true of Socrates is true of the Athenian people. They might appear, as they stood assembled in their Pnyx, sovereign under heaven. But they too recognized the sovereignty of the laws. Law is thus the common spiritual substance of a society, expressed in concrete form, and as such it is the cohesive force and the sovereign of society."[44] A number of modern scholars have taken issue with this interpretative position.[45] But the misconception remains sufficiently entrenched that it is worth taking the time to try to lay out the evidence.

The Athenians typically subordinated law to judgment and aimed at making the "just decision" about anger and pity required by each particular context, using law to help them.[46] It was not the Athenians who invented the idea of the rule of law but Plato and Aristotle. Both philosophers theorized a form of politics that would be based on three ideas in particular: the idea that citizens should always be obedient to the laws and be "slaves" to the laws; the idea that the laws should be changed only very rarely; and the idea that law should be considered as playing the most important role in determining and preserving a city's way of life. The preceding discussion of how the Athenians *used* law has argued the case that the Athenians did not use law in a fashion that is compatible with these three "rule of law" principles. The orators' comments on the value of law and its role in the city give further support to this idea as do the contrasts between the Athenian manner of talking about law and Plato's and Aristotle's approach to the subject.

It is certainly true that the orators saw law as an important phenomenon crucial to the processes of punishing and politics. As evidence of this, we might point out that the orators associated the power of law to the powers of wise men and of oracles. Demosthenes writes, for instance: "You hear, men of the jury, that Solon in the laws and the god in the oracle say the same things" (Dem. 43.67).[47] On one orator's account, enemies of the laws were enemies of the city.[48] Moreover, the laws "hand over" wrongdoers for punishment and as such are analogous to the gods who do the same.[49] The orators could describe law as defining the structure of the city, or argue that the city was arranged according to its laws.[50] Five of the orators, but especially Demosthenes, regularly describe the law as providing not only liberty but also equality and power for the weak.[51] This was partly because law improved the chances of the weaker to carry out their retribution.[52] Notably, the orators stress law as a tool that contributes to the ability of all citizens to carry out punishment.

The case, however, for the importance of the rule of law to Athenian self-understanding is generally based on four fourth-century speeches: Demosthenes' *Against Timocrates* (353), Aeschines' *Against Timarchus* (345), and the two pseudo-Demosthenic speeches, *Against Aristogeiton I and II* (338–324).[53] In the earliest of these speeches, Demosthenes is prosecuting a citizen on charges of having proposed and passed an illegal law. His whole speech is concerned with the question of how the legal order should function and he argues that law is the key to maintaining the democratic way of life: "For I do not think that anyone would say that something is more responsible than the laws for the good things in the city and the freedom of the democracy" (Dem. 24.5). He also argues that the laws give the city its character and that it is necessary to obey them and not to introduce false laws into their company. "All who are wise regard laws as the character of the city. Therefore, it is necessary to work hard in order that they seem as good as possible and to punish those who pollute or corrupt them. . . . What saves the city is the laws. Solon thought law the currency of the city . . . and it is necessary to hate and punish the man who destroys it or introduces counterfeit" (Dem. 24.210–13).

But it turns out that Demosthenes thinks that law matters precisely because it constitutes the courts, which uphold the *politeia*. Laws hand over their own authority to the jurors: "Timocrates' law makes the courts, which it seems are the bond of [*sunechein*] the *politeia*, unauthoritative [*akura*] in regards to inflicting the additional penalties, defined by the laws, for wrongdoings" (Dem. 24.2). In the Demosthenic treatment of the power of law, there is, at a minimum, a tension between the power of the laws and the power of the jurors. He emphasizes the same point again later in the speech.

> And indeed I used to think the legislator needed to legislate about the future, that is, about how to behave and to arrange everything, and about what kinds of penalties it was necessary to have for each wrongdoing. For this is what it is to establish common [*koinous*] laws for the whole citizenry. . . . And laws that are masters make the jury masters. The laws permit them, after hearing the case, to adjust their condemnation to what is necessary for their anger. (Dem. 24.116–18)

Demosthenes' speech argues for the importance of having good laws. It does not tell us much about how he thinks that the jurors should use law once they have taken their seats in the courtroom. His speech also betrays a tension between the idea that laws are the authority in or masters of the city and the idea that jurors and their judgment are.

The next speech in which a strong rule of law argument is to be found is Aeschines' *Against Timarchus* (345). Aeschines argues that "Oligarchy and tyranny are organized according to the characters of their leaders, but only democratic cities are administered according to established laws; and know well that in a democracy it is the laws that protect the body and the constitution" (Aes. 1.4; identical to Aes. 3.6). He argues that the laws should be obeyed once a legislator has established a comprehensive and orderly set of laws:

> I think it is fitting, when we legislate, to consider this: how we will establish laws that are noble and beneficial for the *politeia*, and after we have legislated, it is fitting to obey the established laws, and to punish those who do not obey, if it can be that the affairs of the city will be well. Consider, how much forethought about sobriety Solon employed, the ancient legislator, and Draco, and the other legislators from those times. For first they legislated concerning the sobriety of our children . . . and then for the next of the age-groups. (1.6–10)

But part of the case that Aeschines makes is that it is the Spartans who act according to the rule of law and not the Athenians: "You establish the best laws. But in the assemblies and in the courts, often you lose hold of the speeches on the relevant matter, and are led away by deceit and trickery. The force of the law is relaxing, the democracy is perishing and arguments from custom [*ethos*] are gaining ground. Not so with the Spartans. It is noble to imitate even the virtue of foreigners" (Aes. 1.178–81). Aeschines does argue for the rule of law—for a commitment to following foundational written decrees rather than malleable customary opinion—but he defends that idea of the "rule of law" by referring to the Spartans as an example of those who employ it and by criticizing the Athenians for failing to do so.

In other speeches, Aeschines is willing to act more like a typical Athenian and to shift his focus away from law. He is, for instance, willing to grant that other forces, including the juror's vote and the assemblyman's vote, provide the democracy with its strength. He argues: "The private man rules as king [*basileuei*] in a democratic city by virtue of the law and his vote" (Aes. 3.233). Like Demosthenes, Aeschines displays some ambivalence over whether the laws or the jurors can ultimately be said to rule the city. The citizen's vote must be given as much weight as the law.

The most powerful and rhetorically vigorous argument for the rule of law to be found in the oratorical corpus appears in two of the most atypical speeches in the corpus: *Against Aristogeiton I and II* (only Lycurgus's *Against Leocrates* is equally unusual, if there can be a measure for such things). These two speeches are supposed to have been written in 338–324 or else after the democracy had fallen to Alexander. The date of the speeches itself makes them poor evidence of what was paradigmatic in Athenian politics, but they are nonetheless frequently cited as evidence that the Athenian democrats accepted the rule of law. The speeches are attributed to Demosthenes but most scholars think that this is a spurious attribution.[54] The author, however, was certainly someone who wished to lay an especially heavy stress on law and obedience to the law:

> The whole of human life, men of Athens, whether people dwell in a big city or in a small one, is ordered [*dioikeitai*] according to nature and the laws. Of these, nature is something without regulation and particular to each individual, but the laws are orga-

nized communally [*koinon tetagmenon*] and are the same for everyone. . . . The laws want what is just, noble, and beneficial, and they seek this and when it is found, this is set forth as a communal commandment, equal and identical for all, and this is law. It is fitting for all to obey [the laws] for many reasons, and especially because the law is the discovery and gift of the gods, and the opinion of wise people, and a corrective of all errors voluntary and involuntary [*ton hekousion kai akousion hamartematon*], and the communal bond of the city, in accordance with which it is fitting for everyone in the city to live. (Dem. 25.15–16)

The author also argues that laws should be used to educate people and that punishment should be used to reform people. "All laws are made for the sake of two things, Athenian men—that no one do anything that it is not just to do; and that, those who have transgressed them having been punished, the others are made better" (Dem. 25.17). This is the only oratorical speech to make a case for reformative punishment and the language that is used to make the case is conspicuous: "He is pollution, an unclean beast. Is he not impious, bloodthirsty, unclean, and a sycophant? . . . He is devoted to evil. He is incurable, incurable [*aniaton*]. It is necessary for you all to do as doctors do when they see a cancer or an ulcer or some other incurable bad thing, they burn it or wholly cut it out; thus you should expel this beast, hurling him from the city" (Dem. 25.58, 63, 93, 95). The sequel to this speech includes a similar argument that "The purpose of the lawgiver is to expel bestiality from souls" (Dem. 26.26–27).

This systematic characterization of law and punishment as intended to remedy the diseased and bestial soul of the wrongdoer and his failures of virtue appears *nowhere else* in oratory. Only one Athenian author, Plato, lays a comparable stress on the role of punishment and law in cleansing the soul of the unjust (see chapter 10).[55]

The four speeches are all anomalous not only in all having a strong focus on the law, but also in that they were given in the latter part of the fourth century. Moreover, not one of the four speeches actually supports the argument that the *Athenian citizens* (as opposed to the *speaker*) generally accepted a "rule of law" position. Some Athenians were willing to say that law was the master (*kurios*) of the city. Thus Antiphon calls the decrees, with the laws, *kurioi* of the whole *politeia* (3.1.1). But that was by no means the standard or customary way of describing the position of law in the city. The orators sometimes described the *demos* as being *kurios*,[56] and also the judgments and juries of the courts.[57] The decisions of the courts are even said to be more authoritative than decisions of the council and assembly in one instance.[58] The orators use the word *kurios* to describe the power of a number of institutions in the city; what was true in every case was that whatever institution was said to rule the city was in fact controlled by the *demos*.

Similarly, the laws are sometimes said to "save" or "preserve" the democracy, but law was by no means the only political institution described in this fashion. Lycurgus writes that three things are the most important in ensuring the preservation of democracy: "First is the placement of the laws, second is the vote of the jurors, and third is the judgment handing the wrongdoers over to them. The law was born to say what it is necessary not to do, the accuser to report those liable to penalties from the laws, the jury to punish all whom these two have brought to its attention. And thus both law and the jury's vote are powerless, not strong, without the accuser" (Lyc. 1.3). Lysias claims that the laws share the work of saving the city with the assemblies and with the generalships (14.11). Andocides places the magistrates and the laws on an equal footing: "I think the one salvation [*soterian*] for all is to obey [*peithesthai*] the magistrates [*tois archousi*] and the laws [*kai tois nomois*]" (4.19). Dinarchus calls upon his jury to guard democracy, the law, the people's decrees, and the reports of the council (3.16, 21–22). In another speech, Dinarchus draws a parallel between the laws, the magistrates, and the Athenian citizenry. The orators treated the oaths, the magistrates, the courts, the citizen's vote in jury and assembly, and the gods, as well as the law, as providing strength to or preserving the political system.

As we have seen, a few orators, like Antiphon and the author of *Aristogeiton I and II*, laid more emphasis on law alone when they discussed the question of what preserves the city. And Hyperides, another orator active at the end of the fourth century writes: "Nor must the safety of our citizens depend on those who slander them and truckle to their masters but on the force of law alone" (6.5).[59] But the more typical fourth-century approach to the law was expressed by Demosthenes when he wrote: "Trusting in what, then, and taking strength from what do we risk our money? In you, o jurors, and your laws. . . . But it seems to me that there is no benefit in your laws or contracts, if the one borrowing the money . . . does not fear you or respect the lender" (Dem. 56.2).

The laws were powerful only to extent that the judgments of the jurors were powerful. It was obvious to Athenian citizens that their own judicial power lay behind whatever work their laws did for them. The gods, the laws, and the people in assembly, jury, and magistracies were all masters of the city because all were manifestations of the collective will of the *demos*. The *demos* acted for itself especially when it stood in the assembly and in the courtroom having equipped itself with a range of tools to help it make its judgments. The judgment of the *demos* was the only true *kurios* in the city.

THE RULE OF LAW IN PLATO AND ARISTOTLE

Plato and Aristotle were concerned to revise the definition of a just politics away from the Athenian paradigm.[60] Studies of the political philosophies of the two writers have less frequently recognized the degree to which their approach to law itself was also radical within the Athenian context. Both Plato and Aristotle rejected the Athenian approach to law, which subordinated law to democratic judgment, and attempted to replace it with a "rule of law" paradigm, constructing the earliest extant "rule of law" theories. In this section, I draw primarily on Plato's *Republic*, *Statesman*, and *Laws* and on Aristotle's *Politics* in order to outline (very briefly) how the two philosophers self-consciously rejected the Athenian conceptualization of law on their way to inventing the idea of the "rule of law."

Both Plato and Aristotle begin their arguments for the rule of law by distinguishing a judgment-based politics and a law-based politics. For both Plato and Aristotle the former is a form of politics in which a single person or set of people is able to make all necessary political and judicial decisions as the circumstances arise that mandate decision making, while the latter is a form of politics in which the laws prescribe in advance the sorts of actions to be taken in most cases. Plato explores a politics of judgment in the *Republic* where he discusses the possibility of finding (or educating into existence) a philosopher-king whose knowledge would be the basis for all political decision making.

But the bulk of Plato's argument about the relationship between a politics of judgment and a politics of law appears in the *Statesman* (258b-303c, especially from 291d). The arguments about whether an individual or a set of laws should rule is crucial to the movement of the dialogue as a whole, but for lack of space I will highlight only a few elements of the discussion between the Stranger and young Socrates. The two interlocutors are searching for the form of knowledge (*episteme*) that constitutes true kingly rule (292b-d) and along the way discuss the "the rectitude of ruling without laws" (294a-b). The Stranger argues that law is ultimately incapable of managing a polity in accord with wisdom. According to the Stranger, "Law is always striving to lay down a rule that will last for all time—like an obstinate and ignorant tyrant, who will not allow anything to be done contrary to his appointment—not even in sudden changes of circumstances. But a perfectly simple principle can never be applied to a state of things that is the reverse of simple" (294). A politics of law, the Stranger argues, is not as good as a government based on the judgment of the person who has knowledge (*episteme*). The right form of government is that wherein a wise ruler rules with knowledge and is able to make decisions that fit every circumstance (294a). All other forms of government can be only imitations (*mem-imemenai*) of this single right form of government (*monen orthen politeian*) where the ruler with knowledge rules, even if he rules without law (293e).

Aristotle broaches the topic in book 3 of the *Politics* when he says:

> And the starting point for an investigation [about law] is the question of whether it is more advantageous to be ruled by the best men or by the best laws. Those of the opinion that it is advantageous to be governed by a king think that laws speak only of the general/universal but not of how to organize particulars as they come up, just as in any kind of art it is foolish to rule according to written texts. . . . it is clear that the best constitution is not the one according to written texts and laws, for this reason. (1286a8–15)

Aristotle's distinction between rule by the best people and by the best laws is a distinction between a form of rule where the political leader judges each situation as it comes up and another where the magistrates must carry out the laws. Aristotle concludes this preliminary discussion with the argument that it is, in fact, right for a single person or family to be judge or king whenever one person or family truly excels in virtue. Only then can a politics of judgment be justified.

Although valorizing a politics of judgment, both Plato and Aristotle think that it is unlikely that wise rulers can be found, and so they turn to the task of rehabilitating law.

The Stranger's valorization of a politics of judgment and his critique of law finally leads the young Socrates to ask: "For what possible reason, then, could it be necessary to legislate if law does not comprise the greatest rectitude?" (294c). The Stranger and young Socrates have already agreed that a mass (*plethos*) cannot possibly have the knowledge for politics but only a single person or a few people can (292e). The masses will need a shepherd to guide them. The Stranger now draws upon the analogies of the physician, the sea captain or steersman, and the gymnastic trainer to explain why the citizens, whose knowledge is less than perfect, will use laws. Socrates points out that the knowledgeable doctor cannot sit beside the patient for the whole length of the patient's life; the doctor and other such experts must therefore leave behind instructions or written rules for those times when he must be absent (295b–d). Law must serve as a stand-in for the wisdom of the truly wise ruler.

Aristotle in turn argues that law is needed to rein in human judgment, which, in the unwise, is necessarily corrupted by passion. Based on reason, law is actually a better guide for the unwise than human judgment:

> The thing in which there is absolutely no emotional element is stronger than that in which it is innate; this [emotional element] is not possessed by the law, but it is necessity that every human soul have it. It is preferable for the law to rule rather than for some one of the citizens to rule. . . . The man who recommends that rationality [*nous*] rule seems to think that god and reason only should rule, but the one who recommends that man rule puts forward the wild animal; for this is the sort of thing that desire is, and passion ruins the ruling of even the best men. Law is rationality without desire. (1286a17–20, 128719–32)[61]

Most people are unwise, so for them law is the best guide.

As a third step of their argument, both Plato and Aristotle flesh out the idea of what it means to have law rule in the city such that it manages to subordinate judgment to it. They argue that good laws will be so precise as to make judgment unnecessary, and lawgivers will always begin by writing their laws as specifically as they can *akribos*.[62] For Plato, the laws should be copies of the true particulars of action as far as they admit of being written down (*Statesman* 300). For Aristotle, rightly ordered laws would leave as little decision making as possible to the discretion of the judges (*Rhet.* 1.1.7). Aristotle writes: "It is necessary to make the judge the authority as infrequently as possible except for on the topics of what has happened or will happen. But it is necessary to leave these topics to the judge because the legislator is not able to foresee them in advance" (1.1.7–9). Aristotle's approach to law, like the modern approach to law, aimed to keep juries from law finding and to leave them in a position to make decisions only on matters of fact (Aris. *Rhet.* 1.1.8). Not once in the extant forensic speeches does an Athenian orator use the word *akribos* or *akribeia* to describe what is desirable in law, and modern scholars have often been at a loss for how to deal with the vagueness of Athenian laws, famous for failing to define their terms.[63] But modern legal theorists, like Plato and Aristotle, value precision and "often attempt to limit the amount of 'open texture' a statute may possess by formulating precise definitions of key terms."[64]

Plato and Aristotle also argued that the proper use of law rests on a commitment to constitutionalism. A comprehensive code of laws should be invented at the city's founding and should never or rarely be changed (*Statesman* 297, 300–301). According to Plato, "The philosopher will make laws only after finding a clean surface and outlining a constitution" (*Rep.* 501; cf. *Tim.* 24; *Laws* 957b). Once a city has been given its law code, the people should guard (*phulatto*) the laws as precisely (*akribos*) as possible (*Statesman* 292a) and change them as little as possible. Aristotle criticizes politicians who make laws at random in an ad hoc fashion and praises the true legislator who attempts a comprehensive code. According to Aristotle, "the laws should be made to fit the constitution; not the constitution the laws" (1288b10–40, 1289a13).[65]

In the *Laws* Plato introduces a new political office to the end of having the laws preserved: the guardian of the laws (*nomophulax*) (632c). The dialogue's protagonist argues that citizens should be raised to feel psychologically bound by the laws:

> Once the laws are appropriately ordered, one of the best of the laws would be that which holds that none of the youths should inquire which laws are nobly held and which not; instead with one voice and from one mouth, they should all declare that all the laws are well established because they have been ordained by the gods. Another good law is that, if someone should say otherwise [than that the gods have ordained the laws], those who hear shall not entertain what is said at all. But if one of the old men has opinions concerning the laws, he should make speeches on the subject before a magistrate or someone his own age but not in front of any young man. (634d)

The Athenian Stranger also argues that the work of legislation would be completed only when the founders devise some method by which the laws can be implanted in the souls of citizens with an irreversible quality (*ametastrophon*); for it is *eunomia* in their souls (*en tais psuchais*) that will preserve the laws (*soterian ton nomon*) (960d). In Magnesia, citizens will not expect anything other than to subordinate their judgment to the laws. Magnesia is intended to operate according to "the rule of law" insofar as the Athenian Stranger aims to have the judgment of citizens constrained by the laws and for citizens to be slaves to the laws (698b).

The stress on the comprehensiveness and bindingness of the legal code leads Plato and Aristotle to develop theories of equity to supplement their ethic of a decision making based totally on law. Plato is almost inflexible in his claim that citizens should bend their wills to the laws. But he does argue that changes in the laws will sometimes be necessary because legislators sometimes make mistakes and circumstances sometimes change in ways that invalidate the laws. Thus in the *Statesman* the Stranger argues that it will occasionally be necessary to revise decisions away from legal guidelines:

> *Stranger:* Will the statesman who has knowledge do many things by means of his skill (art) without considering what is written, if he believes that it is better to observe some prescription other than what he wrote out. . . .
>
> *Young Socrates:* Yes.
>
> *Stranger:* And any individual or mass with established laws would also be acting like a statesman if they acted contrary to the laws with a view to something better?
>
> *Young Socrates:* Certainly.
>
> (*Statesman* 300c)

The law can decide only general matters, and so human judgment has to be called in to make decisions on particulars or to revise the law with a view to something better.[66]

According to Aristotle the law will first of all educate the magistrates and then give them the power to judge particulars "according to their judgment" and introduce amendments to the code if necessary (*Pol.* 1287a25—28). Aristotle develops the criteria for amending the law by refining the concept of "equity" in the *Nicomachean Ethics*:

> Equity [*epieikeia*] is justice but not according to the law; rather it is a correction of legal justice. The reason for this is that every law concerns a general (or universal) statement, and yet there are some cases in which is not possible to speak rightly with a universal statement. . . . The law takes in the majority of the cases. . . . When the law prescribes something general, and something happens afterward that is exceptional, then it is right, where the lawgiver has left something out and erred by speaking generally, to correct the omission by speaking as the legislator himself would speak if he were present. (5.10.3, 1137b13)

Aristotle needs to study the relationship between equity and justice because, unlike the Athenians, he has subordinated judgment to law and has asked citizens to focus on enforcing the law rather than on making decisions about justice for themselves.[67]

Aristotle makes this idea of equity central to his *Rhetoric* as well, in the beginning of which he argues that laws should be written so as to leave as few decisions to human beings as possible. But it will sometimes be necessary, he concedes, to argue that the written law of a particular city is unjust and to appeal to equity (*Rhet.* 1.13.13, 1374a2025). Aristotle then defines an appeal to equity an appeal to "common law" (*koinos nomos*), a term that, in tragedy, referred to laws based on the consent of the community. Aristotle ignores this idea and defines "common law" as laws "according to nature," which apply universally and can be discerned by everyone (*koinos nomos, kata phusin, ho manteuontai pantes, Rhet.* 1.13.1, 1373b5–8; also 1.15.6, 1375a25–35). For Aristotle an appeal to the judge's sense of equity should not be an appeal to community norms but to a standard found in nature. Aristotle thus endeavors to separate justice from the community's judgments not only by requiring that citizen-jurors be restricted to finding matters of fact, not law, but also by requiring that equity, the realm of judgment, be based on a standard external to the community and not on the community's customary sense of what was "equitable."

After Aristotle glosses the " law of the community" as the law of nature, he gives an example of what he means by quoting the passage from the *Antigone* in which Antigone describes the laws of the gods as being born neither today nor yesterday but as existing eternally. He glosses Antigone's reference to divine law as a reference to his law of nature, although Antigone herself never once made such an equation. As we saw in Euripides' *Suppliants*, the law of the gods could be treated as being synonymous to the law of mortals based on the consensual community. Antigone's argument that she upholds the laws of the gods is an argument that she upholds religious norms that have traditionally been validated by the community. Aristotle rejects this standard for judging the validity of laws, substitutes "nature" for the community's consensual agreement, and thereby appropriates and reinterprets the language of tragedy and uses it to new ends.

Plato and Aristotle were relatively explicit about the fact that their conceptualizations of the role of law in politics diverged from the Athenian norm, as is evident from how they categorize Athens when they develop their catalogs of different types of political regime. In writers earlier than Plato and Aristotle political regimes were classified according to who ruled them—the one, the few, or the many (e.g., Herodotus). Plato and Aristotle employed this distinction but also observed a conceptually prior division of regimes into those ruled "according to law" and those not ruled "according to law."

The *Statesman* sets up a schema for thinking about politics in which there are seven forms of government (302c–e): an ideal form where a wise ruler carries out a judgment-based politics and six real, nonideal constitutions. These six nonideal forms include three types of regime that are successful (but still imperfect) imitations of the ideal and the three types of regime that are failed imitations of the ideal. The three successful imitations of the ideal are those regimes that achieve rule "according to law" (*kata tous nomous*), regardless of whether they are ruled by the one, the few, or the many. The three failed imitations are those where the one, the few, or the many rule lawlessly or "beyond the laws" (*paranomos*). The distinction between regimes that are beyond the law (*paranomon*) and those that are within the law (*ennomon*) grounds the distinction between legitimate and illegitimate actualizable regimes and is therefore of fundamental importance (302e).[68]

Aristotle's schema is more complicated than Plato's, but it is also based on the distinction between cities ruled "according to law" and cities "not ruled according to law." In the *Politics* he writes: "Where the laws do not rule there is no constitution; the law ought to rule all things, and the magistrates only the particulars, and it is necessary to judge that this arrangement is constitutional government" (1292a30). Aristotle argues that for each type of rule—by the one, few, or many—there are four possible kinds of governmental structure, and so there are twelve types of regime in total. Each set of four includes three types of government that vary according to how magistracies are distributed within the citizenry (for instance, by property qualification, birth qualification, or by lot) but that are all ruled according to law and a fourth kind of regime where the law does not rule (1291b15). Thus in the first three types of democracy and oligarchy, the law rules (*archein ton nomon*, 1291b30), but in the fourth kind of democracy, the people is master and not the law (*kurion d' einai to plethos kai me ton nomon*, 1292a10) and in the fourth kind of oligarchy, the magistrates rule and not the law (*arche me ho nomos all' hoi archontes*, 1292b8).[69] The distinction between cities that are ruled according to law and those that are not ruled according to law, or between cities that used the rule of law and cities that used the rule of judgment, is both prior to and more significant than the division into rule by the one, the few, and the many.

Plato's and Aristotle's distinction between cities that are ruled according to law and cities that are not ruled according to law *is not* a distinction between cities that do and do not have laws. The cities not ruled according to law do in fact have law. This is the most important thing to notice about these cities, but this detail is usually missed.[70] On Plato's account, cities that fail to achieve the rule of law do not guard the laws carefully (292a), violate the laws, act beyond the laws, and act contrary to what has been written (*me kata nomous*; *para ta gegrammena*; *paranomos*) (291–301). These cities have law but use it differently than do the regimes of which Plato approves. On no account do they use law well. On no account are their political systems rightly ordered. Aristotle, unlike Plato is willing to concede that cities that operate with a judgment-based politics can in fact survive decently enough. He writes: "It is not easy for every city to bear nor to endure the fourth kind of democracy [i.e., without the rule of law], . . . unless it is well organized in its laws and customs" (1319b1). Aristotle's fourth type of regime, the regime that is not ruled according to the law, may nonetheless be acknowledged to have organized its laws well.

Both philosophers designated Athens as a city that had law but not the rule of law. In the *Laws*, the Athenian Stranger gives a political history of Athens, describing it as having been constituted, before the Persian Wars, of citizens wishing to live as slaves to the law (698bff.). In the speaker's own day, however, its citizens seek to enslave the law instead (701b). Aristotle makes a similar point about "present day" democracy: "But for a democracy of the form that at the present day is considered to be democracy in the fullest degree (and I mean one of the sort in which the people is sovereign even over the laws), it is advantageous if [they do the following in order to optimize their success]" (1298b15). Like Plato, Aristotle credits the forces of history with having turned Athens into a city where the people and their judgments were superior to the laws. He writes: "Revolutions take place that turn the ancestral form of democracy into one of the most modern kind. Those who desire to rule act as demagogues and bring things to the point where the people are masters [*kurion*] over the laws" (1305a30; cf. 1310a5).

When Plato and Aristotle wrote up their philosophies of the "rule of law," they rejected the Athenian approach to law that treated it as a guide for judgment, as a storehouse of wise opinions that did not need to be drawn up or cataloged with much more precision than is typically used to catalog opinions. The philosophers eschewed an approach to judicial decision making that asked jurors to judge the "just things" rather than only the legal things and that gave jurors wide latitude to decide ethical as well as factual matters. The Athenian commitment to a judgment-based politics was thus undermined.

Plato and Aristotle's theories did not go unnoticed in Athens. As we have seen, unusually strong rule of law arguments turn up in speeches given late in the democracy's life, and the fall of Athens to Macedon led to actual changes in the city's institutions. The new ruler, Demetrius of Phaleron, was a student of Aristotle's and introduced to the city law guards (*nomophulakes*) and "women's officials" (*gunaikonomoi*), both of which were recommended by Plato in the *Laws*. Williams writes of the changes: "After all, Athens' tyrant had received from Aristotle and Theophrastus an education which his later scholarly writings [known by their titles] prove shaped his intellectual interests."[71] Plato and Aristotle's philosophical views impacted politics at least to this extent.

Before the fall of Athens to Macedon, the city proved rather resilient in its ability to use and secure a politics of judgment where law was the tool and not the master of the judges. It is a notorious fact that many fourth-century Athenian laws were said to be Solonian although none (or few) of them actually derived from the historical Solon. The Athenian people made their own judgments about how to order their city and then they attached the legitimating name of the legislator to those judgments.[72] "Solon" was a malleable idea; his importance lay in the power of his name, the name of the absent author, to confirm that a given rule was acceptable to the whole people.[73] The Athenians changed their norms and laws but always called them Solonian to confirm that the laws were the possession of the community as a whole. They did this instead of attempting a true conservatism that worked to preserve some original set of laws. What they continually preserved was the idea that their norms came from the communal store of wisdom.

THE THIRD NORM OF PUBLIC AGENCY: SHAPING THE DEMOCRATIC COMMUNITY

Aristotle's use of the term "common law" to define equity was an appropriation and revision of a concept that was central to Athenian principles of judicial decision making. In tragedy, we saw that characters juxtaposed the "private laws" of the tyrant (*idioi nomoi*) to the "public laws" (*koinoi nomoi*) of the community. The latter could be thought of as being the laws of mortals, the laws of Greece, the laws of the city, or the laws of the gods. But whatever the case, their legitimacy rested on the fact they reflected the community's consensual decision about how to define the norms under which they would live.

Like characters in tragedy, Aristotle also juxtaposed the term "private law" to the term "common law." According to him, however, it was the laws of particular cities, not the laws of the tyrant, that should be thought of as "particular" or "private" (*Rhet.* 1.13.13, 1374a20–26), regardless of whether those laws were written or unwritten. The community's customary and unwritten laws thus become "private" on the Aristotelian paradigm, counter to the tragic paradigm where they were public or shared (*koinos*) and where it was the laws of the tyrant that were called private. In the courts, the Athenians also made a distinction between what was private (*idios*) and what was common (*koinos*), and it was closer to the tragic than to the Aristotelian distinction. The Athenian orator who called his audience's attention to what was "communal" or "shared" (*koinos*) focused their attention on the norms that the community had generated for public life and that it had stored in social memory.

Orators frequently accuse their opponents of having mixed up the categories of private and public by prosecuting with the wrong legal procedure.[74] Thus, Demosthenes worries that Meidias will criticize him for bringing a public prosecution: "It is clear that he will say, when he speaks, that if I had truly suffered the things I say I have, it would have been fitting for me to start a private suit against him but not, by Zeus, to start a public [*demosiai*] trial" (Dem. 21.25). Isocrates similarly accuses a prosecutor of having confused public and private matters when he says: "And I think it is not fitting that they introduce common causes [*koinas aitiois*] into private suits [*idiois*]" (Isoc. 16.2; also 31). And Isaeus generally critizes the Athenians for failing to regulate the categories of public and private: "It is necessary for you not to get accustomed to having public cases [*graphas*] concerning things for which the laws have prescribed private suits [*idias dikas*]" (Isae. 11.28–32).

We have seen already that the prosecutor's personal involvement in a case was necessary in order to justify a prosecution. That personal involvement sufficed as justification in private cases, but in public cases it was necessary but not sufficient for justifying a trial. For instance, Lysias describes a situation in which a public punishment was made void because it had been based on nothing other than personal enmity (9.7).[75]

Ancient and modern writers have expended a good deal of ink arguing about what did justify trying a case by means of a public procedure. Scholars have typically suggested that public procedures were used for cases in which the innocent and helpless needed protection;[76] cases where legal matters were complex (Isae. 11.32); cases where prominent public figures would fight it out in major political battles;[77] and cases where a wrongdoer could not be controlled by the "inorganic" repression of the group but needed to be subjected to the coercion of authorities.[78] All of these suggestions help flesh out the picture of what public cases were like, but they do not tell us what types of case were seen as good opportunities for political battles, for drawing attention to public authority, or for dealing with legal complexity. As it turns out, cases of wrongdoing were selected for trial by a public procedure when they could be used for and were needed for purposes of educating the public and for deterrence. In one case, the public trial of a foreigner is for instance justified purely in terms of its value as an educative experience for the public. "The priest advised you when you were deliberating about how to treat the impious Megarian man. Some people were ordering him to be killed on the spot without a trial but he advised you to hold a trial for the sake of the people generally, which from hearing [*akousantes*] and seeing [*idontes*] [the case] would be more right-minded [*sophronesteroi*]" (Lys. 6.54–55).

As we have seen (chapter 2), *graphe* means written thing, and public procedures called *graphai* both began with a publicly posted written indictment and resulted in the public, as opposed to archival, inscription of a wrongdoing and its punishment.[74] Public cases were memorialized with inscriptions from at least the time of Antiphon who is described as having been penalized with a set of such markers:

> The penalty was assessed as follows: the two prisoners will be delivered to the Eleven; their goods shall be confiscated and a tithe given to the goddess; their houses shall be razed to the ground and stones of record placed upon the sites of both, thus inscribed: Here lived Archeptolemus and Antiphon, the traitors. This sentence is to be inscribed on a pillar of bronze and set up in the same place as the decrees concerning Phrynichus. (ps. Plutarch *Life of Antiphon*).[80]

Andocides, Lycurgus, and Demosthenes also describe such public marking stones.[81] Writing, as we have seen (chapter 3), was understood by the Athenians as an *aide-memoire*, and as a way of fixing narratives in the social memory. The *graphe* was the mode of punishment most associated with writing, and so it had the greatest power to memorialize the acts of wrongdoers and their punishments. The *graphe* was used for cases that the community thought needed to be written into the public memory.[82] The prosecutor of a public case was expected to be self-conscious about his role in crafting Athenian social memory.

The orators themselves suggest that this is a reasonable reading of the purpose of the *graphe*. It is only in public cases (with two exceptions) that orators stress the deterrent effects of punishment and enjoin their audience to make of the punished an example (*paradeigma*) for the future.[83] One speaker argues : "It is necessary, gentlemen, for you to punish [*kolazein*] them not only for the sake of what has happened but also for the sake of an example of the things that are about to be" (Lys. 22.20).[84] Speakers in public cases seem to expect that their case, and the defendant's history, should be inserted into the social memory.[85] Lycurgus in *Against Leocrates* was extremely self-conscious on this front: "But the case before you now does not concern some small part of the affairs of the city nor some small bit of time, but instead this prosecution is on behalf of the whole fatherland and will leave a perpetual memory through all time to your descendants" (7).

In one case, where a public fine has been tacked on to a private case, making the private case in some regard public (a *demosia dike*), the speaker describes the additional penalty as necessary precisely for the sake of deterrence: "It is necessary to make these kinds of trials of the greatest importance; for the private contracts of others, it is necessary to assess how much it is fitting for the plaintiff to receive, but concerning *hubris*, the defendant should pay however much will, for the future, put a stop to his present wantonness [*aselgeias*]" (Isoc. 20.16–17).[86] Public cases, whether *graphai* or *demosiai dikai*, concerned people or activities that had not only damaged the commonwealth but would also harm the security, well-being, and self-identity of the city if allowed to continue without significant and memorialized public repudiation.

The requirement that public prosecutors offer their audiences cases that were suitable for public memorialization led some speakers to suggest that only illustrious wrongdoers should be tried by *graphe*. The prosecutor of Alcibiades' son argues: "If you punish [*kolazete*] men who are unknown [*tous agnotas*], not one among the rest will be improved, no one will know the sentences. But if you punish [*timoresthe*] the most conspicuous [*tous epiphanestatous*] wrongdoers, everyone will learn [*peusontai*]" (Lys. 14.12; cf. 22.5). Later Lysias writes, again in a public case: "You all know the following fact: it is not when you punish [*kolazete*] those who are unable to speak [as public orators] that you provide an example [*paradeigma*] against wronging you. It is when you take justice [*lambanein diken*] from those who are able to speak that all those who are trying to wrong you will stop" (Lys. 27.5; cf. 30.24).

Hyperides defends Euxinippus by chastising his prosecutor for having brought a public charge, an *eisangelia*, against a private citizen who had not engaged in politics: "Once you decided to participate in politics [*politeuesthai*], by Zeus, you should not have tried [*krinein*] private people [*tous idiotas*], nor acted arrogantly against them. Instead, when one of the orators does wrong, prosecute [*krinein*] him, or when some one of the generals does wrong, impeach [*eisangelein*] him. It is possible for these men to harm the city" (Hyp. 4.27). Prosecutors were not supposed to pick on the little guy, and public trials frequently turned into political battles because politicians were well-known people whom it was good to prosecute.

Demosthenes uses the distinction between what was private and what public to express the idea that those who rise to prominence through politics must take especial care to recognize that they have entered the realm where they will be directly impacting the shared life of the city:

> The laws of all cities are concerned with two types of affairs. One type has wholly to do with how we live among ourselves, how we treat one another and associate with each other, and how it is necessary to handle private affairs [*peri ton idion*]. The other type concerns how the man who wishes to be a politician [*politeuesthai*] and claims to care for the city needs to treat [*chresthai*] the community [*toi koinoi*] of the city. (Dem. 24.192)[87]

Communal or public (*koinos*) law was the body of law that called on prosecutors and politicians to be self-conscious about how their actions would impact the city as a whole. The word *koinos*, therefore, referred to the arena where political norms were crafted and the needs of the city as a whole were explicitly defined. In tragedy, the notion of "pollution" was used to explore ideas about the well-being of the community. But only Antiphon, the earliest of the orators whose works are extant, made regular appeals to notions of pollution and cleansing in order to talk about punishment. All of his uses of the trope appear in the context of murder.[88] Fourth-century orators more typically used the trope of the "public" (*demosion* or *koinon*) as opposed to the "private" (*idion*) when they wished to discuss the well-being of the community, and they used the *graphai* and other public procedures for cases in which they needed to, and could, create public memory. The public procedures provided for deterrence by memorializing public anger and judgment.[89] The regeneration of social memory was especially expected to be used by and against those citizens, the politicians, who could teach the most powerful lesson to the community and would be most dangerous to the community. At the end of the day, such public judgments were the source of authority in the city in that they established the common norms that citizens could use to make decisions about their own conduct and according to which they could judge their fellows.

Orators who ventured into the public realm not only acknowledged that their cases touched on matters pertinent to the city's social memory but were also straightforward about their efforts to reshape the content of social memory through their storytelling. In *On the Embassy* Demosthenes says: "It appears to me that the trials are affected as much by the conditions of the hour as by the facts, and I am afraid that the long lapse of time since the embassy has inclined you to forget or to acquiesce in these iniquities. . . . Why am I reminding you [*hupemenesa*] of these things? So you may realize that this wrongdoing comes from Aeschines" (Dem. 19.3, 25). Demosthenes treats his speech as an intervention in social memory, an act that "recalls" what had been "forgotten." In the process of discussing past events the orators sometimes told old stories in new ways. As we saw in the chapter 6, Demosthenes and Lycurgus both narrated the story of the stoning of Lycidas. While Demosthenes emphasized the role of the citizen women in the stoning, Lycurgus emphasized the role of the council members, public officers (Dem. 18.204; Lyc. 1.122; Hdt. 9.5).[90] As we have seen, Lycurgus does this in a speech where he himself was acting as a public officer rather than as an offended victim. His version of the story supports his heterodox definition of the legitimate punisher. The story of past punishment, like the idea of the "sycophant," was a malleable symbol that permitted idiosyncratic interventions in the communal construction of social memory.

Acts of public judgment memorialized the city's ethics of pity and anger. These in turn sustained the city's rules for the distribution of honor and its definitions of desert and justice. Lycurgus emphasizes the idea that public judgments established structures of anger and pity that bound together all the members of the citizenry when he writes: "Though it may not be customary at any other time for members of the jury to set their wives and children beside them in court, at least in a trial for treason, this practice ought to have been sanctioned, so as to bring into full view all those who shared in the danger, as a reminder that they had not been thought [by the defendant to be] deserving of the pity which is common to all [*eleou tou koinou para pasin*]" (1.141).

Anger and pity were the political coin of the city. The distribution of anger and pity allowed for the construction of the relationships between citizens. The "common realm" and the "common laws" were constituted out of these relationships and out of the customary norms that supported them. The fact that the murder courts heard trials sitting in the open air so that the juries would not be with the unclean (Ant. 5.11, 82) represents the way in which a trial could implicate participants in relationships of pity and anger that might even be dangerous. The Athenians desired to avoid that implication in the context of murder, just as no one wished to speak to Orestes when he arrived in Athens on the "Day of the Jugs." When punishments revised networks of anger and pity, they revised the city. The Athenian litigant, acting on his private anger, was also involved, especially in public cases, in trying to define the nature, rules, and norms of his city, or its "constitution."

The city's constitution was made secure not by the institution of law guards or by an effort to keep citizens from questioning the laws. Rather it was made secure by a communal effort to memorialize public decisions. The process of memorializing an act of public judgment implicated the whole city in the networks of social knowledge that controlled the distribution of honor and position in the city. It is, perhaps, no wonder then that the Thirty thought that their efforts to take over the city required them to eradicate democratic social memory. For the short time that the Thirty oligarchs ruled Athens, they not only "got rid of sycophants" but also demolished Athenian memorials and honorific stelai (Tod 98; *IG*ii^2 29).[91] The democrats were equally self-conscious about the importance of communal memory when they returned to power. They reerected the memorials that the oligarchs had torn down (*IG*ii^2 29). The Athenian democrats recognized that their efforts to build the communal memory were central to the maintenance of their democratic order.

Demosthenes saw the nature of democracy as lying precisely in this communal commitment to the common social memory. He writes:

> The difference between oligarchy and democracy is that everyone [*hekastos*] in the oligarchy can undo the past [*ta pepragmena lusai*], and has the authority [*kurios estin*] to establish matters for the future as he sees fit, but in a democracy, the laws advise [*hoi nomoi phrazousi*] us how we ought to treat matters in the future. . . . Timocrates has introduced the injustice of oligarchy into his law, and thinks that he deserves [*exiose*] to have more authority [*kurioteron*] over past events [*peri ton pareleluthoton*] than the jurors who sit in judgment [*katagnonton dikaston*]. (Dem. 24.76)

Law, like social memory, helped memorialize the norms of democratic order so that those norms could give their advice to the jurors in their project of shaping the future. But it was ultimately the jurors who secured the past for the future and held final authority. The jurors, representatives of the whole Athenian *demos*, were the only people who could judge past events and, with the help of the law, they were the ones with authority over the future.

One of the best and longest memorialized of Athenian situations of punishment was the city's response to those who were involved in the wrongdoing of the oligarchy. The democrats ousted the aristocratic clique that ruled the city from 404–403 and afterward not only reerected the memorials that the oligarchs had overturned but also pardoned many of the men associated with the oligarchy by passing an amnesty or moment of "non-remembering." The next chapter explores Athenian methods of executing of punishments and of bringing the processes of punitive memorialization to conclusion. In it, it will be necessary to investigate the paradox of the amnesty: the use of communal "forgetting," as well as remembering, to stabilize the community's response to wrongdoing.

Execution

WAR, PEACE, AND THE FORMALISM OF PUNISHMENT

A finalized punishment establishes, if only temporarily, the fiction that the contestation and subversion of values in the city have ceased. The city seems to be cured of the diseases of anger and social struggle at the moment of punishment. The wish to be clean, to be pure, is a never-to-be fulfilled wish for a truly and perfectly hegemonic system of value. Punishment is a practice through which a community could construct the myth that it is possible to have a system of norms in which all citizens will acquiesce.

The wish to be clean is also a wish for peace or an end to war. Elaine Scarry's *The Body in Pain* offers this analysis of what is at stake when countries war on one another. "The dispute that leads to the war involves a process by which each side calls into question the legitimacy and thereby erodes the reality of the other country's issues, beliefs, ideas, self-conception. Dispute leads relentlessly to war not only because war is an extension and intensification of dispute but because it is a correction and reversal of it."[1] The same applies to wrongdoing and punishment. The wrongdoer opposed his or her own idiosyncratic (or not so idiosyncratic) system of value to that of the city, and the Athenians treated wrongdoing as introducing either the threat of war or war itself to the city. Either the wrongdoer or the city had to change its self-conception and beliefs in order for peace to resume. The city responded to the wrongdoer with a range of relatively more or less "warlike" responses in its effort to reconstitute the peace and establish its vision of the world as authoritative.

Not only in Athens but also elsewhere, punishments restore a peace that has been unsettled by social disruptions and clashes of systems of value when they successfully produce an authoritative judgment, in which citizens acquiesce, about how power can be exercised within the community. Punishments are proved authoritative only when both the wrongdoer and the onlooking citizenry acquiesce in the punishment and cease to contest it. To acquiesce in a punishment is to become quiet about it or to lapse into silence about it. It is to hold one's peace. Punishments become authoritative when they achieve the peace lodged in citizen acquiescence. Even the wrongdoer must be quieted down, for a system of justice cannot confidently sustain its definition of justice in the face of perpetual Promethean protestation.

The moment a punishment is executed is therefore crucial. Citizens and wrongdoers are asked for one last time whether they will protest the act of force imposed on the wrongdoer or whether they will be quiet now. In the moment of execution a punishment is either proved authoritative—in that it garners silence, acquiescence, acceptance, and therefore legitimacy—or is shown not to have authority after all, because citizens and wrongdoer refuse to be silent. The peace that follows punishment does not necessarily confirm a general commitment to the social norms and orders that existed *before* the disruption, but it does confirm a general commitment to the social norms and orders that *were used to produce* the punishment and the principles or norms in accordance with which the judgment decision was made. In a democracy the peace that follows punishment is expected to rest on the wrongdoer's (generally) forced acquiescence and on the community's voluntary acquiescence to the claim that the principles and social norms used to produce the punishment are legitimate and need not (or should not) be contested any further.

In Athens the social disruption that arose from wrongdoing and that necessitated punishment was viewed as a disease that had to be cured. The days, weeks, or months that passed between the moments when a disease was recognized and cured were spent in a long process of negotiation and argument about desert and justice that led eventually to a judgment about how to reorder relationships within the city. The judgment itself, however, was not the final moment of the process of punishing, nor did it complete the cure and cleansing. Cure was achieved by the execution of a punishment that finalized a judgment and proved that social relations had been realigned. "Cure" and "cleansing" were the other names for the peace that was built on the reinvigoration of citizens' acquiescence in the power structure of the regime and its system of value. The silence of acquiescence was one of the most important elements of this cure.

The Athenians had several different types of punishment. Broadly speaking, they fall into two categories: those that treated a clash in a system of values as a temporary *disruption of peacetime* and those that treated a clash as the *all-out struggle of war*. The punishments that suited peacelike contexts aimed to *restore* an old peace. The punishments that suited warlike contexts aimed to *make* a new peace. The former type of punishment explored the possibility of reintegrating the wrongdoer into the community and into the community's hierarchies and systems of value. The latter type of punishment aimed to eliminate the wrongdoer from the community completely and to redefine the boundaries of the community by pushing the wrongdoer beyond them; this was the last resort for solving the problem of the clash of world views. Both types of punishment, however, were finalized when a silence fell upon the struggle of the wrongdoer against the community.

Not every attempted punishment achieved such a complete silence. Those onlookers who wished to contest the legitimacy of a punishment and/or the authority supporting a punishment sometimes refused to be silent. According to Plutarch a Samian named Duris challenged Athenian power by criticizing a Periclean punishment. In his *Life of Pericles*, Plutarch describes the slanders bruited abroad by enemies of the great fifth-century Athenian politician, and he repeats a report that Pericles had punished a group of rebellious Samians in an extremely severe fashion: "Pericles gave the worst of all possible treatments to the Samians; he dragged them into the marketplace [*eis ten agoran*] of Miletus and bound them to the boards [*sanisi prosdesas*] and after they had suffered badly for ten days already, clubbed their heads with wood and then threw out their bodies unburied [*probalein akedeuta ta somata*]" (Plut. *Per.* 28.1–3). According to Plutarch, it was Duris who first narrated the calumnious "tragedy" (*epitragodei*) about what happened to the Samians after they were defeated in a war stemming from their refusal to submit to Athenian command. Whether fact or fiction, the story of the horrific fate of the Samians was ostensibly used by Duris (and is treated by Plutarch) as a story that characterizes Pericles as severe (*omoteta, deinos*) and that therefore casts the Athenians in a bad light. The details of the story reflect how an ancient commentator would analyze penal severity and reveal how a punishment could be divided into component parts. Gernet writes: "Punishment fundamentally entails a certain formalism—we might even say symbolism—one that has survived till very late in our own society and that is naturally more conspicuous in the most ancient societies. It is never idle to ask what is the significance of the rituals that accompany punishment or that are actually involved in executing it."[2] So to the details of Duris's story. Duris's story presents the punishment as divided, formally into four components. First, the Samians are taken into a public place (the marketplace) and displayed. Second, they are bound to a piece of equipment called "the wood." Third, they are tortured and then killed. Finally, their bodies (*somata*) are disposed (*probalein*) without the standard burial rites (*akedeuta*). Scholars writing on ancient Athenian punishment have used this story only to discuss the piece of equipment called "the board." But it is the other elements of the punishment that actually give us information about the nature and severity of the treatment suffered by the Samians: their public exhibition, the physical torture, and the lack of burial. References to the public display and public memorializations of the condemned, to the abuse of the body, and to the problem of burial appear regularly in Athenian descriptions of punishment. In this chapter I begin with a quick synopsis of punishments and who executed them. But then I examine each of the three symbolic elements of Athenian punishment for its semantic weight and social and political relevance.

It is no accident that the narrative structure of Duris's story models the formal structure of Athenian punishment and decisions about what to do with the bodies of the condemned. Duris wishes to criticize the nature and workings of Athenian power; he constructs his story in order to lay bare and make visible the ways in which it worked. The rhetorical device that allows the Samian Duris to make this criticism is the introduction of the body of the condemned to public conversation. Duris's detailed description of what happened to the Samians in his story makes his story unlike most Athenian discussions of punishment. The typical Athenian response to a punishment was to look at the body of the condemned but to say nothing about it. Details about the execution of punishment are generally sparse and can be gleaned only here and there in historical texts. Duris rhetorically holds up the bodies of the dead and says, "Look what has happened to them," and his presentation of the bodies to his audience

breaks the Athenian code of silence—silence about the body of the condemned—that was crucial to maintaining the Athenian system of punishment.
Duris's refusal to be silent about the bodies challenges the justice, legitimacy,
and authority of Pericles' actions.

At the end of this chapter, we will consider another case in which the body of
the condemned was brought before public view in order to challenge the legitimacy of a punishment: Demosthenes' presentation of the disfranchised arbitrator Strato to his jury in his case against Meidias. Demosthenes' methods of
contestation will confirm the important relationship in Athens between the body
of the condemned and silence. Once we understand the nature of the peace built
on such a silence, we will also be able to assess the meaning of the amnesty:
the democracy's response to its greatest enemies, the oligarchs who overthrew
the democratic regime at the end of the fifth century.

THE DETAILS: PUNISHMENTS AND THEIR EXECUTORS

We have detailed evidence of only one execution carried out by an Athenian.
This was the execution of a Persian commander named Artayctes by an Athenian general during wartime and outside of Athens. Herodotus describes the
execution by saying that Artayctes was fastened to "a board" on the headland
where he died from "hanging" there (*pros sanidas pros passaleusantes anekre-
masan*, 7.33, 9.120; 9.122 *anakremasthentos*). Like the Samians, Artayctes died
after having been somehow attached to a "board." It is generally thought that a
device known as the *apotumpanismos* in classical sources was responsible for
these deaths from being "hung" (*anakremasan*), "fastened" (*passaleusantes*), or
"bound" "in the wood" or "to the wood" (*prodeo*; *pros sanidas en toi xuloi*).[3]
Most scholars accept the argument that the *apotumpanismos* provided for a
form of crucifixion in which the wrongdoer was attached to a wooden cross not
by having nails hammered into hands and feet but rather by having iron-collars
fastened around the neck, wrists, and feet; it is possible that the neck collar
could be tightened to cause suffocation.[4] In the early twentieth century, archaeologists unearthed a mass grave at Phaleron that contained seventeen skeletons
who seem to have suffered such a death. Each skeleton had iron collars around
its neck, wrists, and ankles and remnants of wood were attached to the collars.[5]

The punishment of being "fastened" and of being put "in the wood" did not,
however, always lead to death. These phrases were used to describe not only
execution by *apotumpanismos* but also the temporary public exhibition of a
wrongdoer in some sort of device equivalent to the stocks.[6] Thieves, for example, had to spend five days in the device on top of paying a penalty, thanks to
Solon's legislation.[7] In Solon's day, the stocks were called the *podokakke*, according to Lysias, who glosses the word for his fourth-century audience as
meaning "bound in the wood" (*en toi xuloi dedesthai*, 10.16).[8]

It has been suggested that the *apotumpanismos* and the device used for the
stocks may have been one and the same piece of equipment, and the suggestion

is plausible. If the neck collar on the *apotumpanismos* was adjustable, it could have been tightened to cause suffocation, or it could have been left loose so the wrongdoer would hang on display in public but without being in danger of his life.[9] One reference to being put "in the wood" suggests that the collar may well have been adjustable. In Aristophanes' *Thesmophoriazousae* (1001–3), the troublemaker Mnesilochus is put into "the wood" after he has tried to pass at a festival as a woman. He is displayed in all his fancy dress and desperately requests both that he not be exhibited and that he have the "fastens" loosened (*chalason ton helon*) rather than tightened or "hammered in" (*epikroueis*).[10] Similarly, both the Samians and Artayctes were hung on "boards," but the former hung there for ten days without dying while Artayctes seems to have died rather quickly.[11] It is possible that the same piece of machinery was used to exhibit the wrongdoer and to destroy him. The stocks, and only the stocks, were sometimes also described with the more specific phrases "four-holed wood" or "five-holed wood," which might seem to set this device apart from the *apotumpanismos*. But such phrases could equally well describe the device that killed the people found at Phaleron.[12]

The list of punishments used by the Athenians includes other forms of capital punishment: the hemlock made famous (or infamous) by Socrates and, in military contexts, executions by stoning and by sword.[13] House razing and a refusal of burial (*ataphia*) were sometimes used to increase the amount of punishment inflicted on the capital offender. Noncapital offenses were punished with whipping, torture, fines, confiscation of property, public exhibition in the stocks, imprisonment, disfranchisement or the loss of particular political rights (*atimia*), and exile from the city (*phuge* or *atimia*). In the archaic city *atimia* referred to the exile that resulted when a single pursuer chased a single pursued wrongdoer past the borders of their city. By the classical period *atimia* had evolved into more limited forms of disfranchisement—in particular, the loss of the right to speak in political spaces (the assembly and the courts),[14] the loss of the right to enter political spaces (the assembly, courts, *and* agora),[15] the loss of the right to enter specifically religious spaces,[16] the loss of the right to enter the harbor, the loss of the right to cross the Hellespont, and the loss of the right to stay in Attica.[17] Private citizens could punish slaves with imprisonment in a millhouse (Lys. 1.18; Dem. 45.33; Eur. *Cyc.* 240), and the slaves' susceptibility to corporal punishment was a mark of their servility (Dem. 22.55).[18] Whipping and torture were also reserved for slaves (with a few important exceptions), but citizens could suffer any combination of the other penalties.[19]

Magistrates had some responsibility for implementing punishments but most of the work of execution was left to private citizens. As we have seen, male citizens could kill nocturnal thieves, adulterers, certain other wrongdoers caught in the act, murderers who had violated their *atimia*, and those who were caught conspiring against the democracy. The Eleven prison keepers and their subordinate, a slave executioner called the *demokoinos*, supervised executions that resulted from a trial. In the case of executions for murder, the prosecutor was allowed to watch the execution. The Eleven and the *demokoinos* also supervised imprisonment (for those awaiting trial and those punished with a prison sentence) and the "stocks."[20] But for the most part citizens had to execute their own punishments.

The successful prosecutor was responsible for collecting monetary penalties—both those owed to him and those owed to the city.[21] The defendant was supposed to pay his fine voluntarily and he had to give sureties, who would themselves be liable for the fine if the defendant failed to make his deadline. If neither the defendant nor his sureties paid the fine, the prosecutor could simply go to the defendant's house and take items equivalent in value to the damages awarded.[22] A prosecutor who did not think that he was strong enough to do this could carry out another suit, the *dike exoules*, in order to employ the help of public officials in collecting what was due.[23] Those who owed penalties to the city became *atimoi* if they failed to pay by a certain date.[24]

A city official was responsible for seeing that nobody who was *atimos* or disfranchised showed up at the assembly. But, again, the punishment of *atimia* in its many forms generally depended for enforcement on private citizens and on the community at-large rather than on any of the magistrates. The *atimos* was expected to keep himself out of the areas forbidden to him—whether that was the whole city or only its public spaces—but anyone could (presumably) tell the *atimos* to leave areas from which the *atimos* was prohibited. Any citizen could also bring a suit against the *atimos* for the violation of *atimia*, and conviction on such a charge brought a penalty of death. The *polis* as a community enforced *atimia,* and so it was the democratic collective as a whole that in the last resolve backed up financial penalties.

The expectation that wrongdoers would inflict their own *atimia* was such that a defendant in a murder trial was given the chance, after his first speech, to leave the country if he wanted (Dem. 23.69–70), and homicides were supposed to make their own way out of the city, as a sentence of exile for involuntary homicide reveals: "The man convicted of involuntary homicide must leave according to an established road, at certain stated times, and be in exile [*pheugein*] until he is forgiven by some one of the family of the victim. The law concerned with this also prescribes the manner of his return" (Dem. 23.72; cf. 23.31). Even convicted murderers, who were being held in prison while they awaited execution, were expected to make a jailbreak and flee the land (cf. Plato *Crit.* 44b-c). The community itself was the final enforcer of the punishment even in cases of capital punishment. These were the penalties and such were the responsibilities for the enforcement of them. But what did they mean? The first topic that must be explored in an attempt to understand the symbolic formalism of Athenian punishment is social memory.

Two Forms of Memory: Remembering and Forgetting

As we have seen, situations of punishment depended on and were used to create social knowledge. This was especially true in the case of the *graphe*: one of the most important features of the *graphe* was that a conviction under this procedure was followed by the erection of official memorials of punishment.[25] The resulting inscriptions on *stelai* could be called "examples" (*paradeigma*).[26] Wrongdoers themselves could be described as people who had been or whose names had been "written into a stele" (*gegrammenous oun autous amphoterous en tei stelei*) (e.g., Arist. *Rhet.* 1400a32–36; Dem. 47.22).[27] Bronze *stelai* and pillars, however, were by no means the only form of memorial available for the insertion of stories of punishment into the public memory. The convicted wrongdoer was an example (*paradeigma*) and therefore also a memorial. Lycurgus, for instance, says of a general who was punished for failing to bury the dead: "And all of these things happened while you were leading as general, so how do you dare to live and to see the light of the sun, and to intrude on the marketplace, now that you have become a reminder [*hupomnema*] of shame and disgrace for your fatherland." The children of wrongdoers were sometimes subject to their parent's *atimia*, and so they too could serve as reminders of earlier events.[28] The community's networks of social knowledge and social memory were the executioner of reputation not only in the city's public spaces but also across time—some of the force of punishment lay in its guarantee that a wrongdoer would be remembered precisely as a wrongdoer; the city's narrative of his life and not the wrongdoer's would be what persisted in the social memory.

The memorialization of a punishment could occur even before the inscriptions were set up. According to Demosthenes (24.114), binding was inflicted as a penalty so that everybody might see the bound man and so that he would live in disgrace for the rest of his life. We twice hear the argument that an execution should be carried out for public viewing.[29] Aeschines suggests that one of the worst parts of suffering a capital sentence was that one had to look into the jeering face of one's enemy (Aes. 2.181–2). Places of execution could themselves be turned into landmarks in the topography of social memory.[30] Aeschines perpetuates one such spot when he describes the place where an unmarried daughter, after she was caught sleeping around, was walled up with a horse and trampled to death. He says to his jurors: "Even today the foundations of this house stand in your city, and the place [*topos*] is called 'at the horse and girl'" (Aes. 1.182).[31] The city's social memory had its own topography; the landscape helped Athenians to remember their city's social norms.

One punishment, however, served not for remembering but for forgetting. As we have seen, the penalty of *atimia* could include any one of several limitations on a citizen's ability to use public space or to act in accordance with the norms for public action. Such a punishment required that the citizen disappear from the sight of the citizenry, and *atimia* thus required that the city forget about a wrongdoer. Andocides underscores the point when he writes the following about his choice to go into exile: "At the time, I myself understood my misfortune, and I perceived that it would be most pleasant to act in such a way and to set up my daily life somewhere where I would be least likely to be seen by you" (And. 2.10).

The exile lost his community once he was expelled from networks of social memory. He became, in the words of Antiphon, "a beggar in a strange land, an old man without a city" (Ant. 2.2.0). Lysias emphasizes the degree to which exile cuts people off from communal relations when he says: "I will become the most wretched of creatures if I am sent into exile unjustly; I am childless and alone, my house would be desolate, my mother in need of everything, and I would be robbed of my fatherland" (7.41). Not only would he be cut off from his city, but he would be unable to preserve his household. For the fugitive homicide, the matter goes so far that he may no longer be called an Athenian and can be said to have no share in that name (*ton gar phugada to tes poleos ou proseipen onoma, hes ouk esti metousia autoi*, Dem. 23.41). The capacity of the exile to reestablish himself in a foreign city only underscored his complete disappearance from the nexus of social knowledge operative in his home city. His capacity to become a member of another community confirms the extent to which he could be forgotten by his own.[32]

Wrongdoers who stayed in the city and who suffered disfranchisement were also forgotten but in a different sense. They lost their right to prosecute or to defend themselves by trial. Thus they might be wronged at any time without hope of redress. The *atimos* became an invisible man who had lost whatever control he might once have had over the city's networks of social knowledge. His safety depended on his total disappearance from the mind's eye of the citizenry.[33] In one speech we find: "Now that I have been summoned to court by these men, I will run away if I should be convicted unjustly, for how would it be possible for me to mingle with the citizens with any optimism. How could I do that when I already know, if I but think ahead, how eager my opponents are [to act against me] and cannot see how I would manage to get my just rights?" (Lys. 9.21).[34] It is only from those who go into exile that we hear an expectation that their acts will eventually be forgotten because of their departure.[35] Thus *atimia* and exile stand in contrast to other punishments, asking, as they do, that the community forget the wrongdoer.

The *atimos* and exile were like the scapegoats annually sent away from the city during the festival of Thargelion. Orators were explicit about the parallel, as Lysias is here: "Now it is necessary to think that in punishing Andocides and being rid of him, you cleanse the city and that you are escorting out of the city and sending away a *pharmakos*" (Lys. 6.53). Both wrongdoer and scapegoat lost their place in the city and also their standing as Athenians. But the city made sure that it drove out and forgot about those citizens whose social reputations were least worth remembering. The scapegoats chosen by the Athenians were always two of the poorest and most insignificant members of the citizenry. Their forgettable social status qualified them for the ritual role of disappearing forever, bearing with them the burden of the city's ills.[36] Wrongdoers, who were expelled from the city also took away from the city, in their own persons, that which was not worth remembering. They took away everything that could not be called Athenian and left behind only what the city wanted to remember as being Athenian.

The scapegoat festival ritualized a process of "communal forgetting" that was sometimes acted out in certain forms of punishment, and the drama and regularity of the scapegoat ritual teach us an important point about social memory. Every year the Athenians *remembered* to drive out the two scapegoats and to forget about them. Remembering and forgetting happen at the same time, and forgetting is not opposed to remembering but rather another form of remembering.[37] Both are tools to be used in the construction of social memory because memories (whether social or personal) are made as much by what is left out or forgotten as by what is included or remembered. The city had to decide what to leave out of its memory or what to forget, as much as what to remember. Both decisions were crucial to the construction of social memory. A wrongdoer's actions had challenged the city's moral code. That challenge was erased when the wrongdoer was brought in line with the other citizens and submitted to their norms. That submission had to be memorialized in order that the citizenry might be reconfirmed, but the challenge posed to the city by the wrongdoer was also erased when it was simply forgotten and when the wrongdoer disappeared from sight and knowledge. The citizens who forgot the wrongdoer also forgot that their system of value had been challenged or upset, and the stability of their system was thereby restored to them.[38]

The Symbolism of Remembering and Forgetting

The dichotomy between remembering and forgetting, inscribing and expelling, arises in the Athenian "mythohistorical" imagination and its stories about punishment, and this mythohistorical imagination can shed light on the symbolic weight of these dichotomies. From the perspective of fourth-century Athenians, the punishers of myth and pre-democratic history tended especially to inflict four kinds of punishment: stoning, binding, exile, and the precipitation of wrongdoers off cliffs and onto rocks. Stoning, binding, and cases of exile turn up more than once in Homer. As for precipitation, in the *Iliad* Zeus threatens to hurl (*rhipso*) any disobedient god into the deepest chasm beneath the earth (*bathiston hupo chthonos berethron*), which is to say, into Tartarus (8.14). Barkan (1935, 54–56, 92) points out that the stories of the death of Astyanax—the son of Hector and Andromache who was hurled from the walls of Troy after the fall of the city to the Greeks—are based on the idea that precipitation might be a form of execution. All four of these forms of punishment—stoning, binding, exile, and precipitation—appear in tragedy also.[39] Although these four archaic punishments shared a goal, the eradication of a problem found within the community, they differed in respect to the method they employed in effecting that eradication: whether through a process of *containment and consumption* of the wrongdoer *at the center* of the community or through a process of *expulsion* of the wrongdoer *from* the community.

Punishments of containment or consumption are best exemplified by stonings, which, as they are described in tragedy and by Xenophon and Herodotus, generally follow a recognizable pattern. First, the sight of or spreading social knowledge about a wrongdoer inspires a stoning mob. Thus witnesses, who are explicitly and repeatedly said to "see" a wrongdoing, will gather into a stoning mob upon sight of the wrongdoing as a group of herdsmen do when they see Orestes kill a sheep in Euripides' *Iphigeneia in Tauris* (290, 308; cf. Eur. *Or.* 871; Soph. *Aj.* 228, 255), and Euripides describes Helen as fearing that she will be stoned when the Argives see her.[40] Not only visual but also verbal transmissions of social knowledge could inspire a stoning mob. Xenophon tells a story about seeing a group of soldiers rushing off to stone someone; when he stops them to ask whom they are stoning and why, the soldiers respond that a simple hue and cry (*thorubos*) and shouts of "Strike, strike, throw, throw" had helped to rally the crowd (*Ana.* 5.7; cf. Eur. *Or.* 730, 871; Soph. *Aj.* 228; Ar. *Acharn.* 318). On Xenophon's account of the stoning, the soldiers were joining in without having any idea of whom they were stoning or why. Rumor, bare communication of the community's need to exterminate a problem, had brought the soldiers into the mob.[41]

After social knowledge had generated a stoning mob, those holding stones circled (*kukloi*) the wrongdoer and threw not only stones but also curses (Eur. *IT* 331; Hdt. 9.5; and Eur. *Or.* 442–44, 763, by extension). Both the circle and the mob's cursing shouts were an integral part of this form of punishment.[42] Thus, the chorus of Sophocles' *Ajax* abandons Ajax and refuses to support him in his lonely fight against the Atreids precisely because it fears the "stony stoning curse" (*litholeuston Are*) (Soph. *Aj.* 254). A stoning, with its curses, made visible and gave embodiment to the power lodged in networks of social knowledge. The stones and hurled curses are analogous to each other: each expressed the community's desire to enforce its social norms.

The power of the group over the individual that was exemplified by a stoning was sufficient to convince even a hero to modify his behavior. The Euripidean Achilles, for instance, is dissuaded from his efforts to prevent the pre–Trojan War sacrifice of his bride-to-be Iphigeneia because he both hears the cries of the soldiers against him and sees that they are preparing to stone him (*soma leusthenai petroisi*) (Eur. *IA* 1350–51). Achilles is reintegrated to the Greek army by his decision to go along with the sacrifice. His change of heart leads Clytemnestra to remark that "The mob is a fearsome thing of evil" (*to polu gar deinon kakou*, Eur. *IA* 1357). "Fearsome" or "clever" was also the word that Herodotus used to describe the Athenians when they stoned Lycidas. (It is also a central concept in Sophocles' "Ode to Man.")[43] Most important, the stoning mob contained the wrongdoer at the center of the community and, as a punishment of consumption, had the power to reconstitute and transform even the hero's behavior within the community.

Punishments of expulsion did the opposite sort of work and are best exemplified by precipitation, which did not embed a wrongdoer in networks of social memory but removed a problem from the city for good by literally pushing the wrongdoer beyond the community's borders.[44] In Euripides' *Iphigeneia in Tauris*, the king Thoas orders his men to ride along the shores of his land to look for Orestes and Pylades (1423–30). When they find them, they are to hurl (*rhipsai*) them onto the seaside rocks. Later (postclassical) stories of precipitation also emphasize the idea of shores and boundaries. The city of Leucas sacrificed a wrongdoer as a scapegoat to avert evil by hurling (*rhiptesthai*) the criminal from a rock into the sea, according to Strabo. To make sure that the wrongdoer was removed from the community, men stationed below the cliff in boats gathered bits of the wrongdoer (whether living or dead), "such as they could," (*perisozein eis dunamin*), and took the remains beyond the borders (*ton horon exo*) (Strabo 10.2.9). The emphasis on borders in stories of precipitation and expulsion highlights how these punishments aimed to define the boundaries of the community without the wrongdoer.

According to Pausanias, the people of Elis used precipitation, the punishment of boundary crossing, as a grimly appropriate punishment for the crime of boundary crossing itself. The Olympic games were restricted to men, and the people of Elis legislated that any woman found at the games could be thrown off a mountain at the border of the territory of Elis. (It is intriguing that the one woman who was caught at the Olympics was also caught cross-dressing.) Women could also be hurled over the city's boundary precipices if they had been caught merely on the far side of the river bounding the territory of Elis (as if on their way to the Olympics). Pausanias writes: "Along the road to Olympia before you cross the Alpheios River there is the border [*estin horos*] with Skillountos, and here one comes upon a mountain with high cliffs [*petrais hupselais apotomon*]. The law at Elis orders the precipitation [*othein*] of any of the women caught attending the Olympic games or even on the other side of the river Alpheios" (5.67).[45]

The verbs used to denote precipitation, *rhipsai* (cast, throw away, hurl) and *othein* (thrust, shove, force away, repulse, push off) imply a violence of motion, a process in which the convicted wrongdoer becomes an object, a projectile to be sent elsewhere. In Athens, the *atimos* who was seen where he was not meant to be could be driven away (*elauno*) by private citizens.[46] According to the LSJ definition, the verb *elauno* is used in the *Iliad* to describe the whipping and driving of horses (5.366), and in general it describes violent motion and was used to mean "drive" and "set in motion," or "persecute," "plague," and "strike with a weapon but never with a missile." The *atimos* himself became the missile projected outward from the community.

Euripides uses the verb *rhipsai* to describe the precipitation of Astyanax in *Trojan Women*, a play that tells the tale of what happened to the women of Troy after they were captured by the Greeks in the Trojan War. In Euripides' version of Astyanax's death, it is not Andromache but Agamemnon who decides to kill Hector's son by throwing him from the walls of Troy. Agamemnon seeks a total eradication of his enemy by pursuing the complete expulsion of Hector's line from the *polis*. The prospect of the precipitation, the expulsion of the boy from his community's enclosures, inspires Andromache to speak at length about what it means to be cut off from kin and supporters. She understands that the precipitation marks the expulsion of Hector's household from the city and the erasure of a family.

Two different types of power functioned in punishments of containment or consumption and the punishments of expulsion and they can be understood with the help of Seaford's readings of the punishments found in tragedy. In tragedy, daughters and wives are regularly locked up when they are thought to have violated norms of chastity (or other social norms). On Seaford's reading, their families are trying to "reexert control" over them by imprisoning them.[47] Sons, in contrast, "suffer export in uncivilized unbounded space," especially when they are a threat to their fathers.[48] Most famous, the baby Oedipus is sent to be exposed on a mountainside after his father hears the prophecy that his son will grow up to kill him and steal his wife and throne. Punishments of containment or consumption are used as long as it is possible to maintain control over the wrongdoer and in order to modify behavior within the city. But punishments of expulsion aim simply to remove from the city a problem that can no longer be controlled and whose presence in the city is antithetical to the continued existence of the city. Each form of punishment entails a different sort of power. The punishments of containment are a claim by the punisher to be able to control the actions of the punished person completely. This is the power that the ruler exercises over the subject. Punishments of expulsion are an admission by the punisher that he or she does not in fact have control over the wrongdoer. The ruler employs this power against those who are no longer subjects but enemies. Each form of punishment marked the status of the person who was punished relative to the person who carried out the punishment.

The two forms of punishment were not always mutually exclusive and could be combined, mixed, or substituted for one another.[49] In one myth (Konon *FGH* 26F1) after Tennes is accused by his amorous stepmother of making advances, his father locks him in a cask (*kata kleiei*) (as if he were a girl) and sends the cask out to sea (the punishment for a boy). The father also has the stepmother buried alive and has her accomplice stoned. Punishments of expulsion and consumption could similarly be combined within the city. Thus the state debtor, who was inscribed in a *stele*, became *atimos* when he failed to pay by his due date. He was first memorialized at the center of the city and then expelled from the networks of social memory. His expulsion as an *atimos* was memorialized by the same inscription that memorialized his original debt to the state. Each Athenian punishment made use of the elements of expulsion and consumption in different ways and to different degrees.

The two types of power relationships involved in punishments of containment and expulsion also map onto gender roles. The distinction between what happened to daughters and what happened to sons meant that punishments of containment and consumption were associated with the female, a fact that Cantarella uses to explain a curious plot twist in Sophocles' *Antigone*. In that play Creon proclaims that anyone who buries the body of Polyneices will die by stoning, but when Antigone defies his order, Creon substitutes another, more total, punishment of consumption for the stoning. He imprisons Antigone in a cave with just enough food to keep her eventual starvation from counting as murder. A death within the ring of citizens is replaced with the consumption of the starving Antigone within the earth itself. The stoning would have required that Creon rely on the townspeople to carry out the punishment, but the imprisonment is totally within his own control. It marks his power to an even greater degree than the stoning would have and makes Antigone twice a subject: she is both citizen subject to ruler and woman subject to man. Cantarella reads the change of policy as being necessary because the second, more complete form of consumption is more appropriate for a woman.[50]

Punishments of consumption used against men feminized them by marking them as insufficiently powerful to become enemies of the city and to provide a comprehensive challenge to their city's regime. This idea is at the heart of a brief dispute between Aegisthus and the chorus in Aeschylus's *Agamemnon*. After the death of Agamemnon, Clytemnestra and Aegisthus struggle to secure their control over the city of Argos. In the process, Aegisthus comes into conflict with the chorus, which threatens him with stoning, saying: "You will not escape stony curses hurled by the people [*demorripheis eusimous aras*]" (*Ag*. 1615–16). Aegisthus responds by threatening the old men of the chorus in turn not with stoning but with imprisonment, the more intense form of consumption, which was also the woman's penalty. He says, "What makes you think you can speak that way, when you sit at the lower oar and it is those who rule the higher thwart who control the ship [*kratounton ton epi zugoi doros*]. . . . You will soon perceive that it is hard [*baru*] to be taught [*didaskesthai*] at your age, old as you are. . . . Bonds and pangs of hunger are two of the sharpest doctors [*exochotatai / iatromanteis*] available to teach the *phren*" (1617–1623). Aegisthus wants the chorus to stop speaking the way they do, and claims that his punishment of consumption is the best method of teaching and reconstituting wrongdoers, of exerting control over them, of integrating them into his vision for the city. The two threatened punishments of consumption are embedded in a struggle over who will control the political order in the city and over who will sit quietly at the lower oar.

Aegisthus's suggestion that he will use imprisonment against the old men of the chorus is a slur against their maleness. But the chorus lacks political power and therefore has no way to respond other than to try, rhetorically, to invert the insult. In the next line, the old men shout at Aegisthus: "You woman!" (1625). In the city, punishments of containment or consumption forced men to act like women: they forced men to acquiesce in a social order that did not necessarily harmonize with their own views on how the city should be constituted or what their role in the city should be.

The tropes of containment and expulsion also factored into rituals of religious purification. Here too the distinction between the two main types of ritual turns around the question of whether someone or something polluted can be reintegrated to the community. The word *perikathairo* or "purify in a circle" was used to describe cases of purification where the individual would be seated submissively in the middle of an encircling group that would purify him. The purification ritual acted out the idea that the impure individual could be cleansed and reconstituted by being fixed in the heart of the community. Moreover, the individual's seated submissiveness confirmed that the cleansing was bringing the contained individual back in line with community norms. According to Parker, the idea of encirclement was so important to purification that the word *perikathairo* could be used to describe even cases of purification where there was no seated, encircled, and submissive individual.[51]

A second type of purification depended not on encirclement but on expulsion in order to work its cleansing powers. Some rites of purification produced off-scourings or leftover remains from purificatory sacrifices. These leftover sacrificial remnants were still polluted and could not be purified. They had to be expelled from the community, and the expulsion of such polluted remains was described by the word *ekpempo*. According to Hippocrates in *On the Sacred Disease*, "People bury some of the [offscourings] in the ground, they throw some in the sea, and others they carry off to the mountains where nobody can see or tread on them" (Hipp. 148.44–48 J, 1.42G [Loeb 4.40]).[52] Parker adds that offscourings could also be left at the crossroads. The community could cleanse itself by expelling what was polluted and what could not be made pure to any of several distinct removes. The polluted leftovers could be buried somewhere within the land, they could be thrown to the sea from which they might return, they could be left at the crossroads where they might be seen and trod upon, or they could be removed to the mountains, where they would finally be completely absented from the community's networks of sight.

The idea that something might be leftover after a process of purification is a key to understanding punishments of expulsion. Punishments of containment and consumption attempted to reconstitute the wrongdoer within the confines of the city. Such punishments attempted to achieve the wrongdoer's total acquiescence in the community's system of value. Sometimes such total acquiescence could not be brought about. This was the case when the wrongdoer had posed a challenge to the society's norms and structures too great for the person to be reintegrated to the city's social orders. The wrongdoer's continued presence in the city would constitute a leftover form of social disruption, a continued contestation of the Athenian system of value. Such wrongdoers could not be "purified," only expelled. As Parker points out, the word *ekpempo* more frequently refers to exiles, *people* who are driven out of the community, than to offscourings.

Two words were used to denote the polluted leftovers that had to be expelled after a purificatory sacrifice. The general term for such offscourings was *katharmata*, and Dinarchus uses this word to describe Demosthenes when he recommends that the latter be exiled (1.16). But offscourings that were expelled after the purification of, specifically, a house were called *oxuthumia* or "sharp anger."[53] We have already come across the adjective *oxuthumos* in several important contexts—most important, it was used of the Areopagites in Aeschylus's *Eumenides*, of the wasps in Aristophanes' *Wasps*, and of the outspoken type of man preferred by Aristotle in the *Rhetoric* (Aristotle also uses *oxuthumos* to describe excessive anger in the *Nicomachean Ethics*). The wrongdoer who had to be expelled from the community was one who continued to be the subject of a vestigial anger. His or her presence and challenge to the city's system of value was incompatible with peace. What was expelled from the community when the offscourings were expelled, when the offender was expelled, was anger. Communal anger is thus seen to be the emotion that arises against whatever residue of individuality continues to challenge or violate social norms. Punishments of expulsion were thus an admission that the process of integrating citizens into an orderly social hierarchy would produce "leftovers," those people who could never be integrated on the basis of the normative structures used to organize the city. Punishments of expulsion admitted to the impossibility of ever achieving total integration of all citizens into a social order based on a single and perfectly coherent sets of norms. They not only admitted to the permanence of social disruption but also simultaneously required that citizens forget this fact.

If punishments of expulsion and forgetting cleansed the community by removing the wrongdoer and the incurable offscourings of anger from it and by removing the remnants of social disruption, punishments of remembering, punishments of consumption at the center of a community, cleansed the wrongdoer and the community by a process of communal involvement in the reconstitution of the wrongdoer. Cleansing was somehow achieved when the wrongdoer either submitted to community norms or when the wrongdoer's refusal or inability to submit was erased. Either way round *oxuthumia* or sharp anger was removed from the community. In these two ways anger, the disease of wrongdoing and punishment, could be cured. Both containment/memorialization and expulsion/forgetting contributed to the construction of social memory. The two ways of constructing social memory both worked to provide the citizens with a memory of their city's system of value as having achieved the complete integration of all members of the city—even those who might have resisted—into a single social order. The "clean" community was therefore a perfectly harmonious community where the political order had succeeded in installing a single system of value that was or seemed to be consistent across the citizenry. The moment of punishment established and memorialized a momentary and mythical stability where the city's social norms no longer seemed to be under contest. Once again, it is important to note that the two methods of containment and expulsion could sometimes be combined. One orator suggests that a wrongdoer be memorialized with an inscription put up among the offscourings at the crossroads (Hyp. fr. B23, 118).

The parallels between the formalism of purification and the formalism of punishment speak volumes, suggesting that there was a connection between the sacred and the just in Athens despite the fact that glimpses of religious law and religious prescription sneak into oratorical texts only infrequently. The parallel between purification and punishment is to be found not in the role of religion in punishment but rather in the centrality to both purification and punishment of the idea that everything within the walls of the city could and should somehow be made "clean." A moment of punishment approached the status of the sacred because it bespoke the community's desire to be integrated into a pure, harmonious order that would never have its conceptual system of value upset—

although it could be stable and absolutely hegemonic in myth alone—by the leftover, unassimilable forces that arose when individuals tried to subvert, revise, contest, and violate the city's norms and social order. Punishments of consumption sustained the myth of purity by invoking the power of memorialized consensus; punishments of expulsion did so by invoking the power of forgetfulness. Girard has argued that sacrificial rituals and judicial systems play parallel roles in social life. Each aims to prevent social conflict from erupting or raging beyond control.[54] The formalism of Athenian punishment reveals that punishment did indeed carry out the cleansing work of sacrifice.

War, like sacrifice, serves as a model for punishment, but only as a metaphorical model. Citizens liked to use the idea of war to describe situations in which something had gone wrong with their peace. The distinction between war and peace was one of the fundamental conceptual categories used by the Athenians to structure and formalize the execution of punishment (as we shall see in the next section). The parallel between war and torture, as analyzed by Scarry, is useful for exploring the struggles over norms, systems of value, and views of reality that are at stake not only in war but also, in a less systematic way, in punishment.[55] But punishment is not precisely the same thing as war. It consists of a struggle between citizens who once shared and who ostensibly wish to share again a relatively unified self-conception and system of value, not between people who start out as mortal enemies (if anything, civil war would be a closer analogue to punishment than interstate war). Moreover, war is won by means of force; punishment is won not only by means of force but also by means of acquiescence and in terms of a myth of acquiescence. Each therefore yields a different kind of peace. Scarry argues that the bodies of the injured give material reality, in the context of war, to the ideas and belief systems of the winning party. They can be invoked as proof of victory and described in ways that allow the winning side to fix the meaning of its conquest and the reality it desires. The memorialization of war requires the memorialization not only of the victory but also of the struggle, of the moment when a society faced the greatest challenge to its self-conception, a moment symbolized by piles of defeated bodies.

The city has no parallel desire to memorialize the struggle against the wrongdoer when the attack arises from within. A peaceful city wishes to think of itself as having always been and as always being peaceful and harmonious, as having established a system of value that allows for the roles of all citizens in the community to be perfectly integrated with one another. Wrongdoing challenges the myth of the harmonious, stable city. A disruption is evidence of a failure on the city's part and not a challenge over which to triumph. Punishment must memorialize restored harmony and hide the disruption.

The Athenians were silent about the bodies of the condemned when they punished. That silence allowed them to place more emphasis on general communal acquiescence in a system of norms than on the social disruption, struggle, and act of force that had resolved it. This silence was punishment's crucial concluding moment. To hear the silence we must investigate the treatment of the body of the condemned in Athens.

WAR AND PEACE, THE BODY AND SILENCE

During the fifth and fourth centuries, the Athenians carried out capital punishments both in the world of the peacetime city and in the military world of war. The *apotumpanismos* and hemlock were used in the city. The *apotumpanismos* was also used in war. But death by sword and stoning show up exclusively in military contexts. Xenophon's *Hellenica* and *Anabasis*, both of which narrate military ventures, contain not only the stories of stonings discussed earlier but also several stories of people whose throats were cut for wrongdoing.[56] The closest we come to seeing a stoning in the city of Athens is the death of Lycidas during the Persian Wars during the sojourn of the Athenians on Salamis.[57] The closest we come to seeing an execution by sword in the city is when democratic troops cut the throats of pirates and other wrongdoers (*aposphazen*) while they were garrisoned at Phyle during their war efforts against the oligarchs (Lys. 13.77–78). Wartime forms of punishment drew blood, but those used in the peacetime city—*apotumpanismos* and hemlock—did not.[58] The mechanism of the *apotumpanismos*, which employed collars and fastens rather than nails, even seems to have been constructed with an eye to avoiding drawing blood.[59] Thus was the line between peaceful and warlike punishments drawn. The Athenians seem to have distinguished their peacetime punishments not only from the context of bloody war but also from the context of sacrifice.[60] The words used to describe military executions by sword (e.g., *sphageus, aposphazein*) call to mind the vocabulary of sacrifice, and the Athenians not only avoided using these tools when they punished but also prohibited executions on festival days (Aes. 1.16). This fact points again to Girard's argument that judicial punishment comes on the scene after sacrifice as a second attempt to deal with social conflict and violence.

The idea that the Athenians limited themselves to executions that did not draw blood is supported by the fact that two other cities similarly regulated legitimate forms of public execution. According to Herodotus, the Spartans only killed at night (Hdt. 4.146), and Demosthenes reports that the Thracians, in accordance with their custom (*nomimou*), simply did not kill one another at all (23.169). The choices that a city made about how to punish were bound up with the citizenry's identity. A Spartan was someone who could not be executed during the day. An Athenian was someone whose blood could not be drawn during peacetime by a fellow citizen.

The peacetime protection of the body of the citizen distinguished citizens from slaves who could be imprisoned in mills and subjected to blows and whippings as punishment for their crimes.[61] Torture was another wartime tactic.[62] Within the city, the torture of citizens was banned in the late fifth century, but slaves could be tortured throughout the democracy.[63] In this context it is worth remembering that the Greek slave had frequently been a prisoner of war. Slaves (and metics) as foreigners lacked the privileges of peace that protected the body just as they lacked the inviolable right to a trial. The protections of peacetime guarded the citizen's and only the citizen's bodily integrity.

There were, however, situations in which the body of the citizen could be abused. Thieves could be put in the stocks for five days; citizens could be punished with imprisonment. The *apotumpanismos* was probably quite physically painful, and adulterers could be physically abused. As we have seen, an adulterer could be killed when caught in the act. If the adulterer was not killed immediately but was instead brought to trial and convicted, he was put at the mercy of the prosecutor. The prosecutor could treat the adulterer as he pleased in front of the whole court with one restriction: he could not use a knife on him.[64] This legal provision has mystified scholars, but it makes sense if we recognize the importance of ensuring that trials produced bloodless punishments. Fifth- and fourth-century comic references, as well as later Hellenistic references, suggest that after trial adulterers were subjected to depilation or to the insertion of a radish or a skorpios, a kind of poisonous fish, in the rectum. Such forms of physical abuse would have been especially painful because of the "stinging" or "burning" associated with the radishes and fish but they would not necessarily have drawn blood.[65] The contrast between the adulterer's pre and posttrial punishments highlights the degree to which a trial marked a transition from the context of war and bloodiness to the context of peace and bloodlessness. Similarly, military stonings and executions by sword were never preceded by a trial but arose only from the authoritative decision of a military official or from the mass action of the stoning mob.[66] The trial was a ritual that established the existence of a peacetime context and asserted the bodily integrity of the citizen.

Several scholars have rejected the historicity of "radishing" on the grounds that oratorical sources do not yield any explicit references to the forms of corporal abuse suffered by adulterers and comic sources are unlikely to provide useful historical information. Carey, however, has recently pointed out that it would have been uncharacteristic for the orators to discuss the abuse of adulterers openly because they generally resorted to silence and euphemism when discussing sexual matters.[67] Thus Isaeus speaks scornfully of an adulterer who had been caught in adultery and had suffered "what it is fitting for those who do these sorts of things to suffer" (Isae. 8.44). Isaeus never says more specifically what suffering is fitting for an adulterer.[68] A certain openness and freedom with obscene language, sexual language, and scatological language and most particularly with the body was permitted in comedy but not in oratory. Carey argues that we cannot rule out the possibility that Isaeus's vagueness is covering up the obscenity of a practice, radishing, that comedians are willing to discuss.[69]

Theophrastus's discussion of radishes in the *History of Plants* also seems infected by circumlocution. Theophrastus describes the size and shape of radishes and says of them, as he does of no other vegetable, "Their size and shape are clear to everyone because of the use to which they are put" (*HP* 7.2.2).[70] To what use were radishes put that made their size and shape so clear to everyone? The possibility that Theophrastus was referring to radishing cannot be ruled out. What is important here, especially in the example from Isaeus, is simply the observation that the orators tended to speak only indirectly about the penal abuse of the citizen's body. Despite the fact that citizens might suffer the stocks, imprisonment, the *apotumpanismos*, and whatever physical abuse adulterers were subjected to, Demosthenes goes so far as to say that only slaves answered with their bodies for their offenses and that freemen could protect their persons even in the worst cases, since in most cases, the law punished with fines (Dem. 22.54–55).[71]

The orators refrained from discussing not only the noncapital corporal punishment of citizens, but also execution. They eagerly recommended that their opponents suffer the "most extreme penalties," but when it came to actually mentioning an execution, they once again resorted to circumlocution, as Todd points out.[72] Socrates' executioners are referred to as: "Those taking care of this thing" (*ton toutou epimelethenton*, Xen. *Apol.* 7). In another case, the Eleven are instructed "to take the wrongdoer and lead him away and, in the necessary place, do the things that follow from this" (*humeis de labontes kai apagagontes hoi hendeka hou dei ta ek touton prattete*, Xen. *Hell.* 2.3.54–55). The tendency to vagueness reflects a need for silence about what happened to the body of the condemned citizen.

Only five executions (or near executions) of citizens by the *apotumpanismos* are mentioned in Athenian sources, and three of the five are all mentioned in one speech, Lysias's *Against Agoratus*.[73] All three of the executed wrongdoers described by Lysias were not native citizens but had become citizens by decree of the Athenian citizenry. Todd (1997) has argued convincingly that Lysias's open discussion of their deaths by *apotumpanismos* is a way of impugning their social status.[74] As Todd points out, other orators' suggestions that their opponents deserve to die on the *apotumpanismos* also appear only in contexts where an orator is trying to point out that his opponent's citizenship is of doubtful validity.

A similar pattern emerges in respect to torture. Fourth-century sources report three cases where a citizen or freeman was subjected to torture or threatened with torture, despite the law against torturing citizens. Two of the three victims tortured had started life as slaves. The third man had always been free but was also a naturalized and not a native citizen.[75] Citizens whose corporal punishment and torture is reported inevitably turn out not to be "real" citizens after all. Noneuphemistic and open discussion of their corporal sufferings seems to provide a way of making that rhetorical point, and to subject a citizen to corporal punishment proved him to be something less than a citizen. It is no wonder, then, that Glaucon rattles off a string of corporal punishments when asked in Plato's *Republic* to list the worst punishments: whipping, binding, blinding, and execution on a stake (presumably the same thing as being put on or in the wood) (*mastigosetai; streblosetai, dedesetai, ekkauthesetai tophthalmon, teleuton pantakaka pathon anaschinduleuthesetai*, Plato *Rep.* 362a; cf. Hsch. *EM* 100.51).

The citizen defined himself in part with respect to his bodily integrity. Punishments could affect his body provided that they did not draw his blood. But even this much corporal punishment could not be acknowledged. For a citizen to discuss these punishments would have been to admit the violation of his citizenly bodily integrity. If a punished wrongdoer were to break the silence about his body, he would simultaneously be admitting to his own failure to be worthy of citizenship. He had no real choice but to acquiesce in his physical suffering. Citizens received not only protection for their bodies but also the charge to be silent about their bodies. The Athenians honored a silence about the body of the condemned simultaneously to displaying and memorializing citizens in their corporal punishments. The adulterer was physically abused before the whole courtroom. His fellow citizens watched and then acquiesced in a corporal punishment, by saying nothing about it afterward. One condition of peaceful punishments was that they maintain the myth that the citizen body would not be injured. The silence of the condemned and of his fellow citizens about the citizen body confirmed the city's social orders—both the distinction between slave and citizen and the noncontestability of the city's punishments. The citizen who was punished according to the terms of peace received protection for his body but only, to some degree, in return for his silent acquiescence in his punishment.

The greatest silence that could be imposed on wrongdoers was to refuse them burial. References to punishment in Athenian texts reveal a focus not only on remembering or forgetting and on the treatment of body but also on the question of whether to bury the executed wrongdoer. The three formal elements of punishment, with which the chapter began, are not really distinct. Burial was an act of public memorialization, even when carried out by private families, and posed questions about how to use the body for memorialization. The question of whether to bury a wrongdoer was also a decision about whether to treat the wrongdoer like an enemy. A look at the topic of burial elucidates the role of the body and memorialization in drawing the line between peace and war.

Thucydides tells a story in which he contrasts Athenian and Spartan treatment of "enemies" with, implicitly, the Athenian treatment of friends. A crucial distinction between the treatment of an enemy and the treatment of a citizen or friend is that enemies are refused a trial; another key distinction is that enemies are refused burial. The story is this: during an early phase of the Peloponnesian War, two Athenian envoys managed to capture one Corinthian and three Lacedaemonians (2.67.4). The four captives were taken to Athens where they were put to death unjudged (*akritous*) despite their desire to speak in their own defense. The Athenians not only refused to let them speak before killing them but also threw the corpses into a chasm (*authemeron apekteinan pantas kai es pharagga esebalon*). This was done, Thucydides says, in revenge (*amunesthai*) for how the Spartans had treated some Athenian traders. According to the Athenians, the Spartans had caught a group of Athenian and allied traders sailing along the coast of the Peloponnese and had killed the "innocent traders" and then thrown them into a chasm (*apokteinantes kai es pharaggas esbalontes*).

The Spartans had done this, the Athenians thought, as part of a general effort to destroy all those people whom they should capture on the sea as "enemies" (*hos polemious diephtheiron*). To "destroy someone as an enemy" meant to treat him as the Spartans had treated the traders. It meant not only killing someone without a trial but also throwing out his body unburied (*ataphia*).[76]

The Athenians returned the corpses of some executed wrongdoers to their families for burial (e.g., Socrates), but they used *ataphia* for the worst traitors and temple robbers.[77] Phrynichus, Antiphon, and Archeptolemus were all condemned to death and *ataphia* for acts of treachery, and in one case the Athenians even dug up the bodies of a family of sixth-century tyrants and cast their bones over the borders of the land (*scholia* on Ar. *Lys.* 273). Those who suffered a refusal of burial were expelled to the fullest degree from the city; their corpses were cast into the utter oblivion and dishonor of forgetfulness.[78]

Parker argues that *ataphia* must be seen as a deprivation of honor in its extreme form given the importance of the correct treatment of corpses in Athenian thought (cf. Plato *Leg.* 959c). He comments, "One might even conclude that, with their honour, [the unburied wrongdoers] lost the power to pollute. This would lead to the paradox that, while no funeral or tomb is pure except that of the outstanding servant of the community, the only corpse that will not cause pollution if left unburied is that of the public enemy."[79] Pollution was caused when anger spread in the city. The unburied wrongdoer outside the bounds of the city inspired no one to anger. Such corpses, therefore, could not pollute. The unburied wrongdoer was like the offscourings from rites of purification, like the *katharmata* that, as Hippocrates said, should no longer be seen or walked on. The unburied wrongdoer, expelled beyond the borders of the community, was no longer embedded in the city's networks of social memory.

But the city sometimes went to great lengths to memorialize the disappearance of the wrongdoer's body. Sentences of *ataphia* could be supplemented by the requirement that the wrongdoer's property be confiscated, by the requirement that his house be razed, or by the requirement that his children be given permanent *atimia*. Non-Athenian cities also carried out such house razings and frequently converted the demolished property of the wrongdoer to other uses, usually public ones. In non-Athenian cities the wrongdoer's story was quickly erased and written over, his story legible only as in a palimpsest.[80] In Athens, however, the city did not convert the wrongdoer's property to another use and cover up his story. In two of the three cases of house razing for which we have evidence, the Athenians erected plaques and *stelai* on the site of the razed house to memorialize the name of the wrongdoer and the reason for the destruction.[81] The plaque and the property replaced the condemned body and reminded onlookers that the body of the wrongdoer had disappeared.

There were thus three options for the disposal of the body: it could be given back to the family for burial; it could be expelled without memorialization; or the disappearance of the body of the condemned could itself be memorialized. The first option allowed the body to be memorialized. The second option required that it be forgotten. The third option memorialized the requirement that the body be forgotten. These three different levels of remembering and forgetting were central to the structure of punishment.

All three levels of burial and memorialization appear in a story told by Thucydides about Sparta—and on this point Spartan paradigms match the Athenian paradigms for punishment. The traitorous Spartan king Pausanias was caught by the Spartans in an act of treachery, and sought asylum in a Spartan temple (1.134.4).[82] His citizens walled him into the temple where he starved to death. Just before he died, the Spartans pulled him out of the temple, presumably in order to avoid pollution, and the king died on the temple's doorstep rather than inside it. After Pausanias's death, the Spartans made three different decisions about what to do with his body:

> They were about to throw him into the Kaiadas [a cleft in the mountain], as they do with malefactors [*auton emellesan men es ton Kaiadan, houper tous kakourgous, esballein*]. But then they decided to bury him nearby [*epeita edoxe plesion pou katoruxai*]. Later the god at Delphi gave the Lacedaemonians an oracle commanding that they transfer his burial [*ton te taphon husteron . . . metenegkein*] to where he died (and so he now lies in the temple entrance, as what is written on some inscriptions makes clear). (1.134.4)

The story reveals first of all how much attention could be given to the disposal of the corpse. The Spartans had three options for the disposal of the corpse: *ataphia* or exposure in a mountainous region outside the city, described with the phrase *es ton Kaiadan esballein*; burial (*katoruxai*) but in an unspecified place "nearby"; and burial (*taphon*) that would be memorialized with an inscription at a locale central to the city's life. The farther away the body of the wrongdoer was to be sent, the less would it be memorialized. The topography of the city mapped out the topography of social memory. Pausanias's eventual return to the temple doorstep was also his reinstatement as a member of the city.

Like the Spartans, the Athenians could expel wrongdoers from the networks of social memory to different degrees. They had two pits: one being a natural chasm called the *barathron*, which is referred to only in fifth-century sources, and another being a man-made pit called the *orugma*, which appears in two late fourth-century references.[83] Gernet, Glotz, and Cantarella argue that the *barathron* and *orugma* were both used for execution by precipitation. But Thonissen, MacDowell, and Todd are skeptical about this and argue that the *orugma* at least was probably used only for the disposal of corpses.

It is probable that Thonissen, MacDowell, and Todd are right and that the *orugma* was used only for purposes of corpse disposal. In fact, this probably applies to the *barathron* too. Scholarly arguments about the *barathron* have mainly been concerned to uncover the forms of execution used in Athens.[84] But the Athenians were not overwhelmingly concerned with the question, How shall we execute this wrongdoer? They wanted to know, How shall we get rid of the corpse of the wrongdoer whom we have executed? The language of corpse disposal turns out to offer some important and heretofore unconsidered clues about how the *barathron* and the *orugma* were used.

From Homer down to the second century A.D., the vocabulary for death by precipitation is consistent and entirely distinct from the equally consistent vocabulary of corpse disposal. As we have seen, the words used to describe precipitation in Homer, tragedy, and the geographers were *rhipto* and *othein*. Aeschines provides us with the only oratorical instance of either word when he relates a story about an attempted precipitation that occurred during a meeting of the Amphictyonic Council (held either in Delphi or in Thermopylae). Aeschines reports that he intervened when the representatives from Oetaea wanted to hurl the Phokians from a cliff (*othein kata tou kremnou*) for some act of treachery (2.141–143). Demosthenes, in a later speech, reminds the Athenians of this event and warns: "If anyone should testify [before the Amphictyons] about the sacred treasure, he is thrown from a hilltop [*katakremnizetai*]" (Dem. 19.328). The two remarks prove that fourth-century Athenians were familiar with precipitation but only as a method of punishment used *in another city*. They were familiar with precipitation's vocabulary of violent motion, a vocabulary that perhaps even expresses the violence of force necessary to carry out precipitation against a live and struggling victim. But they never used that vocabulary in conjunction with either the *barathron* or the *orugma* nor to describe their own punishments.

The words used for corpse disposal include the verbs *emballo, ekballo,* and *proballo* ("throw in," "throw out") and their related prepositions. The words are used regularly in cases where we are explicitly told that people's bodies were thrown out unburied. Thucydides' story about the treatment of the traders and Spartans and his story about the disposal of the body of Pausanias both contain the phrase "*es ton* [fill in the name of a chasm] *esballein.*" Plutarch uses the word *probalein* to refer to the disposal of corpses. But he also uses the phrase *eisballo eis.* Plato uses the phrase *exballo eis* when describing the disposal of the corpses of executed parricides and matricides across city borders. He writes:

"After the officers and the judges of the magistrates kill them, let them make atonement for the whole city by expelling the naked corpse from the city to the appointed crossroads [*archontes apokteinantes, eis tetagmenen triodon exo tes poleos ekballonton gumnon*] and with all the magistrates' throwing stones at the head of the corpse, each one taking up a stone on behalf of the city [*hai de archai pasai huper holes tes poleos, lithon hekastos pheron, epi ten kephalen tou nekrou ballon apohosiouto ten polin holen*], and after this bearing the body to the borders of the land, by throwing the body out unburied [*meta de touto eis ta tes choras horia pherontes ekballonton toi nomoi ataphon*]. (*Laws* 873b)

Plato wants the bodies disposed "beyond the border" rather than over a precipice or into a chasm, and so he changes the prepositional prefix, from *eis* to *ek*; the prefix indicates the direction of the tossing.

Aristophanes uses an equivalent formulation in the *Knights* when he has one character threaten another with what is presumably a death by *apotumpanismos* to be followed by *ataphia*: "After I have raised you high in the air and hung you by the throat, I will throw you into the *barathron*" (*aras meteoron es to barathron embalo ek tou laruggos ekkremasas, Kn.* 1362–63). The phrase "*es ton* [fill in the name of a chasm] *esballein"* appears with an almost technical regularity in the context of corpse disposal.[85] When it is nothing but a corpse that is tossed into the chasm, it can be tossed or thrown out, like garbage, rather than hurled or thrust. The words *rhipto* and *othein* hint of actions carried out against a resisting, and therefore live, body. The words *emballo, ekballo,* and *proballo* whisper, in contrast, that the act of "throwing" or "tossing" is done to unresisting objects. The word *barathron* is consistently used only with this second set of words. The presence of the person to be executed can be sensed in the vocabulary for precipitation. Only the absence of that person—the presence of a corpse—can be heard in the vocabulary associated with the *barathron*.

There is *no* classical evidence to support the idea that the *barathron* was used for precipitation. The single piece of classical evidence usually adduced to support the argument for precipitation is actually a modern emendation of a text that, in the manuscript version, supports the argument that the *barathron* was used not for execution but for a refusal of burial. In the *Hellenica*, when Xenophon quotes the Decree of Cannonus against traitors, the unemended text reads:

> You all know, men of Athens, that the decree of Cannonus is extremely powerful [*ischurotaton*]. It commands that if anyone does injustice to the people of Athens, he will defend [*apodikein*] himself before the people bound in fetters, and if he is convicted of wrongdoing, [it commands him], slain, to be thrown into the barathron [*apothanonta eis to barathron emblethenai*] and for his property to be confiscated [*demeuthenai*] and for a tenth to be [*einai*] dedicated to the goddess. (Xen. *Hell.* 1.7.20–21)

Dobree reversed the participle and the infinitive in the transliterated phrase so that the last phrase would read not "if he is convicted of wrongdoing, [the law commands him], having died, to be thrown into the *barathron*" but "the law commands him to die by being thrown into the *barathron*" (*apothanein eis to barathron emblethenta*). His decision to emend was based on a gloss on Aristophanes' *Ecclesiazousai* 1089–1090 by the twelfth-century A.D. grammarian Hesychius who explains the line with a reference to the *barathron* as a form of punishment by precipitation.[86] There is, however, no reason to believe the medieval grammarian, since all classical evidence for the use of the phrase *eis embalo* points to the use of the phrase to denote corpse disposal. Moreover, the Decree of Cannonus is concerned with the punishment of traitors and other sources list them as among the class of wrongdoers who could receive *ataphia*. There is no reason to think that the manuscript tradition is faulty, and the Decree of Cannonus probably did stipulate that the wrongdoer should first be killed and then thrown into the *barathron*.[87] This natural chasm and its man-made successor the *orugma* were presumably both used for the disposal of corpses.[88]

Archaeologists have turned up two possible sites that might have been the Athenian "pits." One is a natural chasm near the border of Attica while the other is a man-made excavation at the walls of the city of Athens itself. A *complete* inscription that reads *bar* was found on the horizontal face of a small triangular outcrop on Mt. Beletsi. The outcrop is "overlooking a steep drop at the north side" of a fortification site on the mountain, a western extension of Mt. Parnes, 4.5 kilometers to the west-northwest of Kapandriti, the edge of Attica.[89] The fortification site at Mt. Beletsi would have been occupied at the end of the fifth century. The outcropping is just beside the highest point on the fortification site. It is next to a lookout post, and the inscription points due north, away from Attica, out to the border. If this was the *barathron*, bodies dropped off the ledge on the north side of the fort would have been bodies thrown beyond the furthest outpost of the community's fortifications, beyond the boundaries between peace and war, expelled from the peacetime city. Aristophanes jokes about the fact that the *barathron* was the last piece of Attic earth available to those who are being driven out of the city.

> *Poverty:* You seek to drive us from the land [*ek pases me choras ekbalein*]?
> *Wealth:* Would there not still be the barathron [*oukoun hupoloipon to barathron soi gignetai*]?
>
> (Ar. *Plut.* 431)

If this site was indeed the *barathron*, then the classical democracy would have had guards sitting high up on the hill above where the bodies of wrongdoers lay just as in the *Antigone*, Creon's guards sit on top of a hill with Polyneices' body at its foot (*pedon*).

The search for the *barathron* takes us to the edges of the countryside, but the search for the *orugma* takes us back into town. It takes us, however, only to the outer walls of town, where we find a man-made chasm that cuts the city wall. Wycherly identifies the chasm as a man-made quarry and labels it as one of the pits used by the Athenians for penal purposes.[90] In general, former quarries did play an important role in punishment throughout the ancient world. The Romans used quarries as prisons.[91] Other cities did as well: thus, Athenian troops were enclosed in a quarry on Syracuse in 413 (Thuc. 7.87; Plut. *Nicias*); and in return, the Athenians enclosed their Syracusan enemies in a quarry in the Piraeus (Xen. *Hell.* 1.1.14).

The chasm is on high ground in the deme of Melite and to the northwest of the Hill of the Nymphs. We know that in Plutarch's day the Athenians did in fact dispose of the bodies of wrongdoers in the deme of Melite and presumably in this chasm (Plut. *Them.* 22).[92] But was this former quarry also used for corpse disposal by the Athenians of the classical era? Democratic Athens buried the city's heroes in an honorific cemetery called the Keramikos. This cemetery still existed and was used in Plutarch's day. It thus seems plausible that the (un)burial ground of dishonor might also have survived from the democratic era to Plutarch's day.

The only piece of extended evidence about the fourth-century disposal of wrongdoers is consistent with the identification of the former quarry in the deme of Melite as the *orugma*. A short 150 meters to the north of the chasm, inside the walls of the city, is the road between Athens and the Piraeus. In Plato's *Republic* Socrates tells a story about a man named Leontius who saw the corpses of executed criminals from this road and ran up for a closer look. The bodies were lying under the external side of the north wall (*hupo to borein teichos ektos*) beside the public official (*nekrous para toi demioi keimenous*) (Plato *Rep.* 439E).

The details are all right: The gated-entrance to the city on the Piraeus road was just north of the spot where the North Long Wall met the city walls. Between the gate and the wall, but much closer to the wall, was a chasm splitting the city wall. This chasm and the gap in the city wall were just beside the Hill of the Nymphs. An executioner who had just brought the bodies out of the city and was getting ready to toss them into the pit would have had them just beside the North Long Wall, on its exterior side, and within view of the road from the Piraeus. The bodies would have been approximately 150 meters to the south of the road—well within range to be seen by those passing back and forth on the road between Athens and the Piraeus.

If the preceding identifications are right, the Athenians provided for two stages of expulsion, just as they did when they disposed of offscourings, just as the Spartans did in respect to Pausanias, and just as Plato did in his legislation against the parricide. Wrongdoers thrown into the *orugma* were expelled physically from the city center, through the wall, and into a chasm just on the other side of the wall bounding the heart of Athens. Wrongdoers thrown into the *barathron* were expelled from the whole of Attica. The wrongdoers thrown into the *orugma* could be seen from the road to the Piraeus. The wrongdoers taken out to the mountainous *barathron* could neither be seen nor walked on. A complete silence settled over the body of such a wrongdoer.

A Lysianic speech reveals the ways in which the code of silence bound those who were left behind in the city after a wrongdoer had been executed and his corpse had been disposed of. The speaker describes the demise of two military commanders who were put to death in the early fourth century after a military defeat:

> Nikophemos and Aristophanes were put to death unjudged [*akritoi*]. No one saw them again [*oudeis gar oud' eiden ekeinous*] after they were arrested. For they did not return their bodies [*apedosan*] for burial [*thapsai*], but such was the fearsome misfortune [*deine he sumphora*] that befell them that they were robbed *of this* [i.e., burial] in addition to *that other thing* [i.e., the trial]. But from that business I will now pass; for I cannot accomplish anything there [*alla tauta men easo; ouden gar an perainoimi*]. (Lys. 19.7–8)

Aristophanes and Nikophemos were arrested, and then no one saw them again or knew anything more about them (*oudeis gar oud' eiden ekeinous*). They disappeared from everyone's sight and knowledge precisely because their bodies were not given back for burial. The speaker thus stresses the idea that the Athenians were expelling wrongdoers from the city's networks of social knowledge when they denied wrongdoers a customary burial. He criticizes the *demos* and directly challenges its treatment of the generals until, that is, he lapses into silence— "from this business I will now pass"—and concedes that there is nothing more to say or do. The speaker forgoes his chance to challenge the democracy and instead memorializes the silence into which the men have disappeared. There were in Athens no Antigones who were willing to call attention to the disfigurement and depredations being visited on the corpses of the condemned.

The Athenian silence about the body stands in marked contrast to the treatment of the body of the condemned in the empires of Rome, France, and Britain. Seneca, for instance, complains that his fellow Roman citizens are obsessed with watching things happen to the body. In all three empires the details of the destruction of the body were described, recorded, and made public.[93] The efforts of imperial powers to memorialize the sufferings of the body memorialized the power of the ruler to force his world view on people. In the Athenian case the silence about the body occluded the elements of force involved in punishment and emphasized the degree to which the voluntary acquiescence of the citizenry in a punishment sustained the authority of that punishment. The democracy, the regime built on voluntariness, used a silence about the body, a silence in which condemned and noncondemned alike acquiesced, in order to make all citizens complicit in punishment. The complicity of all citizens in the punishment made the act of power involved in punishment their own and established the penal system of the society as being built on voluntariness, not force. Silence about the body turns out to have a sound and sounds out the willingness of citizens not to contest a punishment. That willingness not to contest a punishment is a statement of approval for the regime, its social orders, and the system of value that have imposed the punishment.

Foucault records a shift from the eighteenth to the nineteenth century in the methods of punishment used in France, Britain, and the United States. Over the same period that empires were being replaced by liberal democracies, the torture of the body was replaced with a focus on reforming the wrongdoer's soul. Foucault calls this the "disappearance of the body as the major target of penal repression"[94] and writes of it:

> In the old system, the body of the condemned man became the king's property, on which the sovereign left his mark and brought down the effects of his power. Now he will be rather the property of society, the object of collective appropriation. . . . In physical torture the example was based on terror: physical fear, collective horror, images that must be engraved on the memories of the spectators, like the brand on the cheek or shoulder of the condemned man. The example is now based on the lesson, the discourse, the decipherable sign, the representation of public morality. It is no longer the terrifying restoration of sovereignty that will sustain the ceremony of punishment, but the reactivation of the code, the collective reinforcements of the link between the idea of crime and the idea of punishment.[95]

As we have seen, punishments in Athens did give the community an opportunity to reestablish its myth of harmony and cleanliness. But I would suggest, *contra* Foucault, that the contrast between imperial and "democratic" punishments does not depend on a disappearance of the body but on the growth of a code of silence about the body.[96] That at least was the case in Athens.

Athenian punishments were followed by two main types of silence about the body. The democrat who suffered corporal punishment could not admit to it. Thus, there were silences in which the punished acquiesced in a refusal to acknowledge the condemned body. The wrongdoer acquiesced in this fashion in order to be reintegrated into the community as a citizen at the price of accepting the city's social norms and of being a symbol of them for his or her fellow citizens. The democrat who was executed, however, and whose body was thrown out, was not an acquiescing citizen. These wrongdoers were forced to be the subject of everyone else's silence. The first kind of silence restored the sovereignty of the city's norms by means of the wrongdoer's acquiescence and reintegration; this silence validated the city's myth of having a harmonious social order. The latter forced silences simply removed from the city that which kept it from being a harmonious whole and reestablished the myth of cleanliness by redrawing boundaries and defining the disease as being "outside" the community in the first place. These forced silences posited a new definition of what constituted the whole community. The principle of "reintegration" defined peace as a condition where that which conflicted with the city could be brought into harmony with it. The principle of "wholeness" defined peace as arising from war over a fundamental incompatibilty between the city's system of belief and the wrongdoer's system where one or the other would simply have to go.

The rest of the chapter investigates the nature of Athenian punishments of reintegration and the nature of punishments that redefined the borders of the "whole community" and also, at last, explains the symbolic weight of fines, imprisonment, *atimia*, and the different modes of execution used in Athens.

Punishments of Reintegration

In *Against Timarchos* Aeschines describes the result of a previous court case as having been that the defendant left court not only fined but also "stoned" (Aes. 1.163). Aeschines must have meant this metaphorically and may well have been referring to the jurors' shouts, the *thorubos* that let the speaker know where he stood with his judges. The image of a stoning captures what happened in the courtroom where jurors circled the defendant in order to listen to his story and communicated back to him their decisions of pity and anger in the *thorubos* of hurled shouts or curses. Like stonings, jury trials produced punishments of containment and consumption, most frequently by reassessing the position of the wrongdoer within networks of social memory. Two questions arise then: what sort of reintegration of the wrongdoer was effected by the memorialization of the metaphorical courtroom "stonings" carried out with private and public fines, imprisonment, and the *atimia* of disfranchisement or exclusion from the city's explicitly political and commercial spaces; and how was this reintegration effected?

The Athenians seem to have had a system for collecting fines from very early in the democracy (Antiphon refers to *kolastai*, the officials in the public treasury who received fines, without making them sound novel). We frequently hear, however, of people who were unable to pay their fines. Monetary penalties do not seem to have been an effective or efficient means of penalization, and yet they were continually in use in democratic Athens. What was the symbolic weight of fines that could justify the continual use of an ineffectual method?[97]

Some scholars have argued that monetary penalties originated in the practice of demanding blood money, or *poine* for murder. This archaic term (from which the words "punishment" and "penalty" ultimately derive) refers to the money that a relative of a murder victim might take to refrain from killing the murderer. If fines did originate in blood money, however, one would expect to see murder punished by fine. But murder was punishable by death from the seventh century to the end of the democracy, and Demosthenes claims that the paying of bloodguilt had long been illegal (Dem. 23.33).

The importance of fines should be seen as deriving not from blood money but from the centrality of reciprocity to Athenian thought. Money was the most tangible marker of exchange, and payment was the easiest way to show that the wrongdoer was giving something up or losing.[98] Moreover, money and writing were linked to one another. In the initial discussion of social knowledge (chapter 2), it was the banker who could claim the privileged position of using written evidence to help his memory because "bankers are accustomed to write out reminders." Contracts had to be recorded, and trade was an impetus to the increased use of writing in the fifth and fourth centuries.[99] Public fines were inscribed and posted in public view by the *kolastai*, and these inscriptions were, like contracts, markers of the realignment of status within the community.[100] Citizens surveyed the markers, their sight became knowledge, and they internalized the new social relations that reconstituted the city. Money served as a tool for assessing value and desert and was suitable language with which to inscribe stories of punishment into social memory.

Financial penalties were useful in that they confirmed the valorization of reciprocity in the city. They were, however, a danger insofar as they threatened equality. Athenian laws legislated specific fines for certain types of wrongdoing, but these fines—although applied equally to all by the laws—did not fall with the same weight on rich and poor. Those who were unable to pay their public fines suffered *atimia* or had to stay in prison until they could pay. Isocrates claims to speak for the poor when he writes in 397: "Although the same penalties are prescribed for all by our laws, not all people run the same risk [*kindunos*] in respect to them. Those who possess wealth [*tois chremata kektemenois*] are in danger of a fine, but those who are poor [*tois d' aporos*], as I am, are in danger of *atimia*" (16.47). The Athenians were extremely sensitive to issues of wealth and class, and so we could reasonably expect that the de facto inequality in punishments would have seemed unjust to the people of Athens.[101]

Athens was not the only city-state to face the problem of penalties that fell with different weight on different wealth classes in the city. According to Aristotle (*Pol.* 1297a20–35), Charondas of Catana solved the difficulty of the unequal weight of nominally equal laws by legislating different financial penalties for different wealth classes. Plato's Athenian Stranger does the same in the *Laws*. The Romans also scaled their penalties according to class: *honestiores* received fines and *humiliores* suffered corporal punishment.[102] But the Athenians refused to employ a solution that would entail writing different laws for different classes and abandoning the goal of *isonomia* or equality before the law. Instead the Athenians seem to have solved the problem of unequal penalization by introducing limited terms of penal imprisonment as substitutes for fines.

Nineteenth-century scholars assumed that the Athenian democrats did not employ penal imprisonment but used imprisonment only to hold those awaiting trial, those awaiting execution, and those unable to pay their fines.[103] As they saw it, brief imprisonment in the stocks occasionally supplemented these penalties, but always as an additional penalty—never as a penalty on its own.[104] Barkan saw in the use of imprisonment as an additional penalty the likelihood of general penal imprisonment and used evidence from the oratorical corpus to make this argument. His argument has been largely ignored—the nineteenth-century interpretation continuing dominant, but a relatively substantial body of evidence suggests that Barkan was right and that the Athenians did develop penal imprisonment.[105] Moreover, the evidence for penal imprisonment also supports the idea that the Athenians probably used imprisonment as a means of rectifying economic inequalities in the city.

The issue of whether the Athenians used penal imprisonment is complicated by vocabulary. In looking for evidence of imprisonment, scholars have primarily looked for places where words for prison appear (*desmoterion, anangkaion, erkte*). They have usually understood the verb *dedesthai* ("to bind") as referring to a temporary form of binding such as was inflicted in the stocks or while someone was awaiting trial.[106] Xenophon, however, twice makes the verb *dedesthai* ("to bind") parallel to *en desmoterioi* ("in prison") (Xen. *Hell.* 7.4.37–8; 5.4.8).[107] Where the verb *dedesthai* appears, we are only infrequently in a position to know whether binding per se or imprisonment is meant. The matter is further complicated by the fact that people were sometimes fettered while they were in prison. This happened in a Spartan prison (Hdt. 9.37.2), and Alcidamas, in *On the Sophists* (17), describes those who are freed from bonds after a long period of time as being "unable to walk like other people, but forced back to the same posture and movements they had to use when they were bound."[108] This must refer to a long imprisonment. We need to keep in mind the possibility that the words "*desmon*" and "*dedesthai*" may refer either to a short period of being bound "in the stocks" or "in fetters" or to longer periods of penal imprisonment.

We know that the Athenians used imprisonment in the military context. Bonds and imprisonment were used as punishments handed out by law (e.g., *zemia kata ton nomon*) in the military for wrongs less serious than treason (*elasso adikemata*) (Aen. Tac. 10.16–20).[109] We also have textual evidence about actual prison buildings that suggests that the prison(s) in Athens probably would have been large enough to hold more people than would have been on remand at any given time.[110] During the oligarchy, the Eleven were capable of receiving in the prison (*desmoterioi*) all the male townsfolk from Eleusis (Xen. *Hell.* 2.4.9), and a report that the oligarchs intended to imprison (*eirxein*) all the relatives of any man serving in the army at Samos who was not of oligarchic persuasion was taken by Athenian troops as credible (Thuc. 8.74). Either act would have required that the city have spaces where large numbers of people could be imprisoned. Other Greek cities also had prisons big enough to hold sizable numbers of prisoners, in one case explicitly more than 100.[111] By the end of the fourth century, the plural *desmoteria* appears in Menander's *Dyskolos* of 317/16, pointing to an increased use of imprisonment in the fourth century.[112]

Those few historians of Athenian democracy who subscribe to the notion that the Athenians used prison as a penalty for citizens (and not just as an additional penalty or as a means of holding a wrongdoer before trial or execution) most frequently rest their case on Socrates' remarks in the *Apology*.[113] There Socrates contemplates four of his possible punishments: imprisonment simple, a fine with imprisonment until payment of the fine, exile, and death. Socrates is said to have said:

> Shall I choose instead of [Meletus's proposal for a penalty] something from those things which I know well are bad, penalizing myself with such a thing? First of all, how about imprisonment [*poteron desmou*]? But why is it necessary for me to live my life in prison [*zen en desmoteroi*], enslaved to every successively appointed magistrate [*douleuonta aei kathistamenei archei*]? Maybe I should be imprisoned [*dedesthai*] for a financial penalty until I pay? (37bc)

Plato depicts Socrates, who is of course a poor man, as not only proposing imprisonment for himself but also as making a very clear distinction between imprisonment resulting from a fine and penal imprisonment. The scene shows that by 399 the idea of prison as punishment was already reasonably well embedded in the workings of the state.

Lysias also makes the distinction between imprisonment attached to a fine and imprisonment simple clear. He writes in 399 that Andocides had proposed that he be punished with a prison sentence if he should fail to deliver his slave for torture.[114] Lysias comments (6.21–22): "He imprisoned himself, having proposed at trial the penalty of bonds [*edesen heauton timesamenos desmou*]. . . . And indeed, how could it not be that one of the gods had destroyed the judgment of this man, who thought it easier to be penalized with imprisonment than with a fine [*rhaon hegesato desmou timesasthai e arguriou*]?"[115]

Lysias describes imprisonment as being worse than a fine, but Andocides himself in *On His Return* of 409/8 (?) describes it as an alternative to be preferred to death: "Although I bore shame before the gods, they seemed to pity me more than did men; when men were wishing to execute me, it was the gods who saved me. My subsequent imprisonment [*desma*] and the amount and kinds of evils I bore with my body [*toi somati eneschomen*], it would take too long for me to tell" (2.15). The same hierarchical ranking of penalties—

fine, imprisonment, death—appears in a speech against Alcibiades where the speaker argues that: "Concerning these things, the law of ostracism appears to me to overdo it and to leave the matter incomplete. For I think this an excessive punishment for private wrongdoing, and for public wrongdoing, I think it a small and worthless penalty, when it is possible to punish with fines and bondage and death [*exon kolazein chremasi kai desmoi kai thanatoi*]" (And. 4.4–5). The bondage mentioned in this passage is of a seriousness to rival a ten-year ostracism. As we have seen already, the vocabulary of binding itself can indeed refer to lodgment in prison. The binding mentioned here must refer to a long prison sentence rather than a few days' bondage in the stocks.

In *Against Timocrates* Demosthenes describes imprisonment as a corporal *penalty (ti pathenai)* distinct from financial penalties (*ti tinein*), and he describes imprisonment as a penalty that the jury can hand out as a sentence (*desmon katagignoskein*).[116] Demosthenes makes these remarks in his prosecution of Timocrates for having proposed and gotten enacted an illegal decree that would allow some wrongdoers to delay going to prison for several months (24.146, 151). The law would have affected only wrongdoers who had been sentenced to a fine with imprisonment until payment, but Demosthenes nonetheless discusses imprisonment as a penalty in its own right as well. Many other citizens (*alloi polloi ton politon*), he says, have had to spend a spell in prison (*menein*), whether because of debt or because of a penalty, and have submitted (*kaitoi kai epi chremasin ede tines edethesan kai epi krisesin, all' homos hupemenon*) (24.132).[117] Demosthenes thus confirms the distinction between the use of punishment to hold people until they had paid their fines and the use of imprisonment to punish people.

Demosthenes' remark that "many others citizens" have spent time in prison is also pointed. Demosthenes is in the process of arguing that Timocrates is trying to find a way for him and his friends to avoid going to jail, as if they are too good for experiences that other citizens must suffer. Demosthenes stresses the fact that even decent citizens have ended up in prison as a way to tell Timocrates that he ought not to think himself above imprisonment. Demosthenes' next words are: "Perhaps it is nauseatingly unpleasant (*aedes*) for me to remind you by name [*onomasti*] of [citizens who have been imprisoned] but it is necessary in order that you, the jury, compare these men before you [Timocrates and his friends] to those others" (24.132). Better men than Timocrates have had to go to prison, Demosthenes argues. But what is important here is that Demosthenes breaks the code of silence about the condemned body of the citizen—and is explicit about the fact that he is doing so. He breaks the silence only in order to prove that Timocrates' friends are not good enough citizens to avoid the disgrace attached to corporal punishment.

The association between imprisonment, women, and slavery presumably marked imprisonment as an exceedingly shameful penalty for a citizen. References to the use of imprisonment in the classical texts support the idea that it was a penalty associated with poverty and/or degradation. Socrates was not the only poor man to consider imprisonment instead of a fine.[118] In Theophrastus's

Characters, the character who is always scrounging for money, dances the *kordax* sober, cannot speak in the assembly, and abuses his mother, is also the one who is regularly caught for theft and is said to "live in prison" on a regular basis, "dwelling more frequently in prison [*keramon*] than in his own house" (6.6). Several orators cast aspersions on their opponents by referring to the fact that they or a relative had spent time in prison.[119]

Although penal imprisonment was degrading, it was the only wartime punishment that was transferred to peacetime contexts.[120] In the sixth century, Solon did two things that paved the way for the growth of penal imprisonment in the city. He abolished the debt slavery by which one citizen could slip into bondage to another. As a result, debtors and convicts who were unable to pay their fines were either made *atimoi* or required to stay in prison until they could pay their fines; Solon had thus ended the debt enslavement of one Athenian to another but had also introduced debt enslavement to the city.[121] Solon also added binding to the arsenal of public penalties by legislating that thieves of certain types must spend five days and five nights in the stocks *in addition* to paying fines.[122] Solon's reforms gave imprisonment and bondage public utility, although prior to his legislation they had been used primarily in the private realm.

In the *Laws* Plato suggests that those citizens of Magnesia who had been imprisoned for their inability to pay fines could be released if they paid *or* if they could persuade the city's officials or the prosecutor that they had spent enough time in prison (857a2–b3). Such a practice may have helped maneuver the Athenian transition from a penal system where imprisonment was used for those who could not pay their fines to a penal system where imprisonment was itself a penalty. Demosthenes describes such a process in *Against Timocrates* when he reminds his jury that an assembly of 6,000 people can be petitioned to take up the question of whether to remit (*aphesis*) the debts of an imprisoned state debtor or to accept a term (or arrangement) (*taxis*) as substitute (46–49). Aristotle (*Pol.* 1261a34) uses the word *taxis* to denote a term spent in office, and so it seems possible that it could also refer to a length of time spent in prison. A court sentence imposing a specific prison sentence would simply anticipate the assembly vote, establishing a *taxis* as a substitute for payment. The poor citizen could hold on to his equality by sacrificing his bodily integrity in some measure, and his sacrifice would be covered by a communal silence. Thus the Athenians set limits on the competitive reciprocity symbolized by fines.

The relative rarity in the oratorical corpus of references to the imposition of imprisonment as a penalty may well testify to the democratic nature of the institution of penal imprisonment. If penal imprisonment primarily affected those insufficiently wealthy to pay a fine, the status of the oratorical corpus as essentially the product of the wealth-elite would explain the emphasis in the speeches on monetary penalties and the obfuscation therein of the debate over imprisonment.[123] Moreover, the suppression of explicit discussion of imprisonment in all but Demosthenes' speech was necessary to allow the orators to maintain the firm distinction between slaves and citizens and between men and women.[124] The silence was necessary to help imprisonment do its work. Imprisonment tempered the system of competitive reciprocity symbolized by financial penalties and, in so doing, helped to sustain the ideology of *isonomia*. It helped produce the oxymoron of a "competitive politics of equality" that dominated Athenian public life, and it reintegrated punished citizens into the politics of the city by mandating a generally observed silence about corporal suffering.

Imprisonment was unusual in being the one penalty that did not ultimately depend for its enforcement on the power of communal knowledge, discourse, and "peer pressure" working through the threat of the "public eye," *atimia*, and private action. The prison building—with its keepers and executioner, the Eleven and the *demokoinos*—could work as a *substitute* for the community and stood as a form of institutional power and control sufficient to effect punishment in its own right. The development of imprisonment, perhaps already when debt-related and definitely when a penalty, marked the actual birth at Athens of a mechanism of *public* retribution that could produce punishments executed entirely by public officials. Athenian democrats, however, attempted to attach the new form of penal power and authority to the power of social knowledge. Demosthenes rouses his jurors to the task of maintaining authority over their prison thus: "Suppose you were told that the prison had been thrown open, and that prisoners [*desmotai*] were escaping. . . . There is not a man, however apathetic, who would not come to the rescue as much as possible" (Dem. 24.208). The belief that social knowledge and communal action ultimately controlled the prison made the Athenian prison acceptable within the peacetime context.

During the regime of the oligarchs, however, the citizens let their control of the prison slip. The oligarchs were associated with frequent use of the prison; the prison was seen as the tool of their power.[125] This association between the oligarchs and imprisonment emphasizes the fact that the power lodged in imprisonment, unlike that lodged in any other Athenian penalty, could be enforced independently of the community and independently of its networks of social memory and social knowledge. The ability of the oligarchs to use the prison contributed to their ability to make the law of Athens into their private possession at the end of the fifth century. The oligarchic use of imprisonment reinscribed the penalty of bondage within a wartime context.

Perhaps the strangest peacetime punishment in Athens was the internal exile of *atimia* by which male citizens were forbidden to enter public spaces. The citizen who suffered disfranchisement was expelled from the political spaces in the city, and he also lost his right to trial, the crucial institution of peacetime. *Atimia* made him someone who could not stand up in jury courts or in the assembly and speak for himself or make claims of desert. This expulsion of the *atimos* was memorialized and he was kept within networks of social knowledge and social memory. *Atimia* as disfranchisement memorialized the exclusion of a male citizen from the public sphere and his relegation to the private sphere. It memorialized his absence from and therefore also silence in the public sphere.

The full weight of the punishment of *atimia* can be seen in the story of Strato, a hapless arbitrator who fell afoul of the arrogant and wealthy Meidias (as Demosthenes portrays him) and as a result suffered an impeachment that resulted in his disenfranchisement. In the course of Demosthenes' long dispute with Meidias, Demosthenes brings Strato into court as a piece of evidence for the case against Meidias and calls him up on the stage to stand beside him as a silent body while he argues:

> This man, O Athenians, is poor perhaps, but not base. As a citizen, this man served in all the campaigns at the proper age and he has not done anything horrible [*deinon*], but now he stands in silence [*siopei*], robbed not only of all other common benefits [*ton allon agathon ton koinon apesteremenos*] but even of being able to speak [*phthengxasthai*] or complain [*odurasthai*]; and it is not even possible for him to tell you whether he has suffered justly or unjustly [*ei dikai' e adika*]. (21.95)

Strato stands in court, silently appearing on stage only when summoned, represented by an angry citizen—and Demosthenes invokes his *orge* repeatedly in the speech (e.g., 21.15, 70, 72, 73)—who runs on at the mouth, as the community memorializes Strato's inability to say for himself what he thought that he deserved. Because he held his peace, Strato did not have to be expelled from the city like the murderer or the traitor. His wrongdoing was such that his public acquiescence in his punishment sufficed to confirm the social order.

Demosthenes, however, undoes this acquiescence by making a point of Strato's silence, of the fact that he has been robbed of the right to speak or complain and talk about justice. Demosthenes' own vociferousness is inspired by his anger just as, according to Aristotle, the hot-tempered man (*oxuthumos*) is also the *parrhesiastikos* or outspoken man (*Rhet.* 2.5.11–12, 1382b). The outspoken man was one who could indulge in the famous Athenian privilege of free speech known as *parrhesia*, the freedom to say any or everything and also to speak as inspired by one's anger. Strato lost the political capacity to act on his anger when he lost his right to enter the public space where arguments about desert were made. But what stung most when one lost the ability to act on anger was not the loss of the emotion but the loss of the privilege of free speech, *parrhesia*, saying everything, and especially saying things about desert, about whether one has suffered justly or unjustly.

In the only comparable scene reported to us, Hyperides calls the prostitute Phryne before the jurors as evidence during his defense of her.[126] Women had to keep their peace in the city, and so Phryne like Strato could not speak. The silence required of women reinforced the city's hierarchies and systems of value, just as Strato's own silence validated the institutions and cultural structures that had brought about his punishment. Hyperides convinces the jury to acquit Phryne by, as the story goes, ripping open her bodice and exposing her to the jury's eyes in order to inspire their pity. Neither Strato nor Phryne was in a position to defend himself or herself. Both needed speaking citizens to break the silences imposed on them, and in both cases vocal orators exposed the silent body in order to make the jury reconsider how the city should treat its members. The woman's position in the political order may be seen as a model for the acquiescence that was also demanded of citizen men when they were punished, and the punished Athenian citizen was forced into a silence such as became a woman. Demosthenes affirms his status as a male citizen when he is not willing to hold his peace in respect to the punishment of Strato and reopens discussions of the (in)justice done to Strato. The contrast between Demosthenes and Strato dramatizes the way in which the silence that followed on a punishment established the fiction that the public contestation of definitions of justice had come to an end.

When silence finally fell upon the disfranchised and the imprisoned, a final and authoritative punishment had been achieved. Now at last we can see what makes monetary penalties unique. Only they did not require permanent silence from the condemned. The citizen who was punished with a fine could return to court and speak again at a later date about his desert and worth as a citizen. Only monetary fines provided for punishment while also confirming the offender and allowing him to continue in his role as a participant in the peaceful processes of reciprocity and exchange that were the privilege of the male citizenry.

PUNISHMENTS THAT REDEFINE THE "WHOLE" COMMUNITY

The Athenians had four methods by which they could redefine the boundaries of the whole community. They could exile people, they could execute them, they could execute them *and* refuse a burial, or they could offer an amnesty. In the second part of this chapter, I took mythical stories of exile as a model for punishments by expulsion, punishments that required the community to forget both the wrongdoer and the wrongdoer's disruption to the peace of the community. In this section I explore historical punishments of expulsion by examining the relative use of the *apotumpanismos* and hemlock as modes of execution, burial, and amnesty.

The discussion of how the Athenians executed people requires clearing some ground for it is generally thought that hemlock was the standard form of punishment. The textual evidence, however, suggests otherwise. The *apotumpanismos* (a form of crucifixion, as discussed earlier) was in use in the fifth and fourth centuries and after the fall of the democracy, but hemlock was only introduced to Athens at the very end of the fifth century.[127] Before then the Athenians did not know how to prepare hemlock for use as an irreversible poison. From Theophrastus's mid-fourth-century perspective, the technological innovation that allowed this was "recent" (*HP* 9.16.8–9). He reports that Thrasyas of Mantineia (with his pupil Alexias) had been the first to work out a method of preparing the plant so that less than one-quarter of an ounce, mixed with other elements, would be poisonous; the work of these scientists does not date earlier than the late fifth century.[128] According to Theophrastus, the people at Keos (who used hemlock to execute their elderly) had also "recently" (*mallon nun e proteron*) contributed their own technological innovation to the preparation of hemlock by figuring out that shredding the hemlock, stripping the outside, taking off the husk, bruising it with the mortar, and putting it through a fine sieve makes death "quick and easy" (*tacheian elaphran*) (9.16.8–9). The earliest reference to hemlock, in Aristophanes' play of 405, mentions precisely the fact that hemlock had to be prepared with a mortar and pestle (Ar. *Frogs* 120–27). The comedian's reference to the technological advance suggests that Aristophanes was making a joke about a new scientific invention just beginning, when he wrote *Frogs*, to make its rounds in Athens.

Most scholars do in fact agree that the "quick and easy" method of killing by hemlock was introduced to Athens only at the end of the fifth century. But two questions remain. First, did the oligarchs introduce the poison as a "quick and *efficient*" form of punishment when they took over the city in 404/3[129] or did the democrats introduce it as a form of "quick and *humane*" punishment?[130] And, second, did the fourth-century Athenians use hemlock as the primary way of punishing, or was it merely a rarely used supplement to the *apotumpanismos*?

The evidence that we have about the two forms of execution in literary sources is very different. First, there is a discrepancy in how the two forms of punishment are treated within oratory. Hemlock is mentioned twice in Lysias and once in Andocides, while references to the *apotympanismos* in oratory appear once in Lysias and once in Demosthenes. All three of the references to hemlock describe punishments handed out by the oligarchs. All of the references to the *apotumpanismos* describe punishments handed out by the *demos*.[131]

There is also a discrepancy in how the two punishments are treated in non-oratorical literature. References to the *apotumpanismos* outside of the orators turn up in several literary genres and appear in Herodotus, Aristophanes, the *Athenian Politeia*, and Athenaeus's description of use of the *apotumpanismos* from A.D. 88.[132] The *apotumpanismos* is also mentioned in Aristotle's *Rhetoric* and in Plato's *Gorgias*, in each case as a detail remarked on only in an offhand fashion.[133] In contrast, discussions of execution by hemlock that occur outside of oratory appear primarily in the specialist literature of the philosophers and in texts where death by hemlock takes on an especial thematic prominence. It is Xenophon who describes the death of Theramenes by hemlock in 404 (Xen. *Hell.* 2.3.54–56), Xenophon and Plato who mention hemlock in describing the death of Socrates in 399 (Xen. *Apol.* 7; Plato *Phaed.* 1187a7–8), and Plutarch who describes the executions of Phocion, Thudippus, Hegemon, Nicocles, and Pythocles in 318 (Plut. *Phoc.* 37–38). We hear about the death of the sophist Prodikos only in the Souda. Otherwise we hear of hemlock in Aristophanes, Theophrastus, Pliny, and Seneca.

Hemlock was typically discussed not as a mode of execution but as a mode of suicide and so it seems at least possible that the attention given to hemlock in the philosophical literature reflects the well-known interest of ancient philosophers in death by suicide. The earliest reference to hemlock sets it in the context of suicide. In Aristophanes' *Frogs* the drug is a way to get to Hades comparable to hanging and to jumping out of a tall building (125), and it is a means of suicide used by noble women in the city (1051). For that matter, Lysias, the orator who spends the most time discussing hemlock, also connects it to suicide; he describes the oligarchs' use of hemlock for executions as "forcing people to be their own murderers" (12.96).

The fourth-century scientist Theophrastus discusses hemlock in several places in his *History of Plants* (9.6, 9.8.3, 9.15.8, 9.16.8–9, 9.20.1). He takes up topics like where it grows (Susa in Asia Minor or other cold and shady spots like Laconia, Crete, Asia, and Megara), how it is prepared, and how to prepare antidotes to it, but always in the context of discussing suicide. Theophrastus makes one exception to his tendency to discusses hemlock in the context of suicide. He describes how the city of Keos used hemlock to thin the ranks of the city's elderly. He makes no mention of any public use of hemlock in Athens despite the fact that he lived and worked there.

Pliny the Elder and Seneca also discuss the Athenian use of hemlock in the context of discussions of suicide and of drugs and their antidotes, and their discussions closely resemble those found in Theophrastus.[134] But Pliny changes Theophrastus's story by adding Athens to Theophrastus's list of suitable spots for gathering hemlock.[135] Pliny is also the first person to claim that the Athenians used hemlock as their regular method of execution. There is good reason to be suspicious about Pliny's claims since Theophrastus would certainly have known if hemlock grew and was regularly used for execution in the city in which he worked. Nor is there any reason for him to have left such information out of his account. The tradition that treats hemlock as being the main method of execution in Athens thus begins only this late.

At the beginning of the sixth century, the Athenians did not have hemlock but had a piece of equipment called the *podokakke* that inflicted a punishment equivalent to the fourth century punishment of being put "in the wood." Being put "in the wood" or "on a board" was also a mode of execution in both the fifth and the fourth century. Execution by hemlock was introduced only at the end of the fifth century, but the death of Socrates in 399 is the last death by hemlock in the city that we hear about from *Athenian* sources. Moreover, technical advances made hemlock easy to use but not inexpensive. At the end of the fourth century hemlock cost twelve drachmae a dose, or roughly one-fourth of the price of an average man's sustenance for a year (Plut. *Phoc.* 36). The expense of hemlock no doubt derives from the fact that hemlock was relatively hard to come by in fourth-century Athens since it grew only in other regions. At the end of the fourth century, those who died by drinking hemlock had to pay for their own dose (Plut. *Phoc.* 36). If all of these factors are taken into consideration, it seems probable that the *apotumpanismos*, which provided for execution "in the wood," was the standard form of execution in Athens from the sixth century down to the fourth century, with changes in the actual mechanism being made over time (as the *podokakke* evolved into another piece of wooden machinery) and with hemlock introduced only as a secondhand optional method of execution for those who could afford to pay for a dosage of the drug that would allow them to commit suicide instead of being executed by the degrading, if bloodless, *apotumpanismos*.[136] But who introduced the poison?

Oratorical references to hemlock suggest that the oligarchs introduced it to the city. As I have said, the only oratorical references to hemlock describe its use by the oligarchs. Andocides remarks that the peace with Sparta had the result that "The Thirty were established, and many of the Athenians died drinking hemlock, and many went into exile" (And. 3.10). Lysias describes how his brother had died by the Thirty's "habitual" order (*toup' ekeinon eithismenon parangelma pinein*) to drink hemlock (Lys. 12.17) and castigates the Thirty for having forced those who had done no wrong to perish by the most shameful and infamous (or unheard of) forms of destruction (*enangkazonto aischistoi kai akleestatoi olethroi apollusthai*, Lys. 13.45). The scholiast to Aristophanes' *Frogs* thought that it was specifically the oligarch Theramenes who had introduced hemlock to Athens, although such evidence is not particularly sound. Hemlock would, however, have suited oligarchic methods in that it was a form of execution that could be carried out by the few against the many because it could be carried out secretly and beyond the purview of the public.[137] If the Thirty did not in fact introduce the public use of hemlock to Athens, they were at least known as its most (in)famous and habitual dispensers.[138]

Plutarch gives us the details of the last execution by hemlock to have taken place in democratic Athens. In 318 a leader of an oligarchic faction in the city named Phocion and four of his friends drank hemlock inside the prison on the day of a public festival (note, that it was a day on which the Athenians were not supposed to be carrying out executions). According to Plutarch, Phocion granted the other condemned men the privilege of drinking the poison first. As a result there was no hemlock left when it was his turn to die, and the executioner demanded that twelve drachmae be paid for the additional hemlock before he would "crush" (*tripsein*) another portion in the mortar. Eventually, Phocion got one of his friends to hand over the fee, interjecting his famous last words: "Is it not even possible to die in Athens without giving a gift to the city?" (*eipon ei mede apothanein Athenesi dorean estin*; Plut. *Phoc.* 36). During Phocion's execution, a festival procession was passing by outside the prison. In the procession was a set of horsemen or the wealthy, elite knights in the city who would have been supporters of Phocion. As they passed the prison, "some of them removed their crowns of honor; others, with tears, looked at the door of the prison [*hoide pros tas thuras dedakrumenoi tes heirktes apeblepsan*]" (Plut. *Phoc.* 37).

In this punishment the public spectacle provided by the *apotumpanismos* was replaced with the silent doors of the prison. In moments of extreme political tension—the execution took place after the fall of the city to Macedon—did the *demos* find it safer to remove the body of the condemned from public view before the wrongdoer had even died? If so, the democrats had learned a lesson from the oligarchs about the use of hemlock. The oligarchs were notorious not only for making people drink hemlock but for making them drink behind prison doors (e.g., Lys. 12.18). On the whole, however, Phocion's burial proved to be a more lasting preoccupation for the Athenians than the method of his execution. The narrative of Phocion's fate concludes thus:

> [After the execution] a decree was passed—as if his enemies still lacked something in their victory [*hosper endeesteron egonismenois tois echthrois*]—that the body of Phocion would be carried over the border [*to soma . . . exorisai*] and that no Athenian should light a fire for his burial cremation [*mede pur enausai medena pros ten taphen*]. Because of this, no friend [*philos*] dared to touch his body, and one Konopion, who habitually took pay to do so such things [*hupourgein eithismenos ta toiauta misthou*], carried the corpse beyond Eleusis, and, getting fire from Megara, burned it. Phocion's wife was present with maidservants and heaped up a mound on the spot and poured libations and, placing the bones in her bodice, she carried them to her house by night and buried [*katoruxe*] them beside her hearth, saying: "Dear hearth, to you I entrust what is left of a good man [*andros agathou*]. Hand them over [*apodos*] to his ancestral sepulchers, when the Athenians come to their senses [*sophronesosi*]." And, in fact, after a short time had passed, and when affairs had led the Athenians to realize what a patron and guardian of sense [*phulaka sophrosunes*] and justice the people had destroyed, they erected a bronze statue of the man and buried his bones with public rites [*ethapsan de demosiois telesi ta osta*]. As for his accusers, the people put one to death, and the other two, who had run from the city [*apodrantas ek tes poleos*], were found by Phocion's son, who punished them [*etimoresato*]. (Plut. *Phoc.* 37–38)

Phocion is condemned to the worst form of treatment: his body will be carried beyond the borders and all Athenians must acquiesce in this expulsion; no Athenian should light a fire for him. All the citizens do acquiesce, but the wife of Phocion refuses to be silent. She can act only in her own household and can speak only to her hearth but that allows her to repatriate Phocion's bones at least partially. Her own act of speech, her refusal to let go of Phocion's body entirely, moves the narrative action forward to the point where the Athenians themselves begin to speak about Phocion as she does. They decide that they were wrong about Phocion's punishment, reverse it, undo its authority, and give Phocion a proper public burial with full honors. His world view is instated as the norm, and the world view that required his expulsion from the city is rejected. His accusers are even put to death. It is as if his expulsion from the city could not be accomplished as long as a total silence was prevented from falling upon his body. Herein lies the structure of punishment: it rests on acquiescence, and the city's self-definition rests on whether citizens will confirm or overturn each particular effort to cloak the body of the condemned in silence.

The manner in which a citizen was executed does not seem to have mattered much to the Athenian democrats (even if it mattered to the philosophers), as long as that death was bloodless. In general, a death at the hands of the *demos* was primarily a subject that was not suitable for speech and was well-cloaked in euphemism. The Athenians did, however, discuss whether an execution should be memorialized and followed by a customary burial. But even if the topic of death at the hands of the *demos* went relatively undiscussed in oratory, it was addressed in spectacle. If the *apotumpanismos* was the same piece of equipment as the stocks, the public display of wrongdoers, a memorializing punishment of reintegration, always also threatened the wrongdoer with execution, a punishment of expulsion. At the center of the city's life, accessible to public view, the public executioner, the *demokoinos* (a slave who worked under the direction of citizens) could, by working the *apotumpanismos*, reintegrate a wrongdoer to the city or begin the process of expulsion with the same piece of penal equipment. The suspended figure of the exhibited wrongdoer, who was fettered into the five-holed wood and transformed into something other than an upright citizen, would constantly have conveyed the threat of execution and with it the question of burial and of whether the wrongdoer would be further transformed into an enemy. The citizens watched this exhibition and were silent about it. If they were not, the city did sometimes slide back and forth between different kinds of punishment; the bones of the condemned man who had been refused burial might after all be returned to Athens. The definition of who was an enemy could be constantly contested and the boundaries of peace constantly redefined as the Athenians attempted to match punishments that were more or less warlike to acts of wrongdoing that were also taken to be more or less warlike.[139] When the silence fell, the contest ceased.

THE AMNESTY

The Thirty oligarchs who took over Athens at the end of the Peloponnesian War upped the ante on the question of how the city should respond to citizens who acted like enemies. The oligarchs had treated the citizens in an extremely "warlike" fashion while they were in power. One of their many crimes, according to Lysias at any rate, seems to have been their regular refusal of customary burials to those whom they executed. Lysias reports his brother's death thus: "After he was carried dead from the prison, they would not allow him to be taken to any one of our three houses, but rented a shed in which to lay him out. [They had all of our property] and although we requested something from out of the many cloaks, they would not give one up for the funeral [*ouk edosan eis ten taphen*]. . . . they drove [*exelasan*] many of the citizens in exile to the enemy, and unjustly subjected many to execution without burial [*pollous d' adikos apokteinantes ataphous epoiesan*]" (12.18, 21). Later in the same speech Lysias adds: "They tore people from their children, parents, and wives, . . . and did not allow them to receive the lawful/customary burial [*oude taphes tes nomizomenes eiasan tuchein*], thinking their own rule [*archen*] to be stronger than the punishments of the gods" (12.96). The oligarchs broke all three of the rules for peace: they executed people without trial, executed them without providing them with reasons for their execution, and refused them burial.

It is not surprising to find them also accused of violating the corporal integrity of citizens. Thucydides describes an Athenian soldier who tells his messmates that at home in Athens the oligarchs had begun to use whipping, the punishment for slaves, as a punishment for citizens also; the other soldiers believe him although the story is a fabrication (*plegais te pantas zemiousi*, Thuc. 8.74.3). With the Thirty, all distinctions between the realm of war that existed beyond the city's borders and the realm of peace that existed inside its walls collapsed. Punishment did not serve to maintain or reestablish "conditions of peace" under the rule of the oligarchs but brought war into the heart of the city.

The democrats eventually managed to oust the oligarchs and their supporters and return to power. At that point they had to decide what to do about the men who had contributed to destroying a large portion of the citizenry by means of hemlock, by denying them trials, and by denying them burial. They did not punish everyone who had been (or who was thought to have been) an oligarchic partisan, but instead decreed a general amnesty, from which they excepted only the Thirty themselves (and a small number of other men who had held important offices under the Thirty).[140] These men were executed.

The oligarchic supporters were, according to the terms of the amnesty, allowed to withdraw from Athens to Eleusis if they so chose.[141] Or they were allowed to stay in Athens after swearing an oath of reconciliation with all of the democratic partisans in which both parties swore, among other things, never to remember (or never to remind one another of) past evils (*mede mnesikakesai medepote*) (1.77–79, 87, 107). The oath was to protect the supporters of the oligarchy from future prosecutions for their deeds under the oligarchy.

In the amnesty we see the Athenians reconstituting the wholeness of their community and the democracy by redrawing the city's border (thanks to the withdrawals to Eleusis) and by reintegrating those who lived within the borders with one another. The boundaries of the "whole" community were redefined by the execution of those citizens whose world views had overturned the very structure of the democracy and the acquiescent departure to Eleusis of those other citizens who refused to give up on the oligarchic experience. In contrast, those who remained in the city were to be reintegrated by means of an oath of "forgetting," an agreement to be silent about what had happened during the civil war.[142]

Analogues to the amnesty are to be found in less significant moments of pardon. The assembly could pardon, and the *kolastai* had the power to charge officials with having imposed illegal fines.[143] If an official was convicted, his conviction meant the condemned's release from his fine. The examples of private pardons and reconciliations are more important, however. Wrongdoers could take sanctuary in a temple or shrine in cases where they expected to suffer death at the hands of a citizen acting in a private punitive capacity.[144] Similarly, the families of the victim could pardon the wrongdoer in homicide cases. Nor were they allowed to change their minds once they had pardoned someone. Thus: "If someone convicts someone of involuntary homicide and has clearly proved him unclean and, after these affairs, forgives him [*aidesetai*] and releases him [*aphei*], he no longer has authority to send him into exile."[145]

Isaeus provides an example of how such a "release" might be effected in a case other than homicide. He describes a trial that was interrupted when the contending parties resolved their differences and came to an agreement (*homol-ogethe*): "I do not think I need to tell you how Leochares begged the jurors and us when the verdict became clear from the votes taken out of the urns, nor do I need to tell you what we could have done to him; but I do need to tell you what was agreed between us at this time. So listen. We agreed with the archons not to count the votes but to mix them together . . . even though, after convicting him of perjury, we could have had him disfranchised."[146]

The amnesty also depended on a moment of agreement like that in the recon-ciliation described by Isaeus. The collective decision to swear off remembering and to respond to the oligarchic takeover with a collective act of "forgetting" was a decision to pass up the opportunity to punish, and Andocides describes it thus:

> Although the opportunity had arisen for you to punish [*genomenon eph' humin tim-oreisthai*], you decided to consider these things past [*egnote ean ta gegenemena*], and you acted to save the city and not for private punishment [*kai peri pleionos epoies-asthe soizein ten polin e tas idias timorias*], and it was decreed that neither party of you was to remember the bad events of the past [*kai edoxe me mnesikakein allelois ton gegenemenon*]. (And. 1.81; cf. Lys. 18.17–19)

The city decided to skip the process of punishing and to move straight to the question of remembering and forgetting. The two parties gathered on the Acropolis and swore pledges to *homonoia* or like-mindedness.

The process of forgetting was carried out with a ceremony that ritualized, formalized, and memorialized the decision not to remember, but the amnesty was somewhat double-edged. It simultaneously validated the oligarchs as mem-bers of the democratic community and stripped them of their right to present their personal interpretations of their honor or to be memorialized for any of their wartime deeds. The Athenians granted the supporters of the oligarchy their lives, but they also refused to give them a chance to put their own case, a chance to argue their desert and to insert their own stories, stories that would have valorized their actions, into the social memory. The amnesty ensured the reestablishment of the democratic system of value through the silence and ac-quiescence of both victor and defeated.

It is seldom pointed out that the 403/2 amnesty was not the first amnesty in Athenian history, or at least, not according to Andocides. He claims that it was modeled on an amnesty sworn after the Persian Wars (And. 1.77, 108–9). The comparison is noteworthy, for the situations that obtained in Athens at the end of both wars were markedly different. The city of Athens was not torn apart by extreme civil strife after the Persian Wars. Andocides describes the first am-nesty thus:

> They fought and were victorious . . . and, having done this deed, they judged it worth-while not to remember ill things that had happened before. Because of these decisions, men who found their city devastated, her temples burned down and walls and houses fallen, achieved rule over Greece by being of one mind with one another [*to allelois homonoien*]. . . . The same things can happen for us, if the citizens should be willing

to be moderate [*sophronein*] and to be of one mind with one another [*homonoein allelois*]. (1.108–9)

In the case of the Persian Wars, war in general and not "civil war" in particular necessitated the amnesty. War sufficed to make necessary an effort to reconstitute the mythical "wholeness" and integrity of the community. Not only after the civil war but also after the Persian Wars, the Athenians had to provide one another with assurances of *homonoia*. They had to reconstruct self-consciously their single shared communal memory in order to make a collective transition from conditions of war to conditions of peace.

Wartime abounded in events that stripped people of their place in social networks and social memory—torturous executions at the hands of enemies who would not even suffer the corpse to be buried, deaths in naval battles like Arginusae and total disappearance into the sea, expulsion from house and home and city, war dead who simply could not be found (e.g., Thuc. 4.44.5). During wartime in Athens it took the funeral oration, which memorialized all soldiers simultaneously and memorialized even those who had left no remains, no bodies at all, to keep the networks of public memory functioning despite the vast ruptures brought about by war. It was important to keep speaking about bodies for as long as the war lasted.[147] The funeral oration memorialized the "unknown soldiers" and thereby memorialized the undesirable acts of *forgetting* produced by war. The amnesty inversely required that the citizens forget the lack of burials, forget the expulsions, and forget the forgetting of war itself.[148] The transition from wartime to peacetime required the amnesty, a willingness to replace the collective memory of acts of war with peacetime paradigms of social memory. The amnesty in effect reconstituted a framework for remembering and established the citizens as having become, once again, a set of people who shared the same minds by forcing the democrats to forget the greatest wrongs of all, the acts of war. The citizens were thereafter allowed to talk only about those social disruptions that did not pose a mortal threat to the city.

The effort to reconstruct the social memory—what to remember and what to forget—required that the Athenians make decisions about what could be discussed and about what topics had to be cloaked in silence. The amnesty established a community that was mythically same-minded because of its agreement to rule certain topics out of the realm of public discussion. It took a great deal of institutional support to make the amnesty work. In the fourth century Athenian citizens kept trying to reopen the topics of discussion closed by the amnesty and tried to prosecute one another for wrongdoings committed during the period of the coup.[149] To prevent this, the Athenians invented a legal procedure called the *paragraphe* by which one could charge that one was being prosecuted in violation of the amnesty.[150] The amnesty, like punishment in general, established a myth that the citizens were all like-minded. In the case of the amnesty, however, the myth had to be reinforced by a law (*paragraphe*) that prevented citizens from reopening discussions that had been closed by a collective act of forgetting. All other forms of punishment, in contrast, primarily rested on the silent acquiescence of the citizens. They rested, in other words, on an agreement in the community about what could be discussed that was already secure. War is over when acquiescence, not force, is enough to sustain authority.

The central principle for action in the Athenian public sphere was that angry honor-sensitive male Athenian citizens should compete with one another on a regular basis but within limits and publicly exchange favor for favor and harm for harm in networks of reciprocity. An elaborate institutional and ideological system supported this principle and made it a viable basis for social organization. The institutional and ideological structures assigned roles to all classes of people in the city—male citizens, female citizens, metics, and slaves—and these roles made the valorization of anger for the male citizens a workable cultural norm. Male citizenship in Athens was valued because it meant that one was able to speak (*phthengxasthai*) or complain (*odurasthai*) and to tell one's fellow citizens whether one has suffered justly or unjustly (*ei dikai' e adika*)— within limits.[151] The political realm was the realm where the city's system of value was defined. Female citizens, metics, and slaves were asked to confirm the system of value established in the political arenas with their silence.

Zeus punished Prometheus by responding to the Titan's increased challenges to his authority with ever more intense forms of punishment. The punishments of the Athenian *demos* were likewise scaled. A male citizen who committed a wrong for which he had to pay a monetary fine could at least, at some later date, have a second chance to say what he was worth. Wrongdoers who had committed crimes deserving of fines broke from the city to such a minor degree that their voices and the power of speech were not taken from them. All of the other punishments required varying degrees of silence from the wrongdoer. Those wrongdoers who were put in the stocks, who were imprisoned, who were disfranchised, or who were granted an amnesty could be reintegrated into the city provided that they acted and behaved in such a way as to confirm the city's system of value. Those wrongdoers who were exiled, executed, or executed and refused burial could not be reintegrated to the city because their challenge to the city's system of value was so extreme.

It was traitors and temple robbers who received the stiffest penalties, punishments that provided for the total erasure of the offender from communal memory by means of execution, *ataphia*, and house razing but also provided for the ensuing recharacterization of the citizen as an offender and for the reinscription of the offender as such in the public memory. The *demos* would erect a plaque, sometimes even in bronze, explaining the wrongdoing of the offender. In its most authoritative punishments, the *demos* articulated its formulation of who and what the offender had been and of what his "desert" had been so thoroughly as to leave the offender no chance to defend himself to posterity and no more opportunity to redefine or to contest his "desert." In bringing both the discussion of desert and the wrongdoer's ability to participate in that discussion to an end, the *demos* stripped the wrongdoer of his citizenship and his manhood. The most powerful punishment was a silencing complete enough to control the future.

The importance of silence to punishment does not apply to Athens alone. The word "appeal" marks precisely the idea that a punishment has not become final or authoritative as long as the condemned still has a voice to call out and say that he or she is suffering unjustly. The United States has recently introduced what are being called maxi-maxi prisons, prisons where prisoners suffer solitary confinement in "administrative segregation" for violations of prison regulations that they have committed while in other prisons. The most striking feature of these prisons is the noises that fill the hallways: a cacophony of shouts, groans, bellows, rattling of door handles, and banging of possessions against walls.[152] No less striking is the silence that falls when the doors to the prison are closed and one stands outside its walls.

PART THREE

Interventions in the Conversation

Plato's Paradigm Shifts

THE SYMBOL OF LEONTIOS

Chapter 9 investigated the ways in which the body of the Athenian condemned was treated to a spectacular silence in Athens. The bodies of wrongdoers were displayed publicly but extant texts include very few direct discussions of such spectacles. Plato was one of the few authors who was willing to discuss the body of the condemned and the silence surrounding it. Like the other authors who challenged such punishments, Plato conjures up the body of the condemned in order to challenge punitive procedures in Athens and the city's political structure more generally. Plato offers us the body of Socrates in the *Phaedo*. In the *Republic* he presents corpses of executed wrongdoers as they lie beside the executioner.[1]

In book 4, Socrates tells this story:

> Once upon a time I heard and believe the following: that Leontios son of Aglaion when he was on his way up from the Piraeus along the outside of the north wall perceived corpses lying beside the executioner. At one and the same time he desired to look at them [*epithumoi*] and was disgusted and repulsed at himself. He struggled over this and covered his head, but was nonetheless overcome by desire and, opening his eyes, he ran to the corpses, as he said, "Look then, you evil-spirits, and fill yourselves with the noble spectacle [*kalou theamatos*]." (439e–40a)

The Platonic rejection of Athenian practices of punishment is perhaps best captured by this story of Leontios and his trip past the bodies of the condemned. A picture is worth a thousand words, and so was the spectacle of the corpses of those condemned by the Athenians to die. Students of rhetoric have long been able to express the ways in which material objects and symbols speak volumes. In chapter 5 I quoted Kenneth Burke's remark that "there is a difference between an abstract term naming the 'idea' of say, security, and a concrete image designed to stand for this idea, and to 'place it before our very eyes.' For one thing, if the image employs the full resources of imagination, it will not represent merely one idea, but will contain a whole bundle of principles, even ones that would be mutually contradictory if reduced to their purely ideational equivalents."[2] In the Athenian context, to look at the spectaclular body of an executed wrongdoer and be quiet about it was to accept an approach to politics and punishment in which the parameters of normative citizen behavior were established by the following key phenomena: anger or *orge*, honor, reciprocity, social knowledge or memory, and a distinction between war and peace. The corpses of the criminals lying beside the road were a symbol of the degree to which Athenian political and public life were based on a valorization of anger that led to the use of reciprocity as a principal for public life, led to the centrality of spectacle to the process of reciprocity, and led even to the exclusion of women from politics. Anyone who could look at the spectacle of the corpses without being (too) discomfited by it accepted the practices of the Athenian regime that culminated in the bodies.

Leontios rejects all these political principles in turning away from the bodies and exhibiting discomfiture. Indeed, the very fact that Socrates had heard the story of Leontios somewhere and that his interlocutors claim to remember it confirms our impression that Leontios's behavior must have been unusual enough to be worth remembering. His discomfiture means that he has distanced himself from the Athenian regime and the ideological habits of mind that made the disposed bodies a "normal" sight in the Athenian landscape. He turns away not only from the dead themselves but from the regime of anger, honor, and reciprocity that landed the bodies there to be the subject of spectacle. Socrates describes Leontios' behavior so as to suggest that citizens should not accept the spectacle, and he thereby effects an initial resignification of the symbol of the corpses, turning their positive political value into a negative one.

Both the figure of the dying Socrates and the figure of the condemned corpses beside the road were meaningful symbols—but they symbolized different sets of principles for Athens than for Plato.

Plato rejected the Athenians' retributive principles of punishment and produced the earliest theory of reformative punishment extant in the Western literary tradition. As we have seen (chapter 3), Plato rejected the most typical Athenian words for punishment (*timoria* and *lambanein diken*), which stressed honor and reciprocity, in favor of the word *kolasis*, which stressed the good of the wrongdoer and which Plato embedded in a thick theory of how a punishment should aim to teach the unvirtuous wrongdoer to be virtuous. Plato not only revised the Athenian vocabulary of punishment but also resignified its central metaphor of disease and cure. On his account, the wrongdoer who had committed an injustice was sick and needed to be cured (cf. especially *Gor.* 477b). He did not use the trope of disease to argue that either the punisher or the community was made ill by and needed to be cured because of an act of wrongdoing. In Plato's usage, it is only the wrongdoer who is sick and only the wrongdoer who needs a cure.

Plato's rejection of a retributive punishment in favor of reformative punishment both entailed and was itself central to a general and comprehensive rejection of Athenian politics and its basis in anger. In the following chapter I take up the Platonic challenge to Athenian conceptions of just punishment and legitimate politics, first by investigating his theories of reformative punishment in the *Protagoras* and the *Gorgias* and then by turning to the *Republic* and the *Laws*. Throughout these texts Plato revises key Athenian concepts by relying on symbols, narratives, and acts of *mimesis*. It will turn out that the narrative about Leontios and his reaction to the corpses of the Athenian condemned is a turning point in the *Republic*'s arguments about anger.

Reform over Reciprocity

It is well known that Plato sought to revise Athenian conceptions of punishment. Socrates and other characters espouse reformative views throughout the early, middle, and late dialogues.[3] Mackenzie (McCabe) and Saunders have both made thorough studies of Plato's reformative theories of punishment, focusing on the *Protagoras*, the *Gorgias*, and the *Laws* to explicate Plato's argument that punishment should aim to teach the unvirtuous wrongdoer how to be virtuous.[4] Virtue can be taught because it is itself a form of knowledge while vice is ignorance.

The famous Socratic paradox that no one knowingly (or voluntarily) does wrong is at the heart of Plato's argument for reformative punishment.[5] All acts of wrongdoing are the result of ignorance. The idea is that everyone who acts is choosing and everyone who chooses is deciding that one action or object of desire is preferable to another and is making a decision about what is the good or right thing to choose in a particular moment. All choices are therefore based on an implicit claim to know what is good and bad. A choice to do an injustice can only be an act of ignorance in which one has momentarily mistaken an "injustice" or "wrong" as something that is "good" to do. The aim of punishment is to deal with the problem of this ignorance by educating (*mathesis*) the wrongdoer about what is truly "good" to do.

Those who notice an act of wrongdoing have a duty to continue to associate with the wrongdoer for the sake of instructing and admonishing that person. If the instruction is a failure, the wrongdoer can be haled to court for punishment or *kolasis*, but that form of punishment should aim to carry on the education by other means.[6] Socrates thus conceptualizes punishing as an activity that a prosecutor should undertake only after having tried to educate the wrongdoer and only with the goal of educating the wrongdoer. Punishment should arise not from anger at the wrongdoer but from concern for the wrongdoer and the state of his or her soul.

Socrates applies such arguments to himself in the *Apology* when he defends himself against Meletus's charge that he has corrupted the youth of Athens:

> Either I do not corrupt [the young] men or I corrupt them involuntarily, so that you [Meletus] are lying either way. But if I corrupt them involuntarily, it is not customary (*nomos*) to drag people here [to court] for the sake of involuntary errors [*ton toiouton akousion hamartematon*], but to take them aside privately and to teach and admonish them [*didaskein kai nouthetein*]. For it is clear that if I learn [*matho*] I will cease from doing whatever I do involuntarily. But you, instead of associating with me and teaching me, were unwilling to do so, and you drag me here, where it is customary to drag those needing punishment not education [*hoi nomos estin eisagein tous kolaseos deomenous all'ou metheseos*]. (26a)

Socrates inverts the whole of the standard Athenian approach to punishment with the small and seemingly innocuous claim that he deserves instruction rather than punishment. In the Athenian context, the victim's and the community's anger generated the need for punishment, but Socrates argues that any claims that will be made about the need for punishment must be based on an assessment of what the wrongdoer's soul needs.[7] Socrates' argument recharacterizes the problem posed by the wrongdoer to the community. No longer does the wrongdoer introduce the threat of a spread of anger. On Socrates' account, acts of wrongdoing show up the community as having failed in respect to the education or *paideia* of the wrongdoer.

People who punish for the sake of irrational passions and for the sake of the past and not for the sake of education are bestial, according to the sophist Protagoras, who makes this point as part of an argument for reformative punishment during a discussion about whether virtue is teachable in the *Protagoras*:

> If you are willing to consider, Socrates, what punishment [*to kolazein*] does to wrongdoers, the phenomenon itself [*auto*] will teach you that people think that it provides for virtue [*areten*]. No one, except for those who punish irrationally [*timoretai alogistos*] like beasts [*therion*], punishes [*kolazei*] wrongdoers with a view to or for the sake of whatever injustice has been done. No, the person who tries to punish [*kolazein*] according to reason [*meta logou*] does not punish [*timoretai*] for the sake of a past injustice [*tou pareleluthotos adikematos*]—for that which is done may not be undone—but rather for the sake of the future in order that the wrongdoer may not do wrong again and that others, when they see this one person being punished, may not do wrong. Since a person who punishes acts with this belief, that person also thinks that virtue is teachable; and punishes for the sake of warding off [*apotropes*] evil. (323d–324b)

Protagoras distinguishes two kinds of punishment: punishment that aims to reform and punishment that attempts to rectify the past.[8] He uses *kolazein* to denote the former and *timoresthai* to denote retributive punishment. *Kolasis* is based on the principle that virtue is teachable, and *timoria* is based on the unreason of a beast. Socrates does not contradict Protagoras on this point although the two are at odds at many other moments in the dialogue. Socrates quibbles with Protagoras's analysis of why virtue is teachable, but never rejects the dichotomy drawn between retributive and reformative punishment. The distinction between irrational retribution and rational reform is central to Plato's analysis of punishment throughout his dialogues.[9]

The distinction drawn by Protagoras includes an implicit rejection of Athenian forms of punishing. On Protagoras's account, people who punish by means of *timoria* and with a view to the past (as the Athenians did) may be considered akin both to wild animals and to irrational (*alogistoi*) creatures. As such, the Athenians, like the wrongdoer, needed to be taught. By setting up Athens as a wild beast that has to be brought to its senses, Protagoras's definitions of retributive and reformative punishment provide a basis for a critique of Athenian politics. In later dialogues Socrates takes up Protagoras's distinction between retributive and reformative punishment and carries out the critique of Athenian politics that it implies.

Socrates challenges the Athenian system of punishment and politics in part by revising its key concepts. The standard Athenian approach to punishment held that to punish someone was to "do badly" to them and that to suffer punishment was therefore a bad thing. In the *Gorgias* Socrates redefines what it means to "suffer punishment."[10] He leads his interlocutors to the point of saying that it is actually a good thing to suffer punishment. In this dialogue we also get the first hints of how an Athenian would react to such criticism and challenges to the standard Athenian practice of punishment.

In the *Gorgias* Plato depicts a sixty-four-year-old Socrates encountering the rhetorician Gorgias, the Athenian Callicles, and their sidekick Polus. The four men embark on a conversation primarily in order to discuss rhetoric and the power of the orator. This power is defined initially in terms of the orator's ability to talk his way out of a judicial conviction and to avoid punishment and being "treated badly," if he should be prosecuted. Socrates soon introduces the question of whether it is in fact good to avoid punishment, and this question leads to the further question of whether being punished is in fact being treated badly. The men set off toward an answer by considering what it means to do or suffer evil. They decide that one should avoid doing evil at all costs and that it is far better to suffer it than to do it, but then they have to decide whether suffering punishment is even suffering something evil at all.

Socrates begins the portion of the discussion that has to do with punishment by pondering the meaning of a typical Athenian phrase for punishment: "to give justice" (*to diken didonai*) (476d). After considering the phrase, Socrates and his interlocutors decide that to "give justice" (*to diken didonai*) means to suffer justice (*dikaia paschei*) at the hands of someone punishing justly (*ho de orthos kolazon dikaios kolazei*). Most people think that to be punished is to suffer something bad, but Socrates argues that to suffer justice or to have something "just" (*dikaia*) done to one is to have something "fair" or "beautiful" (*kala*) done to one. Therefore, the experience of "suffering justice" cannot be thought of as being anything unpleasant or evil (476d–e, 477a); it is instead to have one's life enhanced by justice. Suffering punishment or giving justice is therefore neither unpleasant nor bad. Socrates concludes thus: "So then the person who gives justice, (or who pays the penalty) [*ho diken didous*] suffers something good [*agatha*]?" Punishing, if it is the infliction of justice, cannot be the act of "doing badly" to wrongdoers but is rather to be understood as doing "good things" to them and as providing them with some sort of benefit (*ophelia*) (477a). Socrates thus redefines "giving justice" in such a way as to do away with a key Athenian idea—the idea that being punished is the reciprocal act of "suffering badly" at the hands of someone whom one has treated badly.

Next Socrates takes up the issue of exactly how a person who is punished can be said to benefit and to suffer something "beautiful" from punishment. He asks: "And what will I take this benefit to be [*ten ophelian*]? Is it that one becomes better in one's soul, if one is justly punished [*beltion ten psuchen gignetai, eiper dikaios kolazetai*]?" Socrates gets the response, "quite likely," from his interlocutor and then attempts to specify the form of improvement by turning to medical metaphors. Socrates argues that injustice in the soul is analogous both to poverty and to disease in the body (477bff.). The unjust person should go to the judge to be made well, just as the sick person goes to the doctor to be made well. Medicine "releases us from disease" (*apallattei nosou*), and "justice relieves us from licentiousness [*akolasias*] and injustice [*adikias*]" (478a-b). Justice "is a doctor [*iatrike*] for baseness [*ponerias*] and reforms us [*sophronizei*] and makes people more just" (478a–d).[11]

Socrates thus co-opts the tragic trope of disease but in the process resignifies the trope and reconstitutes its "grammar" so as to designate a different problematic of wrongdoing. The disease involved in punishment is no longer anger, an attack from a source external to the punisher, wrongdoer, and community. Now the disease is baseness (*poneria*), degeneration from within the wrongdoer.[12] No reference to the community is needed in order for the punisher or the philosopher to understand the wrongdoer's disease of licentiousness and injustice. The trope no longer characterizes intersubjectivity in the community nor the problems of the mutual implication of citizens in the problem of a wrongdoing and with the wrongdoer.

Socrates' next move only augments his quarrel with the Athenians over how to approach punishment. He places his argument about punishment within the context of Athenian morality by taking up the subject of helping friends and harming enemies, offering Polus instructions on how to do this. Polus, he argues, must recognize that helping his friends requires that he contribute to the good of their souls. Therefore he must prosecute them when they have done wrong so that they can have a chance to "suffer justice" and be reformed. Polus should use the powers of his rhetoric to ensure that his friends be treated to reformative punishment if they need it. The tools that can be used to "cure" one's friends will be not only words and arguments but even whippings, imprisonment, and fines (480b–d). This leaves Polus having to confront the idea that the orator should not use rhetoric to try to get himself or his friends off the hook; for to help himself or anyone else escape punishment would be to do himself or them an injury.

Polus is floored at the suggestion that this is how the power of the orator should be used. Socrates asks him to confirm their conclusions ("shall this be our statement?") and he responds: "It seems bizarre to me, Socrates [*atopa men . . . emoige dokei*], although perhaps in your opinion it follows from the argument that has preceded" (480d). Polus's ambivalent acceptance of the argument satisfies Socrates and the unflappable philosopher then carries his inversion of Athenian morality one step further by arguing that the best way to harm one's enemies is to let them get off scot-free for wrongdoing.

> Now if we take up the opposite topic, and suppose that it is [in fact] necessary [despite what we argued earlier] to do badly to someone [*kakos poiein*], whether to an enemy or someone else . . . what we have to do is to try with every possible means to act and speak in such a way that he neither gives justice nor appears before a judge. If [the person whom we are trying to harm] should come to trial, it is necessary to contrive a way for our enemy to escape without giving justice. (481a)

In other words, Socrates is arguing that the best way to *harm* an enemy is by making sure that the enemy is *not* punished. At this point in the conversation the Athenian Callicles joins in to express his surprise at the degree to which Socrates has subverted the ordinary paradigms of justice:

> *Callicles:* Tell me, Chaerephon, is Socrates serious about these things or only teasing [*paizei*]?
>
> *Chaerephon:* It seems to me, Callicles, that he is unnaturally or perversely [*huperphuos*] serious; but there is nothing like asking him.
>
> *Callicles:* By god, I want to. Tell me, Socrates, should we take you as presently serious or joking [*paizonta*]? For if you are serious and it happens that the things which you say are true, can it be otherwise than that human life has been turned upside down [or refuted] [*anatetrammenos*]?
>
> (418b–c)

In his argument with Polus Socrates has indeed upended or refuted key principles of Athenian public life. The "rational" punisher whose foremost thought is to educate or reform the diseased wrongdoer has replaced the angry and diseased punisher who would like to rectify a disharmonious and unbalanced social order of honor. The idea that punishing should be done with a view to the past came under attack in the *Protagoras* but the attack has been amplified here. The very idea that one can "do badly" to someone by punishing them in the course of an angry competition over honor has fallen by the wayside. The idea that one should harm one's enemies has not been completely left behind, but it has been turned and twisted so as to present a very strange face to Socrates' interlocutors. Socrates' arguments for a reformative approach to punishment unsettle the Athenian world view to the degree of turning the world upside down. But in this dialogue, the inconceivable is taken to be a playful joke. Here, as elsewhere, when the world is turned upside down it is taken to be but a matter of comedy.[13]

THE ERASURE OF *ORGE*

The Athenian world view (and other Greek world views like it) could not be truly unsettled without an attack on *orge*, the force that drove the system of reciprocity in the city and that was also central to the city's political organization. Nor could it be unsettled without there being some evidence that Socrates was actually having an effect on his Athenian (and non-Athenian) interlocutors. This is the work that Plato saves for the *Republic*.

Mackenzie and Saunders pay little attention to the place of the *Republic* within the corpus of Plato's arguments about reformative punishment. But it is in this dialogue that Socrates effects the revisions of the Athenian conceptualizations of anger that sustain his theory of reformative punishment and that entail a sweeping revision of the conceptual paradigm supporting Athenian political life in general. Moreover, in the *Republic* Socrates is explicit about the fact that he is introducing symbols and stories to make ideas that have been hitherto inconceivable to his audience conceivable. He is explicit about the fact that he is trying to change the topography of the conceptual world underlying his interlocutors' habitual practices and way of life.

Socrates' description of Leontios's inner struggle against the temptation of the Athenian spectacle serves a crucial purpose in the text of the *Republic*. It is the story that Socrates uses to prove to Glaucon that anger is a separate faculty from *eros*. Socrates' story of Leontios's horror at the corpses is a rejection not only of Athenian penal procedures but also of Athenian understandings of anger. After the story concludes with Socrates' imitation of Leontios's shouting at himself, "Go ahead, eyes, feast on the noble spectacle," Socrates glosses his story thus: "This story surely means [*ho logos semainei*] that anger [*ten orgen*] sometimes does battle [*polemein*] against the desires [*tais epithumiais*] as a thing distinct from the thing it battles [*hos allos on alloi*]" (440a). The gloss takes the resignification of the symbol of the body of the condemned one step further.

Socrates claims that Leontios's anger was pulling him not toward the spectacle, as the Athenian conceptualization of anger would require, but away from the spectacle. According to Socrates it is not anger but desire (*epithumia*) that drives people to participate in such spectacles. Socrates' word for desire, *epithumia*, includes not only the desires for food and drink but also sexual desire. Socrates' point—that anger is separate from desire and works against desire— is therefore an innovation and a resignification of the Athenian conceptualization of how *orge* worked. Socrates divides anger from desire, severs two passions that the Athenians considered to be intrinsically linked to one another, and guts the Athenian passion of *orge*, with its isomorphic erotic and iretic elements, of its ambiguities. Socrates' gloss on the story of Leontios is a rejection of the conceptualization of anger employed on the Athenian ideological paradigm and therefore also of the Athenian soul.

Socrates tells Glaucon the story of Leontios as part of his effort to convince Glaucon that the soul is divided into three parts—a rational faculty, a faculty for anger, and a desiring faculty. This idea by no means comes naturally to Glaucon, and Socrates knows it. He introduces the question of how to describe the soul by asking the following question:

> Do we learn with one part, grow angry [*thumoumetha*] with another part of ourselves, and desire [*epithumoumen*] the pleasures of nourishment and generation and whatever is related to them with a third part? Or do we do each of these things with the whole soul when once we set out after something. These are the things that it will be difficult to sort out adequately in conversation. (436a)

Socrates then argues that the soul is in fact tripartite by leading Glaucon through a discussion of cases where people can be seen to be struggling with themselves over some decision—cases where people suffer from what Socrates will call "civil war" of the soul. Thus Socrates discusses situations in which people want to drink something that they know is bad for them (as when the doctor has told you that caffeine is bad for your ulcer). On the basis of examples such as this, Socrates quite easily leads Glaucon to the conclusion that the soul can be said to have, at the very least, two parts: a rational part and a passional part:

> Is there not something in the soul that commands them to drink and something that forbids them to drink, something distinct that overcomes the element commanding them to drink? . . . And surely when what prohibits these things arises it arises from reason [*logismou*] and the impulsions that put up resistance arise from passions and disease [*dia pathematon te kai nosematon*]. . . . It would not be irrational then if we assessed [*axiosomen*] these two forces as being different from one another, calling that part of the soul which reasons the rational element [*logistikon*] and calling that part of the soul with which it lusts [*erai*], hungers, thirsts, and suffers all the flutterings [*eptoetai*] of desire [*epithumias*] in other respects irrational and desiring [*alogiston te kai epithumetikon*]. (439d–440a)

Glaucon agrees with Socrates up to this point in the argument but the next step is a harder sell. Even Socrates is not sure how easy it will be to argue from a soul that is divided into reason and passion to a soul that is divided into reason, anger, and desire. He says: "Let us, then, mark out these two elements as being in the soul. But in respect to the element of the *thumos* [*to de tou thumou*] and that with which we anger [*kai hoi thumoumetha*], is it a third thing or should it be considered to be a twin [*homophues*] to one of the others?" (439d–40a). Glaucon has an answer for Socrates. Anger, he says, might perhaps be identified as being a twin to desire (*isos toi heteroi, toi epithumetikoi*, 439e). Glaucon thus gives Socrates the standard Athenian answer when he says that anger might be identified as twin to the element in the soul that gives rise to lust. He is acknowledging not only that both anger and lust arise from the *thumos* but also the idea that the iretic and erotic passions might be different aspects of a single passion. On Glaucon's view, the *thumos* can be characterized as being a twin of the desiring part of the soul; they have the same nature (*homophues*). Glaucon simply does not think of the soul as being tripartite or of anger as being separate from desire.

It is at this point that Socrates tells the story of Leontios and of how his anger tried to keep his desire in check. The story sets the image of the possibility of the tripartite soul before Glaucon's mind's eye, and does in fact convince him that anger can act in opposition to desire and must therefore be its own faculty. Glaucon can believe in the possibility that anger is its own faculty once he can imagine somebody who acts with his soul organized that way. Glaucon had to see the tripartite soul to believe in it, a point that is crucial to understanding how Socrates uses symbols to revise his interlocutors' habits of mind. Socrates himself will make that point later in the dialogue as we shall see.

The story about Leontios convinces Glaucon that anger is separate from desire, and Socrates notes his success in revising his interlocutor's habitual understanding of how the soul works by commenting on Glaucon's shift of opinion:

But have you understood [*enthumei*] what is happening in regard to this matter? . . .
What is now obvious in respect to the angry or spirited element [*peri thumoeidous*] is
the opposite of what our opinion was recently. Earlier we thought that the spirited
element was the same as the desiring element [*epithumetikon*], but now we see that it
is much more necessary to understand that it takes up arms [*ta hopla*] on the side of
reason [*pros to logistikon*] during the struggles [*staseis*] in the soul. (440e)

Socrates has thus proved that anger is separate from desire counter to his interlocutor's intuitions, and his argument is radical in all possible senses of
the word given how fundamental to Athenian politics were conceptualizations
of desert based on ideas about anger and passion and their inevitable
interconnectedness.

Note too that when Socrates summarizes the conclusions to which he and
Glaucon have come, he casually replaces the word *orge* with *thumoeides*, which
becomes the standard word for the faculty of anger in the Platonic corpus. The
substantive *orge* is used in only three other places in the *Republic*: once to
describe the desires and passions of a "beast" (493a), once to describe the
"humors" or "tempers" of the masses (493d), and once to describe what happens when anger has not been entirely gotten under control (572a). The adjective *orgilos* is used once, and the passion it represents is criticized and set in
opposition to the high-spiritedness of the man who is *thumoeides* (411c). The
word *thumoeides* is a Platonic invention but calls to mind Homeric words, both
for its stress on the *thumos* and because of the suffix *-eides*. There are twenty-
eight instances of it in the *Republic* and only three elsewhere in the Platonic
corpus, highlighting the degree to which this dialogue concerns anger.[14] The
word *thumoeides* generally belongs to the vocabulary of philosophers and scientists, appearing only in Xenophon, Hippocrates, and Aristotle. Socrates has
not only challenged the Athenian conceptualization of anger but he has erased
it. The word *orge* can no longer be used once desire and anger have been
separated from one another. Socrates finalizes the erasure of *orge* by inventing a
new vocabulary of anger to replace it. The Athenian soul has also been replaced
with a new one when what was inconceivable to Glaucon becomes conceivable.

After Socrates uses the story of Leontios to convince Glaucon about the
tripartite soul, he gives another example to emphasize the point that anger responds to the commands of reason in a way that desire does not. This example
also has to do with punishment and once again flies in the face of Athenian
punitive norms. Socrates says:

When a man thinks that he has done wrong, is it not the case that the more noble he
is, the more incapable he will be of growing angry [*orgizesthai*] at hunger, cold, or
any other kind of suffering imposed on him by someone whom he considers to act
justly in treating him thus, and (as I say) his *thumos* will not desire to rise up against
this person . . . but when a man thinks that he has been wronged, won't he boil [*zei*],
grow angry [*chalepainei*] and put [his anger] in league with what seems just . . . and
in noble souls [anger] achieves victory and does not give up before it accomplishes its
aim or dies or else is called back by its own reason even as a dog called back by a

shepherd, and is calmed [*hupo tou logou tou par' hautoi anakletheis praunthei*]. (440c–d)

The person who is punished must submit to the punishment without anger, if the punishment is just.[15] Anger must respond to reason like a sheepdog called back by its shepherd. Socrates in fact models his guardians on such dogs (e.g., 375e). No longer would the citizen who was subjected to punishment inevitably be seen as acting legitimately if he were to carry on feuds of anger with those who had punished him, as in Athens.[16] Anger should not arise automatically at a loss of status. Anger, Socrates argues, should be based on a rational judgment about whether one has been treated justly or unjustly. In other words, anger arises *after* judgment. It is not the warning sign that it is time to judge. It is not the *reason to or inspiration to judge.*

Socrates convinces Glaucon of this point as well but there remains one last piece of work for Socrates to carry out before his arguments about anger will be complete. Socrates has to prove that anger is separate not only from desire but also from reason. This idea turns out to be so intuitive that the proof can be left to Glaucon:

> *Socrates:* Is the *thumos* distinct from reason as well or is it an element of reason so that there are not three elements in the soul but only two, the rational and the desiring? Or are there three elements even as is the case in the city—where there are the moneymakers, the auxiliary guards, and the counselors—so that thus in the soul the third part is this angry-spirited element [*thumoeides*], which is in nature an auxiliary guard of reason unless it is corrupted by a bad upbringing.
>
> *Glaucon:* It is necessarily a third component.
>
> *Socrates:* Yes, if it appears to be distinct from reason even as it appears to be distinct from desire.
>
> *Glaucon:* But that is shown without difficulty [*ou chalepon*]. For one may see this faculty in children who are from their beginnings filled with anger [*thumou*], but some seem never to advance to reason and others only rather late.
>
> *Socrates:* You speak well, and one may also learn that matters are as you say from animals [*therios*].
>
> (440e–441c)

It takes no more than this brief interchange to make the case that anger is separate from reason. The case that anger is separate from reason can be left to Glaucon to make, and he can make it without Socratic help. This is because the standard Athenian idea that anger is part and parcel of the soul's passional faculty is sufficient to prove the case that anger is distinct from reason.[17] In contrast, the standard Athenian understandings of human cognitive and passional experience were not enough to prove that anger was separate from desire.

The separation of anger from desire requires not only a definition of anger and its place in human experience and not only a new vocabulary for anger but also a new vocabulary of desire that will avoid suggesting that desire includes anger. Socrates can no longer use the words *thumos* and *orge* to talk about the body's appetites for sex, food, and drink. As a result, he lays more emphasis on *epithumia* and *hormai* than had been standard in texts written earlier than his dialogues (for *horme*, cf. 439b, 451c, 506e, 511b, 532a, 611e). By the time of Stoic philosophy, *horme* will be the standard word for desire. In book 9 Socrates confirms that he has been troubled by the lack of an obvious name for the desiring part of the soul:

> We said that there was one part of the soul with which a man learns, a part with which he grows angry, and a third part that, because it was made up of many elements [*dia polueidian*], we were unable to denote with a single name belonging properly to it [*heni ouk eschomen onomati proseipein idioi autou*]. Therefore we named [*eponomasamen*] it after that which was greatest and strongest in it; for we called it the desiring part itself [*epithumetikon gar auto keklekamen*] because of the seriousness [*dia sphodroteta*] of its appetites [*epithumion*] for food and drink and sex and all things that follow from these appetites, and also we called it the moneyloving part because such desires are especially satisfied by means of money. (580d–81a)

The Platonic vocabulary of passion—a vocabulary that uses new words for both anger and erotic desire—seals the transition from the Athenian paradigm for thinking about human cognitive and passional experience to the Socratic/Platonic paradigm.

Socrates uses these revisions of vocabulary to seal the conceptual change that he has effected but he also uses symbols. At the end of his final book 9 discussion of the tripartite soul, Socrates suggests that he and his interlocutors will understand the firm division between reason, anger, and desire better if they should "fashion [*plasantes*] a symbol [*eikona*] of the soul out of speech, in order that by looking [*eidei*] at this *eikon* they might see" what he, Socrates, was saying (588c). The icon that Socrates fashions out of speech for his interlocutors to look at is the famous image of the human soul as being one part human for the rational faculty, one part lion for the soul's capacity for anger, and one part many-headed beast for the faculty of desire. Socrates uses his image of the human being who is one part human, one part lion, and one part many-headed beast in order to give his interlocutors a mental picture of what the life of injustice is like. The life of injustice is that in which the human part of the soul is preyed upon by the many-headed beast or by the lion (588d); it is the life lived by people who fail to keep their passions under the control of their reason. The wrongdoer thus suffers the torment of a human being who is mauled by a beast. Socrates' next move is to use this icon to explain why punishment is a boon to wrongdoers:

> How can we say, Glaucon, and on what grounds, that it is profitable to commit injustice, or to be unchaste or to do something shameful through which one becomes a worse person, though acquiring money or some other power? And how can we say that the wrongdoer will profit by escaping notice and not paying a penalty [*kai me didonai diken*]? For will the person who escapes notice not grow worse still? In contrast, the bestial nature of the person who does not escape notice and is punished

[*tou de me lanthanontos kai kolazomenou to men theriodes koimizetai kai hemeroutai*] is cared for and tamed. . . . as a result the entire soul—constituted according to the best nature and possessing moderation and justice in judgment—will be in a more worthy condition [*timioteran hexin*] than a body that possesses strength and beauty with health, in proportion as the soul is more precious [*timiotera*] than the body. (591b)

Punishment tames the beast in the wrongdoer. The argument about the tripartite soul, which is carried out across the whole of the *Republic*, culminates finally in the image of the person as human, lion, or many-headed beast and in the argument that wrongdoers whose souls are put together in this fashion will always want to suffer reformative punishment in order to tame the beast that has control of the soul when he or she commits injustice. Here it is worth interjecting that Leontios's name essentially means "lionlike" and so he was a suitable character to put at the center of a story about anger in the soul. By the end of the *Republic*, Socrates has a symbolic justification for taking Leontios as his central example of how anger should work. The *Republic*'s analysis of and symbols for the tripartite soul justify the claims made elsewhere in that dialogue and others that punishment is good for the wrongdoer. The argument for reformative punishment is thus shown to depend, in the first instance, on the separation of anger from sexual desire and on the rejection of *orge* as a phenomenon upon which to found the organization of human life and politics. The argument for reformative punishment depends on the prior claim that no element of the human psychopassional experience should be valorized to the same level as reason.

Undoing the Athenian "Principle of the Public": The *Republic*

The Athenian "principle of the public" or principle according to which political life was organized was the communal commitment to the spectacle of angry honor-sensitive citizens competing with one another on a regular basis (and within the bounds set by standards of public utility), with women excluded from the realm of anger (speaking ideally) so that the family unit would be free of angry conflicts. Athenian political life to this degree valorized anger and granted it a place in politics. But anger also had to be constrained with a view to its close connection with *eros*. When Socrates redefines the role of anger in human action, he revises not only the place of anger in the political order but also the nature of the political order in general. Socrates argues for a politics that keeps anger outside the walls of the city. The entirety of the *Republic* is largely structured around a rejection and replacement of the political concepts that were connected to the valorization of anger in Athenian politics (and possibly in other political orders; we have seen that some non-Athenians treated *orge* in a manner that paralleled the Athenian treatments). This claim is not a claim that the *Republic* is concerned only with anger or only with Athenian politics; it is rather the claim that an Atheno-centric concern in *this* dialogue provides the context within which Socrates makes a whole slew of arguments about justice that are meant to apply to Athens but also to other cities. It is necessary to look at how Plato treats punishment in this dialogue to understand what he is doing with Athenian politics.

First let me summarize the points made as the dialogue advances. The book begins with Cephalus's assertion that life is better once the passions have been tamed. He argues that "a great peacefulness and freedom attain in old age in respect to all matters concerning such things, when the desires cease and loosen their hold by relaxing, and it is in all respects as Sophocles said, a release [*apellachthai*] from masters who are many and raving" (329c–d). After this initial rejection of passion, the interlocutors take up the topic of justice and move next to an invalidation of the principle of reciprocity. Cephalus wishes to argue that justice is honesty, but his son takes over the argument from him and makes the case that justice is helping friends and harming enemies. This definition of justice does not stand for long because Socrates finally gets the son Polemarchus to agree that it is unjust to harm anyone at all, even an enemy (331e–336a). Thus Athenian reciprocity falls by the wayside in the dialogue's early sections.

Next follows a conversation between Thrasymachus and Socrates in which Socrates establishes his antagonism to an exaggerated Athenian competitiveness and to the use of that competitiveness as a principle for action (Thrasymachus is not, of course, Athenian but he does to large degree say and do things that would have sounded normal in the Athenian courts).[18] During this conversation, Thrasymachus and Socrates describe Athenian competitive paradigms of justice—where everyone is trying to get "more" status and wealth—as "pleonectic," a word that is often translated as "greedy" or as "characterized by a desire to 'overreach'" (344a). The use of the word "pleonectic" to describe competition for status and wealth will pave the way for the dialogue's project of undermining the Athenian valorization of competitiveness. During the course of the conversation, Thrasymachus tries to argue that justice consists of the advantage of the stronger,[19] but eventually gives way before Socrates' insistence that the name of justice cannot be applied to the unjust acts of violence that are carried out by the stronger in order to fulfill their desires. Their conversation concludes when Thrasymachus finally concedes that injustice can in no way be considered a more profitable enterprise than justice (354a).

After the conversation with Thrasymachus, Socrates wants to start the search for justice all over again. Glaucon and Adeimantus each pose Socrates a challenge to get him going. Glaucon tells the story of the shepherd Gyges who found a ring that made him invisible and that therefore made it possible for him to fulfill his desires in any and every way, even by acting against the law and against community norms, without getting caught. Gyges' ring allows him to operate outside the contexts of social networks of sight and communal knowledge and memory. As Glaucon puts it, the unjust man who has nothing to fear from the networks of visuality will rule the city, have any wife he pleases, give his children in marriage to whomever he pleases, have whatever business dealings that he wants and in respect to all these things [*para tauta panta*] he will benefit [*opheleisthai*], profiting from the fact that he is not disheartened by injustice [*kerdainonta toi me duscherainein to adikein*]; he will be successful when he goes to trial, whether in a public or private suit, and will outgrasp his enemies [*pleonektein*] and being greedy [*pleonektounta*] he will be wealthy and help his friends and harm his enemies. (362b–c)

Glaucon thus posits that social memory is the only restraint on an exaggerated Athenian competitiveness and system of reciprocity that is—here he concurs with Socrates—pleonectic. Social knowledge, he implies, is all that keeps Athenian norms from manifesting themselves as *pleonexia*. He asks Socrates whether there is any reason to reject the Athenian habits of competition and reciprocity that are the seeds of *pleonexia* other than fear of the operations of social knowledge.

Adeimantus challenges Socrates by asking him to define justice without doing what fathers usually do in talking about justice to their sons: invoke stories about afterlife punishments and admonish their sons to act justly lest they suffer not only worldly punishments but also those waiting for them after death (363c–e). Adeimantus thus augments Glaucon's request that Socrates prove that justice is intrinsically desirable.

This opening section of the dialogue is a series of conversations in which the name of the interlocutor always reflects the subject matter under discussion. The conversation about passion is carried out by a man named "head," the conversation about reciprocity and harming enemies by a man named "war-leader," the conversation about strife, competition, and the advantage of the stronger by a man named "bold battler," the conversation about social networks of sight and memory by a man named "fierce glaring" or "gray-eyed," and the conversation about the threat of punishment by a man named "where there is no fear." It seems almost too pat to be a relevant detail. Whatever the case, these introductory conversations introduce the parameters for Socrates' discussion of what the just city would be like. It will be a city in which the principles of reciprocity, the valorization of competitiveness, and the powers of social knowledge and memory do not operate. The dialogue is being set up so that the just city will be, by definition, the inverse of Athens.

Before we consider the nature of Socrates' just city, it is worth making note of a few of the details that arise during the conversation between Thrasymachus and Socrates in particular. Thrasymachus and Socrates discuss the topics of desire, strife, and anger during the course of their conversation, but they also act out a drama about anger and punishing. Certain of the details of the drama highlight two things: the degree to which the principles of a competitive politics are being contested by Socrates; and the degree to which Athenian and Socratic principles are really ideational articulations of habitual ways of behaving or habits of mind. Those habits of mind are presented, in this drama, not in the form of analytical statements but in the form of Thrasymachus's exaggerated competitiveness and his desire to hold a penal contest and in Socrates' idiosyncratic way of behaving.

Thrasymachus breaks into the conversation between Polemarchus and Socrates by interrupting, and Socrates accuses him of springing upon them like a wild beast (*therion*) (336b). The accusation anticipates the image of the tripartite soul that Socrates will construct at the end of the dialogue; it also harks back to Protagoras. Thrasymachus will indeed prove to be committed to "beastly" retributive punishment and to have no interest in switching to reformative paradigms. After Thrasymachus breaks into the conversation, Socrates asks Thrasymachus to pity him and Polemarchus rather than being angry or harsh toward them (*eleeisthai . . . e chalepainesthai*) (336e). Socrates thus taps the opposition between anger and pity typically found in forensic oratory and thereby sets his conversation with Thrasymachus in the context of a judicial proceeding. Socrates is the defendant making a plea for pity. He positions Thrasymachus as the prosecutor acting out of anger. The joke is neat since Thrasymachus had written a rhetorical handbook called *Eleoi* or pities. But Thrasymachus does not relax his harshness and instead accuses Socrates of trickery, chastising him for shamming ignorance (337a–b). Next Thrasymachus challenges Socrates to a contest over which of them has a better definition of justice; the loser, he says, will have to pay whatever penalty the winner thinks that he deserves to suffer (*ti axiois pathein*) (337d), just as in the process of *timesis*.

Socrates responds to the challenge the way he does in Plato's *Apology*. He says to Thrasymachus that he is willing to suffer the penalty that is suitable (*prosekei*) for the ignorant: to receive instruction from the wise (337d). Thrasymachus responds: "That's sweet [*hedus*], but in addition to the instruction, you will have to pay silver [*kai apoteison argurion*]" (337d). He insists that Socrates also pay a monetary penalty regardless of whatever instruction he may receive. Thrasymachus is unwilling to give up on the idea of reciprocity, symbolized by the silver, and so the passage enacts the Protagorean opposition between the beast who punishes reciprocally for *timoria* and the calm, rational creature who thinks that punishment should reform.

As the scene unfolds Thrasymachus continues to use courtroom language, and Socrates continues to respond to him by rejecting it. Socrates challenges Thrasymachus's account of justice as being whatever is to the advantage of the stronger, and Thrasymachus calls Socrates a sycophant and says that he does not trust Socrates' use of words (340d). Socrates responds:

> *Socrates:* Do I seem to you to be a sycophant? . . . Do you think that I am acting as an evildoer who is plotting with words in order to damage you [*oiei gar me ex epiboules en tois logois kakourgounta*]?
>
> *Thrasymachus:* I know you are. But you will not sneak past me with your evil deeds nor will you be able to best me openly with speech [*eu men oun oida. . . . oute gar an me lathois kakourgon, oute me lathon biasasthai toi logoi dunaio*].

(341a–b)

Thrasymachus wants to have an open (*me lathon*) hot-blooded contest of force (*biasasthai*), man against man, and he accuses Socrates, who will not participate in that open contest, of employing cunning trickery, evil deeds, and slippery words. Socrates is a sycophant in Thrasymachus's eyes because he refuses to participate in a punitive competition according to the norms of "hot blood."

Socrates offers a second defense to the accusations of sycophancy: "Do you think that I am so mad [*manenai*] as to seek [*xurein*] to subdue a lion [*epicheirin leonta*] and to try to act as a sycophant toward Thrasymachus [*sukophantein Thrasumachon*]?" (341c). Here Socrates implies that the answer to these two questions is no. But as we know, Socrates does use his skill with words to get the Athenian conception of anger under control. Socrates rejects the valorization of anger that drives people to the punitive spectacle and instead puts it firmly beneath the sway of reason and casts it as an emotion that leads people away from the punitive spectacle rather than as one that drives people toward it. Only in book 9 will Socrates finally give a more honest answer to this question. He imagines the angry part of the soul as being represented by a lion, and it becomes clear that Socrates is in fact mad enough to try to subdue lionlike characters like Thrasymachus. But what does that mean in respect to his treatment of Thrasymachus?

The Socratic interventions that lead to the accusations of sycophancy were directed against Thrasymachus's arguments that might makes right and that the life of injustice is more valuable or advantageous than the life of justice. Thrasymachus argues that the unjust man has the greatest power to fill his greedy desire (*lego gar honper nunde elegon, ton megala dunamenon pleonektein*, 344a). This man will be the happiest because he always gets what he wants. Socrates responds by arguing the just person is wise and good and understands the importance of limits and measure, like the excellent musician. The unjust person is ignorant in contrast. Eventually Thrasymachus concedes the point and the result is dramatic. He goes through a transformation that is physiological as well as intellectual.[20]

Socrates reports it thus: "Thrasymachus agreed to all these things nowhere nearly as easily as I describe them, but with resistance and hesitation, and with an incredible amount of sweat, because it was summertime; and then I saw what I had never before seen—Thrasymachus blushing" (350d). Just as Philocleon was physically affected when he was cured of his anger—he cried out that he "was no more"—so Thrasymachus goes through a physiological and a mental transformation simultaneously when he gives up on his pseudoprosecution. The conversation about justice turns out to have an effect on the auditor analogous to the effect of the regimen of the physical trainer on the athlete or the regimen of a doctor on a patient. After the transformation, Thrasymachus launches one last missile and calls Socrates an old woman. After that, he is relatively placid not only for the rest of their conversation but for the rest of the dialogue (350d).

The conversation, however, is not quite over yet, for Socrates must win another point: the idea that injustice causes internal dissension or strife within any group or entity, whether that is a city, a group of thieves, or the soul of the individual (351d). Thrasymachus eventually assents to this second proposition also and thereby paves the way for Socrates to claim later in the dialogue not only that injustice causes strife but also that the presence of strife in the city is itself a sign that injustice exists in the city (351c–352b). This will lead to the idea that one can define the just city by describing a place where there is no strife.[21]

Socrates' first image of the just city, the city that gets called the "city of pigs" by his interlocutors, is precisely a picture of a community that is completely peaceful. The people will loll about on country beds of byrony and myrtle and will eat rough foods—barley, wheat, olives, cheese, and figs—begetting children, singing hymns to the gods, and avoiding war and poverty. They will live in peace and health and die from old age (369c–372c). Such a city, Socrates says, is the only true city (*alethine polis*, 372e).

What is significant about Socrates' decision to take the absence of strife as a starting point from which to define justice in the city and justice in the soul is that he takes this to mean that Athenian competitions will have to go. In the rest of the dialogue it becomes clear that Socrates is willing to designate even penal competitions, which the Athenians treated as introducing a healthy and productive level of rivalry into the city, as "strife." The guardians will be taught not to hate one another and will never be allowed to participate in the exchanges of laughter that provoke violent reactions (388e)—competition among themselves or with the citizens is to be unknown to them.[22] In the just city, Socrates argues, lawsuits (*dikai*) and accusations (*engklemata*) among the citizens will all but vanish, and there will be no more of the quarrels (*astasiastois*) that arise from ownership of property and from having family ties (464d). In Athens 28 cases out of the roughly 120 in the Athenian oratorical corpus had to do with property and family quarrels.

Nor will behavior like Thrasymachus's be acceptable. Thrasymachus's insistence on treating his conversation with Socrates as some kind of court suit makes it an example of the kind of "strife" that the latter wants to get rid of. The depiction of Thrasymachus's aggressiveness serves as an exaggerated portrayal of Athenian competitiveness. It is not limited, manageable, and socially useful but rather a form of behavior that introduces extreme habits of injustice to the city and that must, therefore, be banished from it.

Thrasymachus eventually assents to the proposition that injustice can never be more profitable than justice, and Socrates marks his final victory by thanking Thrasymachus: "For that I have to thank you, Thrasymachus. You became so mild in respect to me when you let go of your temper [*epeide moi praos egenou kai chalepainon epauso*]" (354b). Socrates thanks Thrasymachus not only for having conceded an analytical point but also for having abandoned anger for mildness. What was at stake in the discussion between the two men was not only the specific ideas about justice but also whether Thrasymachus, in the face of Socrates' arguments, would be able to persist in his fierce competitiveness. The drama acted out by Thrasymachus and Socrates allows Plato to redefine Athenian penal competitiveness not as socially useful but as socially destructive and to set the stage for the moment when Socrates will rule such behavior out of the political court entirely.

The Thrasymachean drama makes several other important points as well. The dialogue's arguments about justice are not merely abstract ideas separable from the sphere of human action and activity but rather cannot be disentangled from the particular practices and forms of behavior employed by each interlocutor. When Socrates talks about justice, he is talking about his interlocutors' ways of doing things, which for the *Republic*'s characters means habits of anger, reciprocity, honor, and competition.[23] The drama within the drama of the dialogue posits a link between how people behave on a regular basis and the abstract notions that they will express when asked about justice.

Plato's drama also poses a question about what the intended effect of Socrates' words on those around him is. Socrates himself introduces the question when he twice asks whether people think he is a sycophant (341a–b, c). By the end of the dialogue, Socrates will admit to trying to tame the passion of anger in Thrasymachus and others, but is that also an admission to sycophancy or to an attempt to use words to harm people? Although the full answer to this question is developed only at the end of this chapter, it should be clear by now that Socrates is consistently using words and fashioning his symbols in order to revise concepts that are central to his interlocutors' world views, to force them to conceive of what had been to them inconceivable, and to change their standard forms of behavior. But on Socrates' definitions of harm and benefit, if these changes reform his interlocutors, then he is not doing them any harm. Socrates forces us either to return to his favorite topic—what is harm or injustice and what is benefit or justice?—or else to try to find a way out of the loop of Socratic definitions.

The *Republic* is itself a drama. It poses the question not only of how to define justice but also the question of how efforts to define justice impact the behavior of those people who are engaged in the enterprise of definition. In the dialogue, Socrates regularly chooses to access his interlocutors' habitual definitions of justice by focusing on how they think about punishment. The focus on punishment leads Socrates' interlocutors to challenge him to describe a definition of justice that reverses norms fundamental to Athenian punishment, politics, and life. Socrates agrees to set about redefining the Athenian principle of politics but suggests that he is "mad" to do so. The question about whether Socrates is mad enough to try to tame a lion or to act like a sycophant toward Thrasymachus leaves open the further question, one of the dialogue's central questions, of how we should label the speech acts that Socrates carries out in the Athenian *polis*.

THE JUST CITY AND THE POWER OF THE SYMBOL

Socrates' interlocutors set him a challenge, and then Socrates responds with two images of the just city. The first, as we have seen, is the peaceful, agricultural city, but Socrates' interlocutors want to hear about a city that is both just (and therefore free of strife) and luxurious. Socrates must reject the simple peasant community and theorize a just city with all of the urbane pleasures. His second attempt to describe the just city results in the "republic" with which we are most familiar. The key elements of the just city will be a class of craftsmen, who are responsible for furnishing the city with all it needs, a class of farmers, and the guardians. The guardians themselves will be split into two classes—the actual soldiers, or auxiliaries, and a class of guardian-rulers, the class from which the philosopher-kings will eventually be drawn. The two classes of the guardians (the rulers and the auxiliaries) will live in a camp away from the rest of the citizens, and there they will live according to the principles of communism, without competition, strife, or hatred, and according to principles of strict equality between men and women.

The city will have to fight external wars because of its habits of luxury. The need for the just city to fight wars presents Socrates with his first major problem. The just city must be internally free of strife and any warlike (Thrasymachean) spirit. Yet the guardians will need such a spirit to fight the city's external enemies. Socrates needs some way to keep the warlike spirit of angry competitiveness at the borders of the city without letting it into the city. He therefore turns his attention toward describing how the warrior class can be constituted so as to fight fiercely outside the city while living peacefully within it (374–75). The guardians must be "high-spirited" or able to act with anger (*thumoeides*) (375b), but this makes Socrates worried. He asks the following question: "How can they avoid being savage [*agrioi*] to one another and to the other citizens when they have such a nature? . . . It is necessary for them to be mild [*praous*] to their own people and harsh [*chalepous*] to their enemies" (375c). It will be the guardians' job to be warlike, manly and angry (*andreios* and *thumoeides*, 375b), and severe (*chalepous*, 375c) *in respect to enemies* but to be gentle (*praous*, 375–76) and peaceful *in respect to the citizenry*. (And remember that Thrasymachus's conversion changed him from being harsh to being mild.) The guardians will separate their ability to be manly from how they behave within the city where, like the women of Athens, they will keep their faculty for anger in check. On Athenian terms Socrates feminizes the virtue of the male citizen acting inside the city.[24]

According to Socrates, watchdogs have precisely such a two-sided temperament (375e ff.). They distinguish between foe and friend and treat the former with a warlike aggressiveness and the latter with perfect docility. The guardians should therefore behave like watchdogs. They will have a nature such as allows them to act out the Socratic principle that anger responds to reason like a watchdog to its shepherd. Socrates thus begins his discussion of the just city by positing not only the division of citizens into several classes but also the possibility of keeping angry, manly, Athenian competitiveness at the borders of the city to be employed against enemies but never to be used inside the city. To effect a politics structured this way, he assigns a rigorous education to his guardians with a view to teaching them to maintain a two-sided temperament (375b ff.). That education, discussed in books 2 through 4, teaches the guardians their duties and virtues. The discussion of the education of the guardians reaches its conclusion in the argument about the tripartite soul and the story of Leontios. What is at stake is the possibility of reeducating people to a use of anger different from that of the Athenian paradigm.

Socrates spends a great deal of time talking about the kinds of stories and fictions (or, better, falsehoods)[25] that must be used in educating the guardian children.[26] He educates Glaucon to a new understanding of anger with the story of Leontios and the bodies of the condemned and recommends that the same method—the use of stories about punishment—be used in the education of the guardian children. Socrates takes up the topic of how to educate the children by arguing that the stories that are already part of the Athenian cultural fabric— especially stories that show the gods committing acts of injustice or quarreling or displaying strife—are unacceptable. Children must be told fictions, and whatever fictions they will be told must be censored. Decisions must be made about what will be allowed and what will not be allowed or, rather, about what will be especially condemned—for instance, stories about the mutual attacks of Uranus, Cronus, and Zeus on one another and of Zeus's escape from punishment for his treatment of his father (378a–c). Nor must stories about the wars, hatreds, and quarrels of the gods be admitted into the just city (378b–c). The effort of the educator should instead be to figure out how "we may be able to persuade them that no citizen has ever hated [*apechtheto*] another and that to do so is not holy, and such things are what should be told to children right away by the old men and women, and also as they grow older, and it is necessary for the poets to make stories [*logopoiein*] of this sort" (378c–d). In other words, the guardians must be educated away from any inclination to indulge in angry rivalries or feuds. The poets will no longer be able to tell tales where the gods, as symbols of value, are used to affirm the legitimacy of acting in anger at or hatred for one's fellows. Socrates calls the poets to the task of making new stories (*logopoiein*), of telling new tales, in which ideas of desert and justice will have been reformulated from what they were in Athens.

Next Socrates wants the poets to revise stories that are told about those unfortunate souls who have suffered punishment from the gods. They are to be considered unfortunate no longer. Socrates will require that:

> If a poet should make up a tale about the sufferings [*ta pathe*] of Niobe . . . or about the house of Pelops or the affairs of Troy, he is not allowed to say that these things, or anything like them, are the work of god. Or if they are to be the work of god, it is necessary for him to devise such an explanation as we are even now seeking, and it is necessary for him to say that since the god works justice and the good, they benefited from being punished [*oninanto kolazomenoi*]. But the poet is not allowed to say that those who give justice [*hoi diken didontes*] are unhappy, thanks to the work of god. *But it is permissible to say that the bad are unhappy because they need punishment* (kolaseos) *and that when they give justice* (didontes de diken) *they are being benefited by god.* (380a–b)

Misfortune cannot come from the gods but must be redescribed as arising from guilt or baseness. Punishment in turn will be redescribed as beneficial, and the gods, therefore, as rationally wise punishers who aim to reform. The revised stories will teach the combined lessons of the *Gorgias* and *Protagoras*: that punishment makes the wrongdoer better, is therefore a benefit, and is not to be considered as a "bad thing" to have suffered.

Finally, Socrates also requires that stories about the underworld be revised (and here he is surely cheating in respect to Adeimantus's opening challenge to him). The disheartening descriptions of the afterlife that are current in Socrates' day and age must be forbidden both because they are untrue and because they are injurious to future warriors (386a ff.). In other words, when Socrates sets himself to establishing the rules for what kinds of stories may be used to educate children, he focuses on stories of wrongdoing and punishment. He resignifies the stories and in the process revises the conceptualizations of desert that Athenian narratives of punishment made manifest.

Socrates himself discusses his habit of rereading old stories for new sets of principles, for new conceptualizations of desert and justice. He claims that he, and founders in general, cannot or do not have time to invent new stories reflecting the new Socratic conceptualizations of desert and the Socratic systems of value. But what they do have the power or time to do is to resignify old stories:

> It is fitting for founders [*oikistais*] to know the patterns [*tous men tupous*] according to which the poets must write their mythologies and from which it is necessary for them not to deviate if they make up tales, but it is not necessary for us ourselves to make the stories [*ou men autois ge poeteon muthous*]. . . . In respect to the mythology that we were discussing just now, because we do not know how the truth stands concerning antiquity, we can assimilate the false to the true [*aphomoiountes toi alethei to pseudos*] and make it especially useful in this fashion. (379a, 382d)

Falsehoods are to be assimilated to the truth of the Socratic system of value. These acts of narrative revision must follow a certain principle: the Athenian paradigm of desert, which privileges anger and honor, must be replaced by a Socratic paradigm, which privileges knowledge and virtue. This paradigm is called a *tupos* and the idea seems to be equivalent to the Burkean idea that symbols are built on some general or abstract pattern of principles. In requiring that stories of punishment have a certain "type," the founder will require that stories reflect and show in operation a coherent Socratic conceptualization of authority, justice, and desert. Socrates encourages his poets to do exactly the sort of work that he did in the story of Leontios: resignify a symbol in order to replace the Athenian symbolic order encoded by it with a Socratic symbolic paradigm. Stories that are constructed according to the Socratic *tupos* will encapsulate a set of principles that undergird the new Socratic politics; the Socratic principles will be as easily assimilable as the story is. Book 2 concludes with Glaucon's promise to use the types (*tupoi*) as laws (*nomoi*) (383c).

Socrates recognizes that a single story about punishment instantiates a coherent understanding of a set of social relations, a coherent system of value, and he expects a resignification of a story about punishing to function so as to supplant previous conceptualizations of desert in the minds of the children. As Burke writes: "The symbol might be called a word invented by the artist to specify a particular grouping or pattern or emphasizing of experiences—and the work of art in which the symbol figures might be called a definition of this word. . . . The symbol may also serve to force patterns [of experience] upon the audience, however, the universal experiences being capable of other groupings or patterns than those which characterize a particular reader."[27] A resignification of a single story, a single and particular instantiation of a framework of desert and authority, is expected to produce the realignment of frameworks of desert and authority in the guardians' minds and so of politics in the city at large. One suspects that Socrates uses revision not for lack of an ability to invent stories but because he, like Aristophanes in *Wasps*, recognized that such revision is a more potent tool than invention. The revision of a society's symbols harnesses the power of the old symbols of value to new conceptualizations of value and sets the old symbols to new work.

Socrates' use of fictions to educate the citizens of his just city has troubled commentators because he also argues that his guardians, and the just person in general, must hate falsehood as the gods do. Socrates himself explains the paradox by saying that his guardians and their assistants (and later the philosopher-kings) are to act as if their falsehoods and stories are forms of "medicine" (*pharmakon*, 382d, 389b) that must be used when necessary, for the benefit of the city (*ep' opheleiai tes poleos*, 389b). Not only the storyteller but also the judge and the punisher are frequently enjoined to act like doctors in Platonic dialogues.[28] The implication of the trope is that the "storyteller," as well as the judge and punisher, "cures" those who have the disease of injustice. The stories about the gods, wrongdoing, and punishment that serve as medicine are therefore analogous not only to the prescriptions of the doctor *but also* to the decisions of the judge. Both the stories about punishment and the decisions about punishment "cure" injustice in the soul by making a statement about the proper way to think about desert and by teaching the wrongdoer the "right" system of value. The storyteller who effects a resignification of a symbol that encapsulates principles of authority and desert has the power to effect a cultural paradigm shift and to change "the present order of things." This is Hippocrates' definition of what a *pharmakon* does (*Top. And.* 45),[29] and stories are medicine in this way.

Socrates follows his discussion of the stories that should be used for children with description of one more story that all citizens must come to believe. This is the noble lie. After having laid out the ways in which the guardians can be educated to be warlike and gentle and after forbidding them from engaging in lamentation, exchanges of insult, and quarreling, Socrates introduces the noble lie by asking: "How can we contrive one of those lies that arise out of necessity about which we are just now speaking, in order that one single noble [*gennaion*] lie may persuade the rulers and, if not them, at least the rest of the city?" (414c). The fictions about which they had "just been speaking" were the fictions that served as medicine, and so the noble lie is another *pharmakon*. This cure is the story, the Phoenician tale, to be told to the guardians, auxiliaries, and the rest of the citizens that all the members of the just city are born from earth herself and are born with a nature that is either gold, silver, brass, or iron. Their natures determine their place in the city. Gold is mixed into the race that rules and they are the ones with the most worth (*timiotatoi eisin*, 415a). If a child is born of brass or iron, the guardians "must assign him to a station with respect to what befits his natural worth or honor [*ten tei phusei prosekousan timen*]. If on the contrary these classes produce a child with gold or silver in his composition they will assess his honor and lead him forward [*timesantes anaxousi*] to be a guardian or an auxiliary" (415b–c).

The noble lie gives the guardians a single story on which to base assessments of value, honor (*time*), and desert. This tale puts an end to the possibility that the members of the just city will compete for *time*. Their *time* is rather to be understood as predetermined. According to Socrates it is this story, if it ever comes to be believed, that will finally increase the ability of the citizens to care for one another (415d)—in other words, it is the last stage of a training that will keep the city free of strife, quarrels, insults, *andreia*, and *thumos*. The political principles of Athenian citizens who competed for honor with the possibility of increasing or decreasing their relative status in the city are thus undone by the noble lie that explicitly posits four stable and noncontestable levels of *time* or honor for the citizenry. The noble lie, this final story, establishes nothing other than a system of value, a revised schema for assessing desert, and seals the rejection of the Athenian paradigm for punishment and politics.

By this point in the dialogue, Socrates has undermined Athenian principles of reciprocity, angry competitiveness, and the use of social networks of sight and memory to check unjust behavior, but he has also replaced all of those principles with his own revisions. Punishment benefits the wrongdoer, citizens will always act with mildness to one another, their inclinations to justice will come from within them because of the nature of their education, and honor will be something that is not contestable. Socrates concludes his examination of the education of the guardians by asking what kind of justice is established in the city and in the soul by such an education and by such principles. The answer, in respect to the soul, is that the justice to be found in such a city reflects the citizens' possession of rightly ordered tripartite souls. The justice of this republic reflects, and is built out of, the total erasure of Athenian conceptualizations of anger.

It is at this point in the dialogue that Socrates introduces the story of Leontios. Socrates' use of the story of Leontios conveys to Glaucon not only the tripartite nature of the soul of the citizen of the ideal city but also a new way of looking at Athens. When the *Republic* began, we thought that we knew the nature of the road back to Athens. But after we read the text, the road back to Athens has become something new, a place where we will recoil at the bodies of executed criminals rather than both exulting and being silent about them.[30] Socrates has taught Glaucon a way of thinking about anger, the soul, and the city that should lead him to evaluate negatively the Athenian penal practices that place the bodies of the condemned at the city walls on the road from the Piraeus to Athens. The topography of the Athenian landscape is changed for Glaucon when Socrates resignifies the symbolic value of the bodies of the condemned.

It is only after Socrates has effected a comprehensive revision of the principles underlying Athenian politics and has changed the way we read the topography of the Athenian landscape that he introduces what he considers to be his three most radical proposals: the equality of the guardian women (445–71), the abolition of the family for the guardians (457), and the rule of the philosopher-kings. All three are possible only now that the Socratic system of value—where anger and competition are suppressed—has been fully constructed. Once the political arena is no longer run according to principles of anger, Socrates can argue that men and women do not have different natures, and so they do not need different occupations (454). There is no profession or occupation for the purposes of which a woman's nature is different from a man's since a woman may have a gift for medicine or for music, may be wrathlike or athletic, and may love knowledge or be angry-spirited (455). Wrath is no longer linked to erotic desire and is firmly under the control of reason, so there is no need to worry that women's participation in the processes of anger will turn their *eros* into its unloving inverse.

Moreover, anger will be expressed only outside the city with the result that there is no longer any need to characterize certain ways of handling anger as public rather than private or as male but not female. The line between public and private can be allowed to fade, and the abolition of the family ensures that lawsuits (*dikai*) and accusations (*engklemata*) among the citizens will all but vanish, and there will be no more of the quarrels (*astasiastois*) that arise from ownership of property and from having family ties (464d). In the just city peacefulness and lack of competition will put an end, even, to a need for the courts. Socrates claims that he has shied away from discussing the proposals because of how radical they are (450–51), but the revolutionary novelty of the community of women, abolition of families, and introduction of philosopher-kings reveals instead how revolutionary are Socrates' arguments about anger and the *thumos*. The arguments about anger are the necessary preliminaries to making the "radical" proposals conceivable. The fact that Socrates' arguments about anger could have such radical institutional implications confirms that the idea of anger was at the heart of the conceptual structure on which both Athenian and Platonic approaches to desert and politics are founded.

Socrates' discussion of the education of the philosopher-kings (504–40) reveals the degree to which the justice of the just city will be founded on a suppression of anger. Like the guardians, the philosopher-king must be taught about the right constitution of the soul and the rule that reason should employ anger to govern the desires (540b). But perhaps the most striking moment in the discussion of the philosopher's education arises in the characterization of Socrates. Socrates sets out the course of education that future philosopher-rulers must follow and then takes up the topic of how to identify the students who should be given such a philosophic education. That topic leads him to ponder with dismay the state in which the study of philosophy finds itself in his own time and place. He makes an emphatic statement about the kinds of people who should *not* be allowed to study philosophy. And then he says:

> *Socrates:* In the present moment it is likely that I myself will suffer ridicule.
> *Glaucon:* How?
> *Socrates:* As I spoke, it slipped my mind that we are merely playing [*epaizomen*] and I got pretty tense [*mallon enteinamenos*]. For as I was speaking I was at the same time casting my eyes on philosophy and when I saw how undeservedly [*anaxios*] she has been abused [*propepelakismenen*], I was annoyed [*aganaktesas*] and seemed to myself to say what I said too seriously [*spoudaioteron*] as if I had been angered [*hosper thumotheis*].
> *Glaucon:* This was not the case from my perspective as a listener.
> *Socrates:* But it was from mine as a *rhetor* [speaker].

> (536b–c)

Socrates is very far removed from the *rhetores* of Athens who expressed their own anger and exhorted their juries to anger and pity. He decides that he has spoken too severely out of anger before Glaucon has even noticed that he is getting angry. The philosopher will be so finely attuned to the problem of anger that he can feel and bring a halt to the onset of anger in himself before anyone else even realizes that anger has begun. Even as a *rhetor*, as a speaker and as a persuader, he will not allow anger to slip into his speech. The philosopher is so cognizant of his efforts to maintain internal harmony and to keep the parts of his soul from falling into strife with one another, that he can forestall such strife before it even begins. Anger will never slip out from under the control of reason. The harmonic city free of strife will achieve an equilibrium that is at as little risk of being unsettled as the soul of the properly educated philosopher. Such is, in part, the fruit of the Socratic education.[31]

It should come as no surprise to us, then, that the just city disintegrates precisely when the passions are reintroduced to it. Socrates uses the symbols of the "bee" and the "drone" to tell the story of the just city's degeneration. The bee and the drone introduced *orge* with Hesiod. Now they introduce desire to Socrates' just city. Again, he recognizes the value of the traditional symbol.

As we have seen, the positively valued bee and the negatively valued drone provided a symbolic foundation for a genealogy of the concept of *orge* as it functioned in Athens. That Socrates is content to consider fixed. Hesiod and Aristophanes criticized stingless drones who neither labored nor did the work of anger. Socrates, like Hesiod and Aristophanes, criticizes certain ways of life by suggesting that they are like the lives of drones. He makes no effort to shift the negative valuation attached to the drone, but he does expand the category. Socrates criticizes not only "stingless" drones but also drones with stings, drones who have too much, not too little, Athenian anger. The disintegration of the just city will begin, says Socrates, when the guardians and philosopher-kings fail to assess the value of each citizen—whether they are gold, silver, brass, or iron—

correctly. The failure to maintain the noble lie's patterns of desert and value will breed inequality and disharmony in the city, and, in successive stages, excessive desires of one kind or other will return to the city (547a). The disintegration of the just city thus begins when the Platonic pattern of desert and Platonic system of value are upset. The just city will turn, first of all, into a timocratic city and this city will develop into an oligarchic city, where some people become excessively wealthy and others excessively poor, thanks to the traffic in goods. Here is a section from the discussion, in which Socrates describes the man who has fallen from rich to poor:

> Do you wish that we say about this man that just as a drone [*kephen*] arises in a cell [of the honey-comb] and is a disease for the hive [*smenous nosema*], this type of man in his own home is like the drone and is a disease [*nosema*] to the city . . . and indeed god has made all the flying drones stingless [*akentrous*] while some of those on foot are stingless and some have fearsome stings [*deina kentra*]. And from the stingless ones, beggars result by old age. And from the ones with stings arise all those people called criminals [*kakourgoi*]. . . . In such a city are there not many criminals who are possessed of stings and whom the rulers [*hai archai*] restrain with the stewardship of force [*epimeleiai biai*]. . . .? And we say that such kinds of people arise because of a lack of education [*apaideusian*], bad nurture [*kaken trophen*], and a defect in the constitution [*katastasin tes politeias*]. (552c–e)

The drones without stings beg money from others in order to satisfy the basic physical desires that they are no longer capable of fulfilling on their own. They are like the lazy drones who do not labor in Hesiod and Aristophanes. But Aristophanes' wasps have been recharacterized. The drones with stings attempt to fulfill their desires by acting too aggressively; they can be controlled only by the oversight of magistrates. When drones return to the city, it will not suffice to have old men chastise the young and nursemaids tell them tales. Magistrates will once again have to deal with excessive anger and strife, and the city's policing networks will have to come back into operation. The city's disintegration completes itself when the soul of the just citizen has evolved into a timocratic, oligarchic, democratic, and finally tyrannical soul and when injustice rules and citizens find themselves facing the tyranny of passion and lust (543–75).[32]

Socrates' use of the bee-drone trope to conclude his arguments about the role of anger and desire in his just city reveals the way in which his text is an intervention in the ongoing Athenian cultural conversation about the place of *orge* in political life. Other authors sought to criticize particular uses of *orge* or simply to comment on its centrality to the ethical norms according to which the Athenians structured their social and political life. Plato had Socrates use the symbol not merely in order to critize the Athenian regime of anger but also as part of a rhetorical effort to unsettle that regime.

Socrates' use of symbols is not untheorized by Plato. Both Plato and his Socrates are masters of the rhetorical technique that Aristotle will later describe as "setting things before the eyes" of the audience (e.g., *Rhet.* 3.1.6).[33] Their use of symbols reveals a rhetorician's conviction that abstract ideas must be given embodiment in concrete images and things if they are to be assimilated and if the inconceivable is to be made conceivable. Socrates himself is explicit about his use of symbols to such ends. We will remember that Socrates introduced the imaginative work of fashioning his human being, lion, or many-headed-beast icon by suggesting that he and his interlocutors will better understand the firm division between reason, anger, and desire if they should "fashion [*plasantes*] a symbol [*eikona*] of the soul with speech, in order that by looking [*eidei*] at this *eikon* they might see" what he, Socrates, was saying (588c). The many-headed beast is, of course, the most "fantastical" and "unimaginable" element of the tripartite soul, and Glaucon responds to Socrates' suggestion that they fashion such an image by saying: "That would be the work of a fearsome plastic artist [*deinou plastou*], but nevertheless, since *logos* may be more successfully fashioned [*euplastoteron*] than wax and other such things, let it be fashioned."

To fashion images or icons is to fashion *logos*. It is to reshape language and reason, the realms in which our minds roam, the topographies of the imaginary. Fashioning symbols permits the rhetorician to shape the conceptual possibilities available to an audience and to shift the outer limits of what is conceivable for them. Glaucon accepts the argument for the tripartite soul only once he can imagine Leontios and his actions; but accept the argument he does. Seeing, he believes. Neither Socrates nor the other interlocutors ever suggests that the assorted *institutions* at issue in the *Republic* will be easily fashioned, but here Glaucon suggests (and Socrates seems to agree) that symbolic orders, which are the product of *logos*, are in fact very easily fashioned and revised. The *Republic* revises *logos* and must be considered political to the degree that it not only revises concepts fundamental to Athenian politics but also articulates those revisions in a fashion that makes the revised concepts easily understandable and almost unnoticeably assimilable by those who read the dialogue and become familiar with its symbol world.[34]

In the story of Leontios, Socrates describes a very un-Athenian reaction to a very Athenian sight. He normalizes that un-Athenian reaction for his auditors and makes it comprehensible. With this story, Plato reveals both his interest in changes of ideology and how subtle was his ability to recognize the dominant ideological systems of classical Athens and to replace them with new ones. Socrates' use of the story of Leontios in his efforts to convince Glaucon about the tripartite soul parallels the efforts of the educators to raise the guardian children with a proper understanding of how they should behave by means of stories about punishment. The dialogue concerns not only the education of those children but also the reeducation of Socrates' interlocutors and of Plato's readers. Plato has shown his readers a new road and has diverted us from the standard path back to Athens. Like Socrates, he has done this by making use of the rhetorical power of images, narratives, and "extremely meaningful" and easily assimilable symbols as well as analytic argument. It is precisely through Socrates' use of symbols and skill at constructing symbols that encapsulate whole networks of principles that Plato crafted a text that could intervene in a cultural conversation rather than merely run parallel to it.

Socrates is quite honest throughout the *Republic* about his interest in words, symbols, and the fashioning of *logos*. For that matter, he introduces the need to depict a utopian city as a need to help his audience "see" things better. He introduces his depictions by arguing that the attempt to see justice in the individual is an experience much like trying to read small letters at a distance when one does not have very good eyesight. Socrates suggests to his interlocutors that it would be easier to read the shape of the letters by looking at big versions of them from up close (368d). Socrates then compares himself to a painter in his discussion of whether or not his utopia would be possible:

> "Do you think, then, that he would be any the less a good painter, who, after portraying a pattern of the ideally beautiful man and omitting no touch required for the perfection of the picture, should not be able to prove that it is actually possible for such a man to exist?"
>
> "No by Zeus," he said.
>
> "Then were we not, as we say, trying to create in words the pattern [*paradeigma logoi*] of a true city?"
>
> "Certainly."
>
> "Do you think, then, that our words are any the less well spoken if we find ourselves unable to prove that it is possible for a city to be administered in accordance with our words?"
>
> "That, then, is the truth of the matter." (472c, trans. Cornford)

Socrates claims that his images and his narratives about the just city encapsulate a certain pattern or paradigm just as the children's stories are to be based on a specific *tupos*. Socrates is a master of narrative, mimesis, and the construction of symbols.

The transition to book 10 and the discussion of poetry and visual mimesis therefore by no means changes the subject, as is so often thought. After all, Socrates concludes book 9 with the extraordinary act of mimesis that results in the icon for the tripartite soul and he comments explicitly on his use of a mimetic icon to make a conceptual point. The implausible icon all but demands the discussion of mimesis that follows in book 10. Book 10, with its discussion of the place of mimesis, narrative, and spectacle in the just city returns us to the question that Socrates posed without answer during his conversation with Thrasymachus: to what end does Socrates-Plato use his words and with what effect?

As Halliwell (1988) points out, Socrates' treatment of *mimesis* in book 10 establishes a distinction between those forms of narrative and mimetic art that are problematic and those forms that are not problematic.[35] All forms of mimesis are concerned with truth only in the third remove—the poet or the painter does not really understand the nature of the things he or she represents. God and the artisan who have made the actual thing, which the artist only represents, have truer knowledge. But some forms of *mimesis* have a worse effect on their audience than others. Socrates begins his critique of mimesis by focusing on the nature of the artist, but he soon turns toward a critique of the effect of mimesis on the audience.[36] In this discussion, his central concern is with dramatic spectacles.

Socrates asks which part of the human being (*pros de poion ti esti ton tou anthropou*) is subject to the power (*dunamis*) of *mimesis* (602c). The answer that arises most immediately is that *mimesis* is directed at the power of vision (*opsis*). Tragedy, like Socrates' icons and images, appeals to human beings through their eyes. Insofar as spectacles are aimed at the power of vision, however, it will turn out that they are aimed at the lower part of the soul.[37] *L'oeil peut être se tromper.* The spectator who confronts a representation of something derives opinions from viewing that may differ from the knowledge acquired through reason (602d). For instance, a single object, viewed from near and far, will appear to the eyes be two different lengths, although the mind knows that it is really only one length. A stick that is seen by viewers (*theomenois*) while it is in the water will appear bent, when in reality it is straight (602c). The information provided by the eyes will contradict the information provided by reason and education (602de).

What is true of vision (*he kata ten opsin monon*) also applies to hearing (*e kai kata ten akoen*): spectacle strengthens the power of the elements of the soul that sometimes stand in revolt from reason or in opposition to reason, hence its danger (603a). The problem with spectacle is precisely that it uses vision to cause *stasis* among the three parts of the soul (*hosper kata ten opsin estasiaze*). In particular, spectacle causes *stasis* by rousing the emotions that have been controlled by the regime of the just city.[38] The spectator should, like Leontios, feel disgust at typical Athenian spectacles, but the typical Athenian spectator does not. Instead audiences follow the lamentations of the hero with sympathy (*sumpaschontes*), feeling passion and suffering and growing excited (*spoudazontes*) with the actors (605d). Spectators even praise the poet who can produce these feelings in them (605d). But according to Socrates those people who watch a man (*horonta toiouton andra*), whom they do not think deserves to be emulated (*axioi*), do themselves damage when they settle into enjoyment and praise of the spectacle rather than criticizing it (*chairein te kai epainein*) (605d–e). "The work of poetic mimesis is the same in respect to lust [*aphrodision*] and anger [*thumou*] and all the other desires [*epithumetikon*] and pains and pleasures in the soul, which we say follow along with our every action. For watering these emotions, it nourishes them, when they ought to be dried up, and it makes them our ruler when they ought to be ruled" (606d). Spectacle unsettles the emotional regime of the "just city." Hence its danger.

But not all mimesis has to have this effect. Images, narratives, and mimetic symbols that are built upon the Socratic paradigms and "types" of value do not water the emotions inappropriately but educate citizens' in the proper disposition of them. Spectacles are objectionable, on Socrates' view, precisely when they unsettle the rule of reason in the tripartite soul that *his images* have aimed to establish. Nor does Socrates' worry concern merely the renaissance of passion. Acts of mimesis that rouse the passions have the power to reinvigorate not only Athenian passions but also the principles of Athenian politics that Socrates has tried to erase and replace. In the Athenian *polis* emotion inspired citizens to speak and judge.

The Oceanids pitied the spectacle of Prometheus, as jurors pitied litigants; their emotions led both sets of onlookers to make judgments about desert. The growth of pity and anger led straight to thoughts, arguments, and contests over the definition of justice and about what the legitimate way to assess value might be. Public spectacles not only encouraged the Athenians to react passionally as well as rationally but also encouraged them to be judges about what they saw and to assess the systems of value articulated by the symbols set before them.

The fact that Socrates condemns other people's efforts to impact the imaginary shows only that he is willing to attribute effective force to the poetic ability to put things before people's eyes. If Socrates condemns the tragedians because their images and narratives are powerful and have, in his view, practical and empirical effects on the world, then he must equally consider his own images powerful and pragmatically effective. The difference between the tragedians' images and Socrates' is only that, from Socrates' point of view, his are based on the right *tupos* or general type and encapsulate the right symbolic order. Socrates' images create the right sort of fantasies and therefore create the right sort of mental or ideological topography (the right geography for living in the cave) in the mind of the audience. The tragedians' images do not. Socrates argues for a situation in which the audience is given no images to judge other than Platonic images. Their judgments will always come out the same way in such a situation.

The tragedians' image world has a different result. In the *Laws* Plato tells another tale of the disintegration of a just (or at least of a relatively just city), but this time he tells it through the mouth of a new protagonist, an Athenian Stranger who is having a conversation with some fellow travelers about how to constitute a city from the ground up. In this case the city that disintegrates is Athens and the story serves as a pseudohistory of Athenian politics. The Athenian Stranger does not argue that it is a return of the passions that provides the impetus for the disintegration. Rather, it is spectacle itself that prompts what the stranger calls distintegration.

The Athenian Stranger claims that the Athenians who lived before the Persian Wars were voluntary "slaves to the laws" who bent their will to the laws on all fronts out of reverence (*hekon edouleue tois nomois*, 698b). The Athenians of the Stranger's day and age, however, no longer submit to the laws, and lawlessness (*paranomia*) reigns everywhere. The cause of this change was the effect of certain kinds of music and poetry on the spectators in the theater (700d–e):

> Poets arose who were ignorant of what was just and lawful in music; and they were bacchic and possessed by pleasure more than was necessary . . . and they joined every

kind of music with every other. . . . By making such compositions and using similar forms of dialogue, they inspired in the masses a lawlessness in respect to music and a boldness that made them think that they were sufficient for the task of judgment. As a result the spectators began to voice [their opinions] [*phoneenta egenonto*] after having held their tongues [*aphonon*], as if they understood what was noble or not noble in music, and thus instead of there being an aristocracy in music, some sort of base theatrocracy [*theatrokratia*] sprang up. In music there arose a democracy of free men. (700d–701a)

The Stranger argues that the disintegration occurred because the Athenian audiences at the theater began to take the task of judgment upon themselves. The danger of drama was that it might generate the disintegration of the ideal (or relatively ideal city) by teaching citizens to be their own judges once again. Democracy was theatrocracy.

Socrates' images, narratives, and symbols were intended to undo, or to erase and replace, the Athenian principle of public life: the commitment to all citizens' right to *judge* the spectacle of angry, honor-sensitive citizens competing with one another on a regular basis (and within the bounds set by standards of public utility), with women excluded from the realm of anger (speaking ideally) so that the family unit would be free of angry conflicts. The power of the images can be seen in the case of Glaucon at least, for whom they serve to make the inconceivable conceivable and to prove that anger is separable from desire. Socrates' own efforts in respect to his interlocutors testify to the power of his (and Plato's?) acts of *mimesis*. Socrates' fear of the tragedians' acts of *mimesis* is the necessary fear that their symbols, their images, and narratives might have as much power as his own to undo or unsettle the principles of public life. Plato's Socrates feared lest they undo the ideas supporting the form of politics that he was trying to establish. This was a form of politics where reciprocity and retribution would be illegitimate and where all citizens must recognize the right of the wise to rule because wisdom would not have to compete with the ability to defend one's honor. This political practice would be made possible when anger was recognized as being more easily controlled than the base desires, with the result that reason could gain complete ascendance over anger, its faithful dog. The answer to the question of whether Socrates is a sycophant turns out to depend on whether a desire to undermine and revise Athenian ways of doing things, whether the desire to lead Athenians and others along a road to "elsewhere," constitutes harm. The answer to the question of whether Socrates is a sycophant turns out to depend on whether you buy his arguments.

In the end of the book in the Myth of Er, Socrates concludes by telling Glaucon that he thinks that it is absolutely crucial for everybody to study how to distinguish the good from the evil life in order to know how to choose the best life possible. This they should do by "taking into account all the things that we have said" (*analogizomenon panta ta nun de rhethenta*, 618c).[39] Socrates the *rhetor*, the fashioner of *logos*, enjoins that his interlocutors always take what he has said, his *ta rhethenta*, his stories, arguments, and symbols into account. These are the *pharmaka* by which one conceptualization of desert and system of authority was conjured up out of another in order to replace it and to shift the present order of things.

THE INCURABLES AND THE NECESSITY FOR ANGER/*ORGE* IN THE JUST CITY OF THE *LAWS*

In the *Laws* there is no Socrates but rather a protagonist named the Athenian Stranger who converses with a Spartan and a Cretan in order to try to devise a city, Magnesia, in words from the ground up.[40] In the *Laws*, Plato has his characters outline the actual institutions that they would like to see in the best possible actual state. In the process of outlining these institutions, the Athenian Stranger in no way contradicts three crucial Socratic doctrines: that wisdom should govern the state; that virtue is teachable; and that punishment should reform the wrongdoer and cure the wrongdoer's soul of disease. It is in this text that Plato most specifically elaborates what a reformative system of punishment would look like. Saunders has examined that system extensively and so herein I wish to point out only a few of the particularly noteworthy elements that Saunders passed over. But first a general word about the system of law and punishment used in the *Laws*.

In the *Apology*, *Protagoras*, *Gorgias*, and *Republic*, Socrates discussed his conviction that fellow citizens should teach and persuade one another. In the *Laws,* law must also take on this task.[41]

> When anyone commits any injustice, great or small, the law will teach and compel him either never at all to dare to do the like again, or never voluntarily, or at any rate in a far less degree. . . . Whether this is to be achieved by words or deeds, with pleasures or pains, by honoring or dishonoring, by means of fines or gifts of money, or in whatsoever way at all the law will make a man hate injustice, and love or not hate the nature of the just—this is the task of the noblest laws. (862d)

The laws that are included in the *Laws* come with a prelude that states the reason for the law. This prelude is expected to educate the citizenry into obedience.[42] When it fails, the law then makes use of the threat of punishment to inspire obedience. Punishment itself becomes a third measure to be taken in the effort to educate citizens into obedience to the laws. It is assigned the same educative and reformative tasks as the legal system.

In the context of punishment the legislator, writing his specific laws and drawing up his comprehensive code, must aim, like an archer, at establishing the proper framework for desert:

> And the [wrongdoer] will give justice not for the sake of the wrongdoing [*ouch heneka tou kakourgesai didous ten diken*], for it is not possible for what has happened to be undone [*ou gar to genonos ageneton estai pote*], but so that in the future he himself and all those looking on his punishment will hate injustice [*misesai adikian*]

as much as possible or at least renounce the greater part of such a misfortune. For the sake of all these things and with a view to all these objects it is necessary that the laws aim at justice, like a good archer, for the sake of determining the size of punishment for each thing and especially its desert [*stochazesthai diken tou te megethous tes kolaseos hekaston eneka kai pentelos tes axias*]. (934ab)

Honor, anger, and the Athenian desire to rectify a wrong are no longer at issue or determinative of the size of penalties. Nonetheless, the Athenian Stranger, like the Athenians, is willing to treat the concept of *time* as signifying the guiding political principle of a city. According to the Athenian Stranger: "Honor is, in our view and speaking generally [*time d'estin hemin, hos to holon eipein*], to follow the better, and to make the worse better as much as possible to the same degree as is best able to be accomplished" (728c). Honor has a new definition in Magnesia and the size and type of penalties are thus made to hang on the question of what it takes to cure a wrongdoer rather than on the size of the injustice done to some angry victim (911c).

The legislators will have to seek out and punish, among others, those who exhibit pleonectic desires such as those which Thrasymachus espoused in book 2 of the *Republic*. The Athenian Stranger remarks:

There are some souls that live on earth and that have come to possess unjust profits, and it is clear that since they are like beasts [*theriodeis*], they fall upon the souls of the guardians . . . and seek to persuade them with flattering speeches and with prayers and charms . . . that it is possible to be pleonectic [*exeinai pleonektousi*] in human company without suffering anything severe [*paschein meden chalepon*]. But we say that this error named *pleonexia* is called a disease [*nosema*] in the case of bodies, is called a plague [*loimos*] in respect to seasons and years, and the same thing is injustice [*adikian*] in cities and constitutions with a verbal reorganization [*rhemati meteschematismenon*]. (906b)

Pleonexia is a disease; it is the target of the legislator's punitive cures. The person who suffers from *pleonexia* is like a wild beast. In the *Republic* Socrates gave us a foundational iconography of the soul that legitimated the use of the term "bestial" to apply to the passions. The disease associated with wrongdoing is an inability to keep one's passions under the control of one's reason. The disease of *pleonexia* is also the same thing as injustice, and is defined as such by a "verbal reorganization" carried out not only in this passage but also by the work of the *Republic*. The power of Plato's "sayings" or *rhemata* to establish a new system of desert, to redefine the relationship between justice and desire and between justice, desire, and politics, is what allows the metaphors of disease and pollution to be used here for the pleonectic person. The symbolic system of value that was established in the *Republic* has been transferred to the *Laws* and provides the basis for the legislators' decisions about whom to punish and how.

As far as how to punish is concerned, the Athenian Stranger and his interlocutors set up a rather intricate system of penalties including fines, corporal punishments, limited terms of exile, imprisonment, execution, mutilation of the corpse, and *ataphia.* The Athenian Stranger proposes two forms of punishment in particular that are strikingly different from penalties of the Athenian model. The Athenian Stranger sees no need to acknowledge competitive equality and so is willing to use fines that are staggered by wealth class (e.g., 765c, 743d, 756c, 762b).[43] Also the Stranger recommends a triple-tiered prison system that must have been more extensive than whatever was used in Athens. The prison system is the most interesting element of the Athenian Stranger's system of punishment, and we return to it in a moment.

The legislators should in fact try to cure all cases where a wrongdoer has a curable disease of the soul (862c). For instance, if someone should commit a murder in anger (*thumos*), he would be obliged to go into exile for two years, thereby reforming his own passion (*kolazon ton hautou thumon*, 867c). The Athenian Stranger characterizes those wrongdoers who cannot be reformed not as "unteachable" but rather as "incurable" and says that they are to be put to death and their corpses expelled from the land (862d–863a). The incurable will thus at least serve as an example to others (854e, 862e). Such punishments are forms of cleansing or purges, but the best ones are violent. "The best purge is painful, as are all exceptional medicines [*hosa ton pharmakon toioutotropa*]. This purge carries out punishment by means of a form of justice that employs *timoria*, the goal of which is death or exile. This form of purge customarily releases the city from the greatest wrongdoers who, being incurable, do the greatest damage to the city" (735e). Most punishments should cure, on the account of the Athenian Stranger, and employ *kolasis*. Where cure is impossible, however, the punisher must turn away from using *kolasis* or reformative measures and must turn instead to *timoria*.[44] Just a few paragraphs earlier, the Athenian Stranger had defined the difference between justice and *timoria*. Justice, he argues, can never be considered an experience of "suffering" or of having to submit to something unpleasant, but *timoria* is precisely such suffering (*to pathos*, 728c). The strongest purges must work with the material of suffering, although still applying justice. The Stranger thus faces a problem: the just city must sometimes respond to wrongdoers in such a way that they are subjected to something unpleasant rather than to something "fair, beautiful" and beneficial. How can this fact be reconciled with a commitment to justice that requires never causing harm?

The Stranger effects a reconciliation by arguing that imposing *timoria* on those who are incurable may not benefit them but neither does it harm them. *Timoria* does not make the incurable wrongdoer worse off in respect to his soul. The Stranger argues that the incurable wrongdoer who escapes *timoria* and the one who suffers it are equally wretched (*athlios*). The first wrongdoer is miserable as a result of avoiding *timoria* because the disease persists (*ho men ouk iatreuomenos*). The second wrongdoer suffers *timoria* and is wretched because of having to suffer death or exile, but such a wrongdoer, despite being incurable, is also cured to the degree that his or her destruction (*apollumenos*) allows for the salvation of many other people in the city (*hina heteroi polloi sozontai,*

728bc). Incurable wrongdoers cannot be cured in their own right but they can at least contribute to the general good by becoming an example for the other citizens. They end their lives or depart from the city somewhat better off in respect to their souls on the basis of this contribution to the general good. Punishment of this sort, however, must be called *timoria*, a response to a wrongdoer that aims to destroy the wrongdoer for the good of the city rather than for the good of the wrongdoer.

The worst of the incurables are those who have committed impiety, and the Stranger requires that imprisonment be handed out in every instance of impiety, curable or not. There would be one prison in the *agora* that would hold most wrongdoers. Then there would be a prison called the *sophronisterion*, "a place where people learn moderation," situated near the offices of the city's most important officials. Curable wrongdoers would undergo a process of reeducation in this prison for however long it should take to teach them to learn to love justice. Finally, for those incurables who could not learn, there would be a prison deep in the countryside (*kata ten choran, en toi ton mesogeion desmoterioi*) in the wildest and loneliest spot (*eremos, malista agriotatos topos*, 908–9). There strict rationing would lead to death to be followed by *ataphia* beyond the borders. The name of this prison for the incurables, the Stranger says, will simply be *timoria* (*timorias echon eponumian phemen tina*, 908a). Incurables get sent to a place like Athens.

There will thus be two ways of dealing with wrongdoers in Magnesia: *kolasis* or reform for the curable; and *timoria* and total destruction by consumption for the incurable. A punisher must therefore be able to act in two different ways— as the gentle teacher who reforms on the one hand and on the other hand as punisher who imposes the harsh and painful sentence of *timoria*. Anger arrives in the just city only when the limits of curability, the limits of Socratic punishment have been reached.

> It is necessary for every man to be high-spirited [*thumoeide*] and gentle [*praon*] to the greatest degree possible. For it is not possible to avoid suffering severe treatment from others or treatment that may be difficult to remedy [*chalepa kai dusiata*] nor is it entirely possible to avoid suffering from irremediable acts of injustice [*parapan aniata adikemata*] other than by fighting and victoriously defending oneself and by punishing without pause [*toi meden anieinai kolazonta*]. This no soul can do without a noble *thumos*.
>
> But it is necessary to recognize first, in respect to people who commit curable acts of injustice, that every wrongdoer is an involuntary wrongdoer [*ouch hekon adikos*]. . . .
>
> And the wrongdoer and the person possessed of evil is certainly pitiable. *Thus it is customary* [engkorei] *to pity and to be gentle* [praunein] *to the man possessed of curable evils restraining one's* thumos. . . . *But in dealing with the uncontrollably unspeakably perverse and evil, it is necessary to unleash* orge [ephienai ten orgen]. (731bc; cf. 977d)

The incurables must be subjected to the punishment of *timoria* and so they must be subjected to *orge*. This is the *only* place in the Platonic corpus that Socrates, or one of his substitutes, recommends the use of *orge*. Plato returns to the Athenian paradigm when his protagonist must acknowledge the limits of a rationalist approach to politics and virtue. But he does not return completely. Plato's just punishers will unleash the anger that Platonic philosophy so carefully restrains only when they are ready to push a citizen to the borders of the city. Plato's anger has become an all or nothing proposition; and it is no longer a force that is subject to social negotiation or gradation.[45] His *orge* is a force that only destroys.

There is much more that could be said about the theory and system of punishment that Plato has his characters explore in the *Laws*. But I hope that what I have said shows two points. First, there is the point that the philosophical, rhetorical, and political projects of the *Republic*—where Socrates defines the language of anger, punishment, and politics away from the Athenian paradigm—carry over to the *Laws*. Moreover, Plato's assignment to Socrates of the role of ideal image maker and rhetorician of justice must affect our reading of how Plato conceives of the place of the philosopher in political life. Any assessment of Plato's theory of justice must take account of the ways in which he directly speaks to and revises the Athenian conceptualizations of anger, reciprocity, honor, and social memory.

The second point that I hope to have shown in respect to the *Republic* and at least to have hinted at in respect to the *Laws* is that in both texts Plato treats punishment as being a social practice that reveals the fundamental conceptual structure and system of value according to which the members of a community understand their world and organize their behaviors within that world. Plato depicts Socrates not only as a figure who wishes to revise social orders and practices across the board but also as one who attempts to do so by focusing on the topic of punishment and the topic of how a given society responds to social disruption. Plato grants punishment a central place in his efforts to discuss justice and, in so doing, he makes a claim not unlike Foucault's: that the structure of authority that unifies a group of people into a shared social order and shared reality can be uncovered through an investigation of punishment. That claim is also the theoretical point from which I began my story of punishing in Athens, a story that I have hoped has been read as much for what it says about Athenian politics in general as for what it says about Athenian punishment. Unlike Foucault, Plato also claimed that such an investigation could change the community's shared reality.

CHAPTER 11

Aristotle's Compromises

ON JUSTICE AND DESERT

It must be admitted that Aristotle's treatment of punishment is something of a letdown after the boldness, sweep, and drama of Plato's comprehensive critique of Athenian practices of anger, punishment, politics, and justice. Nonetheless, it is important to take a look at what he has to say about punishment before we turn away entirely from punishment in Athens. Plato's approach to punishment is picked up by Augustine and both philosophers' rejection of anger is replicated in the most influential later-day punitive theories including those of Beccaria, Hobbes, Locke, and Kant. But Aristotle's theory of punishment seems to be one of the roads not taken in the history of philosophy, and his approach to punishment is also unusual and idiosyncratic enough to be enlightening.

Plato's treatment of punishment throughout the dialogues makes the grand point that a system of punishment may be read so as to ascertain a society's way of organizing its politics and its broader conceptualizations of justice. Aristotle's theory of punishment stresses a rhetorically much narrower point but one that is perhaps even more important: any attempt to establish a system of punishment (whether in theory or in practice) is an attempt to establish a system for ascertaining value in a society in such a way that the greater part of a citizenry will acquiesce in the system by which actions are to be evaluated. The effort to achieve acquiescence in a system of value will force the would-be constituter of a system of punishment to make arguments about desert. Aristotle's theory of punishment is important in that it gives us a theory of how to understand the concept of "desert" and the political work that it does. Aristotle not only theorizes the concept "desert" in general, but also makes an argument that any viable system for ascertaining value by means of arguments about desert must take both the good of the wrongdoer and the good of the victim of wrongdoing into account.

As we have seen (chapter 8), Aristotle agrees with Plato that a city should employ the rule of law to ends of virtue. He specifically accepts Plato's formulation of passion as the wild animal that should be ruled by reason, the embodiment of which is to be found in law:[1]

> It is inevitable that the judgment of the individual man will be overpowered by anger [*hup' orges kratethentos*] or by some other passion [*tinos heterou pathous toioutou*]. . . . And the thing in which there is absolutely no emotional element is stronger than that in which it is innate; this [emotional element] is absent from the law, but it is necessarily a part of every human soul. The man who recommends that intellect rule seems to think that god and reason only should rule, but the one who recommends that man

rule puts forward the beast [*therion*]; for that is what desire is [*epithumia*], and passion [*ho thumos*] ruins the rule of even the best men. Law is intellect without desire. (1286a30, 15; 1287a39)

The rule of law provides for a form of politics dictated by reason. Both Plato and Aristotle expect the laws to educate the citizenry. They also to expect that education to fail now and then. When it does, punishment must take over the job begun by law. According to Plato, it is only a reformative approach to punishment that can harmonize with a rationalist politics in which law plays the role of educator. Aristotle agrees with Plato that punishment should reform, and he refers to punishment (*kolasis*) as a medicine (*iatreia/ pharmaka*) for licentiousness (*akolasia*) and injustice (*adikia*) (*NE* 2.3.4, 1104b17).[2] He describes the theory of reformative punishment as what "some people think" and does not—as he often does with common opinion—try to refute the idea (*NE* 10.9.9, 1180a).[3]

Aristotle did not, however, think that a reformative approach sufficed to deal with the problem of wrongdoing in the city, for the problem of anger also had to be solved.[4] In both the *Nicomachean Ethics* and the *Rhetoric* Aristotle tells us that human beings take pleasure in being able to carry out *timoria* (*timoroumenoi, timoreisthai*).[5] Moreover, the anger that inspires punishment is a durable, persistent emotion:

> The bitter-tempered on the other hand are hard to reconcile, and are angry for a long time, because they hold on to their anger; whereas when a man retaliates [*antapodido*] there is an end of the matter: the retribution [*timoria*] stops the anger, replacing the pain of anger with the sweetness of retribution. But if this does not happen, they carry on with the weight—for as their anger is not apparent, no one provides sympathy, and it takes a long time to digest anger inside oneself. (*NE* 4.5.10, 1126a20)

On Aristotle's view, reformative theories of punishment do not take sufficient account of the experiences of the individual angry participants in the process. Citizens will "seek to return ill for ill [*to kakos zetousin*], or good for good, and if they cannot, they think their situation is one of slavery [*ei de me, douleia dokei einai*]" (*NE* 5.5.6, 1132b35). Reformative theories may not suffice to maintain a stable city.

Aristotle is willing to accept the idea that wrongdoing causes problems in the community by poisoning the relationships between citizens with anger.[6] He accepts the need to deal with the claims of the victim side by side with his commitment to reform. One of the idiosyncrasies of Aristotle's discussions of punishment is the frequency with which he places the words *timoria* and *kolasis* together as if they form a single compound noun (like "peanut butter and jelly"); he treats the associated verbs in the same fashion.[7] Aristotle takes a commitment to a rationalized, constitutional politics from Plato, but he also hangs on to some elements of the passional foundations of Athenian politics.[8] He recognized the polity's need to deal with disturbances in citizens' relationships with one another.[9]

Book 5 of the *Nicomachean Ethics* contains Aristotle's famous discussion of justice. The passage offers a theory not only of justice but also of punishment in which Aristotle tries to marry Plato's rationalism to Athens's focus on the good of the victim.[10] Aristotle begins by discussing the nature of justice considered both in its "universal" aspect (Justice with a capital "J" in other words) and in its "particular" aspect. Justice in its universal aspect is complete virtue. It is the ability to act temperately, bravely, liberally, magnanimously, and also justly where that has the specific meaning of not taking more than one's fair share. Moreover, justice in its universal aspect is the exercise of all the virtues not in respect to one's self alone but also in respect to one's neighbor. Aristotle thus defines justice as having to do with relationality and with the treatment of one's fellow citizens (1129b25–1130a1).

The second form of justice, justice in its "particular aspect," has to do with only one of the virtues covered by universal justice (1130b1). Particular justice has to do with "fairness" (*to ison*) and particular injustice is constituted by a desire for "unfair gain," whether of money, honor, or something else (1130a15–30). Like universal justice, particular justice still has as much to do with neighbors as universal justice does.

Universal justice and particular justice (justice as fairness) differ in the kinds of injustice that can be committed in respect to each. Violations of universal justice include wrongs like cowardice and self-indulgence that only indirectly harm the victim. Thus a pair of adulterous lovers harm their spouses indirectly when they commit adultery for the sake of pleasure. Violations of particular justice, in contrast, are always an attempt to gain something *by* harming someone. An adulterer who commits adultery in order to extort money from one of the spouses in exchange for keeping the affair quiet directly harms the extorted spouse with the act of adultery.

Aristotle divides particular justice (justice as fairness) into two types: distributive justice (*to dianemetikon dikaion*) and corrective or diorthotic justice (*to diorthotikon dikaion*). Distributive justice is concerned with the initial distributions of honor and property in the city and with wrongs having to do with honor and property. Because distributive justice concerns the distribution of goods among all citizens, it affects the relations of all citizens to one another, as do violations of distributive justice.

Corrective justice has to do with "private transactions" (*sunallagmata*) that involve only two citizens. These transactions can be either voluntary (contractual or business matters) or involuntary (theft, adultery, poisoning, procuring, enticement of slaves, assassination, false witness, assault, murder, maiming, and abusive language) (1131a1–10).[11] Citizens wrong specific individuals when they carry out contractual violations or any of the violent wrongdoings that fall into the category of involuntary transactions.

Both forms of justice as fairness concern relations between people, but each stresses a different aspect of relationality. Distributive justice emphasizes the ways in which everyone in a given society can be thought of as standing in relation to everyone else. Corrective justice emphasizes the ways in which the two people involved in a single transaction stand in relation to one another. (Aristotle concludes his definitions of the different types of justice with a lengthy summary of the different relationships between citizens involved in each type.)[12]

Aristotle next proceeds to discuss how each kind of justice as fairness (distributive and corrective) is to be effected. He begins by investigating the notion of fairness or equality (*to ison*) that underlies particular justice and argues that both distributive and corrective forms of particular justice will be based on a notion of equality that suits the kind of relationality that pertains in each kind of justice. Aristotle thus aims to define the types of equality that are relevant to distributive and corrective justice respectively.

Aristotle first reaches the conclusion that distributive justice is based on a "geometrical principle" of equality or an equality based on ratios. Each person should stand in relation to her portion of a distributed good as another person does in relation to his. On such a principle, if food were being distributed at a dinner party, guests should get food in differing amounts accordingly as their appetites differed. The hungrier person would get more food; the person with the small appetite, less. Each person's appetite would be equally satisfied despite the fact that guests received different amounts of food. In each case the ratio between the voracity of the appetite and the amount of food served would be the same. Goods such as honor and property should be divided within the citizenry according to this "geometrical principle" of equality.

Aristotle argues that adherence to the principle of equality will contribute to stability and peace in the city. "For battles [*machai*] and accusations [*egklemata*] arise when equals are assigned and possess unequal shares or when those who are not equal are assigned and possess equal shares" (5.3.6–7, 1131a23). Aristotle thus sets himself the task of trying to figure out what principle of distribution according to ratio will, when applied to the city, prevent strife from arising. The question at issue is how to define desert since the idea that equality prevents strife "is clear from the principle of 'according to desert' [*eti ek tou kat' axian touto delon*]. For all agree that justice in distribution needs to be based on some [idea of] desert [*to gar dikaion en tais dianomais homologousi pantes kat' axian tina dein einai*], although all do not mean the same [idea of] desert [*ten mentoi axian ou ten auten legousi pantes (huparchein)*]" (5.3.7, 1131a24–29). Democrats think that property and honor should be distributed according to freedom. Oligarchs think that they should be distributed according to wealth, and the list goes on (ibid.). The struggle over the definition of desert is central to a polity's attempt to define not only punishment but also the nature of its regime.

Aristotle's innovation, however, is not the idea that different classes will have different principles for distribution and desert. His innovation lies in his effort to theorize desert itself. This he does by trying to figure out what kind of claims about human relationality are being made when citizens establish the particular principles of desert and definitions of equality that will guide the distribution of goods in their city. Aristotle's justice aims to show how a certain equality (*isotes*) can be achieved among different people who have different characteristics, possess different things, and live through different experiences. That equality is established by setting up a system of desert that will be generally accepted in the society. The idea that the word "desert" generates equality reveals the following fact about the concept: the word "desert" makes a claim that incommensurable items can nonetheless be compared and can be shown to be not only commensurable but even equal (chicken breasts and dinner guests, or car theft and twenty years in prison). The result of Aristotle's investigation is the recognition that the idea of "desert" enables the work of justice insofar as justice is the task of comparing incommensurables. The idea of "desert" provides grounds for comparing like to unlike and so it provides grounds for relating citizens to one another despite their differences.

The comparison of incommensurable items can be carried out only by means of one of the few tools that allows unlike objects to be compared: analogy. Analogies make comparisons of unlike things by showing some way in which the two unlike things turn out to have something in common. Thus Aristotle argues that justice, which is based on the idea of desert, is "some kind of analogy [or proportion]" (*estin ara to dikaion analogon ti*, 5.3.7, 1131a29–30). Analogy is at the heart of justice because the task of justice is to show how sets of incomparable things may be treated as comparable, equal, or commensurable, and analogies posit a relationship of likeness between things that initially seem unlike one another. Aristotle's explicit attention to the role of analogy in justice highlights the degree to which justice is set the task of dealing with the problem of incommensurability. The idea of "desert" gets past the problem of incommensurability by focusing on some particular characteristic that can be found in all members of a set of incommensurable objects and by setting that characteristic up as a measure between them. The ability of "desert" and its analogies to equalize the unequal prevents strife in the community because people are willing to acquiesce in distributions of goods when they believe that those are carried out on "equal" or "fair" terms. It is also worth pointing out that Aristotle takes analogy to be the root of metaphor in both the *Poetics* and the *Rhetoric*. Justice as fairness or equality must be based on desert; desert— and therefore also justice—is a species of metaphorical thought.

Aristotle's discussion of analogy provides us with a way of thinking about how concepts of desert and justice do their work within a political community. They bring the human capacity for metaphorical thinking to bear in order that the particularity of each citizen's experience may be to some degree overcome and in order that citizens may be brought in relation to one another. But Aristotle does not call a halt at this general discussion. He carries on and makes a case for the specific principles and analogies of desert that he thinks should be used to guide distributive justice on the one hand and corrective justice on the other.

Aristotle decides to base the analogical principle of distributive justice on the idea of "contribution." Each person will receive from the community what he or she has contributed to it: "A distribution [*dianome*] from the communal store of possessions [*apo chrematon koinon*] will follow the same ratio as that between the amounts which the several persons have contributed to the common stock" (5.4.2, 1131b29–31, trans. Rackham). Unjust acts that violate distributive justice violate this form of proportion or analogy (5.4.2, 1131b25–35). Presumably, they must be dealt with by means of corrections to the distribution of property and honor that restore cities to the analogical balance marked out by Aristotle's principle of contribution. This form of justice, based on geometrical equality, takes the relationship of all citizens to one another into account at the same time.

Corrective justice, however, is based on a mathematical principle that deals only with the relationships between pairs of citizens, and it is to this topic—one more directly pertinent to the practice of punishment—that Aristotle moves next. Aristotle has just told us that injustice, in respect to distribution, is a violation of proportion or analogy, and he shifts to the subject of corrective justice by remarking that it too has to do with achieving a "sort" of equality (*ison ti*) (*to adikon . . . para to analogon estin · to d' en tois sunallagmasi dikaion esti men ison ti*). It will turn out that the idea of "desert" (*ta axia*) is also central to organizing a society's response to such violent transactions as theft, adultery, poisoning, procuring, enticement of slaves, assassination, false witness, assault, murder, maiming, and abusive language. The principle of analogy, or the principle of desert that matters in cases of theft, adultery, murder, and assault is not geometric but rather arithmetic (5.4.3, 1132a1–5). The geometric equality of distributive justice made use of ratios (a big hungry person is to three chicken breasts as a small person who has just had a snack is to half a chicken breast). Arithmetic equality uses sums, not ratios. Roughly speaking, it posits that in any given transaction citizens start out with an equal amount of some good (which Aristotle has yet to identify); in an act of wrongdoing, the wrongdoer gains extra portions of this good and the victim loses a portion. The gain and the loss must be equalized (1132a1–10). But what is the good that is equally distributed at some ideal starting point?

In distributive justice, the person who had contributed more honor to the common store would receive more honor, and desert was tied to contribution. But in corrective justice:

> It makes no difference whether an estimable man [*epieikes*] has defrauded an insignificant man [*phaulon*] or whether an insignificant man an estimable man, nor whether it is an estimable or insignificant man that has committed adultery; the law looks only at the nature of the damage [*tou blabous*], treating the parties as equal, and merely asking whether one has done [*ho d' . . . adikei*] and the other suffered injustice [*ho d' adikeitai*], whether one inflicted and the other has sustained damage. Hence the unjust being here the unequal, the judge endeavors to equalize it: inasmuch as when one man has received and the other has inflicted a blow, *the suffering* [to pathos] *and the doing* [he praxis] *of the deed are divided unequally* [dieiretai . . . eis anisa]. And the judge endeavors to make them equal by the penalty or loss [*zemiai*] he imposes, taking away the gain [*kerdos*]. (5.4.3–4, 1132a2–11; trans. Rackham, modified slightly)

In distributive justice, property, honor, and status are distributed among the entire citizenry and therefore are to be considered only in the context of the relationships within the whole city. None of the goods and qualities that are distributed throughout the whole citizenry matters in an act of wrongdoing that involves only two people. Personal characteristics like honor and wealth are therefore to be ignored. The principle of desert involved in corrective justice focuses only on the ways in which the suffering and the doing involved in a given interaction are divided unequally between the two parties involved. In corrective justice it is the good of "agency" that matters. Both parties start out with an equal amount of agency, but a violation of justice disturbs that equality. In an involuntary transaction, one party has suffered or been subject to the violation. The other has done it. The violation of voluntarism undoes the equal distribution of agency between citizens. Corrective justice is therefore concerned with maintaining the equality of citizen interaction. Citizens are not to be made into "subjects" nor are they to make one another into subjects or into those who are acted upon. Justice works to establish the principle that the relationships between citizens must consist not of involuntary interactions but only of voluntary interactions. This idea coincides with an idea that is central to Aristotle's understanding of how a just politics will work. In the just city, citizens live in a regime where they are always able to act voluntarily (cf. esp. *Pol.* 3.4.7, 3.9–10). Corrective justice helps to maintain the social structures necessary for the citizens to live as voluntary actors. The focus of corrective justice is not so much on the people involved in any given situation of wrongdoing and punishment or on their specific emotions or desires (their personal characteristics are to be ignored) but on the wrongdoing itself and its subversion of the conditions necessary for agency. It is not the anger of the victim that motivates the punishment but the general need to maintain a context in which citizens can live as agents rather than as subjects.

Aristotle begins his analysis of the two kinds of justice by acknowledging that what is at issue in a discussion of justice, distribution, and wrongdoing is how to define the principle of desert underpinning justice. The Athenians defined desert as a social concept to be negotiated in terms of honor and emotion in public fora. In the *Republic* Plato sets the criteria of desert with the noble lie and in the *Laws* he leaves it to the legislators to establish on the basis of reason. Instead of following either, Aristotle takes up desert as a philosophical concept, defining it at increasing levels of abstraction as he tries to deal with the fact that "desert" is fundamentally about trying to compare one thing to another, which is unlike it, and to make one thing (a punishment) equal to or fit another (a crime). He is committed to the equality achieved by these comparisons because he thinks such equality, such acts of commensuration, allow the community to avoid strife. The crucial thing that Aristotle recognizes is that strife results when people think that distributions and punishments are *not* handed out according to what they conceive to be the principles defining desert and when people refuse to acquiesce in the equation of "this" to "that." When people do think that goods and agency have been distributed according to desert, their peacefulness, their acquiescence, rests on their acceptance of the form of equality posited by the principle of desert that is operating in their society. In establishing his principles of desert—the principle of contribution and the principle of agency—Aristotle rejected the Athenian focus on anger but accepted the Athenians' commitment to deal with the problem of intersubjectivity and community relations; he shifted away from Plato's attention to the wrongdoer's soul but nonetheless emulated his emphasis on rationality. Aristotle took steps toward both Plato and Athens.

Aristotle's corrective justice is not exactly anger-driven Athenian retribution, however. And Aristotle himself worries that perhaps he has not sufficiently dealt with the victim's desires for reciprocity. His worry manifests itself in the next step of his argument when he turns to consider whether he ought to consider reciprocity as being a part of justice after all. Aristotle invokes the opinion of some people, including the Pythagoreans, that justice is to be defined simply as retaliation (*antipeponthos*) (1132b24). Aristotle dismisses the idea that reciprocity might be a part of either distributive or corrective justice (5.5.2, 1132b24). He also argues that reciprocity sometimes stands in opposition to justice. But then he concedes that reciprocity is nonetheless necessary for maintaining the stability of the community. He writes:

> In the exchange of services, reciprocity is the sort of justice [*to toiouton dikaion to antipeponthos*] that makes a bond in public life [*en men tais koinonias*]. . . . The city remains held together by means of reciprocity according to proportion; for people seek to return ill for ill [*to kakos zetousin*], or good for good, and if they cannot, their situation seems to be one of slavery [*ei de me, douleia dokei einai*]. (*NE* 5.5.6, 1132b30–1133a2; see also *Pol.* 2.1.5, 1261a31)

Reciprocity matters because it provides a bond in the city. Again, Aristotle is concerned with the relationships between people and their relevance to maintaining a stable community where citizens think that they are free. Here he acknowledges, however, that the relationships within the citizenry have to do with agency but even so are also embedded in the city's distributions of honor and property. For instance, Aristotle points out that the man who hits a magistrate will be thought to deserve a greater punishment than one who hits another layman (5.5.4–6, 1132b25–35). Citizens will be concerned not only with agency but also with honor. Aristotle has made an effort to rationalize desert and to turn it into a principle about agency, but he recognizes that the people around him would want to include social assessments in the definitions of desert that they would apply to the wrongs covered by Aristotle's corrective justice.

Distributive justice has to do with the relationships *between all the members of the community* considered at once. Corrective justice has to do with relationships *between two particular people within the community*. In acts of reciprocity the goods that have been distributed at large in the community—property and honor—are exchanged between two people. Reciprocity is thus concerned with the relationships between two citizens as understood within the framework of the larger social context established by patterns of the distribution of goods. It would seem that reciprocity combines the principles of corrective and distributive justice. But Aristotle does not directly address the question of how reciprocity should be linked to the punishments handed out in accordance with his diorthotic justice. Instead, he allows the discussion of reciprocity to evolve into a discussion of commerce. He focuses on how money is a measure that can make different things equal (*to de nomisma hosper metron summetra poiesan isazei*, 5.5.14). Aristotle argues that the need to exchange incommensurable things—for example, a builder's house and shoemaker's shoe—is best effected by means of money precisely because the role of money is to provide a "middle term" by which things can be compared. "And money is somehow a middle term; for it measures all things [*panta gar metrei*]" (5.5.10, 1133a21). He adds: "There would be no community where there is no exchange, and no exchange where there is no equality, and no equality without commensurability [*summetrias*]" (5.5.14, 1133b16–19). Aristotle therefore concludes, like the Athenians, by valuing money as the quintessential tool for dealing with reciprocity. But the Athenians used monetary fines as a symbol for a reciprocity that had already been measured in terms of the anger of the citizen-jurors; money marked the use of human negotiations to achieve decisions on forms of reciprocity measured in human terms. Aristotle in contrast argues that money is itself a medium for making assessments of desert and value. Money, he says (not man), measures all things.

The Athenians were explicit about their use of subjective criteria to assess wrongdoing: discussions of desert were cast in terms of anger and pity. Social memory, with all its malleability, was one of the most important foundations for judgments. Plato and Aristotle both argued for the rule of law and for a conservatism in citizens' approach to their laws. In doing so, each philosopher aimed to establish principles of judgment that would seem to exist outside of the minds of the citizens and practices of the citizenry. Aristotle's discussion of punishment aims to effect a similar shift away from admittedly subjective grounds for judgment and to ostensibly objective grounds for judgment. Aristotle's discussion of corrective justice turned around his emphasis on the need to measure "agency." He thus shifted the focus of punishment away from using the victim's anger as a guide for judgment and to an abstract concept that could be handled mathematically. Despite his shift to abstract and objective measures, he nonetheless aimed to incorporate the needs of the victim into an analysis of wrongdoing. But his discussion of reciprocity makes a similar move from the subjective to the objective. He moves rapidly from the desire of citizens to return ill for ill to a discussion of commerce and trade where money will provide an objective measure of incommensurable things.

The Greek for corrective justice, the word "diorthotic," is an Aristotelian neologism and perhaps reflects Aristotle's attempt to marry the penal ideas of democratic Athens to Platonic ideas. Earlier writers had used related words *diortheuo* and *diorthoo* to mean "to judge rightly" and "to make quite straight, to make up a quarrel." These words all derive from the root *orthos* which means "standing upright" (*Il.* 23.271); "straight" (in relation to a line) (Hes. *Op.* 727); and, in its metaphorical usage, "right, safe, prosperous, true, correct, upright, and just" (*LSJ*). In other words, the idea of straightness could be used to describe the ideas of proper proportion and balance that were central to Athenian understandings of retribution and reciprocity. But the idea of straightness could also be used to describe matters of virtue and good behavior central to Plato.

The question of what sort of punishment was commensurable to wrongdoing elicited different answers from the Athenians, from Plato, and from Aristotle. The Athenians required an angry response that would serve to straighten out a social disruption or quarrel within the community. Plato required a response that would straighten out a certain member of the community and bring that citizen's behavior in line with everyone else's. Aristotle required a response that would preserve the citizens' ability to act as agents without violating one another's agency. All of these ideas were captured in the idea of making human relations "straight" or by the idea of bringing diverse human actions and interests into some sort of harmonization. From the time of archaic writers, justice had been described as a matter of "straightness" while "injustice" was described as a matter of crookedness. But Aristotle has now put the more specific case that the straightness involved in justice has to do with the ability of citizens to make the seemingly incommensurable commensurable in order to foster civic peace.

The Reform of Prometheus and Promethean Rebellion

THE *Prometheus Unbound* is lost to us but for some fragments, the longest of which is to be found in Cicero's *Tusculan Disputations* (45–44 B.C.). Cicero quotes from what is taken to be an opening section of the play. Prometheus has been returned to his rock in the Caucasus and once again he is venting his sufferings:

> Race of Titans, ally of my blood,
> And birthed by heaven,
> Look [*aspicite*] at me tied and bound
> To the bitter rocks, like the ship
> Tied up by scared sailors afraid of the night
> On the horrible-sounding sea. . . .
> Jupiter, son of Saturn, impales me thus,
> And the force of Jupiter took up the hands of Vulcan. . . .
> And I inhabit the fortress of the Furies,
> Transfixed by his cleverness [*transverberatus sollertia*], I am miserable. . . .
> I, wretched, feed [the eagle] who is the custodian of my torment,
> With an eternal misery it befouls me, I, who am alive, [*quae me perenni vivum foedat miseria*].
> For, as you see [*ut videtis*], I am not able to ward the dire bird
> Off my chest because I am constrained by the bonds of Jove.

> (2.23)

Cicero may or may not have doctored the text, since he did revise other quotations from Greek poets. Whatever the case, the text returns us to the spectacle of Prometheus bound on his rock, giving voice to his sufferings (*aspicite, ut videtis*). Cicero, however, does not read the story of the Titan's punishment for the purpose of understanding the challenge that Prometheus poses to Zeus, nor for the purpose of hearing the call for judgment that Prometheus addresses to his audience and spectators, when he calls out for pity. Cicero introduces the quotation when he is midstream in a discussion about how the wise man should respond to pain. The answer will be, of course, that the wise man should respond with a stoic endurance. Cicero takes Prometheus to be an example of a wrongdoer who unvirtuously gives vent to his anguish and does not keep it under control. Prometheus the rebel has been replaced with Prometheus, the merely wretched. The shift is Platonic. In fact, Cicero moves from the quotation to a brief digression on the topic of Plato.

> Do you not see how the poets are bringing about harm [*sed videsne poetae quid mali adferant*]? They bring before us the strongest men lamenting, they weaken our souls,

and [their poems] also are so pleasant that they are not only read but also learned by heart. . . . Thus they were rightly ejected [*eiiciuntur*] from the polity [*civitate*] by Plato [*a Platone*], when he devised that place for his inquiry about what are the best customs and what the best state for a republic. (2.27)

Prometheus, the contester of justice, who is accused of being a *sophist* or clever man in the *Prometheus Bound* by both Kratos and Hermes (62, 944), Prometheus who resembles the Athenian litigant contesting desert in terms of anger and pity, has given place to Prometheus the wretched, an incurable Prometheus who must, with his poet-progenitors, be banished from the best city. In Cicero's reading, Prometheus's claims of desert have, in some sense, given way to Zeus's assessment of him as a rebel deserving of reform, reconstitution, and reeducation. This glimpse of the lamenting Prometheus is essentially our last sight of the Titan in ancient sources. Little else remains from the *Prometheus Unbound* and in our imaginations Prometheus remains forever affixed to his rock. It is a wonder that Cicero preserves even as much of the *Unbound* as he does.

Our parting view of Prometheus would probably be rather different if we had the whole *Unbound*. In the second play it is not Zeus who has the final word but Prometheus. He gains his release, pacifies Zeus, and eventually wins honors from mortals. Prometheus achieves this victory despite Kratos's taunting certitude, at the beginning of the *Prometheus Bound*, that the Titan will never be able to find a way out of his fetters:

> There now, act with hubris, seize the honors of the gods, and go ahead and give them to mortals. Will it be possible for mortals to relieve you in your troubles? The divinities have misnamed you, calling you Prometheus [*pseudonumos se daimones Promethea kalousin*]; for you yourself are in need of some one who can act with forethought [or has Promethean ideas] about the manner in which you will be extricated from this artifice [*auton gar se dei prometheos, / hotoi tropoi tesd' ekkulisthesei technes*]. (Aesch. *PB* 82–87)

But Kratos is wrong to think that Zeus's fetters are strong enough to hold Prometheus. Prometheus turns out to deserve his name after all, for the action of the play, which is pushed forward as Prometheus talks and talks and talks, does eventually lead to his release. It is as a sophist, as a talker, as a clever talker who gains allies by contesting Zeus's assessment of his desert, that Prometheus finds a way to extricate himself from his bonds. Kratos had come closer to understanding Prometheus when earlier in the play he had given the following command to Hephaestus: "Strike more, clamp, leave nothing loose. For he [Prometheus] is fearsome [*deinos*] at finding a way out of even evil impossibilities [*deinos gar heurein kak' amekanon poron*]" (58–59). Prometheus is fearsome and it is his contestation of desert, his ceaseless talking that makes him so.

Kratos, however, had a certain point when he said that Prometheus's forethought was not doing him any good. Prometheus knew from the beginning of the play that he would have to suffer through the ages but that he would eventually be released. He knew that he would come under the total force of necessity even before he was ever punished. Like Kratos, he recognizes that his fore-thought does him no good:

> And what am I saying? I know the whole future exactly.
> Nor will any unexpected trouble come upon me.
> It is necessary for me to bear my allotted fate as if it is easy, recognizing that the
>   might of necessity is incontestable [*hoti to tes anangkes est' aderiton sthenos*].
>
> (101–5)

Prometheus does not stop here, however. The knowledge that he will inevitably be subject to necessity does nothing to quell his desire to speak. In the next two lines he says:

> But in such circumstances it is not possible
> For me to be silent nor for me not to be silent about my fate (*all' oute sigan oute
>   me sigan tuchas / hoion te moi tasd' esti*).
>
> (106–7)

Prometheus's silence would be acquiescence in necessity and in his punish-ment. His speech is an attempt to thwart necessity but it is also a refusal to acquiesce. Prometheus is desperate, caught between two impossibilities: the de-sire to speak and the force of necessity that makes speech pointless. It is his anger that, throughout the play, drives him to speak in the face of necessity. This makes anger—the emotional force that drives Prometheus to contest desert and that throws into question whether Prometheus will acquiesce in Zeus's re-gime—as powerful a force as the necessity that is imposed by the king of the gods, by the Triform Fates, and by the Remembering Furies. Later Prometheus emphasizes once again the powerful counterposition of the forces that drive him to speak and that dissuade him from speaking. "It is painful to speak, painful to be silent" (199–200), he says. Prometheus is caught between the forces within himself and the force of Zeus, but Prometheus cannot resign himself to silence even when he is face to face with necessity. Even then, Prometheus the sophist contests his desert.

Portions of the Promethean myth are also told in the Platonic dialogue *Protagoras*, in which the sophist Protagoras and Socrates argue about whether virtue is teachable and where Protagoras argues for reformative punishment (Plato *Prot.* 320c-322e). Protagoras tells the story of how Prometheus and his brother Epimetheus, or Afterthought, were assigned the task of meting out skills and abilities to all the newly made creatures of the earth. They divvy up the job by deciding that Epimetheus will distribute the assorted goods on offer and that Prometheus will then come along later to assess and rectify his brother's distribution, if necessary. Prometheus discovers, when he arrives to survey his brother's work, that Epimetheus has left human beings naked, without shoes, without beds, and without weapons. He has left them weak, totally vulnerable, totally at the mercy of the comprehensive power of the other animals, totally subject to necessity.

This weakness and vulnerability give rise to Prometheus's theft. He steals not only fire for mortals but also wisdom. With these two tools mortals will be able to make not only clothes, houses, food but also voices and names (*epeita pho-*

nen kai onomata tachu dierthrosato tei technei). Language is to compensate for physical weakness and Zeus adds another gift to this one—the ability to use the language of justice in particular. Zeus sends Hermes to distribute justice and respect (*dike* and *aidos*) to all mortals, so that everyone may participate in political judgment (322d). Thus are human beings made what they are, says Protagoras.

Later Pausanias will credit Prometheus not merely with having given mortals wisdom, voice, and language but even with having fashioned people out of clay (Paus. 10.4.4). It is as if Prometheus has invented human beings entirely—the idea of molding them out of clay—by giving them the gift of *logos*, a tool that Glaucon said was more easily handled, more easily molded, than wax. It is as if he himself has fashioned them by giving them the tool with which to mold themselves and to fashion themselves.

Protagoras's young interlocutor, the audience to his story about the distribution of goods to the animals, is Socrates, who will eventually become a rather fine fashioner of *logoi*, *muthoi*, and icons himself. As does Plato, for that matter. In the *Protagoras* Socrates even claims a Promethean genealogy for himself. The young Socrates precipitates his conversation with the sophist Protagoras, the conversation in which the older man tells the Prometheus myth, by asking Protagoras whether they should hold their discussions about virtue in public or private: "Now consider this matter, whether you think that it is necessary to hold our dialogue on this matter alone just among ourselves or in front of the others?" (316c). Protagoras says that he will speak in front of the others. Like Prometheus, the sophist sets himself up as someone who is willing to speak publicly, who is perhaps willing even to make a spectacle himself. Protagoras rejects Socrates' suggestion that perhaps they should speak privately but commends him for the question: "You correctly take forethought [*promethei*] on my behalf Socrates."

Socrates draws the conversation to a close on another Promethean note. He remarks to Protagoras that their conversation seems to have left them in something of a tangle and that he would like to go through the argument again in order to figure out what virtue (*arete*) is and then to consider again whether it is teachable. He fears lest Epimetheus should bring about their failure by deceiving them, even as he almost brought about human failure with his original distribution of goods. "For," says Socrates, "I prefer Prometheus to Epimetheus in your story, for I use the former and take forethought [*hoi chromenos ego kai promethoumenos*] for the sake of my whole life when I am busy with such matters [i.e., as talking about virtue]." Protagoras, the sophist, had introduced Prometheus to the dialogue, but Socrates, the fashioner of *logoi*, himself claims a lineage from the Titan, sophist, and contester of desert. Protagoras introduces the topic of clever forethought, his gift of language, his willingness to speak at and as a public spectacle, and these are gifts that Socrates can take from the sophist when he claims to prefer Prometheus to Epimetheus.

Socrates may indeed take Prometheus as a model of sorts, but by Cicero's day Prometheus can no longer be presented in such a light. Cicero refers to

Prometheus once more in the *Tusculan Disputations* and quotes lines that we already know from the *Prometheus Bound*. The chorus suggests to Prometheus that he allow words to be the doctors to his wrath. Cicero quotes it thus: "And indeed, Prometheus, I expect you to recognize this, that it is possible for speech to doctor wrath [*mederi posse orationem iracundiae*]" (3.31.76). Cicero does not take the chorus's remark to refer to a desire for punishment that needs to be cured. He takes the disease from which Prometheus suffers to be the disease of baseness. Prometheus is the paradigm only of someone whose soul is diseased and needs curing (*in animorum morbis*). Cicero argues the wretchedness, sorrow, and misery that Prometheus displays will be cured only when he is convinced that it is useless to be overcome by sorrow. The focus on the disease of the soul erases the disease of anger. Later quotations of the Aeschylean text replace the word "anger" (*orges*) with the word "soul" (*psuches*) (Plut. *Consol. ad Apoll.* 102B; Eustathius 696.33).

Similarly, Cicero asks Prometheus to be a stoic mourner of necessity and not an angry talkative judge. In Cicero's Platonized reading of Prometheus, the Athenian process of spectacle is lost to view, the contest over desert is lost to view, the debate itself, about justice, is lost from sight. And yet these erasures, to the degree that we can say they were generated by Plato, arose from a particular and particularly powerful contribution precisely to the conversation about desert and justice in Athens. Cicero's focus on Prometheus's diseased soul rather than on his diseased anger bespeaks the power of Plato's revisions of stories of punishment. For if Prometheus is no longer a model, it is partly because Plato revised stories of punishment so as to transform Prometheus from a rebel, who claimed the right to judge the validity of Zeus's punishment, into the wretched lamenter. The changed appearance of Prometheus reveals the power that lies in fashioning a language that locates concepts at the heart of systems of desert and value and asks people to revise those systems; the change in Prometheus reveals Plato's own Promethean lineage as a contester of desert.

Foucault's *Discipline and Punish* is a recent effort to locate the concepts at the heart of systems of desert and value[1] by a historian who writes not so much histories as "genealogies of power-knowledge."[2] On Foucault's account, any given historical moment should be understood as embodying an ordered set of relations among bodies (human bodies), which can be described as produced by "power-knowledge." The order of the relations among bodies reflects an interpretation of the world as "being a certain way" and, in this sense, is "knowledge." But knowledge works not merely to describe bodies but also, in defining them, puts them in their places and contributes to the work of institutions in keeping them there. Knowledge functions as a power that orders bodies. Insofar as knowledge orders matter and experience, it is *the activity* of keeping bodies in their places. Conversely all the activity of keeping bodies in their places—however it is done and whatever acts of power are used to effect it—can be and must be understood as being subsumed within the rubric of knowledge. All knowing is a form of ordering; all ordering is a form of knowing, regardless of whether the ordering-knowing is accomplished by means of violence, ideology, institutions, culture, or a mixture. Genealogies of power-knowledge analyze knowing and ordering the world as a single "epistemologicojuridical" event;[3] and genealogies analyze every event as having "epistemologicojuridical" ramifications. The dichotomy between violence and ideology breaks down with the introduction of this third category of power. And Foucault writes:

> The subjection is not only obtained by the instruments of violence or ideology; it can also be direct, physical, pitting force against force, bearing on material elements, and yet without involving violence; it may be calculated, organized, technically thought out; it may be subtle, make use neither of weapons nor of terror and yet remain of a physical order. That is to say, there may be a "knowledge" of the body that is not exactly the science of its functioning, and a mastery of its forces that is more than the ability to conquer them: this knowledge and this mastery constitute what might be called the political technology of the body. Of course, this technology is diffuse, rarely formulated in continuous, systematic discourse, it is often made up of bits and pieces; it implements a disparate set of tools or methods. . . . Moreover, it cannot be localized in a particular type of institution or state apparatus. For they have recourse to it; they use, select, or impose certain of its methods. But, in its mechanisms and its effects, it is situated at a quite different level. . . . In short, this power is exercised rather than possessed; it is not the "privilege," acquired or preserved, of the dominant class, but the overall effect of its strategic positions—an effect that is manifested and sometimes extended by the position of those who are dominated.[4]

"Power-knowledge" is a phenomenon that crosses cultural and temporal boundaries, even if the age of liberal democracy has generated what Foucault thinks is a particularly oppressive form of "power-knowledge."

My efforts to understand the construction of authority through the construction of desert map on to Foucault's efforts to understand the workings of power-knowledge. The mechanisms by which authority sustained itself in ancient Athens are different from those operative in eighteenth- and nineteenth-century nation-states, but authority functioned in both political orders. On my account, authority is that which makes a society by binding a group of people together in a mutual acquiescence to a communal set of habitual practices, forms of behavior, and system of value, and *acquiescence* is the complementary *underside* to authority. This acquiescence is generated by means of a mixture of three phenomena, which are distinct in and distinguished *at least* in and by the subjective experience of those who acquiesce: consent or "voluntary" acquiescence, "threats" of force, and force. In respect to the authority involved in punishment, the combined workings of these three phenomena hold in place a socially dominant (i.e., authoritative) "conceptualization of desert" or system of value. Foucault's "subtle" forms of power are at work in generating the acquiescence that helps to hold up authority.

The phenomenon of consent or voluntary acquiescence is the most inexplicable of the three methods used to generate authority. To understand voluntary acquiescence, we have to understand how it is brought about, how people come to accede to particular value claims. "Desert" is relevant in this regard for "desert" is a word that has precisely the role of mobilizing consensual acquiescence in particular structures of authority and in particular distributions of goods. In some sense, "desert" is a word whose definition is an empty set and whose semantic force lies rather in its especial function as trigger to action. Particular conceptualizations of desert fill in the empty set with ideas about "what is deserving" and what kind of action is to be triggered; actors who accept a formulation of "desert" voluntarily acquiesce in the action that results from the practical application of the idea "desert." Throughout the course of this book, we have seen the concepts and categories that the Athenians used in order to establish parameters for the contest over desert that was carried out in the process of punishing. The attempts of citizens to punish resulted in final and authoritative responses to wrongdoing only when citizens could in fact mobilize concepts of desert effectively. By studying contestations of desert, I have precisely been studying the self-conscious efforts of people within one society to understand the concepts and system of value that structured political authority in their community. The structure of authority, of power-knowledge, can be changed by means of the contest over desert.

In the case of Prometheus and of the Athenians, the contest over desert was inspired by subjective feelings of freedom and unfreedom, and of anger and pity. And so, although my investigation of "authority" maps on to Foucault's investigation of "power-knowledge," my reference to "desert" changes the character of the investigation. Speaking about the production of acquiescence with reference to the contest over desert makes subjectivity matter. For it is only the subject who can decide whether he or she is acquiescing consensually.

Foucault argues that, in the face of power-knowledge, our subjectivity is irrelevant because we are objectively unfree bodies whose sense of subjectivity is itself thoroughly ordered by power-knowledge. For him, we are always Prometheus chained to the rock, bound by necessity and equally bound to be aware of the certitude and totality of that necessity. But for Prometheus the question of how to deal with necessity did not end with mere recognition that it cannot be defeated. Prometheus found it difficult to speak and difficult to stay silent and yet spoke. Despite Foucault, we cannot afford to ignore the ways in which subjectivity presses itself upon us. Our subjectivity is relevant to power-knowledge (or authority) precisely *qua* subjectivity, *qua* what motivates the contest over desert, a contest that actually has the power to impact the structure of power-knowledge. Our subjectivity is relevant, regardless of the degree to which it is of our own making, because it generates the contestability, through the struggle over desert, that produces shifts in the particular nature of any given authority structure. Prometheus's words were the only things that gave him the power to change the nature of his chains, the nature of the necessity imposed on him. He spoke in order to say that he would not acquiesce; his speech also affected Zeus's rule and thereby generated a reconstitution of the nature of necessity. In the realm of subjectivity, where we are "selves," we feel free and unfree to varying degrees, even if, as Foucauldian bodies in the realm of objectivity and power-knowledge, we are irrevocably unfree.[5] These feelings of freedom hinge on our assessments of how desert is functioning in our community. Our assessment can generate either a contestation of authority or acquiescence in it.

The figure of the "bee," the trope of moral evaluation that seems to have been permanently fixed in the Athenian conceptual landscape, betrays the force and permanence of authority and also its malleability. Of necessity and by definition, "the bee" symbolized the good or right order, whose definition was delimited by the equally permanent evil of the drone. The permanence of the bee and drone as symbols, respectively, of positive and negative valuations, speak to the ways in which authority, systems of desert, and systems of value inevitably function so as to order the world, to assign relative degrees of worth, and to draw boundaries. But the malleability of the bee and the drone—the opposition between bee and drone could be mapped in one case onto rich and poor, in another case onto male and female, in another case on to a citizen's legitimate anger and a demagogue's wasteful luxuries, and in other cases onto reason and passion—the malleability of the qualities attributed to each positive and negative symbol, and the malleability of the ends to which these categorizations could be directed reveal the ways in which systems of authority are characterized by an inherent contestability. The level of authority in a society and the amount of power invested in the dichotomous division between what is acceptable and what is not acceptable may be unchangeable—the bee is always a bee and not a drone—but the nature of the bee can be redescribed, the nature of the division between what is and is not acceptable transformed.

Selves feel free and unfree to varying degrees depending on the extent to which they acquiesce in authority consensually and the extent to which authority must (in their own eyes) be imposed on them (by threat or by force). In respect to punishment, selves acquiesce in authority consensually to the extent that they accept its formulation of desert. A contest over conceptualizations of desert is therefore a contest in which actors are negotiating the possibilities for and definitions of voluntary acquiescence in their society. It is therefore also a contest to define the level of acquiescence that selves will give to authority. And it is a contest over whether an authoritative system of desert will be based on (subjectively felt) voluntary acquiescence or on (subjectively felt) force or threats of force. In other words, the contest over desert is part of the struggle over acts of freedom and oppression in any given society.

In Athens, this contestability was controlled by limiting the numbers and classes of people who could make claims about desert and speak out about the injustices or justices they were suffering. We heard Demosthenes' commentary on what it would be like to be removed from this contest and to be unable to complain, to give voice, and to say whether one had suffered justly or unjustly. The male Athenian citizen's satisfaction at having the ability to express subjectively based objections to authority and to enter into the contest over desert was at the heart of his sense of what it meant to live in a free and equal political regime. But this freedom for male citizens was enmeshed in a system of authority in which many inhabitants in the city were not permitted to treat their acquiescence as contestable. There may be different levels of subjectively felt freedom and unfreedom within one system of power-knowledge and authority regardless of whether all members of a society are equally unfree. Matters also stand thus when we compare one regime to another. Different forms of power-knowledge, which all produce the same degree of objective unfreedom, may nonetheless, as systems of desert, produce differing degrees of subjective freedom and different combinations of acquiescence, threat, and force. We can engage in power-knowledge in order to have some sort of an impact upon our subjective freedom regardless of whether we can change our objective freedom at all.[6]

The point of making the distinction between the two types of freedom is precisely to prioritize our subjective feelings or thoughts about whether we are free above our "objective" Foucauldian knowledge that, as bodies subject to power-knowledge, we are not free. It is to make the choice of Prometheus to acknowledge necessity and to speak anyway. The former, subjective freedom, is a political phenomenon insofar as it allows of degree and is variable, negotiable, and contestable; the second, objective (un)freedom, is apolitical because it is neither a matter of degree nor variable, neither negotiable nor contestable. Our feelings and thoughts about our freedom lead us to the contest over desert—and when desert is contested, structures of authority can change. Foucault studies the punitive microphysics of power. Pointing out that "conceptualizations of desert" are part of that microphysics of power reintroduces the political world—the world of subjectivity and change—to the realm of power-knowledge.[7] It matters, to use M. Walzer's terms, that selves, if not bodies, can distinguish between Foucault's carceral archipelago and the gulag.[8] It matters, too, that selves, who live in, with, and through language, can find the *loci* of contestability within the conceptual networks supporting systems of authority.

Foucault's own genealogies make use of the political world despite his claim to have left it behind. His genealogies may be understood as introducing elements of the modern conceptualizations of desert and systems of value into political contest, making manifest what had been hidden or not consciously considered. Just by writing about a microphysics of power or forms of unselfconsciously experienced power-knowledge, Foucault transfers power-knowledge from the realm where we engage in authority without noticing to a realm where we engage with authority self-consciously, a thought-act contributing to what is usually termed "resistance." At the end of his career, Foucault expressed some regret that he had not spent more time developing the concept of resistance, and some thinkers have recently begun to do so. Rather than doing that, I posit that wherever we see the concept of desert at work, we can see the realm of power-knowledge, but we can also see its contestability, a contestability that arises precisely from human subjectivity. In other words, I am arguing that the realm of authority or of power-knowledge is the realm of politics to the degree that this authority and power-knowledge are in fact contestable, which is precisely what they are in the struggle over definitions of desert. This struggle begins when we carry out our subjective assessments of freedom and oppression, what Judith Shklar called "the oldest and newest of the theoretical and practical concerns of political theory."[9]

In the *Prometheus Bound*, the Titan—the talkative sophist yoked by necessity to the rock of the Caucasus at the edge of the world, having known that he would be yoked inevitably, the angry challenger who spends an eternity suffering the force of necessity, who is the master of forethought and fashioner of human beings, who leaves it to human beings to use their language to fashion themselves—twice cries out from his chains that it is difficult to speak and difficult to be silent and yet speaks. Foucauldian structures of power-knowledge, even those of which we are unconscious, are already being contested when someone calls out, like Prometheus, "See what injustices I suffer."

Appendixes

The Number of Magistrates in Athens

Our most specific piece of information about the number of *archai* in Athens comes from the following *Ath. Pol.* passage:

> dikastai men gar esan hexakischilioi, toxotai d' hexakosioi kai chilioi kai pros toutois hippeis chilioi kai diakosioi, boule de pentakosioi, kai phrouroi neorion pentakosioi kai pros toutois en tei polei phrouroi n, *archai d' endemoi men eis heptakosious andras* huperorioi d' eis heptakosious. (24.3)

> For there were 6,000 jurors, 1,600 archers, and 1,200 in the cavalry, and the council was 500 people, and there were 500 guardians of the harbors and on top of this 50 guards in the city, and *archai in the city amounted to 700 men* and those abroad amounted to 700.

No modern scholar believes *Ath. Pol.*'s statement that there were 700 *archai* in the city (Hansen 1980a). A.H.M. Jones (1964) comes up with a list of 350 magistrates and Hansen (1980a) comes up with a list of 422–29. There are reasons, however, to doubt these figures and to think that the *Ath. Pol.* number (700) is approximately correct.

Contemporary scholars have compiled their lists of *archai* without including the 500 *bouleutai* or council members, despite the fact that *Ath. Pol.* refers to them as *archai* (*Ath. Pol.* 29.5; 62. 3). Presumably, Jones and Hansen leave the 500 *bouleutai* off their lists because in the previously quoted passage *Ath. Pol.* has already listed the number of *bouleutai* before he says that there are 700 *archai*. It is a mistake, however, not to include the *bouleutai* in the official tally of magistrates.

In addition to the fact that *Ath. Pol.* refers to the *bouleutai* as *archai*, the Greek of the passage cited here indicates that the figure 700 is a *sum* intended to total any *archai* already listed (i.e., the *bouleutai*) with any as yet unmentioned *archai*. Prior to mentioning the 700 *archai*, *Ath. Pol.* has put numbers in the nominative case parallel to the noun that the number modifies: *hexakischilioi*; *hexakosioi kai chilioi*; *chilioi kai diakosioi*; *pentakosioi, pentakosioi*). To say that there are 700 *archai*, however, *Ath. Pol.* uses *eis* with the accusative (*eis heptakosious andras*). Rubincam (1979, 327–37, citing R. Kühner and B. Gerth (*Ausführliche Grammatik der Griechischen Sprache*, vol. 2.1 [Hanover and Leipzig, 1890], p. 469) has found that in Thucydides when the preposition *es* appears with a number in the accusative in a list of figures, it "most commonly designates a limit of some kind" and frequently has a "summary" function, expressing the total obtained by adding together several groups of people or ships (e.g., Thuc. 1.100.1, 3.107.3, 3.114.4, 4.124.1, 6.67.2, 7.19.3, 7.30.3,

7.33.1, 8.44.4). In other words, it is at least possible that the phrase *archai d'* *endemoi men eis heptakosious andras* is used to indicate that *archai* is a collective word meant to include any *archai* who have already been mentioned as well as those that have not yet been mentioned.

If so, any accurate list of magistrates would have to include the *bouleutai*, and A.H.M. Jones' figures should be revised to 850 and Hansen's should be revised to 922–29. But will this mean that *Ath. Pol.* had not overestimated but rather underestimated the number of *archai* in the city? This would be the case only if Jones's 850 and Hansen's 925 are accurate. But I suggest that the figures 850 and 922–29 are in fact too high because of double-counting: some *boule* members fulfilled other functions, in addition to that of *bouleutes*, and therefore had two titles. For instance, 30 *bouleutai* served as *sullogeis tou demou* (discussed later). Hansen's list of magistrates includes 12 magistrates of which he says, "it cannot be precluded that the board is a committee of the Council of 500" (*ten hieropoioi eis panathenaia, anagrapheus, tamia tes boules*). If it is possible that not just these 12 magistrates but rather some number of magistrates nearing on 200 were appointed from within the *boule* (or 100 in respect to Jones's estimates), then *Ath. Pol.*'s estimate of 700 would have been, in fact, correct.

Although no citizen was allowed to hold more than one *arche* at once (heliastic oath, Dem. 24.150), it was possible for an *arche* or magistracy to entail more than one job. The discovery of the Silver Coinage Law after the publication of Rhodes 1972 is reason for reconsidering the issue of how many official hats a *bouleutes* could wear since the law shows 30 *bouleutai* to have served as *sullogeis tou demou*. (It should also be pointed out that since the heliasts did not necessarily do *dokimasiai* for *bouleutai* [Rhodes 1972, 176–77; 1981, 542–43, 615–17], their oath not to appoint people to two offices may not have applied to *bouleutai*.)

To take a modern example, the president of the United States holds only one office, but he or she is also the commander in chief of the armed forces. The president holds a "second set" of powers on the basis of his or her first set of powers. If, in later years, someone should try to determine how many offices there were in the U.S. system, they might well count commander in chief of the armed forces and president as two different positions, although they are not. In the Athenian context, it was possible for a citizen, holding a single *arche*, simultaneously to do the work of being a council member and, as a council member, also to fulfill another function in the city like that of *logistes*. In the *Politics*, Aristotle outlines what the necessary *archai* are in a city: they include superintendence of religious institutions, military institutions, revenue and expenditure, the market, citadel, harbors, countryside, the jury courts, the registration of contracts, collection of fines, custody of prisoners, supervision of accounts and inspections, the auditing of officials, and at last or to complete the matter (*telos*) those offices belonging to the body that meets as a council about the common good (1322b30). In the course of the discussion of these magistracies (1321b5–1323a11; cf. 1321b35; 1322a8), Aristotle remarks that it is possible for several of these powers to be vested in one person, or for one of these powers to be divided among many people. He also describes the council (*boule*) as having control not only over the introduction but also over the execution of business (*he gar aute pollakis echei to telos kai ten eisphoran*, 1322b13). His account also leaves open the possibility that a councillor might fulfill two jobs at once.

We know on the basis of epigraphical evidence that the following officials were appointed out of the *boule*. (Only the 10 *logistai* and the 10 *trieropoioi* were definitely referred to as archai.)

- 10 *logistai* with their ten assessors (*Ath. Pol.* 48.3; 54.2; Pollux 8.99).
- 10 *episkeuastai* (Tod 66; *ATL* A 9, M&L 69, *IG* i^3 71: in the latest text the *boule* does not appoint the *eisagogeis* [line 7] but does appoint the *taktai* [line 8]).
- 10 *trieropoioi* (*Ath. Pol.* 46.2; *IG* i^3 182a.b; cf. schol. Dem. 22.20; Rhodes 1972, 117).
- 3 *bouleutai* to cooperate with Callicrates in drawing up the designs for a temple door (Tod 40 = *IG* i^3 35).
- 5 *bouleutai* (with ten other citizens) appointed to review *horoi* or *orgas* at Eleusis (*IG* ii^2 204.5–12).
- 10 *hieropoioi* (*hieropoioi ek boules, IG* ii^2 1672.279–85 [329/8]; *IG* ii^2 1749.80–84 [341/0]; *IG* ii^2 410 [322/1]; *IG* i^3 82.23–30 [with the verb *diaklerosato*]; *IG* ii^2 334.34–35); *epi to theorikon* (*IG* ii^2 1493; *tous ek tes boules theorous*; Dem. 19.128; cf. Dem. 32.11).
- 30 *sullogeis tou demou* (*IG* ii^2 1425.126–30.) On 30 *sullogeis tou demou* see Lipsius 1915, 30; Rhodes 1972, 21, 129–30; 1981, 520, 527; Hunter 1993, 156–57.
- someone chosen out of the *boule*; *IG* ii^2 1629; cf. Lys. 13.23.
- *tamias ton trieropoion* elected by *boule* (Dem. 22.20, although a scholiast tried to change the text to prevent this reading).

This list shows council members holding approximately eighty other jobs. The question to be answered is whether there is any reason to suppose that more officials may have been appointed from within the *boule* and whether more *bouleutai* may in fact have worn "two hats," so to speak.

I suggest, on the basis of *Ath. Pol.* 46–62, that the following additional officials may also have been chosen out of the *boule*: the 10 *astunomoi*; 10 *agoranomoi*;[1] 10 *metronomoi*; 10 (and later 35) *sitophulakes*; 5 *eisagogeis*, who were responsible for the monthly suits; 10 receivers; the Forty; 5 roadkeepers (cf. Aes. 3.25); 10 *euthunoi* and their twenty assessors.[2] I suggest, on the basis of Dem. 47.22–47, that the 10 *epimeletai neorion* also came from the *boule*. (Since the last claim is plausible only if the reading of *Ath. Pol.* is plausible, I do not argue it at present, and will argue only the case about *Ath. Pol.* 46–62.) Let me point out before I begin that the cases for and against the claim that *bouleutai* could wear two hats stand or fall on the basis of this *Ath. Pol.* passage.

Ath. Pol. sections 42–62 contain a list of magistrates and a description of their duties. The passage is framed and punctuated by summary, organizational paragraphs at 42–43, 47, 55, and 62. These paragraphs reveal the author of *Ath. Pol.* to be especially concerned with how offices were filled. The excerpts that follow provide the organizational skeleton of the passage (the following transla- tions are taken from H. Rackham's translation in the 1952 Loeb edition).

Such, then, are the regulations about the registration of the citizens and about the cadets. All the officials concerned with the regular administration are appointed by lot, except a Treasurer of Military Funds, the Controllers of the Spectacle Fund, and the Superintendent of Wells; these officers are elected by show of hands, and their term of office runs from one Panathenaic Festival to the next. All military officers also are elected by show of hands. The Council is elected by lot, and has five hundred mem- bers, fifty from each tribe. The Presidency is filled by each tribe in turn, in an order settled by lot, each of the first four selected holding the office for thirty-six days and each of the latter six for thirty-five days; for their year is divided into lunar months. (43.1–3)

The Council also shares in the administration of the other offices in most affairs. First there are the ten Treasurers of Athena, elected one from a tribe by lot, from the Five-hundred-bushel class, according to the law of Solon (which is still in force), and the one on whom the lot falls holds office even though he is quite a poor man. (47.1)

These then are the matters administered by the Council. Also ten men are elected by lot as Restorers of Temples, who draw 30 minae from the Receivers and repair the temples that most require it; and ten City Controllers, five of whom hold office in Peiraeus and five in the city. (50.1–2)

These offices, then, are elected by lot and have authority over all the matters stated. As to the officials designated the Nine Archons (*hoi de kaloumenoi ennea archontes*), the mode of their appointment that was originally in force has been stated before; but now the six Lawgivers and their clerk are elected by lot, and also the Archon, King and War-lord, from each tribe in turn. (55.1)

These are the functions of the Nine Archons. They also elect by lot ten men as Stewards of the Games, one from each tribe, who when passed as qualified hold office for four years, and administer the procession of the Panathenaic Festival, and the contest in music, the gymnastic contest and the horse-race, and have the Robe made, and in conjunction with the Council have the vases made, and assign the olive-oil to the competitors. The oil is procured from the sacred trees; and the Archon levies it from the owners of the farms in which the trees are, three quarters of a pint from each trunk. (60.1–2)

They also elect by show of hands all the military officers—ten Generals, formerly one from each tribe, but now from all the citizens together. (61.1)

The officials elected by lot were formerly those elected from the whole tribe to- gether with the Nine Archons and those now elected in the temple of Theseus who used to be divided among the demes; but since the demes began to sell their offices, the latter also are elected by lot from the whole tribe, excepting members of the Council and Guards; these they entrust to the demes. (62.1)

The passage begins with an interest in the distinction between offices assigned by lot and offices that are elected. This distinction, however, is made more precise as the passage progresses. We are asked to distinguish between offices that have always been allotted and the offices of the nine archons, which were once filled by election but are now allotted. These two different types of *allotted* magistrates are then both juxtaposed with the *elected* military officers. The passage thus divides neatly into three sections: offices that have always been allotted (section 1 on table A1), offices that are now allotted with the nine archons but were not always allotted (section II), and elected military offices (section III).[3] The final paragraph confirms that there is a distinction between offices allotted from within a whole tribe and offices allotted from within the demes. The offices of the nine archons are allotted from the whole tribe, the councillors are allotted from the demes, and there has been some slippage in the process for allotting other offices.

But were any of the offices described in the complete passage allotted from within the *boule* itself? It is first worth noting that the passage sets up a parallel between its investigation of the *boule* and its investigation of the archons. In both cases, it first considers tasks that are directly carried out by the *boule* and archons (47.1–50.1 for the *boule* and 55.1–60.1 for the archons). The description of these tasks is then followed by a description of offices and work that is supervised by the *boule* and archons respectively but not, at least in the case of the archons, directly carried out by them. Passage 50.1 should be read as a parallel to passage 60.1. The latter passage describes officials who carried out religious work that was primarily supervised by the *archon basileus*; the paragraphs that precede it describe what the archons themselves do. It is reasonable, therefore, to think that sections 47.1–50.1 concern magistracies that are closely associated with the council. But how many of the magistracies described in this section were actually held by council members?

To answer this question, we need to look at how the passage from 47.1–50.1 describes the process of distributing offices. The verbs are especially important here, and the passage from 47.1–50.1 can itself be divided up into three distinct categories (sections Ia, Ib, and Ic in table A1) on the basis of the different vocabulary used in each part of the passage for describing how offices were filled.

The first group of offices (Ia) is marked by the use of the contracted present passive indicative form *kleroutai* (and the passive *eisi kekleromenoi*). The term is used to describe offices that we know to have been allotted from the whole people. Then there is a marked shift and we are told (Ib) that the *boule* allots ten *logistai* from among themselves (*klerousi logistas de kai ex hauton bouleutai*). The verb *klerousi* is repeated frequently in the list of magistrates that follows. It is interspersed with four uses of the passive *klerountai*, one of which describes the allotment of magistrates (ten *episkeuastai hieron*) whom we know to have been allotted from the *boule*. There is also one usage of the adjective

TABLE A1
Athenian Magistracies Listed in the *Athenaion Politeia*

Particle	Subject	Verb	Complements	Magistracy
I: Allotted Offices				
Ia: Tribal Offices				
de kai	boule	sundiokei	tais allais archais	
	hoi tamiai	kleroutai eisi deka	d' eis ek tes phules	ten treasures of Athena
epeith'	hoi poletai	kleroutai eisi	deka d' eis ek tes phules	ten poletai
de kai	ho basileus	eispherei		
	deka apodektai	eisi kekleromenoi	kata phulas	ten apodektai
Ib: Offices Allotted from within the *Boule*				
de kai	**hoi bouleutai**	**klerousi**	**deka logistas ex hauton**	**ten logistai**
de kai		klerousi	euthunous kai paredrous	ten euthunoi and twenty proedroi
de kai	he boule	dokimazei	tous hippous	
de kai		dokimazei	tous prodromous	
de kai		dokimazei	tous hamiptous	
de	*hoi katalogeis hous an ho demos cheirotonesei deka andras*	*katalegousin*	*tous d' hippeas*	
de	hoi bouleutai	diacheirotonousin	poteron	
kai	he boule	cheirotonesosin		
de pote kai	he boule	ekrinen	ton peplon	
de kai	he boule	dokimazei	tous adunatous	
kai	tamias	estin klerotos	autois	tamias
de kai		sundioikei	tais allais archais ta pleisth'	
men/ oun	ta tauta	estin dioikoumena	hupo tes boules	
de kai	**hieron episkeuastai deka andres**	**klerountai**		**10 hieron episkeuastai**
kai	astunomoi deka	[verb carried over from previous]		10 astunomoi
de kai	agoranomoi	klerountai		10 agoranomoi
de kai	metronomoi	klerountai		10 measure keepers
de kai	sitophulakes	esan . . . klerotoi		35 grain guards

Particle	Subject	Verb	Complements	Magistracy
Ib: *continued*				
de		klerousin	deka epimeletas tou emporiou	10 carers of the harbor
de kai		*kathistasi*	*tous endeka klerotous*	*the Eleven*
de kai		klerousi	eisagogeas e andrea	5 introducers
de kai		klerousi	tettarakonta	the Forty judicial officers
de kai		estin eisangellein eis tous diaitetas		
de kai		klerousi	tasde tas archas	five road-makers, ten logistas, and ten euthunoi
de kai		**klerousi**	**grammatea ton kata prutaneian kaloumenon**	**a secretary for the prytany**
de kai		klerousi	epi tous nomous heteron	a secretary for the laws
Ic: Offices (Mostly Allotted) under the Control of the *Demos*				
de kai	ho demos	cheirotonei	grammatea ton anagnosomen autoi kai tei boulei, kai houtos oudenos esti kurios alla tou anagnonai	a secretary for the assembly
de kai	ho demos	kleroi	deka hieropoious	ten hieropoioi
de kai		kleroi	heterous deka	officials to do sacrifices
de kai		klerousi	eis Salamina archonta	archon to Salamis, demarch for Piraeus
II: Offices Allotted, Appointed, and Installed with the Nine Archons by the Demos				
nun de	[they, the demos]	klerousin	hex thesmothetas etc.	six thesmothetai, secretary, archon, basileus, and polemarchos
no de kai's	*interlude*	*discussion of dokimasiai*		

TABLE A1 (*continued*)

Particle	Subject	Verb	Complements	Magistracy
II: *continued*				
de kai	ho archon kai ho basileus	lambanousi	paredrous	paredroi for archon and basileus
epeita	ho archon	kathistasi	choregous tragoidois	choral producers
de kai		proteron kathistasi		
de kai	archon	kathistesi	choregous eis Delon	
	etc.			
	etc.			
III: Elected Military Offices				
de kai	[they, the *demos*]	cheirotonousi	strategous	generals
de kai		cheirotonousi	taxiarchous deka	taxiarchs
de kai		cheirotonousi	hipparchous duo	hipparchs
de kai		cheirotonousi	phularchous	phylarchs
de kai		cheirotonousi	hipparchon eis Lemnon	hipparch for Lemnos
de kai		cheirotonousi	tamian tes Paralou	a treasurer of the Parales

Note: For the significance of underscoring, boldface type, and italic type to highlight terms in this table, see the discussion in text.

Source: The text used for this table was M. Chambers, ed., *Aristotelis Athenaion Politeia* (Leipzig: Teubner, 1986).

klerotos with the verb "to be." The passage concludes with a return to the active verb *klerousi*, using five in a row. The second to last usage again refers to an office that we know was allotted from within the *boule* (*grammateus ton kata prutaneian*). No change of subject is ever marked for the uses of the verb *klerousi*. If anything, the *boule* is the dominant subject of the passage, since it (or the councillors) are made the subject of a sentence introduced by *de kai* six times. After the closing five uses of *klerousi* we have a drastic change. The next office is described with the phrase "the people elects" (*ho demos cheirotonei*). Section Ic begins with this shift to the singular verb and the *demos* as subject. Three more offices follow before the passage ends. Their modes of distribution are described thus: "the people allots" (*ho demos kleroi*); "it allots" (*kleroi*); "they allot" (*klerousi*). The transition to having the *demos* be the source of the allotments is emphasized and sets up a dramatic contrast to what has come before.

I would argue that in section Ib *Ath. Pol.* has given us a list of magistrates allotted from within the *boule*. The section begins by describing such allotment explicitly. Two other offices on the list are known from other sources to be allotted from within the *boule* and they appear at the middle and end of the list; together the three offices frame the whole passage as concerning offices allotted from within the *boule*. The syntax and structure of the passage suggest that it is reasonable to read the *boule* as the subject of the other allotments described as well. The passage is characterized by an insistent pattern of *de kai*'s used to introduce each new magistracy. The particles emphasize the repetition of verbs in this passage and stress the fact that when *Ath. Pol.* changes verbs it is not for the sake of stylistic variation. We are meant to take this passage as an ordered list. Such a repetition of the unit *de kai* appears nowhere else in any Aristotelian text. Nor does such an insistent repetition of verbs appear anywhere else in the *Ath. Pol.*

Moreover, the one important exception to the verbal pattern in section Ib confirms the idea that the subject of the passage is the *boule* and not the *demos*, as it is often assumed to be. When the Eleven prison guards are described, the adjective *klerotoi* is used, and the plural verb *kathistasi* is used without a subject. We are given: "They install the allotted Eleven" (*kathistasi tous endeka klerotous*). Later in the passage the verb *kathistemi* is used again. *Ath. Pol.* describes the archon and *archon basileus* as selecting or taking (*lambanousi*) secretaries for themselves. Then the archon is described as "installing" the *choregoi* or choral producers. We know from elsewhere (Theoph. *Char.* 26) that the archon did not select the tragic *choregoi*, but he did set them to work and had them work under his jurisdiction. It seems quite likely that the verbal adjective *klerotoi* makes the point that the allotment of the Eleven is carried out elsewhere than in the *boule* and then the word *kathistasi* makes the point that the *boule* set these officers to work and supervised them once they had been allotted by the people. The Eleven were, in fact, allotted from within the whole people, as we know from other sources, and their magistracy is the only one in section Ib whose mode of appointment is attested elsewhere (cf. [Xen.] *Ath. Pol.* 2.2.4 and Arist. *Pol.* 1321b5–1323a11). The language used to describe the Eleven explicitly distinguishes their mode of appointment from the mode of appointment used to fill the other magistracies discussed directly before and after them.

The verbal patterns are laid out in table A1. I would contend that the magistracies described in section Ib and introduced with a *de kai* were, except for the Eleven, allotted from within the *boule* (these are underlined in the table). To highlight different elements of the table, I have put in boldface all offices that we are already certain were filled from within the *boule*. I have put in italics all entries on the list that are isolated interruptions of a subject verb pattern that precedes and follows after them and, therefore, cannot be said to interrupt the subject-verb pattern of the passage as a whole. These coincide with the offices that were not appointed from within the *boule*. If I am correct in my reading of this passage, then *Ath. Pol.*'s claim that there were 700 magistrates would be correct provided that this number is taken to include the *bouleutai*.

Circumstantial evidence provides additional links between some of the offices described in section Ib and the *boule*.

Sitophulakes

a. The grain guardians (*sitophulakes*) carried out work in the fourth century that the *boule insgesamt* carried out earlier. The following references include references to the activities of the *boule* and references to the activities of the *sitophulakes*: *Ath. Pol.* 51.4; Rhodes 1972, 117; Isoc. 17.42, 18.6 (but under oligarchic Ten); Ar. *Kn.* 300–302; And. 2.14 (under oligarchy); Dem. 35.51, 24.11–14; Is. 17.42; Lys. 22.2; *IG* ii² 1623; Hansen 1991a, 193. R. S. Stroud *Hesp.* 43 (1974): 157–88 (= *SEG* 26 [1976–77]: 72.22–26); Dem. 58.5–13.

b. Also, the *sitophulakes* are treated as analogous to the *boule*-selected *sullogeis tou demou* in the silver coinage law (*SEG* 26 [1976–77]: 72).

c. The *sitophulakes* heard accusations about merchants who refused to accept valid coinage (*SEG* 26 [1976–77]: 72.22–26); the *sullogeis tou demou* did as well and supervised the public slave who tested money.

d. In Lys. 22, a *bouleutes* brings a phasis about the grain dealers to the *boule* and it is at least a possibility that Anytos, who testified in the case as a *sitophulax*, was also a member of the council (Lys. 22.9).

Epimeletai *of the harbor*

a. The *epimeletai* of the harbor market are treated as analogous to the *boule*-selected *sullogeis tou demou* in the silver coinage law (*SEG* 26 [1976–77]: 72).

b. The *arche* of the harbor were responsible for merchants' cases at the middle of the fourth century (Xen. *Por.* 3.3; this reference from 355 B.C. is usually taken to refer to the *nautodikai*, but the term "officer" of the harbor is more aptly used if referring to the "carers of the harbor"). Members of the *boule* are to be seen carrying out those functions in *IG* ii² 1631.350–403 where a *boule* member brings an *apographe*. The carers of the harbor could receive accusations about the buying and selling (of grain) (Dem 58.5–13; Dem. 35.51).

c. Dem. 47: *hoi epimelomenoi ton neorion* are made parallel to the *boule* (cf. *IG* ii² 1622.420–22).

d. Suits on naval matters could come before the *boule* (*IG*ii 2.1631.398–401).

Agoranomoi, astunomoi

a. The *agoranomoi* policed buying and selling in general in the market and are equated to the *sitophulakai* (Lys. 22.16) who, as we have seen, were equated to the *sullogeis tou demou*.

b. The *boule* was involved in public building projects (*SEG* 10 [1956] 24.7–13; *IG* ii² 244.28–29).

Metronomoi

a. According to Rhodes (1972, 142), the weights and measures were kept in the *tholos*, which is where the prytany of the *boule* lived, which would mean that the *metronomoi* were associated with the *boule*.

b. The *boule* contributed to the supervision of slaves in charge of the measures (*IG* ii^2 1013.5.45–59). The *boule* took an oath about measures (M&L 45; Lys. 31.2).

c. A late-second-century decree (*IG* ii^2 1013; cf. *Hesp.* 7 [1938]: 27), which refers to the officials concerned with the measures, gives jurisdiction to the *boule*.

The *bouleutai* would have had ample time to do both their work as councillors and some additional job. The use of boards of ten would have allowed magistrates to take turns. Scholars have been puzzled by the fact that texts and epigraphical sources regularly refer to incomplete boards of administrators (cf. Hansen 1980c, 107, 121; e.g., Lys. 22.8). This would not be so puzzling if a boards of administrators were drawn up for the purpose of allowing them to take turns or to substitute for one another (Pl. Com. fr. 166–67; Aes. 3.62; Dem. 58.29: the *boule* as a whole was itself supplied with alternates should someone need to be replaced). Also, some magistracies, as Hansen (1980c, 124) points out about *epimeletai* and *hieropoioi*, would have had duties on only a few days each year. And the *bouleutai* seem to have served at least sometimes on the board of *nomothetai* (And. 1.81–83; cf. Dem. 24.20–27).

The council met approximately 220 days a year (cf. *Ath. Pol.* 43; Sinclair 1988, 225–27), but attendance seems to have been variable (Hansen 1983b, 227–38; Rhodes 1972, 23–39; Dem. 22.35–38). Councillors were required to spend 11–15 days and nights) of every year actually living in the tholos (depending on how many councillors constituted the *trittus* that kept the *epistates* (*Ath. Pol.* 44.1), but Rhodes (1981, 532) expects that even then official duties would have taken them out of the *tholos*. They had to be in Athens throughout the year (Sinclair 1988, 108, 113–14; although they could be sent out of Athens on official duties, Rhodes 1972, 39; Dem. 19.13, 154–55). These requirements are not incompatible with also having to be in, perhaps, the agora for portions of the day or in the Piraeus to see to other administrative tasks. For instance, Lysias describes a group of men chosen out of the *boule* as having to go down to the Piraeus to arrest Agoratus (*hairethentes ton bouleuton*, Lys. 13.23; cf. And. 1.14). The *boule* itself held its meetings in different parts of the city, and Rhodes speculates that, in some cases, full attendance is to be doubted (1972, 23–39).

Another example shows how the *boule* could assume other roles and administrative tasks in an ad hoc fashion: Androtion while councillor had an ad hoc commission appointed to collect arrears of property tax, a job normally carried out by nonbouleutic tax farmers (Sinclair 1988, 113; Dem 22.36–38, 66–73; 24.160–62); the example is, admittedly, problematic since Demosthenes challenged Androtion's maneuver as illegal, but it is at least worth noting that Androtion was able to convince his fellow councillors that setting themselves up as tax collectors was legitimate. In a fourth-century B.C. comic fragment, Sophilus suggested that the *boule* should appoint from itself (*haireisthai hupo tes boules*) two or three *opsonomoi* to improve the state of the fish market (fr. 2 [Kock], ap. Ath. 6.228B). Aeschines (3.29–30) suggested that people who are appointed as commissioners (*epistatai*) of public works in effect become *archai* if their job took more than thirty days. This suggests that the *boule* could assign a task to one of its members that would leave the *bouleutes* in the position of acquiring additional archontic status if the job took more than thirty days.

Scholars have long puzzled over the description of magistrate pay in *Ath. Pol.* 62.2, wondering why the passage describes pay only for the assembly, jurors, *boule*, and for a few specific *archai* but not for the numerous "other" magistrates we hear about in the text and elsewhere. (Arist. *Pol.* 1317b35ff. implies pay for all *archai*.) If those "other" magistrates were in fact drawn from the *boule*, there is no problem because the "missing *archai*" would be covered by the reference to the *boule* (Gabrielsen 1981; but see Hansen 1979, 16–19, for a different view, which Todd 1995, 291, follows).

For a reading of *Ath. Pol.* taking a different position from the one argued in this appendix, see Rhodes 1981. The passages of *Ath. Pol.* (54.7, 46.1, 51.3) that are taken by Rhodes (1981) to be insertions do not affect the reading suggested here. The argument that the offices described in section II do not come from the *boule* is based on two assumptions: the assumption that separate titles always distinguish a new office and the assumption that when the verb *klerousi* appears without a subject in a description of the allotment of officials, the subject should be taken to be "the people." Rhodes (1981, 512, 579–80) for instance, presumes this to be the case. The verb, however, is also used without a subject in places that describe allotments done by the council as confirmed by epigraphical evidence (e.g., *IG* i^3 82.23–30). Since officials could be allotted out of the *boule* (e.g., *Ath. Pol.* 48.4, 51.4), we cannot take for granted that when the word *klerousi* appears it denotes offices allotted by the whole people rather than offices allotted out of the council. Rhodes does not comment on the verb *kathistasi* nor on the summary passage about the relationship between the three kinds of office: those with the nine archons, the offices "from the tribes" that were sold, and the *boule*. Nor does he comment (1981) on the passage that describes magistracy pay.

The Nature and Scope of Arbitration in Athens

In this appendix, I argue that (1) the single phenomenon that we call "arbitration" had two aspects: compromise, where parties could be reconciled, and judgment, where they could not be; (2) that while there are many words denoting one or the other aspects of this process, *dikazein* is unique in denoting *both* parts of the process of dispute resolution and should therefore be translated as "speak so as to resolve a dispute" rather than as "render a judgment"; and 3) in Athens arbitration was carried out more extensively than we have previously thought and in both the fifth and fourth centuries.

In respect to the first point, Scafuro (1997, 120–21) has recently argued not that there were two types of arbitration (as I argue) but rather that there were two separate procedures: reconciliation and arbitration. In doing this, she is attempting to resuscitate a tradition of studying arbitration that died out in 1938 and that has not been replaced with anything else. She has reclaimed the study of compromise reconcialiation for students of ancient judicial decision making. I, however, would like to push the argument farther to say that the process of working reconcialiation was itself a form of arbitration and act of judicial decision making. Scafuro's treatment of arbitration is thorough and very useful (1997). I wish only that it had reached me earlier in my project.

In Athens a distinction existed between arbitrations in which the arbitrator did not take an oath and in which the arbitrator did take an oath. If the arbitrator was trying to work out a compromise settlement for two litigants, he did not take an oath. If he could not work out a compromise and had to make a judgment, then he made the judgment on oath. To work out a compromise agreement was designated by the terms: (*gnonai ta sumpheronta pasin*; *diallattein*; *dialusai* (Karabélias 1997 agrees). To give a judgment was designated by the terms: *ta dikaia diagnonai*; *gignoskein*, *apophaneisthai ta dikaia*. The word *dikazein* could refer to both forms of dispute resolution. (Of a public arbitrator, Dem. 40.16; of private arbitration, Dem. 30.2; 48.8; cf. a judge's decision, Hdt. 1.14; Ant. 5.90; Dem. 21.75; 35.46; Lyc. 1.7). Even at the stage of arbitration, before a case had come to court, it could be referred to as a *dike* (Dem. 40.16, 21.83–84, 52.30–31; *Ath. Pol.* 53.2; cf. Isae. 5.31; Dem. 34.21, 52.14–16). In a private arbitration, disputants could be called *antidikoi* (Theophr. *Char.* 5.3). Lipsius (1915, 222), Gernet (1939, 390–93), and Rhodes (1981, 589) agree that arbitrators had a double function, both working compromises and judging, but they do not link the matter to oaths.

For differences between unoathed and oathed arbitrations, see:

Isae. 5.31–33: "As if we had been wronged only in some minor fashion, we came to an agreement and referred [*epetrepsamen*] the matter to four arbitrators, two of whom we introduced and two of whom they did. In the presence of these men we agreed to abide by whatever they should decide [*emmenein hois an houtoi gnoien*] and we swore an oath to that effect. And the arbitrators said that if they should be able to bring about a compromise [*diallaxai*] without being on oath [*anomotoi*], they would do this, but if not, they themselves would swear an oath and make clear how they think that matters of justice stand in the case [*autoi omosantes apophaneisthai ha dikaia hegounta einai*]."

Dem. 29.58–59: "But after persuading me to refer the matter to Archenos and Dracontides . . . he rejected them when he heard that if they judged these things on oath, they would condemn him [*ei meth' horkou tauta diaitesousi, katagnosontai*]."

Dem. 52.30–31: "This man persuaded the arbitrator [*diaiteten*], selected according to the laws, to arbitrate without being on oath [*anomoton diaitesai*], although I was countering according to the laws that he should arbitrate on oath [*emou diamarturomenou kata tous nomous omosanta diaitan*]. . . . While my father was alive, jurors, Lysitheides would equally not have wronged him either with or without an oath. . . . This is why he explained [the justice of the matter] without being on oath [*dioper anomotos apephenato*]."

Ath. Pol. 53, 55.5: "The forty are competent to judge [*dikazein*] finally in those affairs concerning damages or penalties up to ten drachmae, but they hand over cases exceeding this penalty to the public arbitrators [*diaitetais*]. These arbitrators take them up and, if they are not able to resolve them [*dialusai*], they judge them [*gignoskousi*]; if the judgments [*ta gnosthenta*] are suitable to both parties involved, they stop there, and the case [*he dike*] has an end. . . . For *dokimasia*, the jurors walk to the stone which is the same as the one on which the arbitrators explain their decisions on oath [*eph hou kai hoi diatetai omosantes apophainontai tas diaitas*]."

Arist. Pol. 1285b9–12: "In addition [the kings (*basileis*)] judged private cases [*tas dikas ekrinon*]; and they did this both without taking oaths and on oath; and the oath involved holding the scepter [*touto d' epoioun hoi men ouk omnuontes hoi d' omnuontes, ho d' horkos en tou skeptrou epanatasis*]."

For differences between compromise decisions and judgments, but without reference to oaths, see:

Ath. Pol. 53.2: See earlier quotation.

Isok. 18.10–14: "You must first of all remember that we turned this matter to arbitration not as disputants but according to covenant [*hoti ten diaitan ouk amphisbetountes all' epi rhetois epetrepsamen*]."

Cf. Theophr. *Charac.* 12.13.

Other cases of arbitration: Dem 21.94; 30.1–2; 33.13–15, 30; 34.18–21; 36.15; 37.15–16; 40.10–11, 39–40; 47.6; 48.7–11; 52.14–16; 59.45–48, 65–71; Lys. 32. 2–3; fr. 37.1; Aes. 1.62–63; Isoc. 17.19; Men. *Epi.* 226; Isae. 12.9. Theophr. *Char.* 24.4.

Cases of resolution: Dem. 38.5–6; 36.15, 17; 41.4–5, 29; 42.11–13; 46.6; Isoc. 17.18–19. And. 6.12.

An unusual case: In Isae. 2.29–33 we get oaths from both the litigants and from the judge. The arbitrator promises to take an oath and make a decision, which turns out to be a one-sided judgment decision, but he does so only after the parties themselves swear to interpret his decision as being for the good of all parties despite the fact that it is a one-sided judgment. Rhodes (1981, 620) takes the arbitrator's oath to be a promissory oath guaranteeing that he will take the case.

The word *dikazein* is at the heart of this confusing set of issues involved in arbitration. It is most frequently translated as "to judge" but this translation is problematic. As we have seen, the word could be used of public arbitration (Dem. 40.16) or of private arbitration (Dem. 48.8; cf. 30.2). The word *dikazein* was also used to describe the activities of certain fifth- and fourth-century officials like the Forty, the *basileus*, and the *agoranomoi* (e.g., *Ath. Pol.* 57.25; *IG* i^3 15a.14, 102.24, 104.10, 47.13; Lys. 10.2; Dem. 48.8; cf. Gagarin 1973, 85). Yet when the word *dikazein* is used to describe the powers of such magistrates, it frequently appears in a context where the magistrate *was not* in fact acting as a judge. For instance, the homicide law of Draco includes the provision that in murder cases the *basileus* will carry out some sort of task referred to as *dikazei* and then will hand the case over to the homicide judges who will judge the case (*diagignoskein*) (*IG* i^3 104). The Code of Gortyn makes a distinction between a judicial resolution designated with *dikazein* that is carried out when there is proof and a judicial resolution carried out without proof but with the judges taking oaths and this form of resolution is designated with the phrase *omnunta krinein*.

The word *dikazein* does not seem to be rightly translated by the word "judge" in such cases. Nor can it be translated as "judge" in several other cases. Litigants in classical Athens could be described as putting their claims with the middle form *dikazesthai* (Dem. 39.2; 48.8; 52.15, 27; also *Od.* 11.545; 12.440; Hdt. 1.96; Thuc. 1.77; Plato *Leg.* 845e). The active form was used for "plead a case" at *Il.* 23.570–82; Eur. *Or.* 580. The word could also be used to mean "go to law": Lys. 10.12; 12.4; Dem. 21.26; 22.77; 33.27; 40.12; 55.31; Thuc. 3.44. (cf. Lex. Segueriana 242.19–22; Men. *Epi.*; *Ath. Pol.* 57.25; Dem 19.318; 29.52; 39.2; 40.2, 10–11, 16; 48.8; Ant. 5.9–10; Arist. *Rhet.* 1377a19–21; Aes. *Eum.* 429–72).

In attempting to explain the seemingly anomalous uses of *dikazein*, scholars have typically agreed on two things about the word: *dikazein* refers to a type of *speech*; and *dikazein* refers to a type of speech spoken by a *judge*. What remains disputed is whether what the judge "says" would be a verdict based on his opinion (Talamanca 1979); a verdict based on formal proof (Talamanca 1979 calls this the "traditional view"); someone else's verdict (MacDowell 1978, 32–33, but *contra* Lys. 17.5; *IG*i^3 41e.1–6); a decision on fact only (Ruschenbusch 1982; Heitsch 1989, 71–87); a decision on whether to validate a prior act of self-help (Wolff 1946, 71–76); or a compromise settlement (Gagarin 1973; Gernet 1981a; Thür 1977; 1989, 56). Another way of resolving the problem is to treat the word *dikazein* as an archaic hangover in the fourth century (Lipsius 1915, 55–56; Gernet 1981b, 190).

I would like to suggest that there is still another way to resolve the problem. We have to recognize that not only a judge *but also a litigant* could speak in a way characterized by the word *dikazein*. Moreover, *dikazein* could be used to designate the activity of arbitration, an activity that could involve two different ways of speaking: speaking so as to bring about a compromise and speaking so as to give a judgment decision. All four of these cases—whether a litigant or a judge is described with the word *dikazein* and whether *dikazein* connotes arbitration as compromise or arbitration as judgment—share one element. Each involves a speech act that attempts to resolve a dispute. If we translate *dikazein* as "speak so as to resolve a dispute" or some variation thereof, our problems with the word *dikazein* disappear and it can be explained in all of its instances. A litigant or a judge could speak in such a way as to offer a compromise settlement. For a litigant, this sort of speech would be akin to putting a plea. A judge could also speak so as to resolve a dispute simply by judging the matter (even by making a choice between the litigants' two pleas). In arbitrations there was a slippage between compromise decisions and judgment decisions, and this slippage accounts for the vast variability in the use of the word *dikazein*. When the Athenians needed to specify judgment per se and wanted to distinguish judgment from compromise, the Athenians used words like *krinein* and *diagignoskein* (Talamanca 1979 agrees that these last two words are equivalents).

These different forms of speech—the litigants' speech, the judge's speech, the speech of compromise, and the speech of a judgment decision—had something else in common also. All involved oaths.

1. Litigants could exchange oaths as a way of ending disputes.

Oaths in archaic law (and possibly in Athenian law) were used to end disputes. See Lipsius 1915, 898; Gernet 1981b, 189–90; Mirhady 1991a; 79; 1991b, 22–25; cf. Pollux 8.62 (*lusis tes dikes*); Arist. *Rhet.* 1377a8ff.; Dem. 33.13–14, 39.3–4, 40.10–11, 49.65–67, 59.59–61; Isae. 12.9–10; Aes. 1.46–47.

Oaths supplemented dispute resolution. Cf. Isae. 2.32; 5.31–33; Dem. 29.58–59; 52.14–16; Ant. 6.16. Thür 1970; 1996; Gagarin 1973, 83–84; 1997, 127–28; Talamanca 1979, 117–25. Hunter (1993, 56–61) gives a survey of oaths used at arbitrations as portrayed in the oratorical corpus; cf. Harrison 1971, 15–30; Cole 1996, 227–48. *Contra* are Lipsius 1915, 895–900; Harrison 1971, 150–53; and Bonner 1905, 67–69, 74–79, who take oaths to be rhetorical rather than instrumental.

Litigants made their pleas, their statements of opinion as to how their case should be resolved, in the form of an oath. The litigant's pleas were the *antomosia* (Ant 1.18; Isae. 3.6; 9.1; Dem. 43.3; Lys. 23.13) and oaths in support of indictments were *diomosia*: (Ant. 6.16. cf. Gernet 1981b, 173–76, 192; Gagarin 1997, 125–26).

2. Judges gave decisions on oath or by speaking an oath.
See, for example, *Ath. Pol.* 55.5; Arist. *Pol.* 1285b9–12; Dem. 29.58, 52.30–31.

3. Possible compromise settlements could be expressed by means of oath.
Gagarin (1973, 85) points out that Homeric judges to whom the word *dikazein* is applied generally offer compromise settlements as their way of resolving disputes. He points out, for instance, that in the dispute over the chariot race in the *Iliad* (23.570–82), Menelaos uses the word *dikasein* to describe what he says when he offers a compromise settlement to Antilochus by challenging him to swear an oath (1973, 83–84). Menelaos invites Antilochus to swear that "he did not willingly interfere with Menelaos's chariot by guile." In other words, he invites Antilochus to swear that he caused the problem but that he is not guilty for it. Antilochus responds by asking Menelaos to go easy and by promising to give the disputed mare back, but without *admitting to any guilt.* Thus is a compromise achieved: Menelaos gets his horse; Antilochus does not have to admit to guilt. Thür (1996) argues that the art of oath swearing resided in the ability to offer an oath that was in no literal way untrue (e.g., baby Hermes in the *Homeric Hymns*); this sort of oath would be precisely aimed at satisfying both parties to a dispute and therefore would be aimed at compromise.

It should be pointed out that Menelaos's oath challenge functions simultaneously as an analogue to a litigant's plea, to a judge's attempt to resolve a dispute, and to a compromise suggestion. In other words, in the single act of offering an oath challenge, Menelaos carries out all three of the activities signified by the word *dikazein.* Moreover all of the discrete ways of using oaths coincide with discrete categories of judicial activity described by the word *dikazein.* A speech act that resolves a dispute, a litigant's plea, and a compromise suggestion can all be characterized both as an act of swearing an oath and with the word *dikazein.* Moreover, both "justices" and "oaths" are said to be properly "spoken" if they are "straight." Gagarin (1992, 61–78) analyzes the idea of a straight settlement and makes the case that the Greek idea of justice involves an ad hoc settlement that is adjusted to fit the complex factors of personal status and general notions of fairness on both sides. The word *dikazein* captures the effort to resolve disputes through verbal formulations, formulations that could in fact also take the shape of oaths.

This reading of the verb *dikazein* solves several problems: First, how to read the "trial" scene on Achilles' shield (18.496–510), where the word *dikazein* is syntactically linked to what the litigants are doing; and, second, how to understand cases where magistrates who did not produce final judgments are nonetheless described with the word *dikazein.* For instance, in murder cases where the basileus was described with the word *dikazei* despite the fact that it is the *ephetai* who are said to judge murder cases, there is no reason to think that the *basileus* could not have tried to broker exile deals between the homicide and the victim's family, handing the case over to a murder court only when that effort failed (*IGi*[3] 104). In Dem. 39.22 we hear about this sort of compromise (*lusis*) being carried out for homicide but we are not told specifically who is responsible for production of the resolution.

The last point allows us to address the question of how many magistrates could arbitrate in Athens. For where the word *dikazein* appears, we can at least read it as signifying that magistrates had the power to arrange compromises and perhaps that they had the power to judge. The following officials, in addition to the public arbitrators, thus had the power to arbitrate or to contribute to dispute resolution:

1. The *basileus* (*IG*i^3 104; *Ath. Pol.* 57.2 [on property matters on a comparison to Plato *Laws* 916c]); cf. Dem. 39.22 where a compromise is brought about in a homicide case (*lusis*).

2. The *apodektai* of the Forty, who developed out of the thirty "deme" judges, and who could settle *dikai* involving amounts less than ten drachmae (Rhodes 1972, 147; Harrison 1971; Harrell 1936; *Ath. Pol.* 53.2).

3. Eisagogeis (*Ath. Pol.* 52.2–3).

4. the market (*emporion*) officials (*diairoie ta amphiloga*: Xen. *Por.* 3.3); the *agoranomoi* (Ar. *Wasps* 1406, *Achar.* 723, 968; Harrison 1971, 25–27).

5. *Sitophulakes* (*diagignoskein* up to ten drachmae, *SEG* 26 [1976–77]: 72.22–26).

6. The *boule* (*diadikazein*: ps.-Xen. *Ath. Pol.* 3.4; cf. on property matters on a comparison to Plato *Laws* 916c).

7. Deme officials (cf. Scafuro 1997b).

8. Since the ability to fine up to a certain drachmae amount was equivalent to the ability to settle cases up to that amount in the case of the Forty and the *agoranomoi*, it is possible that all the officials who could fine up to a certain limit also essentially had the power to carry out arbitrations.

In sum, arbitration could be carried out in Athens not only by the public arbitrators invented in 403. Other officials could also arbitrate and contribute to dispute resolution and could do so even before the invention of the public arbitrators. The invention of a board of public arbitrators did not create but only expanded the capacity of the city's administrative apparatus to provide for arbitration. Lipsius (1915) and Steinwenter (1925) agree that before and after the invention of the public arbitrators, other officials could arbitrate, but Harrell (1936), Harrison (1968–71), and Hansen (1975) assume that only public arbitrators could arbitrate. Gernet (1939, 391) calls the idea that the invention of public arbitrators expanded public means of arbitration a bizarre hypothesis. I hope that I have adduced enough evidence to show that the hypothesis is, at least, not bizarre. More magistrates were probably involved in working out compromises—a form of arbitration—than we usually acknowledge.

The Relative Frequency of Penal Words within Each Orator

Orator	tim-root, including (epitim-/ timema)	from kola	didomi diken/lambano diken/etc.	ophlein	zemi-
Antiphon	49 (5/0)	11	23	1	6
Andocides	18 (4/0)	4	6	3	4
Lysias	113 (10/6)	15	78	7	41
Isocrates	20 (2/4)	7	16	5	14
Isaeus	14 (6/2)	2	7	1	9
Demades	7 (3/0)	2	0	0	1
Demosthenes	213 (50/52)	61	238	77	66
Lycurgus	52 (5/1)	16	2	0	7
Aeschines	45 (16/6)	10	12	2	21
Hyperides	13 (1/2)	7	1	0	1
Dinarchus	40 (1/5)	4	8	0	12

Further Argument about the Decree of Cannonus

Not only the grammar of the manuscript version of the Xenophontic quotation of the Decree of Cannonus but also the context in which Xenophon paraphrases the decree support the claim that the reference to the *barathron* in the Decree of Cannonus is in fact a reference to *ataphia*.

The context of the citation is a discussion of the fate of the generals who famously failed to collect the Athenian dead after the battle of Arginousae. In the first book of his *Hellenica*, Xenophon narrates the terrible story of how they were tried and condemned. The case began when a council member brought an accusation against the generals during a session of the *boule*. The council voted to hand the matter over to the assembly, and scheduled a vote to be taken by that body on whether the generals, as a group, were guilty. The proposal decreed that if the generals were found guilty, they were to be sentenced to the following three-part punishment in which the three parts are marked out by parallel infinitives:

1. To punish them with death (*thanatoi zemiosai*).
2. To hand them over to the Eleven (*kai tois hendeka paradounai*).
3. To have their property confiscated, with a tenth part to be (*einai*) dedicated to the goddess (Xen. *Hell.* 1.7.8–10).

The proposal was illegal for it stripped the generals of their right to have individual trials. Socrates, it will be remembered, was then a member of the *boule* and objected to the illegality of the proposal (cf. Plato *Apol.* 32b). But Socrates was not the only person to object. Xenophon reports on the attempts of other citizens to get their fellows to heel to their own legal regulations (Xen. *Hell.* 1.7.11–12). Among the legally minded, was a man named Euryptolemus, who tried to get the Athenians to give the generals a trial.

Euryptolemus argues that the Athenians could try the generals legally according to either of two laws. He introduces his advice by saying: "The advice that I give you is such that, if you follow it, it will not be possible for you to be deceived by me or by anyone else, and since you know the wrongdoers, it will be possible for you to punish them with the form of justice that you desire to inflict [*outh' hup' emou outh' hup' allou oudenos estin exapatethenai humas, kai tous adikountas eidotes kolasesthe hei an boulesthe dikei*]" (Xen. *Hell.* 1.7.19). In other words, Euryptolemos tells the Athenians that he is about to make suggestions for how they should proceed that will allow the Athenians both to act legally and to do exactly as they wish. The implication is that the procedures that he will describe will permit the Athenians to do what they wanted to do in the first place (kill the generals, hand them over to the Eleven, and dedicate confiscated property to the goddess).

Euryptolemos's suggestions are that the Athenians try the generals according to the Decree of Kannonus or according to the law against temple robbers and traitors. The punishments provided for by the Decree of Kannonus was:

1. To be killed.
2. To be thrown into the *barathron*.
3. To have the wrongdoer's property confiscated with a tenth part given to the goddess.

The law against temple robbers and traitors stipulated:

1. Death (not stated explicitly but implicitly required by the second punishment).
2. Not be buried in Attika (*me taphenai en tei Attikei*).
3. For his possessions to be dedicated to the public (*ta de chremata autou demosia einai*).

Death appears in all three punishments as does a postmortem confiscation of property. If the three punishments are in fact parallel, then the phrases "to be handed over to the Eleven," "to be thrown in to the *barathron*," and "not to be buried in Attika" must all denote relatively equivalent treatment of the corpses after death. The third punishment provides for *ataphia* or for something like *ataphia* (burial beyond the borders of Attika). As I argue in the main text, there is good reason to think that the *barathron* was primarily used for corpse disposal. The putative parallelism between the second and third penalties strengthens this argument. Since there is a strong case to think that both the Decree of Kannonus and the law against traitors provided for *ataphia* in some form, then there is also good reason to think that the first penalty did so too. In that case, the phrase "handed over to the Eleven" would also denote the process of handing corpses over to the officials in charge of corpse disposal. *Apodidomi* is in fact the verb used regularly to denote the return of corpses to those who desire to bury them (*apedosan thapsai*, Lys. 19.7–8; Thuc. 1.63.3, 5.74.2, etc.). Can we say that the verb *paradidomi* makes the point that the corpses are not being returned to their "rightful" owners but rather are surrendered to officials for disposal?

Catalog of Cases of Punishing (or Attempts at Punishing) in Tragedy

AESCHYLUS

Suppliant Maidens

1. Murderers by the demos
2. Offender of the gods by the gods
3. Whoever seizes an unwilling bride by Zeus
4. Herald by the king
5. Suppliants by Io

Persians

1. Xerxes and the Persians by Zeus
2. Persians by Athenians
3. Athens by Xerxes

Prometheus Bound

1. Prometheus by Zeus
2. Zeus by Prometheus
3. Io by Hera

Seven against Thebes

1. Citizen by Eteocles
2. Eteocles by Polyneices
3. Eteocles by Oedipus
4. Polyneices by Oedipus
5. Polyneices by the Cadmean powers

Agamemnon

1. Trojans and Paris by Wrath
2. Trojans and Paris by Zeus
3. Chorus by Aegisthus
4. Aegisthus by the people
5. Cassandra by Clytemnestra
6. Agamemnon by Clytemnestra
7. Aegisthus by Clytemnestra
8. Her prophetic implements by Cassandra

9. Clytemnestra by Orestes
10. Aegisthus by the public
11. Citizens by Aegisthus
12. Achaean ships by Fire and Sea
13. Cassandra by Apollo

Libation Bearers

1. Aegisthus by Orestes
2. Clytemnestra by Orestes
3. Orestes by Apollo
4. Meleager by Althaea
5. Lemnian race by gods

Eumenides

1. Orestes by the Furies
2. Clytemnestra by Orestes
3. Athens by the Furies
4. Clytemnestra by the dead

SOPHOCLES

Oedipus Tyrannos

1. Murderer of Laius by Oedipus
2. Oedipus by himself
3. Oedipus by Creon
4. Citizens of Thebes by Oedipus
5. Creon by Oedipus
6. Messenger by herdsman
7. Herdsman by Oedipus
8. Wrongdoer by gods

Oedipus at Colonus

1. Those who use guile by the fates
2. Wrongdoers by the gods
3. Oedipus by Creon
4. Oedipus's descendants by the god
5. Polyneices by Oedipus
6. Oedipus by Thebes
7. Eteocles by Polyneices

Antigone

1. Antigone by Creon
2. Guard by Creon

3. Creon by avenging spirits
4. Argive army by Zeus
5. Lycurgus by Bacchus
6. Unspecified by Hera

Ajax

1. Achaeans by Ajax
2. Odysseus by Ajax
3a. Ajax by Atreids
3b. Chorus by Atreids
4. Teucer by army
5. Ajax by gods
6. Mortals by gods
7. Atreidae by Ajax
8. Ajax by the Greek army
9. Anyone who tries to remove the suppliant child by Teucer
10. Mother of Agamemnon by Atreus

Electra

1a. Clytemnestra by Orestes
1b. Aegisthus by Orestes
2a. Clytemnestra by Electra
2b. Aegisthus by Electra
3. Agamemnon by Clytemnestra
4. Agamemnon by Artemis
5. Orestes by unspecified

Trachiniae

1. Eurytus by Herakles
2. Herakles by Zeus
3. Lichas by a messenger
4. Deianira by Hyllus
5. Deianira by Herakles

Philoctetes

1. Atreidae by Zeus/Philoctetes
2. Neoptolemus by the army

Euripides

Electra

1a. Clytemnestra by Electra and Orestes
1b. Aegisthus by Electra and Orestes

2. Agamemnon by Clytemnestra
3. The sea king's son by Ares
4. The wise by unspecified
5. Aegisthus by unspecified
6. Aegisthus by unspecified

Orestes

1. Tantalus by Zeus
2. Orestes by Eumenides
3. Orestes by gods
3b. Orestes by people
4. Electra by people
5a. Helen by Orestes and Pylades
5b. Menelaus by Orestes and Pylades
6a. Pylades by his father
6b. Pylades by Argos
7. Clytemnestra and Aegisthus by Orestes
8. Agamemnon by Clytemnestra

Iphigeneia at Tauris

1. Orestes by herdsmen
2. Those who stain their hands with blood or touch a wife newly travailed by Artemis
3. Orestes and Pylades by Iphigeneia as temple servant
4. Orestes by Furies
5. Orestes and Pylades by Thoas
6. Temple women by Thoas

Andromache

1. Andromache by Menelaus
2. Hermione by Neoptolemus
3. Neoptolemus by Apollo

Cyclops

1. Cyclops by Odysseus
2. Odysseus by Poseidon

Bacchae

1. Thebes by Dionysos
2a. Dionysos by Pentheus
2b. Dionysos by Pentheus
3. Agave by Dionysos
4. Teiresias by Pentheus
5. Pentheus by Dionysos

6. Citizens by Pentheus
7. Cadmus by Dionysos
8. Actaeon by Artemis
9. Bacchants by the *demos*

Madness of Herakles

1. Amphitryon by unspecified
2. Children of Herakles by Lycus (preemptive act)
3. Herakles by himself
4. Herakles by Hera
5. Herakles by the world
6. Lycus by Herakles

Children of Herakles

1. Children by Argos
2. Eurystheus by Iolaus
3. Eurystheus by Iolaus and Alcmena
4. Athenians by Argives

Phoenician Maidens

1. Citizens by Eteocles/Creon as rulers
2. House of Cadmus by Ares
3. Polyneices by Creon
4. Oedipus by Creon

Suppliants

1. Tydeus by unspecified
2. Creon and Thebans by Theseus and Athens
3a. Theban soldier by the child of an Argive soldier
3b. Theban soldier by second child
4. Thebes by Argive youths

Iphigeneia at Aulis

1. Helen and Paris by Menelaus
2. Agamemnon by Clytemnestra

Rhesus

1. Guards by Hector
2. Odysseus by unspecified

Hecuba

1. Trojans by Achilles
2. Polymestor by Hecuba
3. Hecuba by Polymestor

Trojan Women

1. Achaeans by Athena
2. Agamemnon by Cassandra
3. Cassandra by Trojans
4. Paris by Menelaus
5a. Helen by Menelaus
5b. Aphrodite by Menelaus

Helen

1. Teucer by his father
2. Guards by Theoclymenus
3. Theonoe by Theoclymenus
4. Hades by Demeter

Medea

1. Jason by Medea
2. Medea by Creon
3a. Medea by Aegeus
3b. Aegeus by Medea
4. Talented people by unspecified
5a. Medea by the royal house
5b. Medea by Jason

Ion

1. Mortals by gods
2. Temple handmaids by Xuthus
3a. God by Creusa
3b. Xuthus by Creusa
3c. Ion by Creusa
4. Creusa by rulers of the land

Hippolytus

1. Hippolytus by Aphrodite
2. Nurse by Hippolytus
3. Hippolytus by Theseus
4. Aphrodite by Artemis

Alcestis

1. Zeus by Apollo
2. Apollo by Zeus
3. Admetus by kin of Alcestis

NOTES

PREFACE

1. Gernet 1981d, 240: "One sees that there is nothing quite so illuminating as a walk through the garden of punishments."

2. The word "desert" is a standard Anglo-American English word that, for some reason, has fallen out of pedestrian usage and is found most frequently in philosophical texts. *Webster's New World Dictionary of the American Language* defines "desert" as: "1. the fact of deserving reward or punishment; 2. deserved reward or punishment [to get one's just "deserts"]; 3 the quality of deserving reward; merit." "Desert" is strictly related to the verb "deserve": "to have a right to because of acts or qualities; be worthy of (reward, punishment, etc.); merit."

On the undertheorization of desert in punitive theory, see Duff and Garland 1994, 7.

3. Sagan (1995, 147) coins the word "psychosocial" to describe the ways in which an individual's participation in social practices and ideas interacts with the *individual psyche* (or meets the needs of the individual psyche) and serves to foster *social cohesion*. The word indicates how social cohesion at once supports individual cognitive and psychological mechanisms and needs their support. It does not imply an opinion on the question of whether there can be said to be some sort of social or communal psyche or collective unconscious.

INTRODUCTION

1. Andrews 1994, 43–45, 417–21, 423; Langbein 1974, 129–31, 223; Esmein 1978. According to Langbein's description of the early-nineteenth-century Napoleonic reorganization of the criminal justice system, the public prosecutor's power was a worrying issue. Its reduction was effected by removing investigative and informing powers to the judge so that the prosecutor retained only the role of *poursuite*. The importance of this reform, though, is that the existence of a *public* prosecutor was not something to be challenged by this point. On Rome, see Garnsey 1970; Jones 1972.

2. Baker 1992, 38–40. According to Baker, in the colonies the attorney generals who worked at the colony and county level began to take over all criminal prosecution and to remove that prerogative from private citizens. This seems to have occurred de facto rather than de jure and without the express order to do so from the British attorney general who delegated authority to the colonial attorneys. The use of the private prosecutor in criminal cases in Britain continued until sometime after the colonial regimes had begun to use a public prosecutor. See also Green 1985, 270–71; Langbein 1974, 35–39, 44.

3. Baker 1992, 38–40. See also Friedman 1993, 1–29, on the mystery of the development of a public prosecutor in colonial American law.

4. Baker 1992, 38–40.

5. See Esmein 1978; Andrews 1994; Green 1985; Langbein 1974; Baker 1992.

6. Hart 1995, 5.

7. Green 1985, xviii–xix.

8. Hans and Vidmar 1986, ch. 3.

9. Abramson 1994, 67–76.

10. Ibid.

11. Portman 1995.

12. Green (1985) gives a very careful, thorough, and well-documented history of jury nullification, which my own preliminary primary source research has but confirmed.

13. Pollock and Maitland 1968, 1:152–53; Green 1985; Langbein 1974; Hans and Vidmar 1986, ch. 4.

14. Pollock and Maitland 1968, 2:627; Green 1985; Langbein 1974.

15. Pollock and Maitland 1968, 1:140–55; Green 1985; Langbein 1974.

16. Pollock and Maitland 1968, 2:625–27; Green 1985; Langbein 1974. There was the long-standing rule that jurors were not to eat or drink until they rendered their verdict (Green 1985, 140). Judges also frequently made juries "go back and try again" when they had returned verdicts the judges found unsuitable (Green 1985, 114, 140).

17. Green 1985, 108–14.

18. Ibid., 113–14, where Green cites cases.

19. Ibid., 140.

20. E.g., STAC 4, III, no. 41, which Green describes (1985, 140–41) thus: "The jurors were charged with neglect of duty to find according to 'pregnant evidence' and for 'little dreading the offense of perjury.' Most of the jurors said that they were 'near neighbors' of the parties and the witnesses and knew 'the credit and estimation of every of the same deponents and witnesses, and also some of the said defendants, knowing more of themselves in that matter than was openly given in evidence.'" There is also STAC 5, A4, no. 11, where "jurors gave a very detailed answer reviewing the large body of testimony given against the defendant (for counterfeiting coin) and explaining why it seemed insufficient for conviction."

21. In Elizabeth's reign there were cases of judges, like John Popham, who themselves fined the juries rather than binding them over to the Star Court. These cases served as precedents for the seventeenth-century judges who tried to establish fining as a regular judicial prerogative. See in *The English Reports*: Leonard's Reports (*Sir John Southwel's Case*, 3 Len. 147); Popham's Reports (*Wharton's Case, Watt's Case*, 43 Elizabeth B.R. Rot. 779); Vaughan's Reports (*Bushel's Case*, 124 *English Reports* 1006). *The English Reports* are published volumes and a CD Rom consisting of decisions of the English courts through 1867.

22. Kelyng's fining was challenged but upheld in *Wagstaffe's Case*, which he proceeded to use as precedent for futher fining.

23. Vaughan's Reports (124 *English Reports* 1006).

24. Cited by Abramson (1994, 12, 17). He also points out that the jury takes an oath to decide a case solely "upon the evidence developed at trial."

25. Abramson 1994, 62. The exceptions are Indiana and Maryland (and Kansas from 1971–73). Abramson calls the doctrine "a matter of history everywhere else."

26. It is interesting that Foucault's comparisons of France to Britain and the United States do not take the issue of who could prosecute into account, despite the fact that the historical period covered in *Discipline and Punish* (1991) is that in which Britain was catching up with France and the United States in the use of public prosecution.

27. The phenomenological approach to Athenian punishment generates not only new frameworks for thinking about Athenian history, but also new contributions to long-lived scholarly debates concerning institutional and historical details of the Athenian punitive system, including topics like arbitration, the vocabulary of punishment, slave torture, the distinction between *graphai* and *dikai*, the meaning of "sycophant," radishes, hemlock, the *barathron*, and Aristotle's diorthotic justice. I hope that a methodological shift of

focus can generate not only a new framework for thinking about politics in Athens but also a set of interpretive tools that will be able to contribute to resolving (or advancing the work on) some long-standing questions.

CHAPTER ONE
WHAT IS PUNISHMENT?

1. Studies of Athenian punishment have usually commenced with the questions, What were the punishments? and What did certain crimes receive by way of punishment? See, e.g., Thonissen 1875; Gernet 1982, 27; Harrison 1971, 168–99; MacDowell 1978, 254–58. Even Debrunner Hall (1996) begins here. Cantarella (1991, 7–10) objects to this approach but nonetheless adopts it by asking primarily "What were the symbolic meanings of different forms of execution?"

2. Three disciplines have concerned themselves with punishment and have generated three paradigms for thinking about punishing: the criminological paradigm; the paradigm of juridical philosophy, which primarily concerns itself with the question of whether punishment should be directed at retributive, deterrent, or rehabilitative ends; and sociology.

3. E.g., Weber 1946, 1975.

4. Hudson 1996 summarizes the methodological impacts and developments of the juridical, criminological, and sociological approach, as does Garland 1990. Recent examples in the growing field of punitive sociology include Ignatieff 1978; Garland and Young 1983; Cohen 1985; Garland 1990; Friedman 1993; Bauman 1996.

5. On punishment as drama in general, see Hudson 1996, 93; Foucault 1991, 111–14.

6. Gernet 1981a, 73–111, 143–215, 240–51, 252–76. Gernet never gave the topic of the secular political world its full due in relation to punishment because he was largely focused on the relations between the religious and the political.

The road to interdisciplinary work on ancient texts has been well paved over the course of the century not only by Gernet's work, but also by that of Moses Finley (e.g., 1968), Jean-Pierre Vernant (e.g., 1969), Sally Humphreys (e.g., 1978), and Josiah Ober (1989a).

Each of the last three scholars has put the study of institutions somewhat to the side in order to emphasize the long-overlooked relevance to sociopolitical analyses of *mentalités*, social control, and ideology. In contrast, I hope to be able to link the study of institutions to the study of culture and ideology so that each has equal weight. In order to portray the way in which culture and institution both factor into an attempt to punish, I follow anthropologist Pierre Bourdieu. See note 7.

7. Pierre Bourdieu 1977, 3–71. On Bourdieu's account of "practice," actors engage in a practice (like marriage) in their efforts to produce the results that they personally desire (e.g., improved family status in the community). If they are to succeed, they must be able to deploy the rules governing the practice of marriage in such a way as to accomplish to their own purposes, regardless of whether those rules are established by culture or institution. To describe the practice of marriage is to describe the rules and various strategies that operationalize it. The same can be said about punishment.

I begin from the position that punishing is a practice characterized by the attempt to implement a conception of desert and to make it authoritative. A society's cultural and institutional negotiations of desert produce the rules and strategic tools available for the task of punishing. Going a step beyond Bourdieu, I argue that the rules produced by institutions and the rules produced by culture do not fall into separate categories; rather, they both work to establish a single societal "conceptualization of desert"; this conceptualization of desert may be more or less fluid and contested, depending on the degree to which a harmonization obtains between culture and institution. In fact, I further argue that these conceptions of desert are negotiated and worked out in the very tension between culture and institution. In other words, I claim that the tension between culture and institution is in part the very negotiation of concepts of desert and that this negotiation is what makes culture and institution ultimately inseparable. Culture and institution are each made, to some extent, by the tension with the other that springs up from the inevitable negotiation of desert, a function of language (*logos*) in the Heideggerean sense.

8. This sentence is a rewritten version of a sentence found in Benhabib 1996, 68, although she is discussing a somewhat different subject.

9. Saunders (1991, 21–32), in response to Adkins and Mackenzie.

10. Garland (1990), Cragg (1992), and Hudson (1996) confirm that the philosophers of punishment still employ Flew's, Hart's, and Nozick's definitions. Hart's 1995 definition of punishment (a derivative of Flew's) and Nozick's 1981 definition of the difference between revenge and the punishment of retribution stand out as the rare efforts, since philosophers of punishment have been little given to defining their terms.

11. Hart 1995, 5. Hart's other three criteria are: it must involve pain or other consequences normally considered unpleasant; it must be of an actual or supposed offender for his offense; it must be intentionally administered by an authority constituted by a legal system against which the offense is committed. He adds: "In calling this the standard or central case of punishment I shall relegate to the position of sub-standard or secondary cases the following among many other possibilities: a) Punishments for breaches of legal rules imposed or administered otherwise than by officials (decentralised sanctions); b) Punishments for breaches of non-legal rules or orders (punishments in a family or school)." See also *Black's Law Dictionary*, s.v. "punishment."

12. Nozick 1981, 366–67.

13. Cragg 1992, 16–19. Also, he stresses the lack of "emotion" involved in punishment. See also Vlastos 1991,186–87.

14. Ehrenberg 1969, 21; Thonissen 1875, 69. Bonner and Smith use similar categories (1930, 22–23).

15. See Bonner and Smith 1930, ch. 4, in which the authors even use the play as a source for their *historical* analysis of the Areopagus.

16. See Conacher 1987, 76–82, on Aeschylus's suppression of the traditional "reason" for Artemis's anger.

17. Goldhill (1984, 257) gives a synopsis of the scholarly debate over the dramatic effect of "Athena's vote" and whether it's a tie maker or tie breaker. See also Gagarin 1975.

18. Podlecki 1966, 80–81.

19. Sommerstein 1989b, 21.

20. Kitto 1964, 62, 85.

21. Todd 1995, 79.

22. Cohen 1995, 188. Cf. Meier 1990, 2, 85.

23. On arguments like those of Hunter, Todd, and Cohen, see Herman 1993, 1994a, 1994b, 1996. The definitions of "revenge" and "punishment" do not even capture contemporary penal practices. See the arguments of the sociologist of punishment David Garland (1993, 456–58) on this point.

24. Beginning with Lloyd-Jones's (1983, 94) rejection of the "cliché we have heard all our lives," there has been an outbreak of revisionist readings of the transition. See also Gagarin 1976, 68–71; Zeitlin 1978, 153; Goldhill 1984, 257–80; Cohen 1995, 16.

25. The chorus's answer to Electra is "simply, whoever will kill in return [*antapoktenei*]." Goldhill points out that the chorus thus elides any distinction between a judge and an avenger (1984, 114–15). He also points out that the Furies are described with legal vocabulary and behave in a "legally related" manner before the trial (1984, 228–35). Lest that point be given too much weight, however, Goldhill adds that they are able to do so because of the multivalent meanings of the concept *dike*. See Aesch. *Ag.* 1421. Some critics (Gagarin 1976, 71–75; Vellacott 1984, 116–20) add that the behavior of the Erinyes before and during the trial is altogether calmer, more legal, more "rational" than Apollo's behavior.

26. Zeitlin 1978, 149–84. Also Gagarin 1976, 57–118; Goldhill 1984; and Rocco 1997, ch. 4.

27. Commentators have had little to say about the word *oxuthumos*. In the *Eumenides*, it has a parallel at 473 where *oxumenitou* describes the vengeful passions triggered in murder cases in general.

28. Dindorf (1880, line 517) presumed that the second passage was spurious because of the repetition. Several critics treat the parallelism between the Furies' description of themselves and Athena's description of the Areopagus as I do (Lloyd-Jones 1983, 93; Gagarin 1976, 72–73; Goldhill 1984, 254). Goldhill points out that while both parties must enforce *dike* and must enforce it to the same effect, we cannot actually say that each enforces the same *kind* of *dike* since the word *dike* is so regularly contested in the trilogy.

29. The word *nomos* appears six times in the *Eumenides*. The Erinyes use it three times when they object to Orestes' acquittal, which they conceive to be a defeat of legal order (171, 778, 808). Orestes and Apollo both describe Orestes' purification as a matter of *nomos* (448, 576). The sixth instance is when Athena says that the Areopagus, by engendering fear in citizens, will prevent the pollution of the laws. It should be pointed out, however, that this claim is no different from the claims that the Erinyes themselves make (693) about the form of "law" that they uphold.

30. The name Erinyes is usually understood as linked to *eris* or strife rather than directly to anger. The title Eumenides is not attested until after the fifth century. It seems to come from a list of dramatis personae and from the hypothesis, which reads, "Athena mollified the Erinyes and called them Eumenides." Both of these would have been Hellenistic additions. After the Erinyes have been reconciled to Athena and to Athens, they are referred to as being *euphron, euphron,* and *euphroni* (992, 1030, and 1034 [emendation]), but the word Eumenides, or a cognate, never appears in the play itself. Rather, the reformed avengers are called Semnai Theai. (Theai is an emendation accepted by most scholars.) See Sommerstein 1996, 184; Vellacott, 1984, 116. For a mythological and religious history of the Erinyes, the Semnai Theai, and the Eumenides, see Sommerstein 1989b, 6–12.

31. Sommerstein (1989b, 10) points out that the Erinyes remain ugly although they receive new clothes.

32. See Sidwell 1996, 48; Goldhill 1984, 257–80. The latter makes an especial point of the "with" in Athena's comment. She will "bear with" the anger of the Erinyes (*orgas xunoiso soi*, 848). Even Kitto (1964, 56, 85) points out that the Erinyes keep their avenging function even after the introduction of the Areopagus.

33. A few critics have emphasized the role of authority in the play. Goldhill 1984, 241; Cohen 1995, 18; Sidwell 1996, 44–57.

34. Scholarship had tended to separate this last scene from the rest of the play, either considering it primarily a matter of sacramental ornament or considering the "ethical"

play and the "political" play to be dramatically separate. Dodds (1973a, 45–63) explicitly reknits the play by making an argument that "morals" and "politics" are woven together throughout the play. See also Dover 1957, 230–37; Kagan 1965, 63–64; Goldhill 1984.

35. Cairns (1993, 214) writes about the *Oresteia*: "Punishment implies power, and power which one recognizes as legitimate embodies the *time* that attracts *aidos* and *sebas*." On Cohen's view (1986, 129–41) the Aeschylean Areopagite political order is founded on force and fear.

36. Saunders 1991, 29.

37. I offer a reading of the situation of Prometheus's punishment primarily as a concrete illustration of what would otherwise be, perhaps, an overly abstract point about how the process of punishing works. What follows does not purport to be a complete reading of the play.

Others (Gagarin 1976, 132–40; Saïd 1985, 326–340; Sommerstein 1989b, 24; Meier 1990, 92–93) have also contrasted the *Oresteia* and the *Prometheus*, but usually by placing the emphasis on either punishment or politics. Dodds (1973b, 26–44) deals with both plays in terms of both politics and punishment as two versions of "that old tale of crime and punishment and the beginning of the reign of justice." I have consulted the editions of Paley 1879, Wecklein 1891, Wilamowitz 1913, Mazon 1920, and Thomson 1932. Citations come from Wilamowitz. Secondary literature consulted includes: on the play, Thomson 1966; Gagarin 1976,119–38; Taplin 1977; Griffith 1977; Conacher 1980; Saïd 1985; Bremer 1988; Meier 1990, 96ff.; Bees 1993; Mossman 1996; and Sommerstein 1996, 297–328; on the mythological tradition, Vernant 1969, 19ff.; 1980, 26–44; Triomphe 1992; Brémond 1994. Saïd is perhaps the most useful on all fronts. See also Hes. *Theog.* 521–616 and *Op.* 42–105.

38. The issue of authorship has no bearing on my use of the text, nor is the question of dating problematic in relation to my purposes. But *contra* Aeschylus, see Schmid 1929; Griffith 1977; Lloyd-Jones 1983; Hogan 1989; and Bees 1993. *Pro* Aeschylus, see Dodds 1973b; Scully and Herington 1975; Conacher 1980; Saïd 1985; Hubbard 1991; and Zuntz 1993. Saïd (1985, 9–11) gives a good summary of the dispute. Bees (1993) lays out the issues of dating.

39. Schmid 1929, 32–34. Conacher (1980, 205) refers to the play as static. But more recently, scholars have begun to recognize that the action of the play consists precisely in the struggle, dramatized as a series of conversations, over whether Prometheus's punishment will be taken as authoritative. See Scully and Herington 1975, 9; Gagarin 1976, 133; Sienkewicz 1983–84; Saïd 1985, 297–316; Menzio 1992, 17; Brémond 1994, 74; Sommerstein 1996, 301. Conacher (1980, 35–38) sees the play as set of struggles within Prometheus between speech and silence.

40. Todd 1995, 360.

41. See especially Saïd (1985) for the issue of Zeus's attempt to establish his rule. As several scholars have pointed out, it is important that Aeschylus changes the Hesiodic account to whitewash Prometheus's character. In Aeschylus's version, Prometheus helped Zeus to gain power and stole fire that had been maliciously forbidden. In the Hesiodic account, Prometheus was forbidden from taking the fire because of an earlier trick that Prometheus had already played on Zeus. Furthermore, Hesiod incorporates only the third punishment, the consumption of Prometheus's liver by the eagle, into his poem. Aeschylus, it would seem, is trying to draw out or lengthen the process of punishing. See Scully and Herington 1975; Conacher 1980, 10–19; Saïd 1985, 284–86.

42. Four characters enter together (Kratos, Bia, Hephaestus, and Prometheus), which is unheard of in extant tragedy. In fact, as Taplin (1977, 240–45) points out, there is only one entrance of even three characters simultaneously coming from the same direction (Eur. *Phaeton*) and in that instance, the playwright emphasizes the entrance with the phrase "triple-yoked." Taplin thinks, and I agree, that while the technique is unusual, it is explicable on the basis of the plot. Furthermore, the rarity of such an opening means that the figurative iconography of the tableau produced by the characters would have been all the more striking to the audience.

43. Saïd (1985, 237–69) examines the Homeric and Hesiodic juxtapositions of Kratos and Bia and comes to the conclusion that "Cratos est la souveraineté; bia est la force brutale sur laquelle elle repose." Cf. Vernant 1969, 36–37; Vernant and Vidal-Naquet 1988b, 25–28, 39 (in respect to *Supp.* 315).

44. Bremer 1988, 123. For Dodds (1973b, 33), Kratos represents the "gentleman's gentleman." The issue of Bia's (and Prometheus's) silence in the opening scene is a tricky one. Depending on the date of the play, the number of speaking actors on stage would have been limited to either two or three. Hephaestus, who enters with the two ministers, must speak. In some sense, then, the playwright may not have had the option to have Kratos *and* Bia speak. Nonetheless, it remains significant that the playwright designates Kratos as the speaker. It is theoretically possible that the designation could be the mistake of a later editor, but as Taplin (1977, 240–45) points out, Bia is the "lesser of a fixed pair" (e.g., Hes. *Theog.* 385) and the lesser of such a pair is usually the silent one. Saïd's examination (1985, 237–69) of the use of the pair in the poetic tradition confirms the idea that Bia would be the silent partner. The mythological tradition itself, then, encodes the idea that successful "authority" (Kratos) uses language and can function without the active intervention of force (Bia). In the *Iliad,* Zeus either uses his thunderbolt or comes in person when he decides to use Bia.

45. Cantarella (1991, 38) notices the technical precision of Kratos's language. See also Taplin 1977, 241.

46. Sienkewicz (1983–84, 65–67) recognizes the force of the kinship argument also. Saïd (1985, 297) points out that this claim on the part of Hephaestus is somewhat strange since, on the basis of mythical genealogy, he and Prometheus are scarcely kin.

47. See chapter 4. Also Kitto 1964, 68–70; Dodds 1973b, 41; Goldhill 1984, 217, 240; Meier 1990, 100.

48. In the face of Hephaestus's persistent unwillingness to see the binding as an act of punishment, Kratos simply orders Hephaestus to carry on with his work. Hephaestus answers: "Do not command me overmuch" (*meden engkeleu' agan*). And Kratos responds: "I certainly will command you" (*e men keleuso*). Both characters are explicit: what is at stake in the play is "command," i.e., whether or not Zeus's commands about punishment will be authoritative.

49. See Scarry (1987) on the ways in which pain is made to speak.

50. See note 39.

51. *leusso*: 144, 561, 883; *derkesthai*: 54, 93, 140, 304, 539, 546, 679, 843; *thea*: 69, 69, 118, 302, 304, 690, 802; *esidesthai*: 141, 146, 184, 244, 245, 246, 427, 569, 695, 800, 899, 941, 1093; *omma*: 69, 356, 570, 654, 795, 882, 903; *horao*: 22, 69, 70, 119, 259, 307, 323, 438, 612, 674, 906, 951, 997, 998). Even the lengthiest fragment from *Prometheus Unbound* includes the comment: "Look at me moored! Chained fast to the choppy rock. . . . Zeus's will has become fact" (Cic. *Tusc. Disp.* 2.10.23–24). Interestingly, in the *Poetics* Aristotle makes reference to the *Prometheus Unbound* in order to illustrate the purpose of spectacle in a drama.

52. For Oceanus, see lines 304–10. For Io, 322–29, 581–613.

53. It should be pointed out that while the reactions of the Oceanids, Oceanus, and Io follow the same *dramatic* patterns, they do not follow the same substantive patterns: the Oceanids challenge Zeus's authority from a position of pure sympathy with Prometheus; Oceanus challenges Zeus's legitimacy as well but also recommends that Prometheus submit because Zeus is stronger; and Io queries Prometheus on his punishment from the standpoint of the fellow sufferer.

54. For Oceanus, see 315–21. For Io, 581–613, 618.

55. On narrative overdetermination of Orestes' act in *Libation-Bearers*, see Lesky (1983, 22–24). On narrative overdetermination throughout the *Oresteia*, see Goldhill (1984, 1988).

56. At the end of the play, the Oceanids join Prometheus's side again, rashly or bravely declaring that they will not leave the rock before Zeus blasts it with the thunderbolt. Critics (e.g., Taplin 1977, 252–54, 270–72) have thought that the ending was too abrupt and that the change in the Oceanids is "inscrutable," but Scott (1987, 85–96) makes a persuasive argument for the play as depicting the development of the Oceanids' will and ability to resist. See also Sienkewicz 1983–84.

57. According to Taplin (1977, 268), Hermes' entry is staged in an unusual fashion. Hermes enters thirty-seven lines after the end of the choral song, making this play the only one extant to have a final act *not* opened by an entry. Moreover, if the play was written by Aeschylus, it is the only extant Aeschylean play in which a character (Prometheus), as opposed to the chorus, announces the arrival of another character (Hermes). Also, it would be the only speech in which the announcement is made without use of a proper name. Hermes' entrance, in other words, would have been as dramatically striking as the opening entry of the four characters. Finally, the announcement contains the only Aeschylean use of the phrase *eishoro gar toude*.

58. It might be objected that this play was written sufficiently early in the fifth century that *sophistes* is meant to be taken only in the sense of "wise man" (sardonic) without the negative connotations it has later as "sophist." The first meaning of *sophistes* is no doubt the dominant one in this context. Kratos and Hermes are mocking Prometheus for failing to be clever enough to get himself out of the mess he was in. But in the epilogue I make the case that we are specifically meant to understand that Prometheus, as a *sophistes*, is not only wise and clever but also good with words, and as such is a threat to Zeus's authority that must be repudiated. His ability to challenge Zeus's authority on the basis of his verbal ability shows how the word *sophistes*, with its positive connotations, could slide into the sophist of the negative connotations, the rhetorical trickster.

59. Scully and Herington (1975, 12) go so far as to accuse Hermes of employing brainwashing techniques.

60. Hermes is the "master of bonds" and appears on curse tablets where litigants try to bind their enemies' tongue before trial (Brémond 1994, 53). Essentially the curse of binding used in this sense aims precisely to prevent one's opponent from using rhetoric to put a case about "desert" successfully. Hermes' arrival at the end of the *Prometheus Bound* could therefore be read precisely as symbolizing an effort to put an end to Prometheus's ability to free himself with his tongue by speaking about desert. On the use of bound molten wax curse figures to suggest that the magic of binding gives fake life, see Triomphe 1992, 49–72; Faraone 1993.

61. Prometheus does briefly accept his guilt at one point in the play (*hekon, hekon hemarton*, 266).

62. This should be what happens according to the prediction of Hermes (1048–51),

but, as Taplin (1977, 268–74) points out, the end of the play is, on its own terms, rather obscure. Saïd (1985, 315) equates Bia and the thunderbolt. So does Muellner (1996, 77–78, 130) in the context of the *Iliad*. He also treats the binding of a god as equivalent to the death of an immortal and he treats thunderbolts, caves, and bindings as isomorphs.

63. There is debate over whether there even *was* a trilogy, as well as debate over what the titles of the other plays would have been if they did exist.

64. See Hes. *Theog.* 521–616; *Op.* 42–105. Also there is Hermes' prediction (1007–35) in the *PB*.

65. In Hesiod, the eagle comes every day; in *PB* the eagle is described as *panhemeros* (all-day long or every day?); and in a fragment of *Prometheus Unbound*, the sequel play, the eagle comes every third day only (Cic. *Tusc. Disp.* 2.10.23.25).

66. See Cantarella (1991, 34–40) on Prometheus, Tantalus, and Sisyphus.

67. Prometheus himself suggests that he will not be seen by anyone in Tartarus (*PB* 161–68).

68. See Triomphe (1992, 62) for exposition of the idea that punishments concern definition or "labeling" in the ancient context. For a discussion of labeling, see Hudson 1996, 92–93.

69. Padel 1992,19. The liver was especially associated with anger, fear, and lust (e.g., Aesch. *Ag.* 432, 792; *Eum.* 135; Eur. *Supp.* 599, 919; Soph. *Aj.* 938; Theoc. 13.71); and the liver was associated with bile (Archil. 234W, Plato *Ti.* 71D–E). See chapter 3.

70. Triomphe (1992, 56–68, 70) writes: "Tityos dechiré par les oiseaux—c'est l'homme dechiré par ses desirs, l'angoisse de quelque passion. Le même explication valait d'ailleurs pour Prométhée, justifié par le psychologie organiciste que considerait le foie comme siège des soucis devorants."

71. See Saïd 1985, 233–325.

72. By picking a play in which the punitive authority at stake is that of a tyrant or monarch rather than that of a court, democratic or otherwise, I am making a significant claim: the relation between political authority and punishment, as linked through control of cultural conceptions of desert, remains the same, regardless of regime type. In both tyranny and democracy, the establishment of Kratos or authority and the establishment of a punitive system depends on the establishment of a stable and authoritative conceptualization of desert in which the greater portion of the society acquiesces; the nature of the regime will depend on the way in which the system of desert is established (whether more through force or more through social and ideological harmony) and on the content of the conceptualization of desert. This model of punishment as authority is a stripped-down model. Where authority and punishments are easily finalized, the system of desert is stable; where they are not easily finalized (as in Athens in the cases having to do with the amnesty of 403), the system of desert is unstable. In either case, an examination of punishment is an examination of either the construction or mobilization of a stable system of desert.

73. E.g., 114–152, 177–197, 226–245, 307–321, 330–334, 526–561, 562–565, 578–88, 843–952, 964–65, 1036–39, 1094.

74. The change in the Erinyes in Aeschylus's *Eumenides* consists primarily in the fact that after the institution of the Areopagus, they are actually obliged to formulate and to make explicit the claims of desert on which they base their still angry acts of retribution.

75. My elaboration of "norms of public agency" is compatible with Ober's (e.g., 1994, 159) explorations of "democratic knowledge." See also Schmitt-Pautel 1990 and Herman 1993, 1994a, 1994b, 1996.

76. *New York Times*, Feb. 11, 1997, A1, A12.

77. But Herman (1993, 406–19) reads the case differently (see chapter 7).

CHAPTER TWO
INSTITUTIONAL CONTEXT

1. The traditional date of this reform is 594 B.C. but another school of thought (R. Sealey) puts the reforms in the 570s.

2. See Todd 1995, 100. The creation of *ho boulomenos* must have been meant to *add* noninterested parties to the category of those prosecuting; the addition did not, however, *require* that noninterested parties prosecute. For Solon's political ideas and intentions, see Adkins 1972, 46–57.

3. Todd 1995, 102–9.

4. For a general overview of approaches to Athenian law and an insightful analysis about how to understand the Athenian emphasis on procedure, see Todd 1995. On the criminal approach, see Calhoun 1927 and, for criticism of it, Todd 1995, 109–10.

5. Leaving aside administrative cases of *dokimasia, euthuna,* and cases involving the city's finances (Hyp. 1; Din. 1), there are only two speeches in the extant corpus in which the prosecutor is not personally involved in the case (Lyc. 1; Lys. 22). For the prevalence of personally interested prosecutors, see Osborne 1985a, 51; and my chapters 7 and 8.

6. I have relied to large extent on the compilations of Lipsius 1915; Harrison 1968, 1971; MacDowell 1978; Hansen esp. 1975, 1976, 1987, 1991a; Rhodes 1972; Hunter 1994; and Todd 1995. For the most part, I concur with the combined weight of their analyses of procedure and institutional detail. Where there are substantial disagreements among these scholars, I have tried to outline the debate in the notes and to give my reasons for siding with one or the other interpretation.

7. *egkuklios*: *Ath. Pol.* 43. Rhodes (1981, 512) translates the word as "routine." Cf. Todd 1995, 292, 295–96.

I follow Ober (1989b) in considering the *archai* to stand metonymically for the people as a whole. An example can be found in Lyc. 1.111: "After the friends of the victim caught the murderers and put them in prison, the people [*demos*] noted what had happened, released the prisoners on bond, and held an inquiry after torture." The reference to the *demos* here refers to public officials, probably either the *thesmothetai* or the *Eleven.*

8. The *bouleutai* (councillors) seem to have served at least sometimes on the board of *nomothetai* (And. 1.81–85; cf. Dem. 24.20–27). See Rhodes 1972, 26. This reveals how difficult it is to distinguish executive, legislative, and judicial branches.

9. The nine archonships were offices that had evolved from predemocratic kingships, and each had jurisdiction over specific kinds of legal dispute: the eponymous *archon* (called eponymous by moderns because his name was given to the calendar year) over issues having to do with family or inheritance law (*Ath. Pol.* 56.1); the *basileus* over religious laws (*Ath. Pol.* 57); the *polemarchos* over matters involving foreigners (*Ath. Pol.* 58); and the six *thesmothetai* oversaw accusations that laws were unconstitutional, the bulk of the *graphai* (or public cases), including those against people accused of faking citizenship, bribery, sycophancy, false accusation, and adultery as well as *dikai* (or private cases) involving commercial matters, the mines, and slaves (*Ath. Pol.* 59). The "Eleven," eleven men who acted as supervisors of the prison and of executions, were also of archaic origin.

10. E.g., for *archai* in general, Dem. 35.47; 37.33; for the *boule, Ath. Pol.* 29.5, 62.3. Cf. Todd 1995, 363. The equivalence of the *boule* to the other *archai* would explain *Ath. Pol.* 29.5 where we are told that during the Peloponnesian War, all *archai* were cut off

from pay except the nine archons and the prytanizing members of the *boule*. Or *IG* i^{3}81 (418/17) where the archon and the *boule* exact rents for temple land.

11. *IG* ii^2 1425.126–30; 2821; Rhodes 1972, 21, 129–30; Stroud 1974, 167, lines 5–8 [= *Hesp*. 43 (1974): 157–88]; *IG* ii^2 380.40–42.

12. A reorganization of magistracies and offices in 320/19 after the end of the democracy gave the *agoranomoi* more power (*IG* ii^2 380.10–12). Only for the second century is there evidence that they had their own office (*IG* ii^2 3391). See Wallace 1989 on the reorganization of magistracies.

13. See Todd 1995, 114. See appendix A for further discussion of the sorts of magisterial duties carried out by members of the council.

14. In respect to the subordinates of the *boule*, see Rhodes 1972, 16–29.

15. Hunter 1993, 145–48; Rhodes 1972, 21, 304; *IG* i^3 45.14–17; *Ath. Pol.* 24.3.

16. On *nautodikai* and *xenodikai*, see Lipsius 1915, 86–88; Harrison 1971, 23–25; Cohen 1973; MacDowell 1978, 229–31. For *eisagogeis*, see Harrison 1971, 21–23.

17. Lipsius 1915, 53ff.; Rhodes 1972, 179; MacDowell 1978, 189–90, 235–37; Todd 1995, 78–79, 92. But Carawan (1984) and Hunter (1994) describe the punitive powers of magistrates as minimal, though citing minor exceptions. Cf. Dem. 45.81.

Fining: *archon* (Dem. 21.179, 43.75–79; *Ath. Pol.* 56.7); subordinate to the archon (Ant. 6.3–11; Dem. 21.179); archons (Lys. 30.3); basileus (Lys. 6.21, on emendation); *boule* (And. 4.3; Dem. 24.147; Aes. 1. 35; *Ath. Pol.* 45.1, 49.1; *Hesp.* 43 [1974]: 157–88, lines 32–36; *IG* i^3 4.21–25 [from 485/4 a prytanis is said to fine, but Rhodes 1972, 16–20, says it is not the *prytanis* of the boule]; *IG* i^3 78; *IG* ii^2 1629 [325/4: the assembly grants the *boule* power to punish disorderly trierarchs]; *IG* ii^2 463.25 [307/6: *boule* punishes in respect to buildings [*IG* ii^2 380]; see also Rhodes 1972, 179–207; Gauthier 1971, 44–79); *agoranomoi* (Xen. *Sym.* 2.20; Dem. 43.75; Aes. 1.35 [50 drachmae]); *hieropoioi* from *boule* (*IG* i^3 82.23–30 [up to 50 drachmae]; *IG* i^3 82); *archons* and *proedroi* (Tod 1946–50, no. 11); *proedroi* (Aes. 1.35; Hansen 1991a; 4); *aposteleis* from whole people could punish and imprison (*IG* ii^2 1629); *apodektai* (*Ath. Pol.* 52.11 [10 drachmae]); *Areopagus* (Aes. 2.93); *generals* (Lys. 9.16, 15.5; *Ath. Pol.* 61.2); overseer of *diobelia* (Xen. *Hell.* 1.7.2); *teichopoioi* (Aes. 3.27); *sitophulakes* (*SEG* 26 [1976–77]: 72.22–26, up to 10 drachmae); *any official abused while in office* (Lys. 9.6–9).

18. Cantarella 1991, 110; Morris (1992, 409) says that 5,000 drachmae was enough to feed a family of four for four to seven years in 409. Such a reckoning would make the fines more minimal. Morris does not give a reference for this figure.

19. Scafuro (1997a, 120–21) divides what I am calling "two types" of arbitration into two separate procedures: reconciliation and arbitration. Since 1938, the dominant trend in scholarship has been to ignore reconciliation and to focus only on arbitration as judgment (what Scafuro calls arbitration and what I call *one type* of arbitration). I think that it is important to call both types of decision making (compromise and judgment) "forms of arbitration" because *Ath. Pol.* 53.2–3 makes clear that the Athenians thought of these two elements of dispute resolution as being part of an "arbitrator's" job. Also, I think that it is important to think of them as being two parts of the same process because it helps us to see the links between dispute resolution *qua* compromise and justice *qua* judicial verdict. See Scafuro 1997 for a full treatment of the subject and the history of the arguments. On the bindingness of private arbitrations, see Scafuro 1997a, 123–31.

20. On private and public arbitration in general, see Lipsius 1915, 220–33; Steinwenter 1925; Gernet 1939, 391; Harrell 1936; Harrison 1971, 64–68; MacDowell 1978, 203–9; Rhodes 1981, 589; Hunter 1994, 55–67; Todd 1995, 123–129; Scafuro 1997a. Scafuro (1997a, 392) is in line with most scholars in thinking that the only public arbitra-

tion carried out in Athens was carried out by the Thirty deme judges prior to 401/0 and by the public arbitrators after that time. Please see appendix B for my arguments to the contrary, for arguments about the meaning of *dikazein* and about the extent of public arbitration in Athens, and for a list of the magistrates and officials who could arbitrate.

21. The market (*emporion*) officials (*diairoie ta amphiloga*, Xen. *Por.* 3.3); the fictional *astunomoi* (Plato, *Laws,* e.g., 759a ff.).

22. Scafuro 1997b.

23. *Indicting: archons* (Lys. 5.3; *Ath. Pol.* 56.30–38); the *thesmothetai* (*Ath. Pol.* 59.1); *hieropoioi ek tes boules* (*IG* i³ 82.23–30); *boule* (And. 1.11–18, 64; Xen. *Hell.* 1.7.1–3); *Areopagus* (Dem. 18.132–33). *Presiding: basileus, archon, thesmothetai,* Eleven (Ar. *Ekkl.* 654–56, *Wasps* 1108–9), *polemarchos* (Wade-Gery 1958, 180–200; *IG* i³ 10; 19.164a.24); *boule; sitophulakes, eisagogeis* (*IG* ii² 111, esp. 37–39 [= Tod 142] [364/3: *boule* condemns to death the assassin of an Athenian proxenos in Iulis]; Ant. 6.35–36 [a *choregos* brings an *eisangelia* to the *boule*]; Isoc 17.42; Lys. 14.21, 22.2; Dem. 24.11–14, 47.18–38 [a trierarch hands a case over to the *boule*]; *Ath. Pol.* 40.2; *IG* ii² 1623); *hieropoioi ek tes boules* (*IG* i² 82.23–30); *Areopagus* (Dem. 18.132–33); *syllogeis tou demou* (*SEG* 26 [1976–77] 72.22–26 = *IG* i³ 405). For *nautodikai, xenodikai,* see note 16.

As MacDowell (1978, 237) says, the Athenians did not seem to find it necessary to keep the role of prosecutor and of presiding magistrate distinct. See Todd 1995, 78–79.

24. Aes. 1.35. Cf. Dem. 47.41–43.

25. E.g., Hyp. 5.38; Din. 1; 2.6; Plut. *Mor.* 833–34. See MacDowell 1978, 27–29.

26. Ruschenbusch (1982, 37) argues that most disputes probably ended at the arbitration stage. Scafuro (1997, 130) agrees and stresses the fact that private arbitration would have contributed to this.

27. See *Ath. Pol.* 56–60. See also Todd 1995, 81–82, 273–75.

28. Here is the compromise decision, the first possibility in arbitration (see appendix B).

29. This word is used of decisions in the courts as well; the case is already a *dike* at this point.

30. An indication that the case is already a *dike* even when it is just before an arbitrator.

31. The four of the forty responsible for the tribe(s) involved in the case switch at this point from being judges, as they were before they passed the case to the arbitrators, to being presiding magistrates.

32. For the debate on when and how the Areopagus was restricted in its powers, see Harrison 1971, 36–43; Cantarella 1975; MacDowell 1978, 114–20; Gagarin 1981, 60, 111–15; Wallace 1989; Heitsch 1989, 71–87; Thür 1991; Todd 1995, 81. *Contra* the view I have adopted, see Rhodes 1972. See also Isoc. 7.37; Dem. 23.71, 23.65–70, 54.25; Hyp. 5, fr. 2, 3; Din. 1.4–6; *Ath. Pol.* 3.6, 57.3. For the reforms of Ephialtes in the mid-fifth century in general, see Bonner and Smith 1930, 251; Starr 1990, 25; Hansen 1991a, 37. See also *Ath. Pol.* 25.

33. For the powers of the generals to punish, see Xen. *Hell.* 1.1.15; Lys. 13.67; Dem. 58.55; *IG* ii² 1629.202–10. See also Fernández Nieto 1990, 111–22; Harrison 1971, 31; Hansen 1991a, 244.

34. Cf. Lys. 15.11. In the fourth century, the generals were subject to the same limits in punishing as were the other magistrates. Serious offenses against military discipline were now handled with the following *graphai* in the courts: *astrateias, lipotaxiou, apobeblekenai ten aspida, aponautiou, anaumachiou*. These cases were tried by juries composed of the defendant's fellow soldiers with the general as presiding magistrate. The

general might take the initiative in having the case brought into court, but any of these suits could be initiated by *ho boulomenos*, or, that is, by any citizen who wished (Harrison 1971, 31–32).

35. On the Areopagus, see Wallace 1989, ch. 7.

36. They could present an action called an *apophasis* recommending that someone be put on trial. See Todd 1995, 115. For the investigatory powers of the Areopagus, see Dem. 18.132–33; Din 1.6.5–10; Demades 1.62–63.

37. See note 41. On killing adulterers, see Xen. *Hiero* 3.3; Lys. 1; Dem 23.60, 59.87. On killing traitors, see And. 196–98. *IG* I³ 14. On *hierosulia*, see Xen. *Mem.* 1.2.62; Isoc. 20.6; Lyc. 1.65. At the end of the democracy, *apagoge* could also be used against metics who had left the city in wartime.

38. Several questions are much disputed. (1) Who carried out *apagoge*? Was it a private citizen (Hansen 1976, 13–17; MacDowell 1978, 58; Rhodes 1981, 580–82) or public official (e.g., *Ath. Pol.* 52.1; Lys. 13.23)? (2) Which offenders could be treated this way because they were *kakourgoi* and which offenders could be treated this way by virtue of the "justified killing" clause in the homicide law (Xen. *Hell.* 1.7)? See Gagarin 1978; Hansen 1981, 24; Carawan 1984, 120–22. (3) Do such wrongdoers have to be "caught in the act" (the standard translation of *ep' autophoroi*) (Cohen 1983) or caught "red-handed" with the goods (Todd 1995, 80); or does the crime merely need to be "sufficiently notorious" (Harrison 1971, 225; Harris 1994b)? Hansen (1976, 48–53) argues "in the act" or "in pursuit" or "with the goods" and Rhodes follows him. (4) How frequently did this process result in a summary execution? Was it often (Hansen 1976) or rarely (Carawan 1984)?

39. Todd 1995, 117, citing Hansen 1976, 24.

40. MacDowell 1991, 187; Hansen 1991a. Todd (1995, 56, n. 7) writes: "Athenian laws tended to be classified procedurally according to the officials who deal with them (e.g., Dem. 24.20)."

41. *eisangelia, apographe, menusis, probole, endeixis, apagoge, phasis, ephegesis,* and *apophasis.* I do not discuss *dokimasia, euthuna, diadikasia, enepiskemma,* or *paragrape.* Nor the judicial procedures: *diamarturia, diomosia,* or *anakrisis.* For discussions of these procedures and those mentioned in the text, see Lipsius 1915; Harrison 1968; 1971, 106–33; MacDowell 1978, 211–20; and Todd 1995. For *paragraphe,* see Paoli 1933, 143–64; Wolff 1966a; Ruschenbusch 1982; Katzouros 1989. For *diamarturia,* see Gernet 1927. For *diomosia,* see Ruschenbusch 1960, 146. For *anakrisis,* see Lipsius 1915, 829–44; Dorjahn 1941; Lämmli 1938, 74–128; Harrison 1971; MacDowell 1978; Boegehold 1991. For *apagoge, endeixis,* and *ephegesis*; see Ziebarth 1897; Lipsius 1915, 317–38; MacDowell 1963, 131–33; 1978; Hansen 1976; 1981; Gagarin 1978; 1981; Rhodes 1981; Cohen 1983; 1995; Carawan 1984; Todd 1995, 117–18, 141, 272–76, 284, 330–31; Harris 1994b (And. 1.91–96; Lys. 13.77–78, 85–87; Plato *Apol.* 32b; Isae. 4.28; Dem. 20.156, 23.80, 24.146, 45.81, 58.11; Aes. 1.182; *Ath. Pol.* 29.4).

42. Bonner and Smith (1930, 170) characterize the *graphe* as named for its use of written indictments, in contrast to other forms of procedure that existed when it was invented; see also MacDowell 1978, 32–40; Calhoun 1919, 178; Thomas 1989, 42; Todd 1990, 27, n. 15; 1995, 100. In Dem. 57, we can see the way in which the archaic *dike phonou* led to an oral proclamation. In the fourth century, written claims were posted before trial in both *graphai* and *dikai* taken into court: Isoc. 12.237–38; Dem. 21.103 [of a *graphe*, here, the visibility of the charge is stressed], 58.32; Aes. 1.35; *Ath. Pol.* 48.4–5; Cf. Ar. *Cl.* 770, 1224; *Wasps* 349, 1407, 1418. The prosecuting litigant had to issue summonses in every kind of case (Harrison 1971, 85–94).

43. See note 42.

44. MacDowell 1978, 32–40. For stelai recording confiscations of wrongdoers convicted of mutilating the herms, see *IG* ii 2.1641 face B = *Insc. Dél.* 104–26c; Merritt 1966. On verdicts inscribed in bronze, see Todd 1995, 45–7. There were also *apographai* or "write ups" and "catalogs" of the property of convicted wrongdoers and state debtors liable to confiscation; these catalogs were used to initiate court cases, also called *apographai*, in which the catalogs and the confiscation would essentially be submitted to ratification (Osborne 1985a).

45. On distinctions between public cases and private cases, see Lipsius 1915, 239–48; Harrison 1971, ii.75–78; Hansen 1981, 12–13; Herman 1987; Todd 1995, 99–112. Lipsius tried to distinguish between *dikai kata tinos* and *dikai pros tinos* but scholars presently reject those categories. See also Dem. 21.2–6.

46. Todd 1995, 83.

47. These are the criteria that Harrison (1971, 75–78) and MacDowell (1978, 257–59) use to call most *dikai* private and *graphai* public. Todd thinks (1995, 98) that this distinction has too many exceptions to be useful. I would argue, however, that Harrison and MacDowell are right to point out that the general trend in *dikai* is to emphasize what the prosecutor gets while the trend in *graphai* is to emphasize what the city gets.

48. See Dem. 21.42–44 where a distinction is made between *dikai* that concern only the litigants and *dikai* where a penalty also goes to the *demosion* or public treasury. See also Dem. 18.210, 24.99, 46.26; *Ath. Pol.* 59.5, 67.1. On the private-public distinction, see note 47 and also Lipsius 1915, 239; MacDowell 1978, 57–61; Osborne 1985a, 40; Cohen 1991, 74–77; Hunter 1994, 125. Most recently, Todd (1995, 109–12) has tried to sort out the differences between *dikai* and *graphai*. He points out that in *graphai* penalties were more severe and the prosecutor ran a risk of a fine for failing to get at least 20 percent of the votes. But he decides that it cannot be said that only the *graphe* is used for criminal cases, nor can it be said that the *graphe* is used for all major cases. He comes to the conclusion that *graphai* are for those types of offense in which the community rather than simply the individual is felt to have an interest. I agree with this and expand on it in chapter 8.

49. On the basis of Harrison's (1971, 81) list of suits that are *timetoi* and *atimetoi* and Todd's (1995, 102–9) catalog of suits, we can (very tentatively) estimate that fifteen out of twenty-three *dikai* (or about two-thirds) and eight out of twenty-five *graphai* (or about one-third) were assessed or *timetoi*.

50. On the antiquity of homicide courts as distinct from *dikasteria*, see Ruschenbusch 1960, 132; MacDowell 1963; Gagarin 1981.

51. Throughout the democracy, murder cases were tried in court as *dikai*, a fact that has proved to be something of a scholarly puzzle to those students of Athenian history who have been surprised that murder cases would be considered "private" rather than "public." MacDowell comes to a similar conclusion (1978, 59). Hansen (1981, n. 17) is the lone scholar who supports the possibility that there was a *graphe phonos*, if infrequently used. MacDowell (1963, 130–40) points out that homicides could be tried by *graphe* for violating their *atimia* and argues that the *apagoge* used against murderers effectively provided a public suit for murder. For other approaches to the problem of murder's being a private case, see Gernet 1984, 22; MacDowell 1963, 130–40 (but cf. Ant. 5.9); Todd 1995, 109–10, 272.

52. Todd 1995, 100. Steinwenter (1925) argued that judicial processes developed out of arbitration. Wolff (1946, 34) argued that arbitration and judgment developed as parallel but basically different legal phenomena. Gernet (1981b, 74) agrees with this second position, writing: "There is a discontinuity between the two institutions: the one could

not have been derived from the other through some 'spontaneous evolution.'" Harrison (1971, 18–21, 69–74) tries to combine the two positions. My approach effectively combines both arguments: there was a discontinuity between the idea of getting a single judge to try to work a compromise and/or make a judgment and having a verdict laid down by a collective body. But the forms of judgment used in the two institutional situations are not discontinuous.

53. See Lipsius 1915; Bonner and Smith 1938; Harrison 1971, 72–74; MacDowell 1978, 30. *Contra* is Ruschenbusch 1960. Hansen (1991a, 189) writes: "In early times the magistrates had the power to judge all law-cases (*Ath. Pol.* 3.5)." Cf. Todd (1995, 99) who agrees that *dikai* are archaic but does not address the question of whether they were court cases from their origin.

54. MacDowell 1978, 29–32. Even late in the fourth century, these archons retained jurisdiction over the great majority of *graphai*. For the *heliaia* of the *thesmothetai*: (*IG* i^3 40. 74–76 [446/5]; Ant. 6.21–24; cf. *Ath. Pol.* 68.1). It was only in the mid-fourth century when they took over the jurisdiction of the *xenodikai* and the *nautodikai* that they acquired jurisdiction over most of the *dikai* or private cases eventually assigned to them (MacDowell 1978, 59); this further indicates the extent to which *graphai* were their original terrain. As Stephen Todd points out to me, in Lipsius's classification of actions, there are 10–20 pages each describing *graphai* before the *archon* and *basileus* but 75 pages about *graphai* before the *thesmothetai*, whereas in *dikai* the proportions are largely reversed.

55. If indeed *dikai,* as cases heard before a single judge, preexisted the people's courts, the eventual hearing of *dikai* before courts would have required a specific mechanism for transferring *dikai* from the arbitrator's space to court space. The invention of *ephesis* or appeal is traditionally attributed to Solon based on *Ath. Pol.* 9.1 (Harrison 1971, 69–74, 190–92; Rhodes 1981, 160–62 on *Ath. Pol.* 9.1), but as Hansen (1991a, 189) says, "with how good reason we do not know: it is certainly an anachronism when Aristotle calls *ephesis eis to dikasterion* one of the three Solonian reforms most to the advantage of the *demos* or people." If the *graphe* was in fact invented to be a court case as distinct from a *dike*, then it is unlikely that Solon would have invented *ephesis* at the same moment as he invented the *graphe*. The point of the *graphe* seems to have been to distinguish between court and noncourt cases. Whatever the case for appeal in Solonian Athens, it seems unlikely that the tyrant Peisistratus's thirty circuit judges or judges "according to deme" were subject to appeal procedures. Inscriptions describing the procedures regulating cases in Athenian colonies indicate that *ephesis,* as applied to subject cities, was invented sometime between 470 and 450. Laws written earlier than that do not require transfer of cases to courts in the actual city of Athens while later laws do (Todd 1995, 330). Accordingly, I suggest in the text that it was actually "Cleisthenes" or the politicians of his era who invented *ephesis* in the Athenian context. For the issue of appeal, see Harrison 1971, 190–92; Ehrenberg 1973, 69; MacDowell 1978, 27–30; Sealey 1987, 69; Stanton 1990, 66.

CHAPTER THREE
CULTURAL CONTEXT

1. I make no attempt to give a complete account of Athenian cultural characteristics, but instead set forth those aspects that prove most significant to a consideration of punishment in Athens.

2. For claims about anger, *orge* and otherwise, see (this list is by no means exhaustive) Isoc. 13.1; 20.6–9; And. 1.24; Lys. 1.15; 15.12; 19.6; 29.6; 31.11; Isae. 1.10, 13, 18; 8.37; Dem. 19.265; 21.99; 28.63; 34.19; 35.31; 38.1; 59.51–55; Aes. 2.3; 3.3; Lyc. 1.86, 91–92. For hostility or hatred toward an opponent, see Isoc. 13.1; Lys. 7.20; 13.1; 15.12; Dem. 53.1–3, 15; 54.33; 58.49, 52; 59.1, 14–15. Demosthenes (21.123) tried to rouse his jury with the verbal adjective that expresses necessity: *orgisteon* (it is necessary to be angry!).

In the context of ancient epic, Muellner (1996, 84ff.) identifies *menis* as the *source* of punishment and the actions following from the need to punish, and *cholos* as the *trigger* for the actions. He adds (1996, 187–92) that *menis* comes from an Indo-European root that means "activate the mind." What is true of *menis* is true of *orge*: it is a state of mind from which the unfolding of the punitive drama begins. See also Dover 1974, 182.

Antiphon is the only orator who disavows *orge* or criticizes its constant appearance in the courts without elsewhere claiming anger as a justifiable inspiration to action. In *On the Murder of Herodes* he writes: "All were killed with anger rather than with judgment; . . . first counsel well, and not with anger [*orges*] and slander, as there are no other counselors worse than these. For it is not the case that the angry man [*orgizomenos*] takes good counsel. For this state of mind destroys what guides him, his judgment. The passing of one day after another substantially releases the judgment from anger [*orges*] and finds the truth of events" (5.69, 71, 91).

In one of the rare moments where Demosthenes regrets the priority given to the passions, Demosthenes chastises his fellow citizens for failing simply to love (*philein*) benefactors to the city and to hate its enemies, being led astray by "pity [*eleos*], envy [*phthonos*], anger [*orge*], gratitude [*charisasthai*] and a thousand other things" (Dem. 19.227–28). Demosthenes, also provides the only other lengthy disavowal of anger in the public case *On the Crown*: "Are you not ashamed to introduce a suit for envy [*phthonos*] and not for wrongdoing? . . . Neither for anger [*orgen*] nor for enmity nor for any other thing of this sort should a good and noble citizen think it right for jurors gathered on behalf of the common good [*ton koinon*] to help him, nor should he come to you on behalf of feelings such as these: but he will mostly avoid having such feelings in his nature and, if they are necessary [*anagke*], he will cherish them mildly and moderately" (121.5, 278). But in the same speech, Demosthenes remarks that a man who has willfully done wrong everywhere receives wrath and *timoria* (Dem. 18.274). And elsewhere, he claims himself to have brought a suit out of anger. He also expects to find satisfaction by appearing before the jury: "I wish now to tell you one of the worst things, so that you will see this man's baseness, and I, by venting [*apoduramenos*] before you about what's occurred, will find things easier [*rhaion*]" (45.57; see also 45.4). For other disavowals of anger, see Lys. 25.6–7; 29.2.5; Dem. 22.1.3; Aes. 3.3; Lyc. 1.3.3, 5.7; Demades 1.3, 4.

3. Isoc. 18.42 (*orgizomenoi phainesthe*); 20.3 (*orgizomenoi phainesthe*); 20.22 (*ensemaneisthe ten orgen*); Lys. 12.90 (*deloi esesthe hos orgizomenoi*); Dem. 21.34 (*demosia orge*), 183 (*phainesthe*); 25.27 (*phanesthai orgen*); 41.3. See also Lys. 13.1; 19.6; 29.6; Aes. 2.3 (*aganaktesantes*); 3.107, 198; Lyc. 1.91–92; Demades 1.30. For the anger of collective bodies, see Dem. 21.2, 6 (*demos*); 22.2 (*houtos orgisthesan*, Council of 500); Dem. 59.80 (the Areopagus).

4. Jebb (1914) translates "such dispositions as regulate cities," citing Soph. *Aj.* 639. Segal (1981, 168) translates the phrase as "the temper that governs the towns with law." In Athens the noun *astunomos* was the title of officials who "had the care of the police, streets, and public buildings" (*LSJ*, s.v.). In this ode, wrath is given the role of keeping the community in order but only when it is wrath embedded in "public law." Crane (1989) argues that the ode is a criticism of Creon.

5. There has been much conjecture on the possible spuriousness of *orgas*, because commentators have not understood the phrase, rather than because of any manuscript contradictions or *lacunae*. One late (thirteenth-century) manuscript does replace *orgas* with *hormas*, but this is itself thought to be error or conjecture. Otherwise the manuscript tradition is consistent.

6. Dover (1991, 176) treats *chalepainein*, *aganaktein*, and *orgizomesthai* as equivalent. In Dem. 21.6 *orgizomai* and *aganakto* are synonyms. Compare Dem. 21.2 with Dem. 24.118. See also Dem. 27.63, 34.19, 59.80. Here are some examples of the usage: "When I sailed home, I became aware of and learned about what he had done and was much annoyed [*aganaktesas*] and angry [*chalepos enegkon*], but it was not possible for me to start a private suit for there were none in this time, as you had canceled them because of the war" (Dem. 45.4); "In what way is it not fitting for me to be angry [*diaganaktein*]" (Dem. 28.63). Lysias lists the reasons why he was especially annoyed or angry (*aganakto*) at a defendant (3.3), and Demosthenes uses the same term to describe why Leocrates brought a suit against Poleuktos (*eganaktei*) (41.4).

7. Padel 1992, 26.

8. Considine (1986, 53–56) shows that *menis* (as a noun) applies explicitly to divine wrath. See also Muellner 1996.

9. *LSJ*, s.v.; Chantraine 1968–80, s.v.; Frisk 1960–72, s.v.

10. Theognis: *mneseai*: 98, 1059, 1223, 1303; Herodotus: 1.61.2, 1.73.4, 1.114.5, 1.141.4, 1.156.2, 3.25.1, 3.35.1, 3.52.3–4, 3.131.1, 4.128.1, 6.85.2, 6.128.1, 7.105.1.

11. See chapter 7 for the relation between *charis* and *orge*.

12. In the same section, Aristotle treats the *thumos* and *orge* as forces that bring honor (1369b1–1370b1). See also *De Anima* 403a29–65. On the link between the *thumos* and heroic principles of honor, see also Rickert 1987, 99.

13. Goldhill (1984, 266) examines *orge* in the Oresteia and finds a similar pattern. Cf. Cohen 1995.

14. *Rhet.* 1378a31: "Some pleasure from the hope of punishment follows on every anger." MacLachlan (1993, 137–38) writes (in the context of the *Oresteia*) that the "one and the same act of requital will produce both suffering and satisfaction . . . anger is quickly converted to kharis-joy once it is appeased, satisfied."

15. Arist. *Rhet.* 1378b, quoting *Il.* 18.109. See Blundell 1989, 27.

16. Cf. Pindar *I* 2.35; Eur. *Hel.* 1339; Plut. *Pomp.* 47.

17. *LSJ*, s.v. The link between *orge* and desire or passion comes up in Winkler (1990b, 198). Pindar (*N* 5.32) uses the phrase *knizein orgas*, and the context is sufficiently ambiguous that the sexual connotations of *knizein* may be said to carry weight.

18. On the issue of women's fertility, see also Hipp. *Diseases of Women I* 12, vol. 8, p. 48; also 24.4.7.

19. On plants, see also Hdt. 4.199; Xen. *Oec.* 19.19. The word *orgas* came to mean a "pubescent girl" in Byzantine Greek (Chantraine 1968, s.v.).

20. On Pandora in the *Theogony*, see Loraux 1993, 78.

21. E.g., Stanford 1983. Muellner (1996) points out the need for work on the ancient passions and begins an anthropology of anger in the context of epic, building on the work of Lakoff (1987, esp. a case study on anger on pp. 380–414) and Lakoff and Turner (1989). See also Halperin 1990; Winkler 1990a; 1991 (where he attempts a "passionate psychology"); Foley 1993 (for grief); Gill 1996. There are also Stanford 1983; Walcot 1978; Henderson 1991a, 5, 32–33.

22. See Adkins 1970 for a text that draws on and modifies Snell in useful ways.

23. Respectively from *LSJ*, s.v.: "to consider, to be angry; the soul, mind, temper,

courage, seat of anger." Redfield (1975, 174) writes: "The *thumos* is the seat of the whole practical consciousness, from instant rage and pain to planning and deliberation."

24. Snell 1953; Padel 1992.

25. Padel 1992, ix; Adkins 1970, 37–43. In what follows, I have drawn heavily on Padel 1992, which coincided with and confirmed research that I was doing when I came across it. In using the distinction between what is inside and what is outside the body, I am using a schema that is wholly Padel's. Beyond that, the schematic framework outlined here is, however, wholly mine, and I have no idea whether Padel would agree with it (or with the use to which I put it here), although her research confirms the usefulness of the schematic framework I use here. I do not intend that the framework I outline here be thought to explain all of the instances of *thumos, nous,* and *phren* or an entirely static and stable system of Greek psychology. All of the words used in Greek texts to refer to physiopsychological organs are characterized by a certain indeterminacy, even if they may also seem to have some more regular or core meanings. In the notes that follow, KRS refers to Kirk, Raven, and Schofield 1983.

26. Padel 1992, 3, 12–13. She discusses Plato's concern with the question "what part of the body do we think with" and writes (13, n. 3): "Galen sites intelligence in the brain, spirit in the heart, daring in the liver. This position was only possible after Plato."

27. Padel 1992, esp. 12–48. On heart, ibid., 18–19; on liver ibid., 19–20. *Splanchna*: Ar. *Frogs* 844; Eur. *Hipp.* 118; *Med.* 221.

28. On the *kardia*, Padel 1992, 35.

29. Ibid., esp. 26, 39. Snell's idea that the early Greeks did not conceive of the body as a unity can be replaced with Padel's idea (1992, 44–48) that they conceived of "unity in multiplicity." Homeric poems show us the *functioning* of a body as collection of organs and not simply *the body* as a thing. See Diogenes as reported by Theophrastus *De Sensu* 39ff. (KRS 612, pp. 447–49).

30. On Homeric warriors breathing *menea*, Padel 1992, 26. On other forms of excretion, ibid., 88–98, 105. See Soph. *El.* 310 (breathing out fury); ps.-Arist. *Prob.* 30.1, 953b34–36 (sexual excitement as air or breath [*pneumatodes*] in the penis).

31. Padel (1992, 97) discusses the ways in which wind imagery, erotic imagery, and food and drink imagery merge in Greek thought. Air getting in, Diogenes KRS 602, pp. 442–45, cf. 603; also 612, pp. 447–49; *Il.* 20.222. Wind impregnating, Arist. *HA* 572a13. Wind nourishing, Soph. *Aj.* 558–59. Liquids entering the body, Aesch. *Eum.* 659; *Lib.* 124–28; fr. 25(44)4. On winged words in the form of prophecies, laments, dreams, curses, song, and words simple and on thought that is windlike, see Padel 1992, 92–95, 227–30. Plato *Theat.* 197d–199c), Ar. *Birds* and Ar. *Clouds* use the analogy between *logos* and air thematically. Plutarch (*Q. Conv.* 7.1, 699B), much later, will treat the lungs as a many-holed sieve through which liquids and solids pass.

32. On *menos* and *cholos* (forms of anger) as always being liquids and never organs, Padel 1992, 39. On bile and spleen, Diogenes KRS 615–16, pp. 450–52; ps.-Arist. *Prob.* 30.1, 953b34–36.

33. Padel (1992, 22–3) provides examples of how the innards flow with emotions that behave like liquids. For *menos*, see *Il.* 5.470, 23.468, 22.312; Soph. *Ant.* 1010; Ar. *Wasps* 424; Arist. *Rhet.* 1406a. For sexual desire, Aesch. *Ag.* 1164–66, 743. The quotation is from p. 136.

34. On the phrase "thoughts are hidden in the *nous,*" see Padel 1992, 30–32. An angry speech reveals an angry *nous* (Soph. *El.* 610, Aesch. *Lib.* 390–92). Empedocles argued the blood around the heart is *noema* and so human beings must be considered to "think" with their blood (KRS 349, 394, 392, pp. 289, 311, 310). Diogenes thinks that

we smell with air around the brain and air is *noesis* (KRS 605, pp. 442–45, 612, pp. 447–49). *Cholos* could swell in the *nous*. On the *nous*'s never behaving as a fluid but often behaving as a vessel receiving emotion or sensation, see Padel 1992, 39. *Menos* and *cholos* are the only terms that are not occasionally treated as organs or vessels.

35. Padel 1992, 21, 64, 115–17. The *phrenes* (and the heart) have ears and eyes. The *phren* and *phronema* are frequently wind and breath (ibid., 92ff.). According to Empedocles, *noesan* and perception are different and the latter you do with the *phren* (KRS 396, p. 312; 343, pp. 284–85). Diogenes thought that perception happened through the air (KRS 612, pp. 447–49). Aristotle (*De Anima* 427a22–28, 427b6–7) attacks the preSocratics for thinking that perceiving and thinking (*phronein)* were the same (and that the *phren* was therefore the center of perception).

The *phrenes* can take in not only air but also fire, including vision (Dem. DKA 157; Emp. fr. 84 DK; KRS 389, p. 308) and lightening (*Il.* 16.481, *Od.* 9.301; Aesch. *PB* 363). *Phrenes* are bound by other people's song (e.g., the Erinyes' song, Aesch. *Eum.* 332). Other people's words terrify you in the *phrenes* (*Il.* 19.125; Aesch. *Lib.* 451–52; Eur. *Hipp.* 572–73, 568, 577, 552).

Diogenes thinks that *phronein* requires dry air, and is reduced by sleep and drink (KRS 612, pp. 447–49). Alcaeus describes wine as going into the lungs (fr. 13.1.e, 983n). Odysseus loosens the Cyclops' *phren* with wine (*Od.* 9.362).

On how *cholos* stands in waves against the heart and *phren*, see Padel 1992, 21, 64, 115–17. For the trope of blackness around the *phren*, *Il.* 1.103; Aesch. *Supp.* 785; *Pers.* 115. For anger as generally producing darkening, *Il.* 18.108; Aesch. *Lib.* 413. For *chole* or bile, Archil. 131; Aesch. *Lib.* 184; Hipp. *Aph.* 4.23; *VM* 19; Soph. *Ant.* 1010; Eur. *El.* 828; For *chole* as anger, Ar. *Peace* 66; *Lys.* 465.

36. For associations between the *thumos* and the sea, *Il.* 14.16–20; *Od.* 4.402; Emp. (KRS 394, p. 311). *Thuo* is associated with the sea at *Il.* 23.230; Hes. *Theog.* 109, 131; *Od.* 13.85. *Thuo* is associated with people at *Il.* 1.342, 11.180; Pindar *P* 3.33; Aesch. *Ag.* 1235. It seems significant that in the *Odyssey*, when the *thumos* left the body at death what it left behind was "white bones," or, in other words, when the *thumos* left the body, it left behind dry bones (*Od.* 11.216). See *Il.* 12.386, 13.654, 20.403, 21.386; *Od.* 10.63. See also Padel 1992, 30–32, 39: the *thumos* and *psuche* especially act like vessels filled by breath or fluid (32). The *psuche* is associated with breath, blood, life, and perception, and can be overcome by *eros*. The *psuche* (or soul) also flew away at death. According to the *Iliad,* it flew off like a dream (1.3; *Od.* 11.221–22).

37. On liver as source of anger, Padel 1992, 19. The liver was especially associated with anger, fear, and lust. See *Il.* 20.469; *Od.* 11.578–80; Theoc. 13.71; Aesch. *Ag.* 432, 792; *Eum.* 135; Soph. *Aj.* 938; Eur. *Supp.* 599, 919. For the liver and bile, see Archil. 234w, Plato *Ti.* 71d-e. For *thumos* used for "penis," see Hipponax 10. For *splanchnon* used of womb, see Aesch. *SAT* 1031; Pindar *O* 6.43. For *splanchnon* used of loins, see Soph. *Ant.* 1066. For the womb and testicles as equivalent, see Diogenes KRS 615–16, pp. 450–52. *Thumos* could be the source of *eros* (Eur. *Med.* 8).

38. Hot blood, Arist. *De Anima* 403a29–65. For a sea comparison, see Semon. 7.41–42.

39. We might think of the *thumos* as being the pot that boils when the liquid in it (*cholos* or *chole*) boils. On *thumos* as vessel, Padel 1992, 29. On *thumos* and anger, ibid., 81. For the idea that *cholos* "falls into, is thrown into, or is stored in" *thumos*, see *Il.* 6.326; 9.436, 675; 14.50; Pindar *P* 11.23; Eur. *Med.* 99; Aesch. *PB* 370. For *cholos* as seizing, see *Il.* 1.387, 4.23, 9.553, 18.119; Eur. *Med.* 1266. For *chole* as boiling, see Ar. *Thes.* 468. For *menos* as filling things and boiling, see *Il.* 1.103, 5.470, 22.312, 23.468;

Arist. *Rhet.* 1406a2; Ar. *Wasps* 424. For *menos* and *thumos*, see *Il.* 22.312, 23.468; Plato *Ti.* 70b. For *orge* and *menos* filling, see Ar. *Wasps* 424. And for *thumos* itself as anger, see *Il.* 1.429, 17.254, 9.496; Soph. *OC* 434, 1139; *Med.* 1079. For *thumos* as pondering, see *Il.* 1.193, 2.409, 15.566; Aesch. *PB* 706; Soph. *El.* 1347. Also, the *thumos* could be treated as air or liquid itself. See *Il.* 1.429, 12.386, 16.616, 20.403, 21.386; *Od.* 10.163.

40. E.g., Arist. *De Anima* 403a29–65; Aesch. *Lib.* 625.

41. See notes 34, 35 and 39.

42. Padel (1992, 81, 113) points out that *suncheo*, which means "confuse or trouble," literally means "pour together." It is used with *thumos* (*Il.* 9.612); and with *noos* (*Il.* 24.358). Padel (1992, 81) argues that the Hippocratics saw inner moisture as dangerous; "Spleen and lungs enlarge when fluid is added. Pain happens when liquid and breath enter into the same parts." Heraclitus distinguishes a dry soul from the soul that is moist from drinking (KRS 230–32, pp. 203–5). For *sophron*, see Aesch. *Ag.* 1664; *Lib.* 140; Soph. *Ant.* 492; *Aj.* 132; Ar. *Frogs* 534.

43. Foley 1993; Holst-Warhaft 1992; Dover 1974; 1989, esp. 1–15; Foucault 1978; 1986; Winkler 1990a; 1990b; 1991; Halperin 1990.

44. Foley 1993, 101.

45. Foucault 1978; Cohen 1991; Halperin (1990, 69) writes: "The ethic governing the usage of pleasures takes the form of a kind of calculated economy of sexual spending: limit yourself to what you really need; wait until the most opportune moment to consume; take into account your own social, political and economic status." The same, as we will see (chapter 7), applied to anger.

46. Henderson 1991a, 5: "[There was] a Greek conception of all passions and drives as inborn necessities of life against which one cannot struggle successfully." On necessity and emotions, see chapter 4. See also Foucault 1978; Halperin 1990, 68–69; Padel 1992, 125–29.

47. Halperin 1990, 68; Winkler 1990b, 171–210.

48. On bee stings, Padel 1992, 122.

49. Poliakoff (1987, 104–7) takes up the challenge that Greek or Athenian culture was no more competitive than other cultures. Acknowledging that most other cultures do indeed have a place for competition, Poliakoff argues that "the Greeks distinguished themselves from other cultures in the number and nature of their competitions, and most significantly, in the way they institutionalized rewards and recognition for the victors."

50. The question of whether Athens was a shame or guilt culture does not really matter here; shame and guilt can both serve to enforce the duty to preserve one's honor and either can be triggered by failing to do so in public. On honor, competition, and public spaces in general, see Dodds 1951; Adkins 1960; 1972, 14–21, 60–61; Dover 1974; Gernet 1981b; 1981c; Cantarella 1983; Cohen 1991, 41–69; 1995, chs. 4–5; Williams 1993, ch. 1. We should also note that cooperative virtues are necessary to successful competition in battle and choruses. The question of the extent to which competition factored into political life and the processes of justice has been much debated. Adkins established a distinction between competitive virtues (related to *arete*) and cooperative virtues (related to *dike* or "justice"). See also Zanker 1990 and 1992 on cooperative virtues. But more recently, scholars have also shown the extent to which even the politicians competed with one another as they stood before the people debating policy on the public stage. Ober 1989a; Cohen 1995. As we shall see (chapters 6–8), competition was crucial to Athenian ethics, but only when limited by a set of rules cooperatively constructed.

51. MacLeod 1982, 138–44.

52. Isoc. 16.3, 48; Isae. 1.6; Dem 18.12.4; 21.7, 15; 58.61; Lyc. 1.5. See Vanoyeke (1976, 81) for consideration of *agon* used in regard to both games and trials. See also Todd 1995; Adkins 1960; 1972, 21, 120–27. In arguing that "punishment" in Athens (civic and public as well as private) did have to do with honor, I contradict Herman (1993). I agree with him, however, that the processes of punishment in Athens required a certain "civic virtue" of citizens. I argue throughout this text that Athenian punishment allowed Athenians to carry out competitions of anger and honor but required that they do so in accord with "norms of public agency" which structured their competitions in such a way as to benefit the city.

53. Ant. 6.1 (punishment as *sumphora* which brings *aischune*); And. 2.19; Dem. 43.4; Din. 2.323. See also Ant. 5.18, 95; Isoc. 16.3; Lys. 6.34, 44; 6.1; Dem. 57.1; 59.12; Aes. 1.183; Lyc. 1.91, 97, 129. The mythological etiologies of the Olympic games treat defeat in competition and punishment as analogous events. In some stories, the Olympic games were originally established as a response to murder, pollution, and the need for purification. The loss of honor through a loss in the first Olympic competition would have served to punish the wrongdoer. See Vanoyeke 1976, 71–73, 76; Gernet 1955, ch. 1.

54. The emphasis on reward and punishment as a pair appears consistently in oratory. See And. 2.18; Isoc. 7.22; Lys. 1.19, 26, 34, 35; Dem. 19.177; 24.216; 50.64; Lyc. 1.9, 51, 74.

55. *Time* lost through punishment even threw in doubt the possibility that one could win future crowns and awards (Dem. 51.4). Conversely, a gain of *time* through reward threw in doubt the possibility of being punished at all (Aes. 3.10).

56. See also Dem. 21.72, 23.4, 47.70.

57. Cantarella 1991, 57–62; Todd 1995, 162; Adkins 1972, 15; Blundell 1989, 55.

58. Failure to punish the guilty could be described as lending him advantage and harming the prosecutor (Lyc. 1.145; cf. Lys. 12.100; 13.93; 22.17, 21). See von Reden (1995, 61–67) on *kerdos*. MacLachlan (1993, 16, 108) elucidates the connection between *tinein* ("to pay," a word used for punishment) and *time*.

The scholarly literature (following Gouldner 1965, 49–50) regularly describes competitions in Athens as a "zero-sum game," that is, as a competition where participants are rivals for a good of which there was a limited quantity incapable of expansion. The application of the term "zero-sum game" has been challenged recently by those who argue that the "store" of honor in Athens was actually expandable (Zanker 1990, 1992). Regardless, however, of whether or not the store of honor was expandable, it remains the case that status in Athens was *relative*; one Athenian compared his amount of *time* with another's. If one citizen gained in *time*, then somebody else was relatively farther behind even if the total amount of *time* had increased.

59. *timoria, epitimion, timema, timorema, atimia, timorein, timoreisthai.*

60. Cf. Adkins 1969, 54. In either sense, the words indicate that a person punished lost honor. This loss of honor, according to Lysias among others, was already a matter of shame, even before the redistribution of *time* in the city had been completed in an act of punishment: "With the vote of conviction, you do nothing other than shame [*oneidizete*], but with the penalty you punish [*timoreisthe*] those who have erred" (Lys. 27.16).

61. Cf. Hansen 1976 but Maffi 1983.

62. *tungchano, echo, pascho, parecho, meteimi, ekprasso, eroimen* and *tino* sometimes replace *lambano* or *didomi* and *poine* sometimes replaces *dike*. Nor should we neglect *antiprassomai*.

63. Osborne 1993, 34; Cohen 1995.

64. E.g., Isoc. 18.18; Dem. 52.25. Also *antididomi, antapokteno, antikathnesko, anti-*

tithemi, antidran, antipoieo, antipascho, apotino, ameibomai, ophlein ant' hon, ka-kopatheo, apokteino.

65. Isae. 8.44; Aes. 1.15; 3.121; Lys. 6.13; 13.60; Dem. 19.221, 240; 51.9; 54.23; 59.1.

66. Cf. Gernet 1981a; 1981b; Muellner 1996, 28; Herman 1987; Millet 1991; Blundell 1989; Seaford 1994; von Reden 1995; Konstan 1997. MacLachlan (1993) does do the work of unpacking reciprocity in terms of *charis* or the return of favor for favor.

67. Padel (1995, 180, 182) makes a start by studying negative reciprocity in literary representations.

68. Putnam 1993, 172, who draws on Sahlins 1972. Cf. MacLachlan 1993, 8–12.

69. Seaford 1994, 14–25, esp. n. 19; 204–5.

70. See *Il.* 6.119–23; Edwards 1975, 51–72; Pitt-Rivers 1977; Donlan 1989, 1–6. Bataille (1988, 63–80) reads the unnecessary hyperexpenditure of the potlatch as the point of human existence.

71. Cf. Millett 1991, 31–33; von Reden 1995, 13–24, 79–83.

72. Herman 1987. Cf. Stanton 1995.

73. Konstan 1997.

74. While these models have been primarily applied to positive reciprocity, they also apply to negative reciprocity. Sahlins (1972), Donlan (1981, 154–175), and Seaford (1994, 7) point this out, but there has been little effort to use the model to deal with negative reciprocity.

75. Isoc. 18.61; Dem. 57.65; Hyp. 4.14; Din. 2.3. Or several deaths, Lys. 30.1. The orators do report on noncapital penalties that have been handed down in other cases, but in putting their own case, they either say nothing specific about the penalty that they would like to see imposed on the defendant or request death.

76. *ta eschata*: Isoc. 7.27; Lys. 12.36; Isae. 3.47; Lyc. 1.27; Din. 1.22, 2.11; *ta megista*: Dem. 24.119, 56.10, 59.53; Aes. 1.14.

77. E.g., Lys. 3.17 (*mache*); Aes. 1.64 (*prospolemeo*). See also And. 1.123 and also Dem. 37.36 by vast extension. Inversely, making war could be described in the vocabulary of punishment and suffering defeat could be described as "giving" justice (Aen. Tac. 16.8). The Thucydidean (1.42.1) words *amunesthai* and *boethountai* both of which "shade . . . from self-defense to retaliation" in the military context also appear in the courts. *amunesthai:* Ant. 5.69; And. 1.30, 2.15, 4.38; Lys. 25.18, 26.13, 27.1, 29.54, 30.14, 19.40, 20.30; Dem. 19.180; Din. 1.46, 1.25; Hyp. fr. 17.2. See Blundell 1989, 37, on *amunomai*. See also Ant. 4.1; Isoc. 18.18; Isae. 1.6; Dem. 21.71; 50.64; 54.2, 18; 58.2–3.

78. Poliakoff argues that the incorporation of competitiveness in the city's civic structure helped declaw competitive ferocity. On limits to the struggle for honor, see also Starr 1986; Herman 1987. See Dem. 21.30: "You never deliver anyone of the wrongdoers to some one of his accusers; for when someone is being wronged, you do not impose the *timoria* as the victim of the wrongdoing convinces you to. On the contrary, you establish laws before the acts of wrongdoing and while it is still unclear who will wrong and who will be wronged. What do these laws do? They promise to all citizens in the city that they will take justice for wrongdoing if someone is wronged." See also Dem. 27.65. *Contra* Athenian moderation is the fact that they treated their generals extremely severely. In Hansen's catalog of *eisangelia* cases, many of which were trials of generals for various sorts of military failures, 100 out of 144 resulted in the death penalty (1975, 66–120). Lest we read too much into this, Hansen also points out that one-third of

those death penalties were handed out in cases that arose out of the violation of the Herms and Eleusinian Mysteries.

79. For discussion of the use of this "definitional stop," see Mackenzie (1981, 32) and Blundell (1989, 54).

80. Bedau 1980, 160. Earlier in the century, Treston (1923) tried to divide methods of carrying out *poine* into four categories: socially widespread "orgies" of revenge; limited forms of vendetta; a wergeld system; and a developed state system of distributing penalties. He attributed the second and fourth to the Athenians.

81. Expressions like Antiphon's or like this one from Demosthenes (*axion onta dounai diken*, 30.1) appear throughout oratory.

82. Statements that affirm the value of reciprocity—the idea that to the doer must be done—do not prima facie tell us whether that reciprocal response should be one that "fits" the initial deed or that "outstrips" it.

83. Gernet (1981a, 73–111) discusses the compelling force of the gift and the way in which value regularly involves competition over prestige, honor, desert. Like Gernet, Muellner (1996, 28, 51) employs Mauss' idea of a "total social phenomenon" to describe reciprocity and argues, in paraphrase, that the stability of such a system depends on the means to recalibrate the hierarchy of value and on a clear notion of the equivalences of goods subject to exchange.

84. On visibility, visuality, honor, and shame, see Cairns 1993, 213–14, 235–36, 357, 362, 389–90; Vernant 1995, 19; Redfield 1995, 153–83; Segal 1995, 186.

85. Fentress and Wickham 1992, 88.

86. For the argument about whether it is legitimate to label Athens an "oral society," see esp. Thomas 1989, 1–14. Thomas and Webb (1994, 6) write: "The Greeks' reliance on oral communication not only shaped the process and institutions of their society, but also influenced their conception of speech itself." For "memory studies" as "cultural studies," see Vernant 1969, 51–94; 1983, 75–155; Gernet 1981d, 216–39; Coleman 1992; Tatum and Small 1995a, 149–50; Tatum 1995a, 151–55; 1995b, 167–74; Small 1995b, 156–58.

87. Steiner 1994, 5–6; 63–67. See Havelock 1982, 77–88; Thomas 1992, 65–73, 88–100; Hedrick 1993, 30–38; Thomas and Webb 1994, 8; Jeffery 1976, 25–32. On forgeries see Thomas 1989, 41. In Dem. 33.17 the only check against forgery is a slave's identification of his own handwriting; in Isoc. 17.23–25, there is no test.

88. On the privileged position of sight in Greek culture, see Vernant 1969, 51–94; 1995, 12–13; Gernet 1981c, 216–39.

89. See *Od.* 8.491; Hdt. 1.140; 2.99.1–4; 2.148; Heraclitus fr. 101a. Cf. Hedrick (1993, 17–38) who argues that later Polybius and Strabo value *akoe* over *opsis*.

90. e.g., Democritus, fr. 125; Plato *Theaet.*

91. Thomas 1989, 41; 1992, 62–63.

92. Schepens 1980; Humphreys 1985c, 313–69; Steiner 1994,105. On visuality in Euripides, Aeschylus, and Sophocles, see De Jong 1991, 9–12, 60–63. Scafuro (1994, 157–61) writes that in the context of proving citizenship and kin identity, "the most important evidence for proving identity is that supplied by live witnesses who were present at communal events of personal significance . . . Live witnesses are preferred to deme records." According to Dem. 44.55, hearsay reports could be admitted to court only when they provided evidence from someone who had died.

93. See Bonner 1905, 39–40, 46–53, 58–61; Thomas 1989, 4. Harrison (1971, 153–54) points out that in court the Athenians paid little attention to the "real" evidence of

documents, seals, and handwriting. Dem. 37.44 is an exception. MacDowell (1978, 231–34) discusses the mid-fourth-century introduction of the requirement that contracts brought to court be written.

94. duBois 1991, 75–91.

95. Thomas 1989, 106.

96. Ibid., 123.

97. On the opposition between piecemeal catalogs and a self-consciously preserved past, see O'Higgins 1991, 37–52.

98. E.g., Dem. 49.27, where remembrance of favors done and owed was praiseworthy. See Blundell 1989, 106; MacLachlan 1993, 77–80, 122.

99. Segal (1981, 136–37) also makes this distinction.

100. Only the word *amunomai* (e.g., Dem. 21.75) was limited to acts of punishment that took place outside the courts and that were *not* authoritative and which were, therefore, equivalent to what we call "revenge."

101. Cf. note 59.

102. Cf. note 64.

103. Other financially related punishment words are *tino, poine/poinao, daneismos, misthos, sumphora, thoe, enochos.* On *poine*, see Ruschenbusch 1960, 136–37. I discuss *katagignosko* in chapter 9. While tragedy had many words to describe the *person* who punished or avenged—*alastor, miastor, erinus, arogos, poinator, meniai, ate, timoros, nemesis*—oratory did not employ them.

104. Ant. 3.3.9. Xenophon (*Oec.* 1.5–9, 2.18) uses it simply to mean anything that harms. See Gernet 1984 on religious aspects of the word.

105. IG i^3 102.

106. Cf. 2. Theophr. *CP* 2.14.3–4.

107. "[Of] trees that are chastened [*kolazomenon*] with blows [*plegais*], when this is done to them, all of them, with the fluid drained off, either bear when they had failed to bear or bear finer and more succulent fruit. . . . In the almond, the tree is even said to change from bitter to sweet" (Theophr. *CP* 1.17.9–10).

108. On hubris, see Fisher 1992.

109. Rubinstein (1997) pointed out that the use of the middle forms of some of the verbs for punishing depends on whether the speaker is prosecuting in a public or in a private case.

110. I will take issue with the argument of Seaford (1994, 105) that "the lawcourt replaces (in part, at least) this hostile reciprocity [of direct vengeance] with socially agreed punishment for crime. That is, like commodity-exchange, it replaces a relation between people by an evaluative relation—between crime and its punishment." To the contrary, the activity in the courts remained very much a matter of determining the relations between people. For other discussions of the nature of *dike* and its meaning, see Hirzel 1966 (reprint of 1907), 56–319; Gagarin 1973; 1986; Vlastos 1980, 303–5.

111. Nozick (1981, 371) and Cragg (1992, 3, 14) both acknowledge this modern focus on the recipient of punishment.

112. Dover (1991, 178) agrees that *kolazein* and *timoreisthai* could not be used interchangeably in court.

113. Plato effectively erased the term that focused on the prosecutor's reward from his texts. In its place, he substituted formulations like "the punished happened upon justice [*tungchano*]" or the wrongdoer "was owed justice [*ophliskano*]" (e.g., *Laws* 871e1, 784d7, 945a5, 944e5, 916b7, 843b3; 868b3, 937b5). See Mackenzie 1981; Saunders 1991, ch. 7; Vlastos 1991.

114. *N.E.* 3.5.7, 1113b23–24; 4.5.11, 1126a28–29; 10.9.10, 1180a9–10; *Pol.* 7.12.3, 1332a12. See also *Rhet.* 1.14.3, 1374b25–26.

CHAPTER FOUR
PUNISHMENT AND ITS TRAGIC PROBLEMS

1. Hamilton 1992, 32.

2. Burkert 1985, 238–39; Padel 1992, 182. Call. fr. 178.2; Phot. *Lex.* s.v. *Choes.* Cf. Robertson 1993, 206–8. Ath. 10.49, 437c. Hamilton (1978 and 1992) rejects this etiology for the festival in favor of another on the grounds that the Euripidean source for the etiology is not to be trusted. The etiology that he prefers is nonetheless also a story about the effort of the community of Athens to relieve itself of guilt for a murder so most of the analysis in this chapter would fit regardless.

3. Hamilton (1992, 30–31) also emphasizes the private familial aspects of the festival.

4. On equⲁl measures and slave participation, *IG* ii² 1672.204 (329 B.C.); Callimachus fr. 178.1–5; Schol. Hes. *Op.* 368; Ath. 10.50, 437. The question of whether women joined in the contests is debated. Burkert thinks they did but Robertson (1993, 223) thinks not.

5. Hamilton 1992, 114–18; Burkert 1985, 237.

6. Burkert 1985, 237–28. For silence, see Ath. 7.276c; Plin. 4.613, 643. Callimachus fr. 178; Suda s.v. *Choes*; Ar. *Ach.* 1000–1003. Hamilton (1992) rejects the claims of silence on the basis of the passage describing the Choes in Aristophanes' *Acharnians*. But the revelry displayed in that passage would by no means be incompatible with festival participants' also having a ritual moment of silence around the time that they actually drank.

7. *IG* ii² 1368.10, 127–131 (178 B.C.). See Burkert 1985, 238–39; Padel 1992, 182; Hamilton 1992, 30. See also Phot. *Lex.* s.v. *Choes*, Thuc. 2.15.4; Dem. 59.73.

8. Burkert 1983, 218 n.11; 1985, 238–39; Padel 1992, 182.

9. Hamilton (1992, 31) also stresses the emphasis on the individuation of citizens in the accounts of the festival.

10. Call. fr. 178.2. See Burkert 1983, 218–22.

11. The literature on tragedy is too extensive to cover in its entirety. I have found the following especially useful: Wilamowitz-Moellendorff 1958; Paley 1879; Thomson 1966; Burnett 1976; 1994; Bremer 1988; Brown 1982; 1983; 1991; Crane 1989; 1993; Detienne and Vernant 1978; Diggle 1983; 1990; Easterling 1982; 1990; Foley 1985; 1988; Gagarin 1973; 1975; 1976; Goff 1990; Gill 1996; Goldhill 1984; 1988; 1987; forthcoming; Henderson 1991b; Padel 1992; 1995; Holst-Warhaft 1992; Jebb 1914; de Jong 1991; Keuls 1974; Lattimore 1964; Lloyd-Jones 1983a; Lloyd-Jones and Wilson 1990; Loraux 1985; Meier 1988; 1990; Michelini 1991; 1994; Nussbaum 1986; Pucci 1980; Seaford 1994; C. Segal 1981; E. Segal 1983; Sommerstein, Halliwell, Henderson, and Zimmerman 1993; Vernant 1980; Vernant and Vidal-Naquet 1988a; 1988b; Winkler and Zeitlin 1990; Zeitlin 1978; 1991; 1996.

12. See appendix D for the catalog of the "punitive events" that I culled from the tragedies and use as the basis for this chapter. I cannot promise that the list is comprehensive although it was intended to be. On the regular occurrence of stories of crime, pride, or punishment in tragedy, see Lattimore 1964, 22–35; C. Segal 1981, 51.

13. My approach is not unlike that of Padel (1992, discussed 36–40). See also Lanza 1977.

14. Lakoff 1987, 12–13.

15. For instance, Vernant (e.g., 1969; 1980, 223) treats texts from "Hesiod to Aristotle" as "rational attempts to get rid of polarities and ambivalences." See also C. Segal 1981.

16. Lakoff and Turner 1989. See also Jameson (1984) where Jameson argues that linguists have primarily focused on the categorical conceptualizations implied in nouns and that binary oppositions are highlighted simply because they are the most straightforward and simplest conventional linguistic tropes.

17. Lakoff and Turner 1989, 384: Every "conventional linguistic expression . . . codes[s] a given conceptual metaphor."

18. Ibid., case study 1: "My anger kept building up; he was bursting with anger; I could barely keep it in any more; he was blue in the face; he exploded; she blew up; I could barely contain my rage; his anger welled up." See Muellner 1996, 1–4.

19. Lakoff and Turner 1989, 386. See Jameson (1984) for a general overview of development of the Saussurean approach to linguistic systems.

20. Lakoff 1987, 12, citing Austin 1975, 73.

21. Lakoff 1987, 13, 95–98.

22. See Vernant (e.g., 1969; 1980, 223) who writes: "Within a given society the interrelationships between different combinations of images are governed by certain rules so when a later Greek author takes a mythical model and transforms it, he is still not completely free to recompose it as he will. Even without realizing it, he works along the lines of the 'legendary imagination,' 'traditional associations,' short phrases, mythemes, oppositions, homologies [or in semantic fields]."

23. Halliwell 1991a, 280.

24. The last word appears only once in tragedy, in *Prometheus Bound*, a play with an overabundance of references to disease and sickness. For the trope of disease and cure in that play, cf. Mossman 1996. For the tropes of disease and cure in tragedy in general, cf. Dumortier 1975; Saïd 1985, 168–86.

25. Dumortier 1975, 55–70.

26. On the Furies and disease, cf. C. Segal 1981, 72.

27. Orestes' sickbed is his prison (*anagkaion*) among other things (230).

28. Girard (1992, 20–23, 28–33) treats the idea of pollution and the need for sacrifice precisely as a means of trying to prevent or forestall excessive acts of violence. Parker (1983, 106) agrees: "Pollution appears not as a mess of blood, but as the anger of the victim, or of avenging spirits acting on his behalf, against the man who has robbed him of the life that is his right." Vernant (1980), Padel (1995, 148, 157–164), Vernant and Vidal-Naquet (1988a, 11) agree. But MacDowell (1963, 3–5) doubts the connection between anger/vengeance and purification. His objections would be answered, however, if it is granted that two ideas, which originate in relation to one another, can attain independently ritualized existence. Ritualization of purification could become an independant phenomenon even if conceptually linked to the problems of anger. Gernet (1984, 23) has a different explanation of pollution, as does Adkins (1972, 87) who writes: "'pollution' is the presence (or supposed presence) of any substance, of whatever kind, which is believed to hamper men's relations with the supernatural." Later Stoic thought, deriving a doctrine of emotions from Aristotle, specifically took up the idea that passions (*pathe*) were in fact diseases of the soul (see *NE* 1106, 1105; Cic. *Tusc. Disp.* 4.12.27).

29. Padel (1992, 54–68, 115–17) calls passion, pollution, erotics, and disease a set because all of them are dangerous intrusions on life and self.

30. This is the phrase found in the manuscripts, but Plut. *Consol. ad Apoll.* 102b and Eustathius 696.33 report *psuches*.

31. Girard 1992, 10. Plato (*Crat.* 405) points out that Apollo is considered both god of revenge and god of purification.

32. Winkler 1991, 222, on *eros*. See also Padel 1992, 54–68, 115–17.

33. Padel (1992, 53) also points out that *omotes*, in its biological sense, means "indigestion" and (1995, 53) that anger (*cholos*) is associated with black bile. Cf. Aesch. *Supp.* 265; Soph. *Aj.* 40, 59.

34. *Il.* 4.349, 2.245, 4.411–18, 14.82 (*hupodra idon*).

35. On vision, light, and fire as markers of revenge in Euripides' *Hecuba*, see Zeitlin 1991, 64–74. See also Eur. *Hipp.* 525–26; Aesch. *Lib.* 1058, *Eum.* 54, 832.

36. See also Soph. *Aj.* 228, 255.

37. MacLachlan 1993, 65.

38. In the *Timaeus* (45b–c), Plato describes the eyes as extending out of the body and therefore as being physically affected by the outer world. Likewise, vision affected one physically. See Padel 1992, 42.

39. C. Segal 1995, 186, 191.

40. MacLachlan (1993, 65) describes *charis* as existing in the eyes.

41. Line 16 of the play makes explicit that Medea has transformed *ta philtata* into *echthra*. Also lines 95, 117, 467. On Medea's violation of *philia* in killing her children, see Bongie 1977, 27–56; Walsh 1979, 297.

42. See Soph. *OT* 100, 241, 310; Eur. *IT* 202. See also Eur. *MoH* 1107, 1150, 1220, 1234; *IT* 202. In Eur. *Or.* 480 Orestes' eyes flash lightening. Vernant (1980, 110–30) discusses the conception that the stain of pollution reaches mind as well as hands and involves a defilement associated with the dead man, his anger, and dangerous thirst for vengeance. See also Padel 1992, 123–24.

43. On snakes, see Aesch. *Pers.* 81; Eur. *Or.* 479–80.

44. Aesch. *PB* 515; *Ag.* 155, 179–80; Soph. *Aj.* 1391.

45. Soph. *OC.* 950, 439; Eur. *Phon.* 937; *Alc.* 1165.

46. *On memory* 449b24–25; 451a23–24; 451a27–8; Muellner 1996, 188 n. 35; C. Segal 1981, 135–7; Coleman 1992, 32–33.

47. Parker 1983, 220.

48. See Willink 1986 on this passage.

49. Aesch. *Ag.* 1410, 1415; Soph. *OT* 310; Eur. *PM* 1050; *MoH* 1260, 1388. Parker (1983, 121) argues that any action that restores the normal equilibrium of things becomes a purification.

50. There is an extensive literature dealing with the forms of pollution and disease suffered by both Orestes and Herakles, often treating the two together. Adkins 1966; Ruck 1976; Shelton 1979; Hartigan 1987; Foley 1985.

51. On friendship as a means to reconcile those who are at odds, see Scafuro 1997, 131–38.

52. Ruck (1976, 69) discusses the physical spreading of pollution from Herakles to Theseus. For readings of the play that emphasize *philia,* see Adkins 1966; Hartigan 1987, 129–34. But also Hartigan (1987, 130–32) argues for the ways in which *philia* is ultimately perverted in the *Orestes* and Dunn (1996) and Padilla (1994, 279–302) argue for the perversion of *philia* in the *Herakles*.

53. Cf. Adkins on *philos* and *philia* as denoting precisely those people and those things that have been removed from the agonistic context of hostility that characterizes the outside world.

54. Jebb (1914) compares the charms here to Plato *Phaedr.* 267 and Aesch. *PB* 172. He points out that *epoidai* were used in medical practice where there was an emphasis on curing anger.

55. See Soph. *OT* 100–110; Eur. *El.* 35, 71. Cf. Parker 1983, 311–12.

56. In Euripides' *Suppliants* the word *sphrigonta* describes the *muthon* (speech) that Theseus delivers in anger.

57. On punishment as remedy, see C. Segal 1981, 51, 72, 120, 140.

58. Douglas (1966, 129–58) argued that in communities that are "adequately equipped with practical [penal] sanctions, pollution is not likely to arise." Girard (1992) agrees. Theodorou (1993, 33) suggests that the cure to emotional *nosos* comes from a willingness to accept change. See also MacLachlan 1993, 137–38.

59. Eur. *Med.* 93–94; Soph. *Aj.* 40, 260.

60. Such is the case in Xenophon (*Ana* 7.6.10) when the author reports himself as saying: "If I could see him stoned, I would have no anger and would consider myself paid." On seeing, knowing, and exulting, see also Saunders 1991, 18–19.

61. On taking the wound literally, see Stephens 1995. Newman (1991, 305–10) argues that Philoctetes is reintegrated into the community through "reciprocity and *philia* with Neoptolemus (1402–8)."

62. On necessity, see Schreckenberg 1964. On necessity in *Oresteia*, see Lesky 1983, 22. Foucault's (1978) analysis of sexuality in the ancient world brought to light the way in which sexual desire, with the other human desires for food, drink, and sleep, were all interchangeably part of the "necessities" that applied to human nature. We can now add "anger" to the list of necessities that Halperin (1990, 68) calls "canonical." See Segal (1981, 153) on anger in the *Antigone*. See also Henderson 1991a, 5; Padel 1992, 125–129.

63. The Aeschylean Athena asks why Orestes has killed his mother, and wonders: "Did you kill her fearing [*treon*] someone's wrath [*koton*] or because of some other necessity [*allais anagkais*]?" (Aesch. *Eum.* 426).

64. Aesch. *Supp.* 5 (hate); *Ag.* 1410 (hate), 1635 (hate); Soph. *Ant.* 130; *OC* 950, 960, 439; *Aj.* 41, 114 (pleasure), 5; *El.* 222; Eur. *El.* 111, 766, 1040, 1184, 1260; *Or.* 431; *IT* 1474, 1470–80; *And.* 1165; *Bacc.* 757; *MoH* 842, 1388 (*lupe*); *PM* 937; *CH* 981 (hate). In my attempt to distinguish the punisher's putative motivation, I have not included whatever information is to be gleaned from the semantic distinctions between the different words for punishment. I have relied only on whatever commentary on motivation appears in addition to any penal vocabulary. Accordingly, there is also a set of cases in which the motivation is "unknown," but it is "unknown" only in the sense that the situation of punishment includes no accompanying commentary on motivation. For a desire to make the enemy groan, see Aesch. *PB* 190, 378, 601; *SAT* 895; *Ag.* 700, 1632, 645, 1210; *Lib.* 270, 945; *Eum.* 3; Soph. *Elec.* 4; *Tr.* 269, 1113; Eur. *Or.* 1168; *MoH* 733; *Rh.* 828; *Hel.* 4; *Med.* 171, 1267; *Hec.* 438, 890, 1055, 1118; *Alc.* 1.

65. Aesch. *SAT* 1; Soph. *OT* 7; *Aj.* 7, 1060; *Ant.* 484; Eur. *El.* 338; *MoH* 1260; *CoH* 283; *Med.* 1050, 1362; *Rh.* 828; *Troj. Wom.* 1037.

66. Scarborough (1991, 139–45) elaborates on the meaning of *pharmaka*. See also Padel 1995, 134–35.

67. On poison, passion, shame, and gender, see C. Segal 1981, 60–108. On the wrong done to Creusa as the central charge against Apollo in the play, see Wasserman 1940; Gellie 1984.

68. Girard (1992, 38) also uses Creusa's poison for the sake of discussing the way violence and cleansing are interwoven with one another.

69. Farnell 1977; Bremmer 1983, 299–320; Vernant and Vidal-Naquet 1988a; Griffith 1993 (on scapegoating). See also Hipponax, fr. 4, 5 Bergk; Ar. *Kn.* 1133, 1405; *Frogs* 730–34; *Lys.* 6.5; Lyc. 1.98–99; Men. *Sam.* 481; Plut. *Theseus* 15, 18, 22; Tzetzes Chi-

liades V, 729. It is interesting that Diogenes Laertius places Socrates' birthday on the day of the Thargelia (2.44).

70. For the importance of figs as a symbol for lust, both sexual and angry, and dried figs as a symbol for satisfied anger, see chapter 7.

71. Easterling (1982) on lines 553–54 translates *luterion lupema* as "a pain which brings release." The reading of *lupema* is contested. Campbell suggests *nosema* and Jebb, *lophema*. Stinton (1976) gives a persuasive defense of *luterion lupema*.

72. See Halleran 1988; Pozzi 1994, 585.

73. See Schreckenberg (1964, 505–71) on the relation between slavery and necessity. For the yoke used in respect to punishment, Aesch. *Ag.* 217, 530, 1640; *PB* 107; Eur. *CoH* 885. For the yoke used in respect to slavery, Aesch. *Ag.* 954, 1045, 1071, 1226; *Lib.* 75. See also Segal 1981, 130–31, on the figure of the yoke in Soph. *Aj.* 53–54, 60, 123, 275, 756, 771.

74. Padel 1992, 118.

75. Cf. Winkler 1990a, 87–91; 1991, 227.

76. Apollo describes his punishment by Zeus thus: "The father forced [*enangkasen*] me in punishment for these things to serve a mortal man" (Eur. *Alc.* 28). In Euripides' *Suppliants,* Aethra encourages Theseus "to bring the wrongdoers to necessity [*eis tend' anangken*]" (Eur. *Supp.* 310). Cf. Eur. *And.* 383, 517; *MoH* 1281; *Bacc.* 34; *Tr.* 71–87; Soph. *El.* 240; Aesch. *Eum.* 520, 695.

77. Cf. Aesch. *Ag.* 1620; *Eum.* 200–215; Eur. *Hipp.* 1080; *Hec.* 751; *IA* 1180.

78. There is, in tragedy, a strain of thought that suggests that the cure generated by punishment improves not only the community and the mutual implication of all members of the community in the ills of anger but also the wrongdoer (Aesch. *Ag.* 176–78, 250, 820, 1563–64, 1620; *Eum.* 520, 695; *SAT* 570, 990; *PB* 10, 40, 65, 325, 470; Soph. *Ant.* 960; Eur. *El.* 385, 397). The person who is punished "suffers into wisdom" (*pathei mathos*). For instance, in an interesting verbal twist, Aegisthus says of a citizen who is troubling him that the darkness and hunger [of imprisonment] will see (*epopsetai*) him gentled (Aesch. *Ag.* 1642).

Scholars have argued at length about the nature of the suffering and learning involved. Several have made the argument that the lesson learned by the punished is not an especially moral lesson but rather a practical lesson about how to keep from angering people who have more power than you do (de Romilly 1968, 67–71; Gagarin 1976, 82, 133–36; Dodds 1960, 29; cf. Conacher 1987, 83–85; Saunders 1991, 73–74).

While this does often seem to be the case, a more "reformative" idea—the idea that the person who is punished becomes *sophron* because he or she has learned to know himself better (e.g., Oedipus and Prometheus)—appears in a few instances (Browne 1943, 163–71). The moral improvement experienced by the wrongdoer is not, however, characterized with the trope of disease and cure in tragedy.

79. Muellner 1996, 4, 26.

80. Also Aesch. *Ag.* 1577; *Eum.* 930; Soph. *Ant.* 1315; Eur. *Supp.* 731, 1315; *MoH* 842.

81. Also Eur. *El.* 585. Critias's (or Euripides') *Sisyphus* makes the inverse point that people will cease to believe in "right" and "wrong" if they cease to believe in the gods.

82. Aesch. *PB* 395, 550; *SAT* 725, 895; *Supp. Maid.* 265; *Ag.* 375, 1598; Soph. *OT* 551, 1290; *El.* 610, 1040; Eur. *Hipp.* 1079; *IA* 385, *PM* 933, 1555, 1726; *Sup.* 555; *Troj. Wom.* 71–87. For the importance of sight and the spectacle in a shame culture, see inter alia Williams 1993 and Cairns 1993. For the importance of sight and spectacle in Athens, see chapters 3, 5, 8, and 9.

83. Vernant (1995, 6) writes: "The gods embodied strengths, abilities, virtues, and benefits that men could only obtain in form fleeting and darkened." For all-seeing, see Aesch. *Eum.* 1045; Soph. *OT* 1215; *OC* 280; *El.* 110. Aristophanes parodies this in the *Frogs* 97 (*omma endikon theon*). Also Xen. *Oec.* 12.19 where the master of slaves accomplishes all of his work with his eye (*ophthalmos*). See also Snell 1953, 137–45. For never sleeping, see Soph. *OT* 865. Clytemnestra (Aesch. *Eum.* 95–116) charges the Erinyes with being lesser protectors than gods in a long speech in which she mostly abuses them for having fallen asleep. The Erinyes carry on the theme of their sleep and their failure until line 148. See also MacLeod 1982, 129. For eternity, see de Romilly 1968, 60–71. The two ideas converge in the statement of a Sophoclean chorus that "time" (*chronos*) sees all things (*ho panth' horon*) and finds out the guilty person (Soph. *OT* 1212).

84. E.g., Medea equates new laws with an end of divine power (492–95). See C. Segal 1981, 168–70, on law in *Antigone*; Ostwald 1969; Boedeker 1991, 96.

85. See Dover 1957, 234; Goldhill 1984; 1988; Saïd 1985.

86. For connections drawn between the hubristic and the tyrannical, see Lanza 1977, 95–159; Fisher 1992. For other descriptions of tyrannical behavior, see Eur. *Bacc.* 505, 995, 1015 (*atheon anomon adikon*); *IT* 38; *And.* 11.

87. Crane (1989, 114) remarks: "The classic tyrant bends the *nomoi* to suit his own pleasure."

88. As Theseus and Adrastus have an argument over what a good leader is, Theseus criticizes Adrastus for keeping the law to himself (431–32). See Shaw 1982, 4. Michelini (1994, 235) discusses the importance of equality in Euripides' *Suppliants* and agrees (on the basis of 432) that the tyrant who keeps the law to himself is the definition of "not equal." Sidwell (1996, 44–57) treats Orestes' pollution as a problem for his ability to rule. Cf. the argument of the Erinyes in the Eumenides: "Such are the doings of the younger [*neoteroi*] gods; who rule [*kratountes*] entirely more than is just [*dikas*] a throne dripping blood about its foot, about its head. . . . Seer though he is, at his own bidding, he has stained his sanctuary, honoring mortals [*brotea*] contrary to the law of the gods [*para nomon theon*]. . . . And has destroyed the old apportionments [*palaigeneis de moiras phthiras*]. . . . The citizens must not pollute the laws with evil influences. I counsel them to accept neither anarchy nor tyranny" (92, 695, 778).

89. Shaw (1982, 3–19) agrees that pan-Hellenic law and divine law are equated in the play and discusses the relation of these to hubris and to memory and different forms of written law.

90. Burnett (1976, 5), writing on law in the *Children of Heracles*, argues that two distinctions matter, the distinction between customary law and statue law or law by decree (although it does not matter whether either is written) and a distinction between law that prosecutes and law that protects. As she reads the play, human customary law is equivalent to divine law and opposed to decrees.

91. Ostwald 1969, 55. Shipp (1978, 10) writes: "*Nomos* differs from *themis, rhetra, thesmos* in being secular and popular. If a community is governed by *nomoi*, it cannot at the same time be ruled by other institutions."

92. Scholars (e.g., Lanza and Vegetti 1977; Steiner 1994) have usually approached the tensions about law attested in tragedy from the perspective that what is at issue is the distinction between written and unwritten laws. This is incorrect. *Either* written *or* unwritten law was *unproblematic* as long as it did not have a specific author. Written law is more frequently accused of being problematic in tragedy not because it is per se problematic but because written law can be made the property of a single author or authority

more easily than oral law can be. Written law, if preserved as public property, was not problematic. Eg. Eur. *Supp.* 430.

93. Anonymous Iamblichi 89, 7, 12–14 DK; Solon fr. 4, 9, 11 West; Heraclit. B33; Xen. *Mem.* 1.2.43.

94. The connection between two strophes given here has always seemed to cause problems for commentators and some have emended, objecting to the idea that *hubris* gives birth to the tyrant as opposed to the other way around (e.g., Lloyd-Jones and Wilson 1990). Jebb (1914) accepts the manuscript version and takes the strophe-antistrophe as juxtaposing the laws of Olympus with the tyrant. He reads the strophe as stressing parentage or what gave birth to the laws. He takes 863–70 as treating Olympus as the father with *ektikten* in 870 helping to stress the fact of parentage. He sees the antistrophe, which turns to *hubris*, as establishing an opposition between the laws from Olympus and the act of the tyrant. Sidwell (1992, 106) also sees *hubris* as being what motivates the tyrant to take power, citing Aesch. *Ag.* 1346–47, 1612–13, 1633, and argues that the *asundeton* of 873 means that there is a clear connection between *hubris* and what has come before. I follow Sidwell's argument about the *asundeton*. Cf. Scodel 1982; Carey 1986.

95. Jebb (1914) points out that at Soph. *Ant.* 450 Creon's edicts are opposed to those of Zeus.

96. O'Brien (1978, 68) takes the *aei pote* as conveying infinity in both directions. See de Romilly 1968, 30–32. This is the only passage where Antigone refers to Creon's laws as *nomoi*. Creon himself claims that his decrees are laws. Cf. *Ant.* 191 where Creon says: "I make the city wax [*auxo*] with these laws" and line 383.

97. Indeed, in tragedy, when law is attributed to a specific source *other than* the divine or the Hellenic, it is nearly always associated with the novel and tyrannical. The examples I have used thus far are but the beginning. Here are others: Soph. *OC* 905, 1382; *Aj.* 1129, 1343, 1349–50; *El.* 579–80, 1015, 1043; Eur. *Or.* 487, 527, 571, 941; *Med.* 238, 493, 811, 1000; *Ion* 20, 442, 1312; *Hipp* 91; *IA* 1095; *Hec.* 800, 847, 864. Aesch. *Pers.* 585 (*personomountai = basileia ischus*); *Ag.* 140 (*oikonomos*); Eur. *Hipp.* 1046 (*ouk houto thanei/hosper su sautoi tonde prouthekas nomon*; Wheeler proposed deletion of this line); *Hel.* 1429 (Pelopid law). See also Xen. *Mem.* 1.11.45–50, 4.4.17. For a valorization of "Hellenic law," take Jason's comment to Medea (*Med.* 538): "By bringing you to Greece, I've given you an understanding of justice and the use of law for reasons other than the sake of force [*ischuous*]." Burnett (1976, 5) notices that in Euripides' *Children of Herakles* (194), local Argive law (as opposed to general Hellenic custom) is problematic. Again law is problematic when it belongs to some specific author (or authors).

98. Solon goes into exile from Athens, after writing laws for the city, precisely in order to avoid being made into a *turannos* on the basis of the authority that he had as legislator, according to Plutarch.

99. On law in *Antigone*, see C. Segal (1981, 168–170). Segal also opposes divine and eternal law to secular and civic law. About Creon he writes (169): "He identified *nomoi* with his decrees and indeed with his own personal voice. The whole of his little speech on political philosophy begins and ends with 'I.' Creon's *dike* is 'personal and emotional.'"

100. On the *orgai* of Creon, Antigone, and Haemon in Sophocles' *Antigone*, see C. Segal 1981, 152–54.

101. For the change from poverty to wealth as a metaphor for the hubristic process, see Michelini 1994.

102. Burnett (1976, 5) finds the same thing in the *Children of Heracles* (line 198). See Hdt. 7.104; Eur. *Med.* 536–38; *Or.* 487.

103. My thanks to Leslie Kurke and her work on coinage for some of the language used in this section.

CHAPTER FIVE
INITIATION, PART ONE

1. For a different version of the story of Athenian disbelief in the defeat, see Thuc. 8.1.

2. *LSJ*, s.v., gives the following for *knizo*: "of love," chafe, tease (Hdt. 6.62, Eur. *Med.* 568; Theoc. 5.122); of other feelings, as satiety, anxiety, provoke, tease (Ar. *Wasps* 1286)."

3. On *philia* and *xenia* as such rules, see Adkins 1963.

4. In Pindar's *Olympian* 6, the first gift that Apollo gave to Iamos, the first prophet at Olympia, was the "ability to hear the voice of ignorant falsehoods (*phonan akouein pseudeon agnoton*)" (66).

5. In contrast, hate is aimed at a class, such as that of *anthropos*. Aristotle's use of Cleon as an example of anger has interesting resonances. Cleon was a popular target of political and Aristophanic anger at the end of the fifth century.

6. On investigation, see Fisher 1976, 38; Hunter 1994, 130–34; Todd 1995, 79. All three consider investigation to be a matter left entirely up to private individuals (see Hunter's qualification on p. 3).

7. On evidence in general, see Bonner 1905, 81; Bonner and Smith 1938, 397–403; Lipsius 1915, 866–900; Harrison 1971, 133–54; MacDowell 1978, 242–47; Todd 1995, 26n, 96–97, 128–29. On interrogation, see Carawan 1983.

Evidence was generally given on specific points in the litigant's case (e.g., Dem. 35.14–15; 40.35, 38). After 380, all testimony arrived at court in the form of written statements. In court, the testimony of witnesses, male and female, was primarily used to confirm information provided by the litigant. Cross-examination of a *witness* occurs only once in our extant sources (And. 1.14). Carawan (1983, 210ff.) lists more than twelve examples where the *litigant* (and not a witness) is interrogated at court (including Lys. 12.24–25, 13.6, 22.5; Dem. 57; Isae. fr. 2; Hyp. fr. B55) but several of his examples are merely sets of rhetorical questions rather than factual interrogation (And. 1.99–101; Dem. 35.44–49, 36.19–21; Din 1.83). Isocrates (18.52–56) brought into court a woman that fourteen witnesses had claimed was dead. Demosthenes (21.95) brought a disfranchised arbitrator into court to prove his wretched state.

8. Bonner 1905, 27–37; MacDowell 1978, 243; Todd 1990, 26–27; 1995, 96. E.g., Lys. 32.12; Isae. 3.3; Dem. 39.4, 9; [59].46. Harrison (1971, 136–47) thinks that women's testimony may have been valid in court so long as it was presented by her male *kurios*.

9. Thür 1979; Ruschenbusch 1982; Gagarin 1990; Todd 1990; 1995; Mirhady 1991a; 1991b. For oath challenges involving women, see Isae. 9.24–25, 12.9; Dem. 39.3–9, 52.14, 54.40, 55.27, 59.124. For oath challenges involving men (and no women), see Dem. 29.52, 31.9, 44.55, 46.11, 49.65–66. For an oath challenge involving metics, see Dem. 33.14. Challenges could be used to solicit evidence on particular points (see Dem. 19.146, 25.62, 33.13) or to be conclusive of the suit (see Dem. 39; 40). Scholars dispute whether oath challenges could be used in both private and public cases. Ruschenbusch

(1982, 37) and Todd (1995, 145) think they could be. Mirhady (1991b, 8) thinks challenges could be offered only in private cases.

10. Harrison (1971,139) treats the process of oath challenge as consisting of three separate procedures: summons, the oath of challenge, and the oath disclaiming knowledge. See Thür 1977; Mirhady 1991b, 18; Hunter 1994, 271–91; Todd 1995, 94–97; Gagarin 1996, 3; Ant. 5.9–12; Dem. 29.52, 39.3.4, 49.65, 51.71, 54.1, 56.17–18.

11. See note 10. It should at least be noted that while we know what the witness would have been asked, we have no idea whether she might have answered by giving more information than requested.

12. There is some doubt as to whether a woman's testimony, solicited on oath, ever reached court at all (Johnstone 1997). We have no examples of such quoted testimony. There is a possibility that whenever a woman testified in an oath challenge, her testimony was conclusive of the point of fact or case at issue and so that point of fact would have been dropped from the courtroom trial. See Dem. 19.146, 25.62, 33.13, 39, 40 for the nature of the questions asked, etc.

13. On what women knew, see Hunter 1994, 32–36.

14. See Ant. 1.8–12; 2.4.8; 5.30–32; 6.22–27; And. 1.22, 64; Isoc. 17. 53–55; 21.4; Lys 4.10–17; 7.34–38; Isae. 6.16; 8.9–13, 28–29; Dem. 29.11, 12, 14, 17–21, 25, 38, 55–56; 30.37; 37.42; 47.12, 39; 53.23, 25; 59.121; Aes. 2.126–28; Lyc. 1.28–32; Arist. *Rhet.* 1.15. Slaves could be tortured for their own crimes in addition to having to suffer judicial torture. See Ant. 1.20; Isoc. 17.11–17, 21–22, 49; Dem. 45.61; 46.21; 47.5–17, 35–40; 48.14–18; 52.22; 53.22–25; 54.27–30; 59.120–25; Lyc. 1.28–35, 16–18. Either during the arbitration stage of his *dike* or during the preparatory stage of his *graphe* (*anakrisis*), a litigant could challenge his opponent to produce his slave, whether male or female, and to put a question of fact to the slave while torturing the slave (or while having the public executioner torture the slave). Gagarin (1996) discusses the dispute over whether litigants themselves had to carry out torture. In Isoc. 17.15–17 it was the public executioner (*demokoinos*) who did. For exceptions to the use of slave torture on testifying slaves, see subsequent discussion.

In making the equation between evidential challenges by slave torture and oath challenges, I follow Thür 1977; Hunter 1994, 271–91; Mirhady 1991a, 81; Todd 1995, 96–97; Gagarin 1996, 3; 1997. See Lys. 1.16; Dem. 29.52, 37.44, 39.3–4, 40.15, 45.15–17; 46.21, 47.5–17, 49.55–56.

On slave torture in general, see the preceding references and Soubie 1973, 226; du-Bois 1991; Headlam 1893; 1894; Thür 1977; 1979; 1996; Hunter 1994, 154–84; Cohen 1995, 96–101.

The issues most in dispute in the scholarly literature on slave torture are: (1) whether slave torture ever happened (Harrison [1971, 147–50] and Gagarin [1996] say no); (2) why we don't ever hear of it happening; (3) what sort of testimony it produced; and (4) whether the free and citizens could be tortured. Scholars agree that slaves would have been asked to confirm or disconfirm a point of fact testified to by one of the litigants. Scholars dispute whether a litigant ever would have accepted a challenge, whether acceptance of the challenge was analogous to trial by ordeal, and whether free foreigners or citizens could be tortured in exceptional cases. On my view, there is no reason to think that orators did not accept the challenge (especially given references like Dem. 47.12). Slaves could be asked to testify on points of fact that were not decisive of the case as well as on points of fact that were decisive. Their testimony would either end the case or, more likely, simply require that a particular issue be withdrawn from the case (cf. Lys. 7.34). In either case, we would not expect to hear about slave torture at trial because the point of fact resolved by slave torture would have ceased to be relevant to the trial. We should expect to hear about slave torture only when the challenge was rejected so that the disputed fact remained at issue in the trial.

The nineteenth-century view of slave torture was that it was a way of getting truth from the slaves. Headlam (1893; 1894) argued that slave torture was not a means of collecting evidence but a specimen of ordeal. Gagarin (1990; 1996) reformulates the traditional argument and argues that it was indeed a method of getting truth from slaves and of introducing slave testimony into court, but that such challenges were never actually used. My view, in contrast, is that the oath challenge was a way of excluding the testimony of *the citizen* from court. I am in line with Thür and Mirhady in thinking that an oath challenge was used to have a slave confirm or disconfirm the evidence of a citizen.

In respect to the issue of torture of free and citizen, Bushala (1968, 61–68) argues for the torture of free noncitizens; but Carey (1988) refutes the case rather convincingly (cf. Dem. 39.39; 49.55–56 where the torture of the free is ruled out), as does Hunter (1994, 154, 173–80). For cases of torture of citizens, see And. 2.15; Lys. 13.25, 59–60 (where the torture victim had been born a slave); 6.27; Dem. 18.132–33 (where the torture victim was no longer a citizen when he was tortured); Plut. *Phoc*. 35. For the decreed end to this policy, see And. 1.43–44. For the torture of free noncitizens, see Din. 1.63; Anaximenes 16.1 (14.8–17.2); Plut. *Nicias*. 30; *De garr*. 13. See also Aes. 3.223–24. For the torture of free citizens and noncitizens in homicide cases, see Thuc. 8.92; Ant. 5; Lys 3.

15. On what slaves knew, see Hunter 1994, 94–95.

16. Dem. 37.40–42; For sureties given in the case of the oath challenge of a woman, see Dem 33.13. See Harrison 1971, 147–50; Thür 1977; 1979; Todd 1990; 1995; Mirhady 1991a; Hunter 1994, 91.

17. See [Xen.] *Ath. Pol*. 1.12 who criticizes the degree to which citizens were economically dependent on slaves.

18. Ant. 1.8–10; 6.25–27; Isoc. 17.53–54; Lys. 4.14; 7.34–35; Isae. 8.12–13; Dem. 29.11–15; 30.37; 45.62; 47.8; 49.56–58, 62; 59.122; Lyc. 1.29, 32.

19. Particularly *Pol*. 1259b25–30.

20. Ant. 5.31–32; Isoc. 21.4, 17.54–55; Lys 4.16; Dem. 37.41; Aes. 2.128.

21. Most scholars (e.g., Finley 1968, 95; Thür 1977; duBois 1991) have emphasized the idea that torture establishes the line between slave and citizen more firmly. DuBois (1991) added to that the idea that torture should be read as a process in which male citizens make truth on the basis of their power by taking truth from the body of slaves.

22. Ant. 5.34; And. 1.12; Lys. 1.11–16, 19–20; 5.5 (where slaves are described as making speeches even); Dem. 25.78–80; 45.27. See also Lys. 6.21–22, 7.16–17. See Bonner 1905, 27–37; Hunter 1994, 71–75. Harrison (1968, 171–72; 1971, 147–50) includes theft of public monies as another exception. Sinclair (1988, 28–34) argues that an exception was made in commercial cases as well. MacDowell (1963, 101–9; 1978, 181–83) expresses skepticism about the range of exceptions but says the issue is insoluble. Todd (1990, 26–27; 1995, 96) rejects these exceptions and tells me (personal communication) that R. Osborne has a forthcoming paper in which he argues that *menusis* could be used only in religious cases. Hunter (1994, 70–71) argues that slaves could not volunteer their knowledge.

23. But see Ant. 5.34, where a promise that a testifying slave will receive freedom in exchange for the testimony does not preclude torture.

24. This is a tricky issue. Lys. 5.5 suggests that the worst thing that will happen to a slave for testifying is that he or she would remain enslaved; but in Ant. 5.34 an owner is

said to have killed a slave for testifying against him. In And. 6.22 an owner kills a slave to keep him from informing. For action taken before evidence can be given, see Ant. 5.34; And. 6.22; Isoc. 17.54–55; Lys. 6.22. Cf. Lys. 5.5.

25. Bonner (1905) thought that there was a prejudice against the testimony of metics. *Contra*, cf. Whitehead 1977 and Todd 1995, 96–97, 194–96. Evidence is too scanty to support a firm conclusion, as Whitehead himself points out (1977, 95).

26. Slave narratives from the last few centuries confirm that even a freedman can be subjected to oppression in the extreme. See H. L. Gates Jr., ed., *The Classic Slave Narratives* (Penguin, 1987).

27. Male citizens could be tried for giving false witness, and three such convictions resulted in *atimia*.

28. Todd 1995, 94–97.

29. Hostile witnesses could in fact be brought in by means of the oath challenge. On the use of both hostile and friendly witnesses, see MacDowell 1978, 233–45.

30. See Hyp. 1.10–14: "Is there anything more democratic [*demotikoteron*] in the city than that those able to speak help [*boethein*] those of the citizens who are unable to, when they are in danger [*kinduneuousi*]?" E.g., Lys. 1.23–24, 40–42, 46; 5.1. On the issue of support gathering, see Bonner and Smith 1930, 51; Fisher 1976, 38; Osborne 1985b, 146–48; Todd 1990, 27–28.

31. Harrison (1971) and MacDowell (1978, 244) both marvel over the fact that Athenian male citizens essentially deprived themselves of witnesses.

32. On the agora and gossip, see Ober 1989a, 148–52; Hunter 1994, 96–119. Also Osborne 1985b; Whitehead 1986.

33. Or the public baths. See Dem. 54.6. In Lys. 23.6–7 a citizen wanders around the cheese market looking for people who have information about the wrongdoer whom he is pursuing. See also Ant. 6.

34. The purported "burglars" claim that they were carrying out a legal confiscation on the basis of a prior court sentence.

35. In the same speech in another instance (47.36), a public slave was similarly sent out to find witnesses. Harrison 1971, 147–50; Hunter 1994, 91. See also Xen. *Hell.* 2.3.54–55.

36. Hunter (1994, 70–71) argues that slaves could not volunteer their knowledge.

37. The citizen had participated in the violation of the Mysteries but not in the vandalization of the herms.

38. E.g., Lys. 13.83; Dem. 45.4–6.

39. Scafuro (1997, 392) stresses the fact that private arbitration would have had to become the main way of resolving disputes during such periods.

40. On the contrast between the *xenos* and the *metoikos*, see Todd (1995, 194–96). He writes: "International relations in the ancient Greek world rested on the unstated premise that the natural relationship between independent communities was one of war, until peace had been declared. On this basis, every *xenos* (foreigner) is logically an enemy. . . . The foreigner (as enemy) has in principle no standing within the community, except on the informal basis of individual *xenia*. This need not matter, so long as such aliens remain few or stay for short periods only; but their large-scale and long-term presence from at the latest the start of the classical period called for regularization. The status of metic appears to have been formulated (and indeed gradually formalized) precisely in order to create a position for aliens within the *polis*."

On metics in general, see Paoli 1933, 175–86; Gernet 1955, 162–63; Gauthier 1971; Mossé 1975; Whitehead 1977; MacDowell 1978, 75–78; van Effenterre and van Effenterre 1990; Todd 1995, 194–96. Whitehead (1977, 95) argues that metics had equal status to citizens in their ability to dispense punishment, but were unequal in receiving punishment, in that as they could suffer more severe penalties than citizens did and crimes against metics were punished less severely than crimes against citizens. This latter situation, however, must be taken to mean that they did not have as much power as citizens to prosecute for wrongs done to them.

The issues most disputed in respect to metics are the extent to which they were able to prosecute without the representation of a patron, and whether their privileges and position in the city changed over the course of the democracy. Older scholarship argued that they could bring cases only through the representation of their *prostates* or patron. At *Ath. Pol.* 58.2, the *polemarchos* is described as needing to take cases where there was no *prostates* and as functioning for metics in the same fashion as the *archon* functioned for citizens. Metics could certainly prosecute on their own in *dikai emporikai* and *emmenai dikai* (Paoli 1933, 175–86; Gernet 1938, 1–44; 1955, 162–3; Todd 1995, 193, although Aris. *Pol.* 1275a7–14 claims that metics needed patrons to go to law. See Isoc. 8.53). Whitehead (1977, 96–97) agrees on metics' ability to prosecute in *dikai emporikai* but argues that there were restrictions on their ability to prosecute *graphai*. There are two slim pieces of evidence for a metic's prosecuting in a *graphe* (Dem. 32.29; 59.64–66). We also know that certain forms of *graphai* were restricted to citizen prosecutors (Dem. 21.47, 59.16). According to Dem. 59.66, aliens participating in *graphai* had to give sureties for their appearance in court in all cases, unlike citizens. See Dem. 45.4; Aes. 1.158 (where a *xenos* was brought before the *archon*).

The status of metics in Athenian courts may have changed over the course of the fourth century accordingly as there were variations in the treatment of mercantile business. Mossé (1975) and Whitehead (1977) argue that the status of metics increased in the fourth century. Todd (1995, 199–206) argues that there was no change. See Harrison 1971, 23–25; MacDowell 1978, 224–29. On *nautodikai, xenodikai,* and the transfer of their jurisdiction to the *eisagogeis* presiding over "monthly suits" and to *thesmothetai,* see *IG* i³ 41e; 439.38; 440.89; *IG* ii² 46; 144; Lys. 17.5–6; Xen. *Poroi* 3.3.

41. See note 40.

42. See note 40.

43. Dem. 33.14. See also Dem. 34.18 where a metic serves as an arbitrator for an ex-slave.

44. *IG* i³ 10; 24.5–9; 55.7; 164a.4–5. A *proxenos* was granted by decree privileges against being prosecuted in any of Athens' tribute cities (*IG* ii² 32.9–15; 385.4). See MacDowell 1978, 221–24; Todd 1995, 195–96.

45. Whitehead 1977, 93. See also Todd 1995, 196.

46. One metic is described as feeling safer before an arbitrator than before a court: "Lampis thought it would be easier to say what he wanted before an arbitrator; for it is not the same before you jurors and before an arbitrator. He thought he was safe there before the arbitrator" (Dem. 34.18).

47. Van Effenterre and van Effenterre (1990, 251), Sagan (1995, 44–47), and Todd (1995, 194–96) also draw connections between citizenship, freedom, and the status of the military victor.

48. The Athenians also decreed that no Athenian could be imprisoned, fined, or put to death in one of their tribute cities. See *IG* ii² 32.9–15; 385.4.

49. Gauthier (1971, 144–48) argues from these cases to the Council of 500's possession of summary rights over metics and aliens. See Todd 1995, 196.

50. "He advised you when you were deliberating about the treatment necessary for the impious Megarian man. Others were ordering him to be killed unjudged on the spot,

but he advised you to judge for the sake of people generally, which from hearing [*akousantes*] and seeing [*idontes*] [the case] would be more right-minded [*sophronesteroi*]" (Lys. 6.54–55). "I made it clear to all that I did not speak on behalf of them but to come to the aid of the established laws" (Lys. 22.2–4); Thuc. 3.36–50, esp. 44, 47–48. Gauthier 1971, 144–48.

51. Hunter 1994, 70–75. On slaves in general, see Patterson 1982; Harrison 1968–71; MacDowell 1978; Finley 1968; Todd 1995, 184–94; Hunter 1994.

52. Sinclair (1988, 28–34) argues that slaves could take action in mercantile cases from the mid-fourth century. MacDowell (1978, 82, 181–83) agrees. Todd (1995, 96) rejects. (See note 40 for *dikai emporikai*.) Some slaves did rise to economic prominence in the city as bankers. The question of whether they were allowed extraordinary judicial privileges needs to be addressed.

53. In Ant. 5.31 a slave is accused of falsehood (*katepseusato*).

54. Dem. 21.46–47; Hyp. fr. B37.

55. Isoc. 18.52–40; Dem. 47.68–70, 59.9–10. MacDowell (1963, 17–18) argues on the basis of Demosthenes' speech *Against Evergus* (47) that nonowners *could* prosecute but would have faced public disfavor for doing so.

56. Sinclair 1988, 59–60. Also see MacDowell 1978, 81.

57. See Gagarin 1981; MacDowell 1963.

58. For other formulations of female control, see Isae. 12.5; Xen. *Oec.* 9.23–25; Lys. 23.10–11. On widows, see Hunter 1994, 29–32.

59. E.g., Dem. 50.2. On *kuria*, see Lacey 1968; MacDowell 1978, 84–92; Schaps 1977; Just 1989, 26–41, 45–47; Hunter 1994, ch. 1; Todd 1995, 207–10; Foxhall 1996. On the position of women in the *polis* generally, see MacDowell 1978, 84–108; 1989; Foxhall 1989; Halperin 1990, 219; Patterson 1994; Blundell 1995.

60. On divorce, see Lacey 1968; Harrison 1968; Hunter 1994, ch. 1; Todd 1995, 214–16. Whether women needed help in order to obtain a divorce is unclear. The wife of Alcibiades, Hipparete, tired of her husband's concubines, did, it seems, try on her own to register a divorce with the *basileus* in the agora according to the law (*kata ton nomon*), but Alcibiades forcibly carried her away (And. 4.14). Andocides tells the story as if Alcibiades has interfered inappropriately, but stories involving Alcibiades must be treated as aberrational and his wife is likely to be exceptionally unrepresentative of Athenian women. Cf. Isae. 2.7–8, 8.36.

61. Isae. 10.19–20; 12.9; Dem. 39.4, 56–9; 40.10–11. For a woman being represented at court, see Isae. 3.2–7, 12.9.

62. At *Ath. Pol.* 58.2, the *polemarchos* is described as needing to take cases where there was no *prostates*. Since the office of the *polemarchos* is described as functioning for metics in a fashion similar to how the archon functions for citizens, it seems likely that the archon would step in in the rare cases where a woman was without a *kurios*.

63. See chapter 2 and appendix B.

64. Ant. 6.38–39; Isoc. 17.18–19 (compromise cemented in a temple); Isae. 2.31–32; Dem. 36.15–16 (resolution on Acropolis that keeps people friends rather than enemies); 41.4; 59.45–48, 65–71; also Ar. *Wasps* 1420–24. On the importance of using arbitration to maintain friendship, see Isae. 2.30–33, 5.31–33; Dem. 36.15, 52.30–31; Xen. *Oec.* 11.23–25; Theophr. *Char.* 5.3, 12.13, 24.4; *Ath. Pol* 53. See also Scafuro 1997.

65. Thomas (1989, 1) writes: "Oath-taking was extensively used to mark the transition from private status to public role."

66. Scafuro 1997, 131–38.

67. Only arbitrators who were friends of the disputants, however, provided privacy as well as the possibility of reconciliation; official arbitrators held sessions in public places

with audiences certainly available. (See Dem. 47.12; cf. Dem. 45.17). On private arbitration and privacy, cf. Gernet 1955, 113; Humphreys 1989; Todd 1995, 123–29, 141; Hunter 1994, 62–67. For women, privacy, and reconciliation: Ant. 1.1; Lys. 32.2; Dem. 27.1, 15–16, 53, 65; 33.14; 34.18; 36.15–21; 40.14–19; 44.19; 48.7–11; Xen. *Oec.* 11.23–25; Isae. 1.6–7, 5.3. Cf. Isae. 4.31; Lys. 8.12. For men and privacy: Isoc. 17.18–19.

68. It should be acknowledged also that the speaker's mother wanted to bring a complaint against her father, a situation in which the proscriptions against strife would have been exceptionally strong. But similarly disgrace is attached to acting for a woman in Isae. 7.3, 18–24. See also Lys. 32.12; Isae. 3.3; 12.9; Dem. 29.25–26; 59.46, 47, 71.

Since the presence of women at arbitrations was regularly figured as rare and as resulting from dire necessity, it seems unlikely that citizen women would have found their way into the courtroom on any but an even rarer occasion. Some scholars (e.g., Hall 1995, 1–52) have argued that while women could not appear in court as prosecutors, they could appear as defendants, citing the five cases reported to have been prosecuted against women, the case written by Antiphon against the stepmother and the case against Naeara for which we have speeches, and the cases against Aristagora, Phryne, and Aspasia, of which we have reports.

Firstly, it is worth pointing out that only the stepmother was a citizen, which leaves us with only one extant piece of evidence of the involvement of a citizen woman in a prosecution. In a different but related context, Todd (1997, 113) makes the important point that citizen women and metic or slave women were treated differently in Athens. The rigid gender distinctions that characterized the world of the citizen did not apply to the same extent outside of it. Todd argues that freedwomen, unlike citizen women, could appear in court without representation; he makes this argument on the basis of a set of cases called the Phialai Exeleutherikai (*IG* ii^2 1445–1559, 1553, 1560–78) in which slave owners brought and then dropped prosecutions against former slaves on the charge of failing to show respect. By dropping the charges, the slave owner forced the court to declare the slave free, and this seems to have been a way of making sure that manumitted slaves could be registered officially, with witnesses, as free. Eighty-six women appear on the list of freed people registered this way. But since the cases were dropped before they came to court and the prosecutor was the only person, essentially, who had to take any action, the phenomenon is perhaps an insufficient basis for arguing that the women would have represented themselves in court had they actually had to appear in court.

Only in the case of Phryne are we actually told that the female defendant was in the courtroom (Athen. 590d–e). As her story is related, she did not actually appear before the jurors except for during the brief moment when Hyperides putatively called her forward in order to rip open her dress and expose the beauty of her breasts to the jurors, surely an exceptional case. In Euripides' *Orestes*, Electra is in fact tried in absentia (836–65). For women trying to deal with wrongs outside the courtroom, see Dem. 25.57; also Isae. 3.3; Lys. 1.15.

69. Collier 1976, 91. See also Seaford 1994, 211.

70. Commendable, then, is Iphigeneia who claims not to be angry against the one who killed her (*me thumoumene*) (Eur. *IT* 993).

71. On the position of women as foreigners in the households of men, see Carson (1990, 135–70). See Boedeker (1991, 110–11) on Medea, who has to make a treaty with the whole city of Athens, complete with official libations, before Aegeus will help her (*Med.* 898). Walsh (1979) reads Medea as turning to the public spaces in her pursuit of

honor and as violating the norms of *philia* in the process; her impetus to action, in his view, is that Jason's ambition has destroyed the household. Similarly, Roth (1993, 3) reads the *Oresteia* as dramatizing the corruption of guest-friendship relations (relations of *xenia*), including the guest-friendship relationship between husbands and wives. See also Willink 1988b, 318. (For comments to the effect that *philia* has turned into enmity, cf. *Ag.* 1272; 1273; *Lib.* 234, 173, 615, 906–7, 933).

On the idea that the heroism of women is antithetical to a desirable quiet peace or *hesuchia*, see Michelini 1994, 245–48. On the familiar Greek polarity drawn between marriage and war, see C. Segal 1990b, 109. Joyal (1991, 524) sees a programmatic link with disease in the perversion of *philia*.

72. For commentary on the deceit in Medea's speech, see Knox 1977.

73. Medea's long speech to her *thumos* might be read in the context of her awareness that a woman is supposed to have a different sort of *thumos* than a man. Which direction will her *thumos* go?

74. See Juffras 1991; Huys 1993, 322.

75. The Euripidean Electra is called a man (*arsenas*, 1204), and Knox's (1977) treatment of Medea as a Sophoclean hero whose nature is masculine is widely accepted. On *Hecuba*, see Luschnig 1976; Zeitlin 1991, 60–64. Also Bongie 1977, 28–33; Rickert 1987; Barlow 1989.

76. On manly women conducting revenge, see Huys 1993; Knox 1977; Friedrich 1993, 222.

77. See Schlesier (1993) for maenads as the model for tragedy and Padel (1995 249–59) for a link between maenads, mania, and punishment. See also Zeitlin 1985; Goff 1990, 8; Foley 1993, 107; Padel 1995, 249–59. Hudson (1996, 113) points out the same phenomenon in the modern context and writes: "Why women should be treated more readily as mad and men more readily as bad needs insights beyond those that Marxism has so far offered. . . . females are most usually controlled by non-penal processes and institutions, such as psychiatry and social work (which the evidence would suggest is the case) but men are more readily penalized." She (129–30) posits a continuity between the punishment of crime, control of sexuality, and control of women's lives through psychiatric labeling. Cf. Hutter and Williams 1981.

78. Hecuba uses the following words of herself: *timoreo, timoros*, etc. *Hec.* 749–50, 756, 789–90, 842–43, 882, 1258. Other characters also describe her action with the vocabulary of legitimate punishment (*didonai diken*: Agamemnon, 853; chorus, 1024; Polymestor, 1253). Meridor (1978, 28–35) points out that words associated with *timoria* occur thirty-seven times in the play, despite being rare in other plays. In some sense her act or her designation of a wrongdoing and the need to respond to it "conform[] with standards of Athenian justice."

79. Burnett (1994, 151–64) elaborates at length on the dog imagery. See also, and somewhat *contra*, Zeitlin 1991, 56–60.

80. Lysias says: "If I am exiled, I am most miserable of creatures: I am childless and alone, my house would be alone, my mother left in utter penury, and I should be deprived of my native land" (7.41).

81. Gregory 1991, 108. The meaning of Hecuba's prophesied transformation has been much debated. Luschnig (1976, 227–31) and C. Segal (1990a) emphasize the idea that Hecuba will become a beast rather than mortal. Zeitlin (1991, 62 n. 39) argues that there is too much focus on the idea of bestiality since no bestial qualities are posited of Hecuba's posttransformation state except for the burning gaze. Burnett (1994, 157–58) also challenges the standard bestiality line by arguing that the dog that Hecuba becomes

represents the wild made tame. Nonetheless, as we have seen, a "burning gaze" is an important symbol of the anger of punishment. Burnett does at least agree that the canine qualities and the demons of revenge develop together in the play (158). I would suggest that it is difficult to separate the final image of Hecuba from the earlier image where she and her helpers are likened to a pack of dogs (1077, 1173), an image that is surely meant to convey the bestiality of Hecuba's punishment in some fashion. See also Aesch. *Ag.* 1231–35 where the chorus attaches Clytemnestra's daring and act of punishment to the nature of female monsters. It is noteworthy that the *Maniai, Eumenides, Erinyes,* and *Ate* are all personified as *daughters* of Zeus.

82. Friederich 1993, 230–31.

83. *phoneus:* Aesch. *Ag.* 1309, 1506; Soph. *El.* 778; Eur. *El.* 30; *Med.* 1267; *Ion* 1026. See appendix E for catalog of punitive events found in tragedy.

84. C. Segal 1981, 252.

85. Detienne and Vernant (1978, 27–30), Loraux (1985), and Goldhill (1988) all discuss the connection between womanhood and guile.

86. Detienne and Vernant (1978, 27–29) have a good discussion of *dolos* as providing the weaker competitor with means to overcome the stronger. Cf. Bongie 1977, 39–41.

87. The standard oath formula in treaties includes the promise to act guilelessly (*adolos*).

88. Also, Cassandra describes Clytemnestra as brewing a remedy or poison (*pharmakon*: Aesch. *Ag.* 1261); (cf. *Ion* 1003–5). Agamemnon asks Hecuba if, given her weakness of arm, she will use poison rather than a dagger (Eur. *Hec.* 878). For general associations between women and poison, see Dem. 25.80; Hyp. 3(5).8.4–8; Plut. *Sol.* 21.4–5; Arist. *Magna Moralia* 1188b31–37. Solon allowed citizens to bequeath their property to whomever they chose provided that they did not make their decision under the influence of pain, bondage, *pharmaka*, old age, or the persuasion of a woman (*Nomographus* fr. 4.24–2.6).

89. Seaford (1994, 389–91) discusses the ambiguity of women's gifts, as does Gould (1980, 51–56) and Padel (1995, 161).

90. Burke 1969, 87.

91. Burke 1989, 110.

CHAPTER SIX
INITIATION, PART TWO

1. A term coined on the basis of Herman's work (1993, 1994a, 1994b, 1996) on the place (or lack of a place) for a "Mediterranean" code of honor in classical Athens.

2. [Xen.] *Ath.* 1.10; Dem. 53.16. See MacDowell 1978, 79–83.

3. One citizen, for instance, expressed a worry that his slave might commit suicide after an overly severe punishment (Theophr. *Char.* 12). Another was afraid that his slave might run away (Xen. *Oec.* 3.4). See Hunter 1994, 163. The citizen also had to pay damages and fines imposed on his slaves (Dem. 37.21, 37.51, 53.20, 55.31–32; Hyp. 3.22).

4. Cantarella (1991, 14–16, 40–43, 47–56) examines the role of the head of the household as punisher in myth, looking especially at Odysseus. See also Seaford 1990 for such myths.

5. See Dem. 41.1; 43.1–11, 32–34, 38–42, 55, 59; Dem. 59.51; 80–82. See Lys. 14.28–29 for divorce of a wife for adultery. Divorce was used by husbands as punish-

ment against their wives and by in-laws against one another. The divorce had to be registered in the agora, or made public.

6. The responsibility that citizen men had for punishing their wives further reduces the likelihood that citizen women would be allowed to appear in court. To charge a woman would have been to charge her husband with having failed to punish her himself. Any prosecution against a citizen woman would necessitate that her husband defend not so much her as himself. This is what happens in Apollodorus's *Against Neaera*, where Neaera is charged with having pretended to be a citizen, a misdeed for which Stephanus, her husband, should have divorced her. The speaker admits that the reason for the suit is Theomnestus's hatred of Stephanus. Prosecuting Neaera is a way of getting at Stephanus.

7. See also Dem. 37.33.

8. E.g., Isae.1.6: "I regard it as the worst feature of my present troubles that I am at law with kinsmen against whom it is not noble to defend and revenge oneself." See also Ant. 1.1; Lys. 32.1–3; Isae. 1.6–7; Dem. 27.1.4, 33.14. See also Scafuro 1997, 131–38.

9. E.g., Lys. 8.12.

10. Hunter (1994, ch. 2) catalogs twenty-eight lawsuits among kin, mostly about property and mostly between father's brothers and nephews. Orators involved in such cases regularly claim they know that matters in the family should not be brought to court (see previous note and chapter 5). See also Humphreys 1989.

11. On the length of trials, see Harrison 1971, 156; Todd 1995. Cf. MacDowell (1978, 247–54) and Boegehold (1991, 165–92) on what happened in the courtroom.

12. See chapter 2 and notes on these procedures.

13. See Gagarin 1986, 68; Osborne 1985a, 42–49; Ober 1989a, 198.

14. It should be noted that the Athenians also "punished" inanimate objects; the item (rock, stone, hand of man who had committed suicide) was thrust by law beyond the borders of the state (Aes. 3.244; *Ath. Pol.* 57.4). The trial of inanimate objects provided a publicly recorded explanation of what had caused the death so that someone could not later reopen the case with a false accusation of murder (Boegehold 1995, 50).

15. Blundell (1989, 37) writes: "The Thucydidean (1.42.1) word *amunesthai* shades . . . from self-defense to retaliation." See Ant. 4.1; Isoc. 18.18; Isae.1.6; Dem. 21.71, 54.18, 58.2–3.

16. Cf. Aeschines (3.107) who remarks "Often before now petty causes have been responsible for great evils because there are persons who have the effrontery to beat others; there have been cases where we have become so enraged that wounds, death, exile, and the greatest calamities have resulted."

17. Lys. 1.18; Dem. 45.33.

18. Herman (1993) presents Euphiletos as putting forward an honest and earnest claim to do nothing but act in such a way as to represent the law and civic ideals.

19. E.g., Lysias 1. 37: "Do not take into account, gentlemen, their accusation that I sent the maid to go fetch the young man during the day. Indeed, I, gentlemen, might even think it just [*hegoumen dikaion*] to use any method to catch my wife's corrupter. If he hadn't yet done anything and only words had been spoken, and I had commanded her to fetch him, that would be wrongdoing [*edikoun*]. But if, once he had already done everything and come often to my house, I had used any possible means to catch him, I would consider myself as acting appropriately."

20. E.g., ibid., 41: "It is natural to have friends around when punishing [*etimoreito*]; and do you not think that I should have sent word to my intimate acquaintances in the daytime and bidden them assemble at the house of one of my friends living nearest to me, rather than waiting till the moment of making my discovery to run round in the

night, without knowing whom I should find at home and who was away?" Ibid., 46: "Why did I choose to summon witnesses if I had unjust desires [*adikos epethumoun*]? I could have done it in secrecy."

21. E.g. ibid., 23: "I gathered as many friends as I could." Ibid., 28: "He had not been dragged in from the street, he had not taken refuge at my hearth."

22. Cohen 1991; 1995; Herman 1993; 1994a; 1994b; 1996.

23. I have used MacDowell for the text of the play. For secondary sources, I have referred to Croiset 1909; MacDowell 1971; 1995; Vaio 1971; Reckford 1977; Konstan 1985; Edmunds 1987; Olson 1996.

The question of the play's politics has long been under debate. MacDowell (1971) argued that it was an attack on the courts, but retracted to argue (1995, 177–79) that the play is not political. Edmunds (1987) argued that it was an attack on Cleon. Konstan (1985, 27) writes: "The play expresses a specific political conception of the role of the courts in Athens. A political or ideological perspective on the court system is implicit in the basic narrative and dramatic strategies—'the deep structure'—of the Wasps." Konstan argues that ultimately the play is antidemocratic because only aristocrats can withdraw to a life of leisure. As we shall see, however, the withdrawal of Philocleon to a life of leisure is not treated as a desirable thing in the play. Olson (1996) is alone in arguing for a democratic interpretation of the play that sees it as a criticism of the demagogues and a celebration of the courts. My argument is compatible with Olson's to large degree, although Olson did not address the theme of anger in the play and its relation both to the criticism of the demagogues and the value of the courts. See also Croiset (1909, 89) for Aristophanes' prosecution by Cleon.

24. For an extensive examination of the disease theme, see Sidwell (1990) who thinks the disease is *eros*, MacDowell (1995, 150–80) who thinks it is enthusiasm for law, and Konstan (1985, 32ff.) who thinks it is "a narrow single-mindedness of a passion—detached in the last analysis from the acknowledged public value of its goal." Konstan discusses the anger trope in the play in ways that are compatible with my argument here but without recognizing its democratic implications.

25. See Olson 1996, 130. Sidwell (1990, 12) agrees that Philocleon's disease is linked to the state of the whole Athenian jury system, since his *noson* is an *archaian noson* inborn in the city (line 651).

26. Olson 1996, 132–33.

27. These are the same criticisms of juries that Olson (1996, 134) sees in the play.

28. Sidwell 1989, 271–77.

29. Ibid.

30. MacDowell 1978, 129. Konstan (1985) reads the play as valorizing the life of leisure but the negative results of the symposium are simply too explicit too ignore. Reckford (1977, 296–97) writes: "The cure kills more than it cures. Philocleon loses his identity and suffers psychological death." Olson (1996, 143–44) agrees that the plan has backfired and produced a hubristic Philocleon.

31. Padel 1992, 180.

32. On madness and dancing as ritual cure, see Padel (1995, 134–35).

33. See Reckford 1977, 294; Olson 1996, 137. The standard tendency in the literature on the *Wasps* has been to read its ending as disconnected from the main drama of the play. Sidwell (1990) thinks that "this later outbreak of madness has nothing to do with the original obsession." Even Reckford (1977, 310–12), who sees that Bdelycleon's efforts have backfired, attaches no particular importance to the final scene and describes the ending scenes of dancing as "sheer fun." But Vaio (1971) argued that the play is not

made up of two disconnected parts and Borthwick (1992) points out that the play begins with a traditional dream omen of failure.

34. Reckford 1977, 305, n. 2. On *kentron*, see Henderson 1991a, 122; Padel 1992, 118, 121–22. Reckford (1977, 305–8) argues that the conceit behind the sting is the juror's use of a stylus to draw his penalty line and he suggests an equation of the stylus, sword, sting, and erect phallus.

35. MacDowell (1995, 156) treats the wasps' speech here as having primarily to do with financial issues, particularly their desire for an old-age pension.

36. See Littman (1990, 16) who writes: "From anthropology, we learn that societies that depend on a lineage system for their organization need to maintain 'the interlocking web of social relationships' . . . at all costs in order for the society to survive, and all parts of the social system, including the judicial system, are oriented toward that end." At some level this is true even of tyrannical regimes, so long as the tyrant is at least interested in maintaining the bare existence of a community.

37. According to Isaeus (7.30), the *archon* even had the explicit duty of preventing a family from being extinguished.

38. See Michelini 1994, 244–52. The most dramatic statement of the problem probably comes in the *Madness of Herakles* when the hero comes home but does not leave off his warring and, in a fit of "madness" (969–71, 982–83, 989) and "anger" (549, 562, 526), kills his own children. Padilla (1994) reads the play as showing how paternal violence limits *philia*.

39. Consider this story, where punishment is specifically assigned to the male child: "Thinking his wife pregnant, he enjoined her to tell the child, if a son, that Agoratus had killed his father and that he should take vengeance on behalf of his father [upon coming of age]" (Lys. 13.42). Hunter (1994, 115) writes: "Whatever the role of women in the kinship structure before the advent of the state, it was [after the advent] securely linked to the reproduction of that basic unit [the *oikos*] and with it the social structure." Blundell (1995, 129) writes: "The development of democracy in Athens may have been a parallel phenomenon to the subordination of women, in that both were linked in some degree to the emphasis placed on the economic independence [i.e., self-sufficiency] of the *oikoi*." Foxhall (1989, 31) describes the head of the household as the individual who was empowered to cross the boundary between the household and the community. He "mediated between the changing contexts of public and private life." Hunter (1994, 3–6) discusses the way in which social control functions along a continuum from kin to state. See also Halperin 1990, 219; MacDowell 1978, 84–108; Gould 1980, 53–56. On the "operational unit of oikos," see Patterson 1994 but also MacDowell 1989.

40. In tragedy, Theseus is a lone anomaly in forswearing rage (Eur. *Supp.* 555, 581). As we will see (chapter 10), Socrates did propose that the Athenians take up the first method of putting an end to vendetta. On Socrates' challenge to the Athenian system of anger, honor, and competitive punishment, see Vlastos (1991).

41. Hunter (1994, ch. 2); Humphreys 1989. Consider cases like that by Antiphon, *Against the Stepmother*, in which two half brothers are on opposing sides of a court case.

42. Cf. duBois 1992.

43. Walsh (1979, 294) treats "public roles" as having to do with approval, honor, and blame, unlike private roles in three Euripidean plays.

44. This account of "public" and "private" draws on Cohen (1989; 1991, 148–50) who suggests that the public-private divide has to do with a separation of spheres and roles rather than with total seclusion and isolation. Cf. Foxhall 1989, 31. This allows for a solution to the problem that has puzzled scholars: women clearly spent time in public

on a regular basis despite the powerful rhetoric about public and private; how does this make sense? (See, e.g., Hunter 1994, 33–37.) Notice that when Aristophanes allows women to enter politics in the *Ecclesiazousae*, he also puts an end to public competitions. See also Vernant (1969, 97–158) on the binary opposition between Hestia and Hermes.

45. On women in Greek politics, see MacDowell 1978; Keuls 1993; Sealey 1990; Loraux 1985; 1993; Foxhall 1989; Winkler 1990a; Zeitlin 1978; 1991; 1996; Halperin, Winkler, and Zeitlin 1990; Redfield 1990; Carson 1990; Hunter 1994; Patterson 1994; Blundell 1995. Most efforts to deal with the repression of women in Greek society have involved extensive, careful, and very useful *description* of the ways in which women were isolated and controlled. Herein I attempt *to analyze why* it was that Athenian society was at its basis founded on an exclusion of women from political and public life.

46. Clytemnestra's/woman's wrath in both *oikos* and *doma*: Aesch. *Ag.* 155, 1090, 1100, 1119, 1309, 1364, 1470, 1481, 1533; *Lib.* 13, 34, 50.

47. See Schlesier 1993, 89–114. See also Lys. 8.1 where a similar phrase *epitedeiois anepitedeioi* (those who are "unfriendly to their friends") is used in a discussion of what happens when enmity enters a *philia* group.

48. Orestes (*Lib.* 534) has beseeched the spirit of his father for rule (*kratos*) over the house (*domon*). He gets it with Athena's vote. Athena's speech of acquittal has occasioned much commentary since it (and Apollo's speech [625, 635]) seems to have nothing to do with the merits of the case. E.g., Dover 1957, 236; Dodds 1960, 29; Goldhill 1988, 31; Zeitlin 1978.

49. This reading is based on H. Lloyd-Jones's emendation. The Erinyes/ Semnai Theai are called "metics" several times (*metoikos*: 807, 824, 833, 853, 868, 891, 894, 915). Whitehead (1977, 6) argues that the word means "one who changed his or her home" rather than "with-dweller." Brown (1991), reading the *Antigone*, argues that in that play the word *metoikos* is used primarily as coresident (852, 890) although also connoting "home-changer" in one instance (868). Antigone is also treated in terms of being a *sunoikos/metoikos*. C. Segal (1981, 177–200) discusses this ambiguity and Antigone's position between being male and female, virgin and married.

In reading the *Eumenides*, there is no reason we cannot take the word in both senses, especially since it is linked to and made parallel to *sunoikoi* who are definitely "with-dwellers." The Erinyes who become Semnai Theai have both "changed their home" and learned how to be "with-dwellers." On the red robes, cf. Griffith (1988, 552–53) who cites Phot. s.v. *skaphas* = Men. fr. 166 Koerte.

50. See Loraux (1993, 6–21, 111–43) for the argument that there were no "female Athenians" nor female citizens.

51. The role of *sunoikoi*: *Lib.* 908, 1005; *Eum.* 824, 848–91. On the ritual of marriage as a mediation of difference, see Redfield 1990, 115–22; Halleran 1991, 109–21. In Plutarch (*Coniug. Praec.* 138d) marriage is a ritual that keeps the bride from being *chalepoteta*. Carson (1990, 161) writes: "The ancient wedding undertook systematically, to redeem woman from her original roughness and sourness, and to purify her of chaos, by means of certain very specific ceremonies aimed at the dramatization and reinforcement of female boundaries."

52. Even "the wedding ritual in tragedy tends to be subverted. . . . The wedding . . . expresses the victory of culture over nature. The failure to complete the transition is profoundly anomic and constantly explored in tragedy" (Seaford 1987, 106).

53. The two phenomena of anger and sexual lust are simply not distinct in either men

or women. Padel 1992, 111: " The swelling images of impassioned *splanchna* might seem apt for male sexual organs, but in fact are assimilated to the female *intera*."

54. Hipp. *Diseases of Women I* 12, vol. 8, p. 48; also 24.4.7. On the obligation of women to produce children in order to carry out their obligations of *philia*, see Bongie (1977, 42).

55. See Halleran 1988.

56. This appearance of the word *xunoikoun* (1055) has occasioned some efforts to emend it (e.g., Dawe to *xunipoun*) But Pozzi (1994) and Ormand (1993, 224–27) retain the original. Ormand solves the textual problem by an argument about how destructive forces get into a body from outside.

57. Pozzi 1994, 585. See also Easterling 1982 and C. Segal (1981, 60–108) who discusses the perversion of wedding imagery in Herakles' death scene.

58. Aesch. *Ag.* 45, 220: the Trojan war concerns woman retribution (*gunaikopoinon*); 1454–76: Agamemnon is destroyed by a woman and by strife in the house.

59. Padel (1992, 110–11) discusses the "vital ambiguities in the female model of mind." The reading of the following passage is based on H. Lloyd-Jones's emendation.

60. Carson 1990, 136.

61. The small fragment on Sisyphus is usually taken to be from a play by Critias, but Yunis (1988, 39–46) has argued that it is actually from a Euripidean play by the same name.

62. Faraone argues (1994, 116, 126) that "several types of love magic were believed to reverse traditional gender roles by weakening the male and rendering him more passive and pliable to the demands of the female," and suggests that the danger at issue is that the weakened male would be unfit for political leadership if he gave in to sexual desires too much.

63. C. Segal (1995, 210) writes: "Yet tragedy is no simple part of such a civic spectacle, for with extraordinary openness it enables the city to reflect on what is in conflict with its ideals, what it must exclude or repress, what it fears or labels as alien, unknown, other. In this way, one may understand the tragedian's recurrent dramatization of the power and anger of women in the household." See also Redfield 1995, 154; Padel 1992, 110; Just 1989, 196–216; Sagan 1995, 151.

64. I take the term "collective" to refer *primarily* to the idea of the *demos* and I take collective to be acts of punishment wherein the *demos* was (or could have been) said to be punishing, whether because a full quorum in the assembly was acting or because individual citizens were acting metonymically (with the name of the *demos*).

65. Harrison 1971, 171; MacDowell 1978, 126.

66. Dem. 51.12, 59.86; Aes. 1.183 but Todd says there was no *atimia* for women.

67. Cohen 1991, 72–73. See also the exclusion of cowards from meals in Sparta (Xen. *Lak. Pol.* 9.4–5).

68. This applies to the process of trial by impeachment or *eisangelia*. MacDowell 1978, 61–62. See Ar. *Wasps* 691; *Ath. Pol.* 54.2; Hyp. 5.37–38. See Dem. 47.41.

69. E.g., Lyc. 1.121.

70. Plut. *Cimon* 14.5; *Pericles* 10.6. For Antiphon's appointed prosecutors, see [Plut.] *X. Or.* 833–34; *Ath. Pol.* 46. See also Hansen 1975, 29–36.

71. To some extent, the American colonies (also city-states, really) functioned in the same way. For hue and cry and the service of private citizens as nightwatchmen and constables, see Friedman (1993, 29–32). The principle difference was the early appearance in the colonies of exclusively public prosecution.

72. See chapter 2.

73. *to deinon* and *orge* are linked to one another, e.g., Lys. 22.2.

74. On the importance of the *oikos* in this story, see Patterson (1994, 202–3).

CHAPTER SEVEN
THE NEGOTIATION OF DESERT, PART ONE

1. Winkler 1991, 229. Also see his discussion (pp. 219–28) of a set of prayers known as "anger restraint" prayers.

2. E.g., *Defixionum Tabellae* (Paris, 1904), 100, 102, 108. See Versnel 1990, 72, 64–65.

3. See Versnel, 1990.

4. On anger-restraint curses, see Faraone 1999.

5. Faraone 1991, 11; 1985. See also Faraone 1989.

6. Faraone 1985, 157; 1989, 156.

7. On relation between rhetoric and magic, see de Romilly 1975. On words and magic, see Faraone and Obbink 1991.

8. Carey (1994, 29) also notices this, pointing to the appearance of *orge, misein, aganaktein.* Cf. Dover 1991 on forgiveness as remission of anger.

Pity: E.g., Ant. 1.3; 5.73; 6.9–10 (*charis*); And. 1.6 (*eunoia*); 1.30; 1.141 (*suggnome*); Isoc. 14.52–53; 16.48; 18.62; Isae. 2.44; 5.35; Lys. 3.48; 6.3, 55; 10.22; 18.1; 19.2, 6, 53; 20.34–35 (*eleeate*); 22.21: "You would not be justified in taking pity on them"; 24.1–2, 7; 28.11, 13–14; Dem. 19.65; 21.98, 148; 24.196; 25.81; 27.58–63; 28.20; 53.29: "They claim your pity; give me forgiveness"; 57.1: "Listen to me with goodwill for it is likely that you listen more pityingly to those in danger"; 57.2, 3, 45, 49; 58.69: "Pity us"; Lyc. 1.143–44; Hyp. 3.36; Din. 1.22, 109.

Anger: e.g., Isoc. 18.36; 20.14; Lys. 21.9: "Be angered because of the misfortune"; 10.26–28; 12.90–96; 14.1; 15.9; 25.1; 27.15–16; 28.13–14; 30.23; Isae. 6.56; Dem. 25.27; 40.5: "Be angry"; 18.274; 19.258 (*misein*); 21.127; 22.39 (*orgizesthai*), 64 (*misein*); 24.110, 152–53, 200, 218; 25.26–27, 94; 37.20; 45.20; 51.8–(10); Aes. 1.176, 192–193; 3.198; Lyc. 1.58, 138; Hyp. 5.22; Din. 1.77; 2.4; 3.13, 15; Demades 1.30.

9. Isoc. 18.42 (*orgizomenoi phainesthe*); 20.3 (*orgizomenoi phainesthe*); 20.22 (*ensemaneisthe ten orgen*); Lys. 12.90 (*deloi esesthe hos orgizomenoi*); Dem. 21.183 (*phainesthe*); 25.27 (*phanesetai*).

10. Adkins (1972, 122) writes: "Emotional pleas for pity were notoriously sometimes made in Athenian courts but these speakers seem not to be asking for pity, but rather for admiration for qualities which we should not regard as relevant in court." E.g., Ant. 1.3 (*axios eleeisthai*); 5.73 (*axios eleethenai*); And. 2.6 (*oiktos phthonos axios*); Isoc. 16.48 (*dikaios eleetheien*); 20.14 (*prosekein misein kai koinous echthrous nomizein*); Isae. 6.56 (*axion malista aganaktesai*); Lys. 6.55 (*axioi eleeisthai*); 11.9 (*axion orgisthenai*); 13.1 (*eikotos*); 14.2 (*axia suggnomes*); 14.8 (*orgizesthai dikaios*); 20.21 (*dikaios eleesaite*); 27.11–13 (*axioi*); 28.13–14 (*prosekei orgizesthai*); 31.11 (*axios, dikaion*); Dem. 21.127 (*orthos axian, orgen*); 21.148 (*axiosai suggnomes, philanthropias, charitos*); 21.186 (*axion misein*); 21.196 (*misos phthonos orge axia*); 24.152–53 (*axios tes megistes orges*); 24.200 (*axios orges*); 24.218 (*axion orgisthenai kolasai paradeigma*); 37.20 (*axion chalepainein*); Dem. 44.57 (*axioi orges*); 45.20 (*orges axion*); 54.138 (*prosekes*); Lyc. 1.58, 138 (*eschates orges dikaios*); Aes. 3.260; Din. 1.22 (*prosekein eleou tinos tungchanein*); See also Ant. 1.25.

11. For places where pity and anger are used together, see Ant. 5.73; And. 2.6; Isoc. 18.36–39; Lys. 12.30 (*suggnome*), 80 (*charis*); 15.9; 27.12–15; 28.13–14; 31.11; Dem.

21.98, 186; 24.196; 28.13–14; 29.2. Oratory primarily used the word *eleos* but *oiktos* also appears (e.g., And. 4.6; Dem. 18.41, 19.6, 57.44) and sometimes in opposition to *orge*. *Oiktos* was more common in tragedy (Stanford 1983, 23). Russell (1990, 201) notices *phthonos* and pity as a pair of contraries. See also Carey 1994, 29–33; Plut. *Mor. 790c*.

12. And. 2.9 (*charis, misos*); Dem. 18.274 (*orge, suggnome*); 21.148 (*suggnome, philanthropia, charis*); 21.196 (*misos, phthonos, orge*); 25.81 (*eleos, suggnome, philanthropia*); 29.2 (*phthonos, eleos*).

13. For one of the moments where Demosthenes regrets the priority given to the passions, see chapter 3, note 2.

14. Schofield 1996.

15. Miller 1995, 87–128; 1996.

16. See Triantaphyllopoulos 1975, 26–27.

17. The right to a trial was sometimes violated (e.g., Lys. 19.7–8).

18. Aristotle (*Rhet.* 2.1.8, 1278a–1380b) writes: "The emotions are all those affections which cause men to change their opinion in regard to their judgments, and are accompanied by pleasure and pain; such are anger [*orge*], pity [*eleos*], fear, and all similar emotions and their contraries." Gorg. *Helen*; Thrasymachus *Eleos;* Plato *Phaedrus* 267c. See also Swarney 1993; Carey 1994, 29. For a description of the ways that Roman legal pleaders made similar arguments, see Swarney 1993.

19. On the social function of memory, see Vernant 1969, 51–94; Gernet 1981d, 216–39; Coleman 1992; Tatum and Small 1995a, 149–50; Tatum 1995a 151–55; 1995b, 167–74; Small 1995b, 156–58.

20. Csapo 1993, 27, n. 28: "It may be worthwhile to repeat the *caveat* that 'social representations describe social ideals or protocols, not realities (Winkler, 1990a, 45–48; Halperin 1990, 58–59).' It is not to be supposed that all or even most Greek youths respected the behavioural ideals urged upon them by social representations. They are 'norms,' not in a statistical sense, but as expressions of ideal values to which all real behaviour held some structural relations, whether honoured in the observance or in the breach."

21. See Hunter 1994, 127–38; Cohen 1995; Osborne 1985b. See also Ant. 2.1.8; Isae. 9.16–18; Lys. 14.2; Dem. 53.1.

22. For analogous statements, see Lys. 7.20 (who claims that personal enmities correct civic wrongs); Dem 21.8; 24.8 (I thought myself to have seized upon a most favorable or appropriate moment to help the city and to take *timoria* on behalf of the things I have suffered).

23. The defendant can, in order to delegitimate an accusation, claim that the prosecutor has no personal reason to be angry at him or no true reason for enmity (Lys. 9.13, 16.2).

24. Cf. Lys. 14, 15.

25. Eg., Isoc. 21.1; Lys 14.1–3; 15.12; fr. 78; Isae. 4.1; 6.1; Dem. 22.1.

26. On friends and relatives speaking, see MacDowell 1978, 251.

27. Fisher 1976, 36–37.

28. Isoc. 10.18; Lys. 3.10, 18.18, 39.4; Dem. 18.13, 36.26–27, 37.2.

29. Cf. Dem. 30.29, 33.38, 38.6.

30. E.g., Dem. 36.53–54 where delay is linked to sycophancy and Dem. 18.88 where the orator says: "While acts are recent and known if they are good, they happen upon gratitude [*charitos*], if otherwise, they receive *timorias*." And in Lys. 20.22 we find: "He gave justice . . . straightaway after the deeds when you remembered most of all [*malista ememnesthe*] what had happened."

31. Bonner 1905, 58–65.

32. E.g., Lys. 13.83; Dem. 45.4–6.

33. See also Ober 1989a.

34. Dem. 28.2, 58.59–61. See Carey 1994, 28; Humphreys 1986, 89.

35. Cf. Diomedes (*Il.* 9.33).

36. See Ant. 1.1; Lys. 12.3, 16.20, 19.1; Dem. 27.1–4; 44.1–3.

37. Ant. 1.1; Lys. 3.3; 8.2; cf. Dem. 27.1, 65; 40.1; 41.1; 44.57–59; 45.5; 48.1; 58.59, 61; Isae. 1.6–9; 5.30–32; fr. 6. See Blundell 1989, 38.

38. On *charis* in general, see MacLachlan 1993.

39. MacDowell (1976, 21) and Fisher (1992) have shown how the Athenians considered both youth and wealth to lead to *hubris*, which MacDowell defined as "having energy and power and misusing it self-indulgently." See also MacDowell 1978, 129–32.

40. Todd 1995, 92–94.

41. Osborne 1990, 99–100; Cf. Harvey 1990, 113–14.

42. On sycophants, see Lofberg 1917, 19–25; Harrison 1971, 60–61; MacDowell 1978, 62–66; Osborne 1990, 99–100; Hunter 1994, 126–27. See Lys 13.67; Isae. 11.13, 31; Dem. 21.102–3, 116; 36.54; 38.3, 16, 20; 39.2, 26, 34; 55; 57; 58; Aes. 1; Lyc. 1.31; and Isoc. 15.314–15 on laws against sycophancy.

43. *Patris* appears 81 times in the speech of 150 paragraphs, as opposed to 39 times in the 322 paragraphs of Dem. 18 (*De Corona*), the 24 instances in the 195 paragraphs of Aeschines' *Against Timarchus* and the 10 instances in the 80 paragraph's of Lysias's *Funeral Oration*. These three speeches have the most instances of *patris* after the Lycurgus speech.

44. See Lys. 1.15 where again "a meddler" is contrasted to the person who has private reasons for bringing a case.

45. The only other two speeches in which there is extensive literary quotation are Aeschines' *Against Timarchus* (1.128–29, 144–52), and Demosthenes' *On the False Embassy* (19.243–48, 255–56), a speech in which Demosthenes explicitly uses quotations in order to mock Aeschines' use of literary quotation in *Against Timarchus*.

46. Aes. 3.252–53; Dem. 18.204.

47. Pl. Com. 255; Men. 1071; Henderson 1991. Note that *knizon sukamina* is to ripen figs (L 20.7.14; cf. Ar. *Wasps* 1286).

48. Henderson 1991a, 46–47.

49. E.g., Ar. *Kn.* 708; *Achar.* 995; *Wealth* 1351–53; Pl. Com. 255; Men. 1071; *CA* 1158; Antiphanes 198; Pherecrates 197; Hipponax 124. Henderson 1991a, esp. 4 46–7, 118. Buckheit 1960, 200–204.

50. Henderson 1991a, 118, citing Ar. *Achar.* 158, 160, 1102; *Kn.* 707; *Lys.* 663.

51. See Hipponax, fr. 4 and 5 Bergk; Ar. *Kn.* 1133, 1405; *Frogs* 730–34; Lyc. 1.98–99; Men. *Sam.* 481; Plut. *Theseus* 15, 18, 22; Tzetzes Chiliades 5, 729.

52. Fig wood (and other wild woods) were commonly used for purificatory fires (Parker 1983, 221).

53. On cooking and food as sexual euphemisms, see Henderson 1991a, 129, 142–43.

54. On *kentron*, Henderson 1991a, 122. Padel 1992, 118, 121–22.

55. Reckford 1977, 307. Csapo (1993, 1–28, 115–24), doing work on cockfights, has also found that the *kentron* is a symbol of the "cross-connection between sexual intercourse and physical violence and the intercourse and sport/combat homology."

56. *LSJ*, s.v. According to Henderson, *ischadas* refers only to female genitalia and is never used in a sexual sense in Old Comedy. He therefore rejects Daele's interpretation of *Achar.* 802 as including a reference to the phallus in the word *ischadas*. It seems to

me that Daele is more likely to be right. A related word, *ischanao,* means to "desire eagerly." In Euripides' *Suppliants* the word *sphrigonta* is applied to the *muthon* (speech) that Theseus delivers in anger.

57. Olson (1996, 137) sees a parallel between cession of authority in the house and in the city.

58. On generational conflict in comedy, see Gardner 1989, 59–60.

59. Winkler (1990a, 68; 1991, 221) argues that there was a "system of balances since the prudent householder needs to control eros both in its arousal and in its dispersal."

60. Henderson 1991a, 52, 205; Foucault 1978; Cohen 1991.

61. Ar. *Wasps* 646; Xen. *Cyr.* 4.5.21; cf. *Il.* 4.513, 9.565, where *cholos* is nursed and ripened.

62. For ripeness and plants, see Theophr. *HP* 3.6.9. For ripeness and disease, see Hippocrates, *Acut.* 390. For ripeness and sexuality, see *AP* 12.185, 12.9; Anacreon 432. For *opora,* see Pindar *I* 2.4–5; Aesch. *Supp.* 998, 1015; Alexis fr. 165 Kock.

63. Henderson 1991a, 47.

64. Ibid., 2, 10, 124. Henderson writes, "We note the role of smutty language in sexual aggression . . . in hostility where the motive is exposure of the enemy's hidden parts (degradation)."

65. Isocrates (15.314, 324) discusses the *graphe* against sycophants. The criticisms that orators launch at their opponents for their misuse of anger fit the analytical framework established by the idea of an "economy of spending" anger that is linked to an "economy of spending" of sexual desire. See Lys. 1.28, 25.5; Dem. 58.31–32; Aes. 3.3; Demades 1.1–4. On the general baseness of sycophants, see Lys. 12.5–6; 25.19, 30; Dem. 58.64. The sycophant could misbehave outside the courtroom also; see Aes. 2.145. See Cohen 1991; Foucault 1978; Winkler 1990a; 1990b; 1991.

66. In one Greek city, the *pharmakos,* the ritual scapegoat, was beaten in the genitals with squills and branches of wild figs and sacrificed on fires built with the wood of "wild trees" for which we can probably read "fig trees" (Tzetes. Chiliades 5.734–36). Similarly, there is a tale of a slave in Chaeronea who was beaten away with branches of *vitex agnus castus* in order to drive away a "great hunger"; the fruit and leaves of the tree were considered to be sexual suppressants (Plut. *Mor.* 693). Csapo (1993, 10–22) on cockfights relates the ways in which chickens are seen as being both violent and sex-crazed and have no concept of *kairos.* The triumphant cock is hubristic. In the *Birds,* the sycophants, like the female birds, pluck out the noble cock's feathers, and there is paradigmatic isotopy between the defeated chicken, slave, castrato, and *kinaidos.*

67. See also Dem. 48.6 where he says that it is not the right time for anger (*ouk en kairoi orgizoimen*).

68. On the importance of *hesuchia* or peace and quiet and the prejudice against hubristic activism, see Carter 1986; Michelini 1994. Michelini discusses sycophants as those who "do many things" (*polla prattein*). For a conflation of the oligarchs and sycophants, see Xen. *Hell.* 2.3.22; Lys. 12.4–5, 20; And. 1.99; Theophr. *Char.* 26. For oligarchic overprosecution, see Lys. 12.17; 13.45–54, 56, 66; 26.13; Xen. *Hell.* 2.3.17; Dem. 24.164–66; Aes. 3.220. For a false report of excessive use of whipping, imprisonment, and execution by the oligarchs, see Thuc. 8.74.

69. On the oligarchic regime, see Krentz 1982.

70. On the Thirty's use of "sycophant" as a (literally) catchall word, see Christ 1992, 343–46, citing *Ath. Pol.* 35.3 and Xen. *Hell.* 2.3.12–13.

71. Henderson 1991a, 41.

72. Csapo 1993, 124.

CHAPTER EIGHT
THE NEGOTIATION OF DESERT, PART TWO

1. See also Coleman 1992 for the connection between social memory, the politics of common knowledge, and a politics of rhetoric.

2. E.g., Isae. 9.17–18; Lys. 13.8.

3. E.g., Lys. 3.47, 25.1, 30.6.; Dem. 24.132–38, 29.23; Aes. 1.44–45, 52. Cf. Lys. 12.92, 14.15; Dem. 23.219, 45.87.

4. Gernet 1984, 25. Demosthenes emphasizes an exception to the rule, reminding his audience of how the Athenian citizenry once punished someone with death, even though he was a citizen and the son of a man who had been general (Dem. 34.50). Cf. Dem. 21.176–77; Ant. 5.73. The Romans actually legislated different kinds of penalties for different status classes (cf. Garnsey 1970, 104–50). Gagarin (1986, 106) makes this point in relation to arbitration. Of the *lex talionis*, Vlastos (1991, 182) says: "It aims to put a lid on the extravagance of passion by stipulating that for any given harm, no greater may be inflicted in return."

5. On gossip and moral judgments, Hunter 1994, 101–2.

6. Lys. 12.96; Dem. 24.175; Aes. 1.176; Din. 2.4.

7. Cf. And. 1.108; Dem. 59.71.

8. Abramson (1994, 12, 17) points out that the modern jury takes an oath to decide a case solely "upon the evidence developed at trial." Swarney (1993, 140, 155) on Rome writes: "Viewed superficially from the perspective of modern judicial practice, the obligations of prosecution and defense are simple and straightforward—to establish by direct and concrete evidence that the accused did (or did not) do the deed."

9. *Black's Law Dictionary*, s.v. "Summary Judgment," "Issue," "Issue of fact," "Issue of law," "Genuine Issue."

10. Aristotle writes the following about the Athenian courts: "People often admit having done an action and yet do not admit to the specific terms of an indictment or the crime with which it deals" (*Rhet.* 1374a). In Lys. 29.9, the speaker treats the accused as guilty, arguing about what he deserves rather than about whether he has done the deed, though that, in fact, is unproved. See also Lys. 1, 4, 9; Dem. 34, 38, 52, 54, 56.

11. E.g., Dem. 21. Here is a curious case: "Then you thought the trierarchs who had rented out the trierarchies were responsible in the main for what had happened, and you handed them over to the prison, voting they had betrayed the ships and left their post. Aristophon accused, you judged. But if you had not had a more moderate anger than matched their wrongdoing, nothing could have prevented their being killed" (Dem. 51.8). The trierarchs come to trial only after all the Athenians already think that they, in respect to the facts, are guilty.

12. Aeschines (1.152–53; cf. 1.46–48) complains about this.

13. B. B. Rogers, an English lawyer, writes the following, in tones of frustrated disappointment, in his introduction to his translation of Aristophanes' *Wasps*: "A large assembly can rarely if ever form a fit tribunal for ascertaining facts or deciding questions of law" (London 1906, xxvi–xxvii). MacDowell (1978, 44) commends an orator who "discouraged the irrelevant pleadings and personal attacks. . . to focus. . . on the true merits of the case." Millett (1990, 179) uses the phrase "legal laxity" to refer to the way the Athenian litigants presented their cases.

14. See also Isae. 6.56 (*axion malista aganaktesai*); Dem. 21.175, also 183; 24.152–53 (*axios tes megistes orges*); Lyc. 1.138 (*eschates orges dikaios*). Many other orators make similar comments: Lys. 6.2, 54–55; 29.9; Dem. 34.50–52; Lyc. 1.111; Din. 1.77.

Lysias (12.96) writes: "You should feel the same anger as when you were exiles." All the orators told very specific stories of punishment as well as offering the general injunctions to remember ancestors. E.g., Lys. 18.12–19; Dem. 18.204; 21.71–74; Din. 1.23–24. Thomas (1989) comes across references to past punishments of famous politicians as a "type so common that it forms a rhetorical topos."

15. See chapter 7, note 10 esp.

16. Blundell 1989, 1. Gernet (1984, 32) writes: "Dans la répression provoquée par les cas extremes, on reconnaît toujours la prédominance d'un élément passionnel qui ne laisse pas place à une pensée analytique."

17. L. Rubinstein (1993) argued that references to precedent occur in 49 out of 103 forensic speeches.

18. Worthington (1994, 109, citing Isoc. 4.9–10) points out that it is important for the orator to pick the right historical example.

19. Thomas (1995, 59–67) points out that those who had been memorizers in Crete, for instance, become writers: "Control over the community's past records (written and unwritten) was passed on when writing began to be used by the polis." For the definition of *nomos* and its development, see Shipp 1978; Meier 1990, 173–80; Hansen 1991a; Gregory 1991, 98–102. Cf. Ehrenberg (1946, 74–77) for a discussion of the meanings of *nomos, eunomia,* and *isonomia.* For the argument over the nature of the relationship between custom and written law captured by the word *nomos,* see Shipp 1978; Geschnitzer 1997, 10; and Triantaphyllopoulos 1975, 28–29.

20. On law as proof, see Lipsius 1915, 866–900; Harrison 1971, 134–35; Todd 1995, 58–60.

21. Aeschines (3.31) uses the standard formulation: "I am bringing as my witnesses, the laws, the decrees, and the defendants." Also Isae. 4.15–16, 31; 8.45; Dem. 50.3, 57.

Lipsius and Harrison find the idea strange, which Todd says is justifiable because the idea that law is a form of "proof" is "strange" in the contemporary Anglo-American/European context. See Mirhady 1991b for a discussion of the problem of *atechnai* proofs. In general, on law as proof see Bonner 1905; Lipsius 1915; Harrison 1971, 134–35. Todd 1990, 32; Carey 1994, 26.

22. Litigants pitted their laws against one another just as they pitted their witnesses against one another, and Isocrates argues thus against one opponent: "All the laws support my case; they can cite no law in their favor" (Isoc. 19.15).

23. Todd 1995, 59.

24. Cf. Dem. 18.210, 27.68, 41.25, 52.32, 58.65; Hyp. 3.13. In Dem. 43.71 we find this: "If they had offended the dead man only, jurors, by doing these things, they would have done fearfully, but to a lesser degree; but now they have offended the whole city and broken the laws. You will know this when you hear the law. Read the law."

25. MacDowell (1978, 242) takes essentially the same approach, arguing that the laws were "evidence of what conduct was right or wrong."

26. Similarly Isae. 1.39, 26; 2.26; Lyc. 1.10.

27. Todd 1995, 59.

28. E.g., Lys. 19.64; Isae. 4.31; Dem. 43.84, 48.58; Aes. 1.196, 3.260; Lyc.1.10. This is not exhaustive.

29. This analysis coincides with those of Todd and Harrison. Todd (1995, 50–52) asks: "How did the Athenian *dikastes* determine the law which he was to apply? what were the authoritative sources of law, and how did they relate to each other" He (1995, 53–60) takes up the question of the use of laws as evidence and follows Harrison (1971, 134–35): "His explanation is that the Athenian legal practice drew no clear distinction

between issues of fact and issues of law. Elsewhere (*JHS* 75, 26–35) he is probably closer to the underlying reason: "Statute law has only persuasive and not binding force on an Athenian court. . . . Statute law is seen by at least some litigants as a privilege to which they are entitled rather than as a duty that they had to obey. . . . The basis of judgment is the public concept of what is equitable."

30. Also Aes. 1.160–61: "And the lawgiver is right; for whoever, in his youth, strays away from his ambition to act nobly because of shameful pleasures, he thought it was necessary for him not to be enfranchised when older."

31. Cf. Lys. 9.8, 9, 22; Dem. 47.24.

32. MacDowell (1978, 60) disputes this arguing that every wrongdoing would have had to be brought to court under some legal, if very broad, rubric, such as "treason" or "deceiving the people," etc. But Lys. 31.27: "I hear that this one will say that if [his act] was a crime there should have been a law expressly against it"; Dem. 47.82, 48.58, 56.4. For a case where an Athenian orator tries to use law to establish whether prosecutors are bringing legally valid charges, see Hyp. 4.4.

33. Anger could overrule law even for the sake of an acquittal: "Do not, therefore, be led by anger to absolve the wrongdoer now here before you" (Lys. 6.42).

34. See Ant. 5.15; Isoc. 18.27–39; Dem. 19.283; 58.20, 24; Aes. 3.23.

35. Demosthenes is clearly scoring a rhetorical point here, but if it were the sin of all sins to ignore the laws, then he would not be able to score a rhetorical point by making this kind of argument. Cf. Lysias: "From these men, even if you were wishing to take justice unlawfully [*paranomos*], you would not take justice equivalent to the wrongs they did the city" (Lys. 12.82).

36. Cf. Isoc. 7.33; Lys. 22.2; Din. 1.17.

37. Abramson 1994, 12, 17.

38. Ibid., 12.

39. Ibid., 9.

40. Harris 1994a, 140. The word is used once in this sense, at Isoc. 7.33. Dover (1991, 179) makes an argument that the Athenians did specifically carry out *epieikeia* in courts, but his argument is based on Aristotle's *NE* 1143a19–24 and Plato's *Laws* 757e.

41. Paoli 1933, 72.

42. Humphreys (1991, 17) writing on Athens notes: "Law in practice, in societies that have not acquired the idea of judging by reference to a written code, is flexible and situational." Todd (1995) agrees with her reading of Athenian law as being influenced by such an approach and seconds her view that Athenian law is composed of "on the hoof response to perceived emergencies."

43. A point that Paul Cartledge has made to me in personal communications.

44. Barker 1951, 43.

45. Scholarship is divided on the question of whether Athens operated according to the "rule of law" with the laws superior to popular judgment or according to the superiority of popular judgment. The rule of law camp includes Barker 1951; Ostwald 1969, 98–102; Harris 1994a, 132; Gagarin 1986; Piérart 1987, 37; Sealey 1987, 146; Hansen 1991a, 174. Most recently, Boegehold (1996, 203–14) has argued for a deep legal conservatism in Athens, but he bases his case squarely on all the exceptional and atypical cases in the corpus (Lyc. 1; Dem. 24; Soph. *Ant*; Thuc., 3.37–40; Plato *Crito*). Scholars in this tradition have generally argued that the Athenians "held the rule of law in deep respect and adhered to a form of government that attempted to put that ideal in to practice."

. Among those who accept that the people were sovereign over the laws are Ruschenbusch 1957; Wolin 1994, 37; Murray 1995a, 39; Sinclair 1988; Farrar 1988, 13; Ober 1989a, 98, 301; Humphreys 1991, 17; Todd 1995, 60–63; Mossé 1995; Canfora 1995, 136–39; and Cohen 1995, who points out (34–35) that nobody has taken up the question of what rule of law is in the first place.

46. The phrase "use law" (as opposed to our "apply the law") occurs with some regularity in oratory. E.g., Dem. 20.9. Her[aclides] (*Exc.* 43 Di His.) remarks that the Lycians do not use laws, using the formulation: *nómois ou cherontai.*

47. Also Ant. 6.4–5; Aes. 3.107–21.

48. Din. 1.113.

49. See Ant.1.3, 4.1.7; Dem. 19.1; Aes. 2.184; Lyc. 1.93.

50. Dem. 58.56 (*oikoumene*); 59.115. See Szegedy-Maszak 1978, 199–210.

51. Dem. 21.44–45, 22.30–31, 24.116, 41.12, 42.31, 45.67, 46.12, 51.11, 54.28; but see Dem. 21.112, 123. See Finley (1983, 107) about equality.

52. For passages where law is especially linked to punishment, see Ant. 1.3–4; Isoc. 20.2–3, 19–20; Lys. 1.2; Isae. 9.35–36; Dem. 21.30; 22.30–32; 23.32; 24.215–17; 25.6, 27; 42.15; 54.17, 18; 57.30; 58.65. Several orators attribute to the laws the protection of the body: Isoc. 20.1; Aes. 1.4–5. Lysias (1.19, 26, 34, 35) discusses citizens as acting as representatives of the law. But for passages where law is said to have purposes distinct from punishment, see Lyc. 1.1.5, 93; Dem. 24.92 (provide the city with its strength), 106–116 (make people better), 191–3. Hyp. fr. 210, 213 (provide freedom); Hyp. 6.5. See also Isoc. 16.47.

53. For two additional relatively lengthy statements about law, see Dem. 42.1–2, 13; 59.86.

54. Hansen (1976, 144–52) deals with the authenticity of Demosthenes 25. He decides that rejection of the late fourth-century dating of the speech is unfounded but does not assign the speech to Demosthenes.

55. Demades (1.1) does describe the jury as a doctor that needs to do its examination carefully before prescribing, another remark in a late speech that is Platonic in tenor; interestingly, his formulation puts the jury in the position of the Platonic legislator.

56. Dem. 19.177 (*kurioi* over reward and punishment); 59.12.

57. Ant. 2.2.13; Din. 1.106–7.

58. Dem. 57.56.

59. The fact that this speech is a funeral oration might explain the greater emphasis on law.

60. See Barker 1951; Sinclair 1951; Klosko 1986.

61. It is worth noting that Aristotle (1286a30) focuses on *orge* during the course of this discussion.

62. Plato *Laws: akribeia* 628d, 720c, 762d, 768c, 768d, 769d, 783c, 793d, 807b, 807e, 818e, 838a, 855b, 859b, 867d, 902e, 919e, 930c, 964d, 967b; *Statesman* 295b.

63. On the subject of open texture in Athenian laws, see Harris 1994a, 150, n. 16; Ober 1989a, 144–45.

64. Harris 1994a, 138.

65. Aristotle (1273b30ff.) distinguishes between the person who is a legislator and creates a constitution, and the person who simply makes laws. See Keaney 1992, 39–41. See also, Arist. *Pol.* 1278b9, 1289a15; Plato *Laws* 735a, 751a, 768e; *Ep.* 7 330de, *Ep.* 8356d. Szegedy-Maszak (1978, 199–210) argues that legends of Greek lawgivers spring up late—toward the end of the democracy and after. See also Klosko 1986. 186.

66. For Aristotle's statement of the problem, see *Pol.* 1291b30: "But perhaps someone might say that in compensation for this a single ruler will decide better about particular

cases. Therefore it is clear that on the one hand the ruler must necessarily be a legislator, and that there must be laws laid down, although these must not be sovereign where they go astray—admittedly in all other cases they ought to be sovereign; on the other hand in matters that it is impossible for the law either to decide at all or to decide well. Ought the one best man to govern or all the citizens . . . doing nothing independently of the law except for on matters in regards to which the law must of necessity be deficient?"

67. Sinclair (1951, 179–84) and Ehrenberg (1965, 91–92) notice the importance of equity in Aristotle; see also Lévy 1993. Morrow (1971) points out that Plato's approach to law also required the invention of judicial appeal and suits for *damages* against judges. See Shiner 1987, 173–92 for the contrary view that Aristotle's concept of equity does not look like the modern legal concept. He argues that while Aristotle's concept of *epieikeia* may indeed look like the modern legal concept on its surface, Aristotle did not use a sufficiently concretized concept of law as to require equity.

68. See Sinclair 1951, 192; Klosko 1986, 194–97, 225–34; Barker 1951, 353–63.

69. Aristotle eventually drops the fourth of kind of regime from his analysis, leaving the three acceptable sorts for each type of rule. The disappearance of the fourth kind of democracy and oligarchy, and therefore of the distinction between constitutional and the nonconstitutional regimes, from the analysis that follows allows the distinctions between rule of one, few, and many, and between real cities and the ideal regime, to come to seem to be the most relevant distinctions among systems of government in the Aristotelian *schema*. In most political theory and writings on Plato and Aristotle, it is this distinction between rule of the one, few, and many (or virtuous, rich, and poor) that has primarily been considered. E.g., Barker 1951, 239–68.

70. Lévy (1993, 82) agrees, citing *Pol.* 2.12, 1273b32–33 and *Pol.* 4.6, 1292b25–27, 1293a9–10. Harris (1994a, 138) also agrees.

71. Williams 1982, 182.

72. The many appeals to Solon should be understood in this context; law was recognized as being a form of exceptionally good "opinion," like Solon's opinions. For a description of the appeals to the past as part of conservatism, see Finley 1975, ch. 2; 1983, 133. See also Hansen 1989.

73. On names as providing authority, see Lyotard and Thébaud 1996, 32–33.

74. See Hunter 1994, 56. See also Fisher 1976, 36–37. Blundell 1989, 38.

75. Stephen Todd has pointed out to me that procedural irregularities were involved as well.

76. Fisher (1992) points to Solon's invention of *ho boulomenos* and the *graphe hubreos* as measures intended precisely to restrain the wealthy. Demosthenes (21.44) makes a similar argument. They may well have been intended for such purposes, but whether they succeeded in restraining the elite is another matter. Plutarch (*Solon* 5), at least, seems to think that they did not. Indeed, it is a mistake to emphasize too strongly the role of the *graphe* and the public prosecutor as tools to help those who were too weak to help themselves. The victim, unless acting as the public prosecutor, did not usually receive compensation from a case, *graphe* or other, brought by a public prosecutor (Osborne 1985a, 49). Similarly, the action for *hubris* was always public, and the entire penalty went to the state (MacDowell 1978, 119–131). The *graphe, eisangelia*, and public prosecutor are more immediately the tools that ensure that the state may inflict justice and restore a disturbed balance and order, even if the wronged individual is willing to let a matter slide or to accept compensation out of court or in private arbitration.

77. See Ober 1989a, 327–35. Humphreys (1983a, 238) argues that the *graphe* forced the magistrate to carry out the case.

78. Gernet 1984, 33.

79. For the distinction between public and archival inscription, see Boegehold 1972, 26.

80. This fragment derives from ps.-Plutarch but, since it passes to him by way of Caecilius of Caleacte, is generally taken as genuine. Excerpts are included in *Minor Attic Orators*, vol. 1, ed. K. Maidment, Loeb Classical Library (Cambridge, Mass.: Harvard University Press, 1941).

81. Lyc. 1.117–18, 124, 126: "A pillar in the council chamber commemorates traitors and enemies of the democracy." Lycurgus refers to the same pillar as a *hupomnema*. Dem. 19.271: "The inscription stands right beside brazen Athena; justice was so great and punishment so *entimon* that the *timoriai* were honored with the same position as Pallas Athena's own prize of victory." Also, Din. 2.25 (*grapsantes diarreden*); And. 1.51, 78; Philokrates' confiscation inscription (I. 1749, *Hesp.* 5 [1936]: 393–413). Plut. *Mor.* 843b; Isoc. 16.9; Dem. 9.45. Cf. Aes. 3.258–60 (where a gold crown is the issue in memorialization).

82. Van Effenterre and van Effenterre (1994a, 90) discuss Detienne's contention that in regard to laws: "L'écriture les rend monumentale." The van Effenterres disagree in regard to Cretan laws because the laws were not displayed. But in relation to punishment in Athens, the point of the writing was precisely and explicitly that it be seen and its information remembered. Interestingly, Thomas (1994, 38) describes funerary legislation, contemporary to the arrival of the *graphe*, as evidence of the *polis*'s attempt to extend its control over memorials and memory. The *graphe* seems, indeed, to have been very relevant to that extension of control over public memory.

83. Public cases also made more frequent use of precedent and stories of past punishments, as Rubinstein (1993) pointed out.

84. See also Lys. 6.54; 22.19–22; 30.23–24.

85. E.g., Isoc. 18; 20.16–17; 21.18; Lys. 1.35, 47; 6.54–55; 12.5, 90–92; 14.12, 3, 22 (*kolazein*); 15.9–10; 22.5, 19–20, 45 (*kolazein*); 27.5 (*kolazein*); 28.16; 30.23 (*kolazein*); Dem. 19.105, 232, 270, 284–85, 343; 21.37, 124–25, 227; 22.68; 23.99; 24.143; 34.51–52; 35; 36; 37; 38; 42.15; 45.87; 50.66–67; 51.12; 56.48; 59.77; Aes. 1.89–91. I treat *paragraphai* (Dem. 34, 35, 36, 37, 38; Isoc. 18) as public cases, because although they arise only out of private matters in our extant sources, the *paragraphe* itself concerns the proper use of public institutions and laws and any fine imposed goes to the state. The procedure was introduced in order to sustain the amnesty, and so it seems appropriate to treat it as public (MacDowell 1978, 214–20). (Dem. 33 is a *paragraphe* but it includes no arguments about deterrence or treating the defendant as an example.) I have also treated an antidosis case as public (Dem. 42). Lysias 1 is a private case, but the concepts of deterrence are mobilized not in relation to the defendant's own case but in relation to an adulterer's earlier wrongdoing, with which the speaker is specifically trying to argue that he has dealt in a "public" way; the arguments about deterrence contribute to his unusual rhetorical effort. Dem. 56 and Isoc. 20.16–17 are both private cases in which there is also a public fine, for which fact I classify them as public.

The two exceptions to the rule that arguments about deterrence are made only in public cases are Dem. 50, a private case concerning the performance of trierachies, where the charges are private (*egklemata idia*) but the injuries are common (*koinai*): "If I had come to you arguing with Polycles over some contract or other, the contest would just be between me and Polycles" (Dem. 50.1); and Dem. 54.43, a private case for assault where the prosecutor spends a good deal of time telling his audience that his case could have been a public case. *Paradeigma*: e.g., Dem. 19.105; 21.124, 227; 22.68; 45.87; Aes. 1.89.

86. It should be noted that scholars are uncertain whether this case is a private case or a *graphe hubris*.

87. Harrison 1971, 75; Dem. 21.42–43; 46.26.

88. Ant. 4.3.6, 7. In Antiphon's formulation of disease and remedy, the criminal is a defilement to the city, and the punishment of the criminal cleanses the city (Ant. 2.1.3, 2.1.10–11, 2.3.10–11, 3.1.2, 3.3.11–12). Elsewhere, it remedies (*iatrous genesthai*) the trouble of the prosecutor (Ant. 2.2.13); and the innocent are called clean (*katharon*) (Ant. 4.4.10–11); or a wrongdoer is cleansed (Ant. 6.4–5). Four orators describe punishment as cleansing. The first two attach punishment to retribution and deterrence again: "It required my shame to cure [*iathenai*] Athens" (And. 2.9). Elsewhere, we have: "Now it is necessary to think that in punishing Andocides and being rid of him, you cleanse the city; you are escorting out of the city and sending away a *pharmakos*" (Lys. 6.53). Dem. 25 and 26 treat the wrongdoer as needing to be cleaned. Cf. Aes. 2.148; Dem. 37.59; 47.70; Din. 1.16.

89. Thomas (1989) offers a general discussion of how the democratic institutions propagated an official tradition and democratic theory. Cohen (1989b, 103) argues that definitions of offense existed in the collective consciousness as manifested in jurors and their decisions, which in turn continually redefined offenses.

90. Aes. 3.252 and Lyc. 1.52 also refer to the same story.

91. Some scholars have suggested that the mutilation of the herms should be understood this way as well.

CHAPTER NINE
EXECUTION

1. Scarry 1987, 128 (the text is italicized in Scarry's original).

2. Gernet 1981e, 240.

3. Hdt. 7.33; Plut. *Per.* 28.3; Dem. 21.105 (*monon ou proselosthai*); Ar. *Kn.* 1362–63 (*ek tou laruggos ekkremasas*); Ar. *Wealth* 465–76 (*tumpana kai kuphones*). Another aspect of punishment that people have been interested in is the description of the wrongdoer as seated. See *Dict. Antiq.* IV., figs. 5801–3; Aes. *PB* 1; *Ath. Pol.* 45.1; Dem. 21.105; Lucian *D. Decr.* 1.1; Aned. Bekk. I., p. 219.

4. Keramopoullos 1923, 13; Hunter 1994, 176–80; Todd 1997a.

5. Keramopoullos 1923, 13.

6. In some cases it is impossible to tell whether the phrase means execution or exhibition: Ar. *Eq.* 367–69, 375, 388, 705, 1049 (*desai s' ekeleus' en pentesurrigoi xuloi*).

7. Dem. 24.105, 146; Ar. *Thes.* 930–46. In other cities, Arist. *Pol.* 1306b1–5; Xen. *Hell.* 3.3.11. For this punishment in general: Dem. 24.105, 113, 353; also Lys. 10.15–16. I am not taking these passages as exhaustive of the issue of theft. For a thorough treatment of the issue of theft, see Cohen 1983, esp. 40–44, 63–67.

8. On the *podokakke* in particular, see *Nomographus* fr. 4.24–26 (Solon fr. West); Hyp. 3(5).8.4–8; Plut. *Sol.* 21.4–5.

9. Keramopoullos 1923.

10. As Todd 1997a points out, Mnesilochus is treated and behaves as if he is going to die (Ar. *Thes.* 938, 942, 1098–1135).

11. See Arist. *Rhet.* 2.5.14, 1383a where it is implied that those who are on the *apotumpanismos* (*hoi apotumpanizomenoi*) will not be alive on the morrow.

12. Ar. *Kn.* 1045–49; *Lys.* 679–80. See also Pollux 8.72, 102. Hunter (1994, 176–80) argues that the four-holed and five-holed wood are the stocks or *podokakke*; Gernet (1924, 294–95) argues instead that this refers to the *apotumpanismos*.

13. I argue later that the *barathron* and *orugma* were not used for precipitation but only for the disposal of the corpses of criminals.

14. Dem. 21.95, 22.30.

15. Dem. 21.95, 24.186.

16. Ant. 5.4; Lys. 13.79; Dem. 24.181, 59.86.

17. See Hansen 1976, 55–89. Rhill (1991, 111–12) disputes that there was a change in *atimia* from outlawry to loss of rights.

18. Athenians were protected against imprisonment when they traveled to foreign cities (*IG* ii^2 32.9; 385.4).

19. In general on penalties, see Thonissen 1875; Hager 1879; Glotz 1904a; 1904b; 1929; Lipsius 1915; Gernet 1924; 1955; 1981d; 1981e; 1982; 1984; Harrison 1968; 1971; MacDowell 1978, Hansen esp. 1975; 1976; 1981; Cantarella 1991; Todd 1995; Hunter 1994; Debrunner Hall 1996. On *ataphia,* see Gernet 1924; 1984; Parker 1983; Connor 1985. On house razing, see Connor 1985. On imprisonment, see Barkan 1935; Harrison 1971; Todd 1995; Allen 1997. On *atimia*, see Hansen 1975; Gernet 1924, 294–95; 1982, 11–13; Rhill 1991; Todd 1995, 142. Todd argues that there was no *atimia* for women. But they could be kept out of religious spaces for certain wrongs even if this is never explicitly referred to as *atimia* (Dem 59.87). On *atimia* for children, see Glotz 1904a; Adkins 1972, 43–44; Gernet 1984, 26.

Apotumpanismos: Lys. 13. 55–68 (three cases); Hdt. 7.33, 9.120.4; Arist. *Rhet.* 2.6.27, 1385a10–13; Dem. 21.104–5; *Ath. Pol.* 45.1. References to the hypothetical use of the *apotumpanismos*: Dem. 8.61, 9.61, 10.63, 19.37.

Hemlock: And. 3.10; Lys. 12.17, 96; 18.24, 30; Plato *Phaedo* 116d, 117a-b; Xen. *Hell.* 2.3.54–56; *Apo.* 7.

Stoning: Xen. *Ana.* 5.7, 7.6.10; Hdt. 9.5, 120; Lyc. 1.122; Dem. 18.204.

Sword: Xen. *Hell.* 2.4.26, 3.1.27, 5.1.34, 5.4.14, 6.5.25, 7.4.26; also, Lys. 13.78; Dem. 23.169. An Athenian reference (Dem. 24.139–40) to death by cord (*brochos*) (hanging, presumably) details a Locrian punishment.

Death without *ataphia* for *hierosulia*, traitors, adulterers, and murderers: Xen. *Mem* 1.2.62; Isoc. 20.6; Lyc. 1.65; *IG* i^3 14(= *IG* i^2 10).

Death with *ataphia*: Xen. *Hell.* 1.7.22; Lys. 1.50; Dem. 24.7; Lyc. 1.24, 45, 78, 91, 121, 131, 150; Aes. 3.252; Hyp. 1.20; 3.14, 18, 32–37; 4.18; Din. 1.77. (Some of these cases also include confiscation.)

Confiscation: Dem. 20.40; 22.54–57; 24.50; 47.44; 49.45, 50, 165; 53.27, 2, 28; Xen. *Hell.* 2.3, 1.7; And 1.96; Plut. *Ant.* 834a; Hdt. 6.121; Krateros *FGH* 342F17; Poll. 10.97.

Atimia: And. 1.73; Dem. 23.37, 80; Aes. 3.244; Dem. 21.95; 22.30; 24.186, 181; 59.86; Lys. 13.79; Ant. 5.4.

Death and confiscation: Lys. 18.9, 12–15; 19.31–32 (but in each of these cases confiscation followed as a separate penalty).

Confiscation and *atimia*: Dem. 59.52; *IG* ii^2 43; 125.10ff.

Atimia for children: Ant. fr. b.1.2; And. 1; Isoc. 16.3; Isae. 10.17; Lys. 25.27; Dem. 23.62, 26.11, 57.27, 58.17; *Ath. Pol.* 16.10; *IG* i^3 14; 46.

Death, house razing, and *atimia* for children: Isoc. 16.26; scholia on Ar. *Lys.* 273 and on *Lys.* 313; *FGH* 342f5; ps.-Plut. *Mor.* 834; Lyc. 1.117, 129.

20. For prosecutors watching executions, see Dem. 23.69; Aes. 2.181–2.20. On the Eleven, see Harrison 1968, 17, 150. On the *demios* or *demokoinos*, see MacDowell 1978, 254; Jacob 1979, 81–82. See also Soph. fr. 780; Ant. 1.20; Isoc. 17.15; Lys. 13.56, 22.2; Aes. 1.16; Din. 2.13; *Ath Pol.* 29.4; Plato *Rep.* 443a; *Laws* 987e.

21. The treasury collectors, *kolastai*, citizens who were probably chosen by lot, kept track of all the fines produced by the various *archai*, and could initiate exaction or allow remittance. They maintained the *stelai*, available to public view, on which the names of public debtors were inscribed and scratched out on payment. Despite the power that these officials had, it seems that before the official collecting mechanism could go into motion, those who actually participated in the suit had to inform the Eleven or *kolastai* that their opponent had been found guilty (Dem. 24.196, 58.20). For private action in the context of arbitration, see And. 1.87; Dem. 36.14–16, 37.1.

22. See Hunter 1994.

23. On *praktores* and *dike exoules*, see Harrison 1971; Hunter 1994; Todd 1995, 144.

24. *Atimia* lasted forever if it was punishment in its own right, or until one had paid one's fines, if one were *atimos* for having failed to answer to a monetary punishment.

25. *hupomemneke*: Ant. fr. *App* B; And. 1.51; Dem. 19.27, 24.41; Din. 2.25; Aes. 3.258.

26. E.g., Dem. 20.64. See Hyp. fr. b19(79), b23(118).

27. See Steiner 1994, 105ff., about "reading the man."

28. See Adkins 1972, 43–44; Gernet 1984, 26.

29. Dem. 45.81. See Pollux 8.109, 9, 10. See Dem. 23.69 where the prosecutor is allowed to watch an execution.

30. On landmarks, see D. G. Burnett forthcoming.

31. Demosthenes makes the assembly the site to remember: "And you all saw last year the man arrested out of the assembly by the *thesmothetai*" (Dem. 23.32). Andocides also shows us how places could function as memorials by telling us about the opposite— a case where a place does not, in fact, memorialize any wrongs done. He says: "No one ever, while passing our house, was reminded of having suffered a wrong, whether private or public, done by those of this house" (And. 1.147).

32. Lys. 6.44: "They will be regarded as wicked and impious persons at home even if abroad they should have all their rights as citizens." See Aes. 1.149; Din. 1.58.

33. See Harrison 1971, 171. See also Dem. 21.83–88, 23.44, 33.12.

34. See also Ant. 5.13.

35. Lys. 3.10: "I took the boy and left the city after I thought that enough time had passed for Simon to forget." Wolpert (1995) points out that "forgetting" is not the opposite of "remembering" but only a particular form of "remembering."

36. Ostracism, which expelled those whose reputations were perhaps too great, inverted the paradigm.

37. Wolpert 1995.

38. Girard 1992.

39. Barkan 1935, 54ff., 92. Precipitation: *Il.* 814; Eur. *IT* 1420; *Tr.* 725; Ar. *Frogs* 574; *Clouds* 1450; *Wealth* 31; Thuc. 2.67.4; Plato *Gorg.* 516e. Stoning: *Il.* 3.56–58; *Od.* 16.424–27; Aes. *Ag.* 1611–16; *SAT* 181–99; Soph. *Aj.* 228, 254–59, 728; *Ant.* 31–36; *OC* 421–36; Eur. *Troj. Wom.* 1036–42; *Ion* 1111–12, 1222–25, 1238–41; *Or.* 46–51, 57–59, 442–44, 614, 730–35, 836–65, 907–14, 946–49; *IA* 1350; *IT* 260–400; *Bacch.* 352–57; *COH* 55–60; Ar. *Achar.* 281, 318.

40. Eur. *Or.* 57. In two cases, those instigating the stoning do so in order that the person stoned will be displayed (Xen. *Ana.* 7.6.10; Hdt. 9.120). Xenophon (*Ana.* 5.7)

describes the mob as seeing and setting upon its prey: "They rushed upon him as though a wild boar or a stag had been sighted."

41. See Xen. *Ana.* 6.6.9–12; Soph. *Aj.* 228; Eur. *Or.* 730, 871.

42. Lane and Lane (1994) discuss the spatial metaphor of the center of the people and the form of power involved. See Vernant (1969, 159–81) on the symbolic meanings of circular space. Padel (1995, 102), in discussing madness, describes stoning as marking what was impure within the community or a threat to the community. Cantarella (1991, 80–84) treats a stoning as an act of expiation.

43. Bartsch (1994) drew these connections.

44. Gernet (1982, 11) identifies rock sites near Delphi and near Olympia as having been used for precipitation and makes a case that precipitation was like an ordeal where anyone who did not die upon hitting the rocks was acquitted. "Il y a ici une pensée de devotio, de consécration du coupable aux puissances divines." Pliny (*NH* 4.26.12) attributed precipitation to the Hyperboreans; Strabo (3.3.7) attributed it to the Lusitanians and to the Leukadians (10.2.9).

45. See Eur. *El.* 1270–72, where it is suggested that the Eumenides have their home in this chasm.

46. E.g., Dem. 23.44; 36.59; 38.20; Lyc. 1.129, 133. The word *elauno* appears in the context of a thief in Ar. *Achar.* 1188; in the contest of *miasma* in Aes. *Choe.* 976; *Eum.* 283; and in the context of *agos* in Thuc. 1.126.

47. Seaford 1990. Such imprisoned women of myth include Antigone (who compares herself to Danae and Cleopatra); Arsinoe, daughter of Oinomaos; Hypermestra in myth of Danaids; Sophocles' Tyro; Euripides' Alope, Antiope, Melanippe the Prisoner, and Karya. According to Seaford (1990), citing the Stith Thompson motif-index of folk literature (1989), seclusion of a daughter for the sake of her chastity is a motif that appears in myths and folktales worldwide. Detienne and Vernant (1978, 86–98) consider binding to be isomorphic with womb and tomb imagery.

48. Seaford 1990, 82.

49. Also, Poseidon buries his sons in the earth for raping their mother. Vernant (1969, 97–158) discusses the ways in which the contrast between the inside as female and the outside as male is not always perfectly observed.

50. Cantarella 1991, 27.

51. Parker 1983, 225–27.

52. Parker 1983, 229–30. For *ekpempo* as used for pollution, see Aesch. *Choe.* 98; Soph *OT* 194–97; Aelian *VH* 14.7. Also *Il.* 1.314; Paus. 2.31.8, 8.41.2.

53. For descriptions of *oxuthumia* and house purifications, see Harpocration s.v. and *Et. Magn* s.v.; Theophr. *Char.* 16.7. For sacred laws restricting where they might be thrown out, LSCG 108; *IG* I³ 257 = LSS 4. See Paus. 5.5.10.

54. Girard 1992, 10–38, 68–88.

55. Scarry 1987.

56. E.g., Xen. *Hell.* 2.4.26, 3.1.27, 5.1.34, 5.4.14, 6.5.25, 7.4.26; also, Lys. 13.78; Dem. 23.169.

57. Hdt. 9.5; Lyc. 1.122; Dem. 18.204.

58. Todd (1997, 3) also points out that the punishments were bloodless. Barkan (1935, 64) suggests that the Athenians avoided swords because they loathed the sight of blood.

59. Girard (1992, 38) discusses the danger of blood in the context of wrongdoing and its punishment.

60. In this context, the avoidance of bloodshed might also be an avoidance of impure blood, the blood of sacrificial animals being unpolluted. See Cole 1996, 227–48, and

Gernet 1981c, 167–201, on the importance of knives to courtroom sacrifices and on sacrificial knives as being buried in the ground to make a pledge eternal. See also Girard 1992. See Aes. 3.110–11; Isae. 5.32, 12.9; Dem. 29.26, 33, 56; 39.3–4; 40.210–11; 55.27.

61. For the torture of slaves, judicial and punitive, see Ant. 1.20; Isoc. 17.11–17, 21–22, 49; Dem. 45.61; 46.21; 47.5–17, 35–40; 48.14–18; 52.22; 53.22–25; 54.27–30; 59.120–25; Lyc. 1.28–35, 16–18. For blows, see Dem. 53.16. For the mill, see Lys. 1.18; Dem. 45.33. For the whip, see Aes. 1.35; Xen. *Mem.* 2.1; *IG* ii^2 1362 (Stroud 1974, 158 at lines 30–32). For the general physical abuse of slaves, see, e.g., Ant. 1.20; Lys. 4.10; Dem. 54.4. For all their power over slaves, the citizens did occasionally restrain one another and put limits on one another's punishment of slaves: Dem. 19.197; Ant. 5.69, 48.

62. Hunter (1994, 154, 173–80) discusses the decree ending torture for citizens. See And. 1.43; Lys. 4.14; 13.27, 59; Plut. *Mor.* 509a–c.

63. Several stories show up in military contexts where a punishment is carried out precisely in order to torture (Hdt. 9.120; Dem. 23.169. See Polyb. 2.60.8).

64. Lys. 1.49; Dem. 59.66. For other references to the punishment of adulterers, see Isae. 8.44; Lys. 1.49; Xen. *Mem.* 2.1.5.

65. Cohen 1985, 385–87; Roy 1991, 73–76. Ar. *Clouds* 1083–84 (radishing and depilation); *Wealth* (depilation); *Achar.* 849; Pl. Com., fr. 189 PCG (*Phaon*); Diog. Laert. 2.128; *AP* 9.520; Lucian *De Morte Peregrina*; Alciphron 3.26.4 (= 3.62). Cf. Catullus 15.19; Juvenal 10.137.

66. For military officials, see Xen. *Ana.* 7.6.9–12; *Hell.* 2.4.26. For the mob, see Xen. *Ana.* 5.7.20–30; *Hell.* 1.11.13.

67. Carey 1993, 53–55.

68. See Bain 1991, 53, on euphemism. See Xen. *Mem.* 2.1.5.

69. See also Halliwell 1991a, 280–89; 1991b.

70. The Loeb editor takes this comment to mean, "You all know what radishes are like since we eat them." But the radish is the only plant that receives this sort of commentary during the course of a long discussion of plants, many of which were eaten by the Greeks.

71. See Stroud 1974, 158 at lines 30–32, for an example in which a slave is whipped and a citizen is fined for the same wrongdoing.

72. Todd forthcomimg.

73. For the *apotumpanismos* used in Athens, see Lys. 13.54–56, 66–68, 82–97 (three cases). For when it was almost used, see *Ath. Pol.* 45.1; Dem. 21.104–5. For its use outside Athens, see Hdt. 7.33, 9.120.4; Arist. *Rhet.* 2.6.27 (1385a10–13). As a hypothetical penalty, Dem. 8.61, 9.61, 10.63, 19.137.

74. Todd 1997.

75. For the torture of citizens, see And. 2.15; Lys. 6.27; 13.25, 59–60 (where the torture victim was born a slave); Dem. 18.132–33 (where the torture victim was not a citizen when tortured); Plut. *Phoc.* 35. For the torture of free noncitizens: Din. 1.63; Anaximenes 16.1 (14.8–17.2); Plut. *Nicias.* 30; *De Garr* 13; see Aes. 3.223–24.

76. I think that the uses of parallel verbal forms joined by a *kai* in both of these sentences is a more than strong indicator that the two actions are carried out sequentially and are not two ways of describing the same action.

77. For *ataphia* for traitors and temple robbers, see Xen. *Hell.* 1.7.22. See also Lys. 1.50; Dem. 24.7; Lyc. 1.24, 45, 78, 91, 121, 131, 150; Aes. 3.252; Hyp. 1.20; 3.14, 18, 32–37; 4.18; Din. 1.77. See Segal 1981, 173–76, on tragic violation of rites of burial and

Parker 1983, 46 on *ataphia* in general. Gernet (1981e) thought that the *barathron* (which he understood as being used for precipitation) was used for crimes against religion and against the state.

78. On burial, see Kurtz and Boardman 1971; Morris 1992.

79. Parker 1983, 46, 47.

80. Connor 1985, 79–102.

81. Ibid. For the *ataphia* and razing of the supporters of King Cleomenes of Sparta, see scholia Ar. *Lys.* 313. For *ataphia*, razing, and *stelai* of Phrynichus, Antiphon, and Archeptolemus, see *FGH* 342f5; ps.-Plut. *Mor.* 834.

82. See also Lyc. 1.129 who describes the same story.

83. For the *barathron*, see Hdt. 7.133; Ar. *Wealth.* 574; Xen. *Hell.* 1.7.20; Plato *Gorg.* 516e; Com. Adesp. Nov. (*Comicorum Graecorum Fragmenta*, Austin. 253.10); Sch. Ar. *Wealth* 431. For the word as metaphor, see Dem. 8.45; 25.77. For the *orugma*, see Lyc. 1.121 (*paradounai toi epi tou orugmatos*); Din. 1.62–63 (*tethnasi kata son psephisma duo ton politon, pater kai huios, paradothentes toi epi toi orugmati*). For later references and references to non-Athenian *barathra* and nonpunitive *barathra*, see Arist. *Pr.* 947a19; Aned. Bekk. I, p. 219; Harpocration, *Suidas*; Plut. *Ant.* 834a. For references to precipitation that do not have to do with the *barathron* in Athens, see Aes. 2.142; Dem. 19.327; Paus. 4.18.4, 10.42 (Delphi); Plut. *De Sera* 12.555a; Ael. *VH* 12.18; Serv. ad. Virg. *Aen.* 3.275; Or. *Her.* 15; Hesych. s.v. See Plut. *Praec. Reip. Ger.* 825b; *Pollux* 8, 102.

84. Barkan 1935, 54–57; Gernet 1968, 184; 1981d; 1982, 27; Cantarella 1991, 85. Barkan and Gernet think that precipitation did not occur in the fourth century. *Contra* are Todd 1995, 141; Thonissen 1875; MacDowell 1978, 254. See Parker 1983, 170.

85. See text but also Hdt. 7.133: *embalontes es to barathron*; Thuc. 1.134.4: *es esballein*; Plato *Gorgias* 516e: *eis to barathron embalein epsephisanto*; Ar. *Wealth.* 431: *ek pases me choras ekbalein / oukoun hupoloipon to barathron soi gignetai* (see 1099–1116); Ar. *Frogs* 574: *es to barathron embaloimi se*; Ar. *Clouds* 1450: *embalein es to barathron*; Com. Adesp. Nov. (*Comicorum Graecorum Fragmenta*, Austin. 253.10): *eis to barathron embalein . . .* ; Plut. *Arist.* 3: *eis to barathron embaloien*; Plut. *Them.* 22: *ta somata ton thanatoumenon proballousi*; Thucydides (1.126.12) makes a distinction between driving out the living (*elaunontes tous te zontas*) and throwing out the bones of the dead (*anelontes exebalon ta osta*).

The idea that the word *rhipto* is used for living creatures is supported by the two non-Athenian tales where the word *barathron* (or an analogue) does appear in the context of precipitation, but in both cases the context is mythic rather than historical. In Homer's *Iliad* Zeus threatens to hurl (*rhipso*) any disobedient god into the deepest chasm beneath the earth (*hechi bathiston hupo chthonos esti berethron*) or Tartarus. The gods, of course, would be living when flung down to the netherworld that is lower, even, than Hades. Also, in Pausanias (4.18–19), a Messenian is said to be thrown alive into the Spartan *barathron* and the verb is *rhipto*. The story is a story of a miracle and so scarcely to be taken as historically valid.

86. See Whitehorne 1989, 90–92.

87. For further argument on the text of Xenophon, see appendix D.

88. Keramopollous 1923 agrees.

89. Ober 1987, 205.

90. Wycherly 1978, 269. Daremberg and Saglio 1875 makes the same identification.

91. Peters 1995, 7. Judging from Herz and Waelkens (1988, 1–9, 15) and Dworakowska (1975), there would have been several deep former quarries available to

the Athenians in the fifth and fourth centuries to use as prisons, execution pits, and burial pits. While the Spartans did not use quarries, they did, as we have seen, use a natural chasm as a place to expose the bodies of wrongdoers unburied, but they also used the same chasm or caves connected to it, all produced by an earthquake, as a prison, and Strabo (8.5.7) moves from a discussion of these caves or prisons to a discussion of quarries, as if the one subject leads to the next.

92. Bekker, *Anecdota Graeca* i.219 locates the pit in the deme Keiriadai. The only other piece of information about the location is a scholion on Aristophanes' *Wealth* (431) and Suidas (s.v. *metragurtes*). A scholiast to Aristophanes thought that there was a *barathron* near the Areopagus until the mid-fifth century, when, he says, that the Athenians are said to have filled it in and built the *metroon* and *bouleuterion* above it.

93. Seneca *Epistle* 95, sec. 33. See Bartsch 1994, ch. 2; Foucault 1991.

94. Foucault 1991, 8.

95. Ibid., 109.

96. Another change involves severity. By the fourth century, Draco of the seventh century was reputed to have punished nearly everything with death, and the Athenian punitive system was represented as having become more moderate. Arist. *Pol.* 1274b15–19; Plut. *Sol.* 17. See also Ehrenberg 1973, 57; Stanton 1990, 30–33.

97. Judging from the famous scene on the Shield of Achilles in the *Iliad*, money was involved in punitive exchanges in Homer, though it is impossible to ascertain whether as payment to the judges or as penalty. For discussion of the shield scene in relation to punishment, see Bonner and Smith 1930, 19; Starr 1961, 131; Gagarin 1974; MacDowell 1978, 20; Thür 1996.

98. On the difference between money and coinage, see Millett 1991, 36–37; von Reden 1995, 149–58, 171–76.

99. Thomas 1989, 41. The earliest written contract is attested in Isoc. 17.20 from the first decade of the fourth century.

100. See note 21.

101. See Ober 1989a.

102. See Garnsey 1970, 104–50.

103. Thalheim, in Pauly-Wissowa, s.v. *desmoterion*; R. Dareste [de la Chavanne] 1976, 85; Gilbert 1968, 414. But Thonissen (1875, 114–20) did accept imprisonment.

104. Scholars have usually taken imprisonment to be an additional penalty on the basis of *Ath. Pol.* 67.5.2 but the text does not support the argument. Other forms of penalty that are called additional penalties in this passage (e.g. fines) could also be used as full penalties (e.g., Dem. 21.44, where an additional penalty is monetary).

105. Barkan 1935, 1936. But Harrison (1971, 177) in his appendix discusses and accepts the use of imprisonment as a penalty. See Boegehold 1995, 28; Todd 1995, 140–41. Todd thinks that the use of penal imprisonment is unlikely but writes: "Dem. 25.60–62 implies that on occasion the prison could be moderately full, and it seems unlikely that all these prisoners were simultaneously on remand." Hunter (1994, 144) left the question at issue. See Allen 1997.

106. *Deo* is common already in Homer and used with reference to the binding of horses, wounds, people, and ships. The -*terion* ending (in a different context) appears only once in Homer and once in Hesiod, becoming frequent, however, in the fifth and fourth centuries (Buck and Petersen 1944, esp. 43–47). Other words for "prison" are *heirgmos*, *oikema*, and *keramon*. In late Greek the word *phulake* is also used for "prison." Interestingly, the *Prometheus Bound*, a play that explores the concept of imprisonment as a penalty, was roughly contemporaneous to the construction of the prison,

and writers in later centuries associated the story of Prometheus with the *desmoterion*. Radt 1985, Aes. fr. 202a, concerning *Prometheus Luomenos*. The fragment derives from Philodem. *De Piet. Pap.* Hercul. 1088 III 18. In fr. 204a, from *Prometheus Purkaeus* (The Fire-Kindler), the word fragment *-erion* appears; it is usually restored as *desmoterion*. If the restoration is correct, this is the first instance of the word in our extant sources.

107. Demosthenes (24.146, 151) also uses the verb *dedesthai* to refer to being in prison. See Thuc. 4.41, where the Athenians are said to have bound (*dedesthai*) 292 Spartans but then later the Athenians threaten to "bring out" (*exago*) these Spartans and kill them. The word *exago* suggests that the Spartans were not only fettered but were in fact enclosed somewhere. If that is the case, then the Athenians were able to imprison as many as 300 people at once.

108. Translation from Gagarin and Woodruff 1995.

109. See Thuc. 4.38.5, 4.41.1, 5.18.7, 7.87; Lys. 9.5.3.

110. Todd 1995, 140–41. Mentions of lengthy terms in prison are found at Dem. 24.125, 135; 25.61; Din. 2.2.

111. Thucydides leaves open the possibility that the Athenians may have been able to imprison 292 Spartans (4.41). In Arcadia during a period of stasis in 363, most of the aristocrats from all the region's cities were thrown into prison in the city of Tegea (Xen. *Hell.* 7.4.36). In that case, the prison *desmoterion* was soon full and the public hall (*demosia oikia*) had to be used. Thus, we know that the city of Tegea had a prison and only one prison, but that between the prison and the public hall there was room enough for a large number (*pollous*) of aristocrats from the area. The prison played a part during a period of stasis at Thebes as well, according to Xenophon. The prisoners were let out and armed by one party, providing a force sufficient in number for the party using them to claim its rule in the city (*Hell.* 5.4.8). And in another case (Xen. *Hell.* 5.4.14), we are told that 150 men were released from prison. Aristotle (*Rhet.* 1375a6) describes the Argives as punishing the wrongdoer whose deed forces the city to build a new prison or to make a new law; the implication is that punishing the criminal would require a new prison, an unlikely scenario if prisons are being used only to hold people on remand.

112. Vanderpool (1976, 87) has identified the Poros building in the Agora as "the prison of Socrates" and argues that it was remodeled at the end of the fifth or beginning of the fourth century and again at the end of the fourth century. I do not accept the argument that this building was necessarily "the prison of Socrates" or the argument that it had to be "*the* prison in Athens." But I do accept the argument that this building is of such structure and stone as mark it as a public building and that, of public buildings, it is unique in ways that would befit *a* prison. The argument for the use of imprisonment as a penalty in no way stands or falls on the status of the building. It is worth keeping in mind that the Athenians, like the Spartans and Romans, may well have used quarries or chasms for their prisons. We know that Syracusan prisoners were enclosed (*eirgmenoi*) in a stone quarry in the Piraeus (Xen. *Hell.* 1.1.14). See notes 71 and 72.

113. E.g., Harrison 1971, 177; Barkan 1936, 338–41. Todd (1995, 140) points out that Socrates does this in a piece of fiction.

114. Todd (1995, 140) points out that this is a contingent penalty rather than one proposed in *timesis* and resulting from trial. What matters, however, is simply that imprisonment, as opposed to, say, *atimia*, was proposed as a penalty.

115. MacDowell (1962, appendix d) considers this passage (and the implication of what follows it, that Andocides had a lengthy stay in prison) in comparison with Andocides' own claim (1.64) that he was only in prison for a day as a result of this matter. MacDowell comes to the conclusion that the stories (Lys. 6.21–24, Plut. *Alk.* 21.4–6) of

the friendships that Andocides makes in prison and the denunciations that he makes in order to get out of prison justify accepting that Andocides did have a long stay in prison and lied in his own speech.

116. *katagignoskein thanaton*: Ant. 5.47; And. 1.79 (although this passage is much disputed); Lyc. 1.93; Din. 2.8; 3.21; Hyp. 2.8, *katagignoskein desmon*: And. 4.3–5, 27; 2.16; Dem. 24.12.

117. For other references to prisons, see Hdt. 4.146, 7.96, 139; Lys. 6.21; 13.65; Dem. 25.60–62; 58.6–11; *Ep.* 3.4; Ar. *Frogs* 618; *Eccl.* 1093–94; Strabo 8.5.7 (C367). In Rome, punishments that were handed out in jury courts were allotted specifically according to the crime and status of the defendant, and legal punishments included death, outlawry, monetary fines, torture, and forced labor. The *carcer* was used for those awaiting trial and those awaiting execution. *Custodia* (detention) could also be applied based on a magistrate's power of coercion to prevent trouble. Where *custodia* did become a matter of punishment, it seems to have resulted from the extension of preventative detention and the discretion of *cognitio* judges who could penalize as they wished. Simple imprisonment, however, was never legally recognized as a punishment (Strachan-Davidson 1969, 165; Garnsey 1970, 103, 147–54; Greenridge, 1901, 514–16). In both seventeenth-century England and the American colonies (which, it is worth remembering, were probably comparable to city-states in size for some time), very minimal systems of penal imprisonment functioned and usually arose from systems of debt imprisonment (on the colonies, see Friedman 1993, 48–50).

118. Imprisonment is frequently associated with hunger (e.g., Aes. *Ag.* 820, 1639–42). Several statements in various sources indicate that a city might not always feed its prisoners sufficiently but left them to fend for themselves. In this vein, the Athenian Stranger in Plato's *Laws* (909) wishes to have a prison in Magnesia where strict rationing would lead to death. Whether the same occurred in prisons in Athens is impossible to tell, although the fourth-century comedian Alexis (fr. 220–21.10) refers to a daily prison diet (*diaitan desmoteriou*) as consisting of one clean wheat cake and one cup of water. Creon leaves Antigone only enough food to live for a short while (Soph. *Ant.* 775). In the American colonies at least, debt prisoners had to supply themselves with their own food and in some cases were allowed out of prison to go begging provided that they did not "go out of bounds" or stray more than a certain distance from the prison building, where they had to spend the night (Friedman 1993, 48–49). (Athenian prisoners could apparently be let out too sometimes: Dem. *Ep.* 3.16; Stanford 1983, 14.) The Athenians sometimes treated a prison sentence as potentially a protracted death sentence. A set of surrendering soldiers stipulate, as terms of their surrender, that they not die by imprisonment (Thuc. 7.82.2–3). Ste. Croix (1983, 460, 488) describes the conditions of a Roman *carcer* as dire and frequently causing death.

119. E.g., Dem. *Ep.* 3.16; Lys. 13.

120. For the full argument about the Athenian development of penal imprisonment, see Allen 1997.

121. Barkan 1936, 339; Bonner and Smith 1938, 275; Harrison 1971, 177, 244. For public fines and confiscations, that is, monies owed to the city treasury rather than to another citizen, the instant of a criminal's conviction was the instant in which he became a state debtor, liable to pay his fine (Dem. 22.56, 58.49). If the fine was of a sort in which he had nine months to pay it, the Eleven could drag the debtor to prison at the end of that period if he had not paid. He would stay in prison until he paid. If the fine were due upon conviction, the Eleven could haul the convicted off to prison then and there, where he would stay until he, or his friends, had paid his fine. The problem of debt

enslavement to the city would have been particularly relevant (1) to matters of theft tried by *graphe* and sentenced with fine (on such procedures, see Cohen 1983, 44–49); (2) to matters for which the magistrates imposed fines (they could fine, without taking the matter before a court, up to a certain limit—anywhere from ten to fifty drachmae depending on the magistracy); (3) to matters covered by those few suits that were *atimetoi* and which probably provided for fines (*adikos eirchthenai hos moichon, pseudeggraphes, bouleuseos, moicheias, hetaireseos, proagogeias, argias*); and (4) to fines fixed in *timesis* where the jury purposely set fines at greater levels than the defendant would be able to pay.

122. On the *podokakke*, see the discussion earlier in this chapter

123. Also, we should be aware of Todd's point (1995, 140): "These [oratorical] sources may be unrepresentative, because they tend to concentrate disproportionately on high crimes and misdemeanors."

124. For associations between bound men and the feminine, Ar. *Thes.* 927ff., 1001–7; *Eccl.* 1089–90.

125. On the oligarchs, see Krentz 1982; Thuc. 8.74; Dem. 24.165; Lys. 12.17; 13.54, 56, 66. Lys. 13.45: "You remember those led to prison then because of private enmities . . . and forced to perish by the most shameful and most infamous destruction."

126. Athen. 596d.

127. On the introduction of hemlock at the end of the fifth century, Lipsius (1915, 77) and Bonner (1973, 299) agree. Barkan (1935, 76) and Cantarella (1991, 110) think that only its use changed at the end of the fifth century.

128. *Dictionary of Greek and Roman Biography*, s.v.

129. Hemlock, if less painful than the *apotumpanismos*, was not entirely painless. See Gill (1973, 25–28) on the symptoms it causes.

130. In particular Barkan (1935, 77) and Gernet (1982, 27) describe the invention of hemlock as a move to more humane punishments.

131. For all fourth-century references to hemlock as punishment, see And. 3.10; Lys. 12.17, 96; 18.24, 30; Plato *Phaedo* 116d, 117a–b; Xen. *Hell.* 2.3.54–56; Xen. *Apo.* 7. Other references to hemlock that stress the context of suicide include Ar. *Frogs* 120–27, 1051; Theophr. *HP* 9.6.1; Plato *Lysis* 219e; ps.-Arist. *Prob.* 3.23 (874b); Pliny *NH* 14.7.58, 23.18.30. References to the public use of hemlock: Theophr. *HP* 9.6 (used at Keos to thin ranks of elderly); Pliny *NH* 25.95 (151–54) (claims that the Athenians used hemlock for public punishment); Plut. *Phoc.* 26–36; Wallace 1994, 128, on the *Souda*.

132. Hdt. 7.33, 9.120; Ar. *Wealth* 476; *Thes.* 930–46, 1001–2, 1012; Lys. 13.55, 67–68; Dem. 8.61; 9.61; 10.63; 19.137; 21.104–5; Aes. 2.181–82; Arist. *Rhet.* 2.6.27, 1385a10–13; *Ath. Pol.* 45.1; Athen. 5.214d.

133. In respect to the *Gorgias*, I am assuming that the phrase *teleutan pantakaka pathon anaschinduleuthesetai* refers to the *apotumpanismos*.

134. For discussion of antidotes to hemlock, see Theophr. *HP* 9.6.1; Plato *Lysis* 219e; Pliny *NH* 14.7.58, 23.18.30.

135. Cf. Theophr. *HP* 9.6 and Pliny *NH* 25.95 (151–54). It is interesting that Plutarch also reports that hemlock did not grow very often in the Athenian countryside (*choras*), except for once at the end of the fourth century when there was a "miracle growth" at the altar of Zeus and Athena, which the Athenians took as a portent. All of our stories of execution by hemlock come either from the end of the fifth or from the end of the fourth century. Could this be why stories of "miracle growth" themselves sprang up?

136. Cantarella 1991, 106–16; Todd 1995, 141; Debrunner Hall 1996, 80.

137. See Cantarella 1991, 115.

138. See Lipsius 1915, 77 n. 101; Todd 1997, 6.

139. *Black's Law Dictionary* defines "infamous crime" as determined by the penalty: "It is not the character of the crime but the nature of the punishment [which may be imposed on it] which renders the crime infamous."

140. On the intricacies of the restoration of the democracy, see Krentz 1982; Wolpert 1995.

141. See Krentz 1982; Wolpert 1995.

142. See Loraux (1997) for an extended discussion of the importance of forgetting.

143. On the assembly, see Todd 1995, 163. On the *kolastai*, see Lys. 9.11.

144. And. 2.15–16.

145. Dem. 37.59, 38.22, 43.57.

146. Isae. 5.17–18, 19; also Dem. 53.18.

147. See Scarry 1987.

148. On the funeral oration, see Loraux 1981; Humphreys 1983b. On forgetting, see Loraux 1997.

149. Wolpert 1995.

150. Todd 1995, 136–37.

151. It is worth pointing out that in addition to valuing *astunomous orgas*, Sophocles' chorus praised human beings because of they have taught themselves voice (*pthegme*) (354–55) in the "Ode to Man."

152. ABC News, Nightline Special Report, August 20, 1998.

CHAPTER TEN
PLATO'S PARADIGM SHIFTS

1. The literature on Plato is vast. Nor is this chapter easily situated within the context of any of the standard literature on the Platonic dialogues. I have had recourse to general texts on Plato (Shorey 1903; Taylor 1936; Vlastos 1978a; Annas 1981; Rowe 1984; Kraut 1992). I have consulted texts that have attempted to situate various of Plato's works (particularly the *Republic* and the *Laws*) in their historical context (esp. Havelock 1963; Morrow 1960b; Saunders 1991). I have made use of texts that aim to elucidate the political theory to be found in Plato, whether in particular works or across the board (e.g., Barker 1951; Grene 1965; Sinclair 1951; Strauss 1978; Burnyeat 1976; Gill 1979; 1995; Kagan 1965; Klosko 1986; Laks 1990; Rogers 1991; Saxonhouse 1992; Roberts 1994; Lane 1995; 1998). I have also relied heavily on the thorough and careful work that several scholars have done on punishment in Plato (Adkins 1960; Mackenzie 1981; Saunders 1991; Lucas 1993; Stalley 1995a; 1995b; 1996).

2. Burke 1969, 87.

3. To some degree I will be following Shorey (1903) in this chapter and claiming that certain key ideas appear across early, middle, and late dialogues. For my purposes, what particularly matters is the regular reappearance of an emphasis on the teachability of virtue and the idea that punishment should reform the wrongdoer. Shorey (1903) emphasizes in addition that there are consistencies in the definitions of the virtues, in the discussion of the problem of hedonism, and in a commitment to the inseparability of virtue and happiness. Since my discussion is limited to five Platonic dialogues, I do not need to go so far as Shorey. Nor do I need to defend a claim to the "unity of Plato's" thought. My case rests on the simple fact that, as I show in the text, discussion of reformative punishment appears and reappears as a crucial element of the dialogues that I am discussing. I do not claim that every dialogue treats the subject in the same way or

to the same ends; only that every dialogue I discuss treats the subject of reformative punishment. In fact, I would argue that several of the dialogues have very different ends in discussing punishment. I have arranged my discussion of the dialogues to follow their "chronology" as it is regularly understood to be. I recognize that the *Protagoras* and the *Gorgias* are of ambiguous chronological relationship to one another. In a sense I follow the method of Rowe (1982) who gives a "connected account of Plato's main themes and arguments" moving from one dialogue to the next and picking up threads that each dialogue has brought to the fore. For other approaches, see esp. Sinclair 1951; Adkins 1963; Mackenzie 1981; Laks 1990, 211; Saunders 1991; Lucas 1993.

4. MacKenzie 1981; Saunders 1991.

5. The Socratic paradoxes have been much discussed. See Shorey 1903; Rowe 1984; Mackenzie 1981; Saunders 1991; Stalley 1995a; 1995b; 1996. The debate over the precise senses in which "voluntary" can be understood and over Aristotle's criticism of Plato on this front is not particularly germane to my argument. It suffices for me that on the basis of the paradox that no one does wrong voluntarily, however that is understood, the proper response to wrongdoing is education.

6. Vlastos (1980, 301–20) agrees. See Vlastos (1991, 179–99) for a good discussion of Socrates' rejection of retaliation.

7. Saunders (1991) argues that an important part of Plato's discussion of wrongdoing is precisely a switch from a focus on "crime" to a focus on "souls."

8. On the *Protagoras* on punishment, see Mackenzie 1981; Hubbard and Karnofsky 1982; Saunders 1991; Stalley 1995b. Mackenzie and Saunders treat Protagoras's argument here as being an indication that Protagoras himself held views that punishment should not be retributive. They take the passage as primarily concerning deterrent rather than reformative punishment, however. *Contra* this view Stalley (1995) argues that Protagoras's argument is not necessarily to be understood as that of the historical Protagoras. He also argues that the passage does in fact concern not only deterrence but also the education of the wrongdoer. He points out that what follows next, discussion of the correction of children where their correction is compared to "straightening wood" (325c–d) goes to show that an idea of education is at the heart of Protagoras's claim. I think that Stalley is correct to say that the passage does not merely concern deterrence; the comparison between children and straightening wood of course brings to mind the connection between *kolasis* and pruning.

9. Mackenzie 1981, introd.; Saunders 1991, 5; Lucas 1993; Stalley 1995a.

10. On the *Gorgias* on punishment, see Mackenzie 1981, esp. 108–20, 175–85; McTighe 1984; White 1990; Saunders 1991; Stalley 1996.

11. See Mackenzie 1981, esp. 108ff., 175ff.; McTighe 1984; White 1990; Saunders 1991; Stalley 1996. Stalley (1995a; 1995b; 1996) discusses the additional medical analogies that are to be found in the *Timaeus* and in the *Laws*, citing for the latter 854c–55a, 862e–863c, 934c, 735e, 843d, 941d, 957e. All of these scholars have recognized the importance of the medical trope in this dialogue, but none has connected it to the trope of disease found in tragedy. Dodds (1973c, 111) discusses the way in which internal stasis, excessive anger, etc. are characterized as diseases in Plato (*Sophist* 227d, 228e; *Tim.* 86b–87b).

12. The medical trope appears consistently throughout Plato: *Rep.* 444, 556, 562, 567; *Tim.* 86, 106; *Sophist* 220, 227; *Prot.* 322, 324; *Crat.* 405; *Crito* 48; *Statesman* 295, 296.

13. Anton (1980, 55) also points this out. On *paizein,* see Halliwell 1991a, 280–83. On the comic as turning the world upside down, see Loraux 1993, 181–82.

14. Others have commented on Plato's reintroduction of the archaic term for anger, *thumos*, and on his efforts to banish anger. See Rickert 1987, 99–101; Padel 1992, 28 n. 62.

15. In order to specify the role of reason in restraining anger, Socrates resorts to an image. Reason will be like a "shepherd" holding back the anger that is its "guard dog."

16. Stalley (1996) discusses *Rep.* 440a–d where just people are not angry at their punishments. He argues that both anger and vice are gotten rid of in the just city because the "criminal's anger arising at just punishment will be turned against his own vices." On Plato and curbing emotional excess, see Dodds 1973c, 111; Saunders 1991, 98–99.

17. Penner (1978) argues that Plato's claim to the effect that there are precisely *three* parts of the soul fails. As Penner sees it, Plato fails to distinguish the *thumos* from the rational element and so we are left with a picture of a soul divided only into desire and *thumos* or reason. But Penner's position reflects not the degree to which Plato has failed but rather the success of Plato's argument in separating anger from desire. We no longer think of associating the *thumos* with lust and desire.

18. Several scholars have read Thrasymachus as representing Athenian social values, including Nicholson 1974; Adkins 1960, 238; 1972, 119.

19. On the nature of Thrasymachus's arguments about justice, please see Kerferd 1947–48; Sparshott 1966; Nicholson 1974; Siemsen 1987; Jang 1997. I agree especially with Sparshott's argument that the conversation sets Socrates' defense of cooperation against Thrasymachus's defense of conflict. Thrasymachus's definition of justice presupposes a view of the world where everyone's advantage will conflict. Socrates' attempts to refute Thrasymachus are aimed at his belief in conflict. Kerferd (1947–48) makes the interesting point that Thrasymachus's argument that justice is the interest of the ruler might in fact serve as the basis for a defense of democratic government.

20. Gooch (1987–88) argues that the blushing marks Thrasymachus's "recognition of his own diminishment." He also points out that in Arist. *Prob.* 8.20, 889a20, children are said to blush when they are angry.

21. My emphasis on strife will lead to some conclusions similar to those of Saxonhouse 1992. But I argue that Plato is trying to get rid of competition rather than of diversity.

22. On the link between laughter and *hubris* and the agonistic context, see Halliwell 1991a, 280–83. Also Plato *Laws* 934d–6b, where the Athenian Stranger legislates against ridicule in the city and 935d–6a where he distinguishes between *geloia* with *thumos* and *geloia* without *thumos*.

23. Lear (1992, 194–98) takes up the long-standing position (originated by Bernard Williams) that Plato's use of the analogy between city and soul fails and that it is a mere rhetorical gambit easily seen through. Lear argues that a richer understanding of how Plato understood the movement between internalization of social norms and externalization of norms (which leads to further internalization for other people) provides a strong foundation for taking the analogy seriously. Lear is right to ask us to take the analogy seriously, but we should recognize that it serves a purpose other than discussion of the relation between individual and community. The analogy is in fact a rhetorical gambit but one that Plato expects will be successful *because of* the relation between internalized conceptualization of the orders of life and external behavior and actions. He needs the powerful image of the distinct elements of the city in order to impact his auditors' untangible internal conceptions of the soul.

24. As Socrates puts it elsewhere, he is requiring that his guardians be philosophical (375). On Plato's efforts to restrain the manly, competitive virtues in favor of the quieter,

cooperative virtues, see Adkins 1960, 239. To say that Plato is feminizing the virtue of his citizens is not to say that Plato is putting forward a "feminist position" on politics, as Annas (1976) points out.

25. See Gill 1993.

26. Cf. Lear 1992, esp. 186–87; Havelock 1963.

27. Burke 1969, 110.

28. On Plato's analogies, see Bambrough 1971. For the comparison of doctors and judges, see *Rep.* 406–10, 459.

29. On poetry as a disease and Plato's stories or poetry as a form of medicine, see Havelock 1963, 3–35; Derrida 1968. Derrida (1968, 79) writes (in another context): "Operant par séduction, le *pharmakon* fait sortir des voies des lois générales, naturelles, ou habituelles. Il fait sortir Socrate de son lieu propre et de ses chemins coutumiers."

30. The *Republic* is full of "road" metaphors and starts and ends with them (328e, 614c).

31. Socrates makes one exception to the idea that competition and quarrels will disappear in the just city. In the just city it will not be just to bring actions for assault and outrage, but it will be noble and just for those within a given age-class to defend themselves (*amunesthai*) against assailants of the same age. A problem of assault within an age-group that is dealt with immediately as a fight will have the advantage that if anyone should be angry at someone (*toi thumoito*), he is less likely to push the quarrel to a more intense political level; if he can satisfy (*pleron*) his *thumos* in that more direct way fighting will also force the young men to take care of their bodies (465a–b). Authority to govern and to punish (*kolazein*) the younger men will be given to the older men. After having granted young men the privilege of fighting with one another, Socrates returns to the larger point that his proposals for the just city will secure an end of competitive angry strife. "In all respects these men will live in peace (*eirenen*) with one another thanks to the laws" (465b).

32. Compare this with the reference to bees and wasps in *Phaedo* 81e–82b.

33. Aristotle argues that an idea has been expressed with clarity when it finally appears "before the eyes," a phrase that he repeats over and over in book 3 of the *Rhetoric*. He glosses the phrase "to put before the eyes" thus: "We must now explain the meaning of 'before the eyes' and what must be done to produce this. I mean that things are set before the eyes by words that signify actuality or *energeia*" (3.11.1–5).

34. On the question of whether the *Republic* is to be read as a practical political treatise or as a utopian fantasy that Plato himself expects is no more than a game, I come down on the first side of the matter. But not because I take the *Republic* to be providing a blueprint for politics that Plato, or Socrates in the dialogue, expects that anybody will follow. Rather, I read the *Republic* as being political insofar as it locates the conceptual foundation of the Athenian political system and attempts to revise that conceptual foundation, an attempt based on the recognition of the ways in which ideas and cultural constructs of behavior shape a community and its possibilities for action. The *Republic* is not political in that it gives the Athenians or anyone else a set of institutions but it is political insofar as it gives them a conceptual basis for accepting definitions of anger, the *thumos*, competition, and public peace that are revised away from the Athenian paradigm to such an extent that to accept them means to accept an end to Athenian politics. On the question of Plato's utopianism, see Taylor 1936; Annas 1981; Shorey 1903; Vlastos 1978b; Rogers 1991; Lear 1992.

35. Halliwell 1988.

36. Lear (1992, 209) makes a similar argument. See Havelock 1963, 3–35.

37. In Plato *Tim.* 71d–e the liver is the part of the body that receives images and is influenced by them. As we saw in chapter 2, the liver was also the site of anger and lust.

38. Lear 1992, 209.

39. See Annas 1982; Saunders 1991, ch. 13.

40. Many of the arguments about the *Laws* have centered on whether it stands in contradiction to or in harmony with the *Republic* and, in whichever case, how and why that is so. In general on the text there is Strauss 1983; Burnyeat 1976; Saunders 1975; Laks 1990; Rogers 1991. I find Saunders and Laks the most useful. Also, Pangle usefully emphasizes education, virtue, reform, and piety. On the question of whether the *Laws* is a pragmatic stepdown from the *Republic* or rather its actualization, see Vlastos's comment (1977, 35–36) that Plato has abandoned his metanormative theory of justice. Sinclair (1951, 177) uses a similar formulation. Klosko (1986) and Finley (1983, 124) think it is a "stepdown." Saunders (1991) treats it as a practical version of the good state. Laks (1990, 210–11) comes to the conclusion that there is "a necessary duality, as opposed to a contingent revision, of Plato's political scheme" between the two dialogues.

41. See Bobonich (1991, 365) and Gill (1979, 150) on Plato's preference for persuasion, rather than compulsion, in producing acceptance of the "rule of law."

42. Numerous scholars have pointed out that Plato uses the *Laws* to make a strong argument for maintaining the rule of law in politics when there is no philosopher-king to be found: Sinclair 1951, 194–98; Adkins 1960, 296–99; Morrow 1960b (citing esp. 715d, 766d); Markus 1978; Triantaphyllopoulos 1975, 26–27; Dodds 1973a, 110; 1978; Stalley 1995a, 486; Cohen 1995, 29. Several have taken Plato to be articulating or idealizing what was normal in Greece at this time. E.g., Barker 1951, 89; Morrow 1960b, 591; Klosko 1986, esp. 11–14, 190. André Laks (1990, 222–24) takes a rather subtle and insightful approach to the matter.

43. But see 743d for the Athenian Stranger's general rejection of money, etc.

44. Saunders (1991) also points out that the execution of incurables is *timoria.* On curability versus incurability, see Adkins 1960, 304–12; Saunders 1991. For passages where the medical metaphor appears in the *Laws*, see 857a–864c9; 728b2–c5; 731b3–d5; 735d8–736a3; 793d7–794a2; 854c2–855a2; 864c10–e3; 866d5–868a1; 880d7–881b2; 907e6–909c4; 933e6–934c2; 938b5–6; 941c4–942a4; 944d2–3. On Plato's eschatology, see Saunders 1991, ch. 13.

45. See Mackenzie 1981, 109. Mackenzie's reading of Plato gives him more credit for paying attention to victims than mine does. It should be pointed out that Plato does require that his system of punishment include what is effectively a sphere of civil law where a system of compensation will redress the losses of victims. But they are compensated for their loss rather than cured of their anger, and this is what keeps Plato's account distinct from the Athenian account.

CHAPTER ELEVEN
ARISTOTLE'S COMPROMISES

1. I have found the following texts helpful on Aristotle in general: Ackrill 1989; Adkins 1960, 316–44; Allan 1963; 1965; Barker 1951; Bonner and Smith 1930, 1938; Barnes, Schofield, and Sorabji 1979; Cooper 1996; Edel 1982; Gill 1996; Hardie 1980; Harvey 1965; Irwin 1985; 1988; Jaeger 1957; Johnson 1990; Lear 1995; Lévy 1993; Nussbaum 1986; Piérart 1993; Lord 1982; Lord and O'Connor 1991; Morrow 1960a; Mossé 1969; Ostwald 1996; Panagiotou 1987; Randall 1960; Rorty 1980; Sinclair 1951; von Leyden 1985. On the rule of law in Aristotle, see esp. Weinrib 1987a; 1987b; Cohen

1995, 29; Triantaphyllopoulos 1975, 26–27, 44; and my ch. 8. On punishment and the *Nichomachean Ethics*, book 5, see Nilstun 1981, 6–8; Schütrumpf 1989; Triantaphyllopoulos 1975, 26–27, 44; Martin 1990; Hardie 1980; Sorabji 1978; Thonissen 1875, bk. 4, ch. 3. Most discussions on punishment in Aristotle have focused on how he treats the idea of voluntariness, an idea that Plato spends some time elucidating in the *Laws* (e.g., at 863). My discussion, however, concerns the nature of responses to wrongdoing where an agent has already identified the voluntary actions which count as wrongdoing. Of course, in a fuller treatment of Aristotle on punishment, it would be impossible to put aside the question of voluntariness. I do not discuss it here only because it has played relatively little of a role in our discussion of Athenian punishment. Adkins (1960) gives a thorough treatment of the idea of voluntariness in Athens and in the philosophers.

2. Also like Plato, Aristotle refers to the incurably vicious (*hoi aniatoi*): *NE* 3.12.5, 1119b–10; 5.9.17, 1137a29; 7.7.2, 1150a22. On why the *akolastos* and *akratos* are miserable, see Martin 1990, 188–91.

3. Ross (1966, 189) writes of Aristotle that he incorporates many responses to the Academy, often under the tags of "many say" and "some say" and usually agrees with the Academy unless he says otherwise. Sorabji (1978, 290) does not think that Aristotle accepted Plato's theory of reform although he acknowledges that Aristotle does pay "lip service" to reformative theories. Sorabji thinks, as does Thonissen, that Aristotle's theory of punishment was purely deterrent. While they are right both to point out that Aristotle does not spend as much time elaborating a theory of reform as does Plato and while they are right to point out that Aristotle's system does include elements of deterrence (as did Plato's), they neglect the extent to which Aristotle's comments about punishment relate directly to his comments on *akolasia*. For Aristotle on deterrence, see *NE* 10.9.3, 1179b10; 10.9.6, 1180a5.

4. For Aristotle's attempt to subject anger to the scheme of extremes and means, see Arist. *NE* 1.13.10 On Aristotle on emotion, see Mills 1985; Leighton 1988.

5. *NE* 3.8.12, 1117a7; *Rhet.* 1.11.13, 1370b.

6. Vlastos (1991, 189–90) agrees, and criticizes Aristotle for being willing to acknowledge anger. Mackenzie (1981, 239) argues that this was Plato's project too but that he did not deal with the conflict between reciprocity and reform. Saunders (1991, 351) also argues that Plato recognizes this problem that victims will feel anger, but sees Plato as dealing with it by saying that although people *may* feel anger and glee, they *should* not and the punisher ought always to work to restore friendship between the injured and the injurer. I accept Saunders's view of the matter.

7. *NE* 3.5.7, 4.5.11, 10.9.8; *Rhet.* 1.14.3; *Pol.* 7.12.3.

8. For modern efforts that make an attempt to reconcile the retributive with the reformative, see Acton 1969.

9. Mackenzie (1981, 108), in contrast, argues that Plato pays attention to victims by being thoughtful about moral values, intentions, responsibility, and culpability.

10. The passage is one that commentators have generally found confusing because it introduces new terminology and has a confusing organization of the argument. See Hardie 1980, 188.

11. Despite Aristotle's specific enumeration of the wrongs covered by corrective justice, very few theorists have been willing to read this passage as presenting a theory of punishment. Hardie (1980, 194) writes: "Aristotle's account of judicial redress as the restoration of equality is in one respect surprising, and indeed unsatisfactory. The notions of crime and punishment are not considered." See Weinrib 1987a and Waluchow 1987.

12. Aristotle writes: "Justice is that quality in virtue of which a man is said to be disposed to do by deliberate choice that which is just and when distributing things between himself and another [*houtoi pros allon*], or between two others [*heteroi pros heteron*], not to give too much to himself and too little to his neighbor of what is desirable [*hairetou*], and too little to himself and too much to his neighbor of what is harmful [*blaberou*]; and similarly when he is distributing between two other persons. Hence Injustice is excess and defect: namely in the offender's own case, an excess of anything that is generally speaking beneficial [*ophelimou*] and a deficiency of anything harmful [*blaberous*], . . . and though the result is the same, the deviation from proportion may be in either direction as the case may be. Of the injustice done, the smaller part is the suffering of injustice and the larger part the doing injustice" (5.5.17, 1133b30–1134a8; Rackham's translation).

EPILOGUE
THE REFORM OF PROMETHEUS AND PROMETHEAN REBELLION

1. Walzer 1986, 51–68; Taylor 1986, 69–102.
2. The following account is based on Foucault 1991; 1993; 1980; 1984; and on Hoy 1986 and Dumm 1996.
3. Foucault 1991, 23.
4. Ibid., 26–27.
5. On this point, see Walzer 1986, 51–67; Dumm 1996.
6. See Cohen 1991, 11; Geertz 1973.
7. Walzer 1996, 51–67.
8. Walzer 1986, 62.
9. Shklar 1987, 16; Walzer 1986, 66–67.

APPENDIX A
THE NUMBER OF MAGISTRATES IN ATHENS

1. For their duties, cf. Dem. 20.9; Hyp. 3.14; Xen. *Symp.* 2.20; Lys. 22.16 (where they are called *phulakes* of the *agora* rather than *agoranomoi*). A reorganization of offices in 320/19 after the end of the democracy gave the *agoranomoi* more power in such a way as to suggest that they were perhaps being made distinct from the *boule* for the first time (*IG* ii^2 380.10–12); it is only in the second century that we find evidence that they had their own office (*IG* ii^2 3391). Cf. Wallace (1985) on the reorganization of magistracies after the fall of the democracy.
2. Rhodes (1981, 512) agrees that these came from the *boule*.
3. For information on these offices, cf. Harrison 1971, 27–28. Showing us how financial officers from the tribes could be allotted as a group, Aeschines (3.27) describes a Demosthenic motion in the assembly to hold tribal assemblies so that the members of each tribe could chose supervisors and treasurers for public work (*hekastes ton phulon helesthai*). Aeschines specifically says that the offices chosen to handle public finances are those which the tribes choose (Aes. 3.29–30), confirming the analysis suggested here that the three offices in 47.1 are meant to constitute one category of *arkhai*.

Abramson, J. 1994. *We, the Jury: The Jury System and the Ideal of Democracy.* New York: Basic Books.

Ackrill, J. L. 1989. *Aristotle the Philosopher.* 1981. Reprint, Oxford: Clarendon Press.

Acton, H. B., ed. 1969. *The Philosophy of Punishment: A Collection of Essays.* London: Macmillan.

Adkins, A.W.H. 1960. *Merit and Responsibility.* Oxford: Clarendon Press.

———. " 'Friendship' and 'Self-Sufficiency' in Homer and Aristotle." *CQ* 13, 30–45.

———. "Basic Greek Values in Euripides' *Hecuba* and *Hercules Furens.*" *CQ* 16, 193–219.

———. "Threatening, Abusing and Feeling Angry in the Homeric Poems." *JHS* 89, 7–21.

———. *From the Many to the One.* Ithaca: Cornell University Press.

———. *Moral Values and Political Behaviour in Ancient Greece.* London: Chatto & Windus.

Allan, D. J. 1963. *The Philosophy of Aristotle.* 1952. Reprint, London: Oxford University Press.

———. "Individual and State in the *Ethics* and *Politics.*" In *La "Politique" d'Aristote. Entretiens sur l'antiquité classique* (Geneva) 9, 55–95.

Allen, D. S. 1997. "Imprisonment in Classical Athens." *CQ* 47, 121–35.

Andrews, R. M. 1994. *Law, Magistracy, and Crime in Old Regime Paris, 1735–1789.* Vol. 1: *The System of Criminal Justice.* Cambridge: Cambridge University Press.

Annas, J. 1976. "Plato's *Republic* and Feminism." *Philosophy* 51, 307–21.

———. *An Introduction to Plato's* Republic. Oxford: Clarendon Press.

———. "Plato's Myths of Judgement." *Phronesis* 27, 119–43.

Anton, J. 1980. "Dialectic and Health in Plato's *Gorgias*: Presuppositions and Implications." *Ancient Philosophy 1*, 49–60.

Audollent, A. 1904. *Defixionum Tabellae.* Paris: A. Fontemoing.

Austin, J. L. 1975. *How to Do Things with Words.* 1962. Reprint, Cambridge, Mass.: Harvard University Press.

Bain, D. 1991. "Six Greek Verbs of Sexual Congress." *CQ* 41, 51–77.

Baker, N. V. 1992. *Conflicting Loyalties: Law and Politics in the Attorney General's Office, 1789–1990.* Lawrence: University Press Kansas.

Bambrough, R. 1971. "Plato's Political Analogies." In Vlastos, ed., *Plato II*, 187–205.

Barkan, I. 1935. *Capital Punishment in Ancient Athens.* New York: Arno Press.

———. "Imprisonment as a Penalty in Ancient Athens." *CP* 31, 338–41.

Barker, E. 1951. *Greek Political Theory: Plato and His Predecessors.* 3rd ed. London: Methuen.

Barlow, S. A. 1989. "Stereotype and Reversal in Euripides' *Medea.*" *G&R* 36, 158–71.

Barnes, J., M. Schofield, and R. Sorabji, eds. 1979. *Articles on Aristotle 2: Ethics and Politics.* London: Duckworth.

Bartsch, S. 1994. *Actors in the Audience: Theatricality and Doublespeak from Nero to Hadrian.* Cambridge, Mass.: Harvard University Press.

Bataille, G. 1988. *The Accursed Share: An Essay on General Economy.* Vol. 1: *Consumption.* Trans. R. Hurley. New York: Zone Books.

————. 1991. *The Accursed Share: An Essay on General Economy.* Vols. 2: *The History of Eroticism.* Vol. 3: *Sovereignty.* Trans. R. Hurley. New York: Zone Books.

Baumann, R. A. 1996. *Crime and Punishment in Ancient Rome.* New York: Routledge.

Bedau, H. 1980. "Capital Punishment." In T. Regan, ed., *Matters of Life and Death.* New York: Random House.

Bees, R. 1993. *Zur Datierung des Prometheus Desmotes.* Stuttgart: Teubner.

Benhabib, S., ed. 1996. "Toward a Deliberative Model of Democratic Legitimacy." In Benhabib, ed., *Democracy and Difference: Contesting the Boundaries of the Political,* 67–94. Princeton: Princeton University Press.

Bers, V. 1994. "Tragedy and Rhetoric." In Worthington, ed., *Persuasion,* 176–95.

Betts, J. H., J. T. Hooker, and J. R. Green, eds. 1986. *Studies in Honour of T.B.L. Webster.* Vol. 1. Bristol: Bristol Classical Press.

Blundell, M. W. 1989. *Helping Friends and Harming Enemies.* Cambridge: Cambridge University Press.

Blundell, S. 1995. *Women in Ancient Greece.* London: British Museum Press.

Bobonich, C. 1991. "Persuasion, Compulsion and Freedom in Plato's *Laws.*" *CQ* 41, 365–88.

Boedeker, D. 1991. "Euripides' Medea and the Vanity of *logoi.*" *CP* 86, 95–112.

Boegehold, A. 1972. "The Establishment of a Central Archive at Athens." *AJA* 76, 23–27.

————. 1991. "Three Court Days." In Gagarin, ed., *Symposion 1990,* 165–82.

————. 1995. *The Athenian Agora: Results of Excavations Conducted by the American School of Classical Studies at Athens.* Vol. 28: *The Lawcourts.* Princeton: American School of Classical Studies.

————. 1996. "Resistance to Change in the Law at Athens." In Ober and Hedrick, eds., *Demokratia,* 203–14.

Boegehold, A., and A. Scafuro, eds. 1994. *Athenian Ideology and Civic Identity.* Baltimore: Johns Hopkins University Press.

Bongie, E. B. 1977. "Heroic Elements in the *Medea* of Euripides." *TAPA* 107, 27–56.

Bonner, R. 1905. *Evidence in Athenian Courts.* Chicago: University of Chicago Press.

————. 1907. "The Jurisdiction of Athenian Arbitrators." *CP* 2, 407–18.

————. 1916. "The Institution of Athenian Arbitrators." *CP* 11, 191–95.

Bonner, R. J., and G. Smith. 1930, 1938. *The Administration of Justice from Homer to Aristotle.* Vols. 1, 2. Chicago: University of Chicago Press.

Bonner, T. J. 1973. "The Use of Hemlock for Capital Punishment." In Connor, ed., *Athenian Studies,* 299–302.

Borthwick, E. K. 1992. "Observations on the Opening Scene of Aristophanes' *Wasps.*" *CQ* 42, 274–77.

Bourdieu, P. 1977. *Outline of a Theory of Practice.* Trans. R. Nice. Cambridge: Cambridge University Press.

Bremer, D. 1988. *Aischylos Prometheus in Fesseln.* Frankfurt am Main: Insel Verlag.

Bremmer, J. 1983. "Scapegoat Rituals in Ancient Greece." *HSCP* 87, 299–320.

Brémond, M. 1994. *Le mythe de Prométhée: Les limites de la ruse ou comment apprendre la soumission.* Marseille: Presses Universitaires d'Aix.

Brown, A. L. 1982. "Some Problems in the *Eumenides* of Aeschylus." *JHS* 102, 26–32.

————. 1983. "The Erinyes in the *Oresteia*: Real Life, the Supernatural, and the Stage." *JHS* 103, 13–34.

————. 1991. "Notes on Sophocles' *Antigone.*" *CQ* 41, 325–39.

Browne, R. A. 1943. "Types of Self-Recognition and Self-Reform in Ancient Drama." *AJP* 54, 163–71.

Buck, C. D., and W. Petersen. 1944. *A Reverse Index of Greek Nouns and Adjectives: Arranged by Terminations with Brief Historical Introductions.* Chicago: University of Chicago Press.

Buckheit, V. 1960. "Feigensymbolik im antiken Epigramm." *RhM* 103, 200–230.

Burke, K. 1969. *A Rhetoric of Motives.* Berkeley: University of California Press.

———. 1989. *On Symbols and Society.* Ed. and introd. J. R. Gusfield. Chicago: University of Chicago Press.

Burkert, W. 1983. *Homo necans: The Anthropology of Greek Sacrificial Ritual and Myth.* Trans. P. Bing. Berkeley: University of California Press.

———. 1985. *Greek Religion.* Trans. J. Raffan. Cambridge, Mass.: Harvard University Press.

Burnett, A. 1962. "Human Resistance and Divine Persuasion in Euripides' *Ion.*" *CP* 57, 89–101.

———. 1973. "*Medea* and the Tragedy of Revenge." *CP* 58, 1–24.

———. 1976. "Tribe and City, Custom and Decree in *Children of Heracles.*" *CP* 71, 4–26.

———. 1994. "Hekabe the Dog." *Arethusa* 27, 151–64.

Burnett, D. G. Forthcoming. *El Dorado on Paper.* Chicago: University of Chicago Press.

Burnyeat, M. 1976. "Review of Strauss' *The Argument and Action in Plato's* Laws." *TLS*, no. 3, 865, April 9, 1976, p. 444.

Bushala, E. W. 1968. "Torture of Non-Citizens in Homicide Investigations." *GRBS* 9, 61–68.

Butler, S. 1995. "Racially Based Jury Nullification." *Yale Law Journal* 105, 677–725.

Cairns, D. L. 1993. *Aidos: The Psychology and Ethics of Honour and Shame in Ancient Greek Literature.* Oxford: Clarendon Press.

Calhoun, G. M. 1919. "Oral and Written Pleading in Athenian Courts." *TAPA* 5, 177–93.

———. 1927. *The Growth of Criminal Law in Ancient Greece.* Berkeley: University of California Press.

Canfora, L. 1995. "The Citizen." In Vernant, ed., *The Greeks*, 120–52.

Cantarella, E. 1975. "*Phonos me ek pronoias*: L'elemento soggetive dell' atto illicito nei logografi e nei filosofi." In Modrzejewski, Nörr, and Wolff, eds., *Symposion 1971*, 293–320.

———. 1983. "Spunti di riflessione critice sur *hubris* e *time* in Omero." In Dimakis and Biscardi, eds., *Symposion 1979*, 83–96.

———. 1991. *I supplizi capitali in Grecia e a Roma.* Milan: Rizzoli.

Carawan, E. M. 1983. "*Erotesis*: Interrogation in the Courts of Fourth-Century Athens." *GRBS* 24, 209–26.

———. 1984. "*Akriton apokteinai*: Execution without Trial in 4th Century Athens." *GRBS* 25, 111–22.

Carey, C. 1986. "The Second Stasimon of Sophocles' *Oedipus Tyrannus.*" *JHS* 106, 175–79.

———. 1988. "A Note on Torture in Athenian Homicide Cases." *Historia* 37, 241–45.

———. 1993. "Return of the Radish, or Just When You Thought It Was Safe to Go Back into the Kitchen." *Liverpool Classical Monthly* 18, no. 4, 53–55.

———. 1994. "Rhetorical Means of Persuasion." In Worthington, ed., *Persuasion*, 26–45.

Carson, A. 1990. "Putting Her in Her Place: Woman, Dirt, and Desire." In Halperin, Winkler, and Zeitlin, eds., *Before Sexuality*, 135–70.

Carter, I. 1986. *The Quiet Athenian*. Oxford: Clarendon Press.

Cartledge, P., P. Millett, and S. Todd, eds. 1990. *Nomos: Essays in Athenian Law, Politics and Society*. Cambridge: Cambridge University Press.

Chantraine, P. 1968–80. *Dictionnaire étymologique de la langue grecque*. Paris: Klincksieck.

Christ, M. R. 1992. "Ostracism, Sycophancy, and Deception of the Demos: [Arist] *Ath. Pol.* 43.5." *CQ* 42, 336–46.

Cohen, D. 1983. *Theft in Athenian Law*. Munich: C. H. Beckische Verlag.

———. 1985. "A Note on Aristophanes and the Punishment of Adultery in Athenian Law." *ZRG* 102, 385–87.

———. 1986. "The Theodicy of Aeschylus: Justice and Tyranny in the *Oresteia*." *G&R* 33, 129–41.

———. 1989a. "Seclusion, Separation and the Status of Women in Classical Athens." *G&R* 36, 3–15.

———. 1989b. "The Prosecution of Impiety in Athenian Law." In Thür, ed., *Symposion 1985*, 89–108.

———. 1991. *Law, Sexuality, and Society: The Enforcement of Morals in Classical Athens*. Cambridge: Cambridge University Press.

———. 1995. *Law, Violence, and Community in Classical Athens*. Cambridge: Cambridge University Press.

Cohen, E. E. 1973. *Ancient Athenian Maritime Courts*. Princeton: Princeton University Press.

Cole, S. G. 1996. "Oath Ritual and the Male Community at Athens." In Ober and Hedrick, eds., *Demokratia*, 227–48.

Coleman, J. 1992. *Ancient and Medieval Memories: Studies in the Reconstruction of the Past*. Cambridge: Cambridge University Press.

Collier, J. F. 1976. "Women in Politics." In Rosaldo and Lamphere, eds., *Woman, Culture and Society*, 89–96.

Conacher, D. J. 1980. *Aeschylus'* Prometheus Bound*: A Literary Commentary*. Toronto: University of Toronto Press.

———. 1987. *Aeschylus'* Oresteia*: A Literary Commentary*. Toronto: University of Toronto Press.

Connor, W. R., ed. 1973. *Athenian Studies*. New York: Arno Press.

———. 1985. "The Razing of the House in Greek Society." *TAPA* 115, 79–102.

Considine, P. 1986. "The Etymology of *Menis*." In Betts, Hooker, and Green, eds., *Studies in Honor of T.B.L. Webster*, 7:53–64.

Cooper, J. 1996. "Justice and Rights in Aristotle's *Politics*." *Review of Metaphysics* 49, 859–72.

Cragg, W. 1992. *The Practice of Punishment*. London: Routledge.

Crane, G. 1989. "Creon and the 'Ode to Man' in Sophocles' *Antigone*." *HSCP* 92, 103–116.

———. 1993. "Politics of Consumption and Generosity in the Carpet Scene of the *Agamemnon*." *CP* 88, 117–36.

Croiset, M. 1909. *Aristophanes and the Political Parties at Athens*. London: Macmillan.

Csapo, E. 1993. "Deep Ambivalence: Notes on a Greek Cockfight, Parts I–IV." *Phoenix* 47, 1–28, 115–24.

Daremberg, Ch., and E. Saglio. 1875. *Dictionnaire des antiquités grecques et romaines*. Paris: Hachette.

Dareste de la Chavanne, R. 1976. *La science du droit en Grèce.* 1839. Reprint, New York: Arno Press.

Debrunner Hall, M. D. 1996. "Even Dogs Have Erinyes: Sanctions in Athenian Practice and Thinking." In Foxhall and Lewis, eds., *Greek Law in Its Political Setting,* 75–90.

de Jong, I. 1991. *Narrative in Drama: The Art of the Euripidean Messenger-Speech.* Leiden: E. J. Brill.

de Romilly, J. 1968. *Time in Greek Tragedy.* Ithaca: Cornell University Press.

Derrida, J. 1968. "La pharmacie de Platon." *Tel Quel* 32–33, 1–125.

Detienne, M., and J.-P. Vernant. 1978. *Cunning Intelligence in Greek Culture and Society.* Trans. Janet Lloyd. Sussex: Harvester Press.

Diggle, J. 1983. "On the Manuscripts and the Text of Euripides' *Medea.*" *CQ* 33, 339–57.

———. 1990. "On the *Orestes* of Euripides." *CQ* 40, 100–123.

Dimakis, W. M., and A. Biscardi. 1983. *Symposion 1979: Akten der Gesellschaft für Griechicsche und Hellenistische Rechtsgeschichte.* Cologne: Bohlau Verlag.

Dindorf, W., ed. 1880. *Aeschyli tragoediae.* 1853. Reprint, Leipzig: Teubner.

Dodds, E. R. 1951. *The Greeks and the Irrational.* Berkeley: University of California Press.

———. 1960. "Morals and Politics in the 'Oresteia.'" *Proceedings of the Cambridge Philological Society* 186, 19–31. Reprinted in *The Ancient Concept of Progress,* 45–63.

———. 1973a. *The Ancient Concept of Progress and Other Essays.* Oxford: Oxford University Press.

———. 1973b. "The Prometheus Vinctus and the Progress of Scholarship." In *The Ancient Concept of Progress,* 26–44.

———. 1973c. "Plato and the Irrational." In *The Ancient Concept of Progress,* 106–25.

———. 1978. "Plato and the Irrational Soul." In Vlastos, ed., *Plato II,* 206–29.

Donlan, W. 1981. "Reciprocities in Homer." *CW* 75, 137–75.

———. 1989. "The Unequal Exchange between Glaucus and Diomedes in Light of the Homeric Gift-Economy." *Phoenix* 43, 1–15.

Dorjahn, A. 1941. "On the Athenian Anakrisis." *CP* 36, 182–85.

Douglas, M. 1966. *Purity and Danger: An Analysis of Concepts of Pollution and Taboo.* New York: Praeger.

Dover, K. 1957. "The Political Aspect of Aeschylus' *Eumenides.*" *JHS* 77, 230–37.

———. 1974. *Greek Popular Morality.* Oxford: Basil Blackwell.

———. 1989. *Greek Homosexuality.* 1978. Reprint, Cambridge, Mass.: Harvard University Press.

———. 1991. "Fathers, Sons and Forgiveness." *ICS* 16, 173–82.

duBois, P. 1991. *Torture and Truth.* New York: Routledge.

———. 1992. "Eros and the Woman." *Ramus* 21, 97–116.

Duff, A., ed. 1993. *Punishment.* Aldershot: Dartmouth University Press.

Duff, A., and D. Garland, eds. 1994. *Oxford Readings in Punishment.* Oxford: Oxford University Press.

Dumm, T. L. 1996. *Michel Foucault and the Politics of Freedom.* Thousand Oaks, Calif.: Sage Publications.

Dumortier, J. 1975. *Le vocabulaire médical d'Eschyle et les écrits Hippocratiques.* Paris: Les Belles Lettres.

Dunn, F. M. 1996. *Tragedy's End: Closure and Innovation in Euripidean Drama.* New York: Oxford University Press.

Durkheim, E. 1992. "Two Laws of Penal Evolution." In M. Gane, ed., *The Radical*

Sociology of Durkheim and Mauss. London: Routledge. Originally published in French in *Année Sociologique* (1899–1900).

Dworakowska, A. 1975. *Quarries in Ancient Greece*. Warsaw: Academia Scientarum Polonia.

Dworkin, R. 1977. *Taking Rights Seriously*. Cambridge, Mass.: Harvard University Press.

Easterling, P., ed. 1982. *Sophocles'* Trachiniae. Cambridge: Cambridge University Press.

———. 1990. "Constructing Character in Greek Tragedy." In Pelling, ed., *Characterization and Individuality in Greek Literature*, 83–99.

Edel, A. 1982. *Aristotle and His Philosophy*. London: Croom Helm.

Edmunds, L. 1987. *Cleon, Knights, and Aristophanes' Politics*. New York: Lanham.

Edwards, M. 1975. "Type-Scenes and Homeric Hospitality." *TAPA* 105, 51–72.

Ehrenberg, V. 1946. *Aspects of the Ancient World: Essays and Reviews*. Oxford: Basil Blackwell.

———. 1965. *Polis und Imperium*. Beiträge zum Alten Geschichte. Zurich: Artemis Verlag.

———. 1969. *The Greek State*. 2nd ed. London: Methuen.

———. 1973. *From Solon to Socrates*. 2nd ed. New York: Routledge.

Esmein, A. 1978. *Histoire de la procédure criminelle*. 1887. Reprint, Paris: Eduoard Duchemin.

Euben, P. J., J. R. Wallach, and J. Ober, eds. 1994. *Athenian Political Thought and the Reconstruction of American Democracy*. Ithaca: Cornell University Press.

Faraone, C. A. 1985. "Aeschylus' *humnos desmios: Eum*. 306 and Attic Judicial Curse Tablets." *JHS* 105, 150–54.

———. 1989. "An Accusation of Magic in Classical Athens Ar. *Wasps* 946–48." *TAPA* 119, 149–60.

———. 1991. "The Agonistic Context of Early Greek Binding Spells." In Faraone and Obbink, *Majika Hiera*, 83–97.

———. 1993. "Molten Wax, Spilt Wine and Mutilated Animals." *JHS* 113, 60–80.

———. 1994. "Deianira's Mistake and the Demise of Heracles: Erotic Magic in Sophocles' *Trachiniae*." *Helios* 21, 115–36.

———. 1999. *Ancient Greek Love Magic*. Cambridge, Mass.: Harvard University Press.

Faraone, C. A., and D. Obbink, eds. 1991. *Majika Hiera: Ancient Greek Magic and Religion*. Oxford: Oxford University Press.

Farnell, L. R. 1977. *The Cults of the Greek States*. New York: Cavatzas Brothers.

Farrar, C. 1988. *The Origins of Democratic Thinking: The Invention of Politics in Classical Athens*. Cambridge: Cambridge University Press.

Fentress, J., and C. Wickham. 1992. *Social Memory*. Oxford: Blackwell.

Fernández Nieto, F.J.F. 1990. "La competencia penal de los estrategos." In Nenci and Thür, *Symposion 1988*, 111–22.

Finley, M. I., ed. 1968. *Slavery in Classical Antiquity*. 1960. Reprint, Cambridge: Heffer's.

———. 1975. *The Use and Abuse of History*. London: Chatto & Windus.

———. 1983. *Politics in the Ancient World*. Cambridge: Cambridge University Press.

———. 1985. *Democracy Ancient and Modern*. 2nd ed. New Brunswick: Rutgers University Press.

Fisher, N., ed. 1976. *Social Values in Classical Athens*. London: Dent.

———. 1992. *Hybris: A Study in the Values of Honour and Shame in Ancient Greece*. Warminster: Aris & Phillips.

Foley, H. 1985. *Ritual Irony: Poetry and Sacrifice in Euripides.* Ithaca: Cornell University Press.

———. 1988. "Tragedy and Politics in Aristophanes' *Acharnians.*" *JHS* 108, 33–47.

———. 1993. "The Politics of Tragic Lamentation." In Sommerstein et al., eds., *Tragedy, Comedy and the Polis: Papers from the Greek Drama Conference*, 101–43.

———. 1995. "Tragedy and Democratic Ideology, The Case of Sophocles' *Antigone.*" In Goff, ed., *History, Tragedy, Theory*, 65–84.

Foucault, M. 1978. *The History of Sexuality.* Vol. 1: *An Introduction.* Trans. R. Hurley. New York: Random House.

———. 1984. *The Foucault Reader.* Ed. P. Rabinow. New York: Pantheon Books.

———. 1986. *The History of Sexuality.* Vol. 2: *The Use of Pleasure.* Trans. R. Hurley. New York: Vintage Books.

———. 1991. *Discipline and Punish.* Trans. A. Lane. 1977. Reprint, London: Penguin Books.

Foxhall, L. 1989. "Household, Gender, and Property in Classical Athens." *CQ* 39, 22–44.

———. 1996. "The Law and the Lady: Women and Legal Proceedings in Classical Athens." In Foxall and Lewis, eds., *Greek Law in Its Political Setting*, 133–52.

Foxhall, L., and A.D.E. Lewis, eds. 1996. *Greek Law in Its Political Setting.* Oxford: Clarendon Press.

Friedman, L. M. 1993. *Crime and Punishment in American History.* New York: Basic Books.

Friedrich, R. 1993. "*Medea apolis*: On Euripides' Dramatization of the Crisis of the Polis." In Sommerstein et al., eds., *Tragedy, Comedy and the Polis: Papers from the Greek Drama Conference*, 222–40.

Frisk, H. 1960–72. *Griechisches etymologisches Wörterbuch.* Heidelberg: C. Winter.

Gabrielsen, V. 1981. *Remunerations of state officials in fourth century B.C. Athens.* Odense: Odense University Press.

———. Gagarin, M. 1973. "*Dike* in the *Works and Days.*" *CP* 68, 81–94.

———. 1974. "*Dike* in Archaic Poetry." *CP* 69, 186–97.

———. 1975. "The Vote of Athena." *AJP* 96, 121–27.

———. 1976. *Aeschylean Drama.* Berkeley: University of California Press.

———. 1978. "Self-Defense in Athenian Homicide Law." *GRBS* 19, 111–20.

———. 1981. *Drakon and Early Athenian Homicide Law.* New Haven: Yale University Press.

———. 1986. *Early Greek Law.* Berkeley: University of California Press.

———. 1990. "The Nature of Proofs in Antiphon." *CP* 85, 27–32.

———, ed. 1991. *Symposion 1990: Akten der Gesellschaft für Griechicsche und Hellenistische Rechtsgeschichte.* Cologne: Bohlau Verlag.

———. 1992. "The Poetry of Justice: Hesiod and the Origins of Greek Law." *Ramus* 21, 61–78.

———. 1996. "The Torture of Slaves in Athenian Law." *CP* 91, no. 1, 1–18.

———. 1997. "Oaths and Oath-Challenges in Greek Law." In Thür and Vélissaropoulos-Karakostas, eds., *Symposion 1995*, 125–34.

Gagarin, M., and P. Woodruff, eds. and trans. 1995. *Early Greek Political Thought from Homer to the Sophists.* Cambridge: Cambridge University Press.

Gardner, J. F. 1989. "Aristophanes and Male Anxiety—The Defence of the *Oikos.*" *G&R* 36, 51–62.

Garland, D. 1990. *Punishment and Modern Society.* Oxford: Oxford University Press.

———. 1993. "Sociological Perspectives on Punishment." In Duff, ed., *Punishment* 453–503. Also in *Crime and Justice* 14, 115–65.

Garland, D., and P. Young. 1983. *The Power to Punish: Contemporary Penality and Social Analysis*. London: Heinemann Educational Books.

Garnsey, P. 1970. *Social Status and Legal Privilege in the Roman Empire*. Oxford: Oxford University Press.

Gauthier, P. 1971. "Les XENOI dans les textes atheniens de la seconde moitié du Ve siècle av. J.C." *REG* 84, 44–79.

Geertz, C. 1973. "Thick Description: Toward an Interpretive Theory of Culture." In Geertz, *The Interpretation of Cultures*, 3–30. New York: Harper and Row.

Gellie, G. 1984. "Apollo in the *Ion*." *Ramus* 13, 93–101.

Gernet, L. 1909. "*Authentes*." *REG* 22, 13–22.

———. 1924. "Sur l'exécution capitale." *REG* 37, 261–95.

———. 1938. "Sur les actions commerciales en droit athénien." *REG* 51, 1–44.

———. 1939. "L'institution des arbitres publics à Athènes." *REG* 52, 389–414.

———. 1955. *Droit et société dans la Grèce ancienne*. Paris: Recueil Shirey.

———. 1981a. *The Anthropology of Ancient Greece*. 1968. Trans. J. Hamilton and B. Nagy. Baltimore: Johns Hopkins University Press.

———. 1981b. "The Mythical Idea of Value in Greece." In Gernet, *Anthropology*, 73–111. Also in *Journal de psychol.* 41 (1948): 415–62.

———. 1981c. "Law and Prelaw in Ancient Greece." In Gernet, *Anthropology*, 143–215. Also in *L'Année sociol.* 3 (1948–49): 21–119.

———. 1981d. "The Concept of Time in the Earliest Forms of Law." In Gernet, *Anthropology*, 216–39. Also in *Journal de psychol.* 53 (1956): 378–406.

———. 1981e. "Some Connections between Punishment and Religion in Ancient Greece." In Gernet, *Anthropology*, 240–51. Also in *Ant. Class.* 5 (1936): 329–39.

———. 1981f. "Capital Punishment." In Gernet, *Anthropology*, 252–71. Also in *REG* 37 (1924): 261–93.

———. 1982. *Droit et institutions en Grèce antique*. 1968. Reprint, Paris: Flammarion.

———. 1984. "Le droit pénal de la Grèce ancienne. In Y. Thomas et al., *Du châtiment dans la cité: Supplices corporels et peines de mort dans le monde antique*.

Geschnitzer, F. 1983. "Zur Normenhierarchie im öffentliche Recht der Griechen." In Dimakis and Biscardi, eds., *Symposion 1979*, 141–64.

———. 1997. "Zur Terminologie von 'Gesetz' und 'Recht' in früher Griechisch." In Thür and Vélissaropoulos-Karakostas, eds., *Symposion 1995*, 3–10.

Gilbert, G. 1968. *The Constitutional Antiquities of Sparta and Athens*. 1895. Trans. E. J. Brooks and T. Nickler. London: S. Sonnenschein.

———. Gill, C. 1973. "The Death of Socrates." *CQ* 23, 25–28.

———. 1979. "Plato and Politics: The *Critias* and the *Politicus*." *Phronesis* 24, 148–67.

———. 1993. "Plato on Falsehood—not Fiction." In Gill and Wiseman, eds., *Lies and Fiction*, 38–87.

———. 1995. "Rethinking Constitutionalism in *Statesman* 291–303." In Rowe, ed., *Reading the* Statesman, 292–305.

———. 1996. *Personality in Greek Epic, Tragedy, and Philosophy*. Oxford: Clarendon Press.

Gill, C., and T. P. Wiseman. 1993. *Lies and Fiction in the Ancient World*. Exeter: University of Exeter Press.

Gilula, D. 1983. "Four Deadly Sins? Arist. *Wasps* 74–84." *CQ* 33, 358–62.

Girard, R. 1992. *Violence and the Sacred*. Trans. P. Gregory. Baltimore: Johns Hopkins University Press.

Glotz, G. 1904a. *La solidarité de la famille dans le droit criminel en Grèce*. Paris: Albert Fontemoin.

———. 1904b. *L'ordalie dans la Grèce primitive*. Paris: Fontemoing.

———. 1929. *The Greek City and Its Institutions*. London: Kegan Paul, Trench, Trubner.

Goff, B. E. 1990. *The Noose of Words: Readings of Desire, Violence, and Language in Euripides'* Hippolytus. Cambridge: Cambridge University Press.

———. 1995. *History, Tragedy, Theory: Dialogues on Athenian Drama*. Austin: University of Texas Press.

Goldhill, S. 1984. *Language, Sexuality, Narrative: The Oresteia*. Cambridge: Cambridge University Press.

———. 1987. "The Great Dionysia and Civic Ideology." *JHS* 107, 58–76.

———. 1988. *Reading Greek Tragedy*. 1986. Reprint, Cambridge: Cambridge University Press.

———. Forthcoming. "Greek Drama and Political Theory." In M. Schofield and M. Lane, eds., *Cambridge History of Greek Political Thought*. Cambridge: Cambridge University Press.

Gooch, P. W. 1987–88. "Red Faces in Plato." *CJ* 83, 124–27.

Gould, J. 1980. "Law, Custom and Myth: Aspects of the Social Position of Women in Classical Athens." *JHS* 100, 38–59.

Gouldner, A. 1965. *Enter Plato: Classical Greece and the Origins of Social Theory*. London: Routledge and Kegan Paul.

Grene, D. 1965. *Greek Political Theory: The Image of Man in Thucydides and Plato*. 1950. Reprint, Chicago: University of Chicago, Phoenix Books.

Green, T. A. 1985. *Verdict according to Conscience: Perspectives on the English Criminal Trial Jury, 1200–1800*. Chicago: University of Chicago Press.

Greenidge, A.H.J. 1901. *The Legal Procedure of Cicero's Time*. Oxford: Oxford University Press.

Gregory, J. 1991. *Euripides and the Instruction of the Athenians*. Ann Arbor: University of Michigan Press.

Griffith, M. 1977. *The Authenticity of* "Prometheus Bound." Cambridge: Cambridge University Press.

Griffith, R. D. 1988. "Disrobing in the *Oresteia*." *CQ* 38, 552–53.

———. 1993. "Oedipus Pharmakos? Alleged Scapegoating in Sophocles' *Oedipus the King*." Phoenix 47, 95–114.

Hager, H. 1879. "How Were the Bodies of Criminals at Athens Disposed of after Death?" *AJP* 8, 11.

Hall, E. 1995. "Lawcourt Dramas: The Power of Performance in Greek Forensic Oratory." *BICS* 40, 39–58.

Halleran, M. R. 1988. "Repetition and Irony at Sophocles' *Trachiniae* 574–81." *CP* 83, 129–31.

———. 1991. "Gamos and Destuction in Euripides' *Hippolytos*." *TAPA* 121, 109–21.

Halliwell, S. 1988. *Republic Bk. 10*. With Translation and Commentary. Warminster: Aris & Phillips.

———. 1991a. "The Uses of Laughter in Greek Culture." *CQ* 41, 279–96.

————. 1991b. "Comic Satire and Freedom of Speech in Classical Athens." *JHS* 111, 48–70.

Halperin, D. 1990. *One Hundred Years of Homosexualtiy and Other Essays on Greek Love*. New York: Routledge.

Halperin, D., J. Winkler, and F. Zeitlin, eds. 1990. *Before Sexuality: The Construction of Erotic Experience in the Ancient Greek World*. Princeton: Princeton University Press.

Hamilton, R. 1978. "Prologue, Prophecy, and Plot in Four Plays of Euripides." *AJP* 99, 283–86.

————. 1992. *Choes and Anthesteria: Iconography and Ritual*. Ann Arbor: University of Michigan Press.

Hans, V., and N. Vidmar. 1986. *Judging the Jury*. New York: Plenum Press.

Hansen, M. H. 1975 *Eisangelia: The Sovereignty of the People's Court in Athens in the 4th Century B.C. and the Impeachment of Generals and Politicians*. Odense: Odense University Press.

————. 1976 Apagoge, endeixis, *and* ephegesis *against* kakourgoi, atimoi, *and* pheugontes: *A Study in the Athenian Administration of Justice in the Fourth Century B.C.* Odense: Odense University Press.

————. 1979 "*Misthos* for Magistrates in Classical Athens." *Symbolae Osloenses* 54, 5–22.

————. 1980a. "Seven Hundred *archai* in Classical Athens." *GRBS* 21, 151–73.

————. 1980b. "Perquisites for Magistrates in Fouth-Century Athens." *C&M* 32,105–25.

————. 1981. "The Prosecution of Homicide in Athens: A Reply." *GRBS* 22, 11–30.

————. 1983a. "Two Notes on the Athenian *dikai emporikai*." In Dimakis and Biscardi, eds., *Symposion 1979*, 165–76.

————. 1983b. "Political Activity and the Organization of Attica in the Fourth Century B.C." *GRBS* 24, 227–38.

————. 1987. *The Athenian Assembly in the Age of Demosthenes*. Oxford: Basil Blackwell.

————. 1989. "Solonian Democracy in Fourth-Century Athens." *C&M* 40, 71–100.

————. 1991a. *The Athenian Democracy in the Age of Demosthenes: Structure, Principles, and Ideology*. Oxford: Basil Blackwell.

————. 1991b. "Response to Douglas MacDowell." In Gagarin, ed., *Symposion 1990*, 199–204.

Hardie, W. F. R. 1980. *Aristotle's Ethical Theory*. 1968. Reprint, Oxford: Clarendon Press.

Harrell, H. C. 1936. *Public Arbitration in Athenian Law*. Columbia: University of Missouri Press.

Harris, E. M. 1994a. "Law and Oratory." In Worthington, ed., *Persuasion*, 130–50.

————. 1994b. "'In the Act' or 'Red-Handed': *Apagoge* to the Eleven and *Furtum Manifestum*." In Thür, ed., *Symposion 1985*, 169–84.

Harrison, A.R.W. 1968, 1971. *The Law of Athens*. Vols. 1, 2. Oxford: Clarendon Press.

Hart, H.L.A. 1995. *Punishment and Responsibility: Essays in the Philosophy of Law*. 1968. Reprint, Oxford: Clarendon Press.

Hartigan, K. 1987. "Euripidean Madness: Herakles and Orestes." *G&R* 34, 126–35.

Harvey, D. 1990. "The Sykophant and Sykophancy." In Cartledge, Millett, and Todd, eds., *Nomos*, 103–22.

Harvey, F. D. 1965. "Two Kinds of Equality." *C&M* 26, 101–46.

Havelock, E. 1963. *Preface to Plato*. Cambridge, Mass.: Harvard University Press.

————. 1982. *The Literate Revolution and Its Cultural Consequences.* Princeton: Princeton University Press.

Headlam, J. 1893. "On the *proklesis eis basanon* in Attic Law." *CR* 7, 1–5.

————. 1894. "Slave Torture in Athens." *CR* 8, 136–37.

Hedrick, C. 1993. "The Meaning of Material Culture: Herodotus, Thucydides, and Their Sources." In R. M. Rosen and J. Farrell, eds. *Nomodeiktes: Greek Studies in Honor of Martin Ostwald*, 17–38. Ann Arbor: University of Michigan Press.

Heitsch, E. 1989. "Der Archon Basileus und die Attischen Gerichtshöfe für Tötungsdelikte." In Thür, ed., *Symposion 1985*, 71–87.

Henderson, J. 1991a. *The Maculate Muse.* 1975. Reprint, Oxford: Oxford University Press.

————. 1991b. "Women and the Athenian Dramatic Festivals." *TAPA* 121, 133–47.

Herman, G. 1987. *Ritualised Friendship and the Greek City.* Cambridge: Cambridge University Press.

————. 1993. "Tribal and Civic Codes of Behaviour in Lysias 1." *CQ* 43, 406–19.

————. 1994a. "Honour, Revenge, and the State in Fourth-Century Athens." In W. Eder, ed., *Democracy in Fourth-Century Athens: Decline or Zenith of a Constitution*, 400–413. Stuttgart: Steiner.

————. 1994b. "How Violent Was Athenian Society?" In R. Osborne and S. Hornblower, eds., *Ritual, Finance, Politics: Athenian Democratic Accounts*, 99–117. Oxford: Clarendon Press.

————. 1996. "Ancient Athens and the Values of Mediterranean Society." *Mediterannean Historical Review* 11, 5–36.

Herz, N., and M. Waelkens, eds. 1988. *Classical Marble: Geochemistry, Technology, Trade.* Lucca: NATO Advanced Research Workshop.

Hirzel, R. 1966. *Themis, Dike und verwandtes; ein Beitrag zur Geschichte der Rechtsidee bei den Griechen.* 1907. Reprint, Hildesheim. Gerstenberg Verlag.

Hogan, J. C. 1989. *A Commentary on the Complete Greek Tragedies: Aeschylus.* Chicago: University of Chicago Press.

Holst-Warhaft, G. 1992. *Dangerous Voices: Women's Laments and Greek Literature.* London: Routledge.

Hoy, D. C., ed. 1986. *Foucault: A Critical Reader.* London: Basil Blackwell.

Hubbard, B.A.F., and E. S. Karnofsky. 1982. *Plato's* Protagoras: *A Socratic Commentary.* London: Duckworth.

Hubbard, T. K. 1991. "Recitative Anapests and the Authenticity of *Prometheus Bound*." *AJP* 112, 439–60.

Hudson, B. A. 1996. *Understanding Justice: An Introduction to Ideas, Perspectives, and Controversies in Modern Penal Theory.* Buckingham: Open University Press.

Humphreys, S. 1978. *Anthropology and the Greeks.* London: Routledge.

————. 1983a. "The Evolution of Legal Process in Ancient Attica." In E. Gabba, ed., *Tria Corda: Scritti in onore di Arnaldo Momigliano*, 220–40. Como: Edizioni New Press.

————. 1983b. *The Family, Women, and Death: Comparative Studies.* London: Routledge.

————. 1985a. "Law as Discourse." *History and Anthropology* 1, 241–64.

————. 1985b. "Lycurgus of Butadae: An Athenian Aristocrat." In J. W. Eadie and J. Ober, eds., *The Craft of the Ancient Historian: Essays in Honor of Chester G. Starr*, 199–252. Lanham, Md.: University Press of America.

————. Humphreys, S. 1985c. "Social Relations on Stage: Witnesses in Classical Athens." *History and Anthropology* 1, 313–69.

————. 1986. "Kinship Patterns in the Athenian Courts." *GRBS* 27, 57–92.

————. 1989. "Family Quarrels Dem. 39–40." *JHS* 109, 182–84.

————. 1991. "A Historical Approach to Drakon's Law on Homicide." In Gagarin, ed., *Symposion 1990*, 17–46.

Hunter, V. 1990. "Gossip and the Politics of Reputation in Classical Athens." *Phoenix* 44, 299–325.

————. 1993. "Agnatic Kinship in Athenian Law and Athenian Family Practice: Its Implication for Women." In B. Halperin and D. Hobson, eds., *Law, Politics and Society in the Ancient Mediterranean World*, 100–116. Sheffield: Sheffield Academic Press.

————. 1994. *Policing Athens*. Princeton: Princeton University.

Hutchinson, A. C., and D. Monahan, eds. 1987. *The Rule of Law: Ideal or Ideology.* Toronto: Carswell.

Hutter, B., and G. Williams, eds. 1981. *Controlling Women: The Normal and the Deviant.* London: Croom Helm.

Huys, M. 1993. "Sophocle, *Électre* v. 674–1057: Le revirement d'une héroine sophoclénne aux traits euripidéens." *Mnemosyne* 46, 307–43.

Ignatieff, M. 1978. *A Just Measure of Pain: The Penitentiary in the Industrial Revolution, 1750–1850*. New York: Pantheon.

Irwin, T. 1985. "Moral Science and Political Theory in Aristotle." In P. Cartledge and D. Harvey, eds., *CRUX: Essays in Greek History Presented to G.E.M. de Ste. Croix on His 75th Birthday*. 150–68. Exeter: University of Exeter Press.

————. 1988. *Aristotle's First Principles*. Oxford: Clarendon Press.

Jacob, O. 1979. *Les esclaves publics à Athènes*. 1928. Reprint, New York: Arno Press.

Jaeger, W. 1957. "Aristotle's Use of Medicine as Model of Method in his Ethics." *JHS* 77, 54–61.

Jameson, F. 1984. "The Linguistic Model." In M. Shapiro, ed., *Language and Politics*, 168–194. New York: New York University Press. Reprinted from F. Jameson, *The Prison-House of Language*. Princeton: Princeton University Press, 1972.

Jang, I. H. 1997. "Socrates' Refutation of Thrasymachus." *HPT* 18, 189–206.

Jebb, R. C. 1914. *Sophocles, The Plays and Fragments*. Vols. 1–6. Cambridge: Cambridge University Press.

Jeffery, L. H. 1955. "Further Comments on Archaic Greek Inscriptions." *Annual of the British School at Athens* 50, 67–84.

————. 1976. *Archaic Greece: The City States, c. 700–500 B.C.* New York: St. Martin's Press.

Johnson, C. 1990. *Aristotle's Theory of the State*. Basingstoke: Macmillan.

Johnstone, C. 1997. "Women's Oaths." *Symposion*, 10, 173–99.

Jones, A.H.M. 1964. *Athenian Democracy*. 1957. Reprint, Oxford: Blackwell.

————. 1972. *The Criminal Courts of the Roman Republic and Principate*. Oxford: Basil Blackwell.

Joyal, M. 1991. "Euripides' *Medea* 487–7." *CQ* 41, 524–25.

Juffras, D. M. 1991. "Sophocles' *Electra* 973–85 and Tyrannicide." *TAPA* 121, 99–108.

Just, R. 1989. *Women in Athenian Law and Life*. London: Routledge.

Kagan, D. 1965. *The Great Dialogue: History of Greek Political Thought from Homer to Polybius*. New York: Free Press.

Karabélias, E. 1997. "L'arbitrage privé dans l'Athènes classique." In Thür and Vélissaropoulos-Karakostas, eds., *Symposion 1995*, 135–50.

Katz, M. 1994. "The Character of Tragedy: Women and the Greek Imagination." *Arethusa* 27, 81–104.

Katzouros, P. 1989. "Origine et effets de la paragraphe attique." In Thür, ed., *Symposion 1985*, 119–52.

Keaney, J. J. 1992. *The Composition of Aristotle's* Athenaion Politeia: *Observation and Explanation*. Oxford: Oxford University Press.

Keramopoullos, A. 1923. *Ho apotumpanismos: Sumbole arkhaiologike eis ten historian tou poinikou dikaiou kai ten laographian*. Athens.

Kerferd, G. B. 1947–48. "The Doctrine of Thrasymachus in Plato's *Republic*." *Durham University Journal* 9, 19–27.

Keuls, E. 1974. *The Water Carriers in Hades: A Study of Catharsis through Toil in Classical Antiquity*. Amsterdam: Adolm M. Hakkert.

———. 1993. *The Reign of the Phallus: Sexual Politics in Ancient Athens*. 1985. Reprint, Berkeley: University of California Press.

Kirk, G. S., J. E. Raven, and M. Schofield. 1983. *The Presocratic Philosophers: A Critical History with a Selection of Texts*. Cambridge: Cambridge University Press.

Kitto, H.D.F. 1964. *Form and Meaning in Drama: A Study of Six Greek Plays and of Hamlet*. 2nd ed. London: Methuen.

Klosko, G. 1986. *The Development of Plato's Political Theory*. New York, London: Methuen.

Knox, B. 1977. "The Medea of Euripides: Medea as Sophoclean Hero." *YCS* 25, 193–225.

Konstan, D. 1985. "The Politics of Aristophanes' *Wasps*." *TAPA* 115, 27–46.

———. 1996. "Greek Friendship." *AJP* 117, 71–94.

———. 1997. *Friendship in the Classical World*. Cambridge: Cambridge University Press.

Koumoulides, J. A., ed. 1995. *The Good Idea: Democracy and Ancient Greece*. New Rochelle, N.Y.: Caratzas.

Kraut, R. 1992. *The Cambridge Companion to Plato*. Cambridge: Cambridge University Press.

Krentz, P. 1982. *The Thirty at Athens*. Ithaca: Cornell University Press.

Kurtz, D., and J. Boardman. 1971. *Greek Burial Customs*. Ithaca: Cornell University Press.

Lacey, W. K. 1968. *The Family in Classical Greece*. Ithaca: Cornell University Press.

Lakoff, G. 1987. *Women, Fire, and Dangerous Things: What Categories Reveal about the Mind*. Chicago: University of Chicago Press.

Lakoff, G., and M. Turner. 1989. *More than Cool Reason: A Field Guide to Poetic Metaphor*. Chicago: University of Chicago Press.

Laks, A. 1990. "Legislation and Demiurgy: On the Relationship between Plato's *Republic* and *Laws*." *Classical Antiquity* 9, 209–29.

Lämmli, W. 1938. *Das attische Prozessverfahren in seiner Wirkung auf die Gerichtsrede*. Paderborn: F. Schöningh.

Lane, M. S. 1995. "A New Angle on Utopia: The Political Theory of the *Statesman*." In C. Rowe, ed., *Reading the* Statesman: *Proceedings of the III Symposium Platonicum*, 276–91. Sankt Augustin: Academic Verlag.

———. 1998. *Plato's* Statesman: *A Paradigm of Authority in Time*. Cambridge: Cambridge University Press.

Lane, W. J., and A. M. Lane. 1994. "Athenian Political Thought and the Feminist Politics of Poiesis and Praxis." In Euben, Wallach, and Ober, eds., *Athenian Political Thought*, 265–84.

Langbein, J. H. 1974. *Prosecuting Crime in the Renaissance in England, Germany, and France*. Cambridge, Mass.: Harvard University Press.

Lanza, D. 1977. *Il tiranno e il suo pubblico*. Turin: Einaudi.

Lanza, D., and M. Vegetti. 1977. "L'ideologia della città." In Lanza, Vegetti, Caiani, and Sircana, eds., *L'ideologia della città*, 13–28. Ligouri: Ligouri Editore.

Lattimore, R. 1964. *Story Patterns in Greek Tragedy*. London: Athlone Press.

Lear, J. 1995. *Aristotle: The Desire to Understand*. 1988. Reprint, Cambridge: Cambridge University Press.

———. 1992. "Inside and Outside the *Republic*." *Phronesis* 37, 184–215.

Leighton, S. R. 1988. "Aristotle's Courageous Passions." *Phronesis* 33, 76–99.

Lesky, A. 1983. "Decision and Responsibility." In Segal, ed., *Oxford Readings in Greek Tragedy*, 50–61.

Lévy, E. 1993. "Politeia et politeuma chez Aristote." In Piérart, ed., *Aristote et Athènes*, 65–90.

Lipsius, J. H. 1915. *Das Attische Recht und Rechtsverfahren*. Leipzig. O. R. Reisland.

Littman, R. J. 1990. *Kinship and Politics in Athens, 600–400 B.C.* New York: Peter Lang.

Lloyd-Jones, H. 1983. *The Justice of Zeus*. 2nd ed. Berkeley: University of California Press.

Lloyd-Jones, H., and N. G. Wilson. 1990. *Sophoclea: Studies on the Text of Sophocles*. Oxford: Clarendon Press.

Lofberg, G. 1917. *Sycophancy in Athens*. Menasha, Wis.: Collegiate Press.

Loraux, N. 1981. *L'invention d'Athènes: Histoire de l'oraison funèbre dans la cité classique*. Paris: Editions de l'école des hautes études en sciences sociales.

———. 1985. *Façons tragiques de tuer une femme*. Paris: Hachette.

———. 1993. *The Children of Athena: Athenian Ideas about Citizenship and the Division between the Sexes*. Trans. C. Levine. Princeton: Princeton University Press.

———. 1997. *La cité divisée: L'oubli dans la mémoire d'Athènes*. Paris: Éditions Payot & Rivages.

Lord, C. 1982. *Education and Culture in the Political Thought of Aristotle*. Ithaca: Cornell University Press.

Lord, C., and D. K. O'Connor, eds. 1991. *Essays in the Foundations of Aristotelian Political Science*. Berkeley: University of California Press.

Lucas, J. R. 1993. *Responsibility*. Oxford: Clarendon Press.

Luschnig, C.A.E. 1976. "Euripides' *Hekabe*: The Time Is Out of Joint." *CJ* 71, 227–34.

Lyotard, J.-F., and J.-L. Thébaud. 1996. *Just Gaming*. Trans. Wlad Godzich. Minneapolis: University of Minnesota Press.

MacDowell, D. M. 1962. *Andokides: On the Mysteries*. Oxford: Oxford University Press.

———. 1963. *Athenian Homicide Law in the Age of the Orators*. Manchester: Manchester University Press.

———, ed. 1971. *Aristophanes Wasps*. With introduction and commentary. Oxford: Clarendon Press.

———. 1976. "*Hybris* in Athens." *G&R* 23, 14–31.

———. 1978. *The Law in Classical Athens*. London: Thames and Hudson.

———. 1989. "The *Oikos* in Athenian Law." *CQ* 39, 10–21.

———. 1991. "The Athenian Procedure of Phasis." In Gagarin, ed., *Symposion 1990*, 187–98.

———. 1995. *Aristophanes and Athens: An Introduction to the Plays*. Oxford: Oxford University Press.

Mackenzie, M. M. 1981. *Plato on Punishment*. Cambridge: Cambridge University Press.

MacLachlan, B. 1993. *The Age of Grace: Charis in Early Greek Poetry*. Princeton: Princeton University Press.

MacLeod, C. 1982. "Politics and the *Oresteia*." *JHS* 102, 124–44.

McTighe, K. 1984. "Socrates on Desire for the Good and the Involuntariness of Wrong-Doing: *Gorgias* 446a-468e." *Phronesis* 29, 193–236. Reprinted as "Socrates on Desire for Good and the Involuntariness of Wrongdoing: *Gorgias* 446a-468e." In H. H. Benson, ed., *Essays on the Philosophy of Socrates*, 263–97. Oxford: Oxford University Press, 1992.

Maffi, A. 1983. "Atimazein e pheugein nei poemi omerici." In Dimakis and Biscardi, eds., *Symposion 1979*, 249–60.

Markus, R. A. 1978. "Plato and the Rule of Law." In Vlastos, ed., *Plato II*, 144–65.

Martin, C.F.J. 1990. "On the Alleged Inconsistency in the *Nicomachean Ethics* IX, 4." *JHS* 110, 188–91.

Meier, C. 1988. *Die politische Kunst der griechischen Tragödie*. Munich: Ch. Beck'sche Verlag.

———. 1990. *The Greek Discovery of Politics*. Trans. D. McLintock. Cambridge, Mass.: Harvard University Press.

Menzio, P. 1992. *Prometeo, sofferenza e partecipazione: lettura di Eschilo, Prometeo Incatenato*. Bologna: Patron.

Meridor, R. 1978. "Hecuba's Revenge. Some Observations on Euripides' *Hecuba*." *AJP* 99, 28–35.

Meritt, B. D. 1966. *Inscriptions from the Athenian Agora*. Meridian Conn.: Meridien Gravure.

Michelini, A. 1991. "The Maze of Logos: Euripides' *Suppliants, 163–249*." *Ramus* 20, 16–36.

———. 1994. "Political Themes in Euripides' *Suppliants*." *AJP* 115, 219–52.

Mikalson, J. D. 1991. *Honor Thy Gods: Popular Religion in Greek Tragedy*. Chapel Hill: University of North Carolina Press.

Miller, F., Jr. 1995. *Nature, Justice, and Rights in Aristotle's* Politics. Oxford: Clarendon Press.

———. 1996. "Aristotle and the Origin of Natural Rights." *Review of Metaphysics* 49, 873–908.

Millett, P. 1990. "Sale, Credit and Exchange in Athenian Law and Society." In P. Cartledge, P. Millett, and S. Todd, eds., *Nomos: Essays in Athenian Law, Politics and Society*, pp. 167–94. Cambridge: Cambridge University Press.

———. 1991. *Lending and Borrowing in Ancient Athens*. Cambridge: Cambridge University Press.

Mills, M. J. 1985. "*Phthonos* and Its Related *pathe* in Plato and Aristotle." *Phronesis* 30, 1–12.

Mirhady, D. C. 1991a. "The Oath-Challenge in Athens." *CQ* 41, 78–83.

———. 1991b. "Non-Technical *Pisteis* in Aristotle and Anaximenes." *JHS* 112, 5–28.

Modrzejewski J., D. Nörr, and H. J. Wolff, eds. 1975. *Symposium 1971*. Cologne: Bohlau Verlag.

Morris, I. 1992. *Death-Ritual and Social Structure in Classical Antiquity*. Cambridge: Cambridge University Press.

Morrow, G. 1960a. "Aristotle's Comments on Plato's *Laws*." In I. Düring and G.E.L. Owen, eds., *Aristotle and Plato in the mid-4th Century*, 145–62. Göteburg: Studia Graeca et Latina Gothoburgensia.

———. 1960b. *Plato's Cretan City: A Historical Interpretation of the* Laws. Princeton: Princeton University Press.

———. 1971. "Plato and the Rule of Law." In Vlastos, ed., *Plato II*, 144–65.

Mossé, C. 1969. *Histoire des doctrines politiques en Grèce*. Paris: Presses Universitaires de France.

————. 1975. "Métèques et étrangers à Athènes au IVe–IIIe siècles avant notre ère." In Modrzejewski, Nörr, and Wolff, eds., *Symposion 1971*, 205–14.

Mossé, C. 1995. *Politique et société en Grèce ancienne: Le "modèle" athénien*. Paris: Aubier.

————. Mossman, J. M. 1996. "Chains of Imagery in *Prometheus Bound*." *CQ* 46, no. 1, 58–67.

Muellner, L. 1996. *The Anger of Achilles: Menis in Greek Epic*. Ithaca: Cornell University Press.

Murnaghan, S. 1986. "*Antigone* 904–920 and the Institution of Marriage." *AJP* 107, 192–207.

Murray, O. 1995a. "Liberty and the Ancient Greeks." In Koumoulides, ed., *The Good Idea*, 35–56.

Nenci, G., and G. Thür, eds. 1990. *Symposion 1988: Akten der Gesellschaft für Griechische und Hellenistische Rechtsgschichte*. Cologne: Bohlau Verlag.

Newman, R. J. 1991. "Heroic Resolution: A Note on Sophocles, *Philoctetes* 1405–1406." *CJ* 86, 305–10.

Nicholson, P. P. 1974. "Unravelling Thrasymachus' Arguments in the *Republic*." *Phronesis* 19, 210–32.

Nilstun, T. 1981. *Aristotle on Freedom and Punishment*. Lund, Sweden: Distribution Studentlitteratur.

Nozick, R. 1981. *Philosophical Explanations*. Cambridge, Mass.: Harvard University Press.

Nussbaum, M. 1986. *The Fragility of Goodness: Luck and Ethics in Greek Tragedy and Philosophy*. Cambridge: Cambridge University Press.

Ober, J. 1987. "Pottery and Miscellaneous Artifacts from Attica." *Hesperia* 56, 197–227.

————. 1989a. *Mass and Elite in Democratic Athens: Rhetoric, Ideology, and the Power of the People*. Princeton: Princeton University Press.

————. 1989b. "The Nature of Athenian Democracy." Review of *The Athenian Assembly in the Age of Demosthenes* by Mogens Herman Hansen. *CP* 84, 322–34.

————. 1994. "How to Criticize Democracy in Late Fifth- and Fourth- Century Athens." In Euben, Wallach, and Ober, eds., *Athenian Political Thought*, 147–71.

Ober, J., and C. Hedrick, eds. 1996. *Demokratia: A Conversation on Democracies, Ancient and Modern*. Princeton: Princeton University Press.

O'Brien, J. V. 1978. *Guide to Sophocles' Antigone*. Carbondale: Southern Illinois University Press.

O'Higgins, D. 1991. "Narrators and Narrative in the *Philoctetes* of Sophocles." *Ramus* 20, 37–52.

Olson, S. D. 1996. "Politics and Poetry in Aristophanes' *Wasps*." *TAPA* 126, 129–50.

Ormand, K. 1993. "More Wedding Imagery." *Mnemosyne* 46, 224–27.

Osborne, R. 1985a. "Law in Action in Classical Athens." *JHS* 105, 40–58.

————. 1985b. *Demos: The Discovery of Classical Attika*. Cambridge: Cambridge University Press.

————. 1990. "Vexatious Litigation in Classical Athens." In Cartledge, Millett, and Todd, eds., *Nomos*, 83–102.

————. 1993. "Competitive Festivals and the Polis: A Context for Dramatic Festivals at Athens." In Sommerstein et al., eds., *Tragedy, Comedy and the Polis: Papers from the Greek Drama Conference*, 21–39.

Ostwald, M. 1969. *Nomos and the Beginnings of Athenian Democracy*. Oxford: Clarendon Press.

———. 1996. "Shares and Rights: 'Citizenship' Greek Style and American Style." In Ober and Hedrick, eds., *Demokratia*, 49–61.

Padel, R. 1992. *In and Out of the Mind: Greek Images of the Tragic Self.* Princeton: Princeton University Press.

———. 1995. *Whom Gods Destroy.* Princeton: Princeton University Press.

Padilla, M. W. 1994. "Heroic Paternity in Euripides' *Herakles.*" *Arethusa* 27, 279–302.

Paley, F. A., ed. 1879. *The Tragedies of Aeschylus.* 4th ed., rev. and corrected. London: Wittaker.

Panagiotou, S., ed. 1987. *Justice, Law, and Method in Plato and Aristotle.* Edmonton: Academic Printing and Publishing.

Paoli, V. E. 1933. *Studi sul processo attico.* Padua: Litotipo.

Parker, H., taken as pseudonymous for Francis Neal, by John Jones. 1650. "Reformation in Courts and Cases Testamentary." English Short Title Catalog Record (ESTCR) 206722, Thomason E.616[5].

Parker, R.C.T. 1983. *Miasma: Pollution and Purification in Early Greek Religion.* Oxford: Clarendon Press.

Patterson, C. 1994. "The Case against Neaira and the Public Ideology of the Athenian Family." In Boegehold and Scafuro, eds., *Athenian Identity and Civic Ideology*, 196–215.

Patterson, O. 1982. *Slavery and Social Death: A Comparative Study.* Cambridge, Mass.: Harvard University Press.

Pelling, C., ed. 1990. *Characterization and Individuality in Greek literature.* Oxford: Clarendon Press.

Penner, T. 1978. "Thought and Desire in Plato." In Vlastos, ed., *Plato II*, 96–118.

Peters, E. M. 1995. "Prison before the Prison: The Ancient and Medieval Worlds." In N. Morris and D. J. Rothman, eds., *The Oxford History of the Prison*, 3–48. Oxford: Oxford University Press.

Piérart, M. 1987. "Athènes et ses lois." *Revues des Études Anciennes* 89, 21–37.

———, ed. 1993. *Aristote et Athènes.* Paris: Diffusion de Boccard.

Pitt-Rivers, J. 1977. *The Fate of Shechem, or the Politics of Sex.* Cambridge: Cambridge University Press.

Podlecki, A. 1966. *The Political Background of Aeschylean Tragedy.* Ann Arbor: University of Michigan.

Poliakoff, M. B. 1987. *Combat Sports in the Ancient World: Competition, Violence, and Culture.* New Haven: Yale University Press.

Pollock, F., and F. Maitland. 1968. *The History of English Law.* Vols. 1–2. 1895. Reprint, Cambridge: Cambridge University Press.

Portman, J. 1995. "Three Strikes—The Second Inning." *Nolo News.* http://www.lectlaw.com. April 16, 1999.

Pozzi, D.C. 1994. "Deianeira's Robe: Diction in Sophocles' *Trachiniae.*" *Mnemosyne* 47, 577–85.

Pucci, P. 1980. *The Violence of Pity in Euripides' Medea.* Ithaca: Cornell University Press.

Putnam, R. D. 1993. *Making Democracy Work: Civic Traditions in Modern Italy.* Princeton: Princeton University Press.

Randall, J. H., Jr. 1960. *Aristotle.* New York: Columbia University Press.

Rackham, H., trans. 1952. *Aristotle: The Athenian Constitution; The Eudemian Ethics; On Virtue and Vices.* Cambridge, Mass.: Harvard University Press.

Radt, S. 1985. *Tragicorum Graecorum Fragmenta.* Vols. 1–3. Gottingen.

Reckford, K. J. 1977. "Catharsis and Dream Interpreation in Aristophanes' *Wasps*." *TAPA* 107, 283–312.

Redfield, J. 1975. *Nature and Culture in the* Iliad. Chicago: University of Chicago Press.

———. 1990. "From Sex to Politics: The Rites of Artemis Triklaria and Dionysos Aisymnetes at Patras." In Halperin, Winkler, and Zeitlin, eds., *Before Sexuality*, 115–34.

———. 1995. "Homo Domesticus." In Vernant, ed., *The Greeks*, 153–83.

Rhodes, P. J. 1972. *The Athenian Boule*. Oxford: Clarendon Press.

———. 1981. *A Commentary on the Aristotelian* Athenaion Politeia. Oxford: Clarendon Press.

Rickert, G. A. 1987. "Akrasia and Euripides' *Medea*." *HSCP* 91, 91–118.

Rihll, T. E. 1989. "Lawgivers and Tyrants." *CQ* 39, 277–86.

———. 1991. "EKTHMOROI: Partners in Crime?" *JHS* 111, 101–27.

Roberts, J. T. 1994. *Athens on Trial: The Anti-Democratic Tradition in Western Thought*. Princeton: Princeton University Press.

Robertson, N. 1993. "Athens' Festival of the New Wine." *HSP* 95, 197–250.

Rocco, C. 1997. *Tragedy and Enlightenment*. Berkeley: University of California Press.

Rogers, J. M. 1991. *The Coherence of Ethical and Political Thought in the* Laws *and the* Republic. Ann Arbor: UMI Dissertation Service.

———. 1975. *Magic and Rhetoric in Ancient Greece*. Cambridge, Mass.: Harvard University Press.

Rorty, A. O., ed. 1980. *Essays on Aristotelian Ethics*. Berkeley: University of California Press.

Rosaldo, M. Z., and L. Lamphere, eds. 1976. *Woman, Culture, and Society*. Stanford: Stanford University Press.

Ross, D. 1966. *Aristotle*. 1923. Reprint, London: Methuen.

Roth, D. 1993. "The Theme of Corrupted *Xenia* in Aeschylus' *Oresteia*." *Mnemosyne* 46, 1–17.

Roy, J. 1991. "On Cohen on Radishing." *LCM* 16, 73–76.

Rowe, C. 1984. *Plato*. New York: St. Martin's Press.

———, ed. 1995. "*Reading the* Statesman." In *Proceedings of the III Symposium Platonicum*. 276–91. Sankt Augustin: Academic Verlag.

Rubincam, C. R. 1979. "Thucydides 1.74.1 and the Use of *es* with numerals." *CP* 74, 327–37.

Rubinstein, L. 1993. "Persuasive Precedent." Paper presented at the annual meeting of the American Philological Association.

———. 1997. Paper on friendship groups in oratory presented at the annual meeting of the American Philological Association, New York, December.

Ruck, C. 1976. "Duality and the Madness of Herakles." *Arethusa* 9, 53–75.

Rusche, G., and O. Kircheimer. 1968. *Punishment and Social Structure*. 1939. Reprint, New York: Russell & Russell.

Ruschenbusch, E. 1957. "DIKASTERION PANTON KURION." *Historia* 6, 257–74.

———. 1960. "*Phonos*: Zum Recht Drakons und Seiner Bedeutung für das Werden des Athenischen Staates." *Historia* 9, 129–54.

———. 1982. "Drei Beiträge zur öffentlichen Diaita in Athens." In F.J.F. Fernández Nieto, ed., *Symposion 1982: Akten der Gesellschaft Griechische und Hellenistische Rechtsgeschichte*, 31–40. Cologne: Bohlau Verlag.

Russell, D. A. 1990. "Ethos in Oratory and Rhetoric." In Pelling, ed., *Characterization and Individuality in Greek Literature*, 197–212.

Sagan, E. 1995. "Citizenship as a Form of Psycho-Social Identity." In Koumoulides, ed., *The Good Idea*, 47–60.

Sahlins, M. 1972. *Stone Age Economics*. Chicago: University of Chicago Press.

Saïd, S. 1985. *Sophiste et Tyran: Ou le problème du* Prométhée Enchaîné. Paris: Klincksieck.

Ste. Croix, G. M. de. 1983. *The Class Struggle in the Ancient Greek World from the Archaic Age to the Arab Conquests*. Corrected ed. London: Duckworth.

Saunders, T. J. 1963. "Two Points in Plato's Penal Code." *CQ* 13, 194–99.

———. 1973. "Penology and Eschatology in Plato's *Timaeus* and *Laws*." *CQ* 23, 232–44.

———. 1975. *Bibliography on Plato's* Laws, *1920–1970, with Additional Citations through May 1975*. New York: Arno Press.

———. 1991. *Plato's Penal Code*. Oxford: Clarendon Press.

———. 1996. "Plato on the Treatment of Heretics." In Foxhall and Lewis, eds., *Greek Law in Its Political Setting*, 91–100.

Saxonhouse, A. W. 1992. *Fear of Diversity: The Birth of Political Science in Ancient Greek Thought*. Chicago: University of Chicago Press.

Scafuro, A. C. 1994. "Witnessing and False Witnessing: Proving Citizenship and Kin Identity in Fouth-Century Athens." In Boegehold and Scafuro, eds., *Athenian Ideology and Civic Identity*, 157–95.

———. 1997a. *The Forensic Stage: Settling Disputes in Graeco-Roman New Comedy*. Cambridge: Cambridge University.

———. 1997b. Paper on deme inscriptions presented at the annual meeting of the American Philological Association, New York, December.

Scarborough, J. 1991. "The Pharmacology of Sacred Plants, Herbs, and Roots." In Faraone and Obbink, eds., *Majika Hiera*, 138–74.

Scarry, E. 1987. *The Body in Pain: The Making and Unmaking of the World*. 1985. Reprint, Oxford: Oxford University Press.

Schaps, D. 1977. "The Woman Least Mentioned: Etiquette and Women's Names." *CQ* 27, 323–30.

Schepens, G. 1980. *L'autopsie dans le méthode des historiens grecs du 5e siècle avant J.C.* Brussels: Palais de Academiën.

Schlesier, R. 1993. "Mixtures of Masks: Maenads as Tragic Models." In T. H. Carpenter and C. Faraone, eds., *The Masks of Dionysos*, 89–114. Ithaca: Cornell University Press.

Schmid, W. 1929. *Untersuchungen zum Gefesselten Prometheus*. Tübingen: Beitrager Tübingen.

Schmitt-Pautel, C. 1990. "Collective Activities and the Political in the Greek City." In O. Murray and S.R.F. Price, *The Greek City*, 199–214. Oxford: Clarendon Press.

Schofield, M. 1996. "Sharing in the Constitution." *Review of Metaphysics* 49, 831–58.

Schreckenberg, H. 1964. *Ananke. Untersuchungen zur Geschichte des Wortegebrauchs. Zetemata* 36.

Schütrumpf, E. 1989. "Traditional Elements in the Concept of Hamartia in Aristotle's *Poetics*." *HSP* 92, 137–56.

Scodel, R. 1982. "*HYBRIS* in the Second Stasimon of the *Oedipus Rex*." *CP* 77, 214–23.

Scott, W. C. 1987. "The Development of the Chorus in *Prometheus Bound*." *TAPA* 117, 85–96.

Scully, J., and C. J. Herrington, trans. 1975. *Aeschylus'* Prometheus Bound. New York: Oxford University Press.

Seaford, R. 1987. "The Tragic Wedding." *JHS* 107, 106–30.

———. 1990. "The Imprisonment of Women in Greek Tragedy." *JHS* 110, 76–90.

———. 1994. *Reciprocity and Ritual: Homer and Tragedy in the Developing City-State.* Oxford: Clarendon Press.

Sealey, R. 1987. *The Athenian Republic: Democracy or Rule of Law?* University Park: Pennsylvania State University Press.

———. 1990. *Women and Law in Classical Greece.* Chapel Hill: University of North Carolina Press.

Segal, C. 1981. *Tragedy and Civilization: An Interpretation of Sophocles.* Cambridge, Mass.: Harvard University Press.

———. 1990a. "Golden Armor and Servile Robes: Heroism and Metamorphosis in *Hecuba* of Euripides." *AJP* 111, 304–17.

———. 1990b. "Violence and the Other: Greek, Female, and Barbarian in Euripides' *Hecuba*." *TAPA* 120, 109–31.

———. 1995. "Spectator and Listener." In Vernant, ed., *The Greeks*, 184–217.

Segal, E., ed. 1983. *Oxford Readings in Greek Tragedy.* Oxford: Oxford University Press.

Shaw, M. H. 1982. "The *ethos* of Theseus in the *Suppliant Women*." *Hermes* 110, 3–19.

Shelton, J.A. 1979. "Structural Unity and the Meaning of Euripides' *Herakles*." *Eranos* 77, 101–10.

Shiner, R. 1987. "Aristotle's Theory of Equity." In Panagiotou, ed., *Justice, Law, and Method in Plato and Aristotle*, 173–92.

Shipp, G. 1978. *Nomos "Law."* Sydney: Sydney University Press.

Shklar, J. 1987. "Political Theory and the Rule of Law." In Hutchinson and Monahan, eds., *The Rule of Law*, 1–16.

Shorey, P. 1903. *The Unity of Plato's Thought.* Chicago: University of Chicago Press.

———. 1914. "Plato's *Laws* and the Unity of Plato's Thought." *CP* 9, 345–69.

Sidwell, K. 1989. "The Sacrifice at Aristophanes *Wasps* 860–90." *Hermes* 117, 271–77.

———. 1990. "Was Philokleon Cured? The *NOSOS* Theme in Aristophanes' *Wasps*." *C&M* 41, 9–31.

———. 1992. "The Argument in the Second Stasimon of *Oedipus Tyrannus*." *JHS* 112, 106–22.

———. 1996. "Purificiation and Pollution in Aeschylus' *Eumenides*." *CQ* 46, no. 1, 44–57.

Siemsen, T. 1987. "Thrasymachus' Challenge." *HPTh* 8, 1–19.

Sienkewicz, T. J. 1983–84. "The Chorus of *Prometheus Bound*: Harmony of Suffering." *Ramus* 12–13, 60–73.

Sinclair, R. K. 1988. *Democracy and Participation in Athens.* Cambridge: Cambridge University Press.

Sinclair, T. A. 1951. *History of Greek Political Thought.* London: Routledge.

Small, J. 1995a. "Recent Scientific Advances in the Understanding of Memory." *Helios* 22, 156–58.

———. 1995b. "Artificial Memory and the Writing Habits of the Literate." *Helios* 22, 159–66.

Snell, B. 1953. *The Discovery of the Mind.* Trans. T. G. Rosenmeyer. Oxford: Basil Blackwell.

Sommerstein, A. H. 1989a. "Again Clytemnestra's Weapon." *CQ* 39, 296–301.

———, ed. 1989b. *Aeschylus'* Eumenides. Cambridge: Cambridge University Press.

———. 1996. *Aeschylean Tragedy.* Bari: Levante Editori.

Sommerstein, A. H., S. Halliwell, J. Henderson, and B. Zimmermann, eds. 1993. *Tragedy, Comedy and the Polis: Papers from the Greek Drama Conference, Nottingham, 18–20 July 1990*. Bari: Levante Editori.

Soubie, A. 1973. "Les preuves dans les plaidoyers des orateurs attiques." *RIDA* 20, 171–253.

Sorabji, R. 1978. *Necessity, Cause and Blame*. London: Gerald Duckworth.

Sparshott, F. E. 1966. "Socrates and Thrasymachus." *Phronesis* 50, 421–59.

Stalley, R. F. 1995a. "Punishment in Plato's *Laws*." *History of Political Thought* 16, 476–96.

———. 1995b. "Punishment in Plato's *Protagoras*." *Phronesis* 40, 1–19.

———. 1996. "Punishment and the Physiology of the *Timaeus*." *CQ* 46, no. 2, 357–70.

Stanford, W. B. 1983. *Greek Tragedy and the Emotions: An Introductory Study*. London: Routledge.

Stanton, G. R. 1990. *Athenian Politics, c. 800–500 B.C.* New York: Routledge.

———. 1995. "Aristocratic Obligation in Euripides' *Hekabe*." *Mnemosyne* 48, 11–33.

Starr, C. G. 1961. "The Decline of the Early Greek Kings." *Historia* 10, 2–10.

———. 1986. *Individual and Community: The Rise of the Polis, 800–500 BC*. Oxford: Oxford University Press.

———. 1990. *The Birth of Athenian Democracy: The Assembly in the 5th Century B.C.* Oxford: Oxford University Press.

Steiner, D. T. 1994. *The Tyrant's Writ: Myths and Images of Writing in Ancient Greece*. Princeton: Princeton University Press.

Steinwenter, A. 1925. *Die Streitbeendigung durch Urteil, Schiedsspruch und Vergleich nach griechischen Rechte*. Munich: Beck.

Stephens, J. C. 1995. "The Wound of Philoctetes." *Mnemosyne* 48, 153–68.

Stinton, D. 1976. "Notes on Greek Tragedy," *JHS* 96, 121–45.

Strachan-Davidson, J. L. 1969. *Problems of the Roman Criminal Law*. 1912. Reprint, Amsterdam.

Strauss, L. 1978. *The City and Man*. 1964. Reprint, Chicago: University of Chicago Press.

———. *The Argument and Action of Plato's Laws*. 1975. Reprint, Chicago: University of Chicago.

Stroud, R. S. 1974. "An Athenian Law on Silver Coinage." *Hesperia* 43, 157–88.

Swarney, P. 1993. "Social Status and Social Behaviour as Criteria in Judicial Proceedings in the Late Republic." In B. Halperin and D. Hobson, eds., *Law, Politics and Society in the Ancient Mediterranean World*, 137–55. Sheffield: Sheffield Academic Press.

Szegedy-Maszak, A. 1978. "Legends of the Greek Lawgivers." *GRBS* 19, 199–210.

Talamanca, M. 1979. "*Dikazein e krinein*: alle origine dell'attività giurisdizionale in Grecia." In Wolff, Modrzejewski, and Dimakis, eds. *Symposion 1974*, 103–36.

Taplin, O. 1977. *The Stagecraft of Aeschylus: The Dramatic Use of Exits and Entrances in Greek Tragedy*. Oxford: Clarendon Press.

Tatum, J. 1995a. "Memory in Recent Humanistic Reserch." *Helios* 22, 151–55.

———. 1995b. "Aunt Elvie's Quilt on the Bed of Odysseus: The Role of Artifacts in Natural Memory." *Helios* 22, 167–74.

Tatum, J., and J. Small. 1995a. "Memory and the Study of Classical Antiquity." *Helios* 22, 149–74.

———. 1995b. "Introduction." *Helios* 22, 149–50.

Taylor, A. E. 1936. *Plato, the Man and His Work*. New York: Dial Press.

Taylor, C. 1986. "Foucault on Freedom and Truth." In Hoy, ed., *Foucault: A Critical Reader*, 69–102.

Theodorou, Z. 1993. "Subject to Emotion: Exploring Madness in *Orestes*." *CQ* 43, 32–46.

Thomas, C., and E. Webb. 1994. "From Orality to Rhetoric." In Worthington, ed., *Persuasion*, 3–23.

Thomas, R. 1989. *Oral Tradition and Written Record in Classical Athens*. Cambridge: Cambridge University Press.

————. 1992. *Literacy and Orality in Ancient Greece*. Cambridge: Cambridge University Press.

————. 1994. "Literacy and the City-State in Archaic and Classical Greece." In A. K. Bowman and G. Woolf, eds., *Literacy and Power*, 33–50. Cambridge: Cambridge University Press.

————. 1995. "Written in Stone? Liberty, Equality, Orality, and the Codification of Law." *BICS* 40, 59–74. Reprinted in Foxhall and Lewis, eds., *Greek Law in Its Political Setting*, 9–32.

Thomas, Y., et al. 1984. *Du châtiment dans la cité: Supplices corporels et peines de mort dans le monde antique*. Collection de L'École Française de Rome 79. Paris: Palais Farnèse.

Thompson, S. 1989. *Motif-Index of Folk Literature: A Classification of Narrative Elements in Folk Tales, Ballads, Myths, Fables, Mediaeval Romances, Exempla, Tableaux, Jest Books, and Local Legends*. Bloomington: Indiana University Press.

Thomson, G. 1966. *Aeschylus and Athens: A Study in the Social Origins of Drama*. 1941. Reprint, London: Lawrence & Wishart.

Thonissen, L. 1875. *Le droit pénal de la république athénienne*. Paris: Durand & Lauriel.

Thür, G. 1970. "Zum *dikazein* bei Homer." *ZRG* 87, 426–44.

————. 1977. *Beweisführung vor den Schwurgerichtschen Athens: Die Proklesis zur Basanos*. Vienna: Akademie des Wissenschaft.

————. 1979. "*Proklesis eis basanon*." In Wolff, Modrzejewski, and Dimakis, eds. *Symposion 1974*, 153–74.

————, ed. 1989. *Symposion 1985: Akten der Gesellschaft für Griechische und Hellenistische Rechtsgeschichte*. Cologne: Bohlau Verlag.

————. 1991. "The Jurisdiction of the Areopagus in Homicide Cases." In Gagarin, ed., *Symposion 1990*, 53–72.

————. 1996. "Oaths and Dispute Settlement in Ancient Greek Law." In Foxhall and Lewis, eds., *Greek Law in Its Political Setting*, 57–72.

Thür, G., and J. Vélissaropoulos-Karakostas, eds. 1997. *Symposion 1995: Akten der Gesellschaft für Griechische und Hellenistische Rechtsgeschichte*. Cologne: Bohlau Verlag.

Tod, M. N. 1946–50. *A Selection of Greek Historical Inscriptions*. Vols. 1–2. 2nd ed. Oxford: Clarendon Press.

Todd, S. 1990. "The Purpose of Evidence in Athenian Courts." In Cartledge, Millett, and Todd, eds., *Nomos*, 19–40.

————. 1995. *The Shape of Athenian Law*. 1993. Reprint, Oxford: Oxford University Press.

————. Todd, S. C. (forthcoming). "How to Execute People in Fourth-Century Athens." In J. Edmondson and V. J. Hunter, eds., *Law and Social Status in Classical Athens*. Oxford: Oxford University Press.

————. 1997b. "Status and Gender in Athenian Public Records." In Thür and Vélissaropoulos-Karakostas, eds., *Symposion 1995*, 113–24.

Treston, H. J. 1923. *Poine*. London: Longman, Green.

Triantaphyllopoulos, J. 1975. "Rechtsphilosophie and positives Recht in Griechenland." In Modrzejewski, Nörr, and Wolff, eds., *Symposion 1971*, 23–66.

Triomphe, R. 1992. *Prométhée et Dionysos, ou la Grèce à lueur des torches.* Strasbourg: Université Strasbourg.

Vaio, J. 1971. "Aristophanes' *Wasps*: The Relevance of the Final Scenes." *GRBS* 12, 335–51.

Vanderpool, E. 1976. "The Prison of Socrates." *Illustrated London News* 274, 87–88.

van Effenterre, H., and M. van Effenterre. 1990. "Le controle des étranger dans la cité grecque." In Nenci and Thür, eds., *Symposion 1988*, 251–60.

———. 1994a. "Écrire sur les murs." In H.-J. Gehrke, ed., *Rechtskodifizierung und soziale Normen im interkulturellen Vergleich*, 87–122. Tübingen: Gunter Narr Verlag.

———. 1994b. "Arbitrages Homerique." In Thür, ed., *Symposion 1985*, 3–10.

Vanoyeke, V. 1976. *La naissance des jeux olympiques et le sport dans l'antiquité.* Paris: Les Belles Lettres.

Vellacott, P. 1984. *The Logic of Tragedy: Morals sand Integrity in Aeschylus' Oresteia.* Durham, N.C.: Duke University Press.

Vernant, J-P. 1969. *Mythe et pensé chez les grec: Études de psychologie historique.* 2nd ed. Paris: François Maspero.

———. 1980. *Myth and Society in Ancient Greece.* Trans. J. Lloyd. Sussex: Harvester Press.

———, ed. 1995. *The Greeks.* Trans. C. Lambert and T. L. Fagan. Chicago: University of Chicago.

Vernant, J.-P., and P. Vidal-Naquet. 1988a. *Oedipe et ses mythes.* Brussels: Editions Complexe.

———. 1988b. *Tragedy and Myth in Ancient Greece.* 2nd ed., Trans. J. Lloyd. New York: Zone Books.

Versnel, H. S. 1991. "Beyond Cursing: The Appeal to Justice in Judicial Prayers." In Faraone and Obbink, eds., *Majika Hiera*, 33–59.

Vlastos, G. 1977. *Platonic Studies.* 1973. Reprint, Princeton: Princeton University Press.

———, ed. 1978a. *Plato II: Ethics, Politics, and Philosophy of Art and Religion: A Collection of Critical Essays.* 1971. Reprint, New York: Doubleday.

———. 1978b. "Justice and Happiness in the *Republic*." In Vlastos ed., *Plato II*, 66–95.

———. 1980. "Socrates' Contribution to the Greek Sense of Justice." *Archaiognosia* 1, 301–20.

———. 1991. *Socrates: Ironist and Moral Philosopher.* Cambridge: Cambridge University Press.

von Leyden, W. 1985. *Aristotle on Equality and Justice.* Basingstoke: Macmillan.

von Reden, S. 1995. *Exchange in Ancient Greece.* London: Duckworth.

Wade-Gery, H. T. 1958. "The Judicial Treaty with Phaselis and the History of the Athenian Courts." In *Essays in Greek History.* London: Basil Blackwell.

Walcot, P. 1978. *Envy and the Greeks: A Study of Human Behaviour.* Warminster: Aris & Phillips.

Wallace, R. 1989. *The Areopagus Council to 307 B.C.* 1985. Reprint, Baltimore: Johns Hopkins University Press.

———. 1994. "Private Lives and Public Lives and Public Enemies: Freedom of Thought in Classical Athens." In Boegehold and Scafuro, eds., *Athenian Identity and Civic Ideology*, 127–55.

Walsh, G. B. 1979. "Public and Private in Three Plays of Euripides." *CP* 74, 294–309.

Waluchow, W. J. 1987. "Professor Weinrib on Corrective Justice." In Panagiotou, ed., *Justice, Law, and Method in Plato and Aristotle*, 153–58.

Walzer, M. 1986. "The Politics of Michel Foucault." In Hoy, ed., *Foucault: A Critical Reader*, 51–68.

Wasserman, F. M. 1940. "Divine Violence and Providence in Euripides' *Ion*." *TAPA* 71, 587–604.

Weber, M. 1946. *Essays in Sociology*. Trans., ed., and introd. H. H. Gerth and C. Wright Mills. New York: Oxford University Press.

———. 1975. *The Interpretation of Social Reality*. Ed., and introd. J.E.T. Eldridge. 1971. Reprint, New York: Scribner.

Weinrib, E. 1987a. "Aristotle's Forms of Justice." In Panagiotou, ed., *Justice, Law, and Method in Plato and Aristotle*.

———. 1987b. "The Intelligibility of the Rule of Law." In Hutchinson and Monahan, eds., *The Rule of Law*, 59–84.

White, F. C. 1990. "The Good in Plato's *Gorgias*." *Phronesis* 35, 117–27.

Whitehead, D. 1977. *The Ideology of the Athenian Metic*. Cambridge Philological Society, supp. vol. 4. Cambridge: Cambridge University Press.

———. 1986. *The Demes of Attica, 508/7–ca. 250 B.C.: A Political and Social Study*. Princeton: Princeton University Press.

Whitehorne, J. 1989. "Punishment under the Decree of Cannonus." In Thür, ed., *Symposion 1988*, 89–98.

Wilamowitz-Moellendorff, U. von. 1893. *Aristotles und Athen*. Vols. 1–3. Berlin: Weidmann.

———. 1958. *Aeschyli Tragoediae*. 5th ed. Berlin: August Raabe.

Williams, B. 1993. *Shame and Necessity*. Berkeley: University of California Press.

Williams, J. W. 1982. *Athens without Democracy: The Oligarchy of Phocion and the Tyranny of Demetrius of Phalerum, 322–207 BC*. Ann Arbor: University of Michigan.

Willink, C. W., ed. 1986. *Euripides'* Orestes. Oxford: Clarendon Press.

———. 1988a. "Euripides' *Medea* 1–45, 371–85." *CQ* 38, 313–23.

———. Winkler, J. J. 1990a. *The Constraints of Desire: The Anthropology of Sex and Gender in Ancient Greece*. New York: Routledge.

———. 1990b. "Laying Down the Law: The Oversight of Men's Sexual Behavior in Classical Athens." In Halperin, Winkler, and Zeitlin, eds., *Before Sexuality*, 171–210.

———. 1991. "The Constraints of Eros." In Faraone and Obbink, eds., *Majika Hiera*, 214–43.

Winkler, J., and F. Zeitlin, eds. 1990. *Nothing to Do with Dionysos?* Princeton: Princeton University Press.

Wolff, H. J. 1946. "The Origin of Judicial Litigation among the Greeks." *Traditio* 4, 31–88.

———. 1961. *Beiträge zur Rechtsgeschichte Altgriechenlands und des Hellenistischen Römischen Ägypten*. Weimar: Böhlaus Nachfolger.

———. 1966. *Die attische* Paragraphe: *Ein Beitrag zum Problem der Auflockerung archaïscher Prozessformen*. Weimar: Böhlau.

Wolff, H. J., J. Modzrejewski, and W. M. Dimakis. 1979. *Symposion 1974: Akten der Gesellschaft für Griechicsche und Hellenistische Rechtsgeschichte*. Cologne: Bohlau Verlag.

Wolin, S. 1994. "Norm and Form: The Constitutionalizing of Democracy." In Euben, Wallach, and Ober, eds., *Athenian Political Thought*, 29–58.

Wolpert, A. 1995. "Rebuilding the Walls of Athens: Democratic Ideology, Civic Discourses." Ph.D. dissertation, University of Chicago.

Worthington, I., ed. 1994. *Persuasion*. London: Routledge.

Wycherley, R. E. 1978. *The Stones of Athens*. Princeton: Princeton University Press.

Yunis, H. 1988. "The Debate on Undetected Crime and an Undetected Fragment from Euripides' *Sisyphus*." *ZPE* 75, 39–46.

———. 1989. "Law, Politics, and the *Graphe Paranomon*." *GRBS* 29, 361–82.

Zanker, G. 1990. "Loyalty in the *Iliad*." *Papers of the Leeds International Latin Seminar*, 6, 211–27.

———. 1992. "Sophocles' *Ajax* and the Heroic Values of the *Iliad*." *CQ* 42, 20–25.

Zeitlin, F. 1978. "The Dynamics of Misogyny: Myth and Mythmaking in the Oresteia." *Arethusa* 11, 149–84.

———. 1991. "Euripides' *Hekabe* and the Somatics of Dionysiac Drama." *Ramus* 20, 53–94.

———. 1995. "Art, Memory, and *Kleos*, in Euripides' *Iphigeneia in Aulis*." In Goff, ed., *History, Theory, Tragedy*, 150–98.

———. 1996. *Playing the Other: Gender and Society in Classical Greek literature*. Chicago: University of Chicago Press.

Ziebarth, E. 1897. "Popularklagen mit Delatorenpreaemien nach Griechsichen Recht." *Hermes* 32, 609–28.

Zuntz, G. 1993. "Aeschyli *Prometheus*." *HSPC* 95, 107–12.

Abramson, J., 177
accusations, 7, 99–101; actionable, 102–104; *apagoge*, 46; *eisangelia*, 41, 46, 354n.78; *endeixis*, 46; *ephegesis*, 46; inability of women to make, 104; *phasis*, 43, 46; *probole*, 46, 345n.4; of sycophancy, 157–158; by women, 102
Achilles, 101, 206
acquiescence, 197–98, 223–24, 298; as consensus of community, 93, 212; in *Prometheus Bound*, 30, 33, 295; role of, in construction of authority, 197–98, 200, 209, 231–32, 236–37, 298–99; role of, in democratic punishment, 212, 223–24, 231–32, 240–42; of wrongdoer, 210–11, 216, 238–40. *See also* silence
acquittal, 5, 7; of Orestes, 20
Acropolis, 112, 239
action: anger as, 53–54, 59–60; collective, 141–46, 202, 230; judgments of, 102. *See also* stonings
actors (agents), 16, 17, 35–36, 59, 69, 70–71, 87, 122, 201, 241; Aristotle on the importance of, 287–88, 290–91; critique of women as, 113–18; and Foucault, 299–302; and human agency, 296; impartial judicial, 18; individual vs. collective, 74, 202, 230; and lawmakers, 92; and penal agents, 18, 23, 70; private, 5, 8; public, 5, 20, 40, 135–36; slaves as, 104, 110; strategies of, 17, 34, 45–46, 51, 84, 99, 123, 170; women as, 111–13, 140, 145. *See also* norms of public agency; rhetoric
Adeimantos, 258, 259, 266
adikia, 283
Adkins, A.W.H., 352n.50, 358n.28, 359n.53, 364n.3, 403n.1
adultery: of Eratosthenes, 110, 126–27; of Hippolyta, 101. *See also* wrongdoing
Aegisthus, 19, 83, 87, 209
Aeschines, 203, 219; in *Against Timarchos*, 224; as demagogue, 130–31; on private interests, 152–53; on production of witnesses, 106, 122; on rule of law, 180–81; 194, 373n.16, 384n.30; on stoning of Lycidas, 145, 169, 172, 174, 177
Aeschylus: *Agamemnon*, 19, 20, 21, 116, 118, 209; *Eumenides*, 20, 21, 22, 77, 80, 114, 137, 178; *Libation Bearers*, 19, 21, 118,

137, 138, 139; *Oresteia*, 18, 19, 22, 24, 25, 83, 88, 93, 117, 137, 338n.35, 349n.13; *Prometheus Bound*, 25–33, 89, 294–302, 338n.37; *Prometheus Unbound*, 293
Aethra, 89, 90, 361n.76
Afterlife. *See* Plato; punishment
Agamemnon, 19, 21, 77, 83, 84, 85, 87, 88, 89, 93, 94, 114, 134, 139, 207, 209
Agamemnon, 19, 20, 21, 116, 118
agent. *See* actors
agon, 122. *See* competition; trial
agora: use of in production of witnesses, 106, 169, 136, 280
Agoratus, 152
aidos, 296
aikiai. *See* outrages
Ajax, 84
akolasia, 283
akribeia, 186; in Plato's *Laws*, 385n.62
Alcibiades, 107, 228
Alcmene, 86, 87, 116
allotment, 309–12. *See also* voting
American Civil Liberties Union, 177
American Revolution, 177
amnesty, 200, 232, 237–40, 241; for oligarchs, 196, 238, 239; after Persian Wars, 239. *See also* remembering/forgetting
Amphyctionic Council, 219
amunomai, 125
anakrisis, 103
anangke, 155. *See also* necessity
Anaximenes: on evidence, 175
Andocides, 61, 170, 183, 203, 227, 233, 235, 239; imprisonment of, 227; and penal inscriptions, 192
andreia, 115, 268
Andromache, 204, 207
Andromache, 83
Androtion, 152
anger
—dangers of, 85–86: as cause of pollution, 217; in excess, 90, 93; as revealed in eyes, 78–80
—and *eros*, 54, 102–3, 112, 119, 161–64. *See also* desire; emotion
—felt by: citizens, 60, 151, 231, 378n.8; collective bodies, 136, 145–46, 378n.8; Prometheus, 294–97; women, 51, 113–20. *See also* hot blood

anger (*cont.*)
—language of, 51–52, 75n.18: in oratory, 148–60, 172–77; in comedy, 160–67; in tragedy, 113–18, 294–97. *See also* symbols; *thumoeides*
—and pity, 149–50, 168, 195, 251, 252, 253, 254, 255, 258, 261, 262, 263, 268, 269, 299, 288, 378n.11
—types of: Aristotelian definition of, 117, 283; as *astunomoi orgai*, 51, 93, 94, 348n.4; as *cholos*, 56–58, 76, 83, 351n.35; as *menis*, 52, 76, 84, 348n.2, 349n.8, 350n.30; as *orge*, 9, 10, 11, 17, 19, 20–23, 26, 30, 33–35, 50–57, 149, 197, 224, 348nn.2 and 3, 349nn.6, 12, 17, 21, and 23, 350nn.32 and 34, 353nn.52 and 62, 354n.78, 356n.100; in Plato and the just city, 246–47, 251, 254, 280
—uses of: as aid to memory, 170–71; and control of, 58–59; as evidence, 175; as guided by laws, 174; as measurable and dispensable good, 165, 172–74, 195; by Plato, 281; valorization of, 134, 135, 140, 160, 246, 261. *See also* hotblood
Annas, J. 400n.24
Anthesteria, 73, 95
Antigone, 82, 91, 92, 93, 188, 209, 222; imprisoned, 208
Antigone, 91, 188
Antiphon, 65, 204, 348n.2; in *Against the Stepmother*, 113, 118; 134; on laws as guides, 175, 182; and murder laws, the murder of slaves, and pollution, 111, 176, 183, 192, 194, 388n.88; on youth and necessity, 155, 172
anthropology, 52, 62
apographe, 123
Apollo, 116, 134, 137
Apology, 47, 247, 260, 277
apotumpanismos, 200, 201, 213, 214, 215, 219, 232, 233, 234, 235, 236, 388n.10, 389nn.11 and 12, 392n.73, 397n.132. *See also podokakke*; stocks
appeal, 48, 242
arbitration, 41, 42, 43, 48, 49, 112–13, 123, 334n.27, 346n.52; and numbers of arbitrators, 322; private, 42, 343nn.19 and 20; public, 43, 47, 344nn.26, 29, 30 and 31; role of speech in, 320–321; as spectacle, 66; two types of, 317–322
archai. *See* magistrates
archons. *See* magistrates
Areopagus, 103; Aeschylean, 117, 129, 137; and development of democracy, 19, 20, 21,

22–24, 337n.28; as homicide court and elite power, 43, 45, 47, 48, 344n.32, 345nn.35 and 36, 346n.50
arete, 296
Arginusae, battle of, 42, 240
Argos, 19, 20, 21, 79, 88, 93, 209
aristocracy. *See* elites
Aristophanes: *Birds*, 164; *Clouds*, 164; on drones/wasps, 270–71; *Frogs*, 233; on hemlock, 232, 233, 235; *Knights*, 219; *Peace*, 164; *Thesmophoriasouzae*, 201; *Wasps*, 22, 55, 105, 113, 121, 128–33, 267, 160–62, 163; *Wealth*, 64, 163
Aristotle, 36, 54, 79, 81, 225, 229, 231, 349n.12; on anger, 53, 59, 117; on desert, 282–89; on deterrence, 283; *Nicomachean Ethics*, 187, 283, 284; on pathos, 150; *Politics*, 183, 184–85, 187, 188, 385–86n.66; on punishment, 70, 71, 283–89; on reciprocity and money, 289–90; on reform, 283; *Rhetoric*, 57, 102, 104, 117, 174, 179, 186, 188, 233, 286; on types of regime, 188–89, 190, 254, 386n.69; on voluntariness, 284, 288; on use of symbols, 271–72; 282, 283, 285–91. *See also* "rule of law"
Artayctes, 200, 201
assembly, 6, 40, 42, 44, 46, 49, 58, 229, 230; as *heliaia*, 48
aste, astos, 138
Astyanax, 205; precipitation of, 207
ataphia, 199, 201, 216, 217, 218, 219, 232, 237, 240, 241, 280, 392n.77, 393n.81. *See also* burial
Athena, 114, 137, 178
Athens, fall of, 190
atimia, 202, 203, 204, 224, 227, 390n.24; and fines, 229, 230; of prison sentence, 228; of state debtor, 208, 225
atimos, 116, 142
attorney general, British, 3
Augustine, 282
authority, xi, 33; and authorship, 90–91; conceptual foundations of, 9, 263–77, 298; construction of, 23–24, 30, 145, 168, 177, 197–198; contested, 23, 52, 88, 141, 197–98, 212, 236–37, 299; definition of, 281, 298, 300–301; as discussed in oratory, 182–83; and gender, 117–18; as legitimacy, 23, 51, 88, 101, 116, 124–25, 146; production of truth through, 23; in relation to force, Foucauldian power-knowledge, the *Oresteia*, *Prometheus Bound*, and speech, 23, 25–35, 26–28, 31–33, 231–32, 236–37, 298; revi-

sion of, 277; study of, 298–99; structure of, 141–42
axia, ta, 149–50, 287

Baker, N. V. 333n.2
Barker, E., 179
Bataille, G., 354n.70
Bdelycleon, 128–33, 160–61, 172, 261. *See also* Aristophanes: *Wasps*
Beccaria, C., 282
bees, 53, 55, 59, 352n..48. *See also* symbols: bees/drones as
Benhabib, S., 336n.8
Birds, 164
blood, 213, 214; and blood money, 225
body, 4, 56, 59, 67, 77, 84, 90, 222, 223, 240, 350nn.25, 26, and 29; bones of, 237; of citizens, 213–16, 228–32, 237–38; of the condemned, 200, 213, 219–20, 235–37, 245, 269; in democracy vs. in empire, 223; and emotions, 56–57; rhetoric of the, 199, 214–15, 231–32, 245–46; role of, in punishment and war, 199, 212, 215; silence about, 215–16, 228–32; of slaves, 213–16; of women, 230–32. *See also* blood
boule. See Council of 500
Bourdieu, P: on the practice of punishing, 17, 335n.7
Britain, 3, 5, 6, 7; juries in, 5–8; law in, 177–78; prosecution in, 3, 3n.2
Browne, R. A., 376n.49
burial, 199; customary, 236; as memorialization, 216; public, 236; refusal of, 216–23, 237, 240, 325. *See also* religion
Burke, K., 120, 245, 267
Burnett, A., 362n.90, 363n.97, 371n.81
Burnett, D. G., 390n.30

California, 6
Callicles, 249, 251
Cantarella, E., 335n.1
capital punishment, 63–64, 232–37; and suicide, 235
Carawan, E., 343n.17, 345n.38
Cartledge, P., 384n.43
Cassandra, 85, 93, 118, 372n.88
Cephalus, 258
Cephisiades: as powerless metic, 108
Chaeronea, Battle of, 156
character: use of as evidence, 172
charis, 53, 149; as rhetorical device, 156
Charondas of Catana: laws of 225
Children of Herakles, 83, 116

Choes, 73, 74, 82, 95, 96, 357nn.2, 3, 4, 5, 6, and 7, 358n.9; as Day of the Jugs, 195
cholos, 101, 114
choregos. See magistrates
Cicero, 296; *Tusculan Disputations,* 293–94, 297
citizens, 3, 10, 223–24; behavior of, 165–67; and citizen identity, 213; and corporal punishment, 215, 238; by decree, 215; and disfranchisement, 230; as expelling, 207; and the Furies, 22; as head of *oikos,* 122, 134–38, 140; and imprisonment, 228, 229, 232; integrity of, 216, 241; male, 17, 35, 36, 39, 40, 41, 43, 44, 45, 46, 49, 50–51, 58, 60, 68, 74, 103–4; and manhood, 241; as prosecutors, 72, 122–28, 128–33; as punishers, 40–42, 100, 122–33, 135; and silence, 198; as spectators, 29, 99; as witnesses, 105–106. *See also* citizenship; civic restraint
citizenship, 52, 55, 58–59, 72, 85, 88; definitions of, 17, 241; development of, 111; duties of, 129, 131–32, 142; foundations of, 136–37, 300; as honor, 61; loss of, 203–4; modern vs. ancient, 3; Platonic feminization of, 264; privileges of, 108–9, 134, 213–16, 230–32
"civic restraint," 122, 124–28; in Aristophanes's *Wasps,* 128–33; and social status, 126; for terms of peace, 127–28
civil strife, 197, 212, 239, 240
Cleisthenes, 48
Cleon, 102, 130, 131, 132, 133, 164
Clouds, 164
Clytemnestra, 19, 23, 81, 84, 85, 86, 93, 94, 114, 115, 117–18, 134, 137, 139, 206, 209, 372n.88
Codrus (mythical Athenian king), 50, 159
Cohen, D., 345n.38, 375n.44; on conflict resolution, 127
colonies/allies: judicial treatment of, 108–9
competition/competitiveness, 54–62, 65, 122; and arbitration, 112–13; regulation of, 133, 135–36, 146, 165
consent, 28
Considine, P., 349n.8
constitution
—and downfall of political order, 139, 141, 211, 275, 264–65
—of human beings, 53, 55, 56–59, 272: Platonic version of, 252–57, 269, 270, 275; as political, 141
—of household, 55, 134–41
—of inhabitants of city into collective actor, 141–46: of guardians 269–70

constitution (*cont.*)

—of *polis* as physical space, 51, 221–22, 269

—of sociopolitical order, 17, 85, 88, 90, 145, 195: through memory, 193–96, 225–26, 239–41; and myth of "wholeness," 240; through noble lie, 268; as *politeia*, 180; through punishment, 209, 223–24; role of emotions in, 162, 194, 251; role of law in, 179, role of social norms in, 136–37, 166–67, 210–11; role of speech in, 231–32. *See also* "rule of law"

—of women, "nonpunishers," and philosophers, 55, 99

constitutionalism: Aristotelian theory of, 186; modern 179; Platonic invention of, 186

containment/consumption: and cleansing, 211; against men, 209; and reintegration, 210; stoning as, 206; and women, 208; of wrongdoer, 205, 224. *See also* punishment: formalism of

contracts, 67, 104, 225; and political agreement, 104–5

Conventicles Act, 5, 8

conviction, 5, 6, 37, 38, 40, 203; in a *graphe* trial, 46; of officials, 238; unjust, 202

Corcyra, role of *orge* at, 78

corpses, 216, 217, 218, 222, 223; disposal of, 219, 220

Council of 500, 40, 41, 42, 69, 342n.8, 343nn.14 and 17; on execution of metics, 109; powers of to punish/fine, 41, 142, 144; 157, 165, 171

councillors. *See* magistrates

courts, Athenian popular, 33, 42, 43, 48, 49, 51, 341n.72; as more authoritative than assembly, 182; Delphinion, Palladion, Phreatto, and Prytaneion, 43; on following law, 177; *heliaia*, 48, 49; modern, 171; and witnesses, 67. *See also* Areopagus

Cragg, W., 336n.10, 336n.13

Crane, G., 348n.4

Creon, 91, 92, 93, 208, 348n.4

Creusa, 85, 116, 188, 134

criminology, 15–16, 335nn.2 and 4

Crown Prosecutor Service, 3

Csapo, E., 167, 379n.20

culture, as revealed in tragedy 89; conceptual foundations of, 17, 35, 50–72, 74, 75–76; connections between concepts in, 102; consistency of, 76; contradictions in, 138–41; and "deep structure," 75, 121; and gender, 118, 136–41; production of, 105, 272, 297; relation of to institutions, 8, 39–40, 71–72, 108, 136, 144–46, 269; relation of to literature, 8; relation of symbols to, 245; revision of, 251; role of, in punishment, 35, 36, 50–72

curses, 206

death, 63–64, 200, 232, 236–37, by poison, 118; of Socrates, 234; by stoning, 143–45. *See also* capital punishment; hemlock; suicide

debt, 63

deceit, 116–18

Decree of Cannonus, 220

Deianira, 85, 114, 115, 118, 134, 139

Delphic oracle, 159

Demades, 175

demagogues: in comedy, 130, 132–33. *See also* Cleon

deme, 42

Demetrius of Phaleron, 190

democracy

—common language of, 36, 44, 46, 49, 76, 147, 166: as complement to institutions, 140; and interventions in, 90, 271; and public conversations, 52, 59, 65–68, 71–72, 74; and role in education, 85; and Semonides, 120–21; used to solve problems, 134–41

—principles of, 134, 146, 241: and Aristotle's theory of equality, 285–88; Athenian, 246; as equality, 124, 129, 133, 225–30; and Foucault, 299; and goals of, 90–94, 134, 288; as liberty/freedom, 301–2; as liberty joined with equality, 38, 60–61, 89–90, 94, 130, 283; modern, 36–38, 298; and the relation between equality and law, 180

—and social control, 36, 49, 51, 58–59, 93, 95, 105: over foreigners, 126; and the importance of memory to, 195–96; through institutions, 230; through judgment, 178; through language of sycophancy, 156–67; through obscenity, 164–67; and the role of consent/consensus in, 190–94, 198, 223–24, 239–242; over slaves and women, 110, 300; over social knowledge, 107, 142, 145–46, 191–96, 230; through social memory, 202–5, 258–59; and stoning, 206

—structure of authority in, 38, 105: ambiguities in, 100; and challenges by elites, 44–45, 223–24; and control of penal institutions, 44–45, 223–24; and factions, 235, 236, 238; foundations of, 129, 194; historical development of, 19–20, 44–45, 49, 111; and the power of the citizens, 130; and a pragmatic approach to truth, 104–5; and role of emotions in, 51–52; and role of status and honor in, 127, 128; and slavery, 110–11; in United States, 3–5

demos, 105, 107, 108, 122, 133, 144, 145, 149, 153, 156, 169, 171, 178, 183; as collective, 65; and control of future, 241; power of, 104, 107, 109, 153, 178, 230; as spectators, 65–66, 113, 148, 168–69, 217, 216–17

Demosthenes, 51, 62, 203, 213, 219, 230, 231, 392n.64; *Against Meidias,* 200, 230, 231, 232; *Against Timocrates,* 180, 228, 229; on arbitration, 123, 124–26, 142, 148, 149, 152, 153, 154–59, 170, 172, 173, 174, 176–77; and the authorship of *Against Aristogeiton I and II,* 180, 181–82, 183, 191; on delay and sycophancy, 154–65, 349n.30; 382n.11, 383n.24; on legal protection of slaves, 110, 112; on metics, 368nn.40 and 46; as offscouring, 210; *On the Crown,* 104, 143, 145, 248n.2; *On the Embassy,* 194, 195, 300; on procedures, 123; on public vs. private, 191, 193; on women as witnesses, 103–4, 107, 108

desert, xi

—contest over, 27–30, 34, 59; 71–72, 87, 198: and its centrality to politics, 271, 284–86, 297; as contested in rights language, rhetoric, law, and social memory, 149–51, 168–79; as contested with symbols, 275, 294; as public language, 36, 40; terms for deciding, 65

—definition of, 333n.2: and Aristotle's theory of, 282–89; and formulations/conceptualizations of, 17, 69, 288; in Foucauldian terms, 297–99; and importance of 239–42; in *Prometheus Bound,* 25–35; as redefined by Plato, 266, 277–78; and relation to analogy/metaphor, 286; in terms of anger and pity, 149–51; in terms of money, 225–26

desire or lust, 101, 253–54, 255, 257, 259. *See also* emotion; *epithumia; eros; horme; orge*

desmoterion. See prison

Detienne, M., 117

dikaion, to, dikaia, ta, 149–50, 175, 249

dikastes. See juries

dikazein, 42, 43, 317; meaning of, 319–22

dike, 103; definition of, 39; as *demosia dike,* 192, 193; in *diken didonai,* 249; *emporikai,* 108; 168; in just city, 262, 269; in *lambanein diken,* 62, 69, 71; trial, 39, 43, 46, 47, 48, 53, 54, 337nn.25 and 28, 345nn.42 and 45, 346nn.47, 49, and 51, 347n.55; during war, 108. *See also* justice; private vs. public;

prosecution: private vs. public; prosecutor: public and private

dike exoules, 202, 390n.23

Dinarchus, 23, 124–26, 138, 169, 210; on jurors guarding laws, 183

Dindorf, W., 337n.28

Diodotus: and arguments about justice for foreigners, 109

Dionysus, theater of, 124

disease and remedy, 10, 74, 76, 77, 78, 80, 81, 82, 83, 85, 86, 94, 358nn.24 and 26, 359n.50; anger as, 28, 77–79, 133, 197; grammar of, 76, 77; from jury service, 128; of soul, 182. *See also* metaphor

disfranchisement, 201, 202, 204, 224, 231, 232, 239, 241

dishonor, 50, 60, 61, 215–17, 221, 228, 235. See also *atimia;* honor

disinterested prosecution. *See* prosecution: private vs. public; prosecutor

dispute resolution, 20, 47, 49

disputes, types of: familial, 123, 129, 373n.10; inheritance, 151; in just city, 262; oratorical use of, 153; property, 123

distribution, Aristotelian, of justice, 285–90; commensurability, 288; as commerce metaphor, 290, 299; contribution, 287–88

divorce, 112, 122; general discussion of, 369n.60; in orators, 372n.5

Dodds, E. R., 337n.34

dokimasia, 156

dolos, 101, 116, 372n.86

Donlan, W., 354n.74

Douglas, M., 360n.58

Dover, K., 349n.6

Draco, 48, 111, 181, 394n.96

drones. *See* symbols, bees/drones as

duBois, P., 366n.21

Duris, 198, 199; on the bodies of the executed Samians, 199

Durkheim, E., 16, 17

Dworkin, R., 149

Easterling, P., 361n.71

echthros, 139

economy, of spending. *See* anger; Foucault

Edmunds, L., 374n.23

education: in just city, 264–65, 268, 269, 272; from *kolasis,* 247–48; philosophic, 270; 283

eisangelia, 193

election, 41; of generals, 44. *See also* voting

Electra, 21, 77, 83, 84, 114, 115, 139

Electra (Eur.), 77, 116

Electra (Soph.), 83, 116, 117

eleos, 126, 148, 260

Eleusis: and the Amnesty, 55, 238

Eleven, the, 40, 46, 201, 215, 230, 342n.7, 345n.38

elites, 19, 39, 43, 44, 45, 63, 156, 229, 235; friendship patterns of, 63. *See also* social status; democracy: structure of authority in

emotion, 9, 18, 20, 37, 38, 51, 55, 56, 58, 81, 84, 337n.27, 341n.70, 348n.2, 352n.46, 360n.67; as action, 53–54, 59–60; as cognition, 57; as collective experience, 145, 148–49; as force of destabilization, 77–78, 94, 162, 210–12, 275; as inspiration to speak and judge, 275, 295; as liquid, 52, 54, 56–58; proper use of, 163–65; and sexual desire, 54–55, 57, 59. *See also* anger; body; desire; *eros*; law; pity

enmity, 80, 84, 114–15, 237–38; rejection of as grounds for prosecution, 158. *See also* anger

Ephialtes, 44

epieikeia, 178

Epimetheus (brother of Prometheus), 295, 296

episteme, 184

epithumia, 252, 256

equality. *See* democracy: principles of; *isonomia*

equity: Aristotle on, 187; Athenian use of, 177; modern, 177–78; Plato on, 186–87

equivalence, 63–65; process of determining, 169–70, 173–74. *See also* value

Er, Myth of, 276

Eratosthenes, 37, 38, 110, 126–27, 153

Erectheus, 159

Erinyes, 19–23, 114, 132, 139; as metics, 376n.49; as *Semnai Theai*, 137, 138

eros, 55, 59, 77, 88; and *orge*, 118–19; and the unerotic, 137, 161, 164, 252

eschata, ta, 169

Eteocles, 135

ethical rules. *See* social norms

Eueon: and the definition of legitimate punishment, 124, 125

Eumenides, 20, 21, 22, 77, 80, 114, 137, 178

Eumenides, altar of, 111, 148

eunomia, 186

Euphiletos, 37, 38, 110, 126–27

Euripides, 76, 81; *Andromache*, 83; *Children of Heracles*, 83; *Electra*, 77, 116; *Erectheus*, 159; *Hecuba*, 78, 115–16; *Hippolytus*, 84, 88, 116; *Ion*, 116, 118; *Iphigeneia in Taurus*, 73, 206; *Madness of Heracles*, 78, 89, 116; *Medea*, 78, 114, 116; *Orestes*, 77, 80; *Suppliants*, 188; *Trojan Women*, 207

euthune, 156

evidence, 7, 334n.24, 355n.92 and 93; character as, 172; in Lysias' *Against Eratosthenes*, 127; personal, 67; in Simpson trial, 37; and torture of slaves as, 67; types of, 174; 364n.7, 383n.21; written, 67. *See also* witnesses

excessiveness, 89–94, 128; and the oligarchs, 165–66

execution: personal involvement of prosecutor in, 202, 229–30

expulsion: of Phocion, 236; precipitation as, 206, 207; and religious ritual, 209; and sons, 208; of wrongdoers, 205. *See also* punishment: formalism of

family, 101, 134–41; Athenian, 50, 52; as authority, 24; and burial, 216, 217; children in, 69, 70, 73, 217; clan and, 19; destroyed by anger, 135, 140; disputes within, 123, 129; in drama, 135; of Eratosthenes, 37, 38; as forgiving murderers, 202; kinship structures of, 10, 27; marriage and, 58, 82; of Simpson, 37; and the tragic *oikos*, 138; violation of bonds of, 134

Faraone, C.: on figure of *pharmakon*, 141, 377n.62

fetters, 226

figs. *See* sycophancy; symbols: figs, vines, and orchids as

fines, 201, 224, 225, 228, 229, 230, 241, 396n.121; and equality, 225; and freemen, 215; illegal, 238; importance of, 232; and imprisonment, 229; lawsuits to collect, 202; public, 225; Roman, 226; and silence, 232

Finley, M., 335n.6

foreigners, 102; and enmity, 114–15, 216–17; treatment of, 126; as witnesses, 105. *See also* metics

forgetting. *See* remembering / forgetting

Foucault, M., 9, 223, 334n.26; *Discipline and Punish*, 15, 16, 36, 37, 38, 297, 301; on an economy of spending, 162–63; 281; on passion, 58

Foxhall, L., 375n.39

friendship, 63, 123; as antidote to anger, 82, 112; and witnesses, 106. See also *philia*

funeral oration, 240, 398n.148

Gagarin, M., 345n.38; on slave torture, 365n.14

Garland, D., 336n.10

Gates, H. L., Jr., 367n.26

gaze, the, 78–81, 129, as model for reciprocity, 80–81, 258. *See also* vision
gender, 10, 55, 58, 208, 360n.66; and the constitution of political sphere, 134–41; and deceit, 117–18; and feminized men as tragic monsters, 132; and foreignness, 138; and knowledge, 103–4; Plato on, 264; and "private vs. public," 136; and punishment, 100–102, 111–18, 208–9; and tragedy, 113–18; and women as tragic monsters, 115
Gernet, L., 16, 335n.6, 17, 346n.52, 355n.83, 358n.28, 391nn.44 and 60, 393n.84, 383n.16; on rituals, 199
Girard, R., 77, 212, 213, 358n.28, 359n.31, 360n.68, 391nn.59 and 60; on rituals, 212
Glaucon, 215, 252, 253, 254, 255, 256, 258, 259, 265, 266, 268, 269, 270, 272, 276
gods, 30, 53, 73, 84, 88, 361n.81, 362nn.83, 84, and 89; Anangke, 86; Apollo, 20, 21, 23, 54, 77, 116, 134, 137, 337n.29, 361n.76; Artemis, 19, 88, 89; Athena, 20, 22, 77, 84, 114, 137, 178, 337nn.28, 29, and 32; Bacchus, 73; Demeter, 52, 53; earth, 33; Eumenides, 20, 111, 148; Furies/Erinyes/*Semnai Theai*, 19, 20, 22, 77, 78, 81, 86, 114, 132, 139, 137, 138, 337nn.28, 29, 30, and 31, 362n.83, 376n.49; Hephaestus, 25, 26, 27, 28, 34, 339n.44, 46, and 48; Hera, 26; Hermes, 26, 31, 32, 34, 294, 296, 340nn.57, 58, 59, 60, and 62; Leto, 81; Oceanus and Oceanids, 26, 29, 30, 31, 34, 83, 275, 340nn.52, 53, 54, and 56; Persephone, 52; *Poinae*, 86; Poseidon, 391n.49; Prometheus, 25, 26, 27, 28, 29, 30, 31, 32, 33, 34, 36, 77, 82, 87, 88, 89, 275, 293–97, 294, 299, 301, 302, 338nn.37 and 41, 340nn.53, 58, and 61; Titans, 25, 26, 30, 32, 33, 82, 241, 293, 294, 296, 302; Uranus, 30, 265; Zeus, 25, 26, 27, 28, 30, 31, 32, 34, 77, 87, 88, 90, 114, 118, 129, 191, 265, 294, 295, 296, 205, 227, 237, 241, 338n.41, 340nn.53 and 58, 361n.76
Goldhill, S., 28, 32, 337n.25, 349n.13
Gorgias, 246, 247, 249, 266, 277
gossip, 142, 169
Gouldner, A., 353n.58
grammar: as methodological term, 75; of punishment and anger, 76, 358n.22
graphe, 39, 42, 46, 47, 48, 103, 202, 203, 345n.42, 346nn.47, 48, 49, and 51, 347nn.54 and 55; *hubreos,* 110, 123, 168; for memorialization, 192, 193, 194, 203; during war, 108. *See also* private vs. public; prosecution: private vs. public; prosecutor

Green, T. A., 334n.20
Gregory, J., 116
guardians, Platonic, 186, 190, 262, 267, 268, 269
guest-host relationships, 63, 73–74
guile and deceit: in Euphiletos, 127; in women punishers, 116
guilt, 20, 73, 88
Gyges, ring of, 258

Hades, 29, 233
Halliwell, S., 273–74
Halperin, D., 352n.45
hamartia, 26, 30
Hamilton, R., 357nn.2, 3, and 6
Hansen, M. H., 345n.38, 346n.51, 354n.78, 385n.54
Hardie, W.F.R., 403nn.10 and 11
Harris, E. M., 345n.38; on lack of equity in Athens, 178
Harrison, A.R.W., 345n38, 346nn.47, 49, and 52, 383nn.21 and 29; on slave torture, 365nn.10 and 14, 366n.22
Hart, H.L.A., 336nn.10 and 11
Hector, 205, 207
Hecuba, 78, 79, 115–16
Hecuba, 78, 115–16
Helen, 82, 206
hemlock, 201, 213, 232, 233, 235, 238, 397nn.129, 130, and 131; at Athens, 234, 397n.135; expense of, 234
Henderson, J.: on obscenity, 381n.64; on sexual aggression, 164, 166, 380n.56
Hephaestus, 294
Heracles, 78, 81, 82, 85, 115, 117, 118, 139
Heraclitus, on eye witnesses, 66
Herman, G., 111, 353n.52, 372n.1, 373n.18; on conflict resolution, 127
Hermes, 294, 296
herms: metic's testimony about, 107; mutilation of, 105; slave's testimony about, 105, 107
Herodotus, 79, 200, 205, 206, 213, 233, 349nn.10 and 19; on anger, 53; on eye witnesses, 66, 142, 143, 145
Hesiod: on drones and bees, 119, 133, 270–71; *Theogony,* 55, 337n.41, 341nn.64 and 65; *Works and Days,* 52, 53, 55, 63
Hesychius, on the *barathron,* 220
Hippocratic texts, 54, 217, 254, 349n.18, 352n.42, 377n.54
Hippolyta, as accuser and punisher, 100–102
Hippolytus, 84, 88, 116
Hippolytus, 84, 88, 116

historical sociology, 15–17, 62
historiography, xi-xii, 15–16; of Athens, 19, 20–21
Hobbes, T., 282
ho boulomenos, 39, 50, 342n.2
Homer, 205, 218
homicide. *See* murder; wrongdoing
honor, 50, 59–62; in Aristotle, 287–88; in *Laws*, 278; in *Republic,* 267–68; role of, in democracy, 128–33, 146; role of, in punishment, 69–71, 110. *See also* dishonor; social status
horme, 256
hot blood, 117–18, 124–28, 136; rhetoric of, 154; and sycophancy, 156–65; youth and, 156, 161
household. *See* family
hubris, 70, 91, 362nn.86 and 89, 363n.94; definition of, 89, 125, 131–32, 193
Hudson, B. A., 335n.4, 336n.10, 371n.77
Humphreys, S., 335n.6, 384n.42
Hunter, V., 343n.17, 366n.22, 375n.39
Hyperides, 71, 183, 193, 231

ideology. *See* culture; social norms
idioi nomoi, 190
Iliad, 18, 52, 62, 118, 159, 205, 207, 339n.44, 351nn.36 and 39
impartiality, 18, 20
impiety: slaves' testimony to, 105; in just city, 280. *See also* wrongdoing
imprisonment, 201, 202, 214, 215, 224, 226, 228, 241, 394nn.103–5; at Athens, 226; binding as, 228; as corporal penalty, 228; for debt, 228, 396n.118; enforcement of, 230; history of, 227–30; language of, 227; in Plato, 279–81; possible site of in Athens, 395n.112; and poverty, 228; in United States, 242; use of by oligarchs, 230, 235; as wartime punishment, 229
indictment, 41; for *dike* and *graphe* trials, 46
individuals, 84; expelled from community, 203–5; 205–6; as integrated into community, 141–46, 205–6, 241; position of within community, 60; roles of, 74, 99–102, 143–46, 241. *See also* citizens: male; foreigners; metics; slaves; women
informing, 110
initiation: of individuals into social roles, 74, 161–62; of punishment (*see* punishment)
innards, 33, 56–58, 83, 341n.69, 350nn.26, 27, and 33, 351n.37, 352n.42
inside/outside, of body, 56. *See also* punishment: formalism of

institutions: modern terms for, 39; participation in, 40–42, 45–46; principles embodied by, 17, 40–43, 45–49, 136–37; role of in punishment, 8, 35, 39–49; as substitute for community, 230; use of for authority, 31, 121
integration, 74, 95, 210–12; of inhabitants of *polis,* 141–46. *See also* punishment: formalism of
investigation, 102–3; of murder, 103; by officials, 103, 364n.6; by private citizens, 103
Ion, 116, 134
Ion, 116, 118
Iphigeneia, 139, 206
Iphigeneia in Taurus, 73
Isaeus, 61, 82, 214, 215, 238, 239; on delay of prosecution, 154, 155, 174, 175, 191, 373n.8; on production of witnesses, 105–6, 112
ischas, 160, 161
Isocrates, 50, 60, 61; on pity, 150; on sycophants, 164, 191, 381n.65
isolation, 74, 95; of eros and anger, 140. *See also* punishment: formalism of
isonomia, 23, 60, 225–26, 230. *See also* democracy: principles of; *isonomia*
ison, to, isotes, 284, 285

Jameson, F., 358n.16
Jason, 78, 80, 114–15, 118, 139
Jebb, R. C., 348n.4, 359n.54, 363n.94
judges, 53, 54, 346n.52, 347n.55; in archaic period, 21, 44, 344n.25; in Areopagus, 44; fining the jury, 7, 8; as justices of the peace, 7, 8; as lawmakers, 48; in United States, 8, 37
judgment, 46, 53, 54, 346n.52, 347n.55; by collective, 21, 47–49; culture of, 42; and gender, 21; importance of, 134, 194, 276, 293; and relation to law, 48–49, 175–79, 179–90; role of anger in, 22, 194; rule of vs. rule of law, 185–87, 189; by a single judge, 47–49; and social control, 122, 198. *See also* "rule of law"; spectacle: as inspiration to judge; voting
judicial decisionmaking, 68, 132–33, 168–79; and justice, 178–79; and matters of fact vs. matters of law/ethics, 171–72, 187; overruling law, 176–77; use of anger in, 172–74, 224; use of law in, 172, 174–79; without laws, 176. *See also* equity; jury nullification
juries: ancient vs. modern, 5–8, 38, 171–72, 177–78, 334n.16; Athenian popular, 6, 40, 42, 43, 47, 49, 50, 51, 65, 74, 224, 230,

231; composition of, 5, 6, 43–44; fining of, 6; instruction to, 177; making claims on, 149–51; passions of, 51, 55; pay for, 129, 130, 131; power of acquittal, 8; relation to legislatures, 6, 49, 176–77. *See also* judges; judgment; jury nullification

jury nullification: ancient 5, 6, 8; modern, 5–8, 177, 334n.21

justice, 63–65; contest over, 198, 241–42; definitions of, 62–63, 69, 173–74; definitions of as embodied in culture, 10; definitions of as embodied in institutions, 10, 47–48; as goal, 178–79; language of, 296; process of defining, 147–49, 150, 160; and social relations, 70; as species of metaphorical thought, 286; as straightness, 290–91

Kant, 282
kardia, 56
kata tous nomous, 188
kerdos, 61, 353n.58
kinship, 111, 123
Kitto, H.D.F., 337n.32
knowledge: Foucault on, 297–301; and gender, 103–4; of mob, 107; needed by citizen prosecutor, 50, 99, 102, 107, 154; of past, 66–67, 154, 195–96; production of, 106–7; relation of to anger, 81; relation of to vision and spectacle, 65–66, 79, 113, 206; of slaves and foreigners, 104–5; use of, 169
koinos, 123, 187, 190, 193
kolasis, 69, 70, 71, 246, 247, 248, 279, 280, 283, 356n.107
Konstan, D., 374nn.23 and 24
Kratos and Bia, 25, 26, 27, 28, 29, 31, 32, 34, 294, 339nn.43, 44, and 45, 340n.58,
kurios, 11, 172, 182; as male authority over women, 111–12
Kurke, L., 364n.103

Laks, A., 402n.40
Langbein, J. H., 333n.1
law, 5, 30, 32, 65, 89–94; as ageless/divine/ pan-Hellenic, 90, 92–93; Aristotle on, 190; of community and nature, 187–88, 189, 190, 282–83; critiques of, 185, 187; and desert, 175; as evidence or proof, 174–75; modern use of, 174; as *nomos* and vs. *thesmos*, 90, 91, 337n.29, 362n.90, 363nn.96 and 99; as opinion, 174–75; philosophical treatment of, 183–90; as private possession, 89–91; as public possession, 90–91, 187–88, 190–94; purposes of according to orators, 180, 182, 385n.52; scholarship on, 384–85n.45; and

social memory, 68, 174; subordination of to judgment, 175, 178, 185; in tragedy, 190; and unlawfulness, 8, 88–94, 189, 225, 228, 362n.88, 363nn.94 and 97; use of, 126, 167, 174, 240; and use of anger, 174–76, 178; value of according to orators, 179–83; written vs. unwritten, 67, 90, 150, 176, 191, 193, 362n.92. *See also* judgment; "rule of law"; wrongdoing, types of

Lawrence, Stephen, 3
Laws, 182, 186, 189, 246, 247, 277, 281, 288
Lear, J., 400n.23
Leocrates, prosecution of, 143, 156, 157
Leontios, 221, 245, 246, 252, 253, 257, 265, 266, 268, 272. *See also* body: of the condemned
Leucas, and precipitation, 207
Libation Bearers, 19, 21, 118, 137, 138, 139
liberal democracy, 4, 36
lies/false tales, 100–101, 104; as medicinal, 267; as noble lie, 267–71; in Plato, 265–68. *See also* narratives
liget, 52
Lipsius, J. H., 346n.45, 383n.21
Littman, R. J., 375n.36
Lloyd-Jones, H., 336n.24, 376n.49
Locke, J., 282
logopoios, logopoiein, 100, 265
Loraux, N., on women not seen as citizens, 138
Luschnig, C.A.E., 371n.81
Lycidas, stoning of, 143–45, 147, 194, 213
Lycurgus, 36, 50, 71, 142, 143, 144, 145, 203; *Against Leocrates*, 156–60, 165, 167, 172, 192; on jurors as legislators, 176, 181, 182–83; on law as measure, 175; and oratorical use of inscriptions, 192, 194, 387n.81
Lysias, 50, 51, 69, 95, 110, 148, 149, 200, 203, 227, 233, 237, 392n.64; *Against Agoratus*, 215; on hemlock, 234, 235; on homicide prosecution, 152; on imprisonment, 227; on jurors' anger, 173, 174; on jurors as legislators, 177; on laws as guardians, 191, 192, 193; on metics, 369n.50, 371n.80, 375n.39, 384nn.32 and 35; on personal enmity, 153, 154, 155, 156–58, 169, 171; on unwritten laws, 176

MacDowell, D. M., 344n.23, 345n.38, 346nn.47 and 51, 358n.28, 366n.22; 374nn.23 and 24, 382n.13, 395n.115; on evidence, 383n.25; on *hubris*, 131–32; on orators, 382n.13
Macedon, 190, 235

Mackenzie, M. M., on punishment in Plato, 247, 399n.8, 402n.43, 403n.6
MacLachlan, B., 354n.66, 359n.40
madness, 82, 84
Madness of Herakles, 78, 89
maenad, as tragic trope, 115, 371n.77
magic, vengeance and curse tablets, 147–48; and binding spells, 148; men and, 148; rhetoric as, 147–48; women and, 147
magistrates, 40, 41, 48, 49, 50, 64, 342nn.7 and 10, 343nn.12, 16, and 17; *agoranomos,* 41; archon, 39, 40, 44, 48; *archon basileus,* 43; *archon polemarchos,* 342n.9, 347n.54; *bouleutai* (members of the Council of 500), 305–6; *choregos,* 41, 313; *demokoinos,* 201, 230, 235, 237; *ephetai,* 43; filled by lot, 43; generals, 44, 45, 203, 222, 344nn.33 and 34; as judges, 347n.53; *kolastai,* 224, 238, 390n.21; *logistai, episkeuastai, trieropoioi, hieropoioi, sullogeis tou demou, tamias ton trieropoion, astunomoi, agoranomoi, metronomoi, sitophulakes, eisagogeis, euthunoi, epimeletai neorion,* 305–16; *nomothetai,* 342n.8; number, workload, and pay of, 305–16; power of to prosecute, 344n.23; *sullogeis tou demou,* 41; *thesmothetai,* 40, 48; and treasurers of Athena, 41; *trieropoioi,* 41; powers of, to punish, 41–42, 142. *See also* Eleven, the
Magnesia, 186, 229, 277, 278, 280
mainomai, 115, 119
Mantitheus, 155
Mardonius, 143
marriage, 162; as antidote to anger, 82; as treaty, 114–15, 137–39
Medea, 78, 79, 80, 81, 114–15, 116; as lioness, 116; as Scylla, 116; 118, 134, 139
Medea, 78, 114, 116
Megara, 107
megista, ta, 169
Meidias, 124–25, 191, 200, 230, 231
memorialization. *See* punishment: practice/process of; remembering/forgetting
Menon, the miller, 124, 126
metaphor, metaphors, 75–76, 94, 162; for anger, 60, 74, 94, 162, 163, 164; of bestiality, especially in Plato, 78–79, 248, 256, 260, 278, 399nn.11 and 12, 400n.23, 402n.44; of cleanliness, 210–11; of commerce/exchange for justice, 285–90; functioning of, 163, 167, 278; of harmony, 65, 224; of health, 55, 77–86, 99, 119, 128; of health in Cicero, 297; of health in comedy, 131, 132; of health in modern literature, 197–98, of

health in oratory, 182; of health in Plato, 246, 249–50, 267, 278, 279–81; of necessity, 74, 94; of sexuality, 160–64; of straightness, 290–91; of vision, 74, 94; of war, 197–98, 212, 224. *See also* punishment: formalism of; symbols, symbolism; war/peace
metics, 35, 60, 99, 102, 107–9, 214, 241; in Demosthenes, 368nn.40 and 46; execution of, 109, 137; as prosecutors and witnesses, 105, 107–8; in S. Todd, 367n.40; in wartime, 144, 157. *See also* foreigners
Michelini, A., 362n.88
Miller, F., 149–50
Millett, P., 382n.13
mimesis, 246, 273, 275, 276
misos, 149
mob: as evil, 206; and stoning, 206, 214, 390n.40
moichos, 164
monarchs, 48, 341n.72; just, 93
money, 229; blood money, 225, 394n.97; as language, 225. *See also* contracts; juries: pay for
Morris, I., 343n.18
mortals, 25, 27, 29, 30, 51, 84, 87, 89, 91, 361n.76
Mt. Beletsi, 221
Mt. Parnes, 221
Muellner, L., 340n.62, 348n.2, 349n.21, 355n.83
murder: of Eratosthenes, 110, 126; laws of Draco, 111; pollution from in Antiphon, 194; premeditated vs. unintentional, 108; prosecution for in Lysias, 13, 152; of slaves, 111
Myrtia, as woman bringing accusation, 113
Mysteries, Eleusinian, violation of, 107
myth, 212, 216; of acquiescence, 212; of harmonious order, 212, 223, 224
mythology, 32–33, 122, 205–10

narratives: of accusation, 99–101; anger in, 50–51; about the body, 199–200; of the defendant, 224; of the desert, 65; of individuals, 49, 91–92; as interpretation of reality, 87, 203, 225, 239–40; as medicine, 267, 277; of oligarchs, 239; as precedent, 173–74, 194; of prosecutors, 151–57; in the *Republic,* 259, 265–70; and revisions of social norms, 157–60, 194, 252–53, 297; role of in punishment, 17, 36, 43; use of as scholarly evidence, 102, 145, 216–18; of whipping, 238; of witnesses, 66, 103–7; of women, 119, 125; of the wrongdoer, 217

necessity, 9, 74, 83, 84, 86, 87, 88, 94, 295, 360nn.62 and 63; and anger, 83–84, 86–87, 162; and Foucault, 299; as rhetorical figure, 75, 155–57, 162–63, 294, 297, 299, 300
negotiation, 198
Nicomachean Ethics, 187, 283
nomima, ta, 175
nomophulax, 111, 186, 190. *See also* guardians
nomos, 151, 168, 178; in just city, 266. *See also* law; *tupos*
norms of public agency, 35, 62, 151–67, 168–96; and the past, 68. *See also* action; actors; social norms
nosos, 35, 128, 132, 341n.75, 353n.52. *See also* disease and remedy; metaphor/metaphors: of health
nous, 56, 57, 58, 350nn.25 and 34, 352n.42
novelty, 89
Nozick, R., 336n.10

oath, 239; and challenges for women, 103; as evidence, 174; for men, 364nn.9, 10, and 12; of reconciliation, 238
Ober, J., 335n.6, 341n.75, 342n.7
Oceanids, 275
ochlos, 106–7. *See also demos;* mob
Odysseus, 84
Odyssey, 52, 63, 351n.36
Oedipus, 22, 82, 84, 87, 208
Oedipus at Colonus, 82
Oedipus Tyrannus, 91
offscourings (*katharmata*), 210, 217; disposal of, 222; expelling of, 211; incurable, 211
oikos, 74, 95, 101–2, 112, 122, 204; of Hector, 207; of Phocion, 236. *See also* family
oligarchs, the Thirty, 141, 227, 230, 233, 235, 237, 238, 239, 397n.125; and hemlock, 234, 235; and oligarchy, 180, 200, 233; and sycophants, 165–67, 173, 195; wrongdoing of, 195–96
Olson, S. D., 374n.23
Olympic games, 207
Olympus, 29
omos, 163
oratory, 45, 50, 53, 62, 63, 64, 67, 214, 229, 231, 233, 236, 353n.54, 354n.75, 397n.123; and decorum, 214, 215; language of pity and anger in, 148–51; and language of punishment, 70–72; as product of elite, 229; and relation to tragedy, 76; and the rules for punishment, 124–28; use of quotations from poets in, 159–60
Oresteia, 18, 19, 22, 24, 25, 83, 88, 93, 117, 137, 338n.35, 349n.13

Orestes, 19–22, 23, 73, 74, 80–84, 87, 93, 94, 95, 117–18, 137, 148, 195, 206, 337n.29, 340n.55
Orestes, 77, 80
orge, 101–2; *baruthumon,* 114; diseased, 128; and *eros,* 118–19; as fertility, 164, 252, 255; in households, 138; iretic and erotic, 138, 139, 145, 160, 162, 163; in just city, 270; linked to *deinon,* 378n.73; and *oxuthumia,* 22, 210, 211, 391n.53; in *Prometheus Bound,* 297; in women, 118–21, 139. *See also* anger; desire or lust; emotion
Ormand, K., 377n.56
Osborne, R., 366n.22; on sycophancy, 156
ostracism, 390n.36
outrages, 25, 30, 31, 34, 50, 59
oxuthumos, 22, 117, 210, 211

Padel, R., 56, 132, 350nn.25–29, 350–351nn.30–37, 352n.42, 354n.67, 358n.29, 359n.33
paideia, 248. *See also* education
pain, 28, 31, 88, 339n.49, 352n.42, 361n.71; Aristotle on, 54; and pleasure, 277. *See also* violence
Panathenaic games, 60, 137
Pandora, 55
Paoli, V. E., 178
paragraphe, 240; in orators, 387n.85
pardon, 238
Parker, R., 358n.38
parrhesia, 117, 231. *See also* speech: freedom of
passion. *See* emotion
pathos, 150; in just city, 279; rhetorical technique of, 150
Pausanias, 207, 218, 219, 222, 296
peace. *See* war/peace
Peace, 164
Peleus, 100–102
Peloponnesian War, 108, 216, 237
penal severity, 199
"penal tempers," 16
penalties: *ataphia* (see *ataphia*); binding, 25, 27, 28, 203, 205, 215, 226, 229, 230, 339n.48, 394n.106; blinding, 215; burial alive, 208; confiscation, 201, 217; crucifixion, 200, 232; death by hemlock (*see* hemlock); death by stoning (*see* stoning); death by the sword, 201, 213; depilation, 214; disfranchisement (see *atimia*; disfranchisement); from *dike* trials, 46, 47; execution, 63, 200–203, 213, 215, 217, 222, 224, 228, 232, 233, 236, 238, 240, 241, 335n.1; exile,

penalties (*cont.*)
81, 82, 201, 203, 204, 205, 232, 241; exposure, 218; fines, 4, 25; fines from arbitration,
42; fines of *boule*, 41, 343n.17; fines for juries, 7, 334nn.20 and 21; fines of magistrates, 4; fines from popular courts, 43;
graduated system of, 64; hierarchy of, 34,
227; and honor, 61; house razing, 201, 217,
241; impeachment, 230; imprisonment (*see*
imprisonment); and the orators, 63, 354n.75,
355n.80; precipitation, 205, 206, 207, 218,
219; of prosecutors, 47; public exhibition
(*see* public exhibition); solitary confinement,
242; stoning (*see* stoning); throat cutting,
213; whipping, 201, 215, 237
Penner, T., 400n.17
Pericles, 176, 198, 199, 200
Persians, 129
Persian Wars, 108, 142, 143, 189, 213, 239,
240, 275
personality. *See* constitution: of human beings
persuasion, as solution to anger, 82
Phaedo, 245
Phaleron, mass grave of criminals at, 200
pharmakon, 77, 80, 82, 84, 85, 277, 354nn.66
and 67; in female deceit, 140, 141; in tragedy, 118; used by women and slaves, 140.
See also guile and deceit
pharmakos, 160, 381n.66. *See also* scapegoat
phenomenological method, 10–11, 16, 17,
334n.27
philia, 114, 123, 134, 138–41, 145, 216. *See
also* friendship; witnesses
Philokleon, 113, 128–33, 160–61, 172,
261
Philoctetes, 83
philologoi, 147
philosopher: educated, 270; place of, 281
philosopher-kings, 184, 264, 267
philosophy: analytical, 18; effect of on politics,
190, 281; and language of punishment, 70–
72; of punishment, 282; and a repudiation of
Athens, 184, 188–90; study of, 270. *See
also* Aristotle; Plato
Phocion, 235, 236
Phokians, 219
phonos, 116, 118
phren, 56, 57, 58, 83, 115, 119, 350n.25,
351n.35
Phryne, 231
Phrynichus, *Capture of Miletus*, 79
phthonos, 149
Pindar, 54, 100–102
Piraeus, 100, 156, 221, 222, 245, 269

pits, 222; 391n.45; *barathron*, 218, 219, 221,
222, 393nn.83 and 85, 394n.92; *orugma*,
218, 219, 221, 222; not for precipitation,
220
Pittalakos, and production of witnesses, 106
pity, 9, 10, 29, 30, 73, 126, 148, 224; and anger, 148, 150, 151, 159, 168, 175, 179, 194,
195, 260, 275, 290, 294, 299. *See also* anger; emotion
Plato, 36, 66, 81, 350n.26, 356n.113; on afterlife, 266; on anger 251–57; *Apology*, 47,
227, 247, 249, 260, 277; Athenian reactions
to, 249, 251; on the bodies of the condemned, 245–46; on civil war in the soul,
252–53; on competitiveness, 260, 262; on
gender, 264; *Gorgias*, 233, 246, 247, 249,
266, 277; *Laws*, 183, 186, 189, 226, 229,
246, 247, 277, 281, 288; on mimesis, 273–
77; *Phaedo*, 245; *Protagoras*, 246, 247, 248,
251, 266, 277, 295, 296; on punishment as
education, 71, 121, 135, 147, 179, 247–51,
258, 277–81; *Republic*, 55, 183, 184, 186,
215, 219, 221, 222, 245, 246, 251, 252, 254,
257, 263, 268, 272, 277, 278, 281, 288,
401n.34; and a repudiation of Athenian punishment and politics, 245–51, 258–77; on
separation of anger from desire, 254–56;
Statesman, 183, 184, 185, 187, 188; *Timaeus*, 359n.38; use of symbols, 271–73, 276,
281, 282–84, 293, 297. *See also* "rule of
law"
pleasure, 18, 349n.14, 352n.45; and anger, 54;
and pain, 277; and revenge, 83
pleonexia, 258, 259, 278
plethos, 185
Pliny, 148; on hemlock, 233, 234
Plutarch, 175, 192, 219; on hemlock, 233, 235;
Life of Nicias, 100, 102; *Life of Pericles*,
198, 199
Pnyx, 179
podokakke, 200, 234, 388n.8
Poetics, 286
poison, 232, 235; death by, 118, 140–41; in
tragedy, 372n.88. See also *pharmakon*
Polemarchos (in the *Republic*), 258, 260
polemarchos, 108. *See also* magistrates
Poliakoff, M. B., 352n.49, 354n.78
police, 4; and Scythian archers, 41
polis, 3, 4, 5, 15, 51, 52, 69, 70, 72, 74, 93,
99, 100, 126, 134; and *orge*, 138, 139, 145;
as set of families, 146, 151, 263. *See also*
constitution: of *polis* as physical space
politeia, 172, 180, 181, 182. *See also* constitution; constitutionalism

political theory, xi–xii. *See also* philosophy; "rule of law"

politics

—and effect of wrongdoing/punishment, 32–33, 36, 72, 84, 100, 192–96, 210–11; on control over elites, 133; on establishment of principles of regime, 246

—fluidity in: and abuses of power, 86–94, 237–38; and ambiguity (instability), 30–32, 93, 121, 136–38, 141, 274; effect of competition on, 55, 60–62; and emotions, 10, 58, 148–49, 160–62, 211; and nature of the dynamism, 121, 165, 263, 267, 299; and political participation, 59, 133; stability in, 128, 146

—and language, 9, 44, 68–72, 75–76; and accusation, 125; as ideology, 120–21, 272–73; and revision of central political concepts, 249, 297; and sycophancy, 165–67, 262; and use of metaphor, symbol, and narrative, 88, 253, 263, 265–72, 293–97; and women, 116

—principles of, 36, 167, 198, 242; and basis in justice and desert, 266–67, 271, 284–86; contestability of, 121, 301–2; and emotions as foundation of, 194; legitimacy in, 92–94. *See also* culture: conceptual foundations of

Politics, 183, 184–85, 187, 188, 385–86n.66

pollution, 77–78, 81–82, 90, 94, 95, 96, 217, 218, 358n.28, 359nn.42, 50, and 52, 360n.58, 391nn.52 and 60; from homicide, 238; for murder of slaves, 111; in oratory, 193–94; in philosophy, 279–80; in tragedy, 193. *See also* purification

pololuogoi, 147

Polus, 249, 250, 251

Polyneices, 91, 92, 135, 208

potlatch, 63, 354n.70

poverty, 64, 363n.101

"power-knowledge," 38

Pozzi, D. C., 139

precedent. *See* narratives

"principle of the public," and the construction of a social order, 134–41; definition of, 134, 241; and ideals and utopias, 184, 188–89, 257–63, 276; importance of symbols to, 199; as peace, 146; punishment as instrument of, 9–10, 209; as set of practices, 136; and types of regime, 188–89

prison (Athenian), 41, 202, 225, 229, 230, 235; buildings of, 227, 395nn.111 and 112; silent doors of, 235. *See also* imprisonment

private vs. public, 101, 168, 190–96; and arbitration, 112–13; and deterrence, 191–94; and imprisonment, 229–30; men as mediating, 122, 134–41; Plato on, 269

Prodicus, 233

proklesis eis ton horkon, 103

Prometheus, 25, 26, 27, 28, 29, 30, 31, 32, 33, 34, 36, 77, 82, 87, 88, 89, 241, 338nn.37 and 41, 340nn.53, 58, and 61; as sophist, 294, 299, 301, 302; as spectacle, 275, 293–97. *See also* symbols, symbolism: Prometheus as revisable

Prometheus Bound, 297, 302

Prometheus Unbound, 32, 293–97, 299, 301, 339n.51, 341n.65

proof. *See* evidence; law; social memory; witnesses

prosecution: as competition, 123; critique of rules for, 153, 154–55; delays in, 154; disinterested, 157–60; in France, Prussia, Great Britain, ancient Rome, and American colonies, 3, 333n.1, 396n.117; history of Athenian, 39, 47–49; importance of personal involvement in, 165; justification for participation in, 151–54; language of, 63–64; legitimate, 50–51, 72, 116–18, 168; loss of right to, 204; personally involved, 3–5, 39–40, 151–54, 156–59; private vs. public, 3–5, 39–40, 42, 50–51, 142; procedures of, 123; rhetorical construction of personal involvement in, 157; rules for, 151–56, 157–65, 190–94

prosecutor, 390n.20; as actor, 8, 101; of adultery, 214; Athenian, 10, 36, 39, 41, 42, 43, 46, 47, 49, 50, 59, 65, 72, 201, 204, 229, 342n.5; Athenian magistrates as, 42, 344n.23; Attorney General (British), 3, 333n.2; Crown Prosecutor's Service, 3; District Attorney (U.S.), 3; legitimate, 101; orators as, 168; public and private, 3, 4, 193; and restraint, 64; unsuccessful prosecutors (Athenian), 61

Protagoras, 260, 295, 296

Protagoras, 246, 247, 248, 251, 266, 277, 295, 296; punishment in, 399n.8

proxenoi. See metics

pseudoi logoi, 140. *See also* lies/false tales

psuche, 56, 297, 351n.36; tripartite, 252, 253, 254, 256, 257, 265, 268, 272, 273, 400n.17

public exhibition: of executions, 203; of Mnesilochus, 201; in the stocks, 200; of wrongdoers, 199, 237

punishment

—ancient commentary on, 10, 15, 36, 73–96; in *Iliad*, 18; *Republic* as discussion of, 251, 257–63. *See also* Aristophanes; Aristotle; Plato punishment (*cont.*)

—definitions of, 16, 18–19, 23–24, 60, 72, 118, 281; in Aristotle, 53, 54; as connected to honor and hot blood, 117, 197–98; and descriptions of, 86–88, 129; and "just punishment," 15; as legitimate, 118, 124–28, 135–38; modern definition of, 23–24, 70; and philosophy of, 15; in Plato, 182, 246, 248, 251; and the political basis of, 9–10, 245–46; and principles of, 59

—formalism of, 199–200, 202–5, 210–12, 216–23; as containment/consumption/reintegration, 205–13, 224, 224–32; as expulsion/redefinition of the boundaries of the community, 205–13, 217–23, 224, 232–37; as feminizing/degrading, 209, 228–29; and paradoxes of, 82–83, 118–19; as *pharmaka*, 118–19. *See also* symbols, symbolism

—goals of, 35, 69–71, 211; arguments for, 151; connection to the sacred, 210–13; and deterrence/public education, 191–94; and of memorialization, 205, 212, 225; and metaphoric ideals of, 117, 144–46; oligarchic, 235, 237–38; and the reassessment of honor and reform, 61, 68, 182, 247–51, 260–63. *See also* metaphor, metaphors: of harmony; metaphor, metaphors: of health; remembering/forgetting

—language of, 61–62, 68–72, 109, 116, 125, 356n.103; Platonic, 71, 246, 249, 250, 356nn.112 and 113; *zemia*, 69. See also *kolasis*

—and power, 4, 9, 64, 86–94, 110; abused, 165–67, 228; dangers of, 85–94, 118–19, 134–36; effects of, 69–71, 86–88; effects of on politics, 32–33, 84; of jurors, 130; protests against, 197; and race, 5; and stability, 86; and torture, 25; and violence, 82–83, 85, 86

—practice/process of, 17, 34, 83–85; archaic, 205; and emotion, 18–19, 20–24, 148–49; and finalization, 33–34, 197–98, 205, 210–11, 223–24, 232, 236–37; initiation of, 99–101; memorialization of, 46, 192, 199, 236–37; role of honor in, 110; through Zeus's thunderbolt, 83; timing of, 154–55; and women, 111–18

—rules for: and *sophrosune*, 58; without blood, 214. *See also* blood; "civic restraint"; hot blood; norms of public agency

—stories/narratives of, 65, 68, 205; afterlife, 259, 266; in Demosthenes, 124–25, 143; in drama, 77, 113–18, 137–39; in Herodotus, 143; in the just city, 265, 266, 272; in

Lycurgus, 159; as precedents, 173, 194; Prometheus as, 297

—theoretical models for understanding: as authoritative definition (labeling), 25–35, 210–12, 236–37; as contest, 54–62; 147, 148–49; as exchange, 62–65; as practice and/or process, 17, 25, 34, 63, 198; as reassessment of honor, 61, 68, 71; as retribution, 18; as ritual and/or drama, 16, 17, 33, 34, 334n.5; as standing in opposition to revenge, 18, 21; study of, xi, 9–10, 15–17, 33–34, 38; as war/peace, 64, 125, 197, 212. *See also* Aristotle; Durkheim, E.; Foucault, M.; Saunders, T.; Weber, M.

—types of, 208–9; Aristotelian, 283; in assembly or council, 142; Athens as, 280; capital, 35, 44, 45, 63, 124–25; collective, 142, 143–45; corporal, 3, 124, 125; extra-institutional, 45–46, 50; for family members, 122; and fines for metics, 109, 123; hierarchized, 32–33, 218, 222, 227–28, 241; in the just city, 278–79; in Magnesia, 279–81; by parents, 4–5; in peacetime/wartime, 142–45, 190; by private institutions/prosecutors, 4–5, 50, 201, 345n.37; of wives by husbands, 372n.5, 373n.6; severity of, 199; and slaves, 122; Socratic, 280; special decrees of, 142. *See also* burial; capital punishment; death; penalties; spectacle; individual types of punishment (e.g., fines)

"punitive situations," 35

purification, 209, 217; and anger, 210–12; and punishment, 73, 100, 210–13. *See also* religion

Pylades, 206

Quakers, 5, 8

quarries, as prisons, 221, 393n.91

radish, 214, 215, 392n.70

reason, 9, 18, 20, 56, 58, 91; in Aristotle, 282, 289; with language and logos, 272; as ruling anger, 254, 276; in tripartite soul, 253

Reckford, K. J., 132, 374n.33; on wasps' stings, 161

reciprocity, 30, 50, 62–65, 174, 241; Aristotle on, 289–91; "balanced," 62–63; and citizenship, 108, 229–30; excess in, 88, 125, 134–35; and fines/money, 225–26, 232, 290; "generalized," 62–63; negative, 63–65, 68; Plato on, 258; positive, 62–63, 68; and power, 64; relation of to liberty and equality, 283; and social status, 169–70; unlimited,

63–64; vision as trope for, 79–80. *See also* guest-host relationships

reconciliation, 112–13, 239–40

reforms: Cleisthenic, 48; Platonic, 71; Solonic, 39, 47, 223, 342n.1

religion, 10, 17; and burial, 58, 60, 92, 199, 203, 236, 237; and festivals, 60, 73–75, 85, 97, 128, 235; as protection for slaves, 111; and purification, 209, 210, 211, 217; and ritual cleansing, 85; and sacrifice, 19, 206, 212, 213, 358n.28; and scapegoats, 205. *See also* pollution; purification

remedy, 76, 80, 81, 82, 83, 85, 86, 94, 198, 358n.24, 359n.54, 360n.57, 361n.78. *See also* metaphor, metaphors: of health

remembering/forgetting, 67–68, 196, 204, 205, 240, 390n.35, 398n.148; and amnesty, 237–40; and *ataphia*, 217, 218; and burial, 216–18, 222–23; caused by anger, 81, 119; collective, 239; and expulsion, 210, 212; importance of, 210–12; oath of, 238; and public cases, 192; in punishments, 202–5; and reconciliation, 112; and slaves, 104, 110; symbolism of, 205–13. *See also* burial

Republic, 55, 83, 184, 186, 245, 246, 251, 252, 254, 257, 263, 268, 272, 278, 281, 288

retribution, 18, 31; Cragg, W. on, 19; and *dikephoron,* 21; public, 230. *See* punishment

revenge, 18–20, 34, 216; in history, 19, 20–21; in literature, 19–20, 21–23; and punishment, 22, 23, 24, 336nn.10 and 23, 337n.25, 356n.100; or self-help, 125; and vendetta, 20, 21, 135; as vengeance, 3, 19, 20, 21; W. Cragg on, 19. *See also* punishment

rhemata, rhethenta, ta, rhetor, rhetores, 270, 276, 278

rhetoric: function of, 84, 175, 245; as magic, 147–48; as parallel to rights language, 149–151; Platonic use of, 253, 268–70; and rhetorical handbooks, 150–51, 172, 175; and rights, 149–51; used to challenge social norms, 153, 154, 157–60; used for self-protection, 156–60

Rhetoric, 57, 102, 104, 117, 150, 174, 179, 186, 188, 191, 286

Rhodes, P. J., 345n.38

rights, privileges, protections, 149–50; as justice and desert, 149–50; language of, 149; loss of, 204; of male citizens, 122–33; of metics, 107–9; in modern democracy, 6, 108–9; and right to pity, 194; of slaves, 110–11; to trial by jury, 150; of women, 111–13. *See also* citizenship: privileges of

Roman law: handbooks for, 150; praetorian law, 178

Roth, D., 370n.71

Rowe, C., 398–99n.3

Rubinstein, L., 356n.109, 383n.17, 387n.83

"rule of law," 18–20, 135; as basis for legitimate politics, 188–89, 277, 283; definition of in contrast to politics of judgment, 179, 183–85; invention of by Plato and Aristotle, 183–90; lack of at Athens, 189, 275; requirements for, 185–86; at Sparta, 181

Ruschenbusch, E., 344n.26

Sagan, E., on "pscyhosocial," 333n.3, 368n.47

Sahlins, M., 354n.74

Saïd, S., 339nn.43, 44, and 46

Salamis, 142, 143, 145, 213

Samians, 198, 199, 201

Samos, 227

Saunders, T., 18, 24, 247, 399n.8, 402n.40, 403n.6

scapegoat, 84–86, 160, 204, 206. See also *pharmakos*

Scafuro, A., on arbitration, 317, 343nn.19 and 20, 344n.26, 355n.92, 367n.92

Scarry, E., 197, 212

Schlesier, R., on trope of maenad, 115

Scott, W. C., 340n.56

Seaford, R., 354n.74, 356n.110

Sealey, R., 342n.1

Segal, C., 348n.4, 363n.99; 371n.81, 376n.49, 377n.63

self. *See* constitution: of human beings

self-help, 19, 20, 69. *See also* prosecution; revenge

Semonides, 55; on bee woman, 119–20; on types of women, 119–21

Seneca, 223; on hemlock, 233, 234

Shaw, M., 362nn.88 and 89

Shiner, R., 386n.67

Shklar, J., 302

Shorey, P., 398–99n.3

Sicilian expedition, 100

Sidwell, K., 362n.88, 363n.94, 374nn.24 and 25

silence, 197, 198, 212, 213, 215–16, 222–23, 228, 230, 235, 236, 237–42; Athenian code of, 200; and *atimia,* 230–32; about the body, 216, 222, 223; and disappearance, 217, 222, 240; on execution, 214; and expulsion, 210; as feminine, 231–32; political import of, 228–32; Prometheus's refusal of, 295; refusal of, 236–37, 245–46; on sexual matters, 214; of Strato, 231; two main types, 224. *See also* burial: refusal of

Silver Coinage Law, 306
Simpson, O. J., 37, 38
Sinclair, R. K., 366n.22
Sisyphus, 140, 377n.61
skorpios, 214
slavery, 5, 362n.83; to the city, 229; for debt, 229; and necessity, 216, 240, 361n.73
slaves, 17, 35, 60, 67, 72, 73, 86, 93; and the body, 215; chastisement of, 69; information given by, 100, 102, 107; knowledge of, 107; memories of, 110; and power in knowledge, 109–10; prosecutorial powers of, 109–11; public, 41, 99; as public actors, 110–11; rights and privileges of, 110–11; torture of, 104–5, 201, 213, 214, 227, 238; whipping of, 201, 238, 392n.61; as witnesses, 104–5
social disruption. *See* wrongdoing
social knowledge, 202, 222, 230; construction of, 169. *See also* democracy: common language of
social memory, 46, 50, 65–68, 102, 113; and anger, 170–71, 173, 210–12; construction of, 169, 191–96, 217; of ethical evaluations, 169; and the execution of punishment, 202–5, 224; of facts, 169; importance of public cases for, 191–94; as preserved in poetry, 159; in rumors, 142; use of, 106–7, 166, 168. *See also* law; remembering/forgetting
social norms, 15, 17, 36, 49, 50, 58–59, 62, 68, 72, 92, 93, 95, 96, 197, 198, 203, 206, 208, 210, 216, 224, 231, 236, 241; as constitution of the city, 195; construction of, 150–51; contested, 211; for controlling emotion, 163–65; and cultural change, 120–21, 159, 263; for dealing with wrongdoing, 73–75; encoded in symbols, 245; fully established, 211; imposed by punishment, 87, 193–94, 198, 210–12; for prosecutor, 162; of public agency, 166; relation of wrongdoer to, 211; for sexuality, 162; used to solve political problems, 136–37; violations of, 92; and women, 113, 115. *See also* "civic restraint"; culture; guest-host relationships; hot blood; reciprocity
social relations, 63; as affected by emotion, 162; as affected by punishment, 69–70, 137–41, 225–26; as affected by wrongdoing, 73–75, 78–79; as constitution of the city, 195, 266; as discussed by Aristotle, 284, 285, 289–91; judgments of, 102. *See also* integration; isolation
social status, 69–70; determined by punishment, 208, 225–26; determined in terms of

the emotions of the *demos*, 148–49; effect of on penal strategies, 123, 169–70; as in Plato, 255, 266; and witnesses, 105; and youth, 155–56. *See also* honor
Socrates, 47, 55, 163, 179, 184–85, 187, 221, 245–66, 270, 278, 280, 281, 295, 296; executioners of, 215; on imprisonment, 227
Socratic paradox, 247, 399n.5
Solon, 39, 47, 48, 49, 50, 179, 181, 190, 200, 229, 363n.98
sophist, Prometheus as, 293, 302
Sophocles, 22, 51; *Ajax*, 84, 206; *Antigone*, 91, 188, 208, 258; *Electra*, 83, 116, 117; "Ode to Man" (*Antigone*), 76, 93, 206, 398n.151; *Oedipus at Colonus*, 82; *Oedipus Tyrannus*, 91; *Trachiniae*, 85, 114, 139
sophronisterion, 280
sophrosune, 136, 162
Sorabji, R., 403n.3
Sparshott, F., 400n.19
Sparta, Spartans, 181, 213, 216–19, 222, 235
Spartan law, 159. *See also* "rule of law"
spectacle, 11, 16, 27, 28, 29, 30, 34, 66, 79, 80, 83, 86, 87, 88, 94, 223, 236, 339n.51, 361n.82; and anger, 78–80, 83; as central element of punishment, 199, 245–46, 258, 261; of condemned, 245, 246, 257; as democratic phenomenon, 276; as foundation of social memory, 65–68, 222; as inspiration to judge, 27–30, 275, 293, 297; and the media, 37; Platonic critique of, 274; of Prometheus, 275, 297; responses to, 216, 231–32, 235; stocks as, 235; torture as, 236; trials as, 65
speech: and desert, 299–302; freedom of, 149; impact of on politics, 167, 198, 222–23, 236–37, 263, 278, 294; importance of, 68, 147–48, 200, 230–32, 241; of men for women, 112, 232; need for, 155, 299–302; power of, 298–302; role of in punishment, 149–51, 223–24; in support of a prosecutor, 153–54; in tension with written law, 167; vs. silence of Prometheus, 294–95. *See also* rhetoric
Stalley, R., 399n.11, 400n.16
Statesman, 183, 184, 185, 187, 188
statute of limitations, 154 . *See also* wrongdoing
Steiner, D., 362n.92
Steinwenter, A., 346n.52
stelae, 203, 217, 241
Stephanus, 153
stocks, 197, 202, 215, 216, 224, 238, 240, 241; context of, 198–200; as model, 212; prisoners of, 205, 213, 214, 225

stoning, 142–45, 201, 205, 206, 208, 209, 224; military, 213, 214; not in Athens, 213. *See also* Lycidas; punishment

Strato, 200, 230, 231, 232

structuralism, 75, 358nn.16 and 17

suffering, 26, 83, 361n.78, 214, 87. *See also* violence

suggnome, 149

suicide, 233, 234

suka, suke, etc., 160, 161, 162, 164

sunoikoi, 137

Suppliants, 188

sycophancy, sycophants, 156–67; in comedy, 160–62, 164–67; delayed prosecution as, 156, 379n.30; disinterested prosecution as, 158, 165; and figs, 160–62; language and definition of, 156–59, 160; and Lycurgus (*Against Leocrates*), 159–60; in Lysias's *Against the Grain Dealers*, 158–59; and oligarchs, 165–67; in oratory, 159–60, 381n.65; rhetoric of, 151, 167; of Socrates, 260, 261, 263, 276

symbols, symbolism: of *atimia*, 230–32; bees/drones as, 53, 55, 59, 119, 128–33, 270–71, 300; of democratic power, 105; and fashioning/using symbolic orders, 272, 275, 278, 281, 296; figs, vines, and orchids as, 160–64; of fines, 224–26, 230, 232; functioning of, 167, 245, 266; of gender, 55, 208–9; of imprisonment, 226–30; of *orge*, 55, 59, 119, 133, 160–64; Plato's use of, 252, 256, 265–72; political importance of, 120–21; Prometheus as revisable, 293–97; of punishment, 32–33, 199, 202–205, 205–13; of sexuality, 160–64; Solon as, 190; in stories of past punishment, 194–95; of the wrongdoer's body, 237, 245–46. *See also* Prometheus

system of value, 9, 36, 50, 52, 68, 102; centrality of to politics, 271; confirmation of the, 197–98, 205, 223–24; and cultural change, 120, 159; as inverted during wartime, 144–46; metaphoricity in, 163; Platonic, 266, 269; power of, 145–46; production of, 105, 147–48, 239–42; as represented in symbols, 266–67; threats to, 141, 197–98, 211. *See also* culture: conceptual foundations of

Taplin, O., 339nn.42 and 44, 340n.57

Tartarus, 31, 32, 33, 205, 341n.67

taxis, 229

Tecmessa, 84

Tennes, 208

Thargelion, 85, 204

Thebes, Thebans, 22, 84, 91, 93, 126, 135

theft. *See* Prometheus; wrongdoing

Themistocles, 143

Theognis, on *orge*, 53, 349n.10

Theophrastus, 69, 190, 229, 244; on hemlock, 232, 233, 234; on radishes, 214, 215

Theramenes, 166, 233, 235

Theseus, 82, 88, 90; shrine of, 111

thesmos. See law

thesmothetai, 123

Thetis, 101

Thirty, the. *See* oligarchs

Thomas, R., 369n.65, 383n.19, 387n.82

thorubos, 145, 169, 170, 206, 224, 377n.71; analogous to stoning, 206, 224

Thrasyas of Mantineia, 232

Thrasymachus, 258–64, 273, 278, 400n.19

thria, 160

Thucydides, 78, 107, 109, 216, 218, 219, 237, 354n.77; use of *amunomai* in, 125, 175

thumoeides, 254, 264

thumos, 51, 52, 53, 56, 57, 76, 84, 350n.25, 351nn.36 and 39, 352n.42; of women, 101, 116, 137, 161, 253, 255, 268, 279

Timaeus, 359n.38

Timarchus, 152, 153

time, 126, 128, 144, 268, 278

timesis, 47, 64, 169–70, 260

Timocrates, 195

timoria, 50, 51, 61, 69, 70, 71, 125, 248, 260, 279, 280, 281, 283

Titan, 293, 294, 296, 302

Tityus, 33

Todd, S., 21, 175, 342nn.2 and 4; 345n.38, 346n.48, 347nn.53 and 54, 366n.22, 367n.40, 370n.68, 383n.29, 384n.42, 391n.58, 393n.29, 394n.41, 397n.123; on sycophancy, 156, 160; on witnesses and evidence, 105, 174

topography, 203, 218, 390n.31. *See also* constitution: of *polis* as physical space

torture, 25, 34, 67, 86, 199, 201, 223, 227; of citizens, 210–13, 392n.75; as opposed to punishment, 25, 212; as punishment, 100, 365n.14, 366n.14, 367n.25; of slaves, 104–5, 210–13; and war, 212, 392n.63

Trachiniae, 85, 114, 139

tragedy, 19–20, 21–23, 73–96; family in, 134, 137–39; idea of, 199; list of attempts at punishing made in, 326–31; Platonic critique of, 274, 276; and symbolism of punishment, 208–9; on women as punishers, 113–19 tragic monster: man feminized as, 132; woman as, 115

treason, slaves' testimony about, 105

trial (*agon*), 46, 59, 60, 61, 65, 84, 224; civil, 37; as contest, 147–49, 152; criminal, 37; denial of, 204, 216, 217, 230, 237, 238, 239; importance of, 108, 214, 216; by jury, 38, 42, 43; by ordeal, 7; as ritual, 214. *See also* judicial decisionmaking; juries

Triomphe, R., 33, 341nn.68 and 70

Trojan War, Troy, 19, 67, 78, 139, 205, 207

truth, 7, 23, 67, 77, 100–102, 154, 266, 273; arising from consensus, 104–5, 188, 212. *See also* democracy: and social control

tupos, 266, 273. See also *nomos*

Tyndareus, 81

tyranny, 22, 27, 341n.72; of Zeus, 31, 180

tyrants, 86, 87, 89, 90, 91, 93, 217, 362n.86, 363n.94

Tyrtaios, 159

U.S. government, 5, 6, 242

U.S. supreme court, 118

Uranos, 265

Vaio, J., 374n.33

value, 16, 120, 141, 225–26; Aristotle's theory of, 289–90; assessed in terms of emotions, 148–49, 290–91; and fixity of positive/negative binary, 158, 300; in Foucauldian terms, 297–99; Plato's theory of, 290–91; as represented in symbols, 266, 275. *See also* equivalence

Vanderpool, E., 395n.112

van Effenterre, H., and M. van Effenterre, 387n.82

vendetta, 134–37. *See also* revenge

vengeance. *See* revenge

verdict, 6, 43; false, 7; meaning of, 7; records of, 346n.44; from trial of O. J. Simpson, 37; unanimous, 7

Vernant, J.-P., 335n.6, 358nn.15 and 22, 359n.42

victims, 3, 21, 37, 70, 71, 80, 83, 84, 86; anger of, 71; good, 284; of murder, 225; of precipitation, 219; production of witnesses by, 106, 169, 283; as prosecutors, 39

violence, 83, 85, 86, 207, 219, 258, 358n.28, 360n.68

virtue: as knowledge, 247; as teachable, 248

vision, 29, 66, 74, 75, 78–81, 206, 225, 235; grammar of, 75, 129; networks of, 258; in *Prometheus Bound*, 29, 339n.51; as visibility, 7, 74; as visuality, 78, 79, 203, 204,

209, 355nn.84 and 88, 359nn.35 and 42, 360n.60. *See also* gaze, the; Gyges

Vlastos, G., 382n.4, 403n.6

voluntariness/involuntariness of action, 247, 284

voting, 22, 178; in Areopagus, 20, 22; for generals, 309; in popular juries, 44, 47; on *timesis*, 64; vs. allotment, 309

Walsh, G., 370n.71

Walzer, M., 301

war/peace, 64, 129, 142–46, 197, 212, 214, 224, 238

—and peacetime punishments, 213, 230; boundaries of, 221; as built on silence, 200; context of, 198; as restoring peace, 197, 198

—"the terms of," 101, 119, 122, 125, 128–33, 143; and bloodlessness/the body, 213–16, 237–38; and burial, 216–17, 237; and "civic restraint," 128; as concerned with anger in women, 138–41; and gender, 111–19, 127; in the household, 120; and imprisonment, 229; for slaves, 110–11; and trials, 216

—and wartime: and amnesty, 237–40; prosecution during, 108–9, 129; punishment during, 143–45; and reversal of the terms of peace, 143; treatment of metics during, 126

Wasps, 22, 55, 105, 113, 121, 128–33, 160–62

wealth, 63, 93

Wealth, 64, 163

Weber, M.: phenomenological method of, 16; on punishment, 17

Whitehead, D., 367n.40, 376n.49

Williams, J. W., 190

Winkler, J. J., 147

witnesses: as affected by delay, 154, 206; citizens as, 65–68; as evidence, 174; foreigners as, 105; importance of, 66; metics as, 105; and the production of evidence, 103–7, 127, 169; slaves as, 104–5; testimony of, 7; unidentified bystanders as, 106–7; and the validity of eye-witnesses, 66; women as, 103–4

Wolff, H.J.J., 346n.52

Wolpert, A., 390n.35

women, 17, 22, 35, 54, 55, 73, 79, 85, 93, 203, 205, 213, 225, 241, 349n.18; and chastity, 208; and cold blood, 116–18; as concubines and prostitutes, 58; and containment, 209, 391n.47; in courts, 103–13; as daughters, 122; deceit of, 116; as foreigners, 370–71n.71; and honor (*time*), 16, 99, 102; and imprisonment, 228; in just city, 264; and magic, 147–48; as manlike, 116; as murderesses, 116; political role of, 92, 140,

231–32; as punishers, 111–18, 143, 144, 145; and silence, 231; and suicide, 234; terms of peace for, 112; tragedy, 113–18, 137–39; as tragic monster/maenad, 115; and use of *pharmakon*, 140; virtues of, 115; as witnesses, 103–4; as wives, 101, 137–41

wood, the, 199, 203, 215, 241. See also *apotumpanismos*; *podokakke*; stocks

writing, 66, 67, 192, 355n.87, 387n.82

wrongdoer: after condemnation, 203–5, 207; incurable, as Platonic, 279–81. *See also* dishonor; honor; penalties; symbols, symbolism: of punishment

wrongdoing, 43, 46, 63; Aristotle's definition of, 283, 284; definition of, 197; and deterrence, 191–94; problems caused by, 74, 77–86, 86–94; as social disruption, 42, 198, 210–12; solutions to, 81–86, 95; as violation of honor and social status, 125–26; weight of as measured by anger, 172–73

wrongdoing, types of: administrative, 156; adultery, 38, 43, 46, 63, 110, 122, 142; *aikiai* (*see* outrages); assault, 39; bribery, 7, 39, 69; capital offense, 46; financial, 156; forgery, 355n.87; genuine wrongs, 18; hubris, 39; idleness, 39; impiety, 89, 142; language of, 28; lists of, 15; maltreatment of parents, prostitution, failure to repay public debts, 142; manslaughter, 8; matricide, 19, 20; military desertion, 39; murder or homicide, 8, 37, 38, 39, 44, 46, 48, 49, 81, 89, 93, 142; parricide, 219, 222; perjury, 7, 39; sexual violence, 39; sycophancy, 156, 160–66; temple robbery, 39, 46; theft, 31, 32, 34, 39, 46, 131; treason, 46, 154; unconstitutional laws, 154; vocabulary of, 27, 200, 201, 205, 214, 217, 220, 226, 229, 231, 241

xenia, 101. See also guest-host relationships

xenoi. See metics

Xenophon, 111, 163, 165–66, 254; on emendations in the Decree of Cannonus, 324–25

yoke, 86, 361n.73; bridle, 87

youth, and generational conflict, 161. *See also* social status

Zanker, P., 353n.58

Zeitlin, F., 371n.81

Zeus, 114, 118, 129, 191, 265, 294, 295, 296

DATE DUE

APR 2 4 2003

APR 2 3 REC'D

BOWLING GREEN STATE UNIVERSITY
DISCARDED
LIBRARY

GAYLORD   PRINTED IN U.S.A.

KL 4395 .A43 2000

Allen, Danielle S., 1971-

The world of Prometheus